2012 NATIONAL PLUMBING & HVAC ESTIMATOR

By James A. Thomson

Includes inside the back cover:

- An estimating CD with all the costs in this book, plus,
- An estimating program that makes it easy to use these costs,
- An interactive video guide to the National Estimator program,
- A program that converts your estimates into invoices,
- A program that exports your estimates to QuickBooks Pro.

Quarterly price updates on the Web are free and automatic all during 2012. You'll be prompted when it's time to collect the next update. A connection to the Web is required.

Download all of Craftsman's most popular costbooks for one low price with the Craftsman Site License. http://CraftsmanSiteLicense.com

---

- Turn your estimate into a bid.
- Turn your bid into a contract.
- ConstructionContractWriter.com

Craftsman Book Company
6058 Corte del Cedro / P.O. Box 6500 / Carlsbad, CA 92018

Acknowledgments

The sample "Standard Form Subcontract" and "Subcontract Change Order" forms used in the final section of this book are reprinted with the permission of the publisher, the Associated General Contractors of America (National Office), 1957 E Street NW, Washington, District of Columbia 20006.

Contributing Editor: *Walter James O'Brien*
Cover design by: *Bill Grote*

© 2011 Craftsman Book Company
ISBN 978-1-57218-261-5
Published October 2011 for the year 2012.

Contents

How to Use This Book

This 2012 National Plumbing & HVAC Estimator is a guide to estimating labor and material costs for plumbing, heating, ventilating and air conditioning systems in residential, commercial and industrial buildings.

 Inside the back cover of this book you'll find an envelope with a compact disk. The disk has National Estimator, an easy-to-use estimating program with all the cost estimates in this book. Insert the CD in your computer and wait a few seconds. Installation should begin automatically. (If not, click Start, Settings, Control Panel, double-click Add/Remove Programs and Install.) Select Show Me from the installation menu and Dan will show you how to use National Estimator. When Show Me is complete, select Install Program. When the National Estimator program has been installed, click Help on the menu bar, click Contents, click Print all Topics, click File and click Print Topic to print a 40-page instruction manual for National Estimator.

Costs in This Manual will apply within a few percent on a wide variety of projects. Using the information given on the pages that follow will explain how to use these costs and suggest procedures to follow when compiling estimates. Reading the remainder of this section will help you produce more reliable estimates for plumbing and HVAC work.

 Manhour Estimates in This Book will be accurate for some jobs and inaccurate for others. No manhour estimate fits all jobs because every construction project is unique. Expect installation times to vary widely from job to job, from crew to crew, and even for the same crew from day to day.

There's no way to eliminate all errors when making manhour estimates. But you can minimize the risk of a major error by:

1. Understanding what's included in the manhour estimates in this book, and

2. Adjusting the manhour estimates in this book for unusual job conditions.

The Craft@Hrs Column. Manhour estimates in this book are listed in the column headed *Craft@Hrs*. For example, on page 19 you'll see an estimate for installing a 6 gallon hot water heater. In the *Craft@Hrs* column opposite 6 gallon you'll see:

P1@.500

To the left of the @ symbol you see an abbreviation for the recommended work crew.

Page 7 shows the wage rates and craft codes used in this book.

To the right of the @ symbol you see a number. The number is the estimated manhours (not crew hours) required to install each unit of material listed. In the case of a 6 gallon hot water heater, P1@.500 means that .500 manhours are required to install 1 hot water heater.

Costs in the Labor $ Column are based on manhour estimates in the Craft@Hrs column. Multiply the manhour estimate by the assumed hourly labor cost to find the installation cost in the *Labor $* column. For example, .500 manhours times $34.55 (the average wage for crew P1) is $17.28.

Quarterly price updates on the Web are free and automatic all during 2012. You'll be prompted when it's time to collect the next update. A connection to the Web is required.

Manhour Estimates include all productive labor normally associated with installing the materials described. These estimates assume normal conditions: experienced craftsmen working on reasonably well planned and managed new construction with fair to good productivity. Labor estimates also assume that materials are standard grade, appropriate tools are on hand, work done by other crafts is adequate, layout and installation are relatively uncomplicated, and working conditions don't slow progress.

All manhour estimates include tasks such as:

■ Unloading and storing construction materials, tools and equipment on site.

■ Working no more than two floors above or below ground level.

■ Working no more than 10 feet above an uncluttered floor.

■ Normal time lost due to work breaks.

■ Moving tools and equipment from a storage area or truck not more than 200 feet from the work area.

■ Returning tools and equipment to the storage area or truck at the end of the day.

■ Planning and discussing the work to be performed.

■ Normal handling, measuring, cutting and fitting.

■ Regular cleanup of construction debris.

■ Infrequent correction or repairs required because of faulty installation.

If the work you're estimating won't be done under these conditions, you need to apply a correction factor to adjust the manhour estimates in this book to fit your job.

Applying Correction Factors. Analyze your job carefully to determine whether a labor correction factor is needed. Failure to consider job conditions is probably the most common reason for inaccurate estimates.

Use one or more of the recommended correction factors in Table 1 to adjust for unusual job conditions. To make the adjustment, multiply the manhour estimate by the appropriate conversion factor. On some jobs, several correction factors may be needed. A correction factor less than 1.00 means that favorable working conditions will reduce the manhours required.

Supervision Expense to the installing contractor is not included in the labor cost. The cost of supervision and non-productive labor varies widely from job to job. Calculate the cost of supervision and non-productive labor and add this to the estimate.

Hourly Labor Costs also vary from job to job. This book assumes an average manhour labor cost of $40.47 for plumbers and $39.70 for sheet metal workers. If these hourly labor costs are not accurate for your jobs, adjust the labor costs up or down by an appropriate percentage. Instructions on the next page explains how to make these adjustments. If you're using the National Estimator disk, it's easy to set your own wage rates.

Hourly labor costs in this book include the basic wage, fringe benefits, the employer's contribution to welfare, pension, vacation and apprentice funds, and all tax and insurance charges based on wages. Table 2 at the top of the next page shows how hourly labor costs in this book were calculated. It's important that you understand what's included in the figures in each of the six columns in Table 2. Here's an explanation:

Column 1, the base wage per hour, is the craftsman's hourly wage. These figures are representative of what many contractors are paying plumbers, sheet metal workers and helpers in 2012.

Column 2, taxable fringe benefits, includes vacation pay, sick leave and other taxable benefits. These fringe benefits average about 5.15% of the base wage for many plumbing and HVAC contractors. This benefit is in addition to the base wage.

Condition	Correction Factor
Work in large open areas, no partitions	.85
Prefabrication under ideal conditions, bench work	.90
Large quantities of repetitive work	.90
Very capable tradesmen	.95
Work 300' from storage area	1.03
Work 400' from storage area	1.05
Work 500' from storage area	1.07
Work on 3rd through 5th floors	1.05
Work on 6th through 9th floors	1.10
Work on 10th through 13th floors	1.15
Work on 14th through 17th floors	1.20
Work on 18th through 21st floors	1.25
Work over 21 floors	1.35
Work in cramped shafts	1.30
Work in commercial kitchens	1.10
Work above a sloped floor	1.25
Work in attic space	1.50
Work in crawl space	1.20
Work in a congested equipment room	1.20
Work 15' above floor level	1.10
Work 20' above floor level	1.20
Work 25' above floor level	1.30
Work 30' above floor level	1.40
Work 35' to 40' above floor level	1.50

Table 1 Recommended Correction Factors

Column 3, insurance and employer-paid taxes in percent, shows the insurance and tax rate for the craft workers. The cost of insurance in this column includes workers' compensation and contractor's casualty and liability coverage. Insurance rates vary widely from state to state and depend on a contractor's loss experience. Note that taxes and insurance increase the hourly labor cost by approximately 30%. There is no legal way to avoid these costs.

Column 4, insurance and employer taxes in dollars, shows the hourly cost of taxes and insurance. Insurance and taxes are paid on the costs in both columns 1 and 2.

Column 5, non-taxable fringe benefits, includes employer paid non-taxable benefits such as medical coverage and tax-deferred pension and profit sharing plans. These fringe benefits average 4.55% of the base wage for many plumbing and HVAC contractors.

Column Number	1	2	3	4	5	6
Craft	Base wage per hour	Taxable fringe benefits (at 5.15% of base wage)	Insurance and employer taxes (%)	Insurance and employer taxes ($)	Non-taxable fringe benefits (at 4.55% of base wage)	Total hourly cost used in this book
Laborer	19.83	1.02	32.93%	6.87	0.90	28.62
Plumber	29.88	1.54	24.47%	7.69	1.36	40.47
Sheet Metal Worker	28.92	1.49	26.21%	7.97	1.32	39.70
Operating Engineer	29.35	1.51	25.42%	7.84	1.34	40.04
Sprinkler Fitter	29.35	1.51	25.28%	7.80	1.34	40.00
Electrician	29.27	1.51	20.04%	6.17	1.33	38.28
Cement Mason	25.23	1.30	23.35%	6.19	1.15	33.87

Craft Code	Crew Composition	Average Hourly Cost per Manhour
ER	4 building plumbers, 2 building laborers, 1 operating engineer	37.02
SN	4 building sheet metal workers, 2 building laborers, 1 operating engineer	36.58
P1	1 building plumber and 1 building laborer	34.55
ST	1 sprinkler fitter	40.00
SK	4 sprinkler fitters, 2 building laborers, 1 operating engineer	36.75
SL	1 sprinkler fitter and 1 laborer	34.31
S2	1 building sheet metal worker, 1 building laborer	34.16
BE	1 electrician	38.28
CF	1 cement mason	33.87
SW	1 sheet metal worker	39.70

Table 2 Labor Costs Used in This Book

The employer pays no taxes or insurance on these benefits.

Column 6, the total hourly cost in dollars, is the sum of columns 1, 2, 4, and 5. The labor costs in Column 6 were used to compute costs in the Labor $ column of this book.

Adjusting Costs in the Labor $ Column. The hourly labor costs used in this book may apply within a few percent on many of your jobs. But wage rates may be much higher or lower in some areas. If the hourly costs shown in Column 6 of Table 2 are not accurate for your work, adjust labor costs to fit your jobs.

For example, suppose your hourly labor costs are as follows:

Plumber	$19.00
Laborer	$16.00
Total hourly crew cost	$35.00

Your average cost per manhour would be $17.50 ($35.00 per crew hour divided by 2 because this is a crew of two).

A labor cost of $17.50 is about 50% of the $34.55 labor cost used for crew P1. Multiply costs in the Labor $ column by .50 to find your estimated cost.

For example, notice on page 19 that the labor cost for installing a 6 gallon hot water heater is $17.28 each. If installed by your plumbing crew working at an average cost of $17.50 per manhour, your estimated cost would be 50% of $17.28 or $8.64 per heater.

Adjusting the labor costs in this book will make your estimates much more accurate. Making adjustments to labor costs is both quick and easy if you use the National Estimator disk.

Equipment Cost will vary according to need and application. It typically is $110 per hour for a 10-ton hydraulic truck-mounted crane.

Material Costs in this manual are intended to reflect what medium- to low-volume contractors will be paying in 2012 after applying normal discounts. These costs include charges for delivery to within 25 to 30 miles of the supplier.

Overhead and Profit for the installing contractor are not included in the costs in this manual unless specifically identified in the text. Markup can vary widely with local economic conditions, competition and the installing contractor's operating expenses. Add the markup that's appropriate for your company, the job and the competitive environment.

How Accurate Are These Figures? As accurate as possible considering that the editors don't know your material suppliers, haven't seen the plans or specifications, don't know what building code applies or where the job is, had to project material costs at least six months into the future, and had no record of how much work the crew that will be assigned to the job can handle.

You wouldn't bid a job under those conditions. And I don't claim that all plumbing and HVAC work is done at these prices.

Estimating Is an Art, not a science. There is no one price that applies on all jobs. On many jobs the range between high and low bid will be 10% or more. There's room for legitimate disagreement on what the correct costs are, even when complete plans and specifications are available, the date and site are established, and labor and material costs are identical for all bidders.

No estimate fits all jobs. Good estimates are custom made for a particular project and a single contractor through judgment, analysis and experience. This book is not intended as a substitute for judgment, analysis and sound estimating practice. It's an aid in developing an informed opinion of cost, not an answer book.

Additional Costs to Consider

Here's a checklist of additional costs to consider before submitting any bid.

1. Sales taxes
2. Mobilization costs
3. Payment and performance bond costs
4. Permits and fees
5. Storage container rental costs
6. Utility costs
7. Tool costs
8. Callback costs during warranty period
9. Demobilization costs

Exclusions and Clarifications

Neither the job specifications nor the contract may identify exactly what work should be included in the plumbing and HVAC bid. Obviously, you have to identify what work is included in the job.

The most efficient way to define the scope of the work is to prepare a list of tasks not normally performed by your company and attach that list to each bid submitted. Here's a good list of work that should be excluded from your bid.

Your Bid Should Exclude

Final cleaning of plumbing fixtures

Backings for plumbing fixtures

Toilet room accessories

Electrical work, including motor starters

Electrical wiring and conduit over 100 volts

Temporary utilities

Painting, priming and surface preparation

Structural cutting, patching or repairing

Fire protection and landscape sprinklers

Equipment supports

Surveying and layout of control lines

Removal or stockpiling of excess soil

Concrete work, including forming and rebar

Setting of equipment furnished by others

Equipment, unless shown, and personnel hoisting

Wall and floor blockouts

Pitch pockets

The costs of performance or payment bonds

Site utilities

Asbestos removal or disposal

Contaminated soil removal or disposal

Major increases in copper material prices

Fire dampers not shown on the plans

Your Bid Should Include

Trash sweep-up only. Others haul it away

Site utilities from building to property line only

Piping to 5 feet outside the building only

Plumbing & HVAC permits for your work only

Beware of Price Changes

There's no way to be sure what prices will be in three to six months. All labor, equipment, material and subcontract prices in a bid should be based on costs anticipated when the project is expected to be built, not when the estimate is compiled. That presents a problem. Except for the installation of underground utilities, most plumbing and HVAC work is done six months to a year after the bid is submitted. When possible, get price protection in writing from your suppliers and subcontractors. If your suppliers and subs won't guarantee prices, include an escalation allowance in your bid to cover anticipated price increases.

Material Pricing Conditions

All equipment and material prices quoted by your vendors will be conditional. They usually don't include sales tax and are subject to specific payment and shipping terms. Every estimator should understand the meaning of common shipping terms. They define who pays the freight and who has responsibility for processing freight-damage claims. Here's a summary of important conditions you should understand.

F.O.B. Factory (Free On Board at the Factory): Title passes to the buyer when the goods are delivered by the seller to the freight carrier. The buyer pays the freight and is responsible for freight-damage claims.

F.O.B. Factory F.F.A. (Free On Board at the Factory, Full Freight Allowed): The title passes to the buyer when the goods are delivered by the seller to the freight carrier. The seller pays the freight charges, but the buyer is responsible for freight-damage claims.

F.O.B. (city of destination) (Free On Board to your city): The title passes to the buyer when the goods are delivered by the seller to the freight terminal in the city, or nearest city, of destination. The seller pays the freight and is responsible for freight-damage claims to the terminal. The buyer pays the freight charge and is responsible for freight-damage claims from the terminal to the final destination.

F.O.B. Job Site (Free On Board at job site, or contractor's shop): The title passes to the buyer when the goods are delivered to the job site (or shop). The seller pays the freight and is responsible for freight-damage claims.

F.A.S. Port [of a specific city] (Free Alongside Ship at the nearest port): The title passes to the buyer when goods are delivered to the ship dock or port terminal. The seller pays the freight and is responsible for freight-damage claims to the ship dock or port terminal only. The buyer pays the freight and is responsible for freight-damage claims from the ship dock or port terminal to the designated delivery point.

Obviously, it's to your advantage to instruct all vendors to quote costs F.O.B. the job site or your shop.

Reducing Costs

Most construction specifications allow the use of alternative equipment and materials. It's the estimator's responsibility to select the most cost-effective products. Research and compare your costs before making any decisions. Avoid selecting any material or equipment simply because that's what you've always done.

Don't recommend plastic products such as ABS, PVC, or polypropylene pipe or corrugated flexible ducts until you've checked local code requirements. Most building codes prohibit use of these materials inside public buildings such as schools, care centers and hospitals.

It's wise to select 100% factory-packaged equipment. Beware of equipment labeled "Some assembly required." Field labor costs for mounting loose coils, motors and similar equipment are very high.

Value Engineering

Let's suppose you've submitted a combined plumbing and HVAC bid for $233,000. Your cutthroat competitor put in a bid at $4,000 less, $229,000. Obviously there's no way you're going to get the job. Right?

Not so fast! Maybe value engineering can help you win that contract — while fattening your profit margin.

Suppose the proposal you submitted had two parts. Part I is the bid for $233,000, based entirely on job plans and specs, just the way they were written. But appended to your proposal is Part II, a list of suggestions for saving money without sacrificing any of the capacity or quality designed into the system. Here's an example of what might be in Part II:

1. Deduct for providing pipe hanger spacings per UPC in lieu of specified spacings:
$1,750.00

2. Deduct for reducing heating hot water pipe sizes by using 40 degrees F Delta T in lieu of specified 20 degrees F Delta T: $4,600.00

3. Deduct for providing pressure/temperature taps at air handling units, pumps and chillers in lieu of specified thermometers and pressure gauges:
$875.00

4. Deduct for eliminating water treatment in closed piping systems: $1,800.00

5. Deduct for piping chilled and heating hot water pumps in parallel in lieu of providing 100% standby pumps: $2,900.00

Total deductions: **$11,925.00**

Adopting these suggestions would make you low bidder by nearly $8,000. A saving like that will be tempting to most owners, especially if the owner understands that your suggestions result in a system that is every bit as good and maybe better than the system as originally designed.

You're not offering to undercut the competition. Far from it. You're using knowledge and experience to create better value for the owner. That's called value engineering and it's likely to win the respect of nearly all cost-conscious owners.

Notice that reducing costs is only part of what value engineering is all about. You don't cut costs at the expense of system quality, integrity, capacity or performance.

Don't waste your time, and your client's, by offering to substitute cheaper or lower-quality fixtures or equipment. Any cutthroat contractor with a price list can do that. Recommend the use of inferior materials and you'll be associated with the inferior goods you promote. Some owners consider even the suggestion to be insulting.

The recommendations you make (like most of those in the example) will require design changes. You can expect to be examined (or even challenged) on these points. Be ready to explain and defend each of your suggestions. Convince the client (or the design engineer) that your ideas are based on sound engineering principles and you're well on the way to winning the owner's confidence and the contract.

Now, let's go back to the list and see how we might justify the five value engineering recommendations.

1. **Pipe Hanger Spacing.** The pipe hanger spacings recommended in the Uniform Plumbing Code (UPC) are calculated by experienced, professional structural engineers. The safety factors used in these calculations are very conservative. They've been widely used for many years and have proved to be more than adequate. There's no need for more hangers than the UPC requires.

2. **Changing HHW Delta T.** In hydronic heating systems, heat measured in Btus is pumped to terminal units. The proposed change of the Delta T, from 20 degrees F to 40 degrees F, has no effect whatsoever on how many Btus the system delivers. You're not changing anything but the volume of water being pumped. At lower volume levels, the size of the pump, the pipe and the pipe insulation can all be reduced. Not one of these changes will affect the system's ability to transmit heat. Furthermore, operating costs will also drop, since less pump horsepower will be needed to run the smaller pump.

3. **Thermometers/Pressure Gauges.** Thermometers and pressure gauges installed on or near vibrating machinery have a very short life expectancy. Gauges quickly lose accuracy under harsh conditions. Readings will become less and less reliable. That's potentially dangerous. You can avoid this problem by using insertion-type pressure/temperature taps instead. Store these sensitive gauges in a desk drawer or a tool crib when not in use. Safely stored, they're protected from damage. They'll give accurate readings longer and won't need to be replaced as often. And they're simple to use. Just insert a gauge in one of the conveniently located taps. Make the reading, then remove the gauge and put it away.

4. **Water Treatment.** ITT Bell & Gossett has done studies on corrosion in closed hydronic systems that have a make-up water rate of no more than 5% per year. These studies show that corrosion virtually stops when entrained air is either removed or depleted. No water treatment is needed in this closed system.

5. **100% Standby Pumps.** Two pumps piped and operated in parallel are more economical. Even if one pump fails, the other pump can maintain delivery at 75 to 80% of the designed flow rate. That's usually adequate for emergency operation.

These cost-saving ideas are small, but could tip the balance in your favor. I hope they demonstrate the potential that value engineering has when bidding jobs. Any time you're compiling an estimate, keep an eye out for ways to save money or reduce the owner's cost. Jot a note to yourself about each potential saving you identify. Before submitting the bid, make a list of your alternate suggestions. Maybe best of all, markup on your value engineering suggestions can be higher than your normal markup. If value engineering can cut costs by $10,000, maybe as much as $4,000 of that should end up in your pocket!

Value Engineering: Surplus Materials

Value engineering doesn't begin and end with job plans and specs. Value engineering means getting the most value at the least cost, no matter whether it's value to the owner or value to the contractor. Smart mechanical contractors learn to build extra value into their jobs by controlling shrinkage of materials. Nearly every significant plumbing and HVAC job ends with at least some surplus material on hand. Material left over when the job is done tends to be discarded as waste or hauled off the job in the back of a truck that doesn't have your company name on the door. And why not? It's surplus – not needed. The owner didn't need it. So now it's up for grabs.

Not quite. Let's consider who actually owns that surplus material. When your company has been paid, every piece of material your crew installed belongs to the building owner. But what about those fittings, hangers and valves delivered to the job site but never actually used? Almost certainly, those materials were included in your bid. So aren't they the property of the owner? Not in my opinion. The owner contracted for a mechanical system and (presumably) has one. Unless it's a cost-plus job or a labor-only job, the owner didn't buy materials delivered to the job site. The owner bought a mechanical system and has one – completely separate and apart from any surplus materials. In my mind, the property owner has no more claim to left-over materials than the same owner would have claim to labor hours not expended or equipment not used on the same job.

Unless there's some provision in your contract to the contrary, surplus material belongs to the installing contractor. But your right to that material and the chance of actually getting it back to your shop are two very different propositions. I see recovery of surplus material as a training issue. As a matter of company policy, make it clear to your crews that surplus material belongs to your company. The supervisor on every job should be accountable for recovery of excess material. Every significant job will have at least some surplus. Accounting for that surplus should be part of your routine close-out procedure. Fortunately, it's not difficult. I'll explain.

Control of surplus materials begins with a good checklist, or form. I recommend the Materials, Equipment and Tool form, "MET" for short. A blank MET form appears following this section. Your MET should show both what's delivered to the job site (material, equipment and tools) and surplus "drops" returned to your shop at project close-out. A MET ensures that the estimator, the shop inventory manager and your field supervisor are on the same page. Your MET establishes accountability. Nothing falls through the cracks. Job input equals job output plus returns. Everything delivered to the job and not expended should be returned to your shop.

Here's how it works:

1. Based on the estimate that won you the job, the items needed are purchased for the job and staged for delivery to the job site.

2. As materials, equipment and tools are delivered to the job site, your supervisor completes the first three columns of the MET form: Description, Quantity and Date.

3. As work is completed, the same supervisor completes the four columns under Returned to Inventory: Quantity Returned, Date, Status Code and Value. The status code will be either "RS" (Returned and Salvaged) or "RN" (Returned New).

4. Back at your shop, both RS and RN materials should be restored to inventory.

5. If your company has an inventory manager, have that manager assign the return value to each item returned. If you're using QuickBooks Pro, the "Adjust Inventory" feature can handle this task quite easily. Add two new categories under "Inventory Stock on Hand by Vendor." The first new category is Returned Salvage. The second is Returned New. Be sure the value of RS materials includes the cost of any reconditioning done to restore salvaged materials (such as pumps and boilers) to serviceable condition.

6. Comparing MET deployed to the job site with MET returned to inventory yields MET actually used on the job. That's a very important number to every plumbing and HVAC estimator. Be sure actual usage gets entered on the Project Summary form.

7. When the take-off on your next estimate is complete, compare that materials list with a summary of RS and RN materials on hand from prior jobs.

8. Evaluate which returned materials can be redeployed on the new job.

9. It's a management decision to either (1) charge the new job for the cost of RS and RN materials already on hand, or (2) consider materials on hand as "free" and a competitive advantage in winning the new bid. Either way, RN and RS materials are an asset to your company.

Plumbing and HVAC materials are expensive. Every mechanical contractor has an interest in MET tracking. Everyone in your company should be aware of the need for good materials management. Used correctly, the MET form in this book can help engineer more value into your jobs.

Maximizing the Value of Old Estimates

There should be two profits in every job. The first is money in the bank — a return on time and expenses. The second is what you learn from the job — primarily by comparing the estimate you made with what turns out to be your actual cost. On some jobs, the value of lessons learned may outweigh net revenue.

Every plumbing and HVAC contractor has marginal jobs. That's normal. What *shouldn't* be normal is repeating mistakes. The best way to avoid trouble in your future is to keep track of your past. Keeping old estimates available for reference can help prevent errors on new estimates.

As your file of completed estimates grows, organization becomes more important. You need an easy way to find similar projects with the same components and comparable scope of work. If your estimating file is in QuickBooks Pro, searching by keyword may be enough. Otherwise, I recommend creating a short summary for each completed job, and an index that references all summaries available for comparison. You'll find a blank Project Summary form at the end of this section. To make reference easier, create an index by type of job and equipment used. You may choose to use an alphabetical index based on client name or project ID.

How to complete the Project Summary form is obvious. The many ways to use this form may not be so obvious, so here are a few pointers.

1. Use your index of Project Summary forms to find completed jobs most similar to the job you're bidding. Believe it or not, Project Summary forms with the widest margin of error will be most useful. Ask yourself: Who worked on those projects? Who was the field superintendent? Who were the vendors? Did the errors result from poor estimating or the poor performance of vendors, supervisors or crews? The most common estimating errors occur when (a) inspecting the job site, (b) examining the plans or (c) reading the specifications. What did you miss and why? Look for pitfalls to avoid in the job now being estimated. Identify the biggest two or three mistakes made when bidding that job. Make a notation about each on the Project Summary form.

2. Now look at your bid for the current job. Which mistakes made on a prior job might you expect on this job? Concentrate on the big three oversights to avoid: Inspecting the job site; examining the plans; and reading the specifications.

3. Unless there's a major error in take-off, your estimate of material costs should be within about 5 percent of the actual costs of materials. However, it's common for labor cost estimates to vary 20 percent or more from actual labor costs. This is precisely where data from old jobs comes in handy. If your Project Summary files show that some project types are consistent money-losers, either shift your company's focus to another class of work, factor more contingency into your bids, or find some way to wring inefficiencies out of the labor component. Poor staging, delivery and retrieval procedures drag down labor productivity on any job.

4. Use your file of Project Summary forms to spot any common thread that runs through either money-making jobs or money-losing jobs. For example, if the names of certain subcontractors or vendors are prominent on low-margin jobs, maybe there's a relationship between your profit margin and choice of subs and suppliers. Even the best and most reliable vendors can become complacent if not challenged occasionally.

5. Project Summary forms should note changes and extras identified after the contract was signed — both for which your company was paid and changes done without additional compensation. Projects with changes and extras that exceed about 4 percent of the contract price deserve special scrutiny. Jobs with changes beyond about 4 percent aren't good for business, at least in my opinion. Nearly all changes have a negative impact on your job schedule and require a disproportionate investment of management resources. Too many changes can antagonize the owner and design staff, even if they were responsible for the altered plans. You may know of a mechanical contractor with a reputation for capitalizing on change orders. But I've rarely seen a job plagued with changes that turned into a money-maker for anyone — except the attorneys. Your file of Project Summary forms will show job types that carry change order risk. Before finalizing and submitting any bid, consider whether the job will get mired in disputes over changes and extras. If similar jobs have ended on the courthouse steps, factor that risk into your estimate.

Utility of a Project Summary forms file is limited only by your ingenuity. The important point is to keep and organize the source of your second profit available on every job. What you learn can be more valuable than what you earn.

The Estimating Procedure

Every plumbing and HVAC estimator works under deadline pressure. You'll seldom have the luxury of spending as much time as you would like on an estimate. Estimators who aren't organized waste valuable time and tend to make careless errors. Try to be well-organized and consistent in your approach to estimating. For most projects, I recommend that you follow the procedures listed below and in the order listed:

1. Get a second set of project drawings and specifications for use by your suppliers and subcontractors. Remember that your subs and suppliers need access to the plans and specs and time to prepare their quotes.

2. Study the plans and specs carefully. Highlight important items. Make a list of specific tasks that require labor unit correction factors. The estimate is never complete until you're totally familiar with the project and the applicable construction codes.

3. Get the general contractor or owner to identify the proposed construction schedule and subcontractor lay-down (storage) area. Work schedule and site conditions always affect your costs.

4. Contact all potential suppliers and subcontractors as early as possible. Set a time when each can come to your office to make their take-offs from the spare set of contract documents.

When this important preliminary work is done, or in progress, it's time to begin your detailed take-off.

Guidelines for Good Estimating

You can compile estimates on a legal pad, a printed estimating form or on a computer. Regardless of the method, these guidelines will apply:

List Each Cost Separately on your take-off sheet. Don't combine system estimates, even if the materials are the same type. A combined system estimate may have to be completely redone if materials for one system are changed at a later date. Use the Estimate Detail Sheet on page 16 if you don't already have a good material take-off form.

Use Engineer's Identification Numbers when listing equipment. The word pump without any other description is ambiguous when there are several pumps included in the project.

Don't Forget Labor Adjustment factors if your labor costs are significantly higher or lower than the costs used in this book. See instructions on page 7 for adjusting labor costs.

Use Colored Pencils or highlighters to mark the items you've taken off and listed. Use a different color for each piping or ducting system.

Log Telephone Quotes and other important phone conversations on a telephone quote form. See the sample on page 18.

Project Estimated Costs for labor, material and equipment to the time when the work is expected to be done, not when the job is being estimated.

The only good estimate is a complete estimate. You've probably heard this saying, "He who makes the most mistakes is likely to be low bidder, and live to regret it."

Preparing the Proposal

It's both common courtesy and good business practice to deliver an unpriced copy of your bid or proposal letter to the general contractor three or four days before the bid deadline date. This gives the contractor time to study your proposal and obtain alternate pricing for items you may have excluded. To avoid misunderstandings, make sure your proposals include, as a minimum, the following elements:

1. The complete name and address of the proposed project.

2. Specification title and issue date.

3. A complete listing of drawings and their issue or revision date.

4. A complete list of addenda and their dates of issue.

5. A list of specification section numbers covered by your proposal.

6. A list of exclusions, clarifications and assumptions.

Your final bid can be phoned in or sent by fax, but it should reach the general contractor or owner no more than five or ten minutes before the bid deadline. Prices submitted too early may have to be revised because of last-minute price changes by subcontractors or suppliers.

MET Worksheet
Material, Equipment and Tool Delivery and Surplus Return Record

Project ID _____   Job Location _____

Supervisor _____   Start Date _____

Description of Material, Equipment or Tool Delivered or Returned	Delivered to Job Site		Returned to Inventory			
	Quantity Delivered	Date Delivered	Quantity Returned	Date Returned	Status Code RN or RS	Value at Return

PROJECT SUMMARY

Project ID _____   Job Location _____

Short description _____

Supervisor _____

Index ID _____   Start Date _____

Estimator _____   Client _____

Major vendors _____   Subcontractors _____

_____

Sources of cost deviation _____

_____

Related Projects by ID Number _____

Thumbnail Summary	Labor	Material	Equipment	Subcontract	Deployed RN/RS	Total
Actual cost						
Estimate						
Over/(Under)						
Full Summary						
Bid amount						
Estimated cost						
Projected profit						
Cost overrun						
Bid profit						
Change orders						
Cost of changes						
Total profit						
Total profit with RN/RS						
Redeployment						

Estimate Detail Sheet

Data carried forward from Take-Off Quantity Survey Sheet(s)

Company/Department _____ Estimator _____ Date _____

Project _____ Checked by _____ Date _____

Address _____ Notes:

Job description _____ Estimate # _____

CSI Division/Account _____ Estimate due _____

Item Description	Quantity	Unit	Crew @ MH/Unit	Manhours Ext.	Materials		Labor		Equipment		Subcontract		Total $
					Unit $	Ext. $	Unit $	Ext. $	Unit $	Ext. $	Unit $	Ext. $	
Totals This Sheet				Manhours	Material $		Labor $		Equipment $		Subcontract $		Total $

Carry totals forward to Estimate Summary Sheet

Estimate # _____   Estimate Detail Sheet _____ of _____

Quotation Sheet

Job: _____

Supplier: _____

Salesperson: _____ **Phone No:** _____

Per Plans/Specs: _____ **Freight:** _____ **Terms:** _____

Description	Delivery Time	Price

By: _____

Record of Telephone Conversation

Date:_____ Time:_____ Project:_____

Telecon with:_____

Company:_____ Phone No:_____

Subject:_____

Details of Conversation:_____

_____

_____

_____

_____

_____

_____

_____

_____

_____

_____

_____

_____

_____

_____

_____

_____

_____

_____

_____

_____

_____

By:_____

Description	Craft@Hrs	Unit	Material $	Labor $	Equipment $	Total $

Electric domestic hot water heater, (residential). Set in place only (floor models). Make additional allowances for pipe and electrical connections. (See below)

Description	Craft@Hrs	Unit	Material $	Labor $	Equipment $	Total $
6 gallon						
1.5 KW/110V	P1@.500	Ea	301.00	17.30	—	318.30
10 gallon						
1.5 KW/110V	P1@.500	Ea	336.00	17.30	—	353.30
15 gallon						
1.5 KW/110V	P1@.750	Ea	354.00	25.90	—	379.90
20 gallon						
1.5 KW/110V	P1@.750	Ea	366.00	25.90	—	391.90
30 gallon						
1.5 KW/110V	P1@1.00	Ea	391.00	34.60	—	425.60
40 gallon						
1.5 KW/110V	P1@1.20	Ea	410.00	41.50	—	451.50
50 gallon						
3 KW/110V	P1@1.30	Ea	441.00	44.90	—	485.90
12 gallon						
3 KW/220V	P1@.500	Ea	355.00	17.30	—	372.30
20 gallon						
3 KW/220V	P1@.750	Ea	389.00	25.90	—	414.90
30 gallon						
3 KW/220V	P1@1.00	Ea	425.00	34.60	—	459.60
40 gallon						
3 KW/220V	P1@1.20	Ea	462.00	41.50	—	503.50
50 gallon						
3 KW/220V	P1@1.30	Ea	494.00	44.90	—	538.90

Electric domestic hot water heater, (commercial), 208/240 volt. Set in place only. Make additional allowances for pipe and electrical connections. (See below)

Description	Craft@Hrs	Unit	Material $	Labor $	Equipment $	Total $
96 gallon, 12 kw	P1@1.50	Ea	1,970.00	51.80	—	2,021.80
96 gallon, 18 kw	P1@1.50	Ea	2,670.00	51.80	—	2,721.80
96 gallon, 36 kw	P1@1.50	Ea	2,770.00	51.80	—	2,821.80
120 gallon, 18 kw	P1@2.00	Ea	2,840.00	69.10	—	2,909.10
120 gallon, 36 kw	P1@2.00	Ea	2,920.00	69.10	—	2,989.10
120 gallon, 54 kw	P1@2.00	Ea	3,470.00	69.10	—	3,539.10
120 gallon, 63 kw	P1@2.00	Ea	3,740.00	69.10	—	3,809.10

Gas-fired domestic hot water heater, (residential). Set in place only, Make additional allowances for pipe and combustion venting connections. (See below)

Description	Craft@Hrs	Unit	Material $	Labor $	Equipment $	Total $
30 gallon	P1@1.00	Ea	415.00	34.60	—	449.60
40 gallon	P1@1.00	Ea	672.00	34.60	—	706.60
50 gallon	P1@1.50	Ea	762.00	51.80	—	813.80

Domestic Hot Water Heaters

Description	Craft@Hrs	Unit	Material $	Labor $	Equipment $	Total $

Gas-fired domestic hot water heater, (commercial), standard efficiency. Set in place only, Make additional allowances for pipe and combustion venting connections. (See below)

Description	Craft@Hrs	Unit	Material $	Labor $	Equipment $	Total $
50 gal./95 gph	P1@2.00	Ea	1,860.00	69.10	—	1,929.10
67 gal./106 gph	P1@2.00	Ea	2,200.00	69.10	—	2,269.10
76 gal./175 gph	P1@2.00	Ea	2,950.00	69.10	—	3,019.10
91 gal./291 gph	P1@2.00	Ea	3,550.00	69.10	—	3,619.10

Gas-fired domestic hot water heater, (commercial), energy miser. Set in place only, Make additional allowances for pipe and combustion venting connections. (See below)

Description	Craft@Hrs	Unit	Material $	Labor $	Equipment $	Total $
50 gal./95 gph	P1@2.00	Ea	4,380.00	69.10	—	4,449.10
67 gal./106 gph	P1@2.00	Ea	4,580.00	69.10	—	4,649.10
76 gal./175 gph	P1@2.00	Ea	5,680.00	69.10	—	5,749.10
91 gal./291 gph	P1@2.00	Ea	6,740.00	69.10	—	6,809.10

Tankless natural gas water heaters. Ambient pressure. DOE and UL rated. For residential, multi-dwelling and light commercial potable water applications. Add the cost of piping, tempering valve, circulating pump, controls, and electrical connection, post-installation inspection by both the fire marshal and the mechanical inspector to validate federal, state and local energy tax credits or energy tax credit offsets. For larger arrays (laundries, institutional facilities, food processing plants), develop an estimate based on the required capacity and multiply these costs by the number of heaters required. Rated in Btu's and gallons per minute capacity. (1 Mbh = 1,000 Btu's)

Description	Craft@Hrs	Unit	Material $	Labor $	Equipment $	Total $
19.5–140 Mbh, .75–5.8 Gpm	P1@16.0	Ea	1,520.00	553.00	—	2,073.00
11-199 Mbh, .5-7 Gpm	P1@20.0	Ea	1,790.00	691.00	—	2,481.00
25-235 Mbh .75-9.6 Gpm	P1@20.0	Ea	1,790.00	691.00	—	2,481.00

Tankless electric point-of-use water heaters. Ambient pressure, DOE and UL rated. For residential, multi-dwelling and light commercial potable water applications. Cost does not include piping, tempering valve, circulating pump, controls, storage tank, electrical connection. Add the cost of post-installation inspection by the mechanical inspector to validate federal, state and local energy tax credits or energy tax credit offsets. In rated gallons per minute capacity.

Description	Craft@Hrs	Unit	Material $	Labor $	Equipment $	Total $
5.5 Kw/40 Amp, .75-2 Gpm	P1@4.00	Ea	353.00	138.00	—	491.00
9.5 Kw/50 Amp .75-2.5 Gpm	P1@4.25	Ea	419.00	147.00	—	566.00
19 Kw/100 Amp 1-3.5 Gpm	P1@4.50	Ea	695.00	155.00	—	850.00
28 Kw/120 Amp 1.5-5 Gpm	P1@4.75	Ea	1,270.00	164.00	—	1,434.00

Description	Craft@Hrs	Unit	Material $	Labor $	Equipment $	Total $

Domestic hot water heater connection assembly. Includes supply, return, recirculation and relief piping and fittings (copper), relief and isolation valves. Make additional allowances for gas and venting connections where applicable.

Description	Craft@Hrs	Unit	Material $	Labor $	Equipment $	Total $
3/4" residential	P1@1.75	Ea	308.00	60.50	—	368.50
3/4" commercial	P1@2.25	Ea	414.00	77.70	—	491.70
1" commercial	P1@2.75	Ea	726.00	95.00	—	821.00
1¼" commercial	P1@3.50	Ea	890.00	121.00	—	1,011.00
1½" commercial	P1@3.75	Ea	925.00	130.00	—	1,055.00
2" commercial	P1@4.50	Ea	989.00	155.00	—	1,144.00
2½" commercial	P1@5.75	Ea	2,060.00	199.00	—	2,259.00
3" commercial	P1@6.50	Ea	3,150.00	225.00	—	3,375.00

Domestic water heater combustion vent connection. Make additional allowances for piping distances greater than 25'.

Description	Craft@Hrs	Unit	Material $	Labor $	Equipment $	Total $
2" b-vent	P1@.090	LF	5.25	3.11	—	8.36
3" b-vent	P1@.100	LF	6.50	3.46	—	9.96
4" b-vent	P1@.110	LF	8.65	3.80	—	12.45
6" b-vent	P1@.130	LF	9.85	4.49	—	14.34
Tankless Heater						
Vent kit	P1@2.50	Ea	369.00	86.40	—	455.40
Power vent kit	P1@2.00	Ea	943.00	69.10	—	1,012.10

Water Softener Controllers

Description	Craft@Hrs	Unit	Material $	Labor $	Equipment $	Total $

Water softener, time clock controller. Including brine tank, brine well and pick up tube. Labor includes setting in place, connecting the unit to an existing domestic water distribution system, start up and testing.

Description	Craft@Hrs	Unit	Material $	Labor $	Equipment $	Total $
20,000 grain water softener, TCC	P1@4.50	Ea	505.00	155.00	—	660.00
30,000 grain water softener, TCC	P1@4.50	Ea	538.00	155.00	—	693.00
45,000 grain water softener, TCC	P1@4.50	Ea	598.00	155.00	—	753.00
50,000 grain water softener, TCC	P1@4.75	Ea	675.00	164.00	—	839.00
60,000 grain water softener, TCC	P1@4.75	Ea	797.00	164.00	—	961.00
75,000 grain water softener, TCC	P1@5.00	Ea	855.00	173.00	—	1,028.00
90,000 grain water softener, TCC	P1@5.50	Ea	1,155.00	190.00	—	1,345.00
120,000 grain water softener, TCC	P1@5.75	Ea	1,245.00	199.00	—	1,444.00

Water softener, mechanically metered controller. Including brine tank, brine well and pick up tube. Labor includes setting in place, connecting the unit to an existing domestic water distribution system, start up and testing.

Description	Craft@Hrs	Unit	Material $	Labor $	Equipment $	Total $
20,000 grain water softener, MMC	P1@4.50	Ea	655.00	155.00	—	810.00
30,000 grain water softener, MMC	P1@4.50	Ea	683.00	155.00	—	838.00
45,000 grain water softener, MMC	P1@4.50	Ea	744.00	155.00	—	899.00
50,000 grain water softener, MMC	P1@4.75	Ea	820.00	164.00	—	984.00
60,000 grain water softener, MMC	P1@4.75	Ea	958.00	164.00	—	1,122.00
75,000 grain water softener, MMC	P1@5.00	Ea	1,015.00	173.00	—	1,188.00
90,000 grain water softener, MMC	P1@5.50	Ea	1,315.00	190.00	—	1,505.00
120,000 grain water softener, MMC	P1@5.75	Ea	1,406.00	199.00	—	1,605.00

Description	Craft@Hrs	Unit	Material $	Labor $	Equipment $	Total $

Water softener, electronically metered controller. Including brine tank, brine well and pick up tube. Labor includes setting in place, connecting the unit to an existing domestic water distribution system, start up and testing.

Description	Craft@Hrs	Unit	Material $	Labor $	Equipment $	Total $
20,000 grain water softener, EMC	P1@4.50	Ea	695.00	155.00	—	850.00
30,000 grain water softener, EMC	P1@4.50	Ea	715.00	155.00	—	870.00
45,000 grain water softener, EMC	P1@4.50	Ea	785.00	155.00	—	940.00
50,000 grain water softener, EMC	P1@4.75	Ea	860.00	164.00	—	1,024.00
60,000 grain water softener, EMC	P1@4.75	Ea	998.00	164.00	—	1,162.00
75,000 grain water softener, EMC	P1@5.00	Ea	1,055.00	173.00	—	1,228.00
90,000 grain water softener, EMC	P1@5.50	Ea	1,354.00	190.00	—	1,544.00
120,000 grain water softener, EMC	P1@5.75	Ea	1,446.00	199.00	—	1,645.00

Water softener accessories

Description	Craft@Hrs	Unit	Material $	Labor $	Equipment $	Total $
By-pass valve Manifold	P1@.400	Ea	67.00	13.80	—	80.80
Adapter kit	P1@.200	Ea	18.00	6.91	—	24.91
Turbulator	P1@.400	Ea	33.00	13.80	—	46.80

Iron filter, electronically meter controller. Manganese green sand filter. Labor includes setting in place, connecting the unit to an existing domestic water distribution system, start up and testing.

Description	Craft@Hrs	Unit	Material $	Labor $	Equipment $	Total $
42,000 Iron filter, (1.5 cf media), 5 gpm,	P1@4.00	Ea	657.00	138.00	—	795.00
65,000 Iron filter, (2.0 cf media), 6 gpm	P1@4.50	Ea	777.00	155.00	—	932.00
84,000 Iron filter, (2.5 cf media), 8 gpm	P1@4.75	Ea	830.00	164.00	—	994.00
Replacement green sand media	P1@1.20	CF	38.00	41.50	—	79.50

Iron filter accessories

Description	Craft@Hrs	Unit	Material $	Labor $	Equipment $	Total $
By-pass valve	P1@.400	Ea	67.00	13.80	—	80.80
Air vent	P1@.200	Ea	53.00	6.91	—	59.91
Air controller	P1@.400	Ea	60.00	13.80	—	73.80

Water Softener Accessories

Description	Craft@Hrs	Unit	Material $	Labor $	Equipment $	Total $

Combination iron filter/water softener. Zeolite resins soften water and remove iron and manganese. Controller automatically controls PH level. Labor includes setting in place, connecting the unit to an existing domestic water distribution system, start up and testing.

Description	Craft@Hrs	Unit	Material $	Labor $	Equipment $	Total $
40,000 Iron filter, 1.3 cf media,	P1@4.00	Ea	1,270.00	138.00	—	1,408.00
60,000 Iron filter, 1.7 cf media,	P1@4.50	Ea	1,375.00	155.00	—	1,530.00
80,000 Iron filter, 2.5 cf media,	P1@4.75	Ea	1,995.00	164.00	—	2,159.00

Hot water softener, time clock controller. Brass valve construction. Designed for 150 F. maximum operating temperature. Includes brine tank, brine well and pick up tube. Labor includes setting in place, connecting the unit to an existing domestic water distribution system, start up and testing.

Description	Craft@Hrs	Unit	Material $	Labor $	Equipment $	Total $
20,000 grain hot water softener,	P1@4.50	Ea	1,595.00	155.00	—	1,750.00
30,000 grain hot water softener,	P1@4.50	Ea	1,695.00	155.00	—	1,850.00
40,000 grain hot water softener,	P1@4.50	Ea	1,760.00	155.00	—	1,915.00
60,000 grain hot water softener,	P1@4.75	Ea	2,088.00	164.00	—	2,252.00

Pressure tank, fiberglass wound. Labor includes setting in place, connecting the tank to a domestic water distribution system and testing.

Description	Craft@Hrs	Unit	Material $	Labor $	Equipment $	Total $
Fiberglass pressure tank, 20 gallon	P1@2.00	Ea	249.00	69.10	—	318.10
Fiberglass pressure tank, 30 gallon	P1@2.00	Ea	280.00	69.10	—	349.10
Fiberglass pressure tank, 80 gallon	P1@2.75	Ea	455.00	95.00	—	550.00
Fiberglass pressure tank, 120 gallon	P1@3.50	Ea	600.00	121.00	—	721.00
Brass tank tee assembly, 3/4"	P1@3.50	Ea	30.00	121.00	—	151.00
Brass tank tee assembly, 1"	P1@3.50	Ea	56.00	121.00	—	177.00
Brass tank tee assembly, 1-1/4"	P1@3.50	Ea	96.00	121.00	—	217.00

Description	Craft@Hrs	Unit	Material $	Labor $	Equipment $	Total $

Ultra-violet water disinfection unit. Stainless steel reactor, audible and visible alarm, lamp end-of-life indicator and 7 day override. Gpm rating at 30,000 mj/m2 output. Labor includes setting in place, connecting to the water system and testing.

Description	Craft@Hrs	Unit	Material $	Labor $	Equipment $	Total $
UV system, 1 gpm, 1/4" in/out,	P1@3.00	Ea	191.00	104.00	—	295.00
UV system, 6 gpm, 1/2" in/out,	P1@3.00	Ea	370.00	104.00	—	474.00
UV system, 8 gpm, 3/4" in/out,	P1@4.00	Ea	429.00	138.00	—	567.00
UV system, 12 gpm, 3/4" in/out,	P1@4.00	Ea	548.00	138.00	—	686.00
UV replacement lamp, 20W, 1 gpm	P1@.750	Ea	42.60	25.90	—	68.50
UV replacement lamp, 32W, 6 gpm	P1@.750	Ea	48.20	25.90	—	74.10
UV replacement lamp, 39W, 8-12 gpm	P1@.750	Ea	61.70	25.90	—	87.60
UV replacement ballast, 420 Mv/110V	P1@1.00	Ea	187.00	34.60	—	221.60

Kitchen equipment booster heater

Description	Craft@Hrs	Unit	Material $	Labor $	Equipment $	Total $
1,000 watt	P1@4.00	Ea	526.00	138.00	—	664.00

Dishwasher

Description	Craft@Hrs	Unit	Material $	Labor $	Equipment $	Total $
Built-in	P1@5.00	Ea	765.00	173.00	—	938.00

Garbage disposal

Description	Craft@Hrs	Unit	Material $	Labor $	Equipment $	Total $
1/2 HP	P1@2.00	Ea	160.00	69.10	—	229.10
3/4 HP	P1@2.00	Ea	271.00	69.10	—	340.10

Grease and oil interceptor

Description	Craft@Hrs	Unit	Material $	Labor $	Equipment $	Total $
4 GPM	P1@4.00	Ea	318.00	138.00	—	456.00
10 GPM	P1@5.00	Ea	519.00	173.00	—	692.00
15 GPM	P1@7.00	Ea	774.00	242.00	—	1,016.00
20 GPM	P1@8.00	Ea	937.00	276.00	—	1,213.00

Hair and lint interceptor

Description	Craft@Hrs	Unit	Material $	Labor $	Equipment $	Total $
1½"	P1@.650	Ea	200.00	22.50	—	222.50
2"	P1@.750	Ea	284.00	25.90	—	309.90

All bronze 3/4" to 1-1/2" in-line NPT pump

Description	Craft@Hrs	Unit	Material $	Labor $	Equipment $	Total $
1/12 HP	P1@1.50	Ea	489.00	51.80	—	540.80
1/6 HP	P1@1.50	Ea	730.00	51.80	—	781.80
1/4 HP	P1@1.50	Ea	855.00	51.80	—	906.80

Kitchen Equipment Connections

Description	Craft@Hrs	Unit	Material $	Labor $	Equipment $	Total $
Kitchen appliance gas trim						
1/2"	P1@1.15	Ea	34.50	39.70	—	74.20
3/4"	P1@1.30	Ea	63.00	44.90	—	107.90
1"	P1@1.60	Ea	73.00	55.30	—	128.30
1¼"	P1@2.10	Ea	120.00	72.60	—	192.60
1½"	P1@2.50	Ea	152.00	86.40	—	238.40
2"	P1@3.00	Ea	204.00	104.00	—	308.00
Hot and cold water supply						
1/2"	P1@1.10	Ea	36.70	38.00	—	74.70
3/4"	P1@1.55	Ea	52.00	53.60	—	105.60
1"	P1@1.90	Ea	70.70	65.60	—	136.30
1¼"	P1@2.50	Ea	99.70	86.40	—	186.10
1½"	P1@3.00	Ea	125.00	104.00	—	229.00
Continuous waste						
2-part	P1@.250	Ea	52.20	8.64	—	60.84
3-part	P1@.350	Ea	87.80	12.10	—	99.90
4-part	P1@.450	Ea	114.00	15.50	—	129.50
Indirect waste						
1/2"	P1@1.05	Ea	10.10	36.30	—	46.40
3/4"	P1@1.50	Ea	17.00	51.80	—	68.80
1"	P1@1.90	Ea	27.40	65.60	—	93.00
1¼"	P1@2.15	Ea	40.60	74.30	—	114.90
1½"	P1@2.60	Ea	53.40	89.80	—	143.20
2"	P1@3.00	Ea	81.80	104.00	—	185.80
Kitchen fixture waste tailpiece						
1½"	P1@.100	Ea	11.70	3.46	—	15.16
Kitchen fixture trap with solder bushing						
1½"	P1@.250	Ea	39.20	8.64	—	47.84
2"	P1@.300	Ea	54.60	10.40	—	65.00

Description	Craft@Hrs	Unit	Material $	Labor $	Equipment $	Total $

Water closet, floor mounted, flush tank, white vitreous china, lined tank. Complete with trim. Make additional allowances for rough-in. Based on American Standard Cadet series. ADA means American Disabilities Act compliant. (Wheelchair accessible)

Description	Craft@Hrs	Unit	Material $	Labor $	Equipment $	Total $
Round bowl	P1@2.10	Ea	234.00	72.60	—	306.60
Elongated bowl	P1@2.10	Ea	283.00	72.60	—	355.60
ADA, 18" high	P1@2.10	Ea	384.00	72.60	—	456.60

Water closet, floor mounted, flush valve, white vitreous china. Complete with trim. Make additional allowances for rough-in. Based on American Standard. ADA means American Disabilities Act compliant. (Wheelchair accessible)

Description	Craft@Hrs	Unit	Material $	Labor $	Equipment $	Total $
Elongated bowl	P1@2.60	Ea	365.00	89.80	—	454.80
Elongated bowl, ADA 18" high	P1@2.60	Ea	435.00	89.80	—	524.80
Elongated bowl with a bedpan cleanser	P1@4.10	Ea	634.00	142.00	—	776.00
Elongated bowl, ADA 18" high with a bedpan cleanser	P1@4.10	Ea	685.00	142.00	—	827.00

Water closet, wall hung, flush valve, white vitreous china. Complete with fixture carrier and all trim. Make additional allowances for rough-in. Based on American Standard Afwall series.

Description	Craft@Hrs	Unit	Material $	Labor $	Equipment $	Total $
Elongated bowl	P1@3.55	Ea	583.00	123.00	—	706.00
Elongated bowl with electronic flush valve	P1@3.80	Ea	1,040.00	131.00	—	1,171.00
Elongated bowl with bedpan cleanser	P1@5.05	Ea	842.00	174.00	—	1,016.00
Electronic flush valve, add	P1@.600	Ea	458.00	20.70	—	478.70

Urinal, wall hung, flush valve, white vitreous china. Complete with trim. Make additional allowances for rough-in.

Description	Craft@Hrs	Unit	Material $	Labor $	Equipment $	Total $
Siphon jet type	P1@3.15	Ea	583.00	109.00	—	692.00
Wash out type	P1@3.10	Ea	475.00	107.00	—	582.00
Wash down type	P1@3.00	Ea	335.00	104.00	—	439.00
Urinal carrier, add	P1@.600	Ea	108.00	20.70	—	128.70
Electronic flush valve, add	P1@.600	Ea	378.00	20.70	—	398.70

Urinal, stall type, flush valve, white vitreous china. Complete with trim. Make additional allowances for rough-in.

Description	Craft@Hrs	Unit	Material $	Labor $	Equipment $	Total $
Stall urinal	P1@5.00	Ea	1,140.00	173.00	—	1,313.00

Description	Craft@Hrs	Unit	Material $	Labor $	Equipment $	Total $

Lavatory, wall hung, white vitreous china. Complete with trim and fixture carrier. Make additional allowances for rough-in. ADA means American Disabilities Act compliant. (Wheelchair accessible)

Description	Craft@Hrs	Unit	Material $	Labor $	Equipment $	Total $
Wall hung lav	P1@2.70	Ea	485.00	93.30	—	578.30
Wall hung, ADA	P1@2.70	Ea	708.00	93.30	—	801.30
Fixture carrier	P1@.500	Ea	100.00	17.30	—	117.30

Countertop lavatory, white. Complete with trim. Make additional allowances for rough-in.

Description	Craft@Hrs	Unit	Material $	Labor $	Equipment $	Total $
Vitreous china	P1@2.00	Ea	359.00	69.10	—	428.10
Enameled steel	P1@2.00	Ea	303.00	69.10	—	372.10
Acrylic	P1@2.00	Ea	221.00	69.10	—	290.10

Bathtub, white, 60" x 32". Complete with trim, including shower head. Make additional allowances for rough-in.

Description	Craft@Hrs	Unit	Material $	Labor $	Equipment $	Total $
Enameled steel	P1@2.50	Ea	506.00	86.40	—	592.40
Cast iron	P1@3.50	Ea	732.00	121.00	—	853.00
Fiberglass	P1@2.50	Ea	468.00	86.40	—	554.40
Acrylic	P1@2.50	Ea	500.00	86.40	—	586.40

Tub and shower combination, fiberglass, white. Complete with trim. Make additional allowances for rough-in.

Description	Craft@Hrs	Unit	Material $	Labor $	Equipment $	Total $
One piece	P1@4.50	Ea	1,040.00	155.00	—	1,195.00
Two piece (reno)	P1@5.50	Ea	1,330.00	190.00	—	1,520.00
Four piece (reno)	P1@6.25	Ea	1,420.00	216.00	—	1,636.00

Shower stall, white, 36" x 36". Complete with trim. Make additional allowances for rough-in.

Description	Craft@Hrs	Unit	Material $	Labor $	Equipment $	Total $
Fiberglass One piece	P1@3.50	Ea	649.00	121.00	—	770.00
Fiberglass Three piece	P1@4.25	Ea	834.00	147.00	—	981.00
Acrylic One piece	P1@3.50	Ea	967.00	121.00	—	1,088.00
Acrylic Three piece	P1@4.25	Ea	1,260.00	147.00	—	1,407.00

Shower basin, 36" x 36". Complete with trim (faucet, shower head and strainer). Make additional allowances for rough-in.

Description	Craft@Hrs	Unit	Material $	Labor $	Equipment $	Total $
Fiberglass	P1@2.50	Ea	441.00	86.40	—	527.40
Acrylic	P1@2.50	Ea	475.00	86.40	—	561.40
Molded stone	P1@2.65	Ea	458.00	91.60	—	549.60

Description	Craft@Hrs	Unit	Material $	Labor $	Equipment $	Total $

Kitchen sink, double compartment. Complete with trim. Make additional allowances for rough-in.

Description	Craft@Hrs	Unit	Material $	Labor $	Equipment $	Total $
Stainless steel	P1@2.15	Ea	357.00	74.30	—	431.30
Cast iron	P1@2.50	Ea	468.00	86.40	—	554.40
Acrylic	P1@2.15	Ea	424.00	74.30	—	498.30

Kitchen sink, single compartment. Complete with trim. Make additional allowances for rough-in.

Description	Craft@Hrs	Unit	Material $	Labor $	Equipment $	Total $
Stainless steel	P1@2.00	Ea	302.00	69.10	—	371.10
Cast iron	P1@2.10	Ea	349.00	72.60	—	421.60
Acrylic	P1@2.00	Ea	315.00	69.10	—	384.10

Bar sink. Complete with trim. Make additional allowances for rough-in.

Description	Craft@Hrs	Unit	Material $	Labor $	Equipment $	Total $
Stainless steel	P1@2.00	Ea	271.00	69.10	—	340.10
Acrylic	P1@2.00	Ea	183.00	69.10	—	252.10

Exam room sink. Complete with trim. Make additional allowances for rough-in.

Description	Craft@Hrs	Unit	Material $	Labor $	Equipment $	Total $
Stainless steel	P1@2.10	Ea	392.00	72.60	—	464.60
Acrylic	P1@2.10	Ea	335.00	72.60	—	407.60

Laboratory sink. Complete with trim. Make additional allowances for rough-in.

Description	Craft@Hrs	Unit	Material $	Labor $	Equipment $	Total $
Stainless steel	P1@2.25	Ea	450.00	77.70	—	527.70
Acrylic	P1@2.25	Ea	392.00	77.70	—	469.70

Laundry sink, double compartment. Complete with trim. Make additional allowances for rough-in.

Description	Craft@Hrs	Unit	Material $	Labor $	Equipment $	Total $
Cast iron	P1@3.50	Ea	525.00	121.00	—	646.00
Acrylic	P1@2.25	Ea	231.00	77.70	—	308.70

Laundry sink, single compartment. Complete with trim. Make additional allowances for rough-in.

Description	Craft@Hrs	Unit	Material $	Labor $	Equipment $	Total $
Cast iron	P1@2.75	Ea	455.00	95.00	—	550.00
Acrylic	P1@2.00	Ea	160.00	69.10	—	229.10

Mop sink, floor mounted, 36" x 24". Complete with trim. Make additional allowances for rough-in.

Description	Craft@Hrs	Unit	Material $	Labor $	Equipment $	Total $
Molded stone	P1@2.65	Ea	642.00	91.60	—	733.60
Terrazzo	P1@2.65	Ea	707.00	91.60	—	798.60
Acrylic	P1@2.35	Ea	493.00	81.20	—	574.20

Plumbing Fixtures

Description	Craft@Hrs	Unit	Material $	Labor $	Equipment $	Total $

Slop sink, enameled cast iron with P trap, standard. Complete with trim. Make additional allowances for rough-in.

Description	Craft@Hrs	Unit	Material $	Labor $	Equipment $	Total $
Slop sink with P trap, Std.	P1@3.50	Ea	1,050.00	121.00	—	1,171.00

Floor sink, recessed, enameled steel, white. Add 40% to material prices for acid-resisting finish. Complete with strainer. Make additional allowances for rough-in.

Description	Craft@Hrs	Unit	Material $	Labor $	Equipment $	Total $
9" x 9"	P1@1.00	Ea	90.20	34.60	—	124.80
12" x 12"	P1@1.00	Ea	105.00	34.60	—	139.60
15" x 15"	P1@1.15	Ea	71.50	39.70	—	111.20
18" x 18"	P1@1.25	Ea	93.20	43.20	—	136.40
24" x 24"	P1@1.50	Ea	126.00	51.80	—	177.80

Drinking fountain, refrigerated, stainless steel. Complete with trim. Make additional allowances for rough-in. ADA means American Disabilities Act compliant. (Wheelchair accessible)

Description	Craft@Hrs	Unit	Material $	Labor $	Equipment $	Total $
Free standing	P1@2.00	Ea	1,140.00	69.10	—	1,209.10
Semi recessed	P1@2.50	Ea	1,500.00	86.40	—	1,586.40
Fully recessed	P1@2.50	Ea	2,590.00	86.40	—	2,676.40
Wall hung	P1@2.00	Ea	1,060.00	69.10	—	1,129.10
Wall hung, ADA	P1@2.50	Ea	2,590.00	86.40	—	2,676.40

Drinking fountain, non-refrigerated. Complete with trim. Make additional allowances for rough-in. ADA means American Disabilities Act compliant. (Wheelchair accessible) S.S. means stainless steel.

Description	Craft@Hrs	Unit	Material $	Labor $	Equipment $	Total $
Recessed, china	P1@2.50	Ea	871.00	86.40	—	957.40
Wall hung, china	P1@2.00	Ea	496.00	69.10	—	565.10
Recessed, S.S.	P1@2.50	Ea	989.00	86.40	—	1,075.40
Wall hung, S.S.	P1@2.00	Ea	528.00	69.10	—	597.10
ADA, S.S.	P1@2.50	Ea	910.00	86.40	—	996.40

Description	Craft@Hrs	Unit	Material $	Labor $	Equipment $	Total $

Commercial plumbing fixture rough-in. Includes type L copper supply pipe and DWV copper (to 2½") or cast iron (MJ) DWV (over 2½") drain and vent piping. Make additional allowances for plumbing fixtures and trim. Use these costs for preliminary estimates.

Description	Craft@Hrs	Unit	Material $	Labor $	Equipment $	Total $
Water closet, wall hung, flush valve, with carrier	P1@2.25	Ea	883.00	77.70	—	960.70
Water closet, wall hung, flush valve, no carrier	P1@1.95	Ea	321.00	67.40	—	388.40
Water closet, floor mounted, flush valve	P1@2.75	Ea	714.00	95.00	—	809.00
Water closet, floor mounted, tank type	P1@2.25	Ea	547.00	77.70	—	624.70
Bidet	P1@2.00	Ea	381.00	69.10	—	450.10
Urinal, wall hung, flush valve, with carrier	P1@3.10	Ea	960.00	107.00	—	1,067.00
Urinal, wall hung, flush valve, without carrier	P1@2.35	Ea	547.00	81.20	—	628.20
Lavatory, wall hung, with carrier	P1@2.40	Ea	792.00	82.90	—	874.90
Lavatory	P1@1.90	Ea	381.00	65.60	—	446.60
Sink	P1@1.90	Ea	411.00	65.60	—	476.60
Bath tub	P1@2.35	Ea	587.00	81.20	—	668.20
Shower	P1@2.60	Ea	688.00	89.80	—	777.80
Mop sink	P1@2.40	Ea	487.00	82.90	—	569.90
Slop sink	P1@2.60	Ea	349.00	89.80	—	438.80
Laundry tub	P1@1.95	Ea	414.00	67.40	—	481.40
Wash fountain	P1@2.10	Ea	447.00	72.60	—	519.60
Lab sink, glass drainage	P1@3.80	Ea	1,760.00	131.00	—	1,891.00
Lab sink, acid resistant plastic drainage	P1@2.65	Ea	279.00	91.60	—	370.60
Drinking fountain	P1@2.20	Ea	303.00	76.00	—	379.00
Emergency eyewash and shower	P1@1.75	Ea	115.00	60.50	—	175.50
Washing machine	P1@2.25	Ea	444.00	77.70	—	521.70

Description	Craft@Hrs	Unit	Material $	Labor $	Equipment $	Total $

Commercial plumbing fixture group rough-in. Includes type L copper supply pipe and DWV copper (to 2½") or cast iron (MJ) DWV (over 2½") drain and vent piping. Make additional allowances for plumbing fixtures and trim. Use these costs for preliminary estimates.

Description	Craft@Hrs	Unit	Material $	Labor $	Equipment $	Total $
3 piece washroom group	P1@5.50	Ea	1,090.00	190.00	—	1,280.00
3 piece washroom group back to back	P1@9.75	Ea	1,990.00	337.00	—	2,327.00
Kitchen sink, back to back	P1@2.15	Ea	583.00	74.30	—	657.30
Battery of water closets, floor mounted, tank type, per water closet	P1@1.75	Ea	454.00	60.50	—	514.50
Battery of water closets, floor mounted, flush valve, per water closet	P1@2.20	Ea	593.00	76.00	—	669.00
Battery of water closets, wall hung, flush valve, with carrier, per water closet	P1@1.80	Ea	781.00	62.20	—	843.20
Battery of water closets, wall hung, flush valve, without carrier, per water closet	P1@1.50	Ea	229.00	51.80	—	280.80
Battery of urinals, wall hung, flush valve with carrier, per urinal	P1@2.45	Ea	938.00	84.60	—	1,022.60
Battery of urinals, wall hung, flush valve without carrier, per urinal	P1@1.90	Ea	484.00	65.60	—	549.60
Battery of lavatory basins, wall hung, with carrier, per lavatory	P1@2.00	Ea	729.00	69.10	—	798.10
Battery of lavatory basins, without carrier, per lavatory	P1@1.50	Ea	330.00	51.80	—	381.80

Residential plumbing fixture rough-in. Includes polyethylene (PE) supply pipe and ABS DWV drain and vent piping. Make additional allowances for plumbing fixtures and trim. Use these costs for preliminary estimates.

Description	Craft@Hrs	Unit	Material $	Labor $	Equipment $	Total $
Water closet, floor mounted, tank type	P1@2.00	Ea	126.00	69.10	—	195.10
Bidet	P1@1.85	Ea	94.70	63.90	—	158.60
Lavatory	P1@1.75	Ea	94.70	60.50	—	155.20
Counter sink	P1@1.75	Ea	104.00	60.50	—	164.50
Bathtub	P1@2.10	Ea	94.70	72.60	—	167.30
Shower	P1@2.45	Ea	138.00	84.60	—	222.60
Laundry tub	P1@1.75	Ea	86.20	60.50	—	146.70
Washing machine	P1@2.00	Ea	107.00	69.10	—	176.10

Copper, Type K with Brazed Joints

Type K hard-drawn copper pipe with wrought copper fittings and brazed joints is used in a wide variety of plumbing and HVAC systems such as potable water, heating hot water, chilled water, compressed air, refrigerant and A.C. condensate.

Brazed joints are those made with silver or other alloy filler metals having melting points at, or above, 1,000 degrees F. Maximum working pressure/temperature relationships for brazed joints are approximately as follows:

Maximum Working Pressure (PSIG)*			
Water Temperature	Nominal Pipe Size (inches)		
(degrees F.)	Up to 1	1¼ to 2	2½ to 4
Up to 350	270	190	150

*For copper pipe and solder-type fittings using brazing alloys
melting at, or above 1,000 degrees F.

This section has been arranged to save the estimator's time by including all normally-used system components such as pipe, fittings, valves, hanger assemblies, riser clamps and miscellaneous items under one heading. Additional items can be found under "Plumbing and Piping Specialties." The cost estimates in this section are based on the conditions, limitations and wage rates described in the section "How to Use This Book" beginning on page 5.

Description	Craft@Hrs	Unit	Material $	Labor $	Equipment $	Total $

Type K copper pipe with brazed joints, installed horizontally. Complete installation including six to twelve wrought copper tees and six to twelve wrought copper elbows every 100', and hangers spaced to meet plumbing code (a tee & elbow every 8.3' for ½" dia., a tee and elbow every 16.6' for 4" dia.).

Description	Craft@Hrs	Unit	Material $	Labor $	Equipment $	Total $
1/2"	P1@.117	LF	3.58	4.04	—	7.62
3/4"	P1@.127	LF	6.27	4.39	—	10.66
1"	P1@.147	LF	10.00	5.08	—	15.08
1¼"	P1@.167	LF	13.70	5.77	—	19.47
1½"	P1@.187	LF	16.80	6.46	—	23.26
2"	P1@.217	LF	28.60	7.50	—	36.10
2½"	P1@.247	LF	47.00	8.53	—	55.53
3"	P1@.277	LF	54.20	9.57	—	63.77
4"	P1@.317	LF	99.20	11.00	—	110.20

Copper, Type K with Brazed Joints

Description	Craft@Hrs	Unit	Material $	Labor $	Equipment $	Total $

Type K copper pipe with brazed joints, installed risers. Complete installation including a wrought copper reducing tee every floor and a riser clamp every other floor.

1/2"	P1@.064	LF	3.23	2.21	—	5.44
3/4"	P1@.074	LF	5.83	2.56	—	8.39
1"	P1@.079	LF	8.90	2.73	—	11.63
1¼"	P1@.084	LF	12.30	2.90	—	15.20
1½"	P1@.104	LF	14.50	3.59	—	18.09
2"	P1@.134	LF	24.80	4.63	—	29.43
2½"	P1@.154	LF	37.10	5.32	—	42.42
3"	P1@.174	LF	52.00	6.01	—	58.01
4"	P1@.194	LF	81.20	6.70	—	87.90

Type K copper pipe with brazed joints, pipe only

1/2"	P1@.032	LF	2.57	1.11	—	3.68
3/4"	P1@.035	LF	4.76	1.21	—	5.97
1"	P1@.038	LF	6.01	1.31	—	7.32
1¼"	P1@.042	LF	8.03	1.45	—	9.48
1½"	P1@.046	LF	8.75	1.59	—	10.34
2"	P1@.053	LF	15.60	1.83	—	17.43
2½"	P1@.060	LF	20.40	2.07	—	22.47
3"	P1@.066	LF	26.60	2.28	—	28.88
4"	P1@.080	LF	47.60	2.76	—	50.36

Type K copper 45 degree ell C x C with brazed joints

1/2"	P1@.129	Ea	1.04	4.46	—	5.50
3/4"	P1@.181	Ea	1.97	6.25	—	8.22
1"	P1@.232	Ea	5.82	8.02	—	13.84
1¼"	P1@.284	Ea	7.88	9.81	—	17.69
1½"	P1@.335	Ea	11.70	11.60	—	23.30
2"	P1@.447	Ea	19.20	15.40	—	34.60
2½"	P1@.550	Ea	49.00	19.00	—	68.00
3"	P1@.654	Ea	64.70	22.60	—	87.30
4"	P1@.860	Ea	125.00	29.70	—	154.70

Type K copper 90 degree ell C x C with brazed joints

1/2"	P1@.129	Ea	.60	4.46	—	5.06
3/4"	P1@.181	Ea	1.27	6.25	—	7.52
1"	P1@.232	Ea	4.42	8.02	—	12.44
1¼"	P1@.284	Ea	7.17	9.81	—	16.98
1½"	P1@.335	Ea	10.90	11.60	—	22.50
2"	P1@.447	Ea	19.50	15.40	—	34.90
2½"	P1@.550	Ea	40.50	19.00	—	59.50
3"	P1@.654	Ea	51.20	22.60	—	73.80
4"	P1@.860	Ea	109.00	29.70	—	138.70

Description	Craft@Hrs	Unit	Material $	Labor $	Equipment $	Total $

Type K copper 90 degree ell Ftg x C with brazed joints

Description	Craft@Hrs	Unit	Material $	Labor $	Equipment $	Total $
1/2"	P1@.129	Ea	1.27	4.46	—	5.73
3/4"	P1@.181	Ea	4.19	6.25	—	10.44
1"	P1@.232	Ea	6.28	8.02	—	14.30
1¼"	P1@.284	Ea	8.75	9.81	—	18.56
1½"	P1@.335	Ea	13.10	11.60	—	24.70
2"	P1@.447	Ea	26.30	15.40	—	41.70
2½"	P1@.550	Ea	55.10	19.00	—	74.10
3"	P1@.654	Ea	62.00	22.60	—	84.60
4"	P1@.860	Ea	167.00	29.70	—	196.70

Type K copper tee C x C x C with brazed joints

Description	Craft@Hrs	Unit	Material $	Labor $	Equipment $	Total $
1/2"	P1@.156	Ea	1.03	5.39	—	6.42
3/4"	P1@.204	Ea	2.77	7.05	—	9.82
1"	P1@.263	Ea	10.50	9.09	—	19.59
1¼"	P1@.322	Ea	16.60	11.10	—	27.70
1½"	P1@.380	Ea	24.20	13.10	—	37.30
2"	P1@.507	Ea	38.60	17.50	—	56.10
2½"	P1@.624	Ea	78.30	21.60	—	99.90
3"	P1@.741	Ea	121.00	25.60	—	146.60
4"	P1@.975	Ea	202.00	33.70	—	235.70

Copper, Type K with Brazed Joints

Description	Craft@Hrs	Unit	Material $	Labor $	Equipment $	Total $

Type K copper branch reducing tee C x C x C with brazed joints

Description	Craft@Hrs	Unit	Material $	Labor $	Equipment $	Total $
1/2" x 3/8"	P1@.129	Ea	2.08	4.46	—	6.54
3/4" x 1/2"	P1@.182	Ea	4.85	6.29	—	11.14
1" x 1/2"	P1@.209	Ea	12.30	7.22	—	19.52
1" x 3/4"	P1@.234	Ea	12.30	8.08	—	20.38
1¼" x 1/2"	P1@.241	Ea	18.80	8.33	—	27.13
1¼" x 3/4"	P1@.264	Ea	18.80	9.12	—	27.92
1¼" x 1"	P1@.287	Ea	18.80	9.92	—	28.72
1½" x 1/2"	P1@.291	Ea	22.90	10.10	—	33.00
1½" x 3/4"	P1@.307	Ea	22.90	10.60	—	33.50
1½" x 1"	P1@.323	Ea	22.90	11.20	—	34.10
1½" x 1¼"	P1@.339	Ea	22.90	11.70	—	34.60
2" x 1/2"	P1@.348	Ea	30.80	12.00	—	42.80
2" x 3/4"	P1@.373	Ea	30.80	12.90	—	43.70
2" x 1"	P1@.399	Ea	30.80	13.80	—	44.60
2" x 1¼"	P1@.426	Ea	30.80	14.70	—	45.50
2" x 1½"	P1@.452	Ea	30.80	15.60	—	46.40
2½" x 1/2"	P1@.468	Ea	92.20	16.20	—	108.40
2½" x 3/4"	P1@.485	Ea	92.20	16.80	—	109.00
2½" x 1"	P1@.502	Ea	92.20	17.30	—	109.50
2½" x 1½"	P1@.537	Ea	92.20	18.60	—	110.80
2½" x 2"	P1@.555	Ea	92.20	19.20	—	111.40
3" x 1¼"	P1@.562	Ea	105.00	19.40	—	124.40
3" x 2"	P1@.626	Ea	109.00	21.60	—	130.60
3" x 2½"	P1@.660	Ea	109.00	22.80	—	131.80
4" x 1¼"	P1@.669	Ea	189.00	23.10	—	212.10
4" x 1½"	P1@.718	Ea	189.00	24.80	—	213.80
4" x 2"	P1@.768	Ea	189.00	26.50	—	215.50
4" x 2½"	P1@.819	Ea	189.00	28.30	—	217.30
4" x 3"	P1@.868	Ea	189.00	30.00	—	219.00

Description	Craft@Hrs	Unit	Material $	Labor $	Equipment $	Total $

Type K copper reducer with brazed joints

Description	Craft@Hrs	Unit	Material $	Labor $	Equipment $	Total $
1/2" x 3/8"	P1@.148	Ea	.75	5.11	—	5.86
3/4" x 1/2"	P1@.155	Ea	1.54	5.36	—	6.90
1" x 3/4"	P1@.206	Ea	2.53	7.12	—	9.65
1¼" x 1/2"	P1@.206	Ea	4.25	7.12	—	11.37
1¼" x 3/4"	P1@.232	Ea	4.25	8.02	—	12.27
1¼" x 1"	P1@.258	Ea	4.25	8.91	—	13.16
1½" x 1/2"	P1@.232	Ea	6.50	8.02	—	14.52
1½" x 3/4"	P1@.257	Ea	6.50	8.88	—	15.38
1½" x 1"	P1@.283	Ea	6.50	9.78	—	16.28
1½" x 1¼"	P1@.308	Ea	6.50	10.60	—	17.10
2" x 1/2"	P1@.287	Ea	10.10	9.92	—	20.02
2" x 3/4"	P1@.277	Ea	10.10	9.57	—	19.67
2" x 1"	P1@.338	Ea	10.10	11.70	—	21.80
2" x 1¼"	P1@.365	Ea	10.10	12.60	—	22.70
2" x 1½"	P1@.390	Ea	10.10	13.50	—	23.60
2½" x 1"	P1@.390	Ea	27.50	13.50	—	41.00
2½" x 1¼"	P1@.416	Ea	27.50	14.40	—	41.90
2½" x 1½"	P1@.442	Ea	27.50	15.30	—	42.80
2½" x 2"	P1@.497	Ea	27.50	17.20	—	44.70
3" x 1¼"	P1@.468	Ea	32.10	16.20	—	48.30
3" x 1½"	P1@.493	Ea	32.10	17.00	—	49.10
3" x 2"	P1@.548	Ea	32.10	18.90	—	51.00
3" x 2½"	P1@.600	Ea	32.10	20.70	—	52.80
4" x 2"	P1@.652	Ea	62.00	22.50	—	84.50
4" x 2½"	P1@.704	Ea	62.00	24.30	—	86.30
4" x 3"	P1@.755	Ea	62.00	26.10	—	88.10

Type K copper adapter C x MPT

Description	Craft@Hrs	Unit	Material $	Labor $	Equipment $	Total $
1/2"	P1@.090	Ea	2.02	3.11	—	5.13
3/4"	P1@.126	Ea	2.89	4.35	—	7.24
1"	P1@.162	Ea	7.17	5.60	—	12.77
1¼"	P1@.198	Ea	13.40	6.84	—	20.24
1½"	P1@.234	Ea	15.00	8.08	—	23.08
2"	P1@.312	Ea	19.40	10.80	—	30.20
2½"	P1@.384	Ea	63.10	13.30	—	76.40
3"	P1@.456	Ea	105.00	15.80	—	120.80

Type K copper adapter C x FPT

Description	Craft@Hrs	Unit	Material $	Labor $	Equipment $	Total $
1/2"	P1@.090	Ea	3.08	3.11	—	6.19
3/4"	P1@.126	Ea	5.57	4.35	—	9.92
1"	P1@.162	Ea	8.43	5.60	—	14.03
1¼"	P1@.198	Ea	17.60	6.84	—	24.44
1½"	P1@.234	Ea	21.40	8.08	—	29.48
2"	P1@.312	Ea	32.90	10.80	—	43.70
2½"	P1@.384	Ea	82.70	13.30	—	96.00
3"	P1@.456	Ea	114.00	15.80	—	129.80

Copper, Type K with Brazed Joints

Description	Craft@Hrs	Unit	Material $	Labor $	Equipment $	Total $

Type K copper flush bushing with brazed joints

Description	Craft@Hrs	Unit	Material $	Labor $	Equipment $	Total $
1/2" x 3/8"	P1@.148	Ea	1.88	5.11	—	6.99
3/4" x 1/2"	P1@.155	Ea	3.19	5.36	—	8.55
1" x 3/4"	P1@.206	Ea	8.27	7.12	—	15.39
1" x 1/2"	P1@.206	Ea	9.45	7.12	—	16.57
1¼" x 1"	P1@.258	Ea	9.85	8.91	—	18.76
1½" x 1¼"	P1@.308	Ea	12.50	10.60	—	23.10
2" x 1½"	P1@.390	Ea	23.50	13.50	—	37.00

Type K copper union with brazed joints

Description	Craft@Hrs	Unit	Material $	Labor $	Equipment $	Total $
1/2"	P1@.146	Ea	7.50	5.04	—	12.54
3/4"	P1@.205	Ea	8.98	7.08	—	16.06
1"	P1@.263	Ea	20.10	9.09	—	29.19
1¼"	P1@.322	Ea	36.50	11.10	—	47.60
1½"	P1@.380	Ea	44.90	13.10	—	58.00
2"	P1@.507	Ea	67.00	17.50	—	84.50

Type K copper dielectric union with brazed joints

Description	Craft@Hrs	Unit	Material $	Labor $	Equipment $	Total $
1/2"	P1@.146	Ea	7.04	5.04	—	12.08
3/4"	P1@.205	Ea	7.04	7.08	—	14.12
1"	P1@.263	Ea	14.50	9.09	—	23.59
1¼"	P1@.322	Ea	24.80	11.10	—	35.90
1½"	P1@.380	Ea	34.10	13.10	—	47.20
2"	P1@.507	Ea	47.10	17.50	—	64.60

Type K copper pressure cap with brazed joints

Description	Craft@Hrs	Unit	Material $	Labor $	Equipment $	Total $
1/2"	P1@.083	Ea	.61	2.87	—	3.48
3/4"	P1@.116	Ea	1.25	4.01	—	5.26
1"	P1@.149	Ea	2.82	5.15	—	7.97
1¼"	P1@.182	Ea	4.05	6.29	—	10.34
1½"	P1@.215	Ea	5.91	7.43	—	13.34
2"	P1@.286	Ea	10.70	9.88	—	20.58
2½"	P1@.352	Ea	27.00	12.20	—	39.20
3"	P1@.418	Ea	42.20	14.40	—	56.60
4"	P1@.550	Ea	64.80	19.00	—	83.80

Type K copper coupling with brazed joints

Description	Craft@Hrs	Unit	Material $	Labor $	Equipment $	Total $
1/2"	P1@.129	Ea	.29	4.46	—	4.75
3/4"	P1@.181	Ea	.74	6.25	—	6.99
1"	P1@.232	Ea	2.67	8.02	—	10.69
1¼"	P1@.284	Ea	4.67	9.81	—	14.48
1½"	P1@.335	Ea	6.76	11.60	—	18.36
2"	P1@.447	Ea	10.30	15.40	—	25.70
2½"	P1@.550	Ea	24.20	19.00	—	43.20
3"	P1@.654	Ea	36.90	22.60	—	59.50
4"	P1@.860	Ea	72.30	29.70	—	102.00

Description	Craft@Hrs	Unit	Material $	Labor $	Equipment $	Total $

Class 125 bronze body gate valve, brazed joints

Description	Craft@Hrs	Unit	Material $	Labor $	Equipment $	Total $
1/2"	P1@.240	Ea	16.20	8.29	—	24.49
3/4"	P1@.300	Ea	20.30	10.40	—	30.70
1"	P1@.360	Ea	28.50	12.40	—	40.90
1¼"	P1@.480	Ea	36.00	16.60	—	52.60
1½"	P1@.540	Ea	48.40	18.70	—	67.10
2"	P1@.600	Ea	80.90	20.70	—	101.60
2½"	P1@1.00	Ea	134.00	34.60	—	168.60
3"	P1@1.50	Ea	193.00	51.80	—	244.80

Class 125 iron body gate valve, flanged joints

Description	Craft@Hrs	Unit	Material $	Labor $	Equipment $	Total $
2"	P1@.500	Ea	310.00	17.30	—	327.30
2½"	P1@.600	Ea	418.00	20.70	—	438.70
3"	P1@.750	Ea	454.00	25.90	—	479.90
4"	P1@1.35	Ea	666.00	46.60	—	712.60
5"	P1@2.00	Ea	1,270.00	69.10	—	1,339.10
6"	P1@2.50	Ea	1,270.00	86.40	—	1,356.40

Class 125 bronze body globe valve, with brazed joints

Description	Craft@Hrs	Unit	Material $	Labor $	Equipment $	Total $
1/2"	P1@.240	Ea	30.00	8.29	—	38.29
3/4"	P1@.300	Ea	40.00	10.40	—	50.40
1"	P1@.360	Ea	68.90	12.40	—	81.30
1¼"	P1@.480	Ea	96.90	16.60	—	113.50
1½"	P1@.540	Ea	131.00	18.70	—	149.70
2"	P1@.600	Ea	212.00	20.70	—	232.70

Class 125 iron body globe valve, flanged joints

Description	Craft@Hrs	Unit	Material $	Labor $	Equipment $	Total $
2½"	P1@.650	Ea	351.00	22.50	—	373.50
3"	P1@.750	Ea	421.00	25.90	—	446.90
4"	P1@1.35	Ea	568.00	46.60	—	614.60

200 PSIG iron body butterfly valve, lug type, lever operated

Description	Craft@Hrs	Unit	Material $	Labor $	Equipment $	Total $
2"	P1@.450	Ea	134.00	15.50	—	149.50
2½"	P1@.450	Ea	139.00	15.50	—	154.50
3"	P1@.550	Ea	146.00	19.00	—	165.00
4"	P1@.550	Ea	182.00	19.00	—	201.00

200 PSIG iron body butterfly valve, wafer type, lever operated

Description	Craft@Hrs	Unit	Material $	Labor $	Equipment $	Total $
2"	P1@.450	Ea	122.00	15.50	—	137.50
2½"	P1@.450	Ea	125.00	15.50	—	140.50
3"	P1@.550	Ea	134.00	19.00	—	153.00
4"	P1@.550	Ea	163.00	19.00	—	182.00

Copper, Type K with Brazed Joints

Description	Craft@Hrs	Unit	Material $	Labor $	Equipment $	Total $

Class 125 bronze body 2-piece ball valve, brazed joints

Description	Craft@Hrs	Unit	Material $	Labor $	Equipment $	Total $
1/2"	P1@.240	Ea	7.91	8.29	—	16.20
3/4"	P1@.300	Ea	10.50	10.40	—	20.90
1"	P1@.360	Ea	18.20	12.40	—	30.60
1¼"	P1@.480	Ea	30.30	16.60	—	46.90
1½"	P1@.540	Ea	41.00	18.70	—	59.70
2"	P1@.600	Ea	51.90	20.70	—	72.60
3"	P1@1.50	Ea	355.00	51.80	—	406.80
4"	P1@1.80	Ea	465.00	62.20	—	527.20

Class 125 bronze body swing check valve, brazed joints

Description	Craft@Hrs	Unit	Material $	Labor $	Equipment $	Total $
1/2"	P1@.240	Ea	17.70	8.29	—	25.99
3/4"	P1@.300	Ea	25.40	10.40	—	35.80
1"	P1@.360	Ea	33.30	12.40	—	45.70
1¼"	P1@.480	Ea	47.30	16.60	—	63.90
1½"	P1@.540	Ea	66.70	18.70	—	85.40
2"	P1@.600	Ea	111.00	20.70	—	131.70
2½"	P1@1.00	Ea	223.00	34.60	—	257.60
3"	P1@1.50	Ea	320.00	51.80	—	371.80

Class 125 iron body swing check valve, flanged joints

Description	Craft@Hrs	Unit	Material $	Labor $	Equipment $	Total $
2"	P1@.500	Ea	155.00	17.30	—	172.30
2½"	P1@.600	Ea	197.00	20.70	—	217.70
3"	P1@.750	Ea	245.00	25.90	—	270.90
4"	P1@1.35	Ea	360.00	46.60	—	406.60

Class 125 iron body silent check valve, wafer type

Description	Craft@Hrs	Unit	Material $	Labor $	Equipment $	Total $
2"	P1@.500	Ea	113.00	17.30	—	130.30
2½"	P1@.600	Ea	126.00	20.70	—	146.70
3"	P1@.750	Ea	145.00	25.90	—	170.90
4"	P1@1.35	Ea	194.00	46.60	—	240.60

Class 125 bronze body strainer, threaded joints

Description	Craft@Hrs	Unit	Material $	Labor $	Equipment $	Total $
1/2"	P1@.230	Ea	27.70	7.95	—	35.65
3/4"	P1@.260	Ea	36.40	8.98	—	45.38
1"	P1@.330	Ea	44.60	11.40	—	56.00
1¼"	P1@.440	Ea	62.30	15.20	—	77.50
1½"	P1@.495	Ea	93.80	17.10	—	110.90
2"	P1@.550	Ea	162.00	19.00	—	181.00

Class 125 iron body strainer, flanged joints

Description	Craft@Hrs	Unit	Material $	Labor $	Equipment $	Total $
2"	P1@.500	Ea	124.00	17.30	—	141.30
2½"	P1@.600	Ea	139.00	20.70	—	159.70
3"	P1@.750	Ea	160.00	25.90	—	185.90
4"	P1@1.35	Ea	273.00	46.60	—	319.60

Description	Craft@Hrs	Unit	Material $	Labor $	Equipment $	Total $

Installation of 2-way control valve, threaded joints

1/2"	P1@.210	Ea	—	7.26	—	7.26
3/4"	P1@.275	Ea	—	9.50	—	9.50
1"	P1@.350	Ea	—	12.10	—	12.10
1¼"	P1@.430	Ea	—	14.90	—	14.90
1½"	P1@.505	Ea	—	17.40	—	17.40
2"	P1@.675	Ea	—	23.30	—	23.30
2½"	P1@.830	Ea	—	28.70	—	28.70
3"	P1@.990	Ea	—	34.20	—	34.20

Installation of 3-way control valve, threaded joints

1/2"	P1@.260	Ea	—	8.98	—	8.98
3/4"	P1@.365	Ea	—	12.60	—	12.60
1"	P1@.475	Ea	—	16.40	—	16.40
1¼"	P1@.575	Ea	—	19.90	—	19.90
1½"	P1@.680	Ea	—	23.50	—	23.50
2"	P1@.910	Ea	—	31.40	—	31.40
2½"	P1@1.12	Ea	—	38.70	—	38.70
3"	P1@1.33	Ea	—	46.00	—	46.00

Companion flange, 150 pound cast brass

2"	P1@.290	Ea	370.00	10.00	—	380.00
2½"	P1@.380	Ea	458.00	13.10	—	471.10
3"	P1@.460	Ea	458.00	15.90	—	473.90
4"	P1@.600	Ea	730.00	20.70	—	750.70

Bolt and gasket sets

2"	P1@.500	Ea	3.86	17.30	—	21.16
2½"	P1@.650	Ea	4.51	22.50	—	27.01
3"	P1@.750	Ea	7.67	25.90	—	33.57
4"	P1@1.00	Ea	12.80	34.60	—	47.40

Thermometer with well

7"	P1@.250	Ea	159.00	8.64	—	167.64
9"	P1@.250	Ea	164.00	8.64	—	172.64

Dial type pressure gauge

2½"	P1@.200	Ea	32.70	6.91	—	39.61
3½"	P1@.200	Ea	43.60	6.91	—	50.51

Copper, Type K with Brazed Joints

Description	Craft@Hrs	Unit	Material $	Labor $	Equipment $	Total $

Pressure/temperature tap

Description	Craft@Hrs	Unit	Material $	Labor $	Equipment $	Total $
tap	P1@.150	Ea	15.50	5.18	—	20.68

Hanger with swivel assembly

Description	Craft@Hrs	Unit	Material $	Labor $	Equipment $	Total $
1/2"	P1@.250	Ea	3.74	8.64	—	12.38
3/4"	P1@.250	Ea	4.13	8.64	—	12.77
1"	P1@.250	Ea	4.33	8.64	—	12.97
1¼"	P1@.300	Ea	4.44	10.40	—	14.84
1½"	P1@.300	Ea	4.77	10.40	—	15.17
2"	P1@.300	Ea	4.98	10.40	—	15.38
2½"	P1@.350	Ea	6.78	12.10	—	18.88
3"	P1@.350	Ea	8.37	12.10	—	20.47
4"	P1@.350	Ea	9.19	12.10	—	21.29

Riser clamp

Description	Craft@Hrs	Unit	Material $	Labor $	Equipment $	Total $
1/2"	P1@.100	Ea	2.41	3.46	—	5.87
3/4"	P1@.100	Ea	3.55	3.46	—	7.01
1"	P1@.100	Ea	3.59	3.46	—	7.05
1¼"	P1@.105	Ea	4.31	3.63	—	7.94
1½"	P1@.110	Ea	4.56	3.80	—	8.36
2"	P1@.115	Ea	4.84	3.97	—	8.81
2½"	P1@.120	Ea	5.06	4.15	—	9.21
3"	P1@.120	Ea	5.51	4.15	—	9.66
4"	P1@.125	Ea	7.02	4.32	—	11.34

Type K hard-drawn copper pipe with wrought copper fittings and soft-soldered joints is used in a wide variety of plumbing and HVAC systems such as potable water, heating hot water, chilled water and A.C. condensate.

Soft-soldered joints are those made with solders having melting points in the 350 degree F. to 500 degree F. range. Maximum working pressure/temperature relationships for soft-soldered joints are approximately as follows:

Maximum Working Pressures (PSIG)*				
Soft-solder Type	Water Temperature (degrees F.)	Nominal Pipe Size (inches)		
		Up to 1	1¼ to 2	2½ to 4
50-50 tin-lead**	100	200	175	150
	150	150	125	100
	200	100	90	75
	250	85	75	50
95-5 tin-antimony	100	500	400	300
	150	400	350	275
	200	300	250	200
	250	200	175	150

*For copper pipe and solder-type fittings using soft-solders melting at approximately 350 degrees F. to 500 degrees F.
**The use of any solder containing lead is not allowed in potable water systems.

This section has been arranged to save the estimator's time by including all normally-used system components such as pipe, fittings, valves, hanger assemblies, riser clamps and miscellaneous items under one heading. Additional items can be found under "Plumbing and Piping Specialties." The cost estimates in this section are based on the conditions, limitations and wage rates described in the section "How to Use This Book" beginning on page 5.

Description	Craft@Hrs	Unit	Material $	Labor $	Equipment $	Total $

Type K copper pipe with soft-soldered joints installed horizontally.
Complete installation including six to twelve wrought copper tees and six to twelve wrought copper elbows every 100', and hangers spaced to meet plumbing code (*a tee & elbow every 8.3' for ½" dia., a tee and elbow every 16.6' for 4" dia.*)

1/2"	P1@.112	LF	3.58	3.87	—	7.45
3/4"	P1@.122	LF	6.27	4.22	—	10.49
1"	P1@.142	LF	10.00	4.91	—	14.91
1¼"	P1@.162	LF	13.70	5.60	—	19.30
1½"	P1@.182	LF	16.80	6.29	—	23.09
2"	P1@.212	LF	28.60	7.32	—	35.92
2½"	P1@.242	LF	47.00	8.36	—	55.36
3"	P1@.272	LF	54.20	9.40	—	63.60
4"	P1@.312	LF	99.20	10.80	—	110.00

Copper, Type K with Soft-Soldered Joints

Description	Craft@Hrs	Unit	Material $	Labor $	Equipment $	Total $

Type K copper pipe with soft-soldered joints, installed risers.
Complete installation including a wrought copper reducing tee every floor and a riser clamp every other floor.

Description	Craft@Hrs	Unit	Material $	Labor $	Equipment $	Total $
1/2"	P1@.062	LF	3.23	2.14	—	5.37
3/4"	P1@.072	LF	5.83	2.49	—	8.32
1"	P1@.077	LF	8.90	2.66	—	11.56
1¼"	P1@.082	LF	12.30	2.83	—	15.13
1½"	P1@.102	LF	14.50	3.52	—	18.02
2"	P1@.132	LF	24.80	4.56	—	29.36
2½"	P1@.152	LF	37.10	5.25	—	42.35
3"	P1@.172	LF	52.00	5.94	—	57.94
4"	P1@.192	LF	81.20	6.63	—	87.83

Type K copper pipe with soft-soldered joints, pipe only

Description	Craft@Hrs	Unit	Material $	Labor $	Equipment $	Total $
1/2"	P1@.032	LF	2.57	1.11	—	3.68
3/4"	P1@.035	LF	4.76	1.21	—	5.97
1"	P1@.038	LF	6.01	1.31	—	7.32
1¼"	P1@.042	LF	8.03	1.45	—	9.48
1½"	P1@.046	LF	8.75	1.59	—	10.34
2"	P1@.053	LF	15.60	1.83	—	17.43
2½"	P1@.060	LF	20.40	2.07	—	22.47
3"	P1@.066	LF	26.60	2.28	—	28.88
4"	P1@.080	LF	47.60	2.76	—	50.36

Type K copper 45 degree ell C x C with soft-soldered joints

Description	Craft@Hrs	Unit	Material $	Labor $	Equipment $	Total $
1/2"	P1@.107	Ea	1.04	3.70	—	4.74
3/4"	P1@.150	Ea	1.95	5.18	—	7.13
1"	P1@.193	Ea	5.76	6.67	—	12.43
1¼"	P1@.236	Ea	7.85	8.15	—	16.00
1½"	P1@.278	Ea	11.60	9.60	—	21.20
2"	P1@.371	Ea	19.00	12.80	—	31.80
2½"	P1@.457	Ea	48.90	15.80	—	64.70
3"	P1@.543	Ea	64.50	18.80	—	83.30
4"	P1@.714	Ea	125.00	24.70	—	149.70

Description	Craft@Hrs	Unit	Material $	Labor $	Equipment $	Total $

Type K copper 90 degree ell C x C with soft-soldered joints

Description	Craft@Hrs	Unit	Material $	Labor $	Equipment $	Total $
1/2"	P1@.107	Ea	.62	3.70	—	4.32
3/4"	P1@.150	Ea	1.27	5.18	—	6.45
1"	P1@.193	Ea	4.39	6.67	—	11.06
1¼"	P1@.236	Ea	7.17	8.15	—	15.32
1½"	P1@.278	Ea	10.80	9.60	—	20.40
2"	P1@.371	Ea	19.40	12.80	—	32.20
2½"	P1@.457	Ea	40.20	15.80	—	56.00
3"	P1@.543	Ea	50.90	18.80	—	69.70
4"	P1@.714	Ea	109.00	24.70	—	133.70

Type K copper 90 degree ell Ftg. x C with soft-soldered joint

Description	Craft@Hrs	Unit	Material $	Labor $	Equipment $	Total $
1/2"	P1@.107	Ea	.96	3.70	—	4.66
3/4"	P1@.150	Ea	2.09	5.18	—	7.27
1"	P1@.193	Ea	6.23	6.67	—	12.90
1¼"	P1@.236	Ea	8.66	8.15	—	16.81
1½"	P1@.278	Ea	13.00	9.60	—	22.60
2"	P1@.371	Ea	26.30	12.80	—	39.10
2½"	P1@.457	Ea	55.00	15.80	—	70.80
3"	P1@.543	Ea	61.60	18.80	—	80.40
4"	P1@.714	Ea	125.00	24.70	—	149.70

Type K copper tee C x C x C with soft-soldered joints

Description	Craft@Hrs	Unit	Material $	Labor $	Equipment $	Total $
1/2"	P1@.129	Ea	1.03	4.46	—	5.49
3/4"	P1@.181	Ea	2.77	6.25	—	9.02
1"	P1@.233	Ea	10.40	8.05	—	18.45
1¼"	P1@.285	Ea	16.60	9.85	—	26.45
1½"	P1@.337	Ea	23.80	11.60	—	35.40
2"	P1@.449	Ea	38.40	15.50	—	53.90
2½"	P1@.552	Ea	78.30	19.10	—	97.40
3"	P1@.656	Ea	120.00	22.70	—	142.70
4"	P1@.863	Ea	200.00	29.80	—	229.80

Copper, Type K with Soft-Soldered Joints

Description	Craft@Hrs	Unit	Material $	Labor $	Equipment $	Total $

Type K copper branch reducing tee C x C x C with soft-soldered joints

Description	Craft@Hrs	Unit	Material $	Labor $	Equipment $	Total $
1/2" x 3/8"	P1@.129	Ea	2.08	4.46	—	6.54
3/4" x 1/2"	P1@.182	Ea	4.41	6.29	—	10.70
1" x 1/2"	P1@.195	Ea	8.66	6.74	—	15.40
1" x 3/4"	P1@.219	Ea	8.66	7.57	—	16.23
1¼" x 1/2"	P1@.225	Ea	13.20	7.77	—	20.97
1¼" x 3/4"	P1@.247	Ea	13.20	8.53	—	21.73
1¼" x 1"	P1@.268	Ea	13.20	9.26	—	22.46
1½" x 1/2"	P1@.272	Ea	16.20	9.40	—	25.60
1½" x 3/4"	P1@.287	Ea	16.20	9.92	—	26.12
1½" x 1"	P1@.302	Ea	16.20	10.40	—	26.60
1½" x 1¼"	P1@.317	Ea	16.20	11.00	—	27.20
2" x 1/2"	P1@.325	Ea	21.60	11.20	—	32.80
2" x 3/4"	P1@.348	Ea	21.60	12.00	—	33.60
2" x 1"	P1@.373	Ea	21.60	12.90	—	34.50
2" x 1¼"	P1@.398	Ea	21.60	13.80	—	35.40
2" x 1½"	P1@.422	Ea	21.60	14.60	—	36.20
2½" x 1/2"	P1@.437	Ea	65.20	15.10	—	80.30
2½" x 3/4"	P1@.453	Ea	65.20	15.70	—	80.90
2½" x 1"	P1@.469	Ea	65.20	16.20	—	81.40
2½" x 1½"	P1@.502	Ea	65.20	17.30	—	82.50
2½" x 2"	P1@.519	Ea	65.20	17.90	—	83.10
3" x 1¼"	P1@.525	Ea	73.70	18.10	—	91.80
3" x 2"	P1@.585	Ea	76.50	20.20	—	96.70
3" x 2½"	P1@.617	Ea	76.50	21.30	—	97.80
4" x 1¼"	P1@.625	Ea	100.00	21.60	—	121.60
4" x 1½"	P1@.671	Ea	100.00	23.20	—	123.20
4" x 2"	P1@.718	Ea	100.00	24.80	—	124.80
4" x 2½"	P1@.765	Ea	100.00	26.40	—	126.40
4" x 3"	P1@.811	Ea	100.00	28.00	—	128.00

Description	Craft@Hrs	Unit	Material $	Labor $	Equipment $	Total $

Type K copper reducer with soft-soldered joints

Description	Craft@Hrs	Unit	Material $	Labor $	Equipment $	Total $
1/2" x 3/8"	P1@.124	Ea	.78	4.28	—	5.06
3/4" x 1/2"	P1@.129	Ea	1.44	4.46	—	5.90
1" x 3/4"	P1@.172	Ea	2.53	5.94	—	8.47
1¼" x 1/2"	P1@.172	Ea	4.25	5.94	—	10.19
1¼" x 3/4"	P1@.193	Ea	4.25	6.67	—	10.92
1¼" x 1"	P1@.215	Ea	4.25	7.43	—	11.68
1½" x 1/2"	P1@.193	Ea	6.50	6.67	—	13.17
1½" x 3/4"	P1@.214	Ea	6.50	7.39	—	13.89
1½" x 1"	P1@.236	Ea	6.50	8.15	—	14.65
1½" x 1¼"	P1@.257	Ea	6.50	8.88	—	15.38
2" x 1/2"	P1@.239	Ea	10.10	8.26	—	18.36
2" x 3/4"	P1@.261	Ea	10.10	9.02	—	19.12
2" x 1"	P1@.282	Ea	10.10	9.74	—	19.84
2" x 1¼"	P1@.304	Ea	10.10	10.50	—	20.60
2" x 1½"	P1@.325	Ea	10.10	11.20	—	21.30
2½" x 1"	P1@.325	Ea	27.50	11.20	—	38.70
2½" x 1¼"	P1@.347	Ea	27.50	12.00	—	39.50
2½" x 1½"	P1@.368	Ea	27.50	12.70	—	40.20
2½" x 2"	P1@.414	Ea	27.50	14.30	—	41.80
3" x 2"	P1@.457	Ea	32.10	15.80	—	47.90
3" x 2½"	P1@.500	Ea	32.10	17.30	—	49.40
4" x 2"	P1@.543	Ea	62.00	18.80	—	80.80
4" x 2½"	P1@.586	Ea	62.00	20.20	—	82.20
4" x 3"	P1@.629	Ea	62.00	21.70	—	83.70

Type K copper adapter C x MPT with soft-soldered joint

Description	Craft@Hrs	Unit	Material $	Labor $	Equipment $	Total $
1/2"	P1@.075	Ea	1.85	2.59	—	4.44
3/4"	P1@.105	Ea	2.89	3.63	—	6.52
1"	P1@.134	Ea	7.17	4.63	—	11.80
1¼"	P1@.164	Ea	13.40	5.67	—	19.07
1½"	P1@.194	Ea	15.00	6.70	—	21.70
2"	P1@.259	Ea	19.40	8.95	—	28.35
2½"	P1@.319	Ea	63.10	11.00	—	74.10
3"	P1@.378	Ea	105.00	13.10	—	118.10

Copper, Type K with Soft-Soldered Joints

Description	Craft@Hrs	Unit	Material $	Labor $	Equipment $	Total $

Type K copper adapter C x FPT with soft-soldered joint

Description	Craft@Hrs	Unit	Material $	Labor $	Equipment $	Total $
1/2"	P1@.075	Ea	3.08	2.59	—	5.67
3/4"	P1@.105	Ea	5.57	3.63	—	9.20
1"	P1@.134	Ea	8.43	4.63	—	13.06
1¼"	P1@.164	Ea	17.60	5.67	—	23.27
1½"	P1@.194	Ea	21.40	6.70	—	28.10
2"	P1@.259	Ea	32.90	8.95	—	41.85
2½"	P1@.319	Ea	82.70	11.00	—	93.70
3"	P1@.378	Ea	114.00	13.10	—	127.10

Type K copper flush bushing with soft-soldered joints

Description	Craft@Hrs	Unit	Material $	Labor $	Equipment $	Total $
1/2" x 3/8"	P1@.124	Ea	1.88	4.28	—	6.16
3/4" x 1/2"	P1@.129	Ea	3.19	4.46	—	7.65
1" x 3/4"	P1@.172	Ea	8.27	5.94	—	14.21
1" x 1/2"	P1@.172	Ea	9.45	5.94	—	15.39
1¼" x 1"	P1@.215	Ea	9.85	7.43	—	17.28
1½" x 1¼"	P1@.257	Ea	12.50	8.88	—	21.38
2" x 1½"	P1@.325	Ea	23.50	11.20	—	34.70

Type K copper union with soft-soldered joint

Description	Craft@Hrs	Unit	Material $	Labor $	Equipment $	Total $
1/2"	P1@.121	Ea	7.50	4.18	—	11.68
3/4"	P1@.170	Ea	8.98	5.87	—	14.85
1"	P1@.218	Ea	20.10	7.53	—	27.63
1¼"	P1@.267	Ea	36.50	9.22	—	45.72
1½"	P1@.315	Ea	44.90	10.90	—	55.80
2"	P1@.421	Ea	67.00	14.50	—	81.50

Type K copper dielectric union with soft-soldered joint

Description	Craft@Hrs	Unit	Material $	Labor $	Equipment $	Total $
1/2"	P1@.121	Ea	7.04	4.18	—	11.22
3/4"	P1@.170	Ea	7.04	5.87	—	12.91
1"	P1@.218	Ea	14.50	7.53	—	22.03
1¼"	P1@.267	Ea	24.80	9.22	—	34.02
1½"	P1@.315	Ea	34.10	10.90	—	45.00
2"	P1@.421	Ea	47.10	14.50	—	61.60

Type K copper cap with soft-soldered joint

Description	Craft@Hrs	Unit	Material $	Labor $	Equipment $	Total $
1/2"	P1@.069	Ea	.61	2.38	—	2.99
3/4"	P1@.096	Ea	1.25	3.32	—	4.57
1"	P1@.124	Ea	2.82	4.28	—	7.10
1¼"	P1@.151	Ea	4.05	5.22	—	9.27
1½"	P1@.178	Ea	5.91	6.15	—	12.06
2"	P1@.237	Ea	10.70	8.19	—	18.89
2½"	P1@.292	Ea	27.00	10.10	—	37.10
3"	P1@.347	Ea	42.20	12.00	—	54.20
4"	P1@.457	Ea	64.80	15.80	—	80.60

Description	Craft@Hrs	Unit	Material $	Labor $	Equipment $	Total $

Type K copper coupling with soft-soldered joints

Description	Craft@Hrs	Unit	Material $	Labor $	Equipment $	Total $
1/2"	P1@.107	Ea	.39	3.70	—	4.09
3/4"	P1@.150	Ea	.98	5.18	—	6.16
1"	P1@.193	Ea	2.67	6.67	—	9.34
1¼"	P1@.236	Ea	4.67	8.15	—	12.82
1½"	P1@.278	Ea	6.76	9.60	—	16.36
2"	P1@.371	Ea	10.30	12.80	—	23.10
2½"	P1@.457	Ea	24.20	15.80	—	40.00
3"	P1@.543	Ea	36.90	18.80	—	55.70
4"	P1@.714	Ea	72.30	24.70	—	97.00

Class 125 bronze body gate valve, soft-soldered joints

Description	Craft@Hrs	Unit	Material $	Labor $	Equipment $	Total $
1/2"	P1@.200	Ea	16.10	6.91	—	23.01
3/4"	P1@.249	Ea	20.30	8.60	—	28.90
1"	P1@.299	Ea	28.50	10.30	—	38.80
1¼"	P1@.398	Ea	36.00	13.80	—	49.80
1½"	P1@.448	Ea	48.20	15.50	—	63.70
2"	P1@.498	Ea	80.50	17.20	—	97.70
2½"	P1@.830	Ea	133.00	28.70	—	161.70
3"	P1@1.24	Ea	192.00	42.80	—	234.80

Class 125 iron body gate valve, flanged joints

Description	Craft@Hrs	Unit	Material $	Labor $	Equipment $	Total $
2"	P1@.500	Ea	310.00	17.30	—	327.30
2½"	P1@.600	Ea	418.00	20.70	—	438.70
3"	P1@.750	Ea	454.00	25.90	—	479.90
4"	P1@1.35	Ea	666.00	46.60	—	712.60
5"	P1@2.00	Ea	1,270.00	69.10	—	1,339.10
6"	P1@2.50	Ea	1,270.00	86.40	—	1,356.40

Class 125 bronze body globe valve, with soft-soldered joints

Description	Craft@Hrs	Unit	Material $	Labor $	Equipment $	Total $
1/2"	P1@.200	Ea	30.00	6.91	—	36.91
3/4"	P1@.249	Ea	40.00	8.60	—	48.60
1"	P1@.299	Ea	68.90	10.30	—	79.20
1¼"	P1@.398	Ea	96.90	13.80	—	110.70
1½"	P1@.448	Ea	131.00	15.50	—	146.50
2"	P1@.498	Ea	212.00	17.20	—	229.20

Class 125 iron body globe valve, flanged ends

Description	Craft@Hrs	Unit	Material $	Labor $	Equipment $	Total $
2½"	P1@.600	Ea	351.00	20.70	—	371.70
3"	P1@.750	Ea	421.00	25.90	—	446.90
4"	P1@1.35	Ea	565.00	46.60	—	611.60

Copper, Type K with Soft-Soldered Joints

Description	Craft@Hrs	Unit	Material $	Labor $	Equipment $	Total $

200 PSIG iron body butterfly valve, lug type, lever operated

Description	Craft@Hrs	Unit	Material $	Labor $	Equipment $	Total $
2"	P1@.450	Ea	134.00	15.50	—	149.50
2½"	P1@.450	Ea	139.00	15.50	—	154.50
3"	P1@.550	Ea	146.00	19.00	—	165.00
4"	P1@.550	Ea	182.00	19.00	—	201.00

200 PSIG iron body butterfly valve, wafer type, lever operated

Description	Craft@Hrs	Unit	Material $	Labor $	Equipment $	Total $
2"	P1@.450	Ea	122.00	15.50	—	137.50
2½"	P1@.450	Ea	125.00	15.50	—	140.50
3"	P1@.550	Ea	134.00	19.00	—	153.00
4"	P1@.550	Ea	163.00	19.00	—	182.00

Class 125 bronze body 2-piece ball valve, soft-soldered joints

Description	Craft@Hrs	Unit	Material $	Labor $	Equipment $	Total $
1/2"	P1@.200	Ea	7.91	6.91	—	14.82
3/4"	P1@.249	Ea	9.43	8.60	—	18.03
1"	P1@.299	Ea	18.20	10.30	—	28.50
1¼"	P1@.398	Ea	30.30	13.80	—	44.10
1½"	P1@.448	Ea	41.00	15.50	—	56.50
2"	P1@.498	Ea	51.90	17.20	—	69.10
3"	P1@1.24	Ea	355.00	42.80	—	397.80
4"	P1@1.45	Ea	465.00	50.10	—	515.10

Class 125 bronze body swing check valve, soft-soldered joints

Description	Craft@Hrs	Unit	Material $	Labor $	Equipment $	Total $
1/2"	P1@.200	Ea	17.70	6.91	—	24.61
3/4"	P1@.249	Ea	25.40	8.60	—	34.00
1"	P1@.299	Ea	33.30	10.30	—	43.60
1¼"	P1@.398	Ea	47.30	13.80	—	61.10
1½"	P1@.448	Ea	66.70	15.50	—	82.20
2"	P1@.498	Ea	111.00	17.20	—	128.20
2½"	P1@.830	Ea	223.00	28.70	—	251.70
3"	P1@1.24	Ea	320.00	42.80	—	362.80

Class 125 iron body swing check valve, flanged ends

Description	Craft@Hrs	Unit	Material $	Labor $	Equipment $	Total $
2"	P1@.500	Ea	155.00	17.30	—	172.30
2½"	P1@.600	Ea	197.00	20.70	—	217.70
3"	P1@.750	Ea	245.00	25.90	—	270.90
4"	P1@1.35	Ea	360.00	46.60	—	406.60

Class 125 iron body silent check valve, wafer type

Description	Craft@Hrs	Unit	Material $	Labor $	Equipment $	Total $
2"	P1@.500	Ea	113.00	17.30	—	130.30
2½"	P1@.600	Ea	126.00	20.70	—	146.70
3"	P1@.750	Ea	145.00	25.90	—	170.90
4"	P1@1.35	Ea	194.00	46.60	—	240.60

Description	Craft@Hrs	Unit	Material $	Labor $	Equipment $	Total $

Class 125 bronze body strainer, threaded ends

1/2"	P1@.230	Ea	27.70	7.95	—	35.65
3/4"	P1@.260	Ea	36.40	8.98	—	45.38
1"	P1@.330	Ea	44.60	11.40	—	56.00
1¼"	P1@.440	Ea	62.30	15.20	—	77.50
1½"	P1@.495	Ea	93.80	17.10	—	110.90
2"	P1@.550	Ea	162.00	19.00	—	181.00

Class 125 iron body strainer, flanged ends

2"	P1@.500	Ea	124.00	17.30	—	141.30
2½"	P1@.600	Ea	139.00	20.70	—	159.70
3"	P1@.750	Ea	160.00	25.90	—	185.90
4"	P1@1.35	Ea	273.00	46.60	—	319.60

Installation of copper 2-way control valve, threaded joints

1/2"	P1@.210	Ea	—	7.26	—	7.26
3/4"	P1@.275	Ea	—	9.50	—	9.50
1"	P1@.350	Ea	—	12.10	—	12.10
1¼"	P1@.430	Ea	—	14.90	—	14.90
1½"	P1@.505	Ea	—	17.40	—	17.40
2"	P1@.675	Ea	—	23.30	—	23.30
2½"	P1@.830	Ea	—	28.70	—	28.70
3"	P1@.990	Ea	—	34.20	—	34.20

Installation of copper 3-way control valve, threaded joints

1/2"	P1@.260	Ea	—	8.98	—	8.98
3/4"	P1@.365	Ea	—	12.60	—	12.60
1"	P1@.475	Ea	—	16.40	—	16.40
1¼"	P1@.575	Ea	—	19.90	—	19.90
1½"	P1@.680	Ea	—	23.50	—	23.50
2"	P1@.910	Ea	—	31.40	—	31.40
2½"	P1@1.12	Ea	—	38.70	—	38.70
3"	P1@1.33	Ea	—	46.00	—	46.00

Companion flange, 150 pound cast brass

2"	P1@.290	Ea	370.00	10.00	—	380.00
2½"	P1@.380	Ea	458.00	13.10	—	471.10
3"	P1@.460	Ea	458.00	15.90	—	473.90
4"	P1@.600	Ea	730.00	20.70	—	750.70

Copper, Type K with Soft-Soldered Joints

Description	Craft@Hrs	Unit	Material $	Labor $	Equipment $	Total $

Bolt and gasket sets

Description	Craft@Hrs	Unit	Material $	Labor $	Equipment $	Total $
2"	P1@.500	Ea	3.92	17.30	—	21.22
2½"	P1@.650	Ea	4.60	22.50	—	27.10
3"	P1@.750	Ea	7.84	25.90	—	33.74
4"	P1@1.00	Ea	13.10	34.60	—	47.70

Thermometer with well

Description	Craft@Hrs	Unit	Material $	Labor $	Equipment $	Total $
7"	P1@.250	Ea	159.00	8.64	—	167.64
9"	P1@.250	Ea	164.00	8.64	—	172.64

Dial type pressure gauge

Description	Craft@Hrs	Unit	Material $	Labor $	Equipment $	Total $
2½"	P1@.200	Ea	32.70	6.91	—	39.61
3½"	P1@.200	Ea	43.60	6.91	—	50.51

Pressure/temperature tap

Description	Craft@Hrs	Unit	Material $	Labor $	Equipment $	Total $
tap	P1@.150	Ea	15.50	5.18	—	20.68

Hanger with swivel assembly

Description	Craft@Hrs	Unit	Material $	Labor $	Equipment $	Total $
1/2"	P1@.250	Ea	3.74	8.64	—	12.38
3/4"	P1@.250	Ea	4.13	8.64	—	12.77
1"	P1@.250	Ea	4.33	8.64	—	12.97
1¼"	P1@.300	Ea	4.44	10.40	—	14.84
1½"	P1@.300	Ea	4.77	10.40	—	15.17
2"	P1@.300	Ea	4.98	10.40	—	15.38
2½"	P1@.350	Ea	6.78	12.10	—	18.88
3"	P1@.350	Ea	8.37	12.10	—	20.47
4"	P1@.350	Ea	9.19	12.10	—	21.29

Riser clamp

Description	Craft@Hrs	Unit	Material $	Labor $	Equipment $	Total $
1/2"	P1@.100	Ea	2.41	3.46	—	5.87
3/4"	P1@.100	Ea	3.55	3.46	—	7.01
1"	P1@.100	Ea	3.59	3.46	—	7.05
1¼"	P1@.105	Ea	4.33	3.63	—	7.96
1½"	P1@.110	Ea	4.58	3.80	—	8.38
2"	P1@.115	Ea	4.84	3.97	—	8.81
2½"	P1@.120	Ea	5.09	4.15	—	9.24
3"	P1@.120	Ea	5.52	4.15	—	9.67
4"	P1@.125	Ea	7.03	4.32	—	11.35

Type L hard-drawn copper pipe with wrought copper fittings and brazed joints is used in a wide variety of plumbing and HVAC systems such as potable water, heating hot water, chilled water, compressed air, refrigerant and A.C. condensate.

Brazed joints are those made with silver or other alloy filler metals having melting points at, or above, 1,000 degrees F. Maximum working pressure/temperature relationships for brazed joints are approximately as follows:

Water Temperature (degrees F.)	Maximum Working Pressure (PSIG)*		
	Nominal Pipe Size (inches)		
	Up to 1	1¼ to 2	2½ to 4
Up to 350	270	190	150

*For copper pipe and solder-type fittings using brazing alloys melting at, or above, 1,000 degrees F.

This section has been arranged to save the estimator's time by including all normally-used system components such as pipe, fittings, valves, hanger assemblies, riser clamps and miscellaneous items under one heading. Additional items can be found under "Plumbing and Piping Specialties." The cost estimates in this section are based on the conditions, limitations and wage rates described in the section "How to Use This Book" beginning on page 5.

Description	Craft@Hrs	Unit	Material $	Labor $	Equipment $	Total $

Type L copper pipe with brazed joints installed horizontally. Complete installation including six to twelve wrought copper tees and six to twelve wrought copper elbows every 100', and hangers spaced to meet plumbing code (*a tee & elbow every 8.3' for ½" dia., a tee and elbow every 16.6' for 4" dia.*)

Description	Craft@Hrs	Unit	Material $	Labor $	Equipment $	Total $
1/2"	P1@.116	LF	2.46	4.01	—	6.47
3/4"	P1@.126	LF	3.80	4.35	—	8.15
1"	P1@.146	LF	6.83	5.04	—	11.87
1¼"	P1@.166	LF	9.69	5.74	—	15.43
1½"	P1@.186	LF	13.00	6.43	—	19.43
2"	P1@.216	LF	23.50	7.46	—	30.96
2½"	P1@.246	LF	41.40	8.50	—	49.90
3"	P1@.276	LF	57.30	9.54	—	66.84
4"	P1@.316	LF	82.70	10.90	—	93.60

Copper, Type L with Brazed Joints

Description	Craft@Hrs	Unit	Material $	Labor $	Equipment $	Total $

Type L copper pipe with brazed joints, installed risers.
Complete installation including a wrought copper reducing tee every floor and a riser clamp every other floor.

Description	Craft@Hrs	Unit	Material $	Labor $	Equipment $	Total $
1/2"	P1@.063	LF	2.42	2.18	—	4.60
3/4"	P1@.073	LF	3.82	2.52	—	6.34
1"	P1@.073	LF	6.47	2.52	—	8.99
1¼"	P1@.083	LF	9.14	2.87	—	12.01
1½"	P1@.103	LF	11.40	3.56	—	14.96
2"	P1@.133	LF	29.90	4.60	—	34.50
2½"	P1@.153	LF	32.30	5.29	—	37.59
3"	P1@.173	LF	41.90	5.98	—	47.88
4"	P1@.193	LF	62.30	6.67	—	68.97

Type L copper pipe with brazed joints, pipe only

Description	Craft@Hrs	Unit	Material $	Labor $	Equipment $	Total $
1/2"	P1@.032	LF	1.85	1.11	—	2.96
3/4"	P1@.035	LF	2.93	1.21	—	4.14
1"	P1@.038	LF	4.06	1.31	—	5.37
1¼"	P1@.042	LF	5.82	1.45	—	7.27
1½"	P1@.046	LF	7.43	1.59	—	9.02
2"	P1@.053	LF	12.80	1.83	—	14.63
2½"	P1@.060	LF	18.60	2.07	—	20.67
3"	P1@.066	LF	25.20	2.28	—	27.48
4"	P1@.080	LF	39.60	2.76	—	42.36

Type L copper 45 degree ell C x C with brazed joints

Description	Craft@Hrs	Unit	Material $	Labor $	Equipment $	Total $
1/2"	P1@.129	Ea	1.04	4.46	—	5.50
3/4"	P1@.181	Ea	1.97	6.25	—	8.22
1"	P1@.232	Ea	5.82	8.02	—	13.84
1¼"	P1@.284	Ea	7.88	9.81	—	17.69
1½"	P1@.335	Ea	11.70	11.60	—	23.30
2"	P1@.447	Ea	19.20	15.40	—	34.60
2½"	P1@.550	Ea	49.00	19.00	—	68.00
3"	P1@.654	Ea	64.70	22.60	—	87.30
4"	P1@.860	Ea	125.00	29.70	—	154.70

Type L copper 90 degree ell C x C with brazed joints

Description	Craft@Hrs	Unit	Material $	Labor $	Equipment $	Total $
1/2"	P1@.129	Ea	.60	4.46	—	5.06
3/4"	P1@.181	Ea	1.27	6.25	—	7.52
1"	P1@.232	Ea	4.42	8.02	—	12.44
1¼"	P1@.284	Ea	7.17	9.81	—	16.98
1½"	P1@.335	Ea	10.90	11.60	—	22.50
2"	P1@.447	Ea	19.50	15.40	—	34.90
2½"	P1@.550	Ea	40.50	19.00	—	59.50
3"	P1@.654	Ea	51.20	22.60	—	73.80
4"	P1@.860	Ea	109.00	29.70	—	138.70

Description	Craft@Hrs	Unit	Material $	Labor $	Equipment $	Total $

Type L copper 90 degree ell Ftg. x C with brazed joint

Description	Craft@Hrs	Unit	Material $	Labor $	Equipment $	Total $
1/2"	P1@.129	Ea	.96	4.46	—	5.42
3/4"	P1@.181	Ea	2.10	6.25	—	8.35
1"	P1@.232	Ea	6.28	8.02	—	14.30
1¼"	P1@.284	Ea	8.75	9.81	—	18.56
1½"	P1@.335	Ea	13.10	11.60	—	24.70
2"	P1@.447	Ea	26.30	15.40	—	41.70
2½"	P1@.550	Ea	55.10	19.00	—	74.10
3"	P1@.654	Ea	62.00	22.60	—	84.60
4"	P1@.860	Ea	125.00	29.70	—	154.70

Type L copper tee C x C x C with brazed joints

Description	Craft@Hrs	Unit	Material $	Labor $	Equipment $	Total $
1/2"	P1@.156	Ea	1.03	5.39	—	6.42
3/4"	P1@.204	Ea	2.77	7.05	—	9.82
1"	P1@.263	Ea	10.50	9.09	—	19.59
1¼"	P1@.322	Ea	16.60	11.10	—	27.70
1½"	P1@.380	Ea	24.20	13.10	—	37.30
2"	P1@.507	Ea	38.60	17.50	—	56.10
2½"	P1@.624	Ea	78.30	21.60	—	99.90
3"	P1@.741	Ea	121.00	25.60	—	146.60
4"	P1@.975	Ea	202.00	33.70	—	235.70

Type L copper branch reducing tee C x C x C with brazed joints

Description	Craft@Hrs	Unit	Material $	Labor $	Equipment $	Total $
1/2" x 3/8"	P1@.129	Ea	2.08	4.46	—	6.54
3/4" x 1/2"	P1@.182	Ea	4.41	6.29	—	10.70
1" x 1/2"	P1@.209	Ea	8.66	7.22	—	15.88
1" x 3/4"	P1@.234	Ea	8.66	8.08	—	16.74
1¼" x 1/2"	P1@.241	Ea	13.20	8.33	—	21.53
1¼" x 3/4"	P1@.264	Ea	13.20	9.12	—	22.32
1¼" x 1"	P1@.287	Ea	13.20	9.92	—	23.12
1½" x 1/2"	P1@.291	Ea	16.20	10.10	—	26.30
1½" x 3/4"	P1@.307	Ea	16.20	10.60	—	26.80
1½" x 1"	P1@.323	Ea	16.20	11.20	—	27.40
1½" x 1¼"	P1@.339	Ea	16.20	11.70	—	27.90
2" x 1/2"	P1@.348	Ea	21.60	12.00	—	33.60
2" x 3/4"	P1@.373	Ea	21.60	12.90	—	34.50
2" x 1"	P1@.399	Ea	21.60	13.80	—	35.40
2" x 1¼"	P1@.426	Ea	21.60	14.70	—	36.30
2" x 1½"	P1@.452	Ea	21.60	15.60	—	37.20
2½" x 1/2"	P1@.468	Ea	65.20	16.20	—	81.40
2½" x 3/4"	P1@.485	Ea	65.20	16.80	—	82.00
2½" x 1"	P1@.502	Ea	65.20	17.30	—	82.50
2½" x 1½"	P1@.537	Ea	65.20	18.60	—	83.80
2½" x 2"	P1@.555	Ea	65.20	19.20	—	84.40
3" x 1¼"	P1@.562	Ea	73.70	19.40	—	93.10
3" x 2"	P1@.626	Ea	76.50	21.60	—	98.10
3" x 2½"	P1@.660	Ea	76.50	22.80	—	99.30
4" x 1¼"	P1@.669	Ea	133.00	23.10	—	156.10
4" x 1½"	P1@.718	Ea	133.00	24.80	—	157.80
4" x 2"	P1@.768	Ea	133.00	26.50	—	159.50
4" x 2½"	P1@.819	Ea	133.00	28.30	—	161.30
4" x 3"	P1@.868	Ea	133.00	30.00	—	163.00

Copper, Type L with Brazed Joints

Description	Craft@Hrs	Unit	Material $	Labor $	Equipment $	Total $

Type L copper reducer with brazed joints

Description	Craft@Hrs	Unit	Material $	Labor $	Equipment $	Total $
1/2" x 3/8"	P1@.148	Ea	.75	5.11	—	5.86
3/4" x 1/2"	P1@.155	Ea	1.41	5.36	—	6.77
1" x 3/4"	P1@.206	Ea	2.53	7.12	—	9.65
1¼" x 1/2"	P1@.206	Ea	4.25	7.12	—	11.37
1¼" x 3/4"	P1@.232	Ea	4.25	8.02	—	12.27
1¼" x 1"	P1@.258	Ea	4.25	8.91	—	13.16
1½" x 1/2"	P1@.232	Ea	6.50	8.02	—	14.52
1½" x 3/4"	P1@.257	Ea	6.50	8.88	—	15.38
1½" x 1"	P1@.283	Ea	6.50	9.78	—	16.28
1½" x 1¼"	P1@.308	Ea	6.50	10.60	—	17.10
2" x 1/2"	P1@.287	Ea	10.10	9.92	—	20.02
2" x 3/4"	P1@.277	Ea	10.10	9.57	—	19.67
2" x 1"	P1@.338	Ea	10.10	11.70	—	21.80
2" x 1¼"	P1@.365	Ea	10.10	12.60	—	22.70
2" x 1½"	P1@.390	Ea	10.10	13.50	—	23.60
2½" x 1"	P1@.390	Ea	27.50	13.50	—	41.00
2½" x 1¼"	P1@.416	Ea	27.50	14.40	—	41.90
2½" x 1½"	P1@.442	Ea	27.50	15.30	—	42.80
2½" x 2"	P1@.497	Ea	27.50	17.20	—	44.70
3" x 1¼"	P1@.468	Ea	32.10	16.20	—	48.30
3" x 1½"	P1@.493	Ea	32.10	17.00	—	49.10
3" x 2"	P1@.548	Ea	32.10	18.90	—	51.00
3" x 2½"	P1@.600	Ea	32.10	20.70	—	52.80
4" x 2"	P1@.652	Ea	62.00	22.50	—	84.50
4" x 2½"	P1@.704	Ea	62.00	24.30	—	86.30
4" x 3"	P1@.755	Ea	62.00	26.10	—	88.10

Type L copper adapter C x MPT with brazed joint

Description	Craft@Hrs	Unit	Material $	Labor $	Equipment $	Total $
1/2"	P1@.090	Ea	1.85	3.11	—	4.96
3/4"	P1@.126	Ea	2.89	4.35	—	7.24
1"	P1@.162	Ea	7.17	5.60	—	12.77
1¼"	P1@.198	Ea	13.40	6.84	—	20.24
1½"	P1@.234	Ea	15.00	8.08	—	23.08
2"	P1@.312	Ea	19.40	10.80	—	30.20
2½"	P1@.384	Ea	63.10	13.30	—	76.40
3"	P1@.456	Ea	105.00	15.80	—	120.80

Type L copper adapter C x FPT with brazed joint

Description	Craft@Hrs	Unit	Material $	Labor $	Equipment $	Total $
1/2"	P1@.090	Ea	3.08	3.11	—	6.19
3/4"	P1@.126	Ea	5.57	4.35	—	9.92
1"	P1@.162	Ea	8.43	5.60	—	14.03
1¼"	P1@.198	Ea	17.60	6.84	—	24.44
1½"	P1@.234	Ea	21.40	8.08	—	29.48
2"	P1@.312	Ea	32.90	10.80	—	43.70
2½"	P1@.384	Ea	82.70	13.30	—	96.00
3"	P1@.456	Ea	114.00	15.80	—	129.80

Description	Craft@Hrs	Unit	Material $	Labor $	Equipment $	Total $

Type L copper flush bushing with brazed joints

Description	Craft@Hrs	Unit	Material $	Labor $	Equipment $	Total $
1/2" x 3/8"	P1@.148	Ea	1.88	5.11	—	6.99
3/4" x 1/2"	P1@.155	Ea	3.19	5.36	—	8.55
1" x 3/4"	P1@.206	Ea	8.27	7.12	—	15.39
1" x 1/2"	P1@.206	Ea	9.45	7.12	—	16.57
1¼" x 1"	P1@.258	Ea	9.85	8.91	—	18.76
1½" x 1¼"	P1@.308	Ea	12.50	10.60	—	23.10
2" x 1½"	P1@.390	Ea	23.50	13.50	—	37.00

Type L copper union with brazed joints

Description	Craft@Hrs	Unit	Material $	Labor $	Equipment $	Total $
1/2"	P1@.146	Ea	7.50	5.04	—	12.54
3/4"	P1@.205	Ea	8.98	7.08	—	16.06
1"	P1@.263	Ea	20.10	9.09	—	29.19
1¼"	P1@.322	Ea	36.50	11.10	—	47.60
1½"	P1@.380	Ea	44.90	13.10	—	58.00
2"	P1@.507	Ea	67.00	17.50	—	84.50

Type L copper dielectric union with brazed joints

Description	Craft@Hrs	Unit	Material $	Labor $	Equipment $	Total $
1/2"	P1@.146	Ea	7.04	5.04	—	12.08
3/4"	P1@.205	Ea	7.04	7.08	—	14.12
1"	P1@.263	Ea	14.50	9.09	—	23.59
1¼"	P1@.322	Ea	24.80	11.10	—	35.90
1½"	P1@.380	Ea	34.10	13.10	—	47.20
2"	P1@.507	Ea	47.10	17.50	—	64.60

Type L copper cap with brazed joints

Description	Craft@Hrs	Unit	Material $	Labor $	Equipment $	Total $
1/2"	P1@.083	Ea	.61	2.87	—	3.48
3/4"	P1@.116	Ea	1.25	4.01	—	5.26
1"	P1@.149	Ea	2.82	5.15	—	7.97
1¼"	P1@.182	Ea	4.05	6.29	—	10.34
1½"	P1@.215	Ea	5.91	7.43	—	13.34
2"	P1@.286	Ea	10.70	9.88	—	20.58
2½"	P1@.352	Ea	27.00	12.20	—	39.20
3"	P1@.418	Ea	42.20	14.40	—	56.60
4"	P1@.550	Ea	64.80	19.00	—	83.80

Type L copper coupling with brazed joints

Description	Craft@Hrs	Unit	Material $	Labor $	Equipment $	Total $
1/2"	P1@.129	Ea	.42	4.46	—	4.88
3/4"	P1@.181	Ea	.98	6.25	—	7.23
1"	P1@.232	Ea	2.67	8.02	—	10.69
1¼"	P1@.284	Ea	4.67	9.81	—	14.48
1½"	P1@.335	Ea	6.76	11.60	—	18.36
2"	P1@.447	Ea	10.30	15.40	—	25.70
2½"	P1@.550	Ea	24.20	19.00	—	43.20
3"	P1@.654	Ea	36.90	22.60	—	59.50
4"	P1@.860	Ea	72.30	29.70	—	102.00

Copper, Type L with Brazed Joints

Description	Craft@Hrs	Unit	Material $	Labor $	Equipment $	Total $
Class 125 bronze body gate valve, brazed joints						
1/2"	P1@.240	Ea	16.20	8.29	—	24.49
3/4"	P1@.300	Ea	20.30	10.40	—	30.70
1"	P1@.360	Ea	28.50	12.40	—	40.90
1¼"	P1@.480	Ea	36.00	16.60	—	52.60
1½"	P1@.540	Ea	48.40	18.70	—	67.10
2"	P1@.600	Ea	80.90	20.70	—	101.60
2½"	P1@1.00	Ea	134.00	34.60	—	168.60
3"	P1@1.50	Ea	193.00	51.80	—	244.80
Class 125 iron body gate valve, flanged joints						
2"	P1@.500	Ea	310.00	17.30	—	327.30
2½"	P1@.600	Ea	418.00	20.70	—	438.70
3"	P1@.750	Ea	454.00	25.90	—	479.90
4"	P1@1.35	Ea	666.00	46.60	—	712.60
5"	P1@2.00	Ea	1,270.00	69.10	—	1,339.10
6"	P1@2.50	Ea	1,270.00	86.40	—	1,356.40
Class 125 bronze body globe valve, with brazed joints						
1/2"	P1@.240	Ea	30.00	8.29	—	38.29
3/4"	P1@.300	Ea	40.00	10.40	—	50.40
1"	P1@.360	Ea	68.90	12.40	—	81.30
1¼"	P1@.480	Ea	96.90	16.60	—	113.50
1½"	P1@.540	Ea	131.00	18.70	—	149.70
2"	P1@.600	Ea	212.00	20.70	—	232.70
Class 125 iron body globe valve, flanged joints						
2½"	P1@.650	Ea	351.00	22.50	—	373.50
3"	P1@.750	Ea	421.00	25.90	—	446.90
4"	P1@1.35	Ea	568.00	46.60	—	614.60
200 PSIG iron body butterfly valve, lug type, lever operated						
2"	P1@.450	Ea	134.00	15.50	—	149.50
2½"	P1@.450	Ea	139.00	15.50	—	154.50
3"	P1@.550	Ea	146.00	19.00	—	165.00
4"	P1@.550	Ea	182.00	19.00	—	201.00
200 PSIG iron body butterfly valve, wafer type, lever operated						
2"	P1@.450	Ea	122.00	15.50	—	137.50
2½"	P1@.450	Ea	125.00	15.50	—	140.50
3"	P1@.550	Ea	134.00	19.00	—	153.00
4"	P1@.550	Ea	163.00	19.00	—	182.00

Description	Craft@Hrs	Unit	Material $	Labor $	Equipment $	Total $

Class 125 bronze body 2-piece ball valve, brazed joints

Description	Craft@Hrs	Unit	Material $	Labor $	Equipment $	Total $
1/2"	P1@.240	Ea	7.91	8.29	—	16.20
3/4"	P1@.300	Ea	10.50	10.40	—	20.90
1"	P1@.360	Ea	18.20	12.40	—	30.60
1¼"	P1@.480	Ea	30.30	16.60	—	46.90
1½"	P1@.540	Ea	41.00	18.70	—	59.70
2"	P1@.600	Ea	51.90	20.70	—	72.60
3"	P1@1.50	Ea	355.00	51.80	—	406.80
4"	P1@1.80	Ea	465.00	62.20	—	527.20

Class 125 bronze body swing check valve, brazed joints

Description	Craft@Hrs	Unit	Material $	Labor $	Equipment $	Total $
1/2"	P1@.240	Ea	17.70	8.29	—	25.99
3/4"	P1@.300	Ea	25.40	10.40	—	35.80
1"	P1@.360	Ea	33.30	12.40	—	45.70
1¼"	P1@.480	Ea	47.30	16.60	—	63.90
1½"	P1@.540	Ea	66.70	18.70	—	85.40
2"	P1@.600	Ea	111.00	20.70	—	131.70
2½"	P1@1.00	Ea	223.00	34.60	—	257.60
3"	P1@1.50	Ea	320.00	51.80	—	371.80

Class 125 iron body swing check valve, flanged joints

Description	Craft@Hrs	Unit	Material $	Labor $	Equipment $	Total $
2"	P1@.500	Ea	155.00	17.30	—	172.30
2½"	P1@.600	Ea	197.00	20.70	—	217.70
3"	P1@.750	Ea	245.00	25.90	—	270.90
4"	P1@1.35	Ea	360.00	46.60	—	406.60

Class 125 iron body silent check valve, wafer type

Description	Craft@Hrs	Unit	Material $	Labor $	Equipment $	Total $
2"	P1@.500	Ea	113.00	17.30	—	130.30
2½"	P1@.600	Ea	126.00	20.70	—	146.70
3"	P1@.750	Ea	145.00	25.90	—	170.90
4"	P1@1.35	Ea	194.00	46.60	—	240.60

Class 125 bronze body strainer, threaded joints

Description	Craft@Hrs	Unit	Material $	Labor $	Equipment $	Total $
1/2"	P1@.230	Ea	27.70	7.95	—	35.65
3/4"	P1@.260	Ea	36.40	8.98	—	45.38
1"	P1@.330	Ea	44.60	11.40	—	56.00
1¼"	P1@.440	Ea	62.30	15.20	—	77.50
1½"	P1@.495	Ea	93.80	17.10	—	110.90
2"	P1@.550	Ea	162.00	19.00	—	181.00

Class 125 iron body strainer, flanged joints

Description	Craft@Hrs	Unit	Material $	Labor $	Equipment $	Total $
2"	P1@.500	Ea	124.00	17.30	—	141.30
2½"	P1@.600	Ea	139.00	20.70	—	159.70
3"	P1@.750	Ea	160.00	25.90	—	185.90
4"	P1@1.35	Ea	273.00	46.60	—	319.60

Description	Craft@Hrs	Unit	Material $	Labor $	Equipment $	Total $

Installation of 2-way control valve, threaded joints

Description	Craft@Hrs	Unit	Material $	Labor $	Equipment $	Total $
1/2"	P1@.210	Ea	—	7.26	—	7.26
3/4"	P1@.275	Ea	—	9.50	—	9.50
1"	P1@.350	Ea	—	12.10	—	12.10
1¼"	P1@.430	Ea	—	14.90	—	14.90
1½"	P1@.505	Ea	—	17.40	—	17.40
2"	P1@.675	Ea	—	23.30	—	23.30
2½"	P1@.830	Ea	—	28.70	—	28.70
3"	P1@.990	Ea	—	34.20	—	34.20

Installation of 3-way control valve, threaded joints

Description	Craft@Hrs	Unit	Material $	Labor $	Equipment $	Total $
1/2"	P1@.260	Ea	—	8.98	—	8.98
3/4"	P1@.365	Ea	—	12.60	—	12.60
1"	P1@.475	Ea	—	16.40	—	16.40
1¼"	P1@.575	Ea	—	19.90	—	19.90
1½"	P1@.680	Ea	—	23.50	—	23.50
2"	P1@.910	Ea	—	31.40	—	31.40
2½"	P1@1.12	Ea	—	38.70	—	38.70
3"	P1@1.33	Ea	—	46.00	—	46.00

Companion flange, 150 pound cast brass

Description	Craft@Hrs	Unit	Material $	Labor $	Equipment $	Total $
2"	P1@.290	Ea	365.00	10.00	—	375.00
2½"	P1@.380	Ea	450.00	13.10	—	463.10
3"	P1@.460	Ea	450.00	15.90	—	465.90
4"	P1@.600	Ea	717.00	20.70	—	737.70

Bolt and gasket sets

Description	Craft@Hrs	Unit	Material $	Labor $	Equipment $	Total $
2"	P1@.500	Ea	3.86	17.30	—	21.16
2½"	P1@.650	Ea	4.51	22.50	—	27.01
3"	P1@.750	Ea	7.67	25.90	—	33.57
4"	P1@1.00	Ea	12.80	34.60	—	47.40

Thermometer with well

Description	Craft@Hrs	Unit	Material $	Labor $	Equipment $	Total $
7"	P1@.250	Ea	159.00	8.64	—	167.64
9"	P1@.250	Ea	164.00	8.64	—	172.64

Dial type pressure gauge

Description	Craft@Hrs	Unit	Material $	Labor $	Equipment $	Total $
2½"	P1@.200	Ea	33.10	6.91	—	40.01
3½"	P1@.200	Ea	43.90	6.91	—	50.81

Description	Craft@Hrs	Unit	Material $	Labor $	Equipment $	Total $

Pressure/temperature tap

Description	Craft@Hrs	Unit	Material $	Labor $	Equipment $	Total $
tap	P1@.150	Ea	15.70	5.18	—	20.88

Hanger with swivel assembly

Description	Craft@Hrs	Unit	Material $	Labor $	Equipment $	Total $
1/2"	P1@.250	Ea	3.74	8.64	—	12.38
3/4"	P1@.250	Ea	4.13	8.64	—	12.77
1"	P1@.250	Ea	4.33	8.64	—	12.97
1¼"	P1@.300	Ea	4.44	10.40	—	14.84
1½"	P1@.300	Ea	4.77	10.40	—	15.17
2"	P1@.300	Ea	4.98	10.40	—	15.38
2½"	P1@.350	Ea	6.78	12.10	—	18.88
3"	P1@.350	Ea	8.37	12.10	—	20.47
4"	P1@.350	Ea	9.19	12.10	—	21.29

Riser clamp

Description	Craft@Hrs	Unit	Material $	Labor $	Equipment $	Total $
1/2"	P1@.100	Ea	2.41	3.46	—	5.87
3/4"	P1@.100	Ea	3.55	3.46	—	7.01
1"	P1@.100	Ea	3.59	3.46	—	7.05
1¼"	P1@.105	Ea	4.33	3.63	—	7.96
1½"	P1@.110	Ea	4.58	3.80	—	8.38
2"	P1@.115	Ea	4.84	3.97	—	8.81
2½"	P1@.120	Ea	5.09	4.15	—	9.24
3"	P1@.120	Ea	5.52	4.15	—	9.67
4"	P1@.125	Ea	7.03	4.32	—	11.35

Copper, Type L with Soft-Soldered Joints

Type L hard-drawn copper pipe with wrought copper fittings and soft-soldered joints is used in a wide variety of plumbing and HVAC systems such as potable water, heating hot water, chilled water, and A.C. condensate.

Soft-soldered joints are those made with solders having melting points in the 350 degree F. to 500 degree F. range. Maximum working temperature/pressure relationships for soft-soldered joints are approximately as follows:

	Maximum Working Pressures (PSIG)*			
Soft-solder Type	Water Temperature (degrees F.)	Nominal Pipe Size (inches)		
		Up to 1	1¼ to 2	2½ x 4
50-50 tin-lead**	100	200	175	150
	150	150	125	100
	200	100	90	75
	250	85	75	50
95-5 tin-antimony	100	500	400	300
	150	400	350	275
	200	300	250	200
	250	200	175	150

*For copper pipe and solder-type fittings using soft-solders melting at approximately 350 degrees F. to 500 degrees F.

**The use of any solder containing lead is not allowed in potable water systems.

This section has been arranged to save the estimator's time by including all normally-used system components such as pipe, fittings, valves, hanger assemblies, riser clamps and miscellaneous items under one heading. Additional items can be found under "Plumbing and Piping Specialties." The cost estimates in this section are based on the conditions, limitations and wage rates described in the section "How to Use This Book" beginning on page 5.

Description	Craft@Hrs	Unit	Material $	Labor $	Equipment $	Total $

Type L copper pipe with soft-soldered joints installed horizontally.
Complete installation including eight wrought copper tees and eight wrought copper elbows every 100', and hangers spaced to meet plumbing code. Use these figures for preliminary estimates.

Description	Craft@Hrs	Unit	Material $	Labor $	Equipment $	Total $
1/2"	P1@.111	LF	2.27	3.84	—	6.11
3/4"	P1@.121	LF	3.52	4.18	—	7.70
1"	P1@.141	LF	6.36	4.87	—	11.23
1¼"	P1@.161	LF	9.06	5.56	—	14.62
1½"	P1@.181	LF	12.20	6.25	—	18.45
2"	P1@.211	LF	22.10	7.29	—	29.39
2½"	P1@.241	LF	38.20	8.33	—	46.53
3"	P1@.271	LF	53.40	9.36	—	62.76
4"	P1@.311	LF	77.10	10.70	—	87.80

Description	Craft@Hrs	Unit	Material $	Labor $	Equipment $	Total $

Type L copper pipe with soft-soldered joints, installed risers.
Complete installation including a wrought copper reducing tee every floor and a riser clamp every other floor.

Description	Craft@Hrs	Unit	Material $	Labor $	Equipment $	Total $
1/2"	P1@.061	LF	2.46	2.11	—	4.57
3/4"	P1@.071	LF	3.82	2.45	—	6.27
1"	P1@.076	LF	6.47	2.63	—	9.10
1¼"	P1@.081	LF	9.14	2.80	—	11.94
1½"	P1@.101	LF	11.40	3.49	—	14.89
2"	P1@.131	LF	29.90	4.53	—	34.43
2½"	P1@.151	LF	32.30	5.22	—	37.52
3"	P1@.171	LF	41.90	5.91	—	47.81
4"	P1@.191	LF	62.30	6.60	—	68.90

Type L copper pipe with soft-soldered joints, pipe only

Description	Craft@Hrs	Unit	Material $	Labor $	Equipment $	Total $
1/2"	P1@.032	LF	1.85	1.11	—	2.96
3/4"	P1@.035	LF	2.93	1.21	—	4.14
1"	P1@.038	LF	4.06	1.31	—	5.37
1¼"	P1@.042	LF	5.82	1.45	—	7.27
1½"	P1@.046	LF	7.43	1.59	—	9.02
2"	P1@.053	LF	12.80	1.83	—	14.63
2½"	P1@.060	LF	18.60	2.07	—	20.67
3"	P1@.066	LF	25.20	2.28	—	27.48
4"	P1@.080	LF	39.60	2.76	—	42.36

Type L copper 45 degree ell C x C with soft-soldered joints

Description	Craft@Hrs	Unit	Material $	Labor $	Equipment $	Total $
1/2"	P1@.107	Ea	1.04	3.70	—	4.74
3/4"	P1@.150	Ea	1.97	5.18	—	7.15
1"	P1@.193	Ea	7.11	6.67	—	13.78
1¼"	P1@.236	Ea	9.62	8.15	—	17.77
1½"	P1@.278	Ea	11.70	9.60	—	21.30
2"	P1@.371	Ea	19.20	12.80	—	32.00
2½"	P1@.457	Ea	49.00	15.80	—	64.80
3"	P1@.543	Ea	64.70	18.80	—	83.50
4"	P1@.714	Ea	125.00	24.70	—	149.70

Type L copper 90 degree ell C x C with soft-soldered joints

Description	Craft@Hrs	Unit	Material $	Labor $	Equipment $	Total $
1/2"	P1@.107	Ea	.60	3.70	—	4.30
3/4"	P1@.150	Ea	1.27	5.18	—	6.45
1"	P1@.193	Ea	4.42	6.67	—	11.09
1¼"	P1@.236	Ea	7.17	8.15	—	15.32
1½"	P1@.278	Ea	10.90	9.60	—	20.50
2"	P1@.371	Ea	19.50	12.80	—	32.30
2½"	P1@.457	Ea	40.50	15.80	—	56.30
3"	P1@.543	Ea	51.20	18.80	—	70.00
4"	P1@.714	Ea	109.00	24.70	—	133.70

Copper, Type L with Soft-Soldered Joints

Description	Craft@Hrs	Unit	Material $	Labor $	Equipment $	Total $

Type L copper 90 degree ell Ftg. x C with soft-soldered joint

Description	Craft@Hrs	Unit	Material $	Labor $	Equipment $	Total $
1/2"	P1@.107	Ea	1.27	3.70	—	4.97
3/4"	P1@.150	Ea	4.19	5.18	—	9.37
1"	P1@.193	Ea	6.28	6.67	—	12.95
1¼"	P1@.236	Ea	8.75	8.15	—	16.90
1½"	P1@.278	Ea	13.10	9.60	—	22.70
2"	P1@.371	Ea	26.30	12.80	—	39.10
2½"	P1@.457	Ea	55.10	15.80	—	70.90
3"	P1@.543	Ea	62.00	18.80	—	80.80
4"	P1@.714	Ea	167.00	24.70	—	191.70

Type L copper tee C x C x C with soft-soldered joints

Description	Craft@Hrs	Unit	Material $	Labor $	Equipment $	Total $
1/2"	P1@.129	Ea	1.03	4.46	—	5.49
3/4"	P1@.181	Ea	2.77	6.25	—	9.02
1"	P1@.233	Ea	10.50	8.05	—	18.55
1¼"	P1@.285	Ea	16.60	9.85	—	26.45
1½"	P1@.337	Ea	24.20	11.60	—	35.80
2"	P1@.449	Ea	38.60	15.50	—	54.10
2½"	P1@.552	Ea	78.30	19.10	—	97.40
3"	P1@.656	Ea	121.00	22.70	—	143.70
4"	P1@.863	Ea	202.00	29.80	—	231.80

Type L copper branch reducing tee C x C x C with soft-soldered joints

Description	Craft@Hrs	Unit	Material $	Labor $	Equipment $	Total $
1/2" x 3/8"	P1@.129	Ea	2.08	4.46	—	6.54
3/4" x 1/2"	P1@.182	Ea	4.41	6.29	—	10.70
1" x 1/2"	P1@.195	Ea	8.66	6.74	—	15.40
1" x 3/4"	P1@.219	Ea	8.66	7.57	—	16.23
1¼" x 1/2"	P1@.225	Ea	13.20	7.77	—	20.97
1¼" x 3/4"	P1@.247	Ea	13.20	8.53	—	21.73
1¼" x 1"	P1@.268	Ea	13.20	9.26	—	22.46
1½" x 1/2"	P1@.272	Ea	16.20	9.40	—	25.60
1½" x 3/4"	P1@.287	Ea	16.20	9.92	—	26.12
1½" x 1"	P1@.302	Ea	16.20	10.40	—	26.60
1½" x 1¼"	P1@.317	Ea	16.20	11.00	—	27.20
2" x 1/2"	P1@.325	Ea	21.60	11.20	—	32.80
2" x 3/4"	P1@.348	Ea	21.60	12.00	—	33.60
2" x 1"	P1@.373	Ea	21.60	12.90	—	34.50
2" x 1¼"	P1@.398	Ea	21.60	13.80	—	35.40
2" x 1½"	P1@.422	Ea	21.60	14.60	—	36.20
2½" x 1/2"	P1@.437	Ea	65.20	15.10	—	80.30
2½" x 3/4"	P1@.453	Ea	65.20	15.70	—	80.90
2½" x 1"	P1@.469	Ea	65.20	16.20	—	81.40
2½" x 1½"	P1@.502	Ea	65.20	17.30	—	82.50
2½" x 2"	P1@.519	Ea	65.20	17.90	—	83.10
3" x 1¼"	P1@.525	Ea	73.70	18.10	—	91.80
3" x 2"	P1@.585	Ea	76.50	20.20	—	96.70
3" x 2½"	P1@.617	Ea	76.50	21.30	—	97.80
4" x 1¼"	P1@.625	Ea	133.00	21.60	—	154.60
4" x 1½"	P1@.671	Ea	133.00	23.20	—	156.20
4" x 2"	P1@.718	Ea	133.00	24.80	—	157.80
4" x 2½"	P1@.765	Ea	133.00	26.40	—	159.40
4" x 3"	P1@.811	Ea	133.00	28.00	—	161.00

Description	Craft@Hrs	Unit	Material $	Labor $	Equipment $	Total $

Type L copper reducer with soft-soldered joints

Description	Craft@Hrs	Unit	Material $	Labor $	Equipment $	Total $
1/2" x 3/8"	P1@.124	Ea	.75	4.28	—	5.03
3/4" x 1/2"	P1@.129	Ea	1.41	4.46	—	5.87
1" x 3/4"	P1@.172	Ea	2.53	5.94	—	8.47
1¼" x 1/2"	P1@.172	Ea	4.25	5.94	—	10.19
1¼" x 3/4"	P1@.193	Ea	4.25	6.67	—	10.92
1¼" x 1"	P1@.215	Ea	4.25	7.43	—	11.68
1½" x 1/2"	P1@.193	Ea	6.50	6.67	—	13.17
1½" x 3/4"	P1@.214	Ea	6.50	7.39	—	13.89
1½" x 1"	P1@.236	Ea	6.50	8.15	—	14.65
1½" x 1¼"	P1@.257	Ea	6.50	8.88	—	15.38
2" x 1/2"	P1@.239	Ea	10.10	8.26	—	18.36
2" x 3/4"	P1@.261	Ea	10.10	9.02	—	19.12
2" x 1"	P1@.282	Ea	10.10	9.74	—	19.84
2" x 1¼"	P1@.304	Ea	10.10	10.50	—	20.60
2" x 1½"	P1@.325	Ea	10.10	11.20	—	21.30
2½" x 1"	P1@.325	Ea	27.50	11.20	—	38.70
2½" x 1¼"	P1@.347	Ea	27.50	12.00	—	39.50
2½" x 1½"	P1@.368	Ea	27.50	12.70	—	40.20
2½" x 2"	P1@.414	Ea	27.50	14.30	—	41.80
3" x 2"	P1@.457	Ea	32.10	15.80	—	47.90
3" x 2½"	P1@.500	Ea	32.10	17.30	—	49.40
4" x 2"	P1@.543	Ea	62.00	18.80	—	80.80
4" x 2½"	P1@.586	Ea	62.00	20.20	—	82.20
4" x 3"	P1@.629	Ea	62.00	21.70	—	83.70

Type L copper adapter C x MPT with soft-soldered joint

Description	Craft@Hrs	Unit	Material $	Labor $	Equipment $	Total $
1/2"	P1@.075	Ea	1.85	2.59	—	4.44
3/4"	P1@.105	Ea	2.89	3.63	—	6.52
1"	P1@.134	Ea	7.17	4.63	—	11.80
1¼"	P1@.164	Ea	13.40	5.67	—	19.07
1½"	P1@.194	Ea	15.00	6.70	—	21.70
2"	P1@.259	Ea	19.40	8.95	—	28.35
2½"	P1@.319	Ea	63.10	11.00	—	74.10
3"	P1@.378	Ea	105.00	13.10	—	118.10

Type L copper adapter C x FPT with soft-soldered joint

Description	Craft@Hrs	Unit	Material $	Labor $	Equipment $	Total $
1/2"	P1@.075	Ea	3.08	2.59	—	5.67
3/4"	P1@.105	Ea	5.57	3.63	—	9.20
1"	P1@.134	Ea	8.43	4.63	—	13.06
1¼"	P1@.164	Ea	17.60	5.67	—	23.27
1½"	P1@.194	Ea	21.40	6.70	—	28.10
2"	P1@.259	Ea	32.90	8.95	—	41.85
2½"	P1@.319	Ea	82.70	11.00	—	93.70
3"	P1@.378	Ea	114.00	13.10	—	127.10

Copper, Type L with Soft-Soldered Joints

Description	Craft@Hrs	Unit	Material $	Labor $	Equipment $	Total $

Type L copper flush bushing with soft-soldered joints

Description	Craft@Hrs	Unit	Material $	Labor $	Equipment $	Total $
1/2" x 3/8"	P1@.124	Ea	1.88	4.28	—	6.16
3/4" x 1/2"	P1@.129	Ea	3.19	4.46	—	7.65
1" x 3/4"	P1@.172	Ea	8.27	5.94	—	14.21
1" x 1/2"	P1@.172	Ea	9.45	5.94	—	15.39
1¼" x 1"	P1@.215	Ea	9.85	7.43	—	17.28
1½" x 1¼"	P1@.257	Ea	12.50	8.88	—	21.38
2" x 1½"	P1@.325	Ea	23.50	11.20	—	34.70

Type L copper union with soft-soldered joint

Description	Craft@Hrs	Unit	Material $	Labor $	Equipment $	Total $
1/2"	P1@.121	Ea	7.50	4.18	—	11.68
3/4"	P1@.170	Ea	8.98	5.87	—	14.85
1"	P1@.218	Ea	20.10	7.53	—	27.63
1¼"	P1@.267	Ea	36.50	9.22	—	45.72
1½"	P1@.315	Ea	44.90	10.90	—	55.80
2"	P1@.421	Ea	67.00	14.50	—	81.50

Type L copper dielectric union with soft-soldered joint

Description	Craft@Hrs	Unit	Material $	Labor $	Equipment $	Total $
1/2"	P1@.121	Ea	7.04	4.18	—	11.22
3/4"	P1@.170	Ea	7.04	5.87	—	12.91
1"	P1@.218	Ea	14.50	7.53	—	22.03
1¼"	P1@.267	Ea	24.80	9.22	—	34.02
1½"	P1@.315	Ea	34.10	10.90	—	45.00
2"	P1@.421	Ea	47.10	14.50	—	61.60

Type L copper cap with soft-soldered joint

Description	Craft@Hrs	Unit	Material $	Labor $	Equipment $	Total $
1/2"	P1@.069	Ea	.61	2.38	—	2.99
3/4"	P1@.096	Ea	1.25	3.32	—	4.57
1"	P1@.124	Ea	2.82	4.28	—	7.10
1¼"	P1@.151	Ea	4.05	5.22	—	9.27
1½"	P1@.178	Ea	5.91	6.15	—	12.06
2"	P1@.237	Ea	10.70	8.19	—	18.89
2½"	P1@.292	Ea	27.00	10.10	—	37.10
3"	P1@.347	Ea	42.20	12.00	—	54.20
4"	P1@.457	Ea	64.80	15.80	—	80.60

Type L copper coupling with soft-soldered joints

Description	Craft@Hrs	Unit	Material $	Labor $	Equipment $	Total $
1/2"	P1@.107	Ea	.42	3.70	—	4.12
3/4"	P1@.150	Ea	.98	5.18	—	6.16
1"	P1@.193	Ea	2.67	6.67	—	9.34
1¼"	P1@.236	Ea	4.67	8.15	—	12.82
1½"	P1@.278	Ea	6.76	9.60	—	16.36
2"	P1@.371	Ea	10.30	12.80	—	23.10
2½"	P1@.457	Ea	24.20	15.80	—	40.00
3"	P1@.543	Ea	36.90	18.80	—	55.70
4"	P1@.714	Ea	72.30	24.70	—	97.00

Description	Craft@Hrs	Unit	Material $	Labor $	Equipment $	Total $

Class 125 bronze body gate valve, soft-soldered joints

Description	Craft@Hrs	Unit	Material $	Labor $	Equipment $	Total $
1/2"	P1@.200	Ea	15.40	6.91	—	22.31
3/4"	P1@.249	Ea	19.30	8.60	—	27.90
1"	P1@.299	Ea	27.10	10.30	—	37.40
1¼"	P1@.398	Ea	34.30	13.80	—	48.10
1½"	P1@.448	Ea	46.10	15.50	—	61.60
2"	P1@.498	Ea	77.00	17.20	—	94.20
2½"	P1@.830	Ea	128.00	28.70	—	156.70
3"	P1@1.24	Ea	184.00	42.80	—	226.80

Class 125 iron body gate valve, flanged ends

Description	Craft@Hrs	Unit	Material $	Labor $	Equipment $	Total $
2"	P1@.500	Ea	310.00	17.30	—	327.30
2½"	P1@.600	Ea	418.00	20.70	—	438.70
3"	P1@.750	Ea	454.00	25.90	—	479.90
4"	P1@1.35	Ea	666.00	46.60	—	712.60
5"	P1@2.00	Ea	1,270.00	69.10	—	1,339.10
6"	P1@2.50	Ea	1,270.00	86.40	—	1,356.40

Class 125 bronze body globe valve, with soft-soldered joints

Description	Craft@Hrs	Unit	Material $	Labor $	Equipment $	Total $
1/2"	P1@.200	Ea	30.00	6.91	—	36.91
3/4"	P1@.249	Ea	40.00	8.60	—	48.60
1"	P1@.299	Ea	68.90	10.30	—	79.20
1¼"	P1@.398	Ea	96.90	13.80	—	110.70
1½"	P1@.448	Ea	131.00	15.50	—	146.50
2"	P1@.498	Ea	212.00	17.20	—	229.20

Class 125 iron body globe valve, flanged ends

Description	Craft@Hrs	Unit	Material $	Labor $	Equipment $	Total $
2½"	P1@.600	Ea	351.00	20.70	—	371.70
3"	P1@.750	Ea	421.00	25.90	—	446.90
4"	P1@1.35	Ea	565.00	46.60	—	611.60

200 PSIG iron body butterfly valve, lug type, lever operated

Description	Craft@Hrs	Unit	Material $	Labor $	Equipment $	Total $
2"	P1@.450	Ea	134.00	15.50	—	149.50
2½"	P1@.450	Ea	139.00	15.50	—	154.50
3"	P1@.550	Ea	146.00	19.00	—	165.00
4"	P1@.550	Ea	182.00	19.00	—	201.00

200 PSIG iron body butterfly valve, wafer type, lever operated

Description	Craft@Hrs	Unit	Material $	Labor $	Equipment $	Total $
2"	P1@.450	Ea	122.00	15.50	—	137.50
2½"	P1@.450	Ea	125.00	15.50	—	140.50
3"	P1@.550	Ea	134.00	19.00	—	153.00
4"	P1@.550	Ea	163.00	19.00	—	182.00

Copper, Type L with Soft-Soldered Joints

Description	Craft@Hrs	Unit	Material $	Labor $	Equipment $	Total $

Class 125 bronze body 2-piece ball valve, soft-soldered joints

Description	Craft@Hrs	Unit	Material $	Labor $	Equipment $	Total $
1/2"	P1@.200	Ea	7.91	6.91	—	14.82
3/4"	P1@.249	Ea	10.50	8.60	—	19.10
1"	P1@.299	Ea	18.20	10.30	—	28.50
1¼"	P1@.398	Ea	30.30	13.80	—	44.10
1½"	P1@.448	Ea	41.00	15.50	—	56.50
2"	P1@.498	Ea	51.90	17.20	—	69.10
3"	P1@1.24	Ea	355.00	42.80	—	397.80
4"	P1@1.45	Ea	465.00	50.10	—	515.10

Class 125 bronze body swing check valve, soft-soldered joints

Description	Craft@Hrs	Unit	Material $	Labor $	Equipment $	Total $
1/2"	P1@.200	Ea	17.70	6.91	—	24.61
3/4"	P1@.249	Ea	25.40	8.60	—	34.00
1"	P1@.299	Ea	33.30	10.30	—	43.60
1¼"	P1@.398	Ea	47.30	13.80	—	61.10
1½"	P1@.448	Ea	66.70	15.50	—	82.20
2"	P1@.498	Ea	111.00	17.20	—	128.20
2½"	P1@.830	Ea	223.00	28.70	—	251.70
3"	P1@1.24	Ea	320.00	42.80	—	362.80

Class 125 iron body swing check valve, flanged ends

Description	Craft@Hrs	Unit	Material $	Labor $	Equipment $	Total $
2"	P1@.500	Ea	155.00	17.30	—	172.30
2½"	P1@.600	Ea	197.00	20.70	—	217.70
3"	P1@.750	Ea	245.00	25.90	—	270.90
4"	P1@1.35	Ea	360.00	46.60	—	406.60

Class 125 iron body silent check valve, wafer type

Description	Craft@Hrs	Unit	Material $	Labor $	Equipment $	Total $
2"	P1@.500	Ea	113.00	17.30	—	130.30
2½"	P1@.600	Ea	126.00	20.70	—	146.70
3"	P1@.750	Ea	145.00	25.90	—	170.90
4"	P1@1.35	Ea	194.00	46.60	—	240.60

Class 125 bronze body strainer, threaded ends

Description	Craft@Hrs	Unit	Material $	Labor $	Equipment $	Total $
1/2"	P1@.230	Ea	27.70	7.95	—	35.65
3/4"	P1@.260	Ea	36.40	8.98	—	45.38
1"	P1@.330	Ea	44.60	11.40	—	56.00
1¼"	P1@.440	Ea	62.30	15.20	—	77.50
1½"	P1@.495	Ea	93.80	17.10	—	110.90
2"	P1@.550	Ea	162.00	19.00	—	181.00

Class 125 iron body strainer, flanged ends

Description	Craft@Hrs	Unit	Material $	Labor $	Equipment $	Total $
2"	P1@.500	Ea	123.00	17.30	—	140.30
2½"	P1@.600	Ea	138.00	20.70	—	158.70
3"	P1@.750	Ea	159.00	25.90	—	184.90
4"	P1@1.35	Ea	271.00	46.60	—	317.60

Description	Craft@Hrs	Unit	Material $	Labor $	Equipment $	Total $

Installation of 2-way control valve, threaded joints

Description	Craft@Hrs	Unit	Material $	Labor $	Equipment $	Total $
1/2"	P1@.210	Ea	—	7.26	—	7.26
3/4"	P1@.275	Ea	—	9.50	—	9.50
1"	P1@.350	Ea	—	12.10	—	12.10
1¼"	P1@.430	Ea	—	14.90	—	14.90
1½"	P1@.505	Ea	—	17.40	—	17.40
2"	P1@.675	Ea	—	23.30	—	23.30
2½"	P1@.830	Ea	—	28.70	—	28.70
3"	P1@.990	Ea	—	34.20	—	34.20

Installation of 3-way control valve, threaded joints

Description	Craft@Hrs	Unit	Material $	Labor $	Equipment $	Total $
1/2"	P1@.260	Ea	—	8.98	—	8.98
3/4"	P1@.365	Ea	—	12.60	—	12.60
1"	P1@.475	Ea	—	16.40	—	16.40
1¼"	P1@.575	Ea	—	19.90	—	19.90
1½"	P1@.680	Ea	—	23.50	—	23.50
2"	P1@.910	Ea	—	31.40	—	31.40
2½"	P1@1.12	Ea	—	38.70	—	38.70
3"	P1@1.33	Ea	—	46.00	—	46.00

Companion flange, 150 pound cast brass

Description	Craft@Hrs	Unit	Material $	Labor $	Equipment $	Total $
2"	P1@.290	Ea	360.00	10.00	—	370.00
2½"	P1@.380	Ea	445.00	13.10	—	458.10
3"	P1@.460	Ea	445.00	15.90	—	460.90
4"	P1@.600	Ea	708.00	20.70	—	728.70

Bolt and gasket sets

Description	Craft@Hrs	Unit	Material $	Labor $	Equipment $	Total $
2"	P1@.500	Ea	3.86	17.30	—	21.16
2½"	P1@.650	Ea	4.51	22.50	—	27.01
3"	P1@.750	Ea	7.67	25.90	—	33.57
4"	P1@1.00	Ea	12.80	34.60	—	47.40

Thermometer with well

Description	Craft@Hrs	Unit	Material $	Labor $	Equipment $	Total $
7"	P1@.250	Ea	159.00	8.64	—	167.64
9"	P1@.250	Ea	164.00	8.64	—	172.64

Dial type pressure gauge

Description	Craft@Hrs	Unit	Material $	Labor $	Equipment $	Total $
2½"	P1@.200	Ea	33.10	6.91	—	40.01
3½"	P1@.200	Ea	43.80	6.91	—	50.71

Pressure/temperature tap

Description	Craft@Hrs	Unit	Material $	Labor $	Equipment $	Total $
tap	P1@.150	Ea	15.70	5.18	—	20.88

Copper, Type L with Soft-Soldered Joints

Description	Craft@Hrs	Unit	Material $	Labor $	Equipment $	Total $

Hanger with swivel assembly

Description	Craft@Hrs	Unit	Material $	Labor $	Equipment $	Total $
1/2"	P1@.250	Ea	3.74	8.64	—	12.38
3/4"	P1@.250	Ea	4.13	8.64	—	12.77
1"	P1@.250	Ea	4.33	8.64	—	12.97
1¼"	P1@.300	Ea	4.44	10.40	—	14.84
1½"	P1@.300	Ea	4.77	10.40	—	15.17
2"	P1@.300	Ea	4.98	10.40	—	15.38
2½"	P1@.350	Ea	6.78	12.10	—	18.88
3"	P1@.350	Ea	8.37	12.10	—	20.47
4"	P1@.350	Ea	9.19	12.10	—	21.29

Riser clamp

Description	Craft@Hrs	Unit	Material $	Labor $	Equipment $	Total $
1/2"	P1@.100	Ea	2.41	3.46	—	5.87
3/4"	P1@.100	Ea	3.55	3.46	—	7.01
1"	P1@.100	Ea	3.59	3.46	—	7.05
1¼"	P1@.105	Ea	4.33	3.63	—	7.96
1½"	P1@.110	Ea	4.58	3.80	—	8.38
2"	P1@.115	Ea	4.84	3.97	—	8.81
2½"	P1@.120	Ea	5.09	4.15	—	9.24
3"	P1@.120	Ea	5.52	4.15	—	9.67
4"	P1@.125	Ea	7.03	4.32	—	11.35

Type M hard-drawn copper pipe with wrought copper fittings and brazed joints is used in a wide variety of plumbing and HVAC systems such as potable water, heating hot water and chilled water.

Brazed joints are those made with silver or other alloy filler metals having melting points at, or above, 1,000 degrees F. Maximum working pressure/temperature relationships for brazed joints are approximately as follows:

Maximum Working Pressure (PSIG)*			
Water Temperature (degrees F.)	Nominal Pipe Size (inches)		
	Up to 1	1¼ to 2	2½ to 4
Up to 350	270	190	150

*For copper pipe and solder-type fittings using brazing alloys melting at, or above, 1,000 degrees F.

This section has been arranged to save the estimator's time by including all normally-used system components such as pipe, fittings, valves, hanger assemblies, riser clamps and miscellaneous items under one heading. Additional items can be found under "Plumbing and Piping Specialties." The cost estimates in this section are based on the conditions, limitations and wage rates described in the section "How to Use This Book" beginning on page 5.

Description	Craft@Hrs	Unit	Material $	Labor $	Equipment $	Total $

Type M copper pipe with brazed joints installed horizontally. Complete installation including six to twelve wrought copper tees and six to twelve wrought copper elbows every 100', and hangers spaced to meet plumbing code (*a tee & elbow every 8.3' for ½" dia., a tee and elbow every 16.6' for 4" dia.*).

Description	Craft@Hrs	Unit	Material $	Labor $	Equipment $	Total $
1/2"	P1@.113	LF	1.98	3.90	—	5.88
3/4"	P1@.123	LF	3.07	4.25	—	7.32
1"	P1@.143	LF	6.38	4.94	—	11.32
1¼"	P1@.163	LF	10.80	5.63	—	16.43
1½"	P1@.183	LF	12.80	6.32	—	19.12
2"	P1@.213	LF	26.70	7.36	—	34.06
2½"	P1@.243	LF	39.10	8.40	—	47.50
3"	P1@.273	LF	49.10	9.43	—	58.53
4"	P1@.313	LF	72.30	10.80	—	83.10

Type M copper pipe with brazed joints, installed risers. Complete installation including a wrought copper reducing tee every floor and a riser clamp every other floor.

Description	Craft@Hrs	Unit	Material $	Labor $	Equipment $	Total $
1/2"	P1@.062	LF	1.68	2.14	—	3.82
3/4"	P1@.072	LF	2.73	2.49	—	5.22
1"	P1@.077	LF	5.34	2.66	—	8.00
1¼"	P1@.082	LF	7.88	2.83	—	10.71
1½"	P1@.102	LF	10.40	3.52	—	13.92
2"	P1@.132	LF	13.80	4.56	—	18.36
2½"	P1@.152	LF	29.90	5.25	—	35.15
3"	P1@.172	LF	36.60	5.94	—	42.54
4"	P1@.192	LF	54.40	6.63	—	61.03

Copper, Type M with Brazed Joints

Description	Craft@Hrs	Unit	Material $	Labor $	Equipment $	Total $

Type M copper pipe with brazed joints, pipe only

Description	Craft@Hrs	Unit	Material $	Labor $	Equipment $	Total $
1/2"	P1@.032	LF	1.19	1.11	—	2.30
3/4"	P1@.035	LF	1.94	1.21	—	3.15
1"	P1@.038	LF	3.05	1.31	—	4.36
1¼"	P1@.042	LF	4.58	1.45	—	6.03
1½"	P1@.046	LF	6.42	1.59	—	8.01
2"	P1@.053	LF	11.80	1.83	—	13.63
2½"	P1@.060	LF	16.30	2.07	—	18.37
3"	P1@.066	LF	20.60	2.28	—	22.88
4"	P1@.080	LF	32.90	2.76	—	35.66

Type M copper 45 degree ell C x C with brazed joints

Description	Craft@Hrs	Unit	Material $	Labor $	Equipment $	Total $
1/2"	P1@.129	Ea	1.04	4.46	—	5.50
3/4"	P1@.181	Ea	1.97	6.25	—	8.22
1"	P1@.232	Ea	5.82	8.02	—	13.84
1¼"	P1@.284	Ea	7.88	9.81	—	17.69
1½"	P1@.335	Ea	11.70	11.60	—	23.30
2"	P1@.447	Ea	19.20	15.40	—	34.60
2½"	P1@.550	Ea	49.00	19.00	—	68.00
3"	P1@.654	Ea	64.70	22.60	—	87.30
4"	P1@.860	Ea	125.00	29.70	—	154.70

Type M copper 90 degree ell C x C with brazed joints

Description	Craft@Hrs	Unit	Material $	Labor $	Equipment $	Total $
1/2"	P1@.129	Ea	.59	4.46	—	5.05
3/4"	P1@.181	Ea	1.24	6.25	—	7.49
1"	P1@.232	Ea	4.42	8.02	—	12.44
1¼"	P1@.284	Ea	7.17	9.81	—	16.98
1½"	P1@.335	Ea	10.90	11.60	—	22.50
2"	P1@.447	Ea	19.50	15.40	—	34.90
2½"	P1@.550	Ea	40.50	19.00	—	59.50
3"	P1@.654	Ea	51.20	22.60	—	73.80
4"	P1@.860	Ea	109.00	29.70	—	138.70

Type M copper 90 degree ell Ftg. x C with brazed joints

Description	Craft@Hrs	Unit	Material $	Labor $	Equipment $	Total $
1/2"	P1@.129	Ea	.96	4.46	—	5.42
3/4"	P1@.181	Ea	2.10	6.25	—	8.35
1"	P1@.232	Ea	6.28	8.02	—	14.30
1¼"	P1@.284	Ea	8.75	9.81	—	18.56
1½"	P1@.335	Ea	13.10	11.60	—	24.70
2"	P1@.447	Ea	26.30	15.40	—	41.70
2½"	P1@.550	Ea	55.10	19.00	—	74.10
3"	P1@.654	Ea	62.00	22.60	—	84.60
4"	P1@.860	Ea	125.00	29.70	—	154.70

Description	Craft@Hrs	Unit	Material $	Labor $	Equipment $	Total $

Type M copper tee C x C x C with brazed joints

Description	Craft@Hrs	Unit	Material $	Labor $	Equipment $	Total $
1/2"	P1@.156	Ea	1.03	5.39	—	6.42
3/4"	P1@.204	Ea	2.77	7.05	—	9.82
1"	P1@.263	Ea	10.50	9.09	—	19.59
1¼"	P1@.322	Ea	16.60	11.10	—	27.70
1½"	P1@.380	Ea	24.20	13.10	—	37.30
2"	P1@.507	Ea	38.60	17.50	—	56.10
2½"	P1@.624	Ea	78.30	21.60	—	99.90
3"	P1@.741	Ea	121.00	25.60	—	146.60
4"	P1@.975	Ea	202.00	33.70	—	235.70

Type M copper reducing branch tee C x C x C with brazed joints

Description	Craft@Hrs	Unit	Material $	Labor $	Equipment $	Total $
1/2" x 3/8"	P1@.129	Ea	2.08	4.46	—	6.54
3/4" x 1/2"	P1@.182	Ea	4.41	6.29	—	10.70
1" x 1/2"	P1@.209	Ea	8.66	7.22	—	15.88
1" x 3/4"	P1@.234	Ea	8.66	8.08	—	16.74
1¼" x 1/2"	P1@.241	Ea	13.20	8.33	—	21.53
1¼" x 3/4"	P1@.264	Ea	13.20	9.12	—	22.32
1¼" x 1"	P1@.287	Ea	13.20	9.92	—	23.12
1½" x 1/2"	P1@.291	Ea	16.20	10.10	—	26.30
1½" x 3/4"	P1@.307	Ea	16.20	10.60	—	26.80
1½" x 1"	P1@.323	Ea	16.20	11.20	—	27.40
1½" x 1¼"	P1@.339	Ea	16.20	11.70	—	27.90
2" x 1/2"	P1@.348	Ea	21.60	12.00	—	33.60
2" x 3/4"	P1@.373	Ea	21.60	12.90	—	34.50
2" x 1"	P1@.399	Ea	21.60	13.80	—	35.40
2" x 1¼"	P1@.426	Ea	21.60	14.70	—	36.30
2" x 1½"	P1@.452	Ea	21.60	15.60	—	37.20
2½" x 1/2"	P1@.468	Ea	65.20	16.20	—	81.40
2½" x 3/4"	P1@.485	Ea	65.20	16.80	—	82.00
2½" x 1"	P1@.502	Ea	65.20	17.30	—	82.50
2½" x 1½"	P1@.537	Ea	65.20	18.60	—	83.80
2½" x 2"	P1@.555	Ea	65.20	19.20	—	84.40
3" x 1¼"	P1@.562	Ea	73.70	19.40	—	93.10
3" x 2"	P1@.626	Ea	76.50	21.60	—	98.10
3" x 2½"	P1@.660	Ea	76.50	22.80	—	99.30
4" x 1¼"	P1@.669	Ea	133.00	23.10	—	156.10
4" x 1½"	P1@.718	Ea	133.00	24.80	—	157.80
4" x 2"	P1@.768	Ea	133.00	26.50	—	159.50
4" x 2½"	P1@.819	Ea	133.00	28.30	—	161.30
4" x 3"	P1@.868	Ea	133.00	30.00	—	163.00

Copper, Type M with Brazed Joints

Description	Craft@Hrs	Unit	Material $	Labor $	Equipment $	Total $

Type M copper reducer with brazed joints

Description	Craft@Hrs	Unit	Material $	Labor $	Equipment $	Total $
1/2" x 3/8"	P1@.148	Ea	.75	5.11	—	5.86
3/4" x 1/2"	P1@.155	Ea	1.41	5.36	—	6.77
1" x 3/4"	P1@.206	Ea	2.53	7.12	—	9.65
1¼" x 1/2"	P1@.206	Ea	4.25	7.12	—	11.37
1¼" x 3/4"	P1@.232	Ea	4.25	8.02	—	12.27
1¼" x 1"	P1@.258	Ea	4.25	8.91	—	13.16
1½" x 1/2"	P1@.232	Ea	6.50	8.02	—	14.52
1½" x 3/4"	P1@.257	Ea	6.50	8.88	—	15.38
1½" x 1"	P1@.283	Ea	6.50	9.78	—	16.28
1½" x 1¼"	P1@.308	Ea	6.50	10.60	—	17.10
2" x 1/2"	P1@.287	Ea	10.10	9.92	—	20.02
2" x 3/4"	P1@.277	Ea	10.10	9.57	—	19.67
2" x 1"	P1@.338	Ea	10.10	11.70	—	21.80
2" x 1¼"	P1@.365	Ea	10.10	12.60	—	22.70
2" x 1½"	P1@.390	Ea	10.10	13.50	—	23.60
2½" x 1"	P1@.390	Ea	27.50	13.50	—	41.00
2½" x 1¼"	P1@.416	Ea	27.50	14.40	—	41.90
2½" x 1½"	P1@.442	Ea	27.50	15.30	—	42.80
2½" x 2"	P1@.497	Ea	27.50	17.20	—	44.70
3" x 1¼"	P1@.468	Ea	32.10	16.20	—	48.30
3" x 1½"	P1@.493	Ea	32.10	17.00	—	49.10
3" x 2"	P1@.548	Ea	32.10	18.90	—	51.00
3" x 2½"	P1@.600	Ea	32.10	20.70	—	52.80
4" x 2"	P1@.652	Ea	62.00	22.50	—	84.50
4" x 2½"	P1@.704	Ea	62.00	24.30	—	86.30
4" x 3"	P1@.755	Ea	62.00	26.10	—	88.10

Type M copper adapter C x MPT with brazed joint

Description	Craft@Hrs	Unit	Material $	Labor $	Equipment $	Total $
1/2"	P1@.090	Ea	1.85	3.11	—	4.96
3/4"	P1@.126	Ea	2.89	4.35	—	7.24
1"	P1@.162	Ea	7.17	5.60	—	12.77
1¼"	P1@.198	Ea	13.40	6.84	—	20.24
1½"	P1@.234	Ea	15.00	8.08	—	23.08
2"	P1@.312	Ea	19.40	10.80	—	30.20
2½"	P1@.384	Ea	63.10	13.30	—	76.40
3"	P1@.456	Ea	105.00	15.80	—	120.80

Type M copper adapter C x FPT with brazed joint

Description	Craft@Hrs	Unit	Material $	Labor $	Equipment $	Total $
1/2"	P1@.090	Ea	3.08	3.11	—	6.19
3/4"	P1@.126	Ea	5.57	4.35	—	9.92
1"	P1@.162	Ea	8.43	5.60	—	14.03
1¼"	P1@.198	Ea	17.60	6.84	—	24.44
1½"	P1@.234	Ea	21.40	8.08	—	29.48
2"	P1@.312	Ea	32.90	10.80	—	43.70
2½"	P1@.384	Ea	82.70	13.30	—	96.00
3"	P1@.456	Ea	114.00	15.80	—	129.80

Description	Craft@Hrs	Unit	Material $	Labor $	Equipment $	Total $

Type M copper flush bushing with brazed joints

Description	Craft@Hrs	Unit	Material $	Labor $	Equipment $	Total $
1/2" x 3/8"	P1@.148	Ea	1.88	5.11	—	6.99
3/4" x 1/2"	P1@.155	Ea	3.19	5.36	—	8.55
1" x 3/4"	P1@.206	Ea	8.27	7.12	—	15.39
1" x 1/2"	P1@.206	Ea	9.45	7.12	—	16.57
1¼" x 1"	P1@.258	Ea	9.85	8.91	—	18.76
1½" x 1¼"	P1@.308	Ea	12.50	10.60	—	23.10
2" x 1½"	P1@.390	Ea	23.50	13.50	—	37.00

Type M copper union with brazed joints

Description	Craft@Hrs	Unit	Material $	Labor $	Equipment $	Total $
1/2"	P1@.146	Ea	7.50	5.04	—	12.54
3/4"	P1@.205	Ea	8.98	7.08	—	16.06
1"	P1@.263	Ea	20.10	9.09	—	29.19
1¼"	P1@.322	Ea	36.50	11.10	—	47.60
1½"	P1@.380	Ea	44.90	13.10	—	58.00
2"	P1@.507	Ea	67.00	17.50	—	84.50

Type M copper dielectric union with brazed joints

Description	Craft@Hrs	Unit	Material $	Labor $	Equipment $	Total $
1/2"	P1@.146	Ea	7.04	5.04	—	12.08
3/4"	P1@.205	Ea	7.04	7.08	—	14.12
1"	P1@.263	Ea	14.50	9.09	—	23.59
1¼"	P1@.322	Ea	24.80	11.10	—	35.90
1½"	P1@.380	Ea	34.10	13.10	—	47.20
2"	P1@.507	Ea	47.10	17.50	—	64.60

Type M copper cap with brazed joints

Description	Craft@Hrs	Unit	Material $	Labor $	Equipment $	Total $
1/2"	P1@.083	Ea	.61	2.87	—	3.48
3/4"	P1@.116	Ea	1.25	4.01	—	5.26
1"	P1@.149	Ea	2.82	5.15	—	7.97
1¼"	P1@.182	Ea	4.05	6.29	—	10.34
1½"	P1@.215	Ea	5.91	7.43	—	13.34
2"	P1@.286	Ea	10.70	9.88	—	20.58
2½"	P1@.352	Ea	27.00	12.20	—	39.20
3"	P1@.418	Ea	42.20	14.40	—	56.60
4"	P1@.550	Ea	64.80	19.00	—	83.80

Type M copper coupling with brazed joints

Description	Craft@Hrs	Unit	Material $	Labor $	Equipment $	Total $
1/2"	P1@.129	Ea	.39	4.46	—	4.85
3/4"	P1@.181	Ea	.98	6.25	—	7.23
1"	P1@.232	Ea	2.67	8.02	—	10.69
1¼"	P1@.284	Ea	4.67	9.81	—	14.48
1½"	P1@.335	Ea	6.76	11.60	—	18.36
2"	P1@.447	Ea	10.30	15.40	—	25.70
2½"	P1@.550	Ea	24.20	19.00	—	43.20
3"	P1@.654	Ea	36.90	22.60	—	59.50
4"	P1@.860	Ea	72.30	29.70	—	102.00

Copper, Type M with Brazed Joints

Description	Craft@Hrs	Unit	Material $	Labor $	Equipment $	Total $

Class 125 bronze body gate valve, brazed joints

Description	Craft@Hrs	Unit	Material $	Labor $	Equipment $	Total $
1/2"	P1@.240	Ea	16.20	8.29	—	24.49
3/4"	P1@.300	Ea	20.30	10.40	—	30.70
1"	P1@.360	Ea	28.50	12.40	—	40.90
1¼"	P1@.480	Ea	36.00	16.60	—	52.60
1½"	P1@.540	Ea	48.40	18.70	—	67.10
2"	P1@.600	Ea	80.90	20.70	—	101.60
2½"	P1@1.00	Ea	134.00	34.60	—	168.60
3"	P1@1.50	Ea	193.00	51.80	—	244.80

Class 125 iron body gate valve, flanged ends

Description	Craft@Hrs	Unit	Material $	Labor $	Equipment $	Total $
2"	P1@.500	Ea	310.00	17.30	—	327.30
2½"	P1@.600	Ea	418.00	20.70	—	438.70
3"	P1@.750	Ea	454.00	25.90	—	479.90
4"	P1@1.35	Ea	666.00	46.60	—	712.60
5"	P1@2.00	Ea	1,270.00	69.10	—	1,339.10
6"	P1@2.50	Ea	1,270.00	86.40	—	1,356.40

Class 125 bronze body globe valve, brazed joints

Description	Craft@Hrs	Unit	Material $	Labor $	Equipment $	Total $
1/2"	P1@.240	Ea	30.00	8.29	—	38.29
3/4"	P1@.300	Ea	40.00	10.40	—	50.40
1"	P1@.360	Ea	68.90	12.40	—	81.30
1¼"	P1@.480	Ea	96.90	16.60	—	113.50
1½"	P1@.540	Ea	131.00	18.70	—	149.70
2"	P1@.600	Ea	212.00	20.70	—	232.70

Class 125 iron body globe valve, flanged ends

Description	Craft@Hrs	Unit	Material $	Labor $	Equipment $	Total $
2½"	P1@.650	Ea	351.00	22.50	—	373.50
3"	P1@.750	Ea	421.00	25.90	—	446.90
4"	P1@1.35	Ea	568.00	46.60	—	614.60

200 PSIG iron body butterfly valve, lug type, lever operated

Description	Craft@Hrs	Unit	Material $	Labor $	Equipment $	Total $
2"	P1@.450	Ea	134.00	15.50	—	149.50
2½"	P1@.450	Ea	139.00	15.50	—	154.50
3"	P1@.550	Ea	146.00	19.00	—	165.00
4"	P1@.550	Ea	182.00	19.00	—	201.00

200 PSIG iron body butterfly valve, wafer type, lever operated

Description	Craft@Hrs	Unit	Material $	Labor $	Equipment $	Total $
2"	P1@.450	Ea	122.00	15.50	—	137.50
2½"	P1@.450	Ea	125.00	15.50	—	140.50
3"	P1@.550	Ea	134.00	19.00	—	153.00
4"	P1@.550	Ea	163.00	19.00	—	182.00

Description	Craft@Hrs	Unit	Material $	Labor $	Equipment $	Total $

Class 125 bronze body 2-piece ball valve, brazed joints

Description	Craft@Hrs	Unit	Material $	Labor $	Equipment $	Total $
1/2"	P1@.240	Ea	7.91	8.29	—	16.20
3/4"	P1@.300	Ea	10.50	10.40	—	20.90
1"	P1@.360	Ea	18.20	12.40	—	30.60
1¼"	P1@.480	Ea	30.30	16.60	—	46.90
1½"	P1@.540	Ea	41.00	18.70	—	59.70
2"	P1@.600	Ea	51.90	20.70	—	72.60
3"	P1@1.50	Ea	355.00	51.80	—	406.80
4"	P1@1.80	Ea	465.00	62.20	—	527.20

Class 125 bronze body swing check valve, brazed joints

Description	Craft@Hrs	Unit	Material $	Labor $	Equipment $	Total $
1/2"	P1@.240	Ea	17.70	8.29	—	25.99
3/4"	P1@.300	Ea	25.40	10.40	—	35.80
1"	P1@.360	Ea	33.30	12.40	—	45.70
1¼"	P1@.480	Ea	47.30	16.60	—	63.90
1½"	P1@.540	Ea	66.70	18.70	—	85.40
2"	P1@.600	Ea	111.00	20.70	—	131.70
2½"	P1@1.00	Ea	223.00	34.60	—	257.60
3"	P1@1.50	Ea	320.00	51.80	—	371.80

Class 125 iron body swing check valve, flanged ends

Description	Craft@Hrs	Unit	Material $	Labor $	Equipment $	Total $
2"	P1@.500	Ea	147.00	17.30	—	164.30
2½"	P1@.600	Ea	197.00	20.70	—	217.70
3"	P1@.750	Ea	245.00	25.90	—	270.90
4"	P1@1.35	Ea	360.00	46.60	—	406.60

Class 125 iron body silent check valve, wafer type

Description	Craft@Hrs	Unit	Material $	Labor $	Equipment $	Total $
2"	P1@.500	Ea	113.00	17.30	—	130.30
2½"	P1@.600	Ea	126.00	20.70	—	146.70
3"	P1@.750	Ea	145.00	25.90	—	170.90
4"	P1@1.35	Ea	194.00	46.60	—	240.60

Class 125 bronze body strainer, threaded ends

Description	Craft@Hrs	Unit	Material $	Labor $	Equipment $	Total $
1/2"	P1@.230	Ea	27.70	7.95	—	35.65
3/4"	P1@.260	Ea	36.40	8.98	—	45.38
1"	P1@.330	Ea	44.60	11.40	—	56.00
1¼"	P1@.440	Ea	62.30	15.20	—	77.50
1½"	P1@.495	Ea	93.80	17.10	—	110.90
2"	P1@.550	Ea	162.00	19.00	—	181.00

Class 125 iron body strainer, flanged ends

Description	Craft@Hrs	Unit	Material $	Labor $	Equipment $	Total $
2"	P1@.500	Ea	124.00	17.30	—	141.30
2½"	P1@.600	Ea	139.00	20.70	—	159.70
3"	P1@.750	Ea	160.00	25.90	—	185.90
4"	P1@1.35	Ea	273.00	46.60	—	319.60

Copper, Type M with Brazed Joints

Description	Craft@Hrs	Unit	Material $	Labor $	Equipment $	Total $

Installation of 2-way control valve, threaded joints

Description	Craft@Hrs	Unit	Material $	Labor $	Equipment $	Total $
1/2"	P1@.210	Ea	—	7.26	—	7.26
3/4"	P1@.275	Ea	—	9.50	—	9.50
1"	P1@.350	Ea	—	12.10	—	12.10
1¼"	P1@.430	Ea	—	14.90	—	14.90
1½"	P1@.505	Ea	—	17.40	—	17.40
2"	P1@.675	Ea	—	23.30	—	23.30
2½"	P1@.830	Ea	—	28.70	—	28.70
3"	P1@.990	Ea	—	34.20	—	34.20

Installation of 3-way control valve, threaded joints

Description	Craft@Hrs	Unit	Material $	Labor $	Equipment $	Total $
1/2"	P1@.260	Ea	—	8.98	—	8.98
3/4"	P1@.365	Ea	—	12.60	—	12.60
1"	P1@.475	Ea	—	16.40	—	16.40
1¼"	P1@.575	Ea	—	19.90	—	19.90
1½"	P1@.680	Ea	—	23.50	—	23.50
2"	P1@.910	Ea	—	31.40	—	31.40
2½"	P1@1.12	Ea	—	38.70	—	38.70
3"	P1@1.33	Ea	—	46.00	—	46.00

Companion flange, 150 pound cast brass

Description	Craft@Hrs	Unit	Material $	Labor $	Equipment $	Total $
2"	P1@.290	Ea	365.00	10.00	—	375.00
2½"	P1@.380	Ea	450.00	13.10	—	463.10
3"	P1@.460	Ea	450.00	15.90	—	465.90
4"	P1@.600	Ea	717.00	20.70	—	737.70

Bolt and gasket sets

Description	Craft@Hrs	Unit	Material $	Labor $	Equipment $	Total $
2"	P1@.500	Ea	3.86	17.30	—	21.16
2½"	P1@.650	Ea	4.51	22.50	—	27.01
3"	P1@.750	Ea	7.67	25.90	—	33.57
4"	P1@1.00	Ea	12.80	34.60	—	47.40

Thermometer with well

Description	Craft@Hrs	Unit	Material $	Labor $	Equipment $	Total $
7"	P1@.250	Ea	159.00	8.64	—	167.64
9"	P1@.250	Ea	164.00	8.64	—	172.64

Dial type pressure gauge

Description	Craft@Hrs	Unit	Material $	Labor $	Equipment $	Total $
2½"	P1@.200	Ea	33.10	6.91	—	40.01
3½"	P1@.200	Ea	43.80	6.91	—	50.71

Pressure/temperature tap

Description	Craft@Hrs	Unit	Material $	Labor $	Equipment $	Total $
tap	P1@.150	Ea	15.70	5.18	—	20.88

Description	Craft@Hrs	Unit	Material $	Labor $	Equipment $	Total $

Hanger with swivel assembly

Description	Craft@Hrs	Unit	Material $	Labor $	Equipment $	Total $
1/2"	P1@.250	Ea	3.74	8.64	—	12.38
3/4"	P1@.250	Ea	4.13	8.64	—	12.77
1"	P1@.250	Ea	4.33	8.64	—	12.97
1¼"	P1@.300	Ea	4.44	10.40	—	14.84
1½"	P1@.300	Ea	4.77	10.40	—	15.17
2"	P1@.300	Ea	4.98	10.40	—	15.38
2½"	P1@.350	Ea	6.78	12.10	—	18.88
3"	P1@.350	Ea	8.37	12.10	—	20.47
4"	P1@.350	Ea	9.19	12.10	—	21.29

Riser clamp

Description	Craft@Hrs	Unit	Material $	Labor $	Equipment $	Total $
1/2"	P1@.100	Ea	2.41	3.46	—	5.87
3/4"	P1@.100	Ea	3.55	3.46	—	7.01
1"	P1@.100	Ea	3.59	3.46	—	7.05
1¼"	P1@.105	Ea	4.33	3.63	—	7.96
1½"	P1@.110	Ea	4.58	3.80	—	8.38
2"	P1@.115	Ea	4.84	3.97	—	8.81
2½"	P1@.120	Ea	5.09	4.15	—	9.24
3"	P1@.120	Ea	5.52	4.15	—	9.67
4"	P1@.125	Ea	7.03	4.32	—	11.35

Copper, Type M with Soft-Soldered Joints

Type M hard-drawn copper pipe with wrought copper fittings and soft-soldered joints is used in a wide variety of plumbing and HVAC systems such as potable water, heating hot water, chilled water, and A.C. condensate.

Soft-soldered joints are those made with solders having melting points in the 350 degree F. to 500 degree F. range. Maximum working pressure/temperature relationships for soft-soldered joints are approximately as follows:

Maximum Working Pressures (PSIG)*				
Soft-solder Type	Water Temperature (degrees F.)	Nominal Pipe Size (inches)		
		Up to 1	1¼ to 2	2½ x 4
50-50 tin-lead**	100	200	175	150
	150	150	125	100
	200	100	90	75
	250	85	75	50
95-5 tin-antimony	100	500	400	300
	150	400	350	275
	200	300	250	200
	250	200	175	150

*For copper pipe and solder-type fittings using soft-solders melting at approximately 350 degrees F. to 500 degrees F.

**The use of any solder containing lead is not allowed in potable water systems.

This section has been arranged to save the estimator's time by including all normally-used system components such as pipe, fittings, valves, hanger assemblies, riser clamps and miscellaneous items under one heading. Additional items can be found under "Plumbing and Piping Specialties." The cost estimates in this section are based on the conditions, limitations and wage rates described in the section "How to Use This Book" beginning on page 5.

Description	Craft@Hrs	Unit	Material $	Labor $	Equipment $	Total $

Type M copper pipe with soft-soldered joints installed horizontally.
Complete installation including six to twelve wrought copper tees and six to twelve wrought copper elbows every 100', and hangers spaced to meet plumbing code (*a tee & elbow every 8.3' for ½" dia., a tee and elbow every 16.6' for 4" dia.*).

Description	Craft@Hrs	Unit	Material $	Labor $	Equipment $	Total $
1/2"	P1@.110	LF	1.98	3.80	—	5.78
3/4"	P1@.120	LF	3.07	4.15	—	7.22
1"	P1@.140	LF	6.38	4.84	—	11.22
1¼"	P1@.160	LF	10.80	5.53	—	16.33
1½"	P1@.180	LF	12.80	6.22	—	19.02
2"	P1@.210	LF	26.70	7.26	—	33.96
2½"	P1@.240	LF	39.10	8.29	—	47.39
3"	P1@.270	LF	49.10	9.33	—	58.43
4"	P1@.312	LF	72.30	10.80	—	83.10

Description	Craft@Hrs	Unit	Material $	Labor $	Equipment $	Total $

Type M copper pipe with soft-soldered joints, installed risers.
Complete installation including a wrought copper reducing tee every floor and a riser clamp every other floor.

Description	Craft@Hrs	Unit	Material $	Labor $	Equipment $	Total $
1/2"	P1@.060	LF	1.68	2.07	—	3.75
3/4"	P1@.070	LF	2.73	2.42	—	5.15
1"	P1@.075	LF	5.34	2.59	—	7.93
1¼"	P1@.080	LF	7.88	2.76	—	10.64
1½"	P1@.100	LF	10.40	3.46	—	13.86
2"	P1@.130	LF	13.80	4.49	—	18.29
2½"	P1@.150	LF	29.90	5.18	—	35.08
3"	P1@.170	LF	36.60	5.87	—	42.47
4"	P1@.190	LF	54.40	6.56	—	60.96

Type M copper pipe with soft-soldered joints, pipe only

Description	Craft@Hrs	Unit	Material $	Labor $	Equipment $	Total $
1/2"	P1@.032	LF	1.19	1.11	—	2.30
3/4"	P1@.035	LF	1.94	1.21	—	3.15
1"	P1@.038	LF	3.05	1.31	—	4.36
1¼"	P1@.042	LF	4.58	1.45	—	6.03
1½"	P1@.046	LF	6.42	1.59	—	8.01
2"	P1@.053	LF	11.80	1.83	—	13.63
2½"	P1@.060	LF	16.30	2.07	—	18.37
3"	P1@.066	LF	20.60	2.28	—	22.88
4"	P1@.080	LF	32.90	2.76	—	35.66

Type M copper 45 degree ell C x C with soft-soldered joints

Description	Craft@Hrs	Unit	Material $	Labor $	Equipment $	Total $
1/2"	P1@.107	Ea	1.04	3.70	—	4.74
3/4"	P1@.150	Ea	1.77	5.18	—	6.95
1"	P1@.193	Ea	5.82	6.67	—	12.49
1¼"	P1@.236	Ea	6.56	8.15	—	14.71
1½"	P1@.278	Ea	11.70	9.60	—	21.30
2"	P1@.371	Ea	19.20	12.80	—	32.00
2½"	P1@.457	Ea	49.00	15.80	—	64.80
3"	P1@.543	Ea	64.70	18.80	—	83.50
4"	P1@.714	Ea	125.00	24.70	—	149.70

Type M copper 90 degree ell C x C with soft-soldered joints

Description	Craft@Hrs	Unit	Material $	Labor $	Equipment $	Total $
1/2"	P1@.107	Ea	.55	3.70	—	4.25
3/4"	P1@.150	Ea	1.16	5.18	—	6.34
1"	P1@.193	Ea	4.42	6.67	—	11.09
1¼"	P1@.236	Ea	7.17	8.15	—	15.32
1½"	P1@.278	Ea	10.90	9.60	—	20.50
2"	P1@.371	Ea	19.50	12.80	—	32.30
2½"	P1@.457	Ea	40.50	15.80	—	56.30
3"	P1@.543	Ea	51.20	18.80	—	70.00
4"	P1@.714	Ea	109.00	24.70	—	133.70

Copper, Type M with Soft-Soldered Joints

Description	Craft@Hrs	Unit	Material $	Labor $	Equipment $	Total $

Type M copper 90 degree ell Ftg. x C with soft-soldered joint

Description	Craft@Hrs	Unit	Material $	Labor $	Equipment $	Total $
1/2"	P1@.107	Ea	.96	3.70	—	4.66
3/4"	P1@.150	Ea	2.10	5.18	—	7.28
1"	P1@.193	Ea	6.28	6.67	—	12.95
1¼"	P1@.236	Ea	8.75	8.15	—	16.90
1½"	P1@.278	Ea	13.10	9.60	—	22.70
2"	P1@.371	Ea	26.30	12.80	—	39.10
2½"	P1@.457	Ea	55.10	15.80	—	70.90
3"	P1@.543	Ea	62.00	18.80	—	80.80
4"	P1@.714	Ea	125.00	24.70	—	149.70

Type M copper tee C x C x C with soft-soldered joints

Description	Craft@Hrs	Unit	Material $	Labor $	Equipment $	Total $
1/2"	P1@.129	Ea	.93	4.46	—	5.39
3/4"	P1@.181	Ea	2.52	6.25	—	8.77
1"	P1@.233	Ea	10.50	8.05	—	18.55
1¼"	P1@.285	Ea	16.60	9.85	—	26.45
1½"	P1@.337	Ea	24.20	11.60	—	35.80
2"	P1@.449	Ea	38.60	15.50	—	54.10
2½"	P1@.552	Ea	78.30	19.10	—	97.40
3"	P1@.656	Ea	121.00	22.70	—	143.70
4"	P1@.863	Ea	151.00	29.80	—	180.80

Type M copper branch reducing tee C x C x C with soft-soldered joints

Description	Craft@Hrs	Unit	Material $	Labor $	Equipment $	Total $
1/2" x 3/8"	P1@.129	Ea	2.08	4.46	—	6.54
3/4" x 1/2"	P1@.182	Ea	4.41	6.29	—	10.70
1" x 1/2"	P1@.195	Ea	8.66	6.74	—	15.40
1" x 3/4"	P1@.219	Ea	8.66	7.57	—	16.23
1¼" x 1/2"	P1@.225	Ea	13.20	7.77	—	20.97
1¼" x 3/4"	P1@.247	Ea	13.20	8.53	—	21.73
1¼" x 1"	P1@.268	Ea	13.20	9.26	—	22.46
1½" x 1/2"	P1@.272	Ea	16.20	9.40	—	25.60
1½" x 3/4"	P1@.287	Ea	16.20	9.92	—	26.12
1½" x 1"	P1@.302	Ea	16.20	10.40	—	26.60
1½" x 1¼"	P1@.317	Ea	16.20	11.00	—	27.20
2" x 1/2"	P1@.325	Ea	21.60	11.20	—	32.80
2" x 3/4"	P1@.348	Ea	21.60	12.00	—	33.60
2" x 1"	P1@.373	Ea	21.60	12.90	—	34.50
2" x 1¼"	P1@.398	Ea	21.60	13.80	—	35.40
2" x 1½"	P1@.422	Ea	21.60	14.60	—	36.20
2½" x 1/2"	P1@.437	Ea	65.20	15.10	—	80.30
2½" x 3/4"	P1@.453	Ea	65.20	15.70	—	80.90
2½" x 1"	P1@.469	Ea	65.20	16.20	—	81.40
2½" x 1½"	P1@.502	Ea	65.20	17.30	—	82.50
2½" x 2"	P1@.519	Ea	65.20	17.90	—	83.10
3" x 1¼"	P1@.525	Ea	73.70	18.10	—	91.80
3" x 2"	P1@.585	Ea	76.50	20.20	—	96.70
3" x 2½"	P1@.617	Ea	76.50	21.30	—	97.80
4" x 1¼"	P1@.625	Ea	133.00	21.60	—	154.60
4" x 1½"	P1@.671	Ea	133.00	23.20	—	156.20
4" x 2"	P1@.718	Ea	133.00	24.80	—	157.80
4" x 2½"	P1@.765	Ea	133.00	26.40	—	159.40
4" x 3"	P1@.811	Ea	133.00	28.00	—	161.00

Description	Craft@Hrs	Unit	Material $	Labor $	Equipment $	Total $

Type M copper reducer with soft-soldered joints

Description	Craft@Hrs	Unit	Material $	Labor $	Equipment $	Total $
1/2" x 3/8"	P1@.124	Ea	.75	4.28	—	5.03
3/4" x 1/2"	P1@.129	Ea	1.41	4.46	—	5.87
1" x 3/4"	P1@.172	Ea	2.53	5.94	—	8.47
1¼" x 1/2"	P1@.172	Ea	4.25	5.94	—	10.19
1¼" x 3/4"	P1@.193	Ea	4.25	6.67	—	10.92
1¼" x 1"	P1@.215	Ea	4.25	7.43	—	11.68
1½" x 1/2"	P1@.193	Ea	6.50	6.67	—	13.17
1½" x 3/4"	P1@.214	Ea	6.50	7.39	—	13.89
1½" x 1"	P1@.236	Ea	6.50	8.15	—	14.65
1½" x 1¼"	P1@.257	Ea	6.50	8.88	—	15.38
2" x 1/2"	P1@.239	Ea	10.10	8.26	—	18.36
2" x 3/4"	P1@.261	Ea	10.10	9.02	—	19.12
2" x 1"	P1@.282	Ea	10.10	9.74	—	19.84
2" x 1¼"	P1@.304	Ea	10.10	10.50	—	20.60
2" x 1½"	P1@.325	Ea	10.10	11.20	—	21.30
2½" x 1"	P1@.325	Ea	27.50	11.20	—	38.70
2½" x 1¼"	P1@.347	Ea	27.50	12.00	—	39.50
2½" x 1½"	P1@.368	Ea	27.50	12.70	—	40.20
2½" x 2"	P1@.414	Ea	27.50	14.30	—	41.80
3" x 2"	P1@.457	Ea	32.10	15.80	—	47.90
3" x 2½"	P1@.500	Ea	32.10	17.30	—	49.40
4" x 2"	P1@.543	Ea	62.00	18.80	—	80.80
4" x 2½"	P1@.586	Ea	62.00	20.20	—	82.20
4" x 3"	P1@.629	Ea	62.00	21.70	—	83.70

Type M copper adapter C x MPT with soft-soldered joint

Description	Craft@Hrs	Unit	Material $	Labor $	Equipment $	Total $
1/2"	P1@.075	Ea	1.85	2.59	—	4.44
3/4"	P1@.105	Ea	2.89	3.63	—	6.52
1"	P1@.134	Ea	7.17	4.63	—	11.80
1¼"	P1@.164	Ea	13.40	5.67	—	19.07
1½"	P1@.194	Ea	15.00	6.70	—	21.70
2"	P1@.259	Ea	19.40	8.95	—	28.35
2½"	P1@.319	Ea	63.10	11.00	—	74.10
3"	P1@.378	Ea	105.00	13.10	—	118.10

Type M copper adapter C x FPT with soft-soldered joint

Description	Craft@Hrs	Unit	Material $	Labor $	Equipment $	Total $
1/2"	P1@.075	Ea	3.08	2.59	—	5.67
3/4"	P1@.105	Ea	5.57	3.63	—	9.20
1"	P1@.134	Ea	8.43	4.63	—	13.06
1¼"	P1@.164	Ea	17.60	5.67	—	23.27
1½"	P1@.194	Ea	21.40	6.70	—	28.10
2"	P1@.259	Ea	32.90	8.95	—	41.85
2½"	P1@.319	Ea	82.70	11.00	—	93.70
3"	P1@.378	Ea	114.00	13.10	—	127.10

Copper, Type M with Soft-Soldered Joints

Description	Craft@Hrs	Unit	Material $	Labor $	Equipment $	Total $

Type M copper flush bushing with soft-soldered joints

Description	Craft@Hrs	Unit	Material $	Labor $	Equipment $	Total $
1/2" x 3/8"	P1@.124	Ea	1.88	4.28	—	6.16
3/4" x 1/2"	P1@.129	Ea	3.19	4.46	—	7.65
1" x 3/4"	P1@.172	Ea	8.27	5.94	—	14.21
1" x 1/2"	P1@.172	Ea	9.45	5.94	—	15.39
1¼" x 1"	P1@.215	Ea	9.85	7.43	—	17.28
1½" x 1¼"	P1@.257	Ea	12.50	8.88	—	21.38
2" x 1½"	P1@.325	Ea	23.50	11.20	—	34.70

Type M copper union with soft-soldered joint

Description	Craft@Hrs	Unit	Material $	Labor $	Equipment $	Total $
1/2"	P1@.121	Ea	7.50	4.18	—	11.68
3/4"	P1@.170	Ea	8.98	5.87	—	14.85
1"	P1@.218	Ea	20.10	7.53	—	27.63
1¼"	P1@.267	Ea	36.50	9.22	—	45.72
1½"	P1@.315	Ea	44.90	10.90	—	55.80
2"	P1@.421	Ea	67.00	14.50	—	81.50

Type M copper dielectric union with soft-soldered joint

Description	Craft@Hrs	Unit	Material $	Labor $	Equipment $	Total $
1/2"	P1@.121	Ea	7.04	4.18	—	11.22
3/4"	P1@.170	Ea	7.04	5.87	—	12.91
1"	P1@.218	Ea	14.50	7.53	—	22.03
1¼"	P1@.267	Ea	24.80	9.22	—	34.02
1½"	P1@.315	Ea	34.10	10.90	—	45.00
2"	P1@.421	Ea	47.10	14.50	—	61.60

Type M copper cap with soft-soldered joint

Description	Craft@Hrs	Unit	Material $	Labor $	Equipment $	Total $
1/2"	P1@.069	Ea	.61	2.38	—	2.99
3/4"	P1@.096	Ea	1.25	3.32	—	4.57
1"	P1@.124	Ea	2.82	4.28	—	7.10
1¼"	P1@.151	Ea	4.05	5.22	—	9.27
1½"	P1@.178	Ea	5.91	6.15	—	12.06
2"	P1@.237	Ea	10.70	8.19	—	18.89
2½"	P1@.292	Ea	27.00	10.10	—	37.10
3"	P1@.347	Ea	42.20	12.00	—	54.20
4"	P1@.457	Ea	64.80	15.80	—	80.60

Type M copper coupling with soft-soldered joints

Description	Craft@Hrs	Unit	Material $	Labor $	Equipment $	Total $
1/2"	P1@.107	Ea	.39	3.70	—	4.09
3/4"	P1@.150	Ea	.98	5.18	—	6.16
1"	P1@.193	Ea	2.67	6.67	—	9.34
1¼"	P1@.236	Ea	4.67	8.15	—	12.82
1½"	P1@.278	Ea	6.76	9.60	—	16.36
2"	P1@.371	Ea	10.30	12.80	—	23.10
2½"	P1@.457	Ea	24.20	15.80	—	40.00
3"	P1@.543	Ea	36.90	18.80	—	55.70
4"	P1@.714	Ea	72.30	24.70	—	97.00

Description	Craft@Hrs	Unit	Material $	Labor $	Equipment $	Total $

Class 125 bronze body gate valve with soft-soldered joints

Description	Craft@Hrs	Unit	Material $	Labor $	Equipment $	Total $
1/2"	P1@.200	Ea	16.20	6.91	—	23.11
3/4"	P1@.249	Ea	20.30	8.60	—	28.90
1"	P1@.299	Ea	28.50	10.30	—	38.80
1¼"	P1@.398	Ea	36.00	13.80	—	49.80
1½"	P1@.448	Ea	48.40	15.50	—	63.90
2"	P1@.498	Ea	80.90	17.20	—	98.10
2½"	P1@.830	Ea	134.00	28.70	—	162.70
3"	P1@1.24	Ea	193.00	42.80	—	235.80

Class 125 iron body gate valve with flanged ends

Description	Craft@Hrs	Unit	Material $	Labor $	Equipment $	Total $
2"	P1@.500	Ea	310.00	17.30	—	327.30
2½"	P1@.600	Ea	418.00	20.70	—	438.70
3"	P1@.750	Ea	454.00	25.90	—	479.90
4"	P1@1.35	Ea	666.00	46.60	—	712.60
5"	P1@2.00	Ea	1,270.00	69.10	—	1,339.10
6"	P1@2.50	Ea	1,270.00	86.40	—	1,356.40

Class 125 bronze body globe valve with soft-soldered joints

Description	Craft@Hrs	Unit	Material $	Labor $	Equipment $	Total $
1/2"	P1@.200	Ea	30.00	6.91	—	36.91
3/4"	P1@.249	Ea	40.00	8.60	—	48.60
1"	P1@.299	Ea	68.90	10.30	—	79.20
1¼"	P1@.398	Ea	96.90	13.80	—	110.70
1½"	P1@.448	Ea	131.00	15.50	—	146.50
2"	P1@.498	Ea	212.00	17.20	—	229.20

Class 125 iron body globe valve with flanged ends

Description	Craft@Hrs	Unit	Material $	Labor $	Equipment $	Total $
2½"	P1@.600	Ea	351.00	20.70	—	371.70
3"	P1@.750	Ea	421.00	25.90	—	446.90
4"	P1@1.35	Ea	565.00	46.60	—	611.60

200 PSIG iron body butterfly valve, lug type, lever operated

Description	Craft@Hrs	Unit	Material $	Labor $	Equipment $	Total $
2"	P1@.450	Ea	134.00	15.50	—	149.50
2½"	P1@.450	Ea	139.00	15.50	—	154.50
3"	P1@.550	Ea	146.00	19.00	—	165.00
4"	P1@.550	Ea	182.00	19.00	—	201.00

200 PSIG iron body butterfly valve, wafer type, lever operated

Description	Craft@Hrs	Unit	Material $	Labor $	Equipment $	Total $
2"	P1@.450	Ea	122.00	15.50	—	137.50
2½"	P1@.450	Ea	125.00	15.50	—	140.50
3"	P1@.550	Ea	134.00	19.00	—	153.00
4"	P1@.550	Ea	163.00	19.00	—	182.00

Copper, Type M with Soft-Soldered Joints

Description	Craft@Hrs	Unit	Material $	Labor $	Equipment $	Total $

Class 125 bronze body 2-piece ball valve with soft-soldered joints

Description	Craft@Hrs	Unit	Material $	Labor $	Equipment $	Total $
1/2"	P1@.200	Ea	7.91	6.91	—	14.82
3/4"	P1@.249	Ea	10.50	8.60	—	19.10
1"	P1@.299	Ea	18.20	10.30	—	28.50
1¼"	P1@.398	Ea	30.30	13.80	—	44.10
1½"	P1@.448	Ea	41.00	15.50	—	56.50
2"	P1@.498	Ea	51.90	17.20	—	69.10
3"	P1@1.24	Ea	355.00	42.80	—	397.80
4"	P1@1.45	Ea	465.00	50.10	—	515.10

Class 125 bronze body swing check valve with soft-soldered joints

Description	Craft@Hrs	Unit	Material $	Labor $	Equipment $	Total $
1/2"	P1@.200	Ea	17.70	6.91	—	24.61
3/4"	P1@.249	Ea	25.40	8.60	—	34.00
1"	P1@.299	Ea	33.30	10.30	—	43.60
1¼"	P1@.398	Ea	47.30	13.80	—	61.10
1½"	P1@.448	Ea	66.70	15.50	—	82.20
2"	P1@.498	Ea	111.00	17.20	—	128.20
2½"	P1@.830	Ea	223.00	28.70	—	251.70
3"	P1@1.24	Ea	320.00	42.80	—	362.80

Class 125 iron body swing check valve, flanged ends

Description	Craft@Hrs	Unit	Material $	Labor $	Equipment $	Total $
2"	P1@.500	Ea	155.00	17.30	—	172.30
2½"	P1@.600	Ea	197.00	20.70	—	217.70
3"	P1@.750	Ea	245.00	25.90	—	270.90
4"	P1@1.35	Ea	360.00	46.60	—	406.60

Class 125 iron body silent check valve, wafer type

Description	Craft@Hrs	Unit	Material $	Labor $	Equipment $	Total $
2"	P1@.500	Ea	113.00	17.30	—	130.30
2½"	P1@.600	Ea	126.00	20.70	—	146.70
3"	P1@.750	Ea	145.00	25.90	—	170.90
4"	P1@1.35	Ea	194.00	46.60	—	240.60

Class 125 bronze body strainer, threaded ends

Description	Craft@Hrs	Unit	Material $	Labor $	Equipment $	Total $
1/2"	P1@.230	Ea	27.70	7.95	—	35.65
3/4"	P1@.260	Ea	36.40	8.98	—	45.38
1"	P1@.330	Ea	44.60	11.40	—	56.00
1¼"	P1@.440	Ea	62.30	15.20	—	77.50
1½"	P1@.495	Ea	93.80	17.10	—	110.90
2"	P1@.550	Ea	162.00	19.00	—	181.00

Class 125 iron body strainer, flanged ends

Description	Craft@Hrs	Unit	Material $	Labor $	Equipment $	Total $
2"	P1@.500	Ea	124.00	17.30	—	141.30
2½"	P1@.600	Ea	139.00	20.70	—	159.70
3"	P1@.750	Ea	160.00	25.90	—	185.90
4"	P1@1.35	Ea	273.00	46.60	—	319.60

Description	Craft@Hrs	Unit	Material $	Labor $	Equipment $	Total $

Installation of 2-way control valve, threaded joints

1/2"	P1@.210	Ea	—	7.26	—	7.26
3/4"	P1@.275	Ea	—	9.50	—	9.50
1"	P1@.350	Ea	—	12.10	—	12.10
1¼"	P1@.430	Ea	—	14.90	—	14.90
1½"	P1@.505	Ea	—	17.40	—	17.40
2"	P1@.675	Ea	—	23.30	—	23.30
2½"	P1@.830	Ea	—	28.70	—	28.70
3"	P1@.990	Ea	—	34.20	—	34.20

Installation of 3-way control valve, threaded joints

1/2"	P1@.260	Ea	—	8.98	—	8.98
3/4"	P1@.365	Ea	—	12.60	—	12.60
1"	P1@.475	Ea	—	16.40	—	16.40
1¼"	P1@.575	Ea	—	19.90	—	19.90
1½"	P1@.680	Ea	—	23.50	—	23.50
2"	P1@.910	Ea	—	31.40	—	31.40
2½"	P1@1.12	Ea	—	38.70	—	38.70
3"	P1@1.33	Ea	—	46.00	—	46.00

Companion flange, 150 pound cast brass

2"	P1@.290	Ea	377.00	10.00	—	387.00
2½"	P1@.380	Ea	461.00	13.10	—	474.10
3"	P1@.460	Ea	461.00	15.90	—	476.90
4"	P1@.600	Ea	737.00	20.70	—	757.70

Bolt and gasket sets

2"	P1@.500	Ea	4.08	17.30	—	21.38
2½"	P1@.650	Ea	4.54	22.50	—	27.04
3"	P1@.750	Ea	7.73	25.90	—	33.63
4"	P1@1.00	Ea	12.80	34.60	—	47.40

Thermometer with well

7"	P1@.250	Ea	159.00	8.64	—	167.64
9"	P1@.250	Ea	164.00	8.64	—	172.64

Dial type pressure gauge

2½"	P1@.200	Ea	33.10	6.91	—	40.01
3½"	P1@.200	Ea	43.80	6.91	—	50.71

Pressure/temperature tap

tap	P1@.150	Ea	15.70	5.18	—	20.88

Copper, Type M with Soft-Soldered Joints

Description	Craft@Hrs	Unit	Material $	Labor $	Equipment $	Total $

Hanger with swivel assembly

Description	Craft@Hrs	Unit	Material $	Labor $	Equipment $	Total $
1/2"	P1@.250	Ea	3.74	8.64	—	12.38
3/4"	P1@.250	Ea	4.13	8.64	—	12.77
1"	P1@.250	Ea	4.33	8.64	—	12.97
1¼"	P1@.300	Ea	4.44	10.40	—	14.84
1½"	P1@.300	Ea	4.77	10.40	—	15.17
2"	P1@.300	Ea	4.98	10.40	—	15.38
2½"	P1@.350	Ea	6.78	12.10	—	18.88
3"	P1@.350	Ea	8.37	12.10	—	20.47
4"	P1@.350	Ea	9.19	12.10	—	21.29

Riser clamp

Description	Craft@Hrs	Unit	Material $	Labor $	Equipment $	Total $
1/2"	P1@.100	Ea	2.41	3.46	—	5.87
3/4"	P1@.100	Ea	3.55	3.46	—	7.01
1"	P1@.100	Ea	3.59	3.46	—	7.05
1¼"	P1@.105	Ea	4.33	3.63	—	7.96
1½"	P1@.110	Ea	4.58	3.80	—	8.38
2"	P1@.115	Ea	4.84	3.97	—	8.81
2½"	P1@.120	Ea	5.09	4.15	—	9.24
3"	P1@.120	Ea	5.52	4.15	—	9.67
4"	P1@.125	Ea	7.03	4.32	—	11.35

Hard drawn rigid copper roll-grooved pipe with factory grooved copper fittings is commonly used for domestic or potable water distribution systems.

Maximum operating pressure for fittings is 300 psi (2065kPa). Operating temperature for fittings ranges from -30F to 250F. (-34C – 121C)

Consult manufacturer for pipe pressure and temperature ratings and for the various combinations of pipe, fittings and system applications.

The cost estimates in this section are based on the conditions, limitations and wage rates described in the section "How to Use This Book" beginning on page 5.

Description	Craft@Hrs	Unit	Material $	Labor $	Equipment $	Total $

Type K Copper pipe only, roll grooved, no hangers or fittings

2"	P1@.080	LF	15.40	2.76	—	18.16
2½"	P1@.090	LF	22.50	3.11	—	25.61
3"	P1@.105	LF	30.50	3.63	—	34.13
4"	P1@.145	LF	47.70	5.01	—	52.71
6"	P1@.195	LF	72.80	6.74	—	79.54

Type L Copper pipe only, roll grooved, no hangers or fittings

2"	P1@.070	LF	14.00	2.42	—	16.42
2½"	P1@.070	LF	20.30	2.42	—	22.72
3"	P1@.090	LF	27.40	3.11	—	30.51
4"	P1@.130	LF	42.80	4.49	—	47.29
6"	P1@.180	LF	65.50	6.22	—	71.72

90 degree copper elbow, roll grooved, style #610, (Victaulic)

2"	P1@.410	Ea	83.00	14.20	—	97.20
2½"	P1@.430	Ea	91.30	14.90	—	106.20
3"	P1@.500	Ea	129.00	17.30	—	146.30
4"	P1@.690	Ea	275.00	23.80	—	298.80
6"	P1@1.19	Ea	1,620.00	41.10	—	1,661.10

45 degree copper elbow, roll grooved, style #611, (Victaulic)

2"	P1@.410	Ea	73.00	14.20	—	87.20
2½"	P1@.430	Ea	79.60	14.90	—	94.50
3"	P1@.500	Ea	109.00	17.30	—	126.30
4"	P1@.690	Ea	251.00	23.80	—	274.80
6"	P1@1.19	Ea	1,380.00	41.10	—	1,421.10

Tee, copper, roll grooved, style #620, (Victaulic)

2"	P1@.510	Ea	141.00	17.60	—	158.60
2½"	P1@.540	Ea	150.00	18.70	—	168.70
3"	P1@.630	Ea	225.00	21.80	—	246.80
4"	P1@.860	Ea	498.00	29.70	—	527.70
6"	P1@1.49	Ea	1,850.00	51.50	—	1,901.50

Description	Craft@Hrs	Unit	Material $	Labor $	Equipment $	Total $

Reducing tee, copper, roll grooved, style #625, (Victaulic)

Description	Craft@Hrs	Unit	Material $	Labor $	Equipment $	Total $
2½" x 2"	P1@.540	Ea	232.00	18.70	—	250.70
3" x 2½"	P1@.630	Ea	247.00	21.80	—	268.80
4" x 3"	P1@.860	Ea	580.00	29.70	—	609.70

Reducing tee, copper, roll grooved, style #626, (Victaulic)

Description	Craft@Hrs	Unit	Material $	Labor $	Equipment $	Total $
2½" x 1"	P1@.500	Ea	293.00	17.30	—	310.30
2½" x 1½"	P1@.520	Ea	293.00	18.00	—	311.00
3" x 1½"	P1@.600	Ea	309.00	20.70	—	329.70

Reducer, copper, roll grooved, style #650, (Victaulic)

Description	Craft@Hrs	Unit	Material $	Labor $	Equipment $	Total $
2½" x 2"	P1@.430	Ea	124.00	14.90	—	138.90
3" x 2"	P1@.500	Ea	124.00	17.30	—	141.30
3" x 2½"	P1@.520	Ea	124.00	18.00	—	142.00
4" x 2"	P1@.690	Ea	242.00	23.80	—	265.80
4" x 3"	P1@.720	Ea	242.00	24.90	—	266.90
6" x 3"	P1@1.20	Ea	841.00	41.50	—	882.50

Roll-grooved copper coupling with gasket, style #650, (Victaulic)

Description	Craft@Hrs	Unit	Material $	Labor $	Equipment $	Total $
2"	P1@.300	Ea	40.80	10.40	—	51.20
2 1/2"	P1@.350	Ea	46.00	12.10	—	58.10
3"	P1@.400	Ea	49.80	13.80	—	63.60
4"	P1@.500	Ea	64.10	17.30	—	81.40
5"	P1@.600	Ea	130.00	20.70	—	150.70
6"	P1@.700	Ea	147.00	24.20	—	171.20
8"	P1@.900	Ea	230.00	31.10	—	261.10
10"	P1@1.10	Ea	338.00	38.00	—	376.00
12"	P1@1.35	Ea	507.00	46.60	—	553.60

Flange Adapter, copper, roll grooved, style #641, (Victaulic)

Description	Craft@Hrs	Unit	Material $	Labor $	Equipment $	Total $
2½"	P1@.300	Ea	244.00	10.40	—	254.40
3"	P1@.400	Ea	261.00	13.80	—	274.80
4"	P1@.550	Ea	358.00	19.00	—	377.00

Butterfly Valve, brass, roll grooved, lever handle, style #608, (Victaulic)

Description	Craft@Hrs	Unit	Material $	Labor $	Equipment $	Total $
2½"	P1@.450	Ea	758.00	15.50	—	773.50
3"	P1@.450	Ea	972.00	15.50	—	987.50
4"	P1@.550	Ea	1,320.00	19.00	—	1,339.00

PVC (Polyvinyl Chloride) Schedule 40 pipe with Schedule 40 socket-type fittings and solvent-welded joints is widely used in process, chemical, A.C. condensate, potable water and irrigation piping systems. PVC is available in Type I (normal impact) and Type II (high impact). Type I has a maximum temperature rating of 150 degrees F., and Type II is rated at 140 degrees F.

Consult the manufacturers for maximum pressure ratings and recommended joint solvents for specific applications.

Because of the current unreliability of many plastic valves, most engineers specify standard bronze-body and iron-body valves for use in PVC water piping systems. Plastic valves, however, have to be used in systems conveying liquids that may be injurious to metallic valves.

This section has been arranged to save the estimator's time by including all normally-used system components such as pipe, fittings, valves, hanger assemblies, riser clamps and miscellaneous items under one heading. Additional items can be found under "Plumbing and Piping Specialties." The cost estimates in this section are based on the conditions, limitations and wage rates described in the section "How to Use This Book" beginning on page 5.

Equipment cost, where shown, is $110 per hour for a 10-ton hydraulic truck-mounted crane.

Description	Craft@Hrs	Unit	Material $	Labor $	Equipment $	Total $

Schedule 40 PVC pipe assembly with solvent-weld joints installed horizontally.
Complete installation including three to eight tees and three to eight elbows every 100' and hangers spaced to meet plumbing code (*a tee and elbow every 12' for 1/2" dia., a tee and elbow every 40' for 8" dia.*).

Description	Craft@Hrs	Unit	Material $	Labor $	Equipment $	Total $
½"	P1@.084	LF	1.62	2.90	—	4.52
3/4"	P1@.091	LF	1.95	3.14	—	5.09
1"	P1@.099	LF	2.02	3.42	—	5.44
1¼"	P1@.114	LF	2.12	3.94	—	6.06
1½"	P1@.121	LF	2.41	4.18	—	6.59
2"	P1@.130	LF	2.97	4.49	—	7.46
2½"	P1@.134	LF	4.81	4.63	—	9.44
3"	P1@.146	LF	7.53	5.04	—	12.57
4"	P1@.177	LF	9.53	6.12	—	15.65
6"	P1@.231	LF	16.00	7.98	—	23.98
8"	P1@.236	LF	28.30	8.15	—	36.45

Schedule 40 PVC pipe assembly with solvent-weld joints, installed risers.
Complete installation including a reducing tee every floor and a riser clamp every other.

Description	Craft@Hrs	Unit	Material $	Labor $	Equipment $	Total $
1/2"	P1@.040	LF	.78	1.38	—	2.16
3/4"	P1@.047	LF	1.03	1.62	—	2.65
1"	P1@.052	LF	1.31	1.80	—	3.11
1¼"	P1@.061	LF	1.65	2.11	—	3.76
1½"	P1@.069	LF	2.02	2.38	—	4.40
2"	P1@.077	LF	2.66	2.66	—	5.32
2½"	P1@.088	LF	4.23	3.04	—	7.27
3"	P1@.099	LF	6.43	3.42	—	9.85
4"	P1@.125	LF	8.26	4.32	—	12.58
6"	P1@.202	LF	17.30	6.98	—	24.28
8"	P1@.266	LF	31.90	9.19	—	41.09

PVC, Schedule 40, with Solvent-Weld Joints

Description	Craft@Hrs	Unit	Material $	Labor $	Equipment $	Total $

Schedule 40 PVC pipe with solvent-weld joints

Description	Craft@Hrs	Unit	Material $	Labor $	Equipment $	Total $
1/2"	P1@.020	LF	.43	.69	—	1.12
3/4"	P1@.025	LF	.66	.86	—	1.52
1"	P1@.030	LF	.88	1.04	—	1.92
1¼"	P1@.035	LF	1.08	1.21	—	2.29
1½"	P1@.040	LF	1.28	1.38	—	2.66
2"	P1@.045	LF	1.72	1.55	—	3.27
2½"	P1@.050	LF	2.71	1.73	—	4.44
3"	P1@.055	LF	4.35	1.90	—	6.25
4"	P1@.070	LF	5.07	2.42	—	7.49
5"	P1@.095	LF	8.67	3.28	—	11.95
6"	P1@.120	LF	8.67	4.15	—	12.82
8"	P1@.160	LF	13.50	5.53	—	19.03

Schedule 40 PVC 45 degree ell S x S with solvent-weld joints

Description	Craft@Hrs	Unit	Material $	Labor $	Equipment $	Total $
1/2"	P1@.100	Ea	.69	3.46	—	4.15
3/4"	P1@.115	Ea	1.07	3.97	—	5.04
1"	P1@.120	Ea	1.30	4.15	—	5.45
1¼"	P1@.160	Ea	1.82	5.53	—	7.35
1½"	P1@.180	Ea	2.28	6.22	—	8.50
2"	P1@.200	Ea	3.08	6.91	—	9.99
2½"	P1@.250	Ea	7.69	8.64	—	16.33
3"	P1@.300	Ea	12.00	10.40	—	22.40
4"	P1@.500	Ea	21.40	17.30	—	38.70
5"	P1@.550	Ea	42.40	19.00	—	61.40
6"	P1@.600	Ea	52.90	20.70	—	73.60
8"	P1@.800	Ea	127.00	27.60	—	154.60

Schedule 40 PVC 90 degree ell S x S with solvent-weld joints

Description	Craft@Hrs	Unit	Material $	Labor $	Equipment $	Total $
1/2"	P1@.100	Ea	.44	3.46	—	3.90
3/4"	P1@.115	Ea	.48	3.97	—	4.45
1"	P1@.120	Ea	.83	4.15	—	4.98
1¼"	P1@.160	Ea	1.51	5.53	—	7.04
1½"	P1@.180	Ea	1.60	6.22	—	7.82
2"	P1@.200	Ea	2.52	6.91	—	9.43
2½"	P1@.250	Ea	7.67	8.64	—	16.31
3"	P1@.300	Ea	9.16	10.40	—	19.56
4"	P1@.500	Ea	16.40	17.30	—	33.70
5"	P1@.550	Ea	42.40	19.00	—	61.40
6"	P1@.600	Ea	52.40	20.70	—	73.10
8"	P1@.800	Ea	134.00	27.60	—	161.60

Description	Craft@Hrs	Unit	Material $	Labor $	Equipment $	Total $

Schedule 40 PVC tee S x S x S with solvent-weld joints

Description	Craft@Hrs	Unit	Material $	Labor $	Equipment $	Total $
1/2"	P1@.130	Ea	.55	4.49	—	5.04
3/4"	P1@.140	Ea	.59	4.84	—	5.43
1"	P1@.170	Ea	1.11	5.87	—	6.98
1¼"	P1@.220	Ea	1.75	7.60	—	9.35
1½"	P1@.250	Ea	1.96	8.64	—	10.60
2"	P1@.280	Ea	2.52	9.67	—	12.19
2½"	P1@.350	Ea	10.30	12.10	—	22.40
3"	P1@.420	Ea	13.30	14.50	—	27.80
4"	P1@.560	Ea	24.60	19.30	—	43.90
5"	P1@.710	Ea	59.00	24.50	—	83.50
6"	P1@.840	Ea	85.70	29.00	—	114.70
8"	P1@1.12	Ea	190.00	38.70	—	228.70

Schedule 40 PVC reducing tee S x S x S with solvent-weld joints

Description	Craft@Hrs	Unit	Material $	Labor $	Equipment $	Total $
3/4" x 1/2"	P1@.140	Ea	.69	4.84	—	5.53
1" x 1/2"	P1@.170	Ea	1.30	5.87	—	7.17
1" x 3/4"	P1@.170	Ea	1.93	5.87	—	7.80
1¼" x 1/2"	P1@.220	Ea	1.93	7.60	—	9.53
1¼" x 3/4"	P1@.220	Ea	1.93	7.60	—	9.53
1¼" x 1"	P1@.220	Ea	1.93	7.60	—	9.53
1½" x 1/2"	P1@.250	Ea	3.32	8.64	—	11.96
1½" x 3/4"	P1@.250	Ea	3.32	8.64	—	11.96
1½" x 1"	P1@.250	Ea	3.32	8.64	—	11.96
1½" x 1¼"	P1@.250	Ea	3.32	8.64	—	11.96
2" x 1/2"	P1@.280	Ea	4.75	9.67	—	14.42
2" x 3/4"	P1@.280	Ea	4.75	9.67	—	14.42
2" x 1"	P1@.280	Ea	4.75	9.67	—	14.42
2" x 1¼"	P1@.280	Ea	4.75	9.67	—	14.42
2" x 1½"	P1@.280	Ea	4.75	9.67	—	14.42
2½" x 1"	P1@.350	Ea	9.82	12.10	—	21.92
2½" x 1¼"	P1@.350	Ea	9.82	12.10	—	21.92
2½" x 1½"	P1@.350	Ea	9.82	12.10	—	21.92
2½" x 2"	P1@.350	Ea	9.82	12.10	—	21.92
3" x 2"	P1@.420	Ea	14.60	14.50	—	29.10
3" x 2½"	P1@.420	Ea	14.60	14.50	—	29.10
4" x 2"	P1@.560	Ea	24.60	19.30	—	43.90
4" x 2½"	P1@.560	Ea	24.60	19.30	—	43.90
4" x 3"	P1@.560	Ea	24.60	19.30	—	43.90
5" x 3"	P1@.710	Ea	43.70	24.50	—	68.20
5" x 4"	P1@.710	Ea	43.70	24.50	—	68.20
6" x 3"	P1@.840	Ea	71.60	29.00	—	100.60
6" x 4"	P1@.840	Ea	71.60	29.00	—	100.60
6" x 5"	P1@.840	Ea	71.60	29.00	—	100.60
8" x 4"	P1@1.12	Ea	159.00	38.70	—	197.70
8" x 5"	P1@1.12	Ea	159.00	38.70	—	197.70
8" x 6"	P1@1.12	Ea	159.00	38.70	—	197.70

PVC, Schedule 40, with Solvent-Weld Joints

Description	Craft@Hrs	Unit	Material $	Labor $	Equipment $	Total $
Schedule 40 PVC reducing bushing SPIG x S with solvent-weld joints						
3/4" x 1/2"	P1@.050	Ea	.45	1.73	—	2.18
1" x 1/2"	P1@.060	Ea	.81	2.07	—	2.88
1" x 3/4"	P1@.060	Ea	.81	2.07	—	2.88
1¼" x 1/2"	P1@.080	Ea	1.07	2.76	—	3.83
1¼" x 3/4"	P1@.080	Ea	1.07	2.76	—	3.83
1¼" x 1"	P1@.080	Ea	1.07	2.76	—	3.83
1½" x 1/2"	P1@.100	Ea	1.11	3.46	—	4.57
1½" x 3/4"	P1@.100	Ea	1.11	3.46	—	4.57
1½" x 1"	P1@.100	Ea	1.11	3.46	—	4.57
1½" x 1¼"	P1@.100	Ea	1.11	3.46	—	4.57
2" x 1"	P1@.110	Ea	1.87	3.80	—	5.67
2" x 1¼"	P1@.110	Ea	1.87	3.80	—	5.67
2" x 1½"	P1@.110	Ea	1.87	3.80	—	5.67
2½" x 1¼"	P1@.130	Ea	3.00	4.49	—	7.49
2½" x 1½"	P1@.130	Ea	3.00	4.49	—	7.49
2½" x 2"	P1@.130	Ea	3.00	4.49	—	7.49
3" x 2"	P1@.150	Ea	4.47	5.18	—	9.65
3" x 2½"	P1@.150	Ea	4.47	5.18	—	9.65
4" x 3"	P1@.200	Ea	10.00	6.91	—	16.91
5" x 3"	P1@.250	Ea	19.70	8.64	—	28.34
5" x 4"	P1@.250	Ea	19.70	8.64	—	28.34
6" x 4"	P1@.300	Ea	28.80	10.40	—	39.20
6" x 5"	P1@.300	Ea	28.80	10.40	—	39.20
8" x 4"	P1@.400	Ea	86.10	13.80	—	99.90
8" x 5"	P1@.400	Ea	86.10	13.80	—	99.90
Schedule 40 PVC adapter MPT x S with solvent-weld joints						
1/2"	P1@.060	Ea	.39	2.07	—	2.46
3/4"	P1@.065	Ea	.44	2.25	—	2.69
1"	P1@.070	Ea	.76	2.42	—	3.18
1¼"	P1@.100	Ea	.93	3.46	—	4.39
1½"	P1@.110	Ea	1.26	3.80	—	5.06
2"	P1@.120	Ea	4.11	4.15	—	8.26
2½"	P1@.150	Ea	4.80	5.18	—	9.98
3"	P1@.180	Ea	6.99	6.22	—	13.21
4"	P1@.240	Ea	8.90	8.29	—	17.19
5"	P1@.370	Ea	15.10	12.80	—	27.90
6"	P1@.420	Ea	23.30	14.50	—	37.80
Schedule 40 PVC adapter FPT x S with solvent-weld joints						
1/2"	P1@.110	Ea	.48	3.80	—	4.28
3/4"	P1@.120	Ea	.59	4.15	—	4.74
1"	P1@.130	Ea	.69	4.49	—	5.18
1¼"	P1@.170	Ea	1.08	5.87	—	6.95
1½"	P1@.210	Ea	1.26	7.26	—	8.52
2"	P1@.290	Ea	1.69	10.00	—	11.69
2½"	P1@.330	Ea	4.21	11.40	—	15.61
3"	P1@.470	Ea	8.40	16.20	—	24.60
4"	P1@.630	Ea	15.60	21.80	—	37.40
5"	P1@.890	Ea	24.50	30.70	—	55.20
6"	P1@.970	Ea	34.40	33.50	—	67.90

PVC, Schedule 40, with Solvent-Weld Joints

Description	Craft@Hrs	Unit	Material $	Labor $	Equipment $	Total $

Schedule 40 PVC cap S with solvent-weld joints

Description	Craft@Hrs	Unit	Material $	Labor $	Equipment $	Total $
1/2"	P1@.060	Ea	.39	2.07	—	2.46
3/4"	P1@.065	Ea	.45	2.25	—	2.70
1"	P1@.070	Ea	.69	2.42	—	3.11
1¼"	P1@.100	Ea	1.07	3.46	—	4.53
1½"	P1@.110	Ea	1.08	3.80	—	4.88
2"	P1@.120	Ea	1.31	4.15	—	5.46
2½"	P1@.150	Ea	4.11	5.18	—	9.29
3"	P1@.180	Ea	4.52	6.22	—	10.74
4"	P1@.240	Ea	10.30	8.29	—	18.59
5"	P1@.370	Ea	17.20	12.80	—	30.00
6"	P1@.420	Ea	24.70	14.50	—	39.20

Schedule 40 PVC plug MPT with solvent-weld joints

Description	Craft@Hrs	Unit	Material $	Labor $	Equipment $	Total $
1/2"	P1@.150	Ea	1.14	5.18	—	6.32
3/4"	P1@.160	Ea	1.24	5.53	—	6.77
1"	P1@.180	Ea	2.01	6.22	—	8.23
1¼"	P1@.210	Ea	2.09	7.26	—	9.35
1½"	P1@.230	Ea	2.25	7.95	—	10.20
2"	P1@.240	Ea	2.94	8.29	—	11.23
2½"	P1@.260	Ea	4.04	8.98	—	13.02
3"	P1@.300	Ea	6.11	10.40	—	16.51
4"	P1@.400	Ea	13.90	13.80	—	27.70

Schedule 40 PVC coupling S x S with solvent-weld joints

Description	Craft@Hrs	Unit	Material $	Labor $	Equipment $	Total $
1/2"	P1@.100	Ea	.26	3.46	—	3.72
3/4"	P1@.115	Ea	.39	3.97	—	4.36
1"	P1@.120	Ea	.67	4.15	—	4.82
1¼"	P1@.160	Ea	.93	5.53	—	6.46
1½"	P1@.180	Ea	.97	6.22	—	7.19
2"	P1@.200	Ea	1.52	6.91	—	8.43
2½"	P1@.250	Ea	3.32	8.64	—	11.96
3"	P1@.300	Ea	5.25	10.40	—	15.65
4"	P1@.500	Ea	7.54	17.30	—	24.84
5"	P1@.550	Ea	13.90	19.00	—	32.90
6"	P1@.600	Ea	23.80	20.70	—	44.50
8"	P1@.800	Ea	44.60	27.60	—	72.20

Schedule 40 PVC union S x S with solvent-weld joints

Description	Craft@Hrs	Unit	Material $	Labor $	Equipment $	Total $
1/2"	P1@.125	Ea	3.49	4.32	—	7.81
3/4"	P1@.140	Ea	4.36	4.84	—	9.20
1"	P1@.160	Ea	4.52	5.53	—	10.05
1¼"	P1@.200	Ea	9.32	6.91	—	16.23
1½"	P1@.225	Ea	10.60	7.77	—	18.37
2"	P1@.250	Ea	16.50	8.64	—	25.14
2½"	P1@.275	Ea	24.50	9.50	—	34.00
3"	P1@.300	Ea	30.10	10.40	—	40.50

PVC, Schedule 40, with Solvent-Weld Joints

Description	Craft@Hrs	Unit	Material $	Labor $	Equipment $	Total $

Class 125 bronze body gate valve, threaded ends

Description	Craft@Hrs	Unit	Material $	Labor $	Equipment $	Total $
1/2"	P1@.210	Ea	16.20	7.26	—	23.46
3/4"	P1@.250	Ea	20.30	8.64	—	28.94
1"	P1@.300	Ea	28.50	10.40	—	38.90
1¼"	P1@.400	Ea	36.00	13.80	—	49.80
1½"	P1@.450	Ea	48.40	15.50	—	63.90
2"	P1@.500	Ea	80.90	17.30	—	98.20
2½"	P1@.750	Ea	134.00	25.90	—	159.90
3"	P1@.950	Ea	193.00	32.80	—	225.80

Class 125 iron body gate valve, flanged ends

Description	Craft@Hrs	Unit	Material $	Labor $	Equipment $	Total $
2"	P1@.500	Ea	310.00	17.30	—	327.30
2½"	P1@.600	Ea	418.00	20.70	—	438.70
3"	P1@.750	Ea	454.00	25.90	—	479.90
4"	P1@1.35	Ea	666.00	46.60	—	712.60
5"	ER@2.00	Ea	1,270.00	74.00	31.40	1,375.40
6"	ER@2.50	Ea	1,270.00	92.60	39.30	1,401.90
8"	ER@3.00	Ea	2,090.00	111.00	47.10	2,248.10

Class 125 bronze body globe valve, threaded ends

Description	Craft@Hrs	Unit	Material $	Labor $	Equipment $	Total $
1/2"	P1@.210	Ea	30.00	7.26	—	37.26
3/4"	P1@.250	Ea	40.00	8.64	—	48.64
1"	P1@.300	Ea	57.40	10.40	—	67.80
1¼"	P1@.400	Ea	80.70	13.80	—	94.50
1½"	P1@.450	Ea	109.00	15.50	—	124.50
2"	P1@.500	Ea	176.00	17.30	—	193.30

200 PSIG iron body butterfly valve, lug type, lever operated

Description	Craft@Hrs	Unit	Material $	Labor $	Equipment $	Total $
2"	P1@.450	Ea	134.00	15.50	—	149.50
2½"	P1@.450	Ea	139.00	15.50	—	154.50
3"	P1@.550	Ea	146.00	19.00	—	165.00
4"	P1@.550	Ea	182.00	19.00	—	201.00
5"	ER@.800	Ea	240.00	29.60	12.70	282.30
6"	ER@.800	Ea	293.00	29.60	12.70	335.30
8"	ER@.900	Ea	401.00	33.30	14.10	448.40

200 PSIG iron body butterfly valve, wafer type, lever operated

Description	Craft@Hrs	Unit	Material $	Labor $	Equipment $	Total $
2"	P1@.450	Ea	122.00	15.50	—	137.50
2½"	P1@.450	Ea	125.00	15.50	—	140.50
3"	P1@.550	Ea	134.00	19.00	—	153.00
4"	P1@.550	Ea	163.00	19.00	—	182.00
5"	ER@.800	Ea	217.00	29.60	12.70	259.30
6"	ER@.800	Ea	272.00	29.60	12.70	314.30
8"	ER@.900	Ea	377.00	33.30	14.10	424.40

Description	Craft@Hrs	Unit	Material $	Labor $	Equipment $	Total $
Class 125 bronze body 2-piece ball valve, threaded ends						
1/2"	P1@.210	Ea	7.91	7.26	—	15.17
3/4"	P1@.250	Ea	10.50	8.64	—	19.14
1"	P1@.300	Ea	18.20	10.40	—	28.60
1¼"	P1@.400	Ea	30.30	13.80	—	44.10
1½"	P1@.450	Ea	41.00	15.50	—	56.50
2"	P1@.500	Ea	51.90	17.30	—	69.20
3"	P1@.625	Ea	355.00	21.60	—	376.60
4"	P1@.690	Ea	465.00	23.80	—	488.80
PVC ball valve, solid body, solvent weld joints, EDPM (female socket)						
1/2"	P1@.170	Ea	3.15	5.87	—	9.02
3/4"	P1@.200	Ea	3.57	6.91	—	10.48
1"	P1@.220	Ea	5.20	7.60	—	12.80
1¼"	P1@.280	Ea	5.99	9.67	—	15.66
1½"	P1@.315	Ea	9.98	10.90	—	20.88
2"	P1@.385	Ea	12.50	13.30	—	25.80
PVC ball valve, solid body, threaded joints, EDPM (female pipe thread)						
1/2"	P1@.200	Ea	3.15	6.91	—	10.06
3/4"	P1@.240	Ea	3.57	8.29	—	11.86
1"	P1@.290	Ea	5.20	10.00	—	15.20
1¼"	P1@.390	Ea	5.99	13.50	—	19.49
1½"	P1@.420	Ea	9.98	14.50	—	24.48
2"	P1@.490	Ea	12.50	16.90	—	29.40
PVC ball valve, tru-union, threaded joints, EDPM (female pipe thread)						
1/2"	P1@.200	Ea	3.15	6.91	—	10.06
3/4"	P1@.240	Ea	3.57	8.29	—	11.86
1"	P1@.290	Ea	5.20	10.00	—	15.20
1¼"	P1@.390	Ea	5.99	13.50	—	19.49
1½"	P1@.420	Ea	9.98	14.50	—	24.48
2"	P1@.490	Ea	12.50	16.90	—	29.40
2½"	P1@.520	Ea	77.60	18.00	—	95.60
3"	P1@.590	Ea	179.00	20.40	—	199.40
4"	P1@.630	Ea	331.00	21.80	—	352.80

PVC, Schedule 40, with Solvent-Weld Joints

Description	Craft@Hrs	Unit	Material $	Labor $	Equipment $	Total $

PVC ball valve, union type body, solvent-weld joints, (female socket)

Description	Craft@Hrs	Unit	Material $	Labor $	Equipment $	Total $
1/2"	P1@.185	Ea	3.15	6.39	—	9.54
3/4"	P1@.225	Ea	3.57	7.77	—	11.34
1"	P1@.270	Ea	5.20	9.33	—	14.53
1¼"	P1@.360	Ea	5.99	12.40	—	18.39
1½"	P1@.400	Ea	9.98	13.80	—	23.78
2"	P1@.465	Ea	12.50	16.10	—	28.60
2½"	P1@.490	Ea	77.60	16.90	—	94.50
3"	P1@.540	Ea	179.00	18.70	—	197.70
4"	P1@.600	Ea	331.00	20.70	—	351.70

Class 125 bronze body swing check valve, threaded

Description	Craft@Hrs	Unit	Material $	Labor $	Equipment $	Total $
1/2"	P1@.210	Ea	17.70	7.26	—	24.96
3/4"	P1@.250	Ea	25.40	8.64	—	34.04
1"	P1@.300	Ea	33.30	10.40	—	43.70
1¼"	P1@.400	Ea	47.30	13.80	—	61.10
1½"	P1@.450	Ea	66.70	15.50	—	82.20
2"	P1@.500	Ea	111.00	17.30	—	128.30

Class 125 iron body swing check valve, flanged ends

Description	Craft@Hrs	Unit	Material $	Labor $	Equipment $	Total $
2"	P1@.500	Ea	155.00	17.30	—	172.30
2½"	P1@.600	Ea	197.00	20.70	—	217.70
3"	P1@.750	Ea	245.00	25.90	—	270.90
4"	P1@1.35	Ea	360.00	46.60	—	406.60
5"	ER@2.00	Ea	693.00	74.00	31.40	798.40
6"	ER@2.50	Ea	693.00	92.60	39.30	824.90
8"	ER@3.00	Ea	1,250.00	111.00	47.10	1,408.10

Class 125 iron body silent check valve, wafer type

Description	Craft@Hrs	Unit	Material $	Labor $	Equipment $	Total $
2"	P1@.500	Ea	113.00	17.30	—	130.30
2½"	P1@.600	Ea	126.00	20.70	—	146.70
3"	P1@.750	Ea	145.00	25.90	—	170.90
4"	P1@1.35	Ea	194.00	46.60	—	240.60
5"	ER@2.00	Ea	298.00	74.00	31.40	403.40
6"	ER@2.50	Ea	404.00	92.60	39.30	535.90
8"	ER@3.00	Ea	693.00	111.00	47.10	851.10

Class 125 bronze body strainer, threaded ends

Description	Craft@Hrs	Unit	Material $	Labor $	Equipment $	Total $
1/2"	P1@.210	Ea	27.70	7.26	—	34.96
3/4"	P1@.250	Ea	36.40	8.64	—	45.04
1"	P1@.300	Ea	44.60	10.40	—	55.00
1¼"	P1@.400	Ea	62.30	13.80	—	76.10
1½"	P1@.450	Ea	93.80	15.50	—	109.30
2"	P1@.500	Ea	162.00	17.30	—	179.30

Description	Craft@Hrs	Unit	Material $	Labor $	Equipment $	Total $

Class 125 iron body strainer, flanged ends

Description	Craft@Hrs	Unit	Material $	Labor $	Equipment $	Total $
2"	P1@.500	Ea	124.00	17.30	—	141.30
2½"	P1@.600	Ea	139.00	20.70	—	159.70
3"	P1@.750	Ea	160.00	25.90	—	185.90
4"	P1@1.35	Ea	273.00	46.60	—	319.60
5"	ER@2.00	Ea	554.00	74.00	31.40	659.40
6"	ER@2.50	Ea	554.00	92.60	39.30	685.90
8"	ER@3.00	Ea	937.00	111.00	47.10	1,095.10

Installation of 2-way control valve, threaded joints

Description	Craft@Hrs	Unit	Material $	Labor $	Equipment $	Total $
1/2"	P1@.210	Ea	—	7.26	—	7.26
3/4"	P1@.275	Ea	—	9.50	—	9.50
1"	P1@.350	Ea	—	12.10	—	12.10
1¼"	P1@.430	Ea	—	14.90	—	14.90
1½"	P1@.505	Ea	—	17.40	—	17.40
2"	P1@.675	Ea	—	23.30	—	23.30
2½"	P1@.830	Ea	—	28.70	—	28.70
3"	P1@.990	Ea	—	34.20	—	34.20

Installation of 3-way control valve, threaded joints

Description	Craft@Hrs	Unit	Material $	Labor $	Equipment $	Total $
1/2"	P1@.260	Ea	—	8.98	—	8.98
3/4"	P1@.365	Ea	—	12.60	—	12.60
1"	P1@.475	Ea	—	16.40	—	16.40
1¼"	P1@.575	Ea	—	19.90	—	19.90
1½"	P1@.680	Ea	—	23.50	—	23.50
2"	P1@.910	Ea	—	31.40	—	31.40
2½"	P1@1.12	Ea	—	38.70	—	38.70
3"	P1@1.33	Ea	—	46.00	—	46.00

PVC companion flange

Description	Craft@Hrs	Unit	Material $	Labor $	Equipment $	Total $
2"	P1@.140	Ea	5.47	4.84	—	10.31
2½"	P1@.180	Ea	16.40	6.22	—	22.62
3"	P1@.210	Ea	17.00	7.26	—	24.26
4"	P1@.280	Ea	17.50	9.67	—	27.17
5"	P1@.310	Ea	39.30	10.70	—	50.00
6"	P1@.420	Ea	39.30	14.50	—	53.80
8"	P1@.560	Ea	58.70	19.30	—	78.00

Bolt and gasket sets

Description	Craft@Hrs	Unit	Material $	Labor $	Equipment $	Total $
2"	P1@.500	Ea	3.92	17.30	—	21.22
2½"	P1@.650	Ea	4.60	22.50	—	27.10
3"	P1@.750	Ea	7.84	25.90	—	33.74
4"	P1@1.00	Ea	13.10	34.60	—	47.70
5"	P1@1.10	Ea	21.60	38.00	—	59.60
6"	P1@1.20	Ea	21.60	41.50	—	63.10
8"	P1@1.25	Ea	24.10	43.20	—	67.30

PVC, Schedule 40, with Solvent-Weld Joints

Description	Craft@Hrs	Unit	Material $	Labor $	Equipment $	Total $
Thermometer with well						
7"	P1@.250	Ea	159.00	8.64	—	167.64
9"	P1@.250	Ea	164.00	8.64	—	172.64
Dial type pressure gauge						
2½"	P1@.200	Ea	33.10	6.91	—	40.01
3½"	P1@.200	Ea	43.80	6.91	—	50.71
Pressure/temperature tap						
tap	P1@.150	Ea	15.70	5.18	—	20.88
Hanger with swivel assembly						
1/2"	P1@.250	Ea	3.74	8.64	—	12.38
3/4"	P1@.250	Ea	4.13	8.64	—	12.77
1"	P1@.250	Ea	4.33	8.64	—	12.97
1¼"	P1@.300	Ea	4.44	10.40	—	14.84
1½"	P1@.300	Ea	4.77	10.40	—	15.17
2"	P1@.300	Ea	4.98	10.40	—	15.38
2½"	P1@.350	Ea	6.78	12.10	—	18.88
3"	P1@.350	Ea	8.37	12.10	—	20.47
4"	P1@.350	Ea	9.19	12.10	—	21.29
5"	P1@.450	Ea	13.40	15.50	—	28.90
6"	P1@.450	Ea	15.10	15.50	—	30.60
8"	P1@.450	Ea	19.00	15.50	—	34.50
Riser clamp						
1/2"	P1@.100	Ea	2.41	3.46	—	5.87
3/4"	P1@.100	Ea	3.55	3.46	—	7.01
1"	P1@.100	Ea	3.59	3.46	—	7.05
1¼"	P1@.105	Ea	4.33	3.63	—	7.96
1½"	P1@.110	Ea	4.58	3.80	—	8.38
2"	P1@.115	Ea	4.84	3.97	—	8.81
2½"	P1@.120	Ea	5.09	4.15	—	9.24
3"	P1@.120	Ea	5.52	4.15	—	9.67
4"	P1@.125	Ea	7.03	4.32	—	11.35
5"	P1@.180	Ea	10.10	6.22	—	16.32
6"	P1@.200	Ea	12.20	6.91	—	19.11
8"	P1@.200	Ea	19.80	6.91	—	26.71

PVC, Schedule 80, with Solvent-Weld Joints

PVC (Polyvinyl Chloride) Schedule 80 pipe with Schedule 80 socket-type fittings and solvent-welded joints is widely used in process, chemical, A.C. condensate, potable water and irrigation piping systems. PVC is available in Type I (normal impact) and Type II (high impact). Type I has a maximum temperature rating of 150 degrees F., and Type II is rated at 140 degrees F.

Schedule 80 PVC can be threaded, but it is more economical to use solvent-welded joints.

Manufacturers should be consulted for maximum pressure ratings and recommended joints solvents for specific applications.

Because of the current unreliability of many plastic valves, most engineers specify standard bronze-body and iron-body valves for use in PVC water piping systems. Plastic valves, however, have to be used in systems conveying liquids that may be injurious to metallic valves.

This section has been arranged to save the estimator's time by including all normally-used system components such as pipe, fittings, valves, hanger assemblies, riser clamps and miscellaneous items under one heading. Additional items can be found under "Plumbing and Piping Specialties." The cost estimates in this section are based on the conditions, limitations and wage rates described in the section "How to Use This Book" beginning on page 5.

Equipment cost, where shown, is $110 per hour for a 10-ton hydraulic truck-mounted crane.

Description	Craft@Hrs	Unit	Material $	Labor $	Equipment $	Total $

Schedule 80 PVC pipe assembly with solvent-weld joints installed horizontally.
Complete installation including three to eight tees and three to eight elbows every 100' and hangers spaced to meet plumbing code (*a tee and elbow every 12' for 1/2" dia., a tee and elbow every 40' for 8"dia.*).

Description	Craft@Hrs	Unit	Material $	Labor $	Equipment $	Total $
1/2"	P1@.085	LF	2.19	2.94	—	5.13
3/4"	P1@.093	LF	2.74	3.21	—	5.95
1"	P1@.099	LF	3.02	3.42	—	6.44
1¼"	P1@.115	LF	3.54	3.97	—	7.51
1½"	P1@.117	LF	3.77	4.04	—	7.81
2"	P1@.120	LF	4.80	4.15	—	8.95
2½"	P1@.125	LF	7.89	4.32	—	12.21
3"	P1@.129	LF	10.70	4.46	—	15.16
4"	P1@.161	LF	15.40	5.56	—	20.96
6"	P1@.253	LF	23.30	8.74	—	32.04
8"	P1@.299	LF	38.90	10.30	—	49.20

PVC, Schedule 80, with Solvent-Weld Joints

Description	Craft@Hrs	Unit	Material $	Labor $	Equipment $	Total $

Schedule 80 PVC pipe assembly with solvent-weld joints, installed risers.
Complete installation including a reducing tee every floor and a riser clamp every other.

Description	Craft@Hrs	Unit	Material $	Labor $	Equipment $	Total $
1/2"	P1@.041	LF	1.06	1.42	—	2.48
3/4"	P1@.048	LF	1.54	1.66	—	3.20
1"	P1@.054	LF	1.86	1.87	—	3.73
1¼"	P1@.063	LF	2.18	2.18	—	4.36
1½"	P1@.071	LF	2.85	2.45	—	5.30
2"	P1@.079	LF	3.82	2.73	—	6.55
2½"	P1@.090	LF	6.26	3.11	—	9.37
3"	P1@.101	LF	8.09	3.49	—	11.58
4"	P1@.129	LF	11.60	4.46	—	16.06
6"	P1@.242	LF	20.60	8.36	—	28.96
8"	P1@.296	LF	34.90	10.20	—	45.10

Schedule 80 PVC pipe with solvent-weld joints

Description	Craft@Hrs	Unit	Material $	Labor $	Equipment $	Total $
1/2"	P1@.021	LF	.73	.73	—	1.46
3/4"	P1@.026	LF	.97	.90	—	1.87
1"	P1@.032	LF	1.28	1.11	—	2.39
1¼"	P1@.037	LF	1.50	1.28	—	2.78
1½"	P1@.042	LF	2.02	1.45	—	3.47
2"	P1@.047	LF	2.73	1.62	—	4.35
2½"	P1@.052	LF	4.35	1.80	—	6.15
3"	P1@.057	LF	5.82	1.97	—	7.79
4"	P1@.074	LF	8.58	2.56	—	11.14
6"	P1@.160	LF	16.30	5.53	—	21.83
8"	P1@.190	LF	24.90	6.56	—	31.46

Schedule 80 PVC 45 degree ell S x S with solvent-weld joints

Description	Craft@Hrs	Unit	Material $	Labor $	Equipment $	Total $
1/2"	P1@.105	Ea	3.39	3.63	—	7.02
3/4"	P1@.120	Ea	5.12	4.15	—	9.27
1"	P1@.125	Ea	7.70	4.32	—	12.02
1¼"	P1@.170	Ea	9.83	5.87	—	15.70
1½"	P1@.190	Ea	11.70	6.56	—	18.26
2"	P1@.210	Ea	15.00	7.26	—	22.26
2½"	P1@.262	Ea	31.50	9.05	—	40.55
3"	P1@.315	Ea	38.40	10.90	—	49.30
4"	P1@.520	Ea	69.20	18.00	—	87.20
6"	P1@.630	Ea	86.90	21.80	—	108.70
8"	P1@.840	Ea	188.00	29.00	—	217.00

Description	Craft@Hrs	Unit	Material $	Labor $	Equipment $	Total $

Schedule 80 PVC 90 degree ell S x S with solvent-weld joints

Description	Craft@Hrs	Unit	Material $	Labor $	Equipment $	Total $
1/2"	P1@.105	Ea	1.84	3.63	—	5.47
3/4"	P1@.120	Ea	2.32	4.15	—	6.47
1"	P1@.125	Ea	3.66	4.32	—	7.98
1¼"	P1@.170	Ea	4.97	5.87	—	10.84
1½"	P1@.190	Ea	5.30	6.56	—	11.86
2"	P1@.210	Ea	6.36	7.26	—	13.62
2½"	P1@.262	Ea	14.80	9.05	—	23.85
3"	P1@.315	Ea	16.80	10.90	—	27.70
4"	P1@.520	Ea	25.50	18.00	—	43.50
6"	P1@.630	Ea	72.80	21.80	—	94.60
8"	P1@.840	Ea	198.00	29.00	—	227.00

Schedule 80 PVC tee S x S x S with solvent-weld joints

Description	Craft@Hrs	Unit	Material $	Labor $	Equipment $	Total $
1/2"	P1@.135	Ea	5.07	4.66	—	9.73
3/4"	P1@.145	Ea	5.30	5.01	—	10.31
1"	P1@.180	Ea	6.59	6.22	—	12.81
1¼"	P1@.230	Ea	18.20	7.95	—	26.15
1½"	P1@.265	Ea	18.20	9.16	—	27.36
2"	P1@.295	Ea	22.70	10.20	—	32.90
2½"	P1@.368	Ea	24.70	12.70	—	37.40
3"	P1@.440	Ea	30.90	15.20	—	46.10
4"	P1@.585	Ea	35.80	20.20	—	56.00
6"	P1@.880	Ea	121.00	30.40	—	151.40
8"	P1@1.18	Ea	282.00	40.80	—	322.80

Schedule 80 PVC reducing tee S x S x S with solvent-weld joints

Description	Craft@Hrs	Unit	Material $	Labor $	Equipment $	Total $
3/4" x 1/2"	P1@.145	Ea	5.73	5.01	—	10.74
1" x 1/2"	P1@.175	Ea	6.17	6.05	—	12.22
1" x 3/4"	P1@.175	Ea	6.17	6.05	—	12.22
1¼" x 1/2"	P1@.230	Ea	20.30	7.95	—	28.25
1¼" x 3/4"	P1@.230	Ea	20.30	7.95	—	28.25
1¼" x 1"	P1@.230	Ea	20.30	7.95	—	28.25
1½" x 3/4"	P1@.260	Ea	21.80	8.98	—	30.78
1½" x 1"	P1@.260	Ea	21.80	8.98	—	30.78
1½" x 1¼"	P1@.260	Ea	21.80	8.98	—	30.78
2" x 1/2"	P1@.290	Ea	26.70	10.00	—	36.70
2" x 3/4"	P1@.290	Ea	26.70	10.00	—	36.70
2" x 1"	P1@.290	Ea	26.70	10.00	—	36.70
2" x 1½"	P1@.290	Ea	26.70	10.00	—	36.70
3" x 2"	P1@.430	Ea	37.80	14.90	—	52.70
4" x 2"	P1@.570	Ea	42.90	19.70	—	62.60
4" x 3"	P1@.570	Ea	42.90	19.70	—	62.60
6" x 4"	P1@.850	Ea	145.00	29.40	—	174.40
8" x 4"	P1@1.16	Ea	323.00	40.10	—	363.10
8" x 5"	P1@1.16	Ea	323.00	40.10	—	363.10
8" x 6"	P1@1.16	Ea	323.00	40.10	—	363.10

PVC, Schedule 80, with Solvent-Weld Joints

Description	Craft@Hrs	Unit	Material $	Labor $	Equipment $	Total $

Schedule 80 PVC reducing bushing SPIG x S with solvent-weld joints

Description	Craft@Hrs	Unit	Material $	Labor $	Equipment $	Total $
3/4" x 1/2"	P1@.053	Ea	1.05	1.83	—	2.88
1" x 1/2"	P1@.063	Ea	2.99	2.18	—	5.17
1" x 3/4"	P1@.063	Ea	2.99	2.18	—	5.17
1¼" x 1/2"	P1@.084	Ea	4.79	2.90	—	7.69
1¼" x 3/4"	P1@.084	Ea	4.79	2.90	—	7.69
1¼" x 1"	P1@.084	Ea	4.79	2.90	—	7.69
1½" x 1/2"	P1@.105	Ea	6.36	3.63	—	9.99
1½" x 3/4"	P1@.105	Ea	6.36	3.63	—	9.99
1½" x 1"	P1@.105	Ea	6.36	3.63	—	9.99
1½" x 1¼"	P1@.105	Ea	6.36	3.63	—	9.99
2" x 1"	P1@.116	Ea	9.12	4.01	—	13.13
2" x 1¼"	P1@.116	Ea	9.12	4.01	—	13.13
2" x 1½"	P1@.116	Ea	9.12	4.01	—	13.13
3" x 2"	P1@.158	Ea	25.20	5.46	—	30.66
4" x 2½"	P1@.210	Ea	34.50	7.26	—	41.76
4" x 3"	P1@.210	Ea	34.50	7.26	—	41.76
6" x 3"	P1@.315	Ea	48.20	10.90	—	59.10
6" x 4"	P1@.315	Ea	48.20	10.90	—	59.10
8" x 4"	P1@.420	Ea	117.00	14.50	—	131.50
8" x 6"	P1@.420	Ea	117.00	14.50	—	131.50

Schedule 80 PVC adapter MPT x S with solvent-weld joints

Description	Craft@Hrs	Unit	Material $	Labor $	Equipment $	Total $
1/2"	P1@.063	Ea	3.81	2.18	—	5.99
3/4"	P1@.068	Ea	4.15	2.35	—	6.50
1"	P1@.074	Ea	7.15	2.56	—	9.71
1¼"	P1@.105	Ea	8.44	3.63	—	12.07
1½"	P1@.116	Ea	12.10	4.01	—	16.11
2"	P1@.126	Ea	17.40	4.35	—	21.75
2½"	P1@.158	Ea	20.10	5.46	—	25.56
3"	P1@.189	Ea	22.20	6.53	—	28.73
4"	P1@.252	Ea	39.20	8.71	—	47.91
5"	P1@.385	Ea	54.60	13.30	—	67.90
6"	P1@.435	Ea	126.00	15.00	—	141.00

Schedule 80 PVC adapter FPT x S with solvent-weld joints

Description	Craft@Hrs	Unit	Material $	Labor $	Equipment $	Total $
1/2"	P1@.116	Ea	3.05	4.01	—	7.06
3/4"	P1@.126	Ea	4.52	4.35	—	8.87
1"	P1@.137	Ea	6.62	4.73	—	11.35
1¼"	P1@.179	Ea	10.70	6.18	—	16.88
1½"	P1@.221	Ea	13.10	7.64	—	20.74
2"	P1@.305	Ea	22.90	10.50	—	33.40
2½"	P1@.345	Ea	36.10	11.90	—	48.00
3"	P1@.490	Ea	40.50	16.90	—	57.40
4"	P1@.655	Ea	69.90	22.60	—	92.50
5"	P1@.920	Ea	113.00	31.80	—	144.80
6"	P1@1.10	Ea	138.00	38.00	—	176.00

Description	Craft@Hrs	Unit	Material $	Labor $	Equipment $	Total $

Schedule 80 PVC cap S with solvent-weld joints

Description	Craft@Hrs	Unit	Material $	Labor $	Equipment $	Total $
1/2"	P1@.063	Ea	3.18	2.18	—	5.36
3/4"	P1@.070	Ea	3.30	2.42	—	5.72
1"	P1@.075	Ea	5.88	2.59	—	8.47
1¼"	P1@.105	Ea	7.14	3.63	—	10.77
1½"	P1@.115	Ea	7.14	3.97	—	11.11
2"	P1@.125	Ea	14.10	4.32	—	18.42
2½"	P1@.158	Ea	28.50	5.46	—	33.96
3"	P1@.189	Ea	33.90	6.53	—	40.43
4"	P1@.250	Ea	57.10	8.64	—	65.74
5"	P1@.390	Ea	118.00	13.50	—	131.50
6"	P1@.450	Ea	142.00	15.50	—	157.50

Schedule 80 PVC plug MPT with solvent-weld joints

Description	Craft@Hrs	Unit	Material $	Labor $	Equipment $	Total $
1/2"	P1@.155	Ea	3.08	5.36	—	8.44
3/4"	P1@.165	Ea	3.18	5.70	—	8.88
1"	P1@.190	Ea	3.90	6.56	—	10.46
1¼"	P1@.220	Ea	5.73	7.60	—	13.33
1½"	P1@.240	Ea	6.93	8.29	—	15.22
2"	P1@.255	Ea	7.13	8.81	—	15.94
2½"	P1@.275	Ea	17.90	9.50	—	27.40
3"	P1@.320	Ea	23.20	11.10	—	34.30
4"	P1@.425	Ea	45.20	14.70	—	59.90

Schedule 80 PVC coupling S x S with solvent-weld joints

Description	Craft@Hrs	Unit	Material $	Labor $	Equipment $	Total $
1/2"	P1@.105	Ea	3.23	3.63	—	6.86
3/4"	P1@.120	Ea	4.36	4.15	—	8.51
1"	P1@.125	Ea	4.52	4.32	—	8.84
1¼"	P1@.170	Ea	6.89	5.87	—	12.76
1½"	P1@.190	Ea	7.39	6.56	—	13.95
2"	P1@.210	Ea	7.92	7.26	—	15.18
2½"	P1@.262	Ea	19.50	9.05	—	28.55
3"	P1@.315	Ea	22.40	10.90	—	33.30
4"	P1@.520	Ea	28.20	18.00	—	46.20
6"	P1@.630	Ea	60.20	21.80	—	82.00
8"	P1@.840	Ea	83.00	29.00	—	112.00

Schedule 80 PVC union S x S with solvent-weld joints

Description	Craft@Hrs	Unit	Material $	Labor $	Equipment $	Total $
1/2"	P1@.125	Ea	6.52	4.32	—	10.84
3/4"	P1@.140	Ea	8.98	4.84	—	13.82
1"	P1@.160	Ea	9.46	5.53	—	14.99
1¼"	P1@.200	Ea	18.80	6.91	—	25.71
1½"	P1@.225	Ea	21.30	7.77	—	29.07
2"	P1@.250	Ea	28.90	8.64	—	37.54
2½"	P1@.275	Ea	45.60	9.50	—	55.10
3"	P1@.300	Ea	53.90	10.40	—	64.30

PVC, Schedule 80, with Solvent-Weld Joints

Description	Craft@Hrs	Unit	Material $	Labor $	Equipment $	Total $

Class 125 bronze body gate valve, threaded ends

Description	Craft@Hrs	Unit	Material $	Labor $	Equipment $	Total $
1/2"	P1@.210	Ea	16.20	7.26	—	23.46
3/4"	P1@.250	Ea	20.30	8.64	—	28.94
1"	P1@.300	Ea	28.50	10.40	—	38.90
1¼"	P1@.400	Ea	36.00	13.80	—	49.80
1½"	P1@.450	Ea	48.40	15.50	—	63.90
2"	P1@.500	Ea	80.90	17.30	—	98.20
2½"	P1@.750	Ea	134.00	25.90	—	159.90
3"	P1@.950	Ea	193.00	32.80	—	225.80

Class 125 iron body gate valve, flanged ends

Description	Craft@Hrs	Unit	Material $	Labor $	Equipment $	Total $
2"	P1@.500	Ea	310.00	17.30	—	327.30
2½"	P1@.600	Ea	418.00	20.70	—	438.70
3"	P1@.750	Ea	454.00	25.90	—	479.90
4"	P1@1.35	Ea	666.00	46.60	—	712.60
5"	ER@2.00	Ea	1,270.00	74.00	31.40	1,375.40
6"	ER@2.50	Ea	1,270.00	92.60	39.30	1,401.90
8"	ER@3.00	Ea	2,090.00	111.00	47.10	2,248.10

Class 125 bronze body globe valve, threaded ends

Description	Craft@Hrs	Unit	Material $	Labor $	Equipment $	Total $
1/2"	P1@.210	Ea	30.00	7.26	—	37.26
3/4"	P1@.250	Ea	40.00	8.64	—	48.64
1"	P1@.300	Ea	57.40	10.40	—	67.80
1¼"	P1@.400	Ea	80.70	13.80	—	94.50
1½"	P1@.450	Ea	109.00	15.50	—	124.50
2"	P1@.500	Ea	176.00	17.30	—	193.30

200 PSIG iron body butterfly valve, lug type, lever operated

Description	Craft@Hrs	Unit	Material $	Labor $	Equipment $	Total $
2"	P1@.450	Ea	134.00	15.50	—	149.50
2½"	P1@.450	Ea	139.00	15.50	—	154.50
3"	P1@.550	Ea	146.00	19.00	—	165.00
4"	P1@.550	Ea	182.00	19.00	—	201.00
5"	ER@.800	Ea	240.00	29.60	12.70	282.30
6"	ER@.800	Ea	293.00	29.60	12.70	335.30
8"	ER@.900	Ea	401.00	33.30	14.10	448.40

200 PSIG iron body butterfly valve, wafer type, lever operated

Description	Craft@Hrs	Unit	Material $	Labor $	Equipment $	Total $
2"	P1@.450	Ea	122.00	15.50	—	137.50
2½"	P1@.450	Ea	125.00	15.50	—	140.50
3"	P1@.550	Ea	134.00	19.00	—	153.00
4"	P1@.550	Ea	163.00	19.00	—	182.00
5"	ER@.800	Ea	217.00	29.60	12.70	259.30
6"	ER@.800	Ea	272.00	29.60	12.70	314.30
8"	ER@.900	Ea	377.00	33.30	14.10	424.40

Description	Craft@Hrs	Unit	Material $	Labor $	Equipment $	Total $

Class 125 bronze body 2-piece ball valve, threaded ends

Description	Craft@Hrs	Unit	Material $	Labor $	Equipment $	Total $
1/2"	P1@.210	Ea	7.91	7.26	—	15.17
3/4"	P1@.250	Ea	10.50	8.64	—	19.14
1"	P1@.300	Ea	18.20	10.40	—	28.60
1¼"	P1@.400	Ea	30.30	13.80	—	44.10
1½"	P1@.450	Ea	41.00	15.50	—	56.50
2"	P1@.500	Ea	51.90	17.30	—	69.20
3"	P1@.625	Ea	355.00	21.60	—	376.60
4"	P1@.690	Ea	465.00	23.80	—	488.80

PVC ball valve, solid body, solvent weld joints, EDPM (female socket)

Description	Craft@Hrs	Unit	Material $	Labor $	Equipment $	Total $
1/2"	P1@.170	Ea	3.15	5.87	—	9.02
3/4"	P1@.200	Ea	3.57	6.91	—	10.48
1"	P1@.220	Ea	5.20	7.60	—	12.80
1¼"	P1@.280	Ea	5.99	9.67	—	15.66
1½"	P1@.315	Ea	9.98	10.90	—	20.88
2"	P1@.385	Ea	12.50	13.30	—	25.80

PVC ball valve, solid body, threaded joints, EDPM (female pipe thread)

Description	Craft@Hrs	Unit	Material $	Labor $	Equipment $	Total $
1/2"	P1@.200	Ea	3.15	6.91	—	10.06
3/4"	P1@.240	Ea	3.57	8.29	—	11.86
1"	P1@.290	Ea	5.20	10.00	—	15.20
1¼"	P1@.390	Ea	5.99	13.50	—	19.49
1½"	P1@.420	Ea	9.98	14.50	—	24.48
2"	P1@.490	Ea	12.50	16.90	—	29.40

PVC ball valve, tru-union, threaded joints, EDPM (female pipe thread)

Description	Craft@Hrs	Unit	Material $	Labor $	Equipment $	Total $
1/2"	P1@.200	Ea	3.15	6.91	—	10.06
3/4"	P1@.240	Ea	3.57	8.29	—	11.86
1"	P1@.290	Ea	5.20	10.00	—	15.20
1¼"	P1@.390	Ea	5.99	13.50	—	19.49
1½"	P1@.420	Ea	9.98	14.50	—	24.48
2"	P1@.490	Ea	12.50	16.90	—	29.40
2½"	P1@.520	Ea	77.60	18.00	—	95.60
3"	P1@.590	Ea	179.00	20.40	—	199.40
4"	P1@.630	Ea	331.00	21.80	—	352.80

PVC ball valve, union type body, solvent-weld joints, (female socket)

Description	Craft@Hrs	Unit	Material $	Labor $	Equipment $	Total $
1/2"	P1@.185	Ea	3.15	6.39	—	9.54
3/4"	P1@.225	Ea	3.57	7.77	—	11.34
1"	P1@.270	Ea	5.20	9.33	—	14.53
1¼"	P1@.360	Ea	5.99	12.40	—	18.39
1½"	P1@.400	Ea	9.98	13.80	—	23.78
2"	P1@.465	Ea	12.50	16.10	—	28.60
2½"	P1@.490	Ea	77.60	16.90	—	94.50
3"	P1@.540	Ea	179.00	18.70	—	197.70
4"	P1@.600	Ea	331.00	20.70	—	351.70

PVC, Schedule 80, with Solvent-Weld Joints

Description	Craft@Hrs	Unit	Material $	Labor $	Equipment $	Total $

Class 125 bronze body swing check valve, threaded ends

Description	Craft@Hrs	Unit	Material $	Labor $	Equipment $	Total $
1/2"	P1@.210	Ea	17.70	7.26	—	24.96
3/4"	P1@.250	Ea	25.40	8.64	—	34.04
1"	P1@.300	Ea	33.30	10.40	—	43.70
1¼"	P1@.400	Ea	47.30	13.80	—	61.10
1½"	P1@.450	Ea	66.70	15.50	—	82.20
2"	P1@.500	Ea	111.00	17.30	—	128.30

Class 125 iron body swing check valve, flanged ends

Description	Craft@Hrs	Unit	Material $	Labor $	Equipment $	Total $
2"	P1@.500	Ea	155.00	17.30	—	172.30
2½"	P1@.600	Ea	197.00	20.70	—	217.70
3"	P1@.750	Ea	245.00	25.90	—	270.90
4"	P1@1.35	Ea	360.00	46.60	—	406.60
5"	ER@2.00	Ea	693.00	74.00	31.40	798.40
6"	ER@2.50	Ea	693.00	92.60	39.30	824.90
8"	ER@3.00	Ea	1,250.00	111.00	47.10	1,408.10

Class 125 iron body silent check valve, wafer type

Description	Craft@Hrs	Unit	Material $	Labor $	Equipment $	Total $
2"	P1@.500	Ea	113.00	17.30	—	130.30
2½"	P1@.600	Ea	126.00	20.70	—	146.70
3"	P1@.750	Ea	145.00	25.90	—	170.90
4"	P1@1.35	Ea	194.00	46.60	—	240.60
5"	ER@2.00	Ea	298.00	74.00	31.40	403.40
6"	ER@2.50	Ea	404.00	92.60	39.30	535.90
8"	ER@3.00	Ea	693.00	111.00	47.10	851.10

Class 125 bronze body strainer, threaded ends

Description	Craft@Hrs	Unit	Material $	Labor $	Equipment $	Total $
1/2"	P1@.210	Ea	27.70	7.26	—	34.96
3/4"	P1@.250	Ea	36.40	8.64	—	45.04
1"	P1@.300	Ea	44.60	10.40	—	55.00
1¼"	P1@.400	Ea	62.30	13.80	—	76.10
1½"	P1@.450	Ea	93.80	15.50	—	109.30
2"	P1@.500	Ea	162.00	17.30	—	179.30

Class 125 iron body strainer, flanged ends

Description	Craft@Hrs	Unit	Material $	Labor $	Equipment $	Total $
2"	P1@.500	Ea	165.00	17.30	—	182.30
2½"	P1@.600	Ea	184.00	20.70	—	204.70
3"	P1@.750	Ea	213.00	25.90	—	238.90
4"	P1@1.35	Ea	364.00	46.60	—	410.60
5"	ER@2.00	Ea	738.00	74.00	31.40	843.40
6"	ER@2.50	Ea	738.00	92.60	39.30	869.90
8"	ER@3.00	Ea	1,250.00	111.00	47.10	1,408.10

Description	Craft@Hrs	Unit	Material $	Labor $	Equipment $	Total $

Installation of 2-way control valve, threaded joints

Description	Craft@Hrs	Unit	Material $	Labor $	Equipment $	Total $
1/2"	P1@.210	Ea	—	7.26	—	7.26
3/4"	P1@.275	Ea	—	9.50	—	9.50
1"	P1@.350	Ea	—	12.10	—	12.10
1¼"	P1@.430	Ea	—	14.90	—	14.90
1½"	P1@.505	Ea	—	17.40	—	17.40
2"	P1@.675	Ea	—	23.30	—	23.30
2½"	P1@.830	Ea	—	28.70	—	28.70
3"	P1@.990	Ea	—	34.20	—	34.20

Installation of 3-way control valve, threaded joints

Description	Craft@Hrs	Unit	Material $	Labor $	Equipment $	Total $
1/2"	P1@.260	Ea	—	8.98	—	8.98
3/4"	P1@.365	Ea	—	12.60	—	12.60
1"	P1@.475	Ea	—	16.40	—	16.40
1¼"	P1@.575	Ea	—	19.90	—	19.90
1½"	P1@.680	Ea	—	23.50	—	23.50
2"	P1@.910	Ea	—	31.40	—	31.40
2½"	P1@1.12	Ea	—	38.70	—	38.70
3"	P1@1.33	Ea	—	46.00	—	46.00

PVC companion flange

Description	Craft@Hrs	Unit	Material $	Labor $	Equipment $	Total $
2"	P1@.140	Ea	5.95	4.84	—	10.79
2½"	P1@.180	Ea	17.70	6.22	—	23.92
3"	P1@.210	Ea	18.50	7.26	—	25.76
4"	P1@.280	Ea	19.20	9.67	—	28.87
5"	P1@.310	Ea	42.50	10.70	—	53.20
6"	P1@.420	Ea	42.50	14.50	—	57.00
8"	P1@.560	Ea	63.50	19.30	—	82.80

Bolt and gasket set

Description	Craft@Hrs	Unit	Material $	Labor $	Equipment $	Total $
2"	P1@.500	Ea	3.86	17.30	—	21.16
2½"	P1@.650	Ea	4.51	22.50	—	27.01
3"	P1@.750	Ea	7.64	25.90	—	33.54
4"	P1@1.00	Ea	12.70	34.60	—	47.30
5"	P1@1.10	Ea	21.20	38.00	—	59.20
6"	P1@1.20	Ea	21.20	41.50	—	62.70
8"	P1@1.25	Ea	23.80	43.20	—	67.00

Thermometer with well

Description	Craft@Hrs	Unit	Material $	Labor $	Equipment $	Total $
7"	P1@.250	Ea	159.00	8.64	—	167.64
9"	P1@.250	Ea	164.00	8.64	—	172.64

Dial type pressure gauge

Description	Craft@Hrs	Unit	Material $	Labor $	Equipment $	Total $
2½"	P1@.200	Ea	33.10	6.91	—	40.01
3½"	P1@.200	Ea	43.80	6.91	—	50.71

PVC, Schedule 80, with Solvent-Weld Joints

Description	Craft@Hrs	Unit	Material $	Labor $	Equipment $	Total $

Pressure/temperature tap

Description	Craft@Hrs	Unit	Material $	Labor $	Equipment $	Total $
tap	P1@.150	Ea	15.70	5.18	—	20.88

Hanger with swivel assembly

Description	Craft@Hrs	Unit	Material $	Labor $	Equipment $	Total $
1/2"	P1@.250	Ea	3.74	8.64	—	12.38
3/4"	P1@.250	Ea	4.13	8.64	—	12.77
1"	P1@.250	Ea	4.33	8.64	—	12.97
1¼"	P1@.300	Ea	4.44	10.40	—	14.84
1½"	P1@.300	Ea	4.77	10.40	—	15.17
2"	P1@.300	Ea	4.98	10.40	—	15.38
2½"	P1@.350	Ea	6.78	12.10	—	18.88
3"	P1@.350	Ea	8.37	12.10	—	20.47
4"	P1@.350	Ea	9.19	12.10	—	21.29
5"	P1@.450	Ea	13.40	15.50	—	28.90
6"	P1@.450	Ea	15.10	15.50	—	30.60
8"	P1@.450	Ea	19.00	15.50	—	34.50

Riser clamp

Description	Craft@Hrs	Unit	Material $	Labor $	Equipment $	Total $
1/2"	P1@.100	Ea	2.41	3.46	—	5.87
3/4"	P1@.100	Ea	3.55	3.46	—	7.01
1"	P1@.100	Ea	3.59	3.46	—	7.05
1¼"	P1@.105	Ea	4.33	3.63	—	7.96
1½"	P1@.110	Ea	4.58	3.80	—	8.38
2"	P1@.115	Ea	4.84	3.97	—	8.81
2½"	P1@.120	Ea	5.09	4.15	—	9.24
3"	P1@.120	Ea	5.52	4.15	—	9.67
4"	P1@.125	Ea	7.03	4.32	—	11.35
5"	P1@.180	Ea	10.10	6.22	—	16.32
6"	P1@.200	Ea	12.20	6.91	—	19.11
8"	P1@.200	Ea	19.80	6.91	—	26.71

Polyethylene-Aluminum Pipe with Crimped Joints

Composite pressure pipe is aluminum tube laminated between 2 layers of plastic pipe. It is manufactured and sold in various coiled lengths (200' to 1,000' rolls). The jointing method can be either crimped or compression connections. It will not rust or corrode and because of its flexibility, installations require approximately 40% less fittings. Expansion rates are similar to copper, but its thermal coefficient (heat loss) is over 800 times less than copper. It is also chemically resistant to most acids, salt solutions, alkalis, fats and oils.

Common applications include ice or snow melting systems, radiant floor heating systems, water service tubing, hot & cold domestic water service, chilled water systems, compressed air systems, solar and process piping applications.

Maximum temperature	Maximum pressure	Pipe selection
73 degrees F	200 psi	PE-AL or PEX-AL
140 degrees F	160 psi	PE-AL or PEX-AL
180 degrees F	125 psi	PEX-AL
210 degrees F	115 psi	PEX-AL

PE-AL is the designation for polyethylene-aluminum composite pipe
PEX-AL is the designation for cross linked polyethylene-aluminum composite pipe

Description	Craft@Hrs	Unit	Material $	Labor $	Equipment $	Total $

Cross linked Polyethylene-Aluminum pipe with crimped joints (PEX-AL), pipe only

Description	Craft@Hrs	Unit	Material $	Labor $	Equipment $	Total $
3/8"	P1@.028	LF	.46	.97	—	1.43
1/2"	P1@.028	LF	.68	.97	—	1.65
5/8"	P1@.030	LF	.95	1.04	—	1.99
3/4"	P1@.030	LF	1.34	1.04	—	2.38
1"	P1@.034	LF	2.17	1.17	—	3.34

Polyethylene-Aluminum pipe with crimped joints (PE-AL), pipe only

Description	Craft@Hrs	Unit	Material $	Labor $	Equipment $	Total $
1/2"	P1@.028	LF	.52	.97	—	1.49
5/8"	P1@.030	LF	.72	1.04	—	1.76
3/4"	P1@.030	LF	.95	1.04	—	1.99
1"	P1@.034	LF	1.53	1.17	—	2.70

90 degree brass ell with crimped joints (PEX-AL/PE-AL)

Description	Craft@Hrs	Unit	Material $	Labor $	Equipment $	Total $
1/2"	P1@.080	Ea	1.42	2.76	—	4.18
5/8"	P1@.085	Ea	1.71	2.94	—	4.65
3/4"	P1@.090	Ea	3.30	3.11	—	6.41
1"	P1@.105	Ea	3.60	3.63	—	7.23

90 degree brass ell with crimped joints x male pipe thread (PEX-AL x MPT/PE-AL x MPT)

Description	Craft@Hrs	Unit	Material $	Labor $	Equipment $	Total $
1/2" x 1/2"	P1@.085	Ea	1.55	2.94	—	4.49
1/2" x 3/8"	P1@.095	Ea	1.96	3.28	—	5.24

Polyethylene-Aluminum Pipe with Crimped Joints

Description	Craft@Hrs	Unit	Material $	Labor $	Equipment $	Total $

90 degree brass ell with crimped joints x copper socket (PEX-AL x C/PE-AL x C)

Description	Craft@Hrs	Unit	Material $	Labor $	Equipment $	Total $
1/2"	P1@.085	Ea	1.55	2.94	—	4.49
1/2" x 3/4"	P1@.090	Ea	1.96	3.11	—	5.07
5/8" x 3/4"	P1@.095	Ea	2.13	3.28	—	5.41
3/4"	P1@.095	Ea	1.74	3.28	—	5.02

90 degree brass wingback ell with crimped joints x female pipe thread (PEX-AL x FPT/PE-AL x FPT)

Description	Craft@Hrs	Unit	Material $	Labor $	Equipment $	Total $
1/2"	P1@.085	Ea	3.03	2.94	—	5.97
3/4"	P1@.095	Ea	3.60	3.28	—	6.88

Tee (brass) with crimped joints (PEX-AL/PE-AL)

Description	Craft@Hrs	Unit	Material $	Labor $	Equipment $	Total $
1/2"	P1@.095	Ea	1.51	3.28	—	4.79
5/8"	P1@.105	Ea	1.78	3.63	—	5.41
3/4"	P1@.110	Ea	3.60	3.80	—	7.40
1"	P1@.120	Ea	4.41	4.15	—	8.56

Reducing tee (brass) with crimped joints (PEX-AL/PE-AL)

Description	Craft@Hrs	Unit	Material $	Labor $	Equipment $	Total $
1/2" x 1/2" x 5/8"	P1@.110	Ea	1.78	3.80	—	5.58
1/2" x 1/2" x 3/4"	P1@.115	Ea	2.08	3.97	—	6.05
5/8" x 1/2" x 1/2"	P1@.115	Ea	1.78	3.97	—	5.75
5/8" x 1/2" x 5/8"	P1@.115	Ea	1.78	3.97	—	5.75
5/8" x 5/8" x 1/2"	P1@.115	Ea	1.78	3.97	—	5.75
3/4" x 1/2" x 1/2"	P1@.115	Ea	2.08	3.97	—	6.05
3/4" x 1/2" x 3/4"	P1@.115	Ea	2.22	3.97	—	6.19
3/4" x 3/4" x 1/2"	P1@.115	Ea	2.22	3.97	—	6.19
3/4" x 3/4" x 5/8"	P1@.115	Ea	2.22	3.97	—	6.19
3/4" x 3/4" x 1"	P1@.120	Ea	4.26	4.15	—	8.41
1" x 1/2" x 1/2"	P1@.120	Ea	4.14	4.15	—	8.29
1" x 1/2" x 3/4"	P1@.120	Ea	3.86	4.15	—	8.01
1" x 1/2" x 1"	P1@.120	Ea	4.26	4.15	—	8.41
1" x 3/4" x 1/2"	P1@.120	Ea	4.26	4.15	—	8.41
1" x 3/4" x 3/4"	P1@.120	Ea	4.26	4.15	—	8.41
1" x 3/4" x 1"	P1@.120	Ea	4.26	4.15	—	8.41
1" x 1" x 1/2"	P1@.120	Ea	3.84	4.15	—	7.99
1" x 1" x 3/4"	P1@.120	Ea	4.41	4.15	—	8.56

Coupling (brass) with crimped joints (PEX-AL/PE-AL)

Description	Craft@Hrs	Unit	Material $	Labor $	Equipment $	Total $
1/2"	P1@.080	Ea	.69	2.76	—	3.45
5/8"	P1@.085	Ea	.88	2.94	—	3.82
3/4"	P1@.090	Ea	1.94	3.11	—	5.05
1"	P1@.105	Ea	1.98	3.63	—	5.61

Description	Craft@Hrs	Unit	Material $	Labor $	Equipment $	Total $

Reducing coupling (brass) with crimped joints (PEX-AL/PE-AL)

Description	Craft@Hrs	Unit	Material $	Labor $	Equipment $	Total $
1/2"	P1@.080	Ea	.88	2.76	—	3.64
5/8"	P1@.085	Ea	1.25	2.94	—	4.19
3/4"	P1@.090	Ea	1.32	3.11	—	4.43
1"	P1@.105	Ea	1.63	3.63	—	5.26

Adapter (brass) with crimped joints x male pipe thread (PEX-AL x MPT/PE-AL x MPT)

Description	Craft@Hrs	Unit	Material $	Labor $	Equipment $	Total $
1/2" x 1/2"	P1@.080	Ea	1.05	2.76	—	3.81
1/2" x 3/4"	P1@.085	Ea	1.32	2.94	—	4.26
5/8" x 3/4"	P1@.085	Ea	1.30	2.94	—	4.24
3/4" x 1/2"	P1@.090	Ea	1.78	3.11	—	4.89
3/4" x 3/4"	P1@.090	Ea	1.89	3.11	—	5.00
3/4" x 1"	P1@.105	Ea	3.03	3.63	—	6.66
1" x 1"	P1@.105	Ea	3.30	3.63	—	6.93

Adapter (brass) with crimped joints x female pipe thread (PEX-AL x FPT/PE-AL x FPT)

Description	Craft@Hrs	Unit	Material $	Labor $	Equipment $	Total $
1/2" x 1/2"	P1@.080	Ea	1.09	2.76	—	3.85
1/2" x 3/4"	P1@.085	Ea	1.51	2.94	—	4.45
5/8" x 3/4"	P1@.085	Ea	1.51	2.94	—	4.45
3/4" x 1/2"	P1@.090	Ea	1.78	3.11	—	4.89
3/4" x 3/4"	P1@.090	Ea	1.96	3.11	—	5.07
3/4" x 1"	P1@.105	Ea	3.27	3.63	—	6.90
1" x 1"	P1@.105	Ea	3.60	3.63	—	7.23

Adapter (brass) with crimped joints x copper fitting (spigot) (PEX-AL x C ftg/PE-AL x C ftg)

Description	Craft@Hrs	Unit	Material $	Labor $	Equipment $	Total $
1/2" x 1/2"	P1@.080	Ea	1.25	2.76	—	4.01
1/2" x 3/4"	P1@.085	Ea	1.53	2.94	—	4.47
5/8" x 3/4"	P1@.085	Ea	1.51	2.94	—	4.45
3/4" x 3/4"	P1@.090	Ea	3.03	3.11	—	6.14
1" x 1"	P1@.105	Ea	3.60	3.63	—	7.23

Adapter (brass) with crimped joints x copper socket (PEX-AL x C/PE-AL x C)

Description	Craft@Hrs	Unit	Material $	Labor $	Equipment $	Total $
1/2" x 1/2"	P1@.080	Ea	1.05	2.76	—	3.81
1/2" x 3/4"	P1@.085	Ea	1.54	2.94	—	4.48
5/8" x 3/4"	P1@.085	Ea	1.60	2.94	—	4.54
3/4" x 1/2"	P1@.090	Ea	1.72	3.11	—	4.83
3/4" x 3/4"	P1@.090	Ea	2.48	3.11	—	5.59
3/4" x 1"	P1@.105	Ea	3.60	3.63	—	7.23
1" x 1"	P1@.105	Ea	4.14	3.63	—	7.77

Polyethylene-Aluminum Pipe with Crimped Joints

Description	Craft@Hrs	Unit	Material $	Labor $	Equipment $	Total $
Cap (brass) with crimped joints (PEX-AL/PE-AL)						
1/2"	P1@.060	Ea	.47	2.07	—	2.54
5/8"	P1@.065	Ea	.66	2.25	—	2.91
3/4"	P1@.070	Ea	.88	2.42	—	3.30
1"	P1@.085	Ea	1.09	2.94	—	4.03
Mini ball valve (brass) with crimped joints (PEX-AL/PE-AL)						
1/2" x 3/8" straight	P1@.150	Ea	5.53	5.18	—	10.71
1/2" x 3/8" angle	P1@.150	Ea	5.09	5.18	—	10.27
1/2" x copper	P1@.150	Ea	5.83	5.18	—	11.01
1/2" x MPT	P1@.150	Ea	6.14	5.18	—	11.32
1/2"	P1@.150	Ea	6.49	5.18	—	11.67
1/2" x comp	P1@.150	Ea	6.58	5.18	—	11.76
5/8"	P1@.165	Ea	9.24	5.70	—	14.94
5/8" x 3/4" copper	P1@.170	Ea	7.37	5.87	—	13.24
5/8" x 3/4" MPT	P1@.170	Ea	8.09	5.87	—	13.96
3/4"	P1@.170	Ea	9.93	5.87	—	15.80
3/4" x copper	P1@.170	Ea	9.35	5.87	—	15.22
Balancing valve (brass) with crimped joints (PEX-AL/PE-AL)						
1/2" x copper	P1@.150	Ea	38.00	5.18	—	43.18
1/2" x MPT	P1@.150	Ea	43.80	5.18	—	48.98
Manifolds (headers) copper with crimped joints (PEX-AL)						
3 - 1/2" outlets	P1@.750	Ea	31.90	25.90	—	57.80
3 - 5/8" outlets	P1@.750	Ea	36.10	25.90	—	62.00
4 - 1/2" outlets	P1@.850	Ea	40.90	29.40	—	70.30
4 - 5/8" outlets	P1@.850	Ea	47.30	29.40	—	76.70
5 - 1/2" outlets	P1@1.00	Ea	52.40	34.60	—	87.00
6 - 1/2" outlets	P1@1.20	Ea	59.40	41.50	—	100.90
8 - 1/2" outlets	P1@1.45	Ea	84.70	50.10	—	134.80
10 - 1/2" outlets	P1@1.65	Ea	109.00	57.00	—	166.00
12 - 1/2" outlets	P1@1.85	Ea	132.00	63.90	—	195.90
Manifolds (headers) copper with mini ball valves and crimped joints (PEX-AL)						
3 - 1/2" outlets	P1@.750	Ea	118.00	25.90	—	143.90
3 - 5/8" outlets	P1@.750	Ea	142.00	25.90	—	167.90
4 - 1/2" outlets	P1@.850	Ea	154.00	29.40	—	183.40
4 - 5/8" outlets	P1@.850	Ea	187.00	29.40	—	216.40
5 - 1/2" outlets	P1@1.00	Ea	195.00	34.60	—	229.60
6 - 1/2" outlets	P1@1.20	Ea	223.00	41.50	—	264.50

Description	Craft@Hrs	Unit	Material $	Labor $	Equipment $	Total $

Crimp rings, nickel plated soft copper

Description	Craft@Hrs	Unit	Material $	Labor $	Equipment $	Total $
1/2"	P1@.000	Ea	.18	—	—	.18
5/8"	P1@.000	Ea	.19	—	—	.19
3/4"	P1@.000	Ea	.22	—	—	.22
1"	P1@.000	Ea	.33	—	—	.33

Replacement O-rings

Description	Craft@Hrs	Unit	Material $	Labor $	Equipment $	Total $
1/2"	P1@.000	Ea	.12	—	—	.12
5/8"	P1@.000	Ea	.12	—	—	.12
3/4"	P1@.000	Ea	.18	—	—	.18
1"	P1@.000	Ea	.18	—	—	.18

Pipe hangers (polypropylene)

Description	Craft@Hrs	Unit	Material $	Labor $	Equipment $	Total $
1/2"	P1@.050	Ea	.06	1.73	—	1.79
5/8"	P1@.050	Ea	.06	1.73	—	1.79
3/4"	P1@.050	Ea	.06	1.73	—	1.79
1"	P1@.050	Ea	.08	1.73	—	1.81

Pipe clips (nail clips)

Description	Craft@Hrs	Unit	Material $	Labor $	Equipment $	Total $
1/2"	P1@.030	Ea	.13	1.04	—	1.17
5/8"	P1@.030	Ea	.20	1.04	—	1.24
1"	P1@.030	Ea	.46	1.04	—	1.50

Miscellaneous tools

Description	Craft@Hrs	Unit	Material $	Labor $	Equipment $	Total $
Crimp tool	P1@.000	Ea	266.00	—	—	266.00
Beveling tool	P1@.000	Ea	5.40	—	—	5.40
Reaming tool	P1@.000	Ea	32.30	—	—	32.30
Pipe bender kit	P1@.000	Ea	663.00	—	—	663.00
Bending spring	P1@.000	Ea	28.70	—	—	28.70
Pipe cutter	P1@.000	Ea	19.40	—	—	19.40

Polyethylene-Aluminum Pipe with Compression Joints

Composite pressure pipe is aluminum tube laminated between 2 layers of plastic pipe. It is manufactured and sold in various coiled lengths (200' to 1000' rolls). The jointing method can be either crimped or compression connections. It will not rust or corrode and because of its flexibility, installations require approximately 40% less fittings. Installed like soft copper, it can be supported every 8.2 feet where applicable. Expansion rates are similar to copper, but its thermal coefficient (heat loss) is over 800 times less than copper. It is also chemically resistant to most acids, salt solutions, alkalis, fats and oils.

Common applications include ice or snow melting systems, radiant floor heating systems, water service tubing, hot & cold domestic water service, chilled water systems, compressed air systems, solar and process piping applications.

Maximum temperature	Maximum pressure	Pipe selection
73 degrees F	200 psi	PE-AL or PEX-AL
140 degrees F	160 psi	PE-AL or PEX-AL
180 degrees F	125 psi	PEX-AL
210 degrees F	115 psi	PEX-AL

PE-AL is the designation for polyethylene-aluminum composite pipe
PEX-AL is the designation for cross linked polyethylene-aluminum composite pipe

Description	Craft@Hrs	Unit	Material $	Labor $	Equipment $	Total $

Cross linked Polyethylene-Aluminum pipe with compression joints (PEX-AL), pipe only

Description	Craft@Hrs	Unit	Material $	Labor $	Equipment $	Total $
3/8"	P1@.028	LF	.42	.97	—	1.39
1/2"	P1@.028	LF	.63	.97	—	1.60
5/8"	P1@.030	LF	.85	1.04	—	1.89
3/4"	P1@.030	LF	1.21	1.04	—	2.25
1"	P1@.034	LF	1.94	1.17	—	3.11

Polyethylene-Aluminum pipe with compression joints (PE-AL), pipe only

Description	Craft@Hrs	Unit	Material $	Labor $	Equipment $	Total $
1/2"	P1@.028	LF	.51	.97	—	1.48
5/8"	P1@.030	LF	.68	1.04	—	1.72
3/4"	P1@.030	LF	.92	1.04	—	1.96
1"	P1@.034	LF	1.47	1.17	—	2.64

90 degree brass ell with compression joints (PEX-AL/PE-AL)

Description	Craft@Hrs	Unit	Material $	Labor $	Equipment $	Total $
1/2"	P1@.092	Ea	2.97	3.18	—	6.15
5/8"	P1@.098	Ea	4.13	3.39	—	7.52
3/4"	P1@.104	Ea	6.03	3.59	—	9.62
1"	P1@.121	Ea	10.60	4.18	—	14.78

90 degree brass ell with compression joints x male pipe thread (PEX-AL x MPT/PE-AL x MPT)

Description	Craft@Hrs	Unit	Material $	Labor $	Equipment $	Total $
1/2" x 1/2"	P1@.098	Ea	4.65	3.39	—	8.04
1/2" x 3/4"	P1@.105	Ea	5.64	3.63	—	9.27
3/4" x 3/4"	P1@.109	Ea	5.20	3.77	—	8.97

Description	Craft@Hrs	Unit	Material $	Labor $	Equipment $	Total $

90 degree brass ell with compression joints x copper socket (PEX-AL x C/PE-AL x C)

Description	Craft@Hrs	Unit	Material $	Labor $	Equipment $	Total $
1/2"	P1@.098	Ea	2.54	3.39	—	5.93
1/2" x 3/4"	P1@.109	Ea	2.70	3.77	—	6.47
5/8" x 3/4"	P1@.112	Ea	3.22	3.87	—	7.09
3/4"	P1@.115	Ea	4.87	3.97	—	8.84

90 degree brass wingback ell with compression joints x female pipe thread (PEX-AL x FPT/PE-AL x FPT)

Description	Craft@Hrs	Unit	Material $	Labor $	Equipment $	Total $
1/2"	P1@.098	Ea	2.20	3.39	—	5.59
5/8"	P1@.105	Ea	3.77	3.63	—	7.40
3/4"	P1@.115	Ea	5.78	3.97	—	9.75

Tee (brass) with compression joints (PEX-AL/PE-AL)

Description	Craft@Hrs	Unit	Material $	Labor $	Equipment $	Total $
1/2"	P1@.109	Ea	3.63	3.77	—	7.40
5/8"	P1@.121	Ea	5.83	4.18	—	10.01
3/4"	P1@.127	Ea	8.64	4.39	—	13.03
1"	P1@.141	Ea	14.30	4.87	—	19.17

Reducing tee (brass) with compression joints (PEX-AL/PE-AL)

Description	Craft@Hrs	Unit	Material $	Labor $	Equipment $	Total $
5/8" x 5/8" x 1/2"	P1@.138	Ea	5.34	4.77	—	10.11
3/4" x 1/2" x 3/4"	P1@.138	Ea	7.59	4.77	—	12.36
3/4" x 3/4" x 1/2"	P1@.138	Ea	7.76	4.77	—	12.53
3/4" x 1/2" x 3/4"	P1@.138	Ea	6.88	4.77	—	11.65
3/4" x 3/4" x 5/8"	P1@.138	Ea	7.84	4.77	—	12.61
1" x 1/2" x 1/2"	P1@.142	Ea	11.70	4.91	—	16.61
1" x 1" x 1/2"	P1@.142	Ea	15.70	4.91	—	20.61
1" x 3/4" x 3/4"	P1@.142	Ea	8.83	4.91	—	13.74
1" x 1" x 3/4"	P1@.142	Ea	13.60	4.91	—	18.51

Coupling (brass) with compression joints (PEX-AL/PE-AL)

Description	Craft@Hrs	Unit	Material $	Labor $	Equipment $	Total $
3/8"	P1@.090	Ea	2.51	3.11	—	5.62
1/2"	P1@.092	Ea	2.74	3.18	—	5.92
5/8"	P1@.098	Ea	3.72	3.39	—	7.11
3/4"	P1@.104	Ea	5.53	3.59	—	9.12
1"	P1@.121	Ea	9.93	4.18	—	14.11

Reducing coupling (brass) with compression joints (PEX-AL/PE-AL)

Description	Craft@Hrs	Unit	Material $	Labor $	Equipment $	Total $
5/8" x 1/2"	P1@.092	Ea	3.28	3.18	—	6.46
3/4" x 1/2"	P1@.098	Ea	4.95	3.39	—	8.34
3/4" x 5/8"	P1@.104	Ea	4.79	3.59	—	8.38
1" x 3/4"	P1@.121	Ea	6.66	4.18	—	10.84

Cap (brass) with compression joints (PEX-AL/PE-AL)

Description	Craft@Hrs	Unit	Material $	Labor $	Equipment $	Total $
1/2"	P1@.069	Ea	1.84	2.38	—	4.22
5/8"	P1@.075	Ea	2.54	2.59	—	5.13
3/4"	P1@.081	Ea	3.33	2.80	—	6.13
1"	P1@.098	Ea	4.95	3.39	—	8.34

Polyethylene-Aluminum Pipe with Compression Joints

Description	Craft@Hrs	Unit	Material $	Labor $	Equipment $	Total $
Mini ball valve (brass) with compression joints (PEX-AL/PE-AL)						
1/2" x 3/8" straight	P1@.173	Ea	6.69	5.98	—	12.67
1/2" x 3/8" angle	P1@.173	Ea	6.30	5.98	—	12.28
1/2" x copper	P1@.173	Ea	6.27	5.98	—	12.25
1/2" x MPT	P1@.173	Ea	6.60	5.98	—	12.58
1/2"	P1@.173	Ea	7.37	5.98	—	13.35
5/8"	P1@.173	Ea	9.74	5.98	—	15.72
5/8" x 3/4" copper	P1@.196	Ea	7.59	6.77	—	14.36
5/8" x 3/4" MPT	P1@.196	Ea	8.14	6.77	—	14.91
3/4"	P1@.196	Ea	9.05	6.77	—	15.82
3/4" x copper	P1@.196	Ea	9.41	6.77	—	16.18
Balancing valve (brass) with compression joints (PEX-AL/PE-AL)						
1/2" x copper	P1@.173	Ea	42.00	5.98	—	47.98
1/2" x MPT	P1@.173	Ea	46.60	5.98	—	52.58
Crimp rings, nickel plated soft copper						
1/2"	P1@.000	Ea	.18	—	—	.18
5/8"	P1@.000	Ea	.20	—	—	.20
3/4"	P1@.000	Ea	.23	—	—	.23
1"	P1@.000	Ea	.34	—	—	.34
Replacement O-rings						
1/2"	P1@.000	Ea	.12	—	—	.12
5/8"	P1@.000	Ea	.12	—	—	.12
3/4"	P1@.000	Ea	.18	—	—	.18
1"	P1@.000	Ea	.18	—	—	.18
Pipe hangers (polypropylene)						
1/2"	P1@.050	Ea	.06	1.73	—	1.79
5/8"	P1@.050	Ea	.06	1.73	—	1.79
3/4"	P1@.050	Ea	.06	1.73	—	1.79
1"	P1@.050	Ea	.08	1.73	—	1.81
Pipe clips (nail clips)						
1/2"	P1@.030	Ea	.13	1.04	—	1.17
5/8"	P1@.030	Ea	.20	1.04	—	1.24
1"	P1@.030	Ea	.46	1.04	—	1.50
Miscellaneous tools						
Crimp tool	P1@.000	Ea	266.00	—	—	266.00
Beveling tool	P1@.000	Ea	5.40	—	—	5.40
Reaming tool	P1@.000	Ea	32.30	—	—	32.30
Pipe bender kit	P1@.000	Ea	477.00	—	—	477.00
Bending spring	P1@.000	Ea	39.90	—	—	39.90
Pipe cutter	P1@.000	Ea	19.40	—	—	19.40

Description	Craft@Hrs	Unit	Material $	Labor $	Equipment $	Total $

Water meters, turbine type. Including brass connection unions

Description	Craft@Hrs	Unit	Material $	Labor $	Equipment $	Total $
1/2"	P1@.500	Ea	121.00	17.30	—	138.30
3/4"	P1@.500	Ea	195.00	17.30	—	212.30
1"	P1@.650	Ea	263.00	22.50	—	285.50
1½"	P1@.700	Ea	706.00	24.20	—	730.20
2"	P1@.800	Ea	1,040.00	27.60	—	1,067.60
3"	P1@.900	Ea	1,620.00	31.10	—	1,651.10
4"	P1@.975	Ea	3,020.00	33.70	—	3,053.70

Water meters, compound type. Including brass connection unions

Description	Craft@Hrs	Unit	Material $	Labor $	Equipment $	Total $
2"	P1@.800	Ea	2,560.00	27.60	—	2,587.60
3"	P1@.900	Ea	3,330.00	31.10	—	3,361.10
4"	P1@.975	Ea	5,470.00	33.70	—	5,503.70

Water meter by-pass and connection assembly. Includes three isolation ball valves, two tees, two 90 degree elbows, 10' of Type L copper pipe and standard support devices. Make additional allowances for the cost of the water meter.

Description	Craft@Hrs	Unit	Material $	Labor $	Equipment $	Total $
1/2"	P1@1.00	Ea	83.10	34.60	—	117.70
3/4"	P1@1.50	Ea	126.00	51.80	—	177.80
1"	P1@1.95	Ea	217.00	67.40	—	284.40
1½"	P1@2.45	Ea	400.00	84.60	—	484.60
2"	P1@3.25	Ea	588.00	112.00	—	700.00
3"	P1@5.50	Ea	1,750.00	190.00	—	1,940.00
4"	P1@6.75	Ea	2,980.00	233.00	—	3,213.00

Backflow preventers-reduced pressure. Including valves and test ports

Description	Craft@Hrs	Unit	Material $	Labor $	Equipment $	Total $
3/4"	P1@1.00	Ea	305.00	34.60	—	339.60
1"	P1@1.25	Ea	377.00	43.20	—	420.20
1½"	P1@2.00	Ea	606.00	69.10	—	675.10
2"	P1@2.15	Ea	754.00	74.30	—	828.30
2½"	P1@4.00	Ea	2,730.00	138.00	—	2,868.00
3"	P1@4.75	Ea	3,610.00	164.00	—	3,774.00
4"	P1@6.00	Ea	4,110.00	207.00	—	4,317.00
6"	P1@7.95	Ea	4,490.00	275.00	—	4,765.00

Backflow preventers-reduced pressure. Including integral ball valves and test ports

Description	Craft@Hrs	Unit	Material $	Labor $	Equipment $	Total $
1/2"	P1@.900	Ea	185.00	31.10	—	216.10
3/4"	P1@1.00	Ea	219.00	34.60	—	253.60
1"	P1@1.25	Ea	274.00	43.20	—	317.20
1¼"	P1@1.50	Ea	402.00	51.80	—	453.80
1½"	P1@2.00	Ea	437.00	69.10	—	506.10
2"	P1@2.15	Ea	492.00	74.30	—	566.30

Plumbing and Piping Specialties

Description	Craft@Hrs	Unit	Material $	Labor $	Equipment $	Total $

Backflow preventers, double check valve assembly. Including integral ball valves and test ports

Description	Craft@Hrs	Unit	Material $	Labor $	Equipment $	Total $
1/2"	P1@1.00	Ea	139.00	34.60	—	173.60
3/4"	P1@1.00	Ea	153.00	34.60	—	187.60
1"	P1@1.25	Ea	185.00	43.20	—	228.20
1¼"	P1@1.95	Ea	312.00	67.40	—	379.40
1½"	P1@2.00	Ea	322.00	69.10	—	391.10
2"	P1@2.15	Ea	392.00	74.30	—	466.30
2½"	P1@2.95	Ea	1,610.00	102.00	—	1,712.00
3"	P1@3.45	Ea	2,050.00	119.00	—	2,169.00
4"	P1@3.95	Ea	2,780.00	136.00	—	2,916.00
6"	P1@5.75	Ea	4,680.00	199.00	—	4,879.00

Vacuum breakers, atmospheric. Female pipe thread

Description	Craft@Hrs	Unit	Material $	Labor $	Equipment $	Total $
1/4"	P1@.350	Ea	48.50	12.10	—	60.60
1/2"	P1@.350	Ea	67.60	12.10	—	79.70
3/4"	P1@.350	Ea	82.70	12.10	—	94.80

Vacuum breakers, hose connection. Male/female hose thread, polished brass

Description	Craft@Hrs	Unit	Material $	Labor $	Equipment $	Total $
1/2"	P1@.150	Ea	20.60	5.18	—	25.78
3/4"	P1@.150	Ea	25.10	5.18	—	30.28

Suction diffusers

Description	Craft@Hrs	Unit	Material $	Labor $	Equipment $	Total $
2"	P1@1.25	Ea	284.00	43.20	—	327.20
3"	P1@2.50	Ea	477.00	86.40	—	563.40
4"	P1@3.25	Ea	609.00	112.00	—	721.00
6"	P1@4.80	Ea	860.00	166.00	—	1,026.00
8"	P1@5.95	Ea	1,610.00	206.00	—	1,816.00
10"	P1@6.75	Ea	2,190.00	233.00	—	2,423.00

Triple duty valves

Description	Craft@Hrs	Unit	Material $	Labor $	Equipment $	Total $
2"	P1@1.25	Ea	377.00	43.20	—	420.20
3"	P1@2.50	Ea	510.00	86.40	—	596.40
4"	P1@3.25	Ea	922.00	112.00	—	1,034.00
6"	P1@4.80	Ea	1,510.00	166.00	—	1,676.00
8"	P1@5.95	Ea	2,230.00	206.00	—	2,436.00
10"	P1@6.75	Ea	3,280.00	233.00	—	3,513.00

In-line circulating pump, all bronze. 115 volt, including flange kit

Description	Craft@Hrs	Unit	Material $	Labor $	Equipment $	Total $
1/25 HP	P1@1.50	Ea	361.00	51.80	—	412.80
1/16 HP	P1@1.55	Ea	455.00	53.60	—	508.60
1/12 HP	P1@1.60	Ea	628.00	55.30	—	683.30
1/6 HP	P1@1.75	Ea	1,070.00	60.50	—	1,130.50
1/4 HP	P1@1.95	Ea	1,600.00	67.40	—	1,667.40
1 HP	P1@2.25	Ea	1,850.00	77.70	—	1,927.70
1½ HP	P1@2.85	Ea	2,240.00	98.50	—	2,338.50

Description	Craft@Hrs	Unit	Material $	Labor $	Equipment $	Total $

In-line circulating pump, iron body. 115 volt, including flange kit

Description	Craft@Hrs	Unit	Material $	Labor $	Equipment $	Total $
1/25 HP	P1@1.50	Ea	177.00	51.80	—	228.80
1/16 HP	P1@1.55	Ea	198.00	53.60	—	251.60
1/12 HP	P1@1.60	Ea	372.00	55.30	—	427.30
1/6 HP	P1@1.75	Ea	632.00	60.50	—	692.50
1/4 HP	P1@1.95	Ea	732.00	67.40	—	799.40
1 HP	P1@2.25	Ea	858.00	77.70	—	935.70
1½ HP	P1@2.85	Ea	1,130.00	98.50	—	1,228.50

Primed steel cam-lock non-fire rated access doors

Description	Craft@Hrs	Unit	Material $	Labor $	Equipment $	Total $
8" x 8"	P1@.400	Ea	62.10	13.80	—	75.90
12" x 12"	P1@.500	Ea	71.40	17.30	—	88.70
16" x 16"	P1@.600	Ea	87.90	20.70	—	108.60
18" x 18"	P1@.800	Ea	101.00	27.60	—	128.60
24" x 24"	P1@1.25	Ea	149.00	43.20	—	192.20
36" x 36"	P1@1.60	Ea	275.00	55.30	—	330.30
Add for Allen key lock		Ea	4.50	—	—	4.50
Add for cylinder lock		Ea	11.10	—	—	11.10

Primed steel cam-lock 1-1/2 hour fire rated access doors

Description	Craft@Hrs	Unit	Material $	Labor $	Equipment $	Total $
8" x 8"	P1@.400	Ea	229.00	13.80	—	242.80
12" x 12"	P1@.500	Ea	240.00	17.30	—	257.30
16" x 16"	P1@.600	Ea	284.00	20.70	—	304.70
18" x 18"	P1@.800	Ea	289.00	27.60	—	316.60
24" x 24"	P1@1.25	Ea	404.00	43.20	—	447.20
24" x 36"	P1@1.50	Ea	523.00	51.80	—	574.80
48" x 48"	P1@2.00	Ea	809.00	69.10	—	878.10
Add for cylinder lock		Ea	11.40	—	—	11.40

Threaded automatic air vent

Description	Craft@Hrs	Unit	Material $	Labor $	Equipment $	Total $
Float type	P1@.150	Ea	11.60	5.18	—	16.78
35 PSIG	P1@.150	Ea	76.10	5.18	—	81.28
150 PSIG	P1@.150	Ea	125.00	5.18	—	130.18

Threaded manual air vent

Description	Craft@Hrs	Unit	Material $	Labor $	Equipment $	Total $
175 PSIG	P1@.150	Ea	7.21	5.18	—	12.39

150 pound forged steel slip-on companion flange, welding type

Description	Craft@Hrs	Unit	Material $	Labor $	Equipment $	Total $
2½"	P1@.610	Ea	40.10	21.10	—	61.20
3"	P1@.730	Ea	40.10	25.20	—	65.30
4"	P1@.980	Ea	55.30	33.90	—	89.20
6"	ER@1.47	Ea	73.00	54.40	23.10	150.50
8"	ER@1.77	Ea	135.00	65.50	27.90	228.40
10"	ER@2.20	Ea	225.00	81.40	34.70	341.10
12"	ER@2.64	Ea	336.00	97.70	41.40	475.10

Plumbing and Piping Specialties

Description	Craft@Hrs	Unit	Material $	Labor $	Equipment $	Total $

150 pound forged steel companion flange, threaded

2"	P1@.290	Ea	43.10	10.00	—	53.10
2½"	P1@.380	Ea	64.70	13.10	—	77.80
3"	P1@.460	Ea	72.00	15.90	—	87.90
4"	P1@.600	Ea	96.00	20.70	—	116.70
6"	ER@.680	Ea	142.00	25.20	10.60	177.80
8"	ER@.760	Ea	196.00	28.10	11.90	236.00

300 pound forged steel slip-on companion flange, welding type

2½"	P1@.810	Ea	46.00	28.00	—	74.00
3"	P1@.980	Ea	46.00	33.90	—	79.90
4"	P1@1.30	Ea	67.40	44.90	—	112.30
6"	ER@1.95	Ea	123.00	72.20	30.60	225.80
8"	ER@2.35	Ea	173.00	87.00	37.10	297.10
10"	ER@2.90	Ea	285.00	107.00	45.70	437.70
12"	ER@3.50	Ea	456.00	130.00	55.00	641.00

PVC companion flange

2"	P1@.140	Ea	4.70	4.84	—	9.54
2½"	P1@.180	Ea	14.20	6.22	—	20.42
3"	P1@.210	Ea	14.70	7.26	—	21.96
4"	P1@.280	Ea	15.20	9.67	—	24.87
5"	P1@.310	Ea	34.00	10.70	—	44.70
6"	P1@.420	Ea	34.00	14.50	—	48.50
8"	P1@.560	Ea	50.40	19.30	—	69.70

Bolt and gasket set

2"	P1@.500	Ea	4.03	17.30	—	21.33
2½"	P1@.650	Ea	4.70	22.50	—	27.20
3"	P1@.750	Ea	7.99	25.90	—	33.89
4"	P1@1.00	Ea	13.40	34.60	—	48.00
5"	P1@1.10	Ea	15.40	38.00	—	53.40
6"	P1@1.20	Ea	15.40	41.50	—	56.90
8"	P1@1.25	Ea	20.00	43.20	—	63.20
10"	P1@1.70	Ea	23.90	58.70	—	82.60
12"	P1@2.20	Ea	32.10	76.00	—	108.10

Dielectric union, brazed joints

1/2"	P1@.146	Ea	16.40	5.04	—	21.44
3/4"	P1@.205	Ea	16.40	7.08	—	23.48
1"	P1@.263	Ea	34.00	9.09	—	43.09
1¼"	P1@.322	Ea	58.20	11.10	—	69.30
1½"	P1@.380	Ea	79.40	13.10	—	92.50
2"	P1@.507	Ea	109.00	17.50	—	126.50

Description	Craft@Hrs	Unit	Material $	Labor $	Equipment $	Total $
125/150# galvanized ASME expansion tank						
15 gallon	P1@1.75	Ea	287.00	60.50	—	347.50
30 gallon	P1@2.00	Ea	516.00	69.10	—	585.10
40 gallon	P1@2.35	Ea	573.00	81.20	—	654.20
60 gallon	P1@2.65	Ea	777.00	91.60	—	868.60
80 gallon	P1@2.95	Ea	1,440.00	102.00	—	1,542.00
100 gallon	P1@3.25	Ea	1,720.00	112.00	—	1,832.00
120 gallon	P1@3.50	Ea	1,860.00	121.00	—	1,981.00
Expansion tank fitting						
3/4"	P1@.300	Ea	67.20	10.40	—	77.60
Lead roof pipe flashing						
1½"	P1@.250	Ea	31.60	8.64	—	40.24
2"	P1@.250	Ea	41.60	8.64	—	50.24
3"	P1@.250	Ea	48.30	8.64	—	56.94
4"	P1@.250	Ea	53.10	8.64	—	61.74
6"	P1@.350	Ea	68.10	12.10	—	80.20
8"	P1@.400	Ea	86.10	13.80	—	99.90
Roof flashing, 20" x 20"						
Pitched roof, neoprene						
all pipe	P1@.300	Ea	20.90	10.40	—	31.30
Pitched roof, aluminum/neoprene						
all pipe	P1@.300	Ea	22.20	10.40	—	32.60
Flat roof, aluminum/neoprene						
all pipe	P1@.300	Ea	42.10	10.40	—	52.50
Braided stainless steel pipe connector, solder ends, brazed joints						
1/2"	P1@.240	Ea	53.20	8.29	—	61.49
3/4"	P1@.300	Ea	70.50	10.40	—	80.90
1"	P1@.360	Ea	91.40	12.40	—	103.80
1¼"	P1@.480	Ea	106.00	16.60	—	122.60
1½"	P1@.540	Ea	121.00	18.70	—	139.70
2"	P1@.600	Ea	162.00	20.70	—	182.70
Braided stainless steel pipe connector, threaded joints						
1/2"	P1@.210	Ea	60.00	7.26	—	67.26
3/4"	P1@.250	Ea	64.90	8.64	—	73.54
1"	P1@.300	Ea	70.00	10.40	—	80.40
1¼"	P1@.400	Ea	71.40	13.80	—	85.20
1½"	P1@.450	Ea	96.80	15.50	—	112.30
2"	P1@.500	Ea	125.00	17.30	—	142.30

Plumbing and Piping Specialties

Description	Craft@Hrs	Unit	Material $	Labor $	Equipment $	Total $

Braided stainless steel pipe connector, flanged joints

Description	Craft@Hrs	Unit	Material $	Labor $	Equipment $	Total $
2"	P1@.500	Ea	143.00	17.30	—	160.30
2½"	P1@.630	Ea	177.00	21.80	—	198.80
3"	P1@.750	Ea	229.00	25.90	—	254.90
4"	P1@1.50	Ea	299.00	51.80	—	350.80
6"	P1@2.50	Ea	544.00	86.40	—	630.40
8"	P1@3.00	Ea	1,210.00	104.00	—	1,314.00

Galvanized steel band pipe hanger

Description	Craft@Hrs	Unit	Material $	Labor $	Equipment $	Total $
1/2"	P1@.250	Ea	1.87	8.64	—	10.51
3/4"	P1@.250	Ea	1.87	8.64	—	10.51
1"	P1@.250	Ea	1.87	8.64	—	10.51
1¼"	P1@.300	Ea	1.98	10.40	—	12.38
1½"	P1@.300	Ea	2.10	10.40	—	12.50
2"	P1@.300	Ea	2.20	10.40	—	12.60
2½"	P1@.350	Ea	2.70	12.10	—	14.80
3"	P1@.350	Ea	3.10	12.10	—	15.20
4"	P1@.350	Ea	3.93	12.10	—	16.03
6"	P1@.450	Ea	6.18	15.50	—	21.68
8"	P1@.450	Ea	9.19	15.50	—	24.69

Trapeze pipe hanger

Description	Craft@Hrs	Unit	Material $	Labor $	Equipment $	Total $
24"	P1@1.00	Ea	43.20	34.60	—	77.80
36"	P1@1.25	Ea	55.10	43.20	—	98.30
48"	P1@1.50	Ea	83.70	51.80	—	135.50

Wall bracket support with anchors and bolts

Description	Craft@Hrs	Unit	Material $	Labor $	Equipment $	Total $
6" x 6"	P1@.600	Ea	20.30	20.70	—	41.00
8" x 8"	P1@.650	Ea	23.30	22.50	—	45.80
10" x 10"	P1@.700	Ea	26.30	24.20	—	50.50
12" x 12"	P1@.800	Ea	31.70	27.60	—	59.30
15" x 15"	P1@.950	Ea	36.60	32.80	—	69.40
18" x 18"	P1@1.10	Ea	51.60	38.00	—	89.60
24" x 24"	P1@1.60	Ea	74.70	55.30	—	130.00

Galvanized U-bolts with nuts

Description	Craft@Hrs	Unit	Material $	Labor $	Equipment $	Total $
1/2"	P1@.160	Ea	1.59	5.53	—	7.12
3/4"	P1@.165	Ea	1.59	5.70	—	7.29
1"	P1@.170	Ea	1.75	5.87	—	7.62
1¼"	P1@.175	Ea	2.00	6.05	—	8.05
1½"	P1@.180	Ea	2.40	6.22	—	8.62
2"	P1@.190	Ea	2.57	6.56	—	9.13
2½"	P1@.210	Ea	3.97	7.26	—	11.23
3"	P1@.250	Ea	4.59	8.64	—	13.23
4"	P1@.300	Ea	5.20	10.40	—	15.60
6"	P1@.400	Ea	8.12	13.80	—	21.92

Description	Craft@Hrs	Unit	Material $	Labor $	Equipment $	Total $
Nail-on wire pipe hooks						
1/2"	P1@.100	Ea	.09	3.46	—	3.55
3/4"	P1@.100	Ea	.11	3.46	—	3.57
1"	P1@.100	Ea	.12	3.46	—	3.58
Galvanized steel pipe sleeves						
1"	P1@.120	Ea	3.97	4.15	—	8.12
1¼"	P1@.125	Ea	4.41	4.32	—	8.73
1½"	P1@.125	Ea	4.99	4.32	—	9.31
2"	P1@.130	Ea	5.37	4.49	—	9.86
2½"	P1@.150	Ea	5.46	5.18	—	10.64
3"	P1@.180	Ea	5.58	6.22	—	11.80
4"	P1@.220	Ea	6.34	7.60	—	13.94
5"	P1@.250	Ea	7.91	8.64	—	16.55
6"	P1@.270	Ea	8.54	9.33	—	17.87
8"	P1@.270	Ea	9.82	9.33	—	19.15
10"	P1@.290	Ea	11.40	10.00	—	21.40
12"	P1@.310	Ea	15.50	10.70	—	26.20
14"	P1@.330	Ea	28.90	11.40	—	40.30
Dial-type pressure gauge						
2½"	P1@.200	Ea	32.70	6.91	—	39.61
3½"	P1@.200	Ea	43.40	6.91	—	50.31
Riser clamp						
1/2"	P1@.100	Ea	2.41	3.46	—	5.87
3/4"	P1@.100	Ea	3.55	3.46	—	7.01
1"	P1@.100	Ea	3.59	3.46	—	7.05
1¼"	P1@.105	Ea	4.33	3.63	—	7.96
1½"	P1@.110	Ea	4.58	3.80	—	8.38
2"	P1@.115	Ea	4.84	3.97	—	8.81
2½"	P1@.120	Ea	5.09	4.15	—	9.24
3"	P1@.120	Ea	5.52	4.15	—	9.67
4"	P1@.125	Ea	7.03	4.32	—	11.35
5"	P1@.180	Ea	10.10	6.22	—	16.32
6"	P1@.200	Ea	12.20	6.91	—	19.11
8"	P1@.200	Ea	19.80	6.91	—	26.71
10"	P1@.250	Ea	29.40	8.64	—	38.04
12"	P1@.250	Ea	34.90	8.64	—	43.54
15 PSIG float and thermostatic steam trap, threaded						
3/4"	P1@.250	Ea	285.00	8.64	—	293.64
1"	P1@.300	Ea	285.00	10.40	—	295.40
1¼"	P1@.400	Ea	343.00	13.80	—	356.80
1½"	P1@.450	Ea	644.00	15.50	—	659.50
2"	P1@.500	Ea	826.00	17.30	—	843.30

Plumbing and Piping Specialties

Description	Craft@Hrs	Unit	Material $	Labor $	Equipment $	Total $

15 PSIG inverted bucket steam trap, threaded joints

Description	Craft@Hrs	Unit	Material $	Labor $	Equipment $	Total $
1/2"	P1@.210	Ea	165.00	7.26	—	172.26
3/4"	P1@.250	Ea	406.00	8.64	—	414.64
1"	P1@.300	Ea	581.00	10.40	—	591.40
1¼"	P1@.400	Ea	969.00	13.80	—	982.80
1½"	P1@.450	Ea	969.00	15.50	—	984.50
2"	P1@.500	Ea	1,450.00	17.30	—	1,467.30

Thermometer with well

Description	Craft@Hrs	Unit	Material $	Labor $	Equipment $	Total $
7"	P1@.250	Ea	159.00	8.64	—	167.64
9"	P1@.250	Ea	164.00	8.64	—	172.64

Class 125 bronze body 2-piece ball valve, brazed joints

Description	Craft@Hrs	Unit	Material $	Labor $	Equipment $	Total $
1½"	P1@.240	Ea	7.91	8.29	—	16.20
3/4"	P1@.300	Ea	10.50	10.40	—	20.90
1"	P1@.360	Ea	18.20	12.40	—	30.60
1¼"	P1@.480	Ea	30.30	16.60	—	46.90
1½"	P1@.540	Ea	41.00	18.70	—	59.70
2"	P1@.600	Ea	51.90	20.70	—	72.60
3"	P1@1.50	Ea	355.00	51.80	—	406.80
4"	P1@1.80	Ea	465.00	62.20	—	527.20

Class 125 bronze body 2-piece ball valve, soft-soldered joints

Description	Craft@Hrs	Unit	Material $	Labor $	Equipment $	Total $
1/2"	P1@.200	Ea	7.91	6.91	—	14.82
3/4"	P1@.249	Ea	10.50	8.60	—	19.10
1"	P1@.299	Ea	18.20	10.30	—	28.50
1¼"	P1@.308	Ea	30.30	10.60	—	40.90
1½"	P1@.498	Ea	41.00	17.20	—	58.20
2"	P1@.498	Ea	51.90	17.20	—	69.10
3"	P1@1.24	Ea	355.00	42.80	—	397.80
4"	P1@1.45	Ea	465.00	50.10	—	515.10

Class 125 bronze body 2-piece ball valve, threaded joints

Description	Craft@Hrs	Unit	Material $	Labor $	Equipment $	Total $
1/2"	P1@.210	Ea	7.91	7.26	—	15.17
3/4"	P1@.250	Ea	10.50	8.64	—	19.14
1"	P1@.300	Ea	18.20	10.40	—	28.60
1¼"	P1@.400	Ea	30.30	13.80	—	44.10
1½"	P1@.450	Ea	41.00	15.50	—	56.50
2"	P1@.500	Ea	51.90	17.30	—	69.20
3"	P1@.625	Ea	355.00	21.60	—	376.60
4"	P1@.690	Ea	465.00	23.80	—	488.80

Description	Craft@Hrs	Unit	Material $	Labor $	Equipment $	Total $

Class 150, 600 pound W.O.G. bronze body 2-piece ball valve, threaded joints

1/2"	P1@.210	Ea	12.90	7.26	—	20.16
3/4"	P1@.250	Ea	21.00	8.64	—	29.64
1"	P1@.300	Ea	26.70	10.40	—	37.10
1¼"	P1@.400	Ea	33.40	13.80	—	47.20
1½"	P1@.450	Ea	45.00	15.50	—	60.50
2"	P1@.500	Ea	57.00	17.30	—	74.30

Bronze body circuit balance valve

1/2"	P1@.210	Ea	63.60	7.26	—	70.86
3/4"	P1@.250	Ea	67.60	8.64	—	76.24
1"	P1@.300	Ea	78.40	10.40	—	88.80
1¼"	P1@.400	Ea	97.50	13.80	—	111.30
1½"	P1@.400	Ea	123.00	13.80	—	136.80
2"	P1@.500	Ea	173.00	17.30	—	190.30
2½"	P1@1.75	Ea	654.00	60.50	—	714.50
3"	P1@2.50	Ea	1,010.00	86.40	—	1,096.40
4"	P1@3.15	Ea	1,720.00	109.00	—	1,829.00

200 PSIG iron body butterfly valve, lug type, lever operated

2"	P1@.450	Ea	134.00	15.50	—	149.50
2½"	P1@.450	Ea	139.00	15.50	—	154.50
3"	P1@.550	Ea	146.00	19.00	—	165.00
4"	P1@.505	Ea	182.00	17.40	—	199.40
6"	ER@.800	Ea	293.00	29.60	12.70	335.30
8"	ER@.800	Ea	401.00	29.60	12.70	443.30
10"	ER@.900	Ea	557.00	33.30	14.10	604.40
12"	ER@1.00	Ea	729.00	37.00	15.70	781.70

200 PSIG iron body butterfly valve, wafer type, lever operated

2"	P1@.450	Ea	122.00	15.50	—	137.50
2½"	P1@.450	Ea	125.00	15.50	—	140.50
3"	P1@.550	Ea	134.00	19.00	—	153.00
4"	P1@.550	Ea	163.00	19.00	—	182.00
6"	ER@.800	Ea	272.00	29.60	12.70	314.30
8"	ER@.800	Ea	377.00	29.60	12.70	419.30
10"	ER@.900	Ea	527.00	33.30	14.10	574.40
12"	ER@1.00	Ea	692.00	37.00	15.70	744.70

Class 125 bronze body swing check valve, with brazed joints

1/2"	P1@.240	Ea	17.70	8.29	—	25.99
3/4"	P1@.300	Ea	25.40	10.40	—	35.80
1"	P1@.360	Ea	33.30	12.40	—	45.70
1¼"	P1@.480	Ea	47.30	16.60	—	63.90
1½"	P1@.540	Ea	66.70	18.70	—	85.40
2"	P1@.600	Ea	111.00	20.70	—	131.70
2½"	P1@1.00	Ea	223.00	34.60	—	257.60
3"	P1@1.50	Ea	320.00	51.80	—	371.80

Description	Craft@Hrs	Unit	Material $	Labor $	Equipment $	Total $

Class 125 bronze body swing check valve with soft-soldered joints

Description	Craft@Hrs	Unit	Material $	Labor $	Equipment $	Total $
1/2"	P1@.200	Ea	17.70	6.91	—	24.61
3/4"	P1@.249	Ea	25.40	8.60	—	34.00
1"	P1@.299	Ea	33.30	10.30	—	43.60
1¼"	P1@.398	Ea	47.30	13.80	—	61.10
1½"	P1@.448	Ea	66.70	15.50	—	82.20
2"	P1@.498	Ea	111.00	17.20	—	128.20
2½"	P1@.830	Ea	223.00	28.70	—	251.70
3"	P1@1.24	Ea	320.00	42.80	—	362.80

Class 125 bronze body swing check valve, threaded joints

Description	Craft@Hrs	Unit	Material $	Labor $	Equipment $	Total $
1/2"	P1@.210	Ea	17.70	7.26	—	24.96
3/4"	P1@.250	Ea	25.40	8.64	—	34.04
1"	P1@.300	Ea	33.30	10.40	—	43.70
1¼"	P1@.400	Ea	47.30	13.80	—	61.10
1½"	P1@.450	Ea	66.70	15.50	—	82.20
2"	P1@.500	Ea	111.00	17.30	—	128.30

Class 300 bronze body swing check valve, threaded joints

Description	Craft@Hrs	Unit	Material $	Labor $	Equipment $	Total $
1/2"	P1@.210	Ea	59.90	7.26	—	67.16
3/4"	P1@.250	Ea	70.90	8.64	—	79.54
1"	P1@.300	Ea	86.60	10.40	—	97.00
1¼"	P1@.400	Ea	125.00	13.80	—	138.80
1½"	P1@.450	Ea	180.00	15.50	—	195.50
2"	P1@.500	Ea	250.00	17.30	—	267.30

Class 125 iron body swing check valve, flanged joints

Description	Craft@Hrs	Unit	Material $	Labor $	Equipment $	Total $
2"	P1@.500	Ea	155.00	17.30	—	172.30
2½"	P1@.600	Ea	197.00	20.70	—	217.70
3"	P1@.750	Ea	245.00	25.90	—	270.90
4"	P1@1.35	Ea	360.00	46.60	—	406.60
6"	ER@2.50	Ea	699.00	92.60	39.30	830.90
8"	ER@3.00	Ea	1,250.00	111.00	47.10	1,408.10
10"	ER@4.00	Ea	2,060.00	148.00	62.90	2,270.90
12"	ER@4.50	Ea	2,790.00	167.00	70.80	3,027.80

Class 250 iron body swing check valve, flanged joints

Description	Craft@Hrs	Unit	Material $	Labor $	Equipment $	Total $
2"	P1@.500	Ea	401.00	17.30	—	418.30
2½"	P1@.600	Ea	467.00	20.70	—	487.70
3"	P1@.750	Ea	581.00	25.90	—	606.90
4"	P1@1.35	Ea	712.00	46.60	—	758.60
6"	ER@2.50	Ea	1,380.00	92.60	39.30	1,511.90
8"	ER@3.00	Ea	2,540.00	111.00	47.10	2,698.10

Description	Craft@Hrs	Unit	Material $	Labor $	Equipment $	Total $

Class 125 iron body silent check valve, wafer type

Description	Craft@Hrs	Unit	Material $	Labor $	Equipment $	Total $
2"	P1@.500	Ea	113.00	17.30	—	130.30
2½"	P1@.600	Ea	126.00	20.70	—	146.70
3"	P1@.750	Ea	145.00	25.90	—	170.90
4"	P1@1.35	Ea	194.00	46.60	—	240.60
5"	P1@2.00	Ea	298.00	69.10	—	367.10
6"	P1@2.50	Ea	404.00	86.40	—	490.40
8"	P1@3.00	Ea	693.00	104.00	—	797.00

Class 125 iron body silent check valve, flanged joints

Description	Craft@Hrs	Unit	Material $	Labor $	Equipment $	Total $
2"	P1@.500	Ea	113.00	17.30	—	130.30
2½"	P1@.600	Ea	131.00	20.70	—	151.70
3"	P1@.750	Ea	147.00	25.90	—	172.90
4"	P1@1.35	Ea	193.00	46.60	—	239.60
6"	ER@2.50	Ea	347.00	92.60	39.30	478.90
8"	ER@3.00	Ea	625.00	111.00	47.10	783.10
10"	ER@4.00	Ea	970.00	148.00	62.90	1,180.90

Class 250 iron body silent check valve, flanged joints

Description	Craft@Hrs	Unit	Material $	Labor $	Equipment $	Total $
2"	P1@.500	Ea	168.00	17.30	—	185.30
2½"	P1@.600	Ea	193.00	20.70	—	213.70
3"	P1@.750	Ea	215.00	25.90	—	240.90
4"	P1@1.35	Ea	292.00	46.60	—	338.60
6"	ER@2.50	Ea	512.00	92.60	39.30	643.90
8"	ER@3.00	Ea	932.00	111.00	47.10	1,090.10
10"	ER@4.00	Ea	1,470.00	148.00	62.90	1,680.90

Class 125 bronze body gate valve, solder ends

Description	Craft@Hrs	Unit	Material $	Labor $	Equipment $	Total $
1/2"	P1@.240	Ea	16.20	8.29	—	24.49
3/4"	P1@.300	Ea	20.30	10.40	—	30.70
1"	P1@.360	Ea	28.50	12.40	—	40.90
1¼"	P1@.480	Ea	36.00	16.60	—	52.60
1½"	P1@.540	Ea	48.40	18.70	—	67.10
2"	P1@.600	Ea	80.90	20.70	—	101.60
2½"	P1@1.00	Ea	134.00	34.60	—	168.60
3"	P1@1.50	Ea	193.00	51.80	—	244.80

Class 125 bronze body gate valve, threaded joints

Description	Craft@Hrs	Unit	Material $	Labor $	Equipment $	Total $
1/2"	P1@.210	Ea	16.20	7.26	—	23.46
3/4"	P1@.250	Ea	20.30	8.64	—	28.94
1"	P1@.300	Ea	28.50	10.40	—	38.90
1¼"	P1@.400	Ea	36.00	13.80	—	49.80
1½"	P1@.450	Ea	48.40	15.50	—	63.90
2"	P1@.500	Ea	80.90	17.30	—	98.20
2½"	P1@.750	Ea	134.00	25.90	—	159.90
3"	P1@.950	Ea	193.00	32.80	—	225.80

Plumbing and Piping Specialties

Description	Craft@Hrs	Unit	Material $	Labor $	Equipment $	Total $

Class 300 bronze body gate valve, threaded joints

Description	Craft@Hrs	Unit	Material $	Labor $	Equipment $	Total $
1/2"	P1@.210	Ea	33.00	7.26	—	40.26
3/4"	P1@.250	Ea	43.10	8.64	—	51.74
1"	P1@.300	Ea	52.30	10.40	—	62.70
1¼"	P1@.400	Ea	71.20	13.80	—	85.00
1½"	P1@.450	Ea	89.80	15.50	—	105.30
2"	P1@.500	Ea	132.00	17.30	—	149.30
2½"	P1@.750	Ea	270.00	25.90	—	295.90
3"	P1@.950	Ea	383.00	32.80	—	415.80

Class 125 iron body gate valve, flanged joints

Description	Craft@Hrs	Unit	Material $	Labor $	Equipment $	Total $
2"	P1@.500	Ea	258.00	17.30	—	275.30
2½"	P1@.600	Ea	349.00	20.70	—	369.70
3"	P1@.750	Ea	378.00	25.90	—	403.90
4"	P1@1.35	Ea	554.00	46.60	—	600.60
6"	ER@2.50	Ea	1,060.00	92.60	39.30	1,191.90
8"	ER@3.00	Ea	1,740.00	111.00	47.10	1,898.10
10"	ER@4.00	Ea	2,850.00	148.00	62.90	3,060.90
12"	ER@4.50	Ea	3,940.00	167.00	70.80	4,177.80

Class 250 iron body gate valve, flanged joints

Description	Craft@Hrs	Unit	Material $	Labor $	Equipment $	Total $
2"	P1@.500	Ea	452.00	17.30	—	469.30
2½"	P1@.600	Ea	326.00	20.70	—	346.70
3"	P1@.750	Ea	413.00	25.90	—	438.90
4"	P1@1.35	Ea	699.00	46.60	—	745.60
6"	ER@2.50	Ea	1,300.00	92.60	39.30	1,431.90
8"	ER@3.00	Ea	2,010.00	111.00	47.10	2,168.10
10"	ER@4.00	Ea	3,590.00	148.00	62.90	3,800.90
12"	ER@4.50	Ea	5,840.00	167.00	70.80	6,077.80

Class 125 bronze body globe valve, brazed joints

Description	Craft@Hrs	Unit	Material $	Labor $	Equipment $	Total $
1/2"	P1@.240	Ea	30.00	8.29	—	38.29
3/4"	P1@.300	Ea	40.00	10.40	—	50.40
1"	P1@.360	Ea	57.40	12.40	—	69.80
1¼"	P1@.480	Ea	80.70	16.60	—	97.30
1½"	P1@.540	Ea	109.00	18.70	—	127.70
2"	P1@.600	Ea	176.00	20.70	—	196.70

Class 125 bronze body globe valve, soft-soldered joints

Description	Craft@Hrs	Unit	Material $	Labor $	Equipment $	Total $
1/2"	P1@.200	Ea	30.00	6.91	—	36.91
3/4"	P1@.249	Ea	40.00	8.60	—	48.60
1"	P1@.299	Ea	57.40	10.30	—	67.70
1¼"	P1@.398	Ea	80.70	13.80	—	94.50
1½"	P1@.448	Ea	109.00	15.50	—	124.50
2"	P1@.498	Ea	176.00	17.20	—	193.20

Description	Craft@Hrs	Unit	Material $	Labor $	Equipment $	Total $

Class 125 bronze body globe valve, threaded ends

Description	Craft@Hrs	Unit	Material $	Labor $	Equipment $	Total $
1/2"	P1@.210	Ea	30.00	7.26	—	37.26
3/4"	P1@.250	Ea	40.00	8.64	—	48.64
1"	P1@.300	Ea	57.40	10.40	—	67.80
1¼"	P1@.400	Ea	80.70	13.80	—	94.50
1½"	P1@.450	Ea	109.00	15.50	—	124.50
2"	P1@.500	Ea	176.00	17.30	—	193.30

Class 300 bronze body globe valve, threaded joints

Description	Craft@Hrs	Unit	Material $	Labor $	Equipment $	Total $
1/2"	P1@.210	Ea	56.50	7.26	—	63.76
3/4"	P1@.250	Ea	71.80	8.64	—	80.44
1"	P1@.300	Ea	102.00	10.40	—	112.40
1¼"	P1@.400	Ea	148.00	13.80	—	161.80
1½"	P1@.450	Ea	197.00	15.50	—	212.50
2"	P1@.500	Ea	273.00	17.30	—	290.30

Class 125 iron body globe valve, flanged joints

Description	Craft@Hrs	Unit	Material $	Labor $	Equipment $	Total $
2"	P1@.500	Ea	207.00	17.30	—	224.30
2½"	P1@.600	Ea	321.00	20.70	—	341.70
3"	P1@.750	Ea	385.00	25.90	—	410.90
4"	P1@1.35	Ea	518.00	46.60	—	564.60
6"	ER@2.50	Ea	908.00	92.60	39.30	1,039.90
8"	ER@3.00	Ea	1,400.00	111.00	47.10	1,558.10
10"	ER@4.00	Ea	2,120.00	148.00	62.90	2,330.90

Class 250 iron body globe valve, flanged joints

Description	Craft@Hrs	Unit	Material $	Labor $	Equipment $	Total $
2"	P1@.500	Ea	455.00	17.30	—	472.30
2½"	P1@.600	Ea	566.00	20.70	—	586.70
3"	P1@.750	Ea	673.00	25.90	—	698.90
4"	P1@1.35	Ea	928.00	46.60	—	974.60
6"	ER@2.50	Ea	1,830.00	92.60	39.30	1,961.90
8"	ER@3.00	Ea	4,070.00	111.00	47.10	4,228.10

Class 125 bronze body strainer, threaded joints

Description	Craft@Hrs	Unit	Material $	Labor $	Equipment $	Total $
1/2"	P1@.230	Ea	27.70	7.95	—	35.65
3/4"	P1@.260	Ea	36.40	8.98	—	45.38
1"	P1@.330	Ea	44.60	11.40	—	56.00
1¼"	P1@.440	Ea	62.30	15.20	—	77.50
1½"	P1@.495	Ea	93.80	17.10	—	110.90
2"	P1@.550	Ea	162.00	19.00	—	181.00

Class 125 iron body strainer, flanged joints

Description	Craft@Hrs	Unit	Material $	Labor $	Equipment $	Total $
2"	P1@.500	Ea	113.00	17.30	—	130.30
2½"	P1@.600	Ea	127.00	20.70	—	147.70
3"	P1@.750	Ea	147.00	25.90	—	172.90
4"	P1@1.35	Ea	251.00	46.60	—	297.60
6"	ER@2.50	Ea	508.00	92.60	39.30	639.90
8"	ER@3.00	Ea	858.00	111.00	47.10	1,016.10

Description	Craft@Hrs	Unit	Material $	Labor $	Equipment $	Total $

Class 250 iron body strainer, flanged joints

Description	Craft@Hrs	Unit	Material $	Labor $	Equipment $	Total $
2"	P1@.500	Ea	194.00	17.30	—	211.30
2½"	P1@.600	Ea	212.00	20.70	—	232.70
3"	P1@.750	Ea	249.00	25.90	—	274.90
4"	P1@1.35	Ea	441.00	46.60	—	487.60
6"	ER@2.50	Ea	706.00	92.60	39.30	837.90
8"	ER@3.00	Ea	1,290.00	111.00	47.10	1,448.10

Installation of 2-way control valve, threaded joints

Description	Craft@Hrs	Unit	Material $	Labor $	Equipment $	Total $
1/2"	P1@.210	Ea	—	7.26	—	7.26
3/4"	P1@.250	Ea	—	8.64	—	8.64
1"	P1@.300	Ea	—	10.40	—	10.40
1¼"	P1@.400	Ea	—	13.80	—	13.80
1½"	P1@.450	Ea	—	15.50	—	15.50
2"	P1@.500	Ea	—	17.30	—	17.30
2½"	P1@.830	Ea	—	28.70	—	28.70
3"	P1@.990	Ea	—	34.20	—	34.20

Installation of 2-way control valve, flanged joints

Description	Craft@Hrs	Unit	Material $	Labor $	Equipment $	Total $
2"	P1@.500	Ea	—	17.30	—	17.30
2½"	P1@.600	Ea	—	20.70	—	20.70
3"	P1@.750	Ea	—	25.90	—	25.90
4"	P1@1.35	Ea	—	46.60	—	46.60
6"	P1@2.50	Ea	—	86.40	—	86.40
8"	P1@3.00	Ea	—	104.00	—	104.00
10"	P1@4.00	Ea	—	138.00	—	138.00
12"	P1@4.50	Ea	—	155.00	—	155.00

Installation of 3-way control valve, threaded joints

Description	Craft@Hrs	Unit	Material $	Labor $	Equipment $	Total $
1/2"	P1@.260	Ea	—	8.98	—	8.98
3/4"	P1@.365	Ea	—	12.60	—	12.60
1"	P1@.475	Ea	—	16.40	—	16.40
1¼"	P1@.575	Ea	—	19.90	—	19.90
1½"	P1@.680	Ea	—	23.50	—	23.50
2"	P1@.910	Ea	—	31.40	—	31.40
2½"	P1@1.12	Ea	—	38.70	—	38.70
3"	P1@1.33	Ea	—	46.00	—	46.00

Description	Craft@Hrs	Unit	Material $	Labor $	Equipment $	Total $

Installation of 3-way control valve, flanged joints

2"	P1@.910	Ea	—	31.40	—	31.40
2½"	P1@1.12	Ea	—	38.70	—	38.70
3"	P1@1.33	Ea	—	46.00	—	46.00
4"	P1@2.00	Ea	—	69.10	—	69.10
6"	P1@3.70	Ea	—	128.00	—	128.00
8"	P1@4.40	Ea	—	152.00	—	152.00
10"	P1@5.90	Ea	—	204.00	—	204.00
12"	P1@6.50	Ea	—	225.00	—	225.00

Lever handled gas valve, threaded joints

1/2"	P1@.210	Ea	25.90	7.26	—	33.16
3/4"	P1@.250	Ea	28.70	8.64	—	37.34
1"	P1@.300	Ea	35.80	10.40	—	46.20
1¼"	P1@.400	Ea	47.80	13.80	—	61.60
1½"	P1@.450	Ea	64.30	15.50	—	79.80
2"	P1@.500	Ea	93.80	17.30	—	111.10

Plug-type gas valve, flanged joints, lubricated

2"	P1@.500	Ea	204.00	17.30	—	221.30
2½"	P1@.600	Ea	331.00	20.70	—	351.70
3"	P1@.750	Ea	463.00	25.90	—	488.90
4"	P1@1.35	Ea	635.00	46.60	—	681.60
6"	P1@2.50	Ea	1,130.00	86.40	—	1,216.40

3/4" hose bibb

Low quality	P1@.350	Ea	10.60	12.10	—	22.70
Med. quality	P1@.350	Ea	15.30	12.10	—	27.40
High quality	P1@.350	Ea	20.30	12.10	—	32.40

Water pressure reducing valve, threaded joints, 25-75 PSI

1/2"	P1@.210	Ea	93.30	7.26	—	100.56
3/4"	P1@.250	Ea	120.00	8.64	—	128.64
1"	P1@.300	Ea	198.00	10.40	—	208.40
1¼"	P1@.400	Ea	240.00	13.80	—	253.80
1½"	P1@.450	Ea	343.00	15.50	—	358.50
2"	P1@.500	Ea	544.00	17.30	—	561.30

Water hammer arrester, threaded joints

1/2"	P1@.160	Ea	45.00	5.53	—	50.53
3/4"	P1@.190	Ea	52.20	6.56	—	58.76
1"	P1@.230	Ea	133.00	7.95	—	140.95
1¼"	P1@.300	Ea	154.00	10.40	—	164.40
1½"	P1@.340	Ea	221.00	11.70	—	232.70
2"	P1@.380	Ea	336.00	13.10	—	349.10

Plumbing and Piping Specialties

Description	Craft@Hrs	Unit	Material $	Labor $	Equipment $	Total $
Carbon steel weldolet, Schedule 40						
1/2"	P1@.330	Ea	14.50	11.40	—	25.90
3/4"	P1@.500	Ea	14.90	17.30	—	32.20
1"	P1@.670	Ea	15.60	23.10	—	38.70
1¼"	P1@.830	Ea	18.90	28.70	—	47.60
1½"	P1@1.00	Ea	18.90	34.60	—	53.50
2"	P1@1.33	Ea	20.80	46.00	—	66.80
2½"	P1@1.67	Ea	45.80	57.70	—	103.50
3"	P1@2.00	Ea	52.00	69.10	—	121.10
4"	P1@2.67	Ea	67.10	92.20	—	159.30
6"	P1@4.00	Ea	277.00	138.00	—	415.00
8"	P1@4.80	Ea	408.00	166.00	—	574.00
10"	P1@6.00	Ea	564.00	207.00	—	771.00
12"	P1@7.20	Ea	693.00	249.00	—	942.00

Description	Craft@Hrs	Unit	Material $	Labor $	Equipment $	Total $
Carbon steel weldolet, Schedule 80						
1/2"	P1@.440	Ea	16.00	15.20	—	31.20
3/4"	P1@.670	Ea	16.40	23.10	—	39.50
1"	P1@.890	Ea	17.90	30.70	—	48.60
1¼"	P1@1.11	Ea	22.50	38.40	—	60.90
1½"	P1@1.33	Ea	22.50	46.00	—	68.50
2"	P1@1.77	Ea	24.30	61.20	—	85.50
2½"	P1@2.22	Ea	54.40	76.70	—	131.10
3"	P1@2.66	Ea	55.90	91.90	—	147.80
4"	P1@3.55	Ea	124.00	123.00	—	247.00
6"	P1@5.32	Ea	390.00	184.00	—	574.00
8"	P1@6.38	Ea	520.00	220.00	—	740.00

Description	Craft@Hrs	Unit	Material $	Labor $	Equipment $	Total $
Carbon steel threadolet, Schedule 40						
3/4"	P1@.330	Ea	8.99	11.40	—	20.39
1"	P1@.440	Ea	9.98	15.20	—	25.18
1¼"	P1@.560	Ea	13.90	19.30	—	33.20
1½"	P1@.670	Ea	15.60	23.10	—	38.70
2"	P1@.890	Ea	18.20	30.70	—	48.90
2½"	P1@1.11	Ea	56.10	38.40	—	94.50

Description	Craft@Hrs	Unit	Material $	Labor $	Equipment $	Total $
Carbon steel threadolet, Schedule 80						
1/2	P1@.300	Ea	13.40	10.40	—	23.80
3/4"	P1@.440	Ea	14.80	15.20	—	30.00
1"	P1@.590	Ea	18.40	20.40	—	38.80
1¼"	P1@.740	Ea	82.50	25.60	—	108.10
1½"	P1@.890	Ea	82.50	30.70	—	113.20
2"	P1@1.18	Ea	108.00	40.80	—	148.80

Cast Iron, DWV, Service Weight, No-Hub with Coupled Joints

Service weight cast iron soil pipe with hub-less coupled joints is widely used for non-pressurized underground and in-building drain, waste and vent (DWV) systems.

This section has been arranged to save the estimator's time by including all normally-used system components such as pipe, fittings, hanger assemblies and riser clamps under one heading. Additional items can be found under "Plumbing and Piping Specialties." The cost estimates in this section are based on the conditions, limitations and wage rates described in the section "How to Use This Book" beginning on page 5.

Equipment cost, where shown, is $110 per hour for a 10-ton hydraulic truck-mounted crane.

Description	Craft@Hrs	Unit	Material $	Labor $	Equipment $	Total $

DWV cast iron no-hub (MJ) horizontal pipe assembly.
Horizontally hung in a building. Assembly includes fittings, couplings, hangers and rod. Based on a reducing wye and a 45 degree elbow every 15 feet and a hanger every 6 feet for 2" pipe. A reducing wye and a 45 degree elbow every 40 feet and a hanger every 8 feet for 10" pipe. *(Distance between fittings in the pipe assembly increases as pipe diameter increases.)* Use these figures for preliminary estimates.

Description	Craft@Hrs	Unit	Material $	Labor $	Equipment $	Total $
2"	P1@.130	LF	10.20	4.49	—	14.69
3"	P1@.160	LF	11.10	5.53	—	16.63
4"	P1@.190	LF	13.20	6.56	—	19.76
6"	ER@.220	LF	25.60	8.14	3.50	37.24
8"	ER@.260	LF	49.00	9.63	4.10	62.73
10"	ER@.310	LF	76.10	11.50	5.00	92.60

DWV cast iron no-hub (MJ), pipe only

Description	Craft@Hrs	Unit	Material $	Labor $	Equipment $	Total $
2"	P1@.050	LF	5.59	1.73	—	7.32
3"	P1@.060	LF	6.67	2.07	—	8.74
4"	P1@.080	LF	8.69	2.76	—	11.45
6"	ER@.110	LF	16.20	4.07	—	20.27
8"	ER@.130	LF	30.10	4.81	—	34.91
10"	ER@.140	LF	52.40	5.18	—	57.58

DWV cast iron no-hub 1/8 bend

Description	Craft@Hrs	Unit	Material $	Labor $	Equipment $	Total $
2"	P1@.250	Ea	6.47	8.64	—	15.11
3"	P1@.350	Ea	8.46	12.10	—	20.56
4"	P1@.500	Ea	10.70	17.30	—	28.00
6"	ER@.650	Ea	34.40	24.10	10.30	68.80
8"	ER@.710	Ea	91.90	26.30	11.20	129.40
10"	ER@.800	Ea	137.00	29.60	12.70	179.30

Cast Iron, DWV, Service Weight, No-Hub with Coupled Joints

Description	Craft@Hrs	Unit	Material $	Labor $	Equipment $	Total $

DWV cast iron no-hub 1/4 bend

Description	Craft@Hrs	Unit	Material $	Labor $	Equipment $	Total $
2"	P1@.250	Ea	7.92	8.64	—	16.56
3"	P1@.350	Ea	9.84	12.10	—	21.94
4"	P1@.500	Ea	15.00	17.30	—	32.30
6"	ER@.650	Ea	36.40	24.10	10.30	70.80
8"	ER@.710	Ea	141.00	26.30	11.20	178.50
10"	ER@.710	Ea	154.00	26.30	11.20	191.50

DWV cast iron no-hub long sweep 1/4 bend

Description	Craft@Hrs	Unit	Material $	Labor $	Equipment $	Total $
2"	P1@.250	Ea	13.80	8.64	—	22.44
3"	P1@.350	Ea	16.60	12.10	—	28.70
4"	P1@.500	Ea	26.30	17.30	—	43.60
5"	ER@.580	Ea	48.40	21.50	9.20	79.10
6"	ER@.650	Ea	58.90	24.10	10.30	93.30

DWV cast iron no-hub low heel outlet 1/4 bend

Description	Craft@Hrs	Unit	Material $	Labor $	Equipment $	Total $
3"	P1@.470	Ea	14.00	16.20	—	30.20
4"	P1@.650	Ea	17.00	22.50	—	39.50

DWV cast iron no-hub closet bend

Description	Craft@Hrs	Unit	Material $	Labor $	Equipment $	Total $
3"	P1@.350	Ea	32.30	12.10	—	44.40
4"	P1@.500	Ea	33.10	17.30	—	50.40

DWV cast iron no-hub closet flange

Description	Craft@Hrs	Unit	Material $	Labor $	Equipment $	Total $
4" x 3"	P1@.500	Ea	47.30	17.30	—	64.60

DWV cast iron no-hub P-trap

Description	Craft@Hrs	Unit	Material $	Labor $	Equipment $	Total $
2"	P1@.250	Ea	12.80	8.64	—	21.44
3"	P1@.350	Ea	39.90	12.10	—	52.00
4"	P1@.500	Ea	49.20	17.30	—	66.50
6"	ER@.650	Ea	175.00	24.10	10.30	209.40

DWV cast iron no-hub wye

Description	Craft@Hrs	Unit	Material $	Labor $	Equipment $	Total $
2"	P1@.380	Ea	10.10	13.10	—	23.20
3"	P1@.520	Ea	14.10	18.00	—	32.10
4"	P1@.700	Ea	22.10	24.20	—	46.30
6"	ER@.900	Ea	59.70	33.30	14.10	107.10
8"	ER@1.15	Ea	152.00	42.60	18.20	212.80
10"	ER@1.50	Ea	364.00	55.50	23.70	443.20

Cast Iron, DWV, Service Weight, No-Hub with Coupled Joints

Description	Craft@Hrs	Unit	Material $	Labor $	Equipment $	Total $

DWV cast iron no-hub reducing wye

Description	Craft@Hrs	Unit	Material $	Labor $	Equipment $	Total $
3" x 2"	P1@.470	Ea	13.50	16.20	—	29.70
4" x 2"	P1@.600	Ea	18.10	20.70	—	38.80
4" x 3"	P1@.650	Ea	19.10	22.50	—	41.60
6" x 2"	ER@.770	Ea	48.50	28.50	12.10	89.10
6" x 3"	ER@.770	Ea	52.60	28.50	12.10	93.20
6" x 4"	ER@.800	Ea	51.70	29.60	12.50	93.80
8" x 2"	ER@1.00	Ea	123.00	37.00	15.70	175.70
8" x 3"	ER@1.00	Ea	125.00	37.00	15.70	177.70
8" x 4"	ER@1.00	Ea	127.00	37.00	15.70	179.70
8" x 6"	ER@1.10	Ea	132.00	40.70	17.40	190.10

DWV cast iron no-hub combination upright wye and 1/8 bend

Description	Craft@Hrs	Unit	Material $	Labor $	Equipment $	Total $
2"	P1@.380	Ea	25.10	13.10	—	38.20
3"	P1@.520	Ea	40.30	18.00	—	58.30
4"	P1@.700	Ea	53.20	24.20	—	77.40

DWV cast iron no-hub combination upright reducing wye and 1/8 bend

Description	Craft@Hrs	Unit	Material $	Labor $	Equipment $	Total $
3" x 2"	P1@.470	Ea	43.80	16.20	—	60.00
4" x 2"	P1@.600	Ea	52.10	20.70	—	72.80
4" x 3"	P1@.650	Ea	54.60	22.50	—	77.10

DWV cast iron no-hub double wye

Description	Craft@Hrs	Unit	Material $	Labor $	Equipment $	Total $
2"	P1@.500	Ea	31.10	17.30	—	48.40
3"	P1@.700	Ea	31.50	24.20	—	55.70
4"	P1@.950	Ea	48.90	32.80	—	81.70
6"	ER@1.10	Ea	169.00	40.70	17.40	227.10
8"	ER@1.45	Ea	310.00	53.70	22.80	386.50

DWV cast iron no-hub double reducing wye

Description	Craft@Hrs	Unit	Material $	Labor $	Equipment $	Total $
3" x 2"	P1@.520	Ea	31.10	18.00	—	49.10
4" x 2"	P1@.740	Ea	43.30	25.60	—	68.90
4" x 3"	P1@1.00	Ea	44.70	34.60	—	79.30
6" x 4"	ER@1.75	Ea	167.00	64.80	27.50	259.30

DWV cast iron no-hub combination wye and 1/8 bend

Description	Craft@Hrs	Unit	Material $	Labor $	Equipment $	Total $
2"	P1@.380	Ea	19.40	13.10	—	32.50
3"	P1@.520	Ea	27.70	18.00	—	45.70
4"	P1@.700	Ea	44.20	24.20	—	68.40
6"	ER@.900	Ea	151.00	33.30	14.10	198.40
8"	ER@1.15	Ea	303.00	42.60	17.60	363.20

Cast Iron, DWV, Service Weight, No-Hub with Coupled Joints

Description	Craft@Hrs	Unit	Material $	Labor $	Equipment $	Total $
DWV cast iron no-hub combination reducing wye and 1/8 bend						
3" x 2"	P1@.470	Ea	23.50	16.20	—	39.70
4" x 2"	P1@.600	Ea	35.80	20.70	—	56.50
4" x 3"	P1@.650	Ea	38.30	22.50	—	60.80
6" x 2"	ER@.770	Ea	170.00	28.50	12.10	210.60
6" x 3"	ER@.770	Ea	180.00	28.50	12.10	220.60
6" x 4"	ER@.800	Ea	184.00	29.60	12.70	226.30
8" x 4"	ER@1.20	Ea	335.00	44.40	18.90	398.30
DWV cast iron no-hub double combination wye and 1/8 bend						
2"	P1@.500	Ea	33.60	17.30	—	50.90
3"	P1@.700	Ea	54.10	24.20	—	78.30
4"	P1@.950	Ea	66.60	32.80	—	99.40
DWV cast iron no-hub double combination reducing wye and 1/8 bend						
3" x 2"	P1@.600	Ea	38.10	20.70	—	58.80
4" x 2"	P1@1.25	Ea	60.10	43.20	—	103.30
4" x 3"	P1@1.35	Ea	62.90	46.60	—	109.50
DWV cast iron no-hub sanitary tee (TY)						
2"	P1@.380	Ea	11.70	13.10	—	24.80
3"	P1@.520	Ea	14.10	18.00	—	32.10
4"	P1@.700	Ea	23.20	24.20	—	47.40
6"	ER@.900	Ea	70.80	33.30	14.10	118.20
8"	ER@1.15	Ea	186.00	42.60	18.20	246.80
DWV cast iron no-hub reducing sanitary tee (TY)						
3" x 2"	P1@.470	Ea	13.40	16.20	—	29.60
4" x 2"	P1@.600	Ea	17.90	20.70	—	38.60
4" x 3"	P1@.650	Ea	20.50	22.50	—	43.00
6" x 2"	ER@.770	Ea	56.10	28.50	12.10	96.70
6" x 3"	ER@.770	Ea	53.00	28.50	12.10	93.60
6" x 4"	ER@.800	Ea	57.50	29.60	12.70	99.80
8" x 3"	ER@1.00	Ea	147.00	37.00	15.70	199.70
8" x 4"	ER@1.00	Ea	144.00	37.00	15.70	196.70
8" x 6"	ER@1.10	Ea	152.00	40.70	17.40	210.10
DWV cast iron no-hub tapped sanitary tee (tapped TY)						
2" x 1½"	P1@.200	Ea	32.90	6.91	—	39.81
2" x 2"	P1@.250	Ea	32.90	8.64	—	41.54
3" x 2"	P1@.350	Ea	41.90	12.10	—	54.00
4" x 2"	P1@.425	Ea	49.70	14.70	—	64.40
6" x 2"	ER@.700	Ea	128.00	25.90	11.00	164.90

Cast Iron, DWV, Service Weight, No-Hub with Coupled Joints

Description	Craft@Hrs	Unit	Material $	Labor $	Equipment $	Total $

DWV cast iron no-hub test tee

Description	Craft@Hrs	Unit	Material $	Labor $	Equipment $	Total $
2"	P1@.370	Ea	41.60	12.80	—	54.40
3"	P1@.520	Ea	58.90	18.00	—	76.90
4"	P1@.750	Ea	75.00	25.90	—	100.90
6"	ER@1.12	Ea	269.00	41.50	17.60	328.10
8"	ER@1.25	Ea	487.00	46.30	19.60	552.90

DWV cast iron no-hub cross (double TY)

Description	Craft@Hrs	Unit	Material $	Labor $	Equipment $	Total $
2"	P1@.500	Ea	33.10	17.30	—	50.40
3"	P1@.700	Ea	35.30	24.20	—	59.50
4"	P1@.950	Ea	50.70	32.80	—	83.50
6"	ER@1.30	Ea	189.00	48.10	20.40	257.50

DWV cast iron no-hub reducing cross (double TY)

Description	Craft@Hrs	Unit	Material $	Labor $	Equipment $	Total $
3" x 2"	P1@.600	Ea	31.20	20.70	—	51.90
4" x 2"	P1@.900	Ea	43.10	31.10	—	74.20
4" x 3"	P1@.900	Ea	44.20	31.10	—	75.30
6" x 4"	ER@1.20	Ea	172.00	44.40	18.90	235.30
8" x 4"	ER@1.50	Ea	435.00	55.50	23.70	514.20

DWV cast iron no-hub reducer

Description	Craft@Hrs	Unit	Material $	Labor $	Equipment $	Total $
2"	P1@.120	Ea	6.51	4.15	—	10.66
3"	P1@.130	Ea	7.00	4.49	—	11.49
4"	P1@.150	Ea	10.40	5.18	—	15.58
6"	ER@.200	Ea	27.80	7.40	3.10	38.30
8"	ER@.400	Ea	71.50	14.80	6.30	92.60
10"	ER@.650	Ea	110.00	24.10	10.30	144.40

DWV cast iron no-hub cap

Description	Craft@Hrs	Unit	Material $	Labor $	Equipment $	Total $
2"	P1@.125	Ea	3.98	4.32	—	8.30
3"	P1@.175	Ea	6.81	6.05	—	12.86
4"	P1@.250	Ea	8.88	8.64	—	17.52
6"	ER@.375	Ea	16.80	13.90	5.90	36.60
8"	ER@.500	Ea	31.10	18.50	7.90	57.50
10"	ER@.750	Ea	48.00	27.80	11.90	87.70

MJ (mechanical joint) coupling with gasket (labor included with fittings)

Description	Craft@Hrs	Unit	Material $	Labor $	Equipment $	Total $
2"	--@--	Ea	7.70	—	—	7.70
3"	--@--	Ea	8.42	—	—	8.42
4"	--@--	Ea	9.05	—	—	9.05
6"	--@--	Ea	24.60	—	—	24.60
8"	--@--	Ea	45.80	—	—	45.80
10"	--@--	Ea	63.50	—	—	63.50

Cast Iron, DWV, Service Weight, No-Hub with Coupled Joints

Description	Craft@Hrs	Unit	Material $	Labor $	Equipment $	Total $

Hanger with swivel assembly

Description	Craft@Hrs	Unit	Material $	Labor $	Equipment $	Total $
2"	P1@.400	Ea	6.33	13.80	—	20.13
3"	P1@.450	Ea	8.17	15.50	—	23.67
4"	P1@.450	Ea	10.10	15.50	—	25.60
5"	P1@.500	Ea	15.60	17.30	—	32.90
6"	P1@.500	Ea	17.40	17.30	—	34.70
8"	P1@.550	Ea	22.90	19.00	—	41.90
10"	P1@.650	Ea	29.90	22.50	—	52.40

Riser clamp

Description	Craft@Hrs	Unit	Material $	Labor $	Equipment $	Total $
2"	P1@.115	Ea	5.08	3.97	—	9.05
3"	P1@.120	Ea	5.80	4.15	—	9.95
4"	P1@.125	Ea	7.38	4.32	—	11.70
5"	P1@.180	Ea	10.60	6.22	—	16.82
6"	P1@.200	Ea	12.80	6.91	—	19.71
8"	P1@.200	Ea	20.80	6.91	—	27.71
10"	P1@.250	Ea	30.90	8.64	—	39.54

Cast Iron, DWV, Service Weight, Hub & Spigot with Gasketed Joints

Service weight hub and spigot cast iron soil pipe with gasketed joints is widely used for non-pressurized underground and in-building drain, waste and vent (DWV) systems.

This section has been arranged to save the estimator's time by including all normally-used system components such as pipe, fittings, valves, hanger assemblies and riser clamps under one heading. Additional items can be found under "Plumbing and Piping Specialties." The cost estimates in this section are based on the conditions, limitations and wage rates described in the section "How to Use This Book" beginning on page 5.

Equipment cost, where shown, is $110 per hour for a 10-ton hydraulic truck-mounted crane.

Description	Craft@Hrs	Unit	Material $	Labor $	Equipment $	Total $

DWV cast iron pipe, hub and spigot, gasketed joints

Description	Craft@Hrs	Unit	Material $	Labor $	Equipment $	Total $
2"	P1@.060	LF	9.59	2.07	—	11.66
3"	P1@.070	LF	10.60	2.42	—	13.02
4"	P1@.090	LF	13.90	3.11	—	17.01
6"	ER@.110	LF	26.50	4.07	1.70	32.27
8"	ER@.140	LF	44.50	5.18	2.20	51.88
10"	ER@.180	LF	71.10	6.66	2.80	80.56
12"	ER@.230	LF	91.80	8.51	3.70	104.01
15"	ER@.280	LF	138.00	10.40	4.40	152.80

DWV cast iron 1/8 bend, hub and spigot, gasketed joints

Description	Craft@Hrs	Unit	Material $	Labor $	Equipment $	Total $
2"	P1@.300	Ea	11.10	10.40	—	21.50
3"	P1@.400	Ea	15.30	13.80	—	29.10
4"	P1@.550	Ea	21.40	19.00	—	40.40
6"	ER@.700	Ea	53.90	25.90	11.00	90.80
8"	ER@1.15	Ea	127.00	42.60	18.20	187.80
10"	ER@1.25	Ea	172.00	46.30	19.60	237.90
12"	ER@2.25	Ea	399.00	83.30	35.50	517.80
15"	ER@2.50	Ea	668.00	92.60	39.30	799.90

DWV cast iron 1/4 bend, hub and spigot, gasketed joints

Description	Craft@Hrs	Unit	Material $	Labor $	Equipment $	Total $
2"	P1@.300	Ea	12.40	10.40	—	22.80
3"	P1@.400	Ea	19.20	13.80	—	33.00
4"	P1@.550	Ea	33.60	19.00	—	52.60
6"	ER@.900	Ea	63.80	33.30	14.10	111.20
8"	ER@1.15	Ea	170.00	42.60	18.20	230.80
10"	ER@1.25	Ea	238.00	46.30	19.60	303.90
12"	ER@2.25	Ea	498.00	83.30	35.50	616.80
15"	ER@2.50	Ea	1,000.00	92.60	39.30	1,131.90

DWV cast iron heel inlet 1/4 bend, hub and spigot, gasketed joints

Description	Craft@Hrs	Unit	Material $	Labor $	Equipment $	Total $
3" x 2"	P1@.550	Ea	23.30	19.00	—	42.30
4" x 2"	P1@.700	Ea	28.40	24.20	—	52.60

Cast Iron, DWV, Service Weight, Hub & Spigot with Gasketed Joints

Description	Craft@Hrs	Unit	Material $	Labor $	Equipment $	Total $

DWV cast iron 1/16 bend, hub and spigot, gasketed joints

Description	Craft@Hrs	Unit	Material $	Labor $	Equipment $	Total $
2"	P1@.300	Ea	7.07	10.40	—	17.47
3"	P1@.400	Ea	11.80	13.80	—	25.60
4"	P1@.550	Ea	16.40	19.00	—	35.40
6"	ER@.700	Ea	27.50	25.90	11.00	64.40
8"	ER@1.15	Ea	96.80	42.60	18.20	157.60

DWV cast iron closet bend, hub and spigot, gasketed joints

Description	Craft@Hrs	Unit	Material $	Labor $	Equipment $	Total $
4" x 4"	P1@.400	Ea	41.00	13.80	—	54.80

DWV cast iron closet flange, hub and spigot, gasketed joints

Description	Craft@Hrs	Unit	Material $	Labor $	Equipment $	Total $
4" x 2"	P1@.075	Ea	13.30	2.59	—	15.89
4" x 3"	P1@.100	Ea	18.30	3.46	—	21.76
4" x 4"	P1@.125	Ea	23.80	4.32	—	28.12

DWV cast iron regular P-trap, hub and spigot, gasketed joints

Description	Craft@Hrs	Unit	Material $	Labor $	Equipment $	Total $
2"	P1@.300	Ea	47.40	10.40	—	57.80
3"	P1@.400	Ea	65.90	13.80	—	79.70
4"	P1@.550	Ea	102.00	19.00	—	121.00
6"	ER@.700	Ea	223.00	25.90	11.00	259.90
8"	ER@1.15	Ea	659.00	42.60	18.20	719.80
10"	ER@2.00	Ea	904.00	74.00	31.40	1,009.40

DWV cast iron sanitary tee, (TY) hub and spigot, gasketed joints

Description	Craft@Hrs	Unit	Material $	Labor $	Equipment $	Total $
2"	P1@.400	Ea	22.80	13.80	—	36.60
3"	P1@.600	Ea	39.90	20.70	—	60.60
4"	P1@.750	Ea	79.90	25.90	—	105.80
6"	ER@.900	Ea	183.00	33.30	14.10	230.40
8"	ER@1.50	Ea	266.00	55.50	21.50	343.00

DWV cast iron sanitary reducing tee, (TY) hub and spigot, gasketed joints

Description	Craft@Hrs	Unit	Material $	Labor $	Equipment $	Total $
3" x 2"	P1@.400	Ea	32.30	13.80	—	46.10
4" x 2"	P1@.650	Ea	84.40	22.50	—	106.90
4" x 3"	P1@.700	Ea	84.40	24.20	—	108.60
6" x 2"	ER@.750	Ea	113.00	27.80	11.80	152.60
6" x 3"	ER@.800	Ea	113.00	29.60	12.70	155.30
6" x 4"	ER@.850	Ea	113.00	31.50	13.40	157.90

DWV cast iron sanitary tapped tee, (tapped TY) hub and spigot, gasketed joints

Description	Craft@Hrs	Unit	Material $	Labor $	Equipment $	Total $
2"	P1@.300	Ea	19.50	10.40	—	29.90
3"	P1@.400	Ea	28.70	13.80	—	42.50
4"	P1@.550	Ea	28.40	19.00	—	47.40

Cast Iron, DWV, Service Weight, Hub & Spigot with Gasketed Joints

Description	Craft@Hrs	Unit	Material $	Labor $	Equipment $	Total $

DWV cast iron combination wye and 1/8 bend, hub and spigot, gasketed joints

2"	P1@.400	Ea	20.20	13.80	—	34.00
3"	P1@.600	Ea	30.50	20.70	—	51.20
4"	P1@.750	Ea	42.30	25.90	—	68.20
5"	ER@.850	Ea	79.60	31.50	13.40	124.50
6"	ER@.900	Ea	101.00	33.30	14.10	148.40

DWV cast iron combination reducing wye and 1/8 bend, hub and spigot, gasketed joints

3" x 2"	P1@.550	Ea	22.80	19.00	—	41.80
4" x 2"	P1@.650	Ea	31.20	22.50	—	53.70
4" x 3"	P1@.700	Ea	36.30	24.20	—	60.50
5" x 2"	ER@.700	Ea	64.20	25.90	11.00	101.10
5" x 4"	ER@.800	Ea	76.20	29.60	12.70	118.50
6" x 2"	ER@.750	Ea	65.10	27.80	11.80	104.70
6" x 3"	ER@.750	Ea	69.20	27.80	11.80	108.80
6" x 4"	ER@.800	Ea	72.60	29.60	12.70	114.90

DWV cast iron combination double wye and 1/8 bend, hub and spigot, gasketed joints

2"	P1@.500	Ea	38.60	17.30	—	55.90
3"	P1@.750	Ea	52.80	25.90	—	78.70
4"	P1@.950	Ea	75.10	32.80	—	107.90
6"	ER@1.10	Ea	258.00	40.70	17.30	316.00

DWV cast iron combination double reducing wye and 1/8 bend, hub and spigot, gasketed joints

3" x 2"	P1@.550	Ea	42.50	19.00	—	61.50
4" x 2"	P1@.650	Ea	53.30	22.50	—	75.80
4" x 3"	P1@.700	Ea	60.50	24.20	—	84.70
6" x 4"	ER@.800	Ea	169.00	29.60	12.70	211.30

DWV cast iron wye, hub and spigot, gasketed joints

2"	P1@.400	Ea	18.60	13.80	—	32.40
3"	P1@.600	Ea	32.20	20.70	—	52.90
4"	P1@.750	Ea	42.80	25.90	—	68.70
6"	ER@.900	Ea	103.00	33.30	14.10	150.40
8"	ER@1.50	Ea	230.00	55.50	23.70	309.20
10"	ER@2.00	Ea	386.00	74.00	31.40	491.40
12"	ER@2.50	Ea	869.00	92.60	39.30	1,000.90
15"	ER@3.00	Ea	1,720.00	111.00	47.10	1,878.10

Cast Iron, DWV, Service Weight, Hub & Spigot with Gasketed Joints

Description	Craft@Hrs	Unit	Material $	Labor $	Equipment $	Total $
DWV cast iron reducing wye, hub and spigot, gasketed joints						
4" x 2"	P1@.650	Ea	32.30	22.50	—	54.80
4" x 3"	P1@.700	Ea	39.70	24.20	—	63.90
6" x 2"	ER@.750	Ea	82.40	27.80	11.80	122.00
6" x 3"	ER@.750	Ea	82.40	27.80	11.80	122.00
6" x 4"	ER@.800	Ea	83.40	29.60	12.70	125.70
8" x 4"	ER@1.35	Ea	192.00	50.00	21.20	263.20
8" x 6"	ER@1.45	Ea	204.00	53.70	22.80	280.50
10" x 4"	ER@1.85	Ea	330.00	68.50	29.20	427.70
10" x 6"	ER@1.90	Ea	340.00	70.30	29.90	440.20
10" x 8"	ER@1.95	Ea	363.00	72.20	30.80	466.00
12" x 6"	ER@2.35	Ea	614.00	87.00	37.10	738.10
12" x 8"	ER@2.40	Ea	673.00	88.80	37.70	799.50
12" x 10"	ER@2.45	Ea	726.00	90.70	38.70	855.40
15" x 6"	ER@2.85	Ea	992.00	106.00	44.90	1,142.90
15" x 8"	ER@2.85	Ea	1,000.00	106.00	44.90	1,150.90
15" x 10"	ER@2.90	Ea	1,120.00	107.00	45.70	1,272.70
15" x 12"	ER@2.95	Ea	1,130.00	109.00	46.50	1,285.50
DWV cast iron double wye, hub and spigot, gasketed joints						
2"	P1@.500	Ea	24.20	17.30	—	41.50
3"	P1@.750	Ea	42.00	25.90	—	67.90
4"	P1@.950	Ea	58.20	32.80	—	91.00
6"	ER@1.10	Ea	135.00	40.70	17.30	193.00
8"	ER@1.85	Ea	333.00	68.50	29.20	430.70
10"	ER@2.50	Ea	466.00	92.60	39.30	597.90
12"	ER@2.75	Ea	674.00	102.00	43.50	819.50
15"	ER@3.50	Ea	2,040.00	130.00	55.00	2,225.00
DWV cast iron reducing double wye, hub and spigot, gasketed joints						
3" x 2"	P1@.550	Ea	35.50	19.00	—	54.50
4" x 2"	P1@.650	Ea	43.30	22.50	—	65.80
4" x 3"	P1@.700	Ea	48.00	24.20	—	72.20
6" x 4"	ER@.800	Ea	102.00	29.60	12.70	144.30
DWV cast iron reducer, hub and spigot, gasketed joints						
3"	P1@.150	Ea	12.40	5.18	—	17.58
4"	P1@.200	Ea	32.30	6.91	—	39.21
6"	ER@.320	Ea	50.40	11.80	5.00	67.20
8"	ER@.350	Ea	107.00	13.00	5.50	125.50
10"	ER@.570	Ea	225.00	21.10	9.00	255.10
12"	ER@.620	Ea	299.00	23.00	9.70	331.70
15"	ER@1.12	Ea	553.00	41.50	17.60	612.10

Cast Iron, DWV, Service Weight, Hub & Spigot with Gasketed Joints

Description	Craft@Hrs	Unit	Material $	Labor $	Equipment $	Total $
Gaskets for hub and spigot joints						
2"	--@--	Ea	2.91	—	—	2.91
3"	--@--	Ea	3.85	—	—	3.85
4"	--@--	Ea	4.90	—	—	4.90
5"	--@--	Ea	7.52	—	—	7.52
6"	--@--	Ea	7.92	—	—	7.92
8"	--@--	Ea	17.20	—	—	17.20
10"	--@--	Ea	26.70	—	—	26.70
12"	--@--	Ea	33.90	—	—	33.90
15"	--@--	Ea	40.50	—	—	40.50
Hanger with swivel assembly						
2"	P1@.400	Ea	6.35	13.80	—	20.15
3"	P1@.450	Ea	8.21	15.50	—	23.71
4"	P1@.450	Ea	10.20	15.50	—	25.70
5"	P1@.500	Ea	15.60	17.30	—	32.90
6"	P1@.500	Ea	17.50	17.30	—	34.80
8"	P1@.550	Ea	22.90	19.00	—	41.90
10"	P1@.650	Ea	30.30	22.50	—	52.80
12"	P1@.750	Ea	41.70	25.90	—	67.60
15"	P1@.850	Ea	55.40	29.40	—	84.80
Riser clamp						
2"	P1@.115	Ea	5.08	3.97	—	9.05
3"	P1@.120	Ea	5.80	4.15	—	9.95
4"	P1@.125	Ea	7.38	4.32	—	11.70
5"	P1@.180	Ea	10.60	6.22	—	16.82
6"	P1@.200	Ea	12.80	6.91	—	19.71
8"	P1@.200	Ea	20.80	6.91	—	27.71
10"	P1@.250	Ea	30.90	8.64	—	39.54
12"	P1@.250	Ea	38.40	8.64	—	47.04

Copper, DWV with Soft-Soldered Joints

Copper drainage tubing is used for non-pressurized above grade, interior building drain, waste and vent (DWV) systems.

Because of its thin walls, it must be handled carefully and protected from damage during building construction.

This section has been arranged to save the estimator's time by including all normally-used system components such as pipe, fittings, hanger assemblies and riser clamps under one heading. Additional items can be found under "Plumbing and Piping Specialties." The cost estimates in this section are based on the conditions, limitations and wage rates described in the section "How to Use This Book" beginning on page 5.

Description	Craft@Hrs	Unit	Material $	Labor $	Equipment $	Total $

DWV copper pipe assembly, installed horizontally. Assembly includes fittings, couplings, hangers and rod. Based on a reducing wye and a 45 degree elbow every 12 feet for 1¼" pipe. A reducing wye and a 45 degree elbow every 25 feet for 4" pipe, and hangers spaced to meet plumbing code.

Description	Craft@Hrs	Unit	Material $	Labor $	Equipment $	Total $
1¼"	P1@.130	LF	12.60	4.49	—	17.09
1½"	P1@.132	LF	12.80	4.56	—	17.36
2"	P1@.137	LF	16.30	4.73	—	21.03
3"	P1@.179	LF	29.30	6.18	—	35.48
4"	P1@.202	LF	54.70	6.98	—	61.68

DWV copper pipe assembly, installed risers. Complete installation including a reducing tee every floor and a riser clamp every other.

Description	Craft@Hrs	Unit	Material $	Labor $	Equipment $	Total $
1¼"	P1@.069	LF	9.74	2.38	—	12.12
1½"	P1@.074	LF	11.00	2.56	—	13.56
2"	P1@.086	LF	15.00	2.97	—	17.97
3"	P1@.110	LF	29.10	3.80	—	32.90
4"	P1@.134	LF	48.70	4.63	—	53.33

DWV copper pipe, soft-soldered joints

Description	Craft@Hrs	Unit	Material $	Labor $	Equipment $	Total $
1¼"	P1@.040	LF	5.02	1.38	—	6.40
1½"	P1@.045	LF	6.36	1.55	—	7.91
2"	P1@.050	LF	8.36	1.73	—	10.09
3"	P1@.060	LF	13.20	2.07	—	15.27
4"	P1@.070	LF	16.90	2.42	—	19.32

DWV copper 1/8 bend, soft-soldered joints

Description	Craft@Hrs	Unit	Material $	Labor $	Equipment $	Total $
1¼"	P1@.170	Ea	6.28	5.87	—	12.15
1½"	P1@.200	Ea	5.79	6.91	—	12.70
2"	P1@.270	Ea	10.50	9.33	—	19.83
3"	P1@.400	Ea	25.90	13.80	—	39.70
4"	P1@.540	Ea	107.00	18.70	—	125.70

Copper, DWV with Soft-Soldered Joints

Description	Craft@Hrs	Unit	Material $	Labor $	Equipment $	Total $

DWV copper 1/4 bend, soft-soldered joints

Description	Craft@Hrs	Unit	Material $	Labor $	Equipment $	Total $
1¼"	P1@.170	Ea	7.07	5.87	—	12.94
1½"	P1@.200	Ea	8.07	6.91	—	14.98
2"	P1@.270	Ea	13.00	9.33	—	22.33
3"	P1@.400	Ea	34.20	13.80	—	48.00
4"	P1@.540	Ea	165.00	18.70	—	183.70

DWV copper closet flange, soft-soldered joints

Description	Craft@Hrs	Unit	Material $	Labor $	Equipment $	Total $
4" x 3"	P1@.680	Ea	33.50	23.50	—	57.00
4" x 4"	P1@.980	Ea	41.40	33.90	—	75.30

DWV copper P-trap, soft-soldered joints

Description	Craft@Hrs	Unit	Material $	Labor $	Equipment $	Total $
1¼"	P1@.240	Ea	47.70	8.29	—	55.99
1½"	P1@.240	Ea	41.50	8.29	—	49.79
2"	P1@.240	Ea	63.30	8.29	—	71.59
3"	P1@.320	Ea	182.00	11.10	—	193.10

DWV copper sanitary tee, (TY) soft-soldered joints

Description	Craft@Hrs	Unit	Material $	Labor $	Equipment $	Total $
1½"	P1@.240	Ea	14.60	8.29	—	22.89
2"	P1@.320	Ea	20.00	11.10	—	31.10
3"	P1@.490	Ea	69.30	16.90	—	86.20
4"	P1@.650	Ea	174.00	22.50	—	196.50

DWV copper sanitary cross, soft-soldered joints

Description	Craft@Hrs	Unit	Material $	Labor $	Equipment $	Total $
1½"	P1@.640	Ea	97.40	22.10	—	119.50
2"	P1@.900	Ea	141.00	31.10	—	172.10
3"	P1@1.36	Ea	398.00	47.00	—	445.00

DWV copper combination wye and 1/8 bend, soft-soldered joints

Description	Craft@Hrs	Unit	Material $	Labor $	Equipment $	Total $
1½"	P1@.240	Ea	30.90	8.29	—	39.19
2"	P1@.320	Ea	52.80	11.10	—	63.90
3"	P1@.490	Ea	174.00	16.90	—	190.90
4"	P1@.650	Ea	392.00	22.50	—	414.50

DWV copper wye, soft-soldered joints

Description	Craft@Hrs	Unit	Material $	Labor $	Equipment $	Total $
1½"	P1@.240	Ea	24.00	8.29	—	32.29
2"	P1@.320	Ea	34.50	11.10	—	45.60
3"	P1@.490	Ea	86.50	16.90	—	103.40
4"	P1@.650	Ea	174.00	22.50	—	196.50

DWV copper cleanout with threaded plug

Description	Craft@Hrs	Unit	Material $	Labor $	Equipment $	Total $
1¼"	P1@.100	Ea	12.20	3.46	—	15.66
1½"	P1@.160	Ea	18.20	5.53	—	23.73
2"	P1@.230	Ea	23.70	7.95	—	31.65

Copper, DWV with Soft-Soldered Joints

Description	Craft@Hrs	Unit	Material $	Labor $	Equipment $	Total $

DWV copper female adapter

Description	Craft@Hrs	Unit	Material $	Labor $	Equipment $	Total $
1½"	P1@.130	Ea	9.41	4.49	—	13.90
2"	P1@.170	Ea	17.90	5.87	—	23.77
3"	P1@.230	Ea	71.40	7.95	—	79.35
4"	P1@.300	Ea	122.00	10.40	—	132.40

DWV copper male adapter

Description	Craft@Hrs	Unit	Material $	Labor $	Equipment $	Total $
1½"	P1@.130	Ea	10.70	4.49	—	15.19
2"	P1@.170	Ea	12.80	5.87	—	18.67
3"	P1@.230	Ea	62.50	7.95	—	70.45
4"	P1@.300	Ea	105.00	10.40	—	115.40

DWV copper soil adapter (copper x MJ)

Description	Craft@Hrs	Unit	Material $	Labor $	Equipment $	Total $
2"	P1@.170	Ea	15.30	5.87	—	21.17
3"	P1@.250	Ea	31.30	8.64	—	39.94
4"	P1@.320	Ea	58.60	11.10	—	69.70

DWV copper test cap, soft-soldered joint

Description	Craft@Hrs	Unit	Material $	Labor $	Equipment $	Total $
1½"	P1@.100	Ea	.36	3.46	—	3.82
2"	P1@.130	Ea	.51	4.49	—	5.00
3"	P1@.200	Ea	.65	6.91	—	7.56
4"	P1@.250	Ea	1.37	8.64	—	10.01

DWV copper test tee, soft-soldered joints

Description	Craft@Hrs	Unit	Material $	Labor $	Equipment $	Total $
1½"	P1@.200	Ea	35.10	6.91	—	42.01
2"	P1@.270	Ea	45.80	9.33	—	55.13
3"	P1@.400	Ea	123.00	13.80	—	136.80

DWV copper fitting reducer, soft-soldered joints

Description	Craft@Hrs	Unit	Material $	Labor $	Equipment $	Total $
1½"	P1@.100	Ea	5.79	3.46	—	9.25
2"	P1@.140	Ea	7.42	4.84	—	12.26
3"	P1@.200	Ea	25.90	6.91	—	32.81
4"	P1@.270	Ea	41.20	9.33	—	50.53

DWV copper coupling, soft-soldered joints

Description	Craft@Hrs	Unit	Material $	Labor $	Equipment $	Total $
1¼"	P1@.170	Ea	3.08	5.87	—	8.95
1½"	P1@.200	Ea	3.55	6.91	—	10.46
2"	P1@.270	Ea	5.08	9.33	—	14.41
3"	P1@.400	Ea	9.41	13.80	—	23.21
4"	P1@.540	Ea	37.00	18.70	—	55.70

Description	Craft@Hrs	Unit	Material $	Labor $	Equipment $	Total $

Hanger with swivel assembly

Description	Craft@Hrs	Unit	Material $	Labor $	Equipment $	Total $
1¼"	P1@.300	Ea	4.44	10.40	—	14.84
1½"	P1@.300	Ea	4.77	10.40	—	15.17
2"	P1@.300	Ea	4.98	10.40	—	15.38
3"	P1@.350	Ea	8.37	12.10	—	20.47
4"	P1@.350	Ea	9.19	12.10	—	21.29

Riser clamp

Description	Craft@Hrs	Unit	Material $	Labor $	Equipment $	Total $
1¼"	P1@.105	Ea	4.33	3.63	—	7.96
1½"	P1@.110	Ea	4.58	3.80	—	8.38
2"	P1@.115	Ea	4.84	3.97	—	8.81
3"	P1@.120	Ea	5.52	4.15	—	9.67
4"	P1@.125	Ea	7.03	4.32	—	11.35

ABS, DWV with Solvent-Weld Joints

ABS (Acrylonitrile Butadiene Styrene) ASTM D 2661-73 is made from various grades of rubber-based resins and is primarily used for non-pressurized drain, waste and vent (DWV) systems.

ABS can also be used for low-temperature (100 degree F. maximum) water distribution systems, but consult the manufacturers for the proper ASTM type, maximum pressure limitations and recommended joint solvent.

The current Uniform Plumbing Code (UPC) states in Sections 401 and 503 that "ABS piping systems shall be limited to those structures where combustible construction is allowed." This does not preclude its use for underground DWV systems.

This section has been arranged to save the estimator's time by including all normally-used system components such as pipe, fittings, hanger assemblies and riser clamps under one heading. The cost estimates in this section are based on the conditions, limitations and wage rates described in the section "How to Use This Book" beginning on page 5.

Description	Craft@Hrs	Unit	Material $	Labor $	Equipment $	Total $
ABS DWV pipe with solvent-weld joints						
1½"	P1@.020	LF	1.00	.69	—	1.69
2"	P1@.025	LF	1.58	.86	—	2.44
3"	P1@.030	LF	2.76	1.04	—	3.80
4"	P1@.040	LF	4.48	1.38	—	5.86
6"	P1@.055	LF	8.28	1.90	—	10.18
ABS DWV 1/8 bend with solvent-weld joints						
1½"	P1@.120	Ea	.95	4.15	—	5.10
2"	P1@.125	Ea	1.71	4.32	—	6.03
3"	P1@.175	Ea	4.14	6.05	—	10.19
4"	P1@.250	Ea	7.82	8.64	—	16.46
6"	P1@.325	Ea	61.90	11.20	—	73.10
ABS DWV 1/8 street bend with solvent-weld joints						
1½"	P1@.060	Ea	1.05	2.07	—	3.12
2"	P1@.065	Ea	1.99	2.25	—	4.24
3"	P1@.088	Ea	4.40	3.04	—	7.44
4"	P1@.125	Ea	12.10	4.32	—	16.42
6"	P1@.163	Ea	60.80	5.63	—	66.43
ABS DWV 1/4 bend with solvent-weld joints						
1½"	P1@.120	Ea	1.16	4.15	—	5.31
2"	P1@.125	Ea	1.96	4.32	—	6.28
3"	P1@.175	Ea	4.94	6.05	—	10.99
4"	P1@.250	Ea	11.30	8.64	—	19.94
6"	P1@.325	Ea	63.90	11.20	—	75.10
ABS DWV closet bend with solvent-weld joints						
3" x 4"	P1@.250	Ea	16.70	8.64	—	25.34
ABS DWV closet flange with solvent-weld joints						
4"	P1@.125	Ea	7.54	4.32	—	11.86

Description	Craft@Hrs	Unit	Material $	Labor $	Equipment $	Total $

ABS DWV P-trap with solvent-weld joints

Description	Craft@Hrs	Unit	Material $	Labor $	Equipment $	Total $
1½"	P1@.150	Ea	3.47	5.18	—	8.65
2"	P1@.190	Ea	8.58	6.56	—	15.14
3"	P1@.260	Ea	20.40	8.98	—	29.38
4"	P1@.350	Ea	39.50	12.10	—	51.60

ABS DWV sanitary tee (TY) with solvent-weld joints

Description	Craft@Hrs	Unit	Material $	Labor $	Equipment $	Total $
1½"	P1@.150	Ea	1.66	5.18	—	6.84
2"	P1@.190	Ea	3.84	6.56	—	10.40
3"	P1@.260	Ea	7.40	8.98	—	16.38
4"	P1@.350	Ea	15.60	12.10	—	27.70
6"	P1@.450	Ea	71.40	15.50	—	86.90

ABS DWV reducing sanitary tee (TY) with solvent-weld joints

Description	Craft@Hrs	Unit	Material $	Labor $	Equipment $	Total $
2" x 1½"	P1@.160	Ea	2.79	5.53	—	8.32
3" x 1½"	P1@.210	Ea	4.77	7.26	—	12.03
3" x 2"	P1@.235	Ea	5.30	8.12	—	13.42
4" x 2"	P1@.300	Ea	15.30	10.40	—	25.70
4" x 3"	P1@.325	Ea	18.20	11.20	—	29.40

ABS DWV double sanitary tee (TY) with solvent-weld joints

Description	Craft@Hrs	Unit	Material $	Labor $	Equipment $	Total $
1½"	P1@.210	Ea	5.10	7.26	—	12.36
2"	P1@.250	Ea	7.67	8.64	—	16.31
3"	P1@.350	Ea	12.10	12.10	—	24.20
4"	P1@.475	Ea	47.90	16.40	—	64.30

ABS DWV combination wye and 1/8 bend with solvent-weld joints

Description	Craft@Hrs	Unit	Material $	Labor $	Equipment $	Total $
1½"	P1@.150	Ea	10.10	5.18	—	15.28
2"	P1@.190	Ea	13.10	6.56	—	19.66
3"	P1@.260	Ea	17.60	8.98	—	26.58
4"	P1@.350	Ea	30.70	12.10	—	42.80

ABS DWV combination reducing wye and 1/8 bend with solvent-weld joints

Description	Craft@Hrs	Unit	Material $	Labor $	Equipment $	Total $
2" x 1½"	P1@.160	Ea	14.50	5.53	—	20.03
3" x 1½"	P1@.210	Ea	22.20	7.26	—	29.46
3" x 2"	P1@.235	Ea	15.50	8.12	—	23.62
4" x 2"	P1@.300	Ea	28.10	10.40	—	38.50
4" x 3"	P1@.325	Ea	33.10	11.20	—	44.30

ABS, DWV with Solvent-Weld Joints

Description	Craft@Hrs	Unit	Material $	Labor $	Equipment $	Total $

ABS DWV bushing with solvent-weld joints

Description	Craft@Hrs	Unit	Material $	Labor $	Equipment $	Total $
2" x 1½"	P1@.062	Ea	.87	2.14	—	3.01
3" x 1½"	P1@.088	Ea	4.31	3.04	—	7.35
3" x 2"	P1@.088	Ea	3.08	3.04	—	6.12
4" x 2"	P1@.125	Ea	6.23	4.32	—	10.55
4" x 3"	P1@.125	Ea	6.23	4.32	—	10.55
6" x 4"	P1@.163	Ea	31.10	5.63	—	36.73

ABS DWV FIP adapter

Description	Craft@Hrs	Unit	Material $	Labor $	Equipment $	Total $
1½"	P1@.080	Ea	1.31	2.76	—	4.07
2"	P1@.085	Ea	2.42	2.94	—	5.36
3"	P1@.155	Ea	5.73	5.36	—	11.09
4"	P1@.220	Ea	10.90	7.60	—	18.50
6"	P1@.285	Ea	42.00	9.85	—	51.85

ABS DWV test cap

Description	Craft@Hrs	Unit	Material $	Labor $	Equipment $	Total $
1½"	P1@.030	Ea	.66	1.04	—	1.70
2"	P1@.040	Ea	1.06	1.38	—	2.44
3"	P1@.050	Ea	1.67	1.73	—	3.40
4"	P1@.090	Ea	2.64	3.11	—	5.75

ABS DWV cleanout plug

Description	Craft@Hrs	Unit	Material $	Labor $	Equipment $	Total $
1½"	P1@.090	Ea	3.06	3.11	—	6.17
2"	P1@.120	Ea	4.48	4.15	—	8.63
3"	P1@.240	Ea	7.98	8.29	—	16.27
4"	P1@.320	Ea	17.30	11.10	—	28.40
6"	P1@.450	Ea	55.10	15.50	—	70.60

ABS DWV cleanout tee with solvent-weld joints

Description	Craft@Hrs	Unit	Material $	Labor $	Equipment $	Total $
1½"	P1@.120	Ea	4.74	4.15	—	8.89
2"	P1@.125	Ea	7.67	4.32	—	11.99
3"	P1@.175	Ea	12.70	6.05	—	18.75
4"	P1@.250	Ea	26.00	8.64	—	34.64

ABS DWV wye with solvent-weld joints

Description	Craft@Hrs	Unit	Material $	Labor $	Equipment $	Total $
1½"	P1@.150	Ea	2.22	5.18	—	7.40
2"	P1@.190	Ea	4.14	6.56	—	10.70
3"	P1@.260	Ea	7.67	8.98	—	16.65
4"	P1@.350	Ea	17.70	12.10	—	29.80
6"	P1@.450	Ea	74.80	15.50	—	90.30

ABS DWV reducing wye with solvent-weld joints

Description	Craft@Hrs	Unit	Material $	Labor $	Equipment $	Total $
2" x 1½"	P1@.160	Ea	3.84	5.53	—	9.37
3" x 1½"	P1@.210	Ea	5.36	7.26	—	12.62
3" x 2"	P1@.235	Ea	6.00	8.12	—	14.12
4" x 2"	P1@.300	Ea	12.90	10.40	—	23.30
4" x 3"	P1@.325	Ea	16.10	11.20	—	27.30
6" x 4"	P1@.400	Ea	61.90	13.80	—	75.70

Description	Craft@Hrs	Unit	Material $	Labor $	Equipment $	Total $

ABS DWV reducer with solvent-weld joints

Description	Craft@Hrs	Unit	Material $	Labor $	Equipment $	Total $
2" x 1½"	P1@.125	Ea	.87	4.32	—	5.19
3" x 1½"	P1@.150	Ea	4.31	5.18	—	9.49
3" x 2"	P1@.150	Ea	3.08	5.18	—	8.26
4" x 2"	P1@.185	Ea	6.23	6.39	—	12.62
4" x 3"	P1@.210	Ea	6.16	7.26	—	13.42

ABS DWV coupling with solvent-weld joints

Description	Craft@Hrs	Unit	Material $	Labor $	Equipment $	Total $
1½"	P1@.120	Ea	.74	4.15	—	4.89
2"	P1@.125	Ea	1.09	4.32	—	5.41
3"	P1@.175	Ea	2.53	6.05	—	8.58
4"	P1@.250	Ea	4.60	8.64	—	13.24
6"	P1@.325	Ea	27.20	11.20	—	38.40

Hanger with swivel assembly

Description	Craft@Hrs	Unit	Material $	Labor $	Equipment $	Total $
1½"	P1@.300	Ea	4.77	10.40	—	15.17
2"	P1@.300	Ea	4.98	10.40	—	15.38
3"	P1@.350	Ea	8.37	12.10	—	20.47
4"	P1@.350	Ea	9.19	12.10	—	21.29
6"	P1@.450	Ea	15.10	15.50	—	30.60

Riser clamp

Description	Craft@Hrs	Unit	Material $	Labor $	Equipment $	Total $
1½"	P1@.110	Ea	4.58	3.80	—	8.38
2"	P1@.115	Ea	4.84	3.97	—	8.81
3"	P1@.120	Ea	5.52	4.15	—	9.67
4"	P1@.125	Ea	7.03	4.32	—	11.35
6"	P1@.130	Ea	12.20	4.49	—	16.69

Galvanized steel pipe sleeves

Description	Craft@Hrs	Unit	Material $	Labor $	Equipment $	Total $
2"	P1@.130	Ea	6.34	4.49	—	10.83
2½"	P1@.150	Ea	6.47	5.18	—	11.65
3"	P1@.180	Ea	6.62	6.22	—	12.84
4"	P1@.220	Ea	7.52	7.60	—	15.12
5"	P1@.250	Ea	9.37	8.64	—	18.01
6"	P1@.270	Ea	10.10	9.33	—	19.43

Lead roof pipe flashing

Description	Craft@Hrs	Unit	Material $	Labor $	Equipment $	Total $
1½"	P1@.250	Ea	31.60	8.64	—	40.24
2"	P1@.250	Ea	41.60	8.64	—	50.24
3"	P1@.250	Ea	48.30	8.64	—	56.94
4"	P1@.250	Ea	53.10	8.64	—	61.74
6"	P1@.350	Ea	68.10	12.10	—	80.20

PVC, DWV with Solvent-Weld Joints

PVC (Polyvinyl Chloride) meets ASTM – D3034, D3212, F1336, F679 & CSA 182.2 (CSA - Canadian Standards Association – similar to UL – Underwriters Laboratories). The applications for PVC DWV have increased in number due to the unique flame spread characteristics of their compounds, as well as the development of new fire stop devices for use with combustible piping systems.

PVC will not rust, pit or degrade when exposed to moisture and is extremely resistant to a broad range of corrosive agents.

PVC DWV is suitable for sewer, vent and storm water drainage applications in both below and above grade applications.

When penetrating a vertical or horizontal fire separation (fire rated wall or floor) with combustible piping, certified fire stop devices must be used in compliance with local and national codes.

PVC DWV is not permitted in a ceiling space used as a return air plenum and is not permitted in a vertical shaft. PVC DWV has a flame spread rating of 15.

This section has been arranged to save the estimator's time by including all normally-used system components such as pipe, fittings, hanger assemblies and riser clamps under one heading. The cost estimates in this section are based on the conditions, limitations and wage rates described in the section "How to Use This Book" beginning on page 5.

Description	Craft@Hrs	Unit	Material $	Labor $	Equipment $	Total $

PVC DWV pipe with solvent-weld joints

Description	Craft@Hrs	Unit	Material $	Labor $	Equipment $	Total $
1½"	P1@.021	LF	1.06	.73	—	1.79
2"	P1@.026	LF	1.92	.90	—	2.82
3"	P1@.032	LF	4.07	1.11	—	5.18
4"	P1@.042	LF	4.99	1.45	—	6.44
6"	P1@.058	LF	8.97	2.00	—	10.97

PVC DWV 90 degree elbow with solvent-weld joints

Description	Craft@Hrs	Unit	Material $	Labor $	Equipment $	Total $
1½"	P1@.126	Ea	1.07	4.35	—	5.42
2"	P1@.131	Ea	2.50	4.53	—	7.03
3"	P1@.184	Ea	6.58	6.36	—	12.94
4"	P1@.263	Ea	13.00	9.09	—	22.09
6"	P1@.341	Ea	54.60	11.80	—	66.40

PVC DWV 90 degree street elbow with solvent-weld joints

Description	Craft@Hrs	Unit	Material $	Labor $	Equipment $	Total $
1½"	P1@.063	Ea	1.76	2.18	—	3.94
2"	P1@.068	Ea	2.99	2.35	—	5.34
3"	P1@.092	Ea	8.73	3.18	—	11.91
4"	P1@.131	Ea	21.10	4.53	—	25.63
6"	P1@.171	Ea	77.20	5.91	—	83.11

PVC DWV 45 degree elbow with solvent-weld joints

Description	Craft@Hrs	Unit	Material $	Labor $	Equipment $	Total $
1½"	P1@.126	Ea	1.38	4.35	—	5.73
2"	P1@.131	Ea	1.67	4.53	—	6.20
3"	P1@.184	Ea	4.19	6.36	—	10.55
4"	P1@.263	Ea	10.60	9.09	—	19.69
6"	P1@.341	Ea	64.30	11.80	—	76.10

Description	Craft@Hrs	Unit	Material $	Labor $	Equipment $	Total $

PVC DWV wye with solvent-weld joints

Description	Craft@Hrs	Unit	Material $	Labor $	Equipment $	Total $
1½"	P1@.158	Ea	2.59	5.46	—	8.05
2"	P1@.200	Ea	5.74	6.91	—	12.65
3"	P1@.273	Ea	9.49	9.43	—	18.92
4"	P1@.368	Ea	15.50	12.70	—	28.20
6"	P1@.473	Ea	61.00	16.30	—	77.30

PVC DWV reducing wye with solvent-weld joints

Description	Craft@Hrs	Unit	Material $	Labor $	Equipment $	Total $
2" x 1½"	P1@.168	Ea	4.98	5.80	—	10.78
3" x 1½"	P1@.221	Ea	5.71	7.64	—	13.35
3" x 2"	P1@.247	Ea	8.21	8.53	—	16.74
4" x 2"	P1@.315	Ea	15.90	10.90	—	26.80
4" x 3"	P1@.341	Ea	18.80	11.80	—	30.60
6" x 3"	P1@.473	Ea	69.40	16.30	—	85.70
6" x 4"	P1@.473	Ea	73.90	16.30	—	90.20

PVC DWV sanitary tee (TY) with solvent-weld joints

Description	Craft@Hrs	Unit	Material $	Labor $	Equipment $	Total $
1½"	P1@.158	Ea	1.84	5.46	—	7.30
2"	P1@.200	Ea	3.39	6.91	—	10.30
3"	P1@.273	Ea	7.30	9.43	—	16.73
4"	P1@.368	Ea	13.90	12.70	—	26.60
6"	P1@.473	Ea	76.50	16.30	—	92.80

PVC DWV reducing sanitary tee (TY) with solvent-weld joints

Description	Craft@Hrs	Unit	Material $	Labor $	Equipment $	Total $
2" x 1½"	P1@.168	Ea	2.65	5.80	—	8.45
3" x 1½"	P1@.221	Ea	4.56	7.64	—	12.20
3" x 2"	P1@.247	Ea	6.12	8.53	—	14.65
4" x 2"	P1@.315	Ea	13.40	10.90	—	24.30
4" x 3"	P1@.341	Ea	15.40	11.80	—	27.20
6" x 3"	P1@.473	Ea	58.70	16.30	—	75.00
6" x 4"	P1@.473	Ea	58.70	16.30	—	75.00

PVC DWV double wye with solvent-weld joints

Description	Craft@Hrs	Unit	Material $	Labor $	Equipment $	Total $
2" x 1½"	P1@.263	Ea	7.49	9.09	—	16.58
3" x 2"	P1@.368	Ea	15.20	12.70	—	27.90
4" x 3"	P1@.473	Ea	49.60	16.30	—	65.90
6" x 4"	P1@.578	Ea	59.90	20.00	—	79.90

PVC DWV closet flange with solvent-weld joints, adjustable with test plate

Description	Craft@Hrs	Unit	Material $	Labor $	Equipment $	Total $
4" x 3"	P1@.131	Ea	13.00	4.53	—	17.53

PVC DWV closet flange with solvent-weld joints, non-adjustable with test plate

Description	Craft@Hrs	Unit	Material $	Labor $	Equipment $	Total $
4" x 3"	P1@.131	Ea	9.79	4.53	—	14.32

PVC, DWV with Solvent-Weld Joints

Description	Craft@Hrs	Unit	Material $	Labor $	Equipment $	Total $

PVC DWV closet flange with solvent-weld joints, non-adjustable without test plate

Description	Craft@Hrs	Unit	Material $	Labor $	Equipment $	Total $
4" x 3"	P1@.131	Ea	8.91	4.53	—	13.44

PVC DWV closet flange with solvent-weld joints, adjustable, offset without test plate

Description	Craft@Hrs	Unit	Material $	Labor $	Equipment $	Total $
4" x 3"	P1@.170	Ea	19.10	5.87	—	24.97

PVC DWV P-trap with solvent-weld joints

Description	Craft@Hrs	Unit	Material $	Labor $	Equipment $	Total $
1½"	P1@.160	Ea	4.17	5.53	—	9.70
2"	P1@.200	Ea	10.20	6.91	—	17.11
3"	P1@.285	Ea	24.00	9.85	—	33.85
4"	P1@.370	Ea	47.10	12.80	—	59.90
6"	P1@.580	Ea	180.00	20.00	—	200.00

PVC DWV bushing with solvent-weld joints

Description	Craft@Hrs	Unit	Material $	Labor $	Equipment $	Total $
2" x 1½"	P1@.062	Ea	.86	2.14	—	3.00
3" x 2"	P1@.088	Ea	2.52	3.04	—	5.56
4" x 3"	P1@.125	Ea	5.29	4.32	—	9.61
6" x 4"	P1@.163	Ea	27.30	5.63	—	32.93

PVC DWV FIP adapter

Description	Craft@Hrs	Unit	Material $	Labor $	Equipment $	Total $
1½"	P1@.080	Ea	1.16	2.76	—	3.92
2"	P1@.085	Ea	2.03	2.94	—	4.97
3"	P1@.155	Ea	4.92	5.36	—	10.28
4"	P1@.220	Ea	9.58	7.60	—	17.18
6"	P1@.285	Ea	43.30	9.85	—	53.15

PVC DWV MIP adapter

Description	Craft@Hrs	Unit	Material $	Labor $	Equipment $	Total $
1½"	P1@.080	Ea	1.28	2.76	—	4.04
2"	P1@.085	Ea	2.12	2.94	—	5.06
3"	P1@.155	Ea	4.37	5.36	—	9.73
4"	P1@.220	Ea	11.70	7.60	—	19.30
6"	P1@.285	Ea	21.50	9.85	—	31.35

PVC DWV coupling with solvent-weld joints

Description	Craft@Hrs	Unit	Material $	Labor $	Equipment $	Total $
1½"	P1@.120	Ea	.61	4.15	—	4.76
2"	P1@.125	Ea	.96	4.32	—	5.28
3"	P1@.175	Ea	2.24	6.05	—	8.29
4"	P1@.250	Ea	4.71	8.64	—	13.35
6"	P1@.325	Ea	23.00	11.20	—	34.20

Description	Craft@Hrs	Unit	Material $	Labor $	Equipment $	Total $

PVC DWV reducer with solvent-weld joints

Description	Craft@Hrs	Unit	Material $	Labor $	Equipment $	Total $
2" x 1½"	P1@.125	Ea	1.42	4.32	—	5.74
3" x 2"	P1@.150	Ea	4.29	5.18	—	9.47
4" x 3"	P1@.185	Ea	5.59	6.39	—	11.98
6" x 4"	P1@.210	Ea	56.50	7.26	—	63.76

PVC DWV in-line cleanout with solvent-weld joints

Description	Craft@Hrs	Unit	Material $	Labor $	Equipment $	Total $
1½"	P1@.120	Ea	5.33	4.15	—	9.48
2"	P1@.125	Ea	9.12	4.32	—	13.44
3"	P1@.175	Ea	13.40	6.05	—	19.45
4"	P1@.250	Ea	27.90	8.64	—	36.54
6" x 4"	P1@.250	Ea	95.20	8.64	—	103.84
6"	P1@.250	Ea	95.20	8.64	—	103.84

PVC DWV end cleanout

Description	Craft@Hrs	Unit	Material $	Labor $	Equipment $	Total $
1½"	P1@.090	Ea	2.34	3.11	—	5.45
2"	P1@.120	Ea	3.81	4.15	—	7.96
3"	P1@.240	Ea	7.73	8.29	—	16.02
4"	P1@.320	Ea	14.40	11.10	—	25.50
6"	P1@.450	Ea	50.10	15.50	—	65.60

PVC DWV fitting end cleanout

Description	Craft@Hrs	Unit	Material $	Labor $	Equipment $	Total $
1½"	P1@.090	Ea	2.23	3.11	—	5.34
2"	P1@.120	Ea	4.41	4.15	—	8.56
3"	P1@.240	Ea	5.15	8.29	—	13.44
4"	P1@.320	Ea	11.00	11.10	—	22.10
6"	P1@.450	Ea	57.10	15.50	—	72.60

Hanger with swivel assembly

Description	Craft@Hrs	Unit	Material $	Labor $	Equipment $	Total $
1½"	P1@.300	Ea	6.08	10.40	—	16.48
2"	P1@.300	Ea	6.36	10.40	—	16.76
3"	P1@.350	Ea	10.70	12.10	—	22.80
4"	P1@.350	Ea	11.70	12.10	—	23.80
6"	P1@.450	Ea	19.10	15.50	—	34.60

Riser clamp

Description	Craft@Hrs	Unit	Material $	Labor $	Equipment $	Total $
1½"	P1@.110	Ea	4.58	3.80	—	8.38
2"	P1@.115	Ea	4.84	3.97	—	8.81
3"	P1@.120	Ea	5.52	4.15	—	9.67
4"	P1@.125	Ea	7.03	4.32	—	11.35
6"	P1@.130	Ea	12.20	4.49	—	16.69

PVC, DWV with Solvent-Weld Joints

Description	Craft@Hrs	Unit	Material $	Labor $	Equipment $	Total $

Galvanized steel pipe sleeves

2"	P1@.130	Ea	6.34	4.49	—	10.83
2½"	P1@.150	Ea	6.47	5.18	—	11.65
3"	P1@.180	Ea	6.62	6.22	—	12.84
4"	P1@.220	Ea	7.52	7.60	—	15.12
5"	P1@.250	Ea	9.37	8.64	—	18.01
6"	P1@.270	Ea	10.10	9.33	—	19.43

Lead roof pipe flashing

1½"	P1@.400	Ea	33.10	13.80	—	46.90
2"	P1@.450	Ea	43.70	15.50	—	59.20
3"	P1@.500	Ea	50.50	17.30	—	67.80
4"	P1@.550	Ea	55.90	19.00	—	74.90

PVC, DWV with Gasketed Bell and Spigot Joints

PVC (Polyvinyl Chloride) is polymerized vinyl chloride produced from acetylene and anhydrous hydrochloric acid.

PVC sewer pipe (ASTM D-3034) 10' lay length, is for underground installation and is used primarily to convey sewage and rain water. It is of the bell & spigot type with joints made water-tight by means of an elastomeric gasket (o-ring) factory-installed in the hub end of the pipe and fittings.

This section includes pipe and all commonly-used fittings. Additional items can be found under "Plumbing and Piping Specialties." The cost estimates in this section are based on the conditions, limitations, and wage rates described in the section "How to Use This Book" beginning on page 5.

Description	Craft@Hrs	Unit	Material $	Labor $	Equipment $	Total $

PVC SDR35 sewer pipe with bell and spigot gasketed joints

Description	Craft@Hrs	Unit	Material $	Labor $	Equipment $	Total $
4"	P1@.050	LF	3.95	1.73	—	5.68
6"	P1@.070	LF	8.67	2.42	—	11.09
8"	P1@.090	LF	13.80	3.11	—	16.91
10"	P1@.110	LF	19.30	3.80	—	23.10
12"	P1@.140	LF	24.30	4.84	—	29.14
15"	P1@.180	LF	35.90	6.22	—	42.12
18"	P1@.230	LF	55.80	7.95	—	63.75

PVC sewer pipe 1/16 bend B x B with bell and spigot gasketed joints

Description	Craft@Hrs	Unit	Material $	Labor $	Equipment $	Total $
4"	P1@.320	Ea	18.30	11.10	—	29.40
6"	P1@.400	Ea	35.80	13.80	—	49.60
8"	P1@.480	Ea	105.00	16.60	—	121.60
10"	P1@.800	Ea	286.00	27.60	—	313.60
12"	P1@1.06	Ea	374.00	36.60	—	410.60
15"	P1@1.34	Ea	992.00	46.30	—	1,038.30
18"	P1@1.60	Ea	1,440.00	55.30	—	1,495.30

PVC sewer pipe 1/16 bend B x S with bell and spigot gasketed joints

Description	Craft@Hrs	Unit	Material $	Labor $	Equipment $	Total $
4"	P1@.320	Ea	17.40	11.10	—	28.50
6"	P1@.400	Ea	34.20	13.80	—	48.00
8"	P1@.480	Ea	110.00	16.60	—	126.60
10"	P1@.800	Ea	281.00	27.60	—	308.60
12"	P1@1.06	Ea	363.00	36.60	—	399.60
15"	P1@1.34	Ea	793.00	46.30	—	839.30
18"	P1@1.60	Ea	1,210.00	55.30	—	1,265.30

PVC sewer pipe 1/8 bend B x B with bell and spigot gasketed joints

Description	Craft@Hrs	Unit	Material $	Labor $	Equipment $	Total $
4"	P1@.320	Ea	18.40	11.10	—	29.50
6"	P1@.400	Ea	37.00	13.80	—	50.80
8"	P1@.480	Ea	99.20	16.60	—	115.80
10"	P1@.800	Ea	267.00	27.60	—	294.60
12"	P1@1.06	Ea	394.00	36.60	—	430.60
15"	P1@1.34	Ea	873.00	46.30	—	919.30
18"	P1@1.60	Ea	1,400.00	55.30	—	1,455.30

PVC, DWV with Gasketed Bell and Spigot Joints

Description	Craft@Hrs	Unit	Material $	Labor $	Equipment $	Total $

PVC sewer pipe 1/8 bend B x S with bell and spigot gasketed joints

Description	Craft@Hrs	Unit	Material $	Labor $	Equipment $	Total $
4"	P1@.320	Ea	16.50	11.10	—	27.60
6"	P1@.400	Ea	33.00	13.80	—	46.80
8"	P1@.480	Ea	99.20	16.60	—	115.80
10"	P1@.800	Ea	264.00	27.60	—	291.60
12"	P1@1.06	Ea	382.00	36.60	—	418.60
15"	P1@1.34	Ea	685.00	46.30	—	731.30
18"	P1@1.60	Ea	1,160.00	55.30	—	1,215.30

PVC sewer pipe 1/4 bend B x B with bell and spigot gasketed joints

Description	Craft@Hrs	Unit	Material $	Labor $	Equipment $	Total $
4"	P1@.320	Ea	26.20	11.10	—	37.30
6"	P1@.400	Ea	48.70	13.80	—	62.50
8"	P1@.480	Ea	133.00	16.60	—	149.60
10"	P1@.800	Ea	452.00	27.60	—	479.60
12"	P1@1.06	Ea	581.00	36.60	—	617.60
15"	P1@1.34	Ea	1,230.00	46.30	—	1,276.30
18"	P1@1.60	Ea	2,080.00	55.30	—	2,135.30

PVC sewer pipe 1/4 bend B x S with bell and spigot gasketed joints

Description	Craft@Hrs	Unit	Material $	Labor $	Equipment $	Total $
4"	P1@.320	Ea	24.20	11.10	—	35.30
6"	P1@.400	Ea	51.30	13.80	—	65.10
8"	P1@.480	Ea	140.00	16.60	—	156.60
10"	P1@.800	Ea	447.00	27.60	—	474.60
12"	P1@1.06	Ea	564.00	36.60	—	600.60
15"	P1@1.34	Ea	1,110.00	46.30	—	1,156.30
18"	P1@1.60	Ea	1,930.00	55.30	—	1,985.30

PVC sewer pipe coupling B x B with bell and spigot gasketed joints

Description	Craft@Hrs	Unit	Material $	Labor $	Equipment $	Total $
4"	P1@.320	Ea	22.60	11.10	—	33.70
6"	P1@.400	Ea	45.20	13.80	—	59.00
8"	P1@.480	Ea	77.00	16.60	—	93.60
10"	P1@.800	Ea	169.00	27.60	—	196.60
12"	P1@1.06	Ea	248.00	36.60	—	284.60
15"	P1@1.34	Ea	513.00	46.30	—	559.30
18"	P1@1.60	Ea	100.00	55.30	—	155.30

PVC sewer pipe wye B x B x B with bell and spigot gasketed joints

Description	Craft@Hrs	Unit	Material $	Labor $	Equipment $	Total $
4"	P1@.480	Ea	30.60	16.60	—	47.20
6"	P1@.600	Ea	70.20	20.70	—	90.90
8"	P1@.720	Ea	194.00	24.90	—	218.90
10"	P1@1.20	Ea	564.00	41.50	—	605.50
12"	P1@1.59	Ea	801.00	54.90	—	855.90
15"	P1@2.01	Ea	1,400.00	69.40	—	1,469.40
18"	P1@2.40	Ea	2,450.00	82.90	—	2,532.90

Description	Craft@Hrs	Unit	Material $	Labor $	Equipment $	Total $

PVC sewer pipe wye B x S x B with bell and spigot gasketed joints

Description	Craft@Hrs	Unit	Material $	Labor $	Equipment $	Total $
10"	P1@1.20	Ea	557.00	41.50	—	598.50
12"	P1@1.59	Ea	793.00	54.90	—	847.90
15"	P1@2.01	Ea	1,290.00	69.40	—	1,359.40
18"	P1@2.40	Ea	2,260.00	82.90	—	2,342.90

PVC sewer pipe reducing wye B x B x B with bell and spigot gasketed joints

Description	Craft@Hrs	Unit	Material $	Labor $	Equipment $	Total $
6" x 4"	P1@.560	Ea	62.50	19.30	—	81.80
8" x 4"	P1@.640	Ea	92.70	22.10	—	114.80
8" x 6"	P1@.680	Ea	111.00	23.50	—	134.50
10" x 4"	P1@.960	Ea	281.00	33.20	—	314.20
10" x 6"	P1@1.00	Ea	286.00	34.60	—	320.60
10" x 8"	P1@1.04	Ea	452.00	35.90	—	487.90
12" x 4"	P1@1.22	Ea	407.00	42.20	—	449.20
12" x 6"	P1@1.26	Ea	419.00	43.50	—	462.50
12" x 8"	P1@1.30	Ea	625.00	44.90	—	669.90
12" x 10"	P1@1.46	Ea	760.00	50.40	—	810.40
15" x 4"	P1@1.50	Ea	614.00	51.80	—	665.80
15" x 6"	P1@1.54	Ea	727.00	53.20	—	780.20
15" x 8"	P1@1.58	Ea	821.00	54.60	—	875.60
15" x 10"	P1@1.74	Ea	980.00	60.10	—	1,040.10
15" x 12"	P1@1.87	Ea	1,100.00	64.60	—	1,164.60
18" x 4"	P1@1.76	Ea	1,400.00	60.80	—	1,460.80
18" x 6"	P1@1.80	Ea	1,420.00	62.20	—	1,482.20
18" x 8"	P1@1.84	Ea	1,490.00	63.60	—	1,553.60
18" x 10"	P1@2.00	Ea	1,650.00	69.10	—	1,719.10
18" x 12"	P1@2.13	Ea	1,780.00	73.60	—	1,853.60
18" x 15"	P1@2.27	Ea	1,900.00	78.40	—	1,978.40

PVC sewer pipe reducing wye B x S x B with bell and spigot gasketed joints

Description	Craft@Hrs	Unit	Material $	Labor $	Equipment $	Total $
10" x 4"	P1@.960	Ea	273.00	33.20	—	306.20
10" x 6"	P1@1.00	Ea	288.00	34.60	—	322.60
10" x 8"	P1@1.04	Ea	465.00	35.90	—	500.90
12" x 4"	P1@1.22	Ea	413.00	42.20	—	455.20
12" x 6"	P1@1.26	Ea	419.00	43.50	—	462.50
12" x 8"	P1@1.30	Ea	616.00	44.90	—	660.90
12" x 10"	P1@1.46	Ea	749.00	50.40	—	799.40
15" x 4"	P1@1.50	Ea	627.00	51.80	—	678.80
15" x 6"	P1@1.54	Ea	711.00	53.20	—	764.20
15" x 8"	P1@1.58	Ea	832.00	54.60	—	886.60
15" x 10"	P1@1.74	Ea	953.00	60.10	—	1,013.10
15" x 12"	P1@1.87	Ea	1,110.00	64.60	—	1,174.60
18" x 4"	P1@1.76	Ea	1,320.00	60.80	—	1,380.80
18" x 6"	P1@1.80	Ea	1,420.00	62.20	—	1,482.20
18" x 8"	P1@1.84	Ea	1,490.00	63.60	—	1,553.60
18" x 10"	P1@2.00	Ea	1,650.00	69.10	—	1,719.10
18" x 12"	P1@2.13	Ea	1,780.00	73.60	—	1,853.60
18" x 15"	P1@2.27	Ea	1,900.00	78.40	—	1,978.40

PVC, DWV with Gasketed Bell and Spigot Joints

Description	Craft@Hrs	Unit	Material $	Labor $	Equipment $	Total $

PVC sewer pipe tee-wye B x B x B with bell and spigot gasketed joints

Description	Craft@Hrs	Unit	Material $	Labor $	Equipment $	Total $
4"	P1@.480	Ea	34.20	16.60	—	50.80
6"	P1@.600	Ea	86.40	20.70	—	107.10
6" x 4"	P1@.560	Ea	73.70	19.30	—	93.00
8" x 4"	P1@.640	Ea	93.60	22.10	—	115.70
8" x 6"	P1@.680	Ea	108.00	23.50	—	131.50

PVC sewer pipe tee B x S x B with bell and spigot gasketed joints

Description	Craft@Hrs	Unit	Material $	Labor $	Equipment $	Total $
10"	P1@1.20	Ea	471.00	41.50	—	512.50
12"	P1@1.59	Ea	652.00	54.90	—	706.90
15"	P1@2.01	Ea	1,040.00	69.40	—	1,109.40
18"	P1@2.40	Ea	1,950.00	82.90	—	2,032.90

PVC sewer pipe reducing tee B x S x B with bell and spigot gasketed joints

Description	Craft@Hrs	Unit	Material $	Labor $	Equipment $	Total $
10" x 4"	P1@.960	Ea	300.00	33.20	—	333.20
10" x 6"	P1@1.00	Ea	311.00	34.60	—	345.60
10" x 8"	P1@1.04	Ea	487.00	35.90	—	522.90
12" x 4"	P1@1.22	Ea	367.00	42.20	—	409.20
12" x 6"	P1@1.26	Ea	374.00	43.50	—	417.50
12" x 8"	P1@1.30	Ea	515.00	44.90	—	559.90
12" x 10"	P1@1.46	Ea	616.00	50.40	—	666.40
15" x 4"	P1@1.50	Ea	595.00	51.80	—	646.80
15" x 6"	P1@1.54	Ea	625.00	53.20	—	678.20
15" x 8"	P1@1.58	Ea	639.00	54.60	—	693.60
15" x 10"	P1@1.74	Ea	749.00	60.10	—	809.10
15" x 12"	P1@1.87	Ea	821.00	64.60	—	885.60
18" x 4"	P1@1.76	Ea	1,500.00	60.80	—	1,560.80
18" x 6"	P1@1.80	Ea	1,540.00	62.20	—	1,602.20
18" x 8"	P1@1.84	Ea	1,620.00	63.60	—	1,683.60
18" x 10"	P1@2.00	Ea	1,670.00	69.10	—	1,739.10
18" x 12"	P1@2.13	Ea	1,740.00	73.60	—	1,813.60
18" x 15"	P1@2.27	Ea	1,850.00	78.40	—	1,928.40

Description	Craft@Hrs	Unit	Material $	Labor $	Equipment $	Total $

PVC sewer pipe reducer S x B with bell and spigot gasketed joints

Description	Craft@Hrs	Unit	Material $	Labor $	Equipment $	Total $
6" x 4"	P1@.360	Ea	33.00	12.40	—	45.40
8" x 4"	P1@.400	Ea	89.90	13.80	—	103.70
8" x 6"	P1@.440	Ea	101.00	15.20	—	116.20
10" x 4"	P1@.560	Ea	237.00	19.30	—	256.30
10" x 6"	P1@.600	Ea	243.00	20.70	—	263.70
10" x 8"	P1@.640	Ea	289.00	22.10	—	311.10
12" x 4"	P1@.690	Ea	311.00	23.80	—	334.80
12" x 6"	P1@.730	Ea	319.00	25.20	—	344.20
12" x 8"	P1@.770	Ea	367.00	26.60	—	393.60
12" x 10"	P1@.930	Ea	407.00	32.10	—	439.10
15" x 4"	P1@.830	Ea	524.00	28.70	—	552.70
15" x 6"	P1@.870	Ea	542.00	30.10	—	572.10
15" x 8"	P1@.910	Ea	616.00	31.40	—	647.40
15" x 10"	P1@1.07	Ea	616.00	37.00	—	653.00
15" x 12"	P1@1.20	Ea	710.00	41.50	—	751.50
18" x 8"	P1@1.04	Ea	760.00	35.90	—	795.90
18" x 10"	P1@1.20	Ea	770.00	41.50	—	811.50
18" x 12"	P1@1.33	Ea	774.00	46.00	—	820.00
18" x 15"	P1@1.47	Ea	793.00	50.80	—	843.80

PVC sewer pipe adapter B x S with bell and spigot gasketed joints

Description	Craft@Hrs	Unit	Material $	Labor $	Equipment $	Total $
4"	P1@.320	Ea	19.30	11.10	—	30.40
6"	P1@.400	Ea	35.80	13.80	—	49.60
8"	P1@.480	Ea	91.70	16.60	—	108.30
10"	P1@.800	Ea	114.00	27.60	—	141.60
12"	P1@1.06	Ea	174.00	36.60	—	210.60
15"	P1@1.34	Ea	262.00	46.30	—	308.30
18"	P1@1.60	Ea	575.00	55.30	—	630.30

PVC sewer pipe cap with bell and spigot gasketed joints

Description	Craft@Hrs	Unit	Material $	Labor $	Equipment $	Total $
4"	P1@.160	Ea	11.80	5.53	—	17.33
6"	P1@.200	Ea	22.00	6.91	—	28.91
8"	P1@.240	Ea	59.50	8.29	—	67.79
10"	P1@.400	Ea	186.00	13.80	—	199.80
12"	P1@.530	Ea	281.00	18.30	—	299.30
15"	P1@.670	Ea	454.00	23.10	—	477.10
18"	P1@.800	Ea	652.00	27.60	—	679.60

PVC sewer pipe test plug with bell and spigot gasketed joints

Description	Craft@Hrs	Unit	Material $	Labor $	Equipment $	Total $
4"	P1@.160	Ea	8.89	5.53	—	14.42
6"	P1@.200	Ea	13.60	6.91	—	20.51
8"	P1@.240	Ea	48.70	8.29	—	56.99
10"	P1@.400	Ea	161.00	13.80	—	174.80
12"	P1@.530	Ea	193.00	18.30	—	211.30
15"	P1@.670	Ea	382.00	23.10	—	405.10
18"	P1@.800	Ea	529.00	27.60	—	556.60

Polypropylene, Schedule 40, with Heat-Fusioned Joints

Polypropylene is used almost exclusively for acid and laboratory drain, waste and vent (DWV) systems.

Joints are made by applying low-voltage current to electrical resistance coils imbedded in propylene collars, which are slipped over the ends of the pipe, then inserted into the hubs of the fittings. Compression clamps are placed around the assemblies and tightened to compress the joints prior to applying electrical current from the power unit to fuse the joint.

This section has been arranged to save the estimator's time by including all normally-used system components such as pipe, fittings, hanger assemblies, and riser clamps under one heading. The cost estimates in this section are based on the conditions, limitations and wage rates described in the section "How to Use This Book" beginning on page 5.

Description	Craft@Hrs	Unit	Material $	Labor $	Equipment $	Total $

Schedule 40 DWV polypropylene pipe with heat-fusioned joints

Description	Craft@Hrs	Unit	Material $	Labor $	Equipment $	Total $
1½"	P1@.050	LF	5.60	1.73	—	7.33
2"	P1@.055	LF	7.60	1.90	—	9.50
3"	P1@.060	LF	13.60	2.07	—	15.67
4"	P1@.080	LF	19.40	2.76	—	22.16
6"	P1@.110	LF	35.00	3.80	—	38.80

Schedule 40 DWV polypropylene 1/8 bend with heat-fusioned joints

Description	Craft@Hrs	Unit	Material $	Labor $	Equipment $	Total $
1½"	P1@.350	Ea	20.40	12.10	—	32.50
2"	P1@.400	Ea	24.90	13.80	—	38.70
3"	P1@.450	Ea	45.40	15.50	—	60.90
4"	P1@.500	Ea	51.50	17.30	—	68.80
6"	P1@.750	Ea	142.00	25.90	—	167.90

Schedule 40 DWV polypropylene 1/4 bend with heat-fusioned joints

Description	Craft@Hrs	Unit	Material $	Labor $	Equipment $	Total $
1½"	P1@.350	Ea	20.60	12.10	—	32.70
2"	P1@.400	Ea	25.40	13.80	—	39.20
3"	P1@.450	Ea	43.50	15.50	—	59.00
4"	P1@.500	Ea	69.20	17.30	—	86.50
6"	P1@.750	Ea	171.00	25.90	—	196.90

Schedule 40 DWV polypropylene long sweep 1/4 bend with heat-fusioned joints

Description	Craft@Hrs	Unit	Material $	Labor $	Equipment $	Total $
1½"	P1@.350	Ea	21.00	12.10	—	33.10
2"	P1@.400	Ea	29.40	13.80	—	43.20
3"	P1@.450	Ea	49.90	15.50	—	65.40
4"	P1@.500	Ea	71.40	17.30	—	88.70

Schedule 40 DWV polypropylene P-trap with heat-fusioned joints

Description	Craft@Hrs	Unit	Material $	Labor $	Equipment $	Total $
1½"	P1@.500	Ea	40.40	17.30	—	57.70
2"	P1@.560	Ea	56.20	19.30	—	75.50
3"	P1@.630	Ea	102.00	21.80	—	123.80
4"	P1@.700	Ea	182.00	24.20	—	206.20

Description	Craft@Hrs	Unit	Material $	Labor $	Equipment $	Total $

Schedule 40 DWV polypropylene sanitary tee (TY) with heat-fusioned joints

Description	Craft@Hrs	Unit	Material $	Labor $	Equipment $	Total $
1½"	P1@.500	Ea	25.40	17.30	—	42.70
2"	P1@.560	Ea	30.80	19.30	—	50.10
3"	P1@.630	Ea	51.20	21.80	—	73.00
4"	P1@.700	Ea	92.10	24.20	—	116.30

Schedule 40 DWV polypropylene reducing sanitary tee (TY) with heat-fusioned joints

Description	Craft@Hrs	Unit	Material $	Labor $	Equipment $	Total $
2" x 1½"	P1@.510	Ea	30.80	17.60	—	48.40
3" x 1½"	P1@.530	Ea	53.40	18.30	—	71.70
3" x 2"	P1@.580	Ea	57.20	20.00	—	77.20
4" x 2"	P1@.650	Ea	82.30	22.50	—	104.80
4" x 3"	P1@.700	Ea	85.50	24.20	—	109.70
6" x 4"	P1@.850	Ea	156.00	29.40	—	185.40

Schedule 40 DWV polypropylene combination wye and 1/8 bend with heat-fusioned joints

Description	Craft@Hrs	Unit	Material $	Labor $	Equipment $	Total $
1½"	P1@.500	Ea	34.20	17.30	—	51.50
2"	P1@.560	Ea	45.80	19.30	—	65.10
3"	P1@.630	Ea	72.60	21.80	—	94.40
4"	P1@.700	Ea	103.00	24.20	—	127.20

Schedule 40 DWV polypropylene combination reducing wye and 1/8 bend with heat-fusioned joints

Description	Craft@Hrs	Unit	Material $	Labor $	Equipment $	Total $
2" x 1½"	P1@.500	Ea	40.80	17.30	—	58.10
3" x 1½"	P1@.520	Ea	60.40	18.00	—	78.40
3" x 2"	P1@.570	Ea	65.50	19.70	—	85.20
4" x 2"	P1@.580	Ea	90.60	20.00	—	110.60
4" x 3"	P1@.630	Ea	94.90	21.80	—	116.70

Schedule 40 DWV polypropylene wye with heat-fusioned joints

Description	Craft@Hrs	Unit	Material $	Labor $	Equipment $	Total $
1½"	P1@.500	Ea	26.20	17.30	—	43.50
2"	P1@.560	Ea	37.30	19.30	—	56.60
3"	P1@.630	Ea	65.50	21.80	—	87.30
4"	P1@.700	Ea	94.90	24.20	—	119.10
6"	P1@1.05	Ea	240.00	36.30	—	276.30

Polypropylene, Schedule 40, with Heat-Fusioned Joints

Description	Craft@Hrs	Unit	Material $	Labor $	Equipment $	Total $

Schedule 40 DWV polypropylene reducing wye with heat-fusioned joints

Description	Craft@Hrs	Unit	Material $	Labor $	Equipment $	Total $
2" x 1½"	P1@.510	Ea	36.50	17.60	—	54.10
3" x 2"	P1@.580	Ea	60.90	20.00	—	80.90
4" x 2"	P1@.600	Ea	87.80	20.70	—	108.50
4" x 3"	P1@.650	Ea	91.40	22.50	—	113.90
6" x 2"	P1@.900	Ea	154.00	31.10	—	185.10
6" x 3"	P1@.900	Ea	156.00	31.10	—	187.10
6" x 4"	P1@.950	Ea	157.00	32.80	—	189.80

Schedule 40 DWV polypropylene female adapter with heat-fusioned joints

Description	Craft@Hrs	Unit	Material $	Labor $	Equipment $	Total $
1½"	P1@.280	Ea	12.70	9.67	—	22.37
2"	P1@.330	Ea	17.20	11.40	—	28.60
3"	P1@.350	Ea	28.60	12.10	—	40.70
4"	P1@.400	Ea	54.80	13.80	—	68.60

Schedule 40 DWV polypropylene male adapter with heat-fusioned joints

Description	Craft@Hrs	Unit	Material $	Labor $	Equipment $	Total $
1½"	P1@.280	Ea	12.50	9.67	—	22.17
2"	P1@.330	Ea	15.20	11.40	—	26.60
3"	P1@.350	Ea	25.10	12.10	—	37.20
4"	P1@.400	Ea	52.00	13.80	—	65.80

Schedule 40 DWV polypropylene cleanout adapter with heat-fusioned joints

Description	Craft@Hrs	Unit	Material $	Labor $	Equipment $	Total $
1½"	P1@.210	Ea	13.30	7.26	—	20.56
2"	P1@.280	Ea	15.70	9.67	—	25.37
3"	P1@.430	Ea	29.20	14.90	—	44.10
4"	P1@.640	Ea	50.10	22.10	—	72.20
6"	P1@.850	Ea	86.40	29.40	—	115.80

Schedule 40 DWV polypropylene plug with heat-fusioned joints

Description	Craft@Hrs	Unit	Material $	Labor $	Equipment $	Total $
1½"	P1@.060	Ea	4.62	2.07	—	6.69
2"	P1@.065	Ea	5.04	2.25	—	7.29
3"	P1@.070	Ea	8.82	2.42	—	11.24
4"	P1@.090	Ea	9.90	3.11	—	13.01

Schedule 40 DWV polypropylene coupling with heat-fusioned joints

Description	Craft@Hrs	Unit	Material $	Labor $	Equipment $	Total $
1½"	P1@.350	Ea	16.20	12.10	—	28.30
2"	P1@.400	Ea	20.00	13.80	—	33.80
3"	P1@.450	Ea	25.60	15.50	—	41.10
4"	P1@.500	Ea	36.50	17.30	—	53.80
6"	P1@.750	Ea	58.20	25.90	—	84.10

Polypropylene, Schedule 40, with Heat-Fusioned Joints

Description	Craft@Hrs	Unit	Material $	Labor $	Equipment $	Total $

Schedule 40 DWV polypropylene reducer with heat-fusioned joints

Description	Craft@Hrs	Unit	Material $	Labor $	Equipment $	Total $
2" x 1½"	P1@.360	Ea	17.20	12.40	—	29.60
3" x 2"	P1@.410	Ea	19.70	14.20	—	33.90
4" x 2"	P1@.430	Ea	43.70	14.90	—	58.60
4" x 3"	P1@.450	Ea	44.90	15.50	—	60.40

Schedule 40 DWV polypropylene flange with heat-fusioned joints

Description	Craft@Hrs	Unit	Material $	Labor $	Equipment $	Total $
2"	P1@.350	Ea	56.30	12.10	—	68.40
3"	P1@.380	Ea	117.00	13.10	—	130.10
4"	P1@.430	Ea	152.00	14.90	—	166.90
6"	P1@.630	Ea	199.00	21.80	—	220.80

Schedule 40 DWV polypropylene bolt and gasket set

Description	Craft@Hrs	Unit	Material $	Labor $	Equipment $	Total $
2"	P1@.500	Ea	5.54	17.30	—	22.84
2½"	P1@.650	Ea	5.87	22.50	—	28.37
3"	P1@.750	Ea	6.16	25.90	—	32.06
4"	P1@1.00	Ea	11.20	34.60	—	45.80

Hanger with swivel assembly

Description	Craft@Hrs	Unit	Material $	Labor $	Equipment $	Total $
1½"	P1@.300	Ea	4.77	10.40	—	15.17
2"	P1@.300	Ea	4.98	10.40	—	15.38
3"	P1@.350	Ea	8.37	12.10	—	20.47
4"	P1@.350	Ea	9.19	12.10	—	21.29
6"	P1@.450	Ea	15.10	15.50	—	30.60

Riser clamp

Description	Craft@Hrs	Unit	Material $	Labor $	Equipment $	Total $
1½"	P1@.110	Ea	4.58	3.80	—	8.38
2"	P1@.115	Ea	4.84	3.97	—	8.81
3"	P1@.120	Ea	5.52	4.15	—	9.67
4"	P1@.125	Ea	7.03	4.32	—	11.35
6"	P1@.200	Ea	12.20	6.91	—	19.11

Pipe sleeve

Description	Craft@Hrs	Unit	Material $	Labor $	Equipment $	Total $
2"	P1@.130	Ea	7.14	4.49	—	11.63
2½"	P1@.150	Ea	7.25	5.18	—	12.43
3"	P1@.180	Ea	7.43	6.22	—	13.65
4"	P1@.220	Ea	8.44	7.60	—	16.04
5"	P1@.250	Ea	10.50	8.64	—	19.14
6"	P1@.270	Ea	11.30	9.33	—	20.63
8"	P1@.270	Ea	13.10	9.33	—	22.43

Lead roof pipe flashing

Description	Craft@Hrs	Unit	Material $	Labor $	Equipment $	Total $
1½"	P1@.250	Ea	33.30	8.64	—	41.94
2"	P1@.250	Ea	44.30	8.64	—	52.94
3"	P1@.250	Ea	50.80	8.64	—	59.44
4"	P1@.250	Ea	56.40	8.64	—	65.04

Floor, Area, Roof and Planter Drains

Description	Craft@Hrs	Unit	Material $	Labor $	Equipment $	Total $

Floor drain, cast iron or plastic body, nickel-bronze grate. Add for rough-in (P trap, fittings, hangers, etc.).

Description	Craft@Hrs	Unit	Material $	Labor $	Equipment $	Total $
3" x 2"	P1@.500	Ea	141.00	17.30	—	158.30
5" x 3"	P1@.500	Ea	176.00	17.30	—	193.30
6" x 4"	P1@.500	Ea	227.00	17.30	—	244.30
8" x 6"	P1@.500	Ea	302.00	17.30	—	319.30

Area drain, cast iron or plastic body, cast iron grate. Add for rough-in (P trap, fittings, hangers, etc.).

Description	Craft@Hrs	Unit	Material $	Labor $	Equipment $	Total $
10" x 3"	P1@.650	Ea	302.00	22.50	—	324.50
12" x 4"	P1@.650	Ea	329.00	22.50	—	351.50
14" x 6"	P1@.700	Ea	354.00	24.20	—	378.20

Roof and overflow drain, cast iron or plastic body, with plastic dome, flow control weir and deck clamp. Add for rough-in (pipe, fittings, hangers, etc.).

Description	Craft@Hrs	Unit	Material $	Labor $	Equipment $	Total $
8" x 3"	P1@1.50	Ea	404.00	51.80	—	455.80
10" x 4"	P1@1.50	Ea	427.00	51.80	—	478.80
12" x 6"	P1@1.65	Ea	427.00	57.00	—	484.00

Planter drain, cast iron. Add for rough-in (pipe, fittings, hangers, etc.).

Description	Craft@Hrs	Unit	Material $	Labor $	Equipment $	Total $
2"	P1@1.00	Ea	77.70	34.60	—	112.30
3"	P1@1.10	Ea	89.60	38.00	—	127.60
4"	P1@1.15	Ea	109.00	39.70	—	148.70
6"	P1@1.25	Ea	158.00	43.20	—	201.20

Planter drain, plastic. Add for rough-in (pipe, fittings, hangers, etc.).

Description	Craft@Hrs	Unit	Material $	Labor $	Equipment $	Total $
4"	P1@.800	Ea	23.70	27.60	—	51.30
5"	P1@1.00	Ea	25.10	34.60	—	59.70
6"	P1@1.05	Ea	41.20	36.30	—	77.50
8"	P1@1.10	Ea	62.90	38.00	—	100.90

Description	Craft@Hrs	Unit	Material $	Labor $	Equipment $	Total $

Cleanout, in-line, (Barrett) cast iron, (MJ) brass plug. Add for MJ couplings.

2"	P1@.350	Ea	66.00	12.10	—	78.10
3"	P1@.350	Ea	84.40	12.10	—	96.50
4"	P1@.400	Ea	119.00	13.80	—	132.80
6"	P1@.400	Ea	420.00	13.80	—	433.80

Cleanout, in-line, (Barrett) ABS/PVC

2"	P1@.300	Ea	18.40	10.40	—	28.80
3"	P1@.300	Ea	29.80	10.40	—	40.20
4"	P1@.350	Ea	54.00	12.10	—	66.10
6"	P1@.350	Ea	210.00	12.10	—	222.10
8"	P1@.400	Ea	407.00	13.80	—	420.80
10"	P1@.550	Ea	502.00	19.00	—	521.00

Cleanout, end of line (Malcolm), cast iron body, brass top. Add for MJ coupling.

2" raised	P1@.250	Ea	23.70	8.64	—	32.34
2" recessed	P1@.250	Ea	59.30	8.64	—	67.94
3" raised	P1@.250	Ea	27.70	8.64	—	36.34
3" recessed	P1@.300	Ea	86.90	10.40	—	97.30
4" raised	P1@.300	Ea	37.00	10.40	—	47.40
4" recessed	P1@.350	Ea	113.00	12.10	—	125.10
6" raised	P1@.350	Ea	117.00	12.10	—	129.10
6" recessed	P1@.400	Ea	216.00	13.80	—	229.80
8" raised	P1@.450	Ea	252.00	15.50	—	267.50

Cleanout, end-of-line (Malcolm), ABS/PVC

2"	P1@.250	Ea	9.82	8.64	—	18.46
3"	P1@.250	Ea	16.40	8.64	—	25.04
4"	P1@.300	Ea	29.80	10.40	—	40.20
6"	P1@.300	Ea	125.00	10.40	—	135.40
8"	P1@.400	Ea	225.00	13.80	—	238.80
10"	P1@.450	Ea	258.00	15.50	—	273.50
12"	P1@.550	Ea	302.00	19.00	—	321.00

Fire Protection Sprinklers

Description	Craft@Hrs	Unit	Material $	Labor $	Equipment $	Total $

Complete wet sprinkler system (square foot costs).

System includes subcontractors' overhead and profit. Cost includes design drawings, zone and supervision valves, sprinkler heads, pipe, and connection to water supply service. Make additional allowances if a fire pump is required. Costs are based on ordinary hazard coverage (110 sf per head). Coverage density can vary depending on room sizes and/or hazard rating. Use these costs for preliminary estimates.

Description		Unit	Material $	Labor $	Equipment $	Total $
Exposed piping to 5,000		SF	—	—	—	4.44
Exposed piping 5,000-15,000		SF	—	—	—	3.74
Exposed piping over 15,000		SF	—	—	—	3.33
Concealed piping to 5,000		SF	—	—	—	4.13
Concealed piping 5,000-15,000		SF	—	—	—	3.56
Concealed piping over 15,000		SF	—	—	—	2.79
Add for dry system		%	—	—	—	20.0

Complete wet sprinkler system (per head costs).

Cost includes sprinkler heads, sprinkler mains, branch piping, and supports. Make additional allowances for zone and supervision valves, alarms, connection to water service and fire pump when required. Costs are based on ordinary hazard 155 degree heads. Use these costs for preliminary estimates.

Description		Unit	Material $	Labor $	Equipment $	Total $
Upright heads to 5,000 SF		Ea	—	—	—	309.00
Upright heads 5,000 to 15,000 SF		Ea	—	—	—	295.00
Upright heads over 15,000 SF		Ea	—	—	—	280.00
Pendent heads to 5,000 SF		Ea	—	—	—	469.00
Pendent heads 5000 to 15,000 SF		Ea	—	—	—	390.00
Pendent heads over 15,000 SF		Ea	—	—	—	330.00

Supervision (zone) valves, flanged.

Add for alarm trim if required.

Description	Craft@Hrs	Unit	Material $	Labor $	Equipment $	Total $
2½" OS&Y gate valve	SL@1.70	Ea	298.00	58.30	—	356.30
3" OS&Y gate vlv	SL@1.80	Ea	315.00	61.80	—	376.80
4" OS&Y gate vlv	SL@2.20	Ea	363.00	75.50	—	438.50
6" OS&Y gate vlv	SL@2.80	Ea	558.00	96.10	—	654.10
8" OS&Y gate vlv	SL@3.50	Ea	888.00	120.00	—	1,008.00
2½" butterfly valve (lug)	SL@.600	Ea	453.00	20.60	—	473.60
3" butterfly vlv	SL@.700	Ea	457.00	24.00	—	481.00
4" butterfly vlv	SL@.850	Ea	468.00	29.20	—	497.20
6" butterfly vlv	SL@1.15	Ea	649.00	39.50	—	688.50
8" butterfly vlv	SL@1.85	Ea	968.00	63.50	—	1,031.50

Description	Craft@Hrs	Unit	Material $	Labor $	Equipment $	Total $

Supervision (zone) valves, grooved. Add for alarm trim if required

Description	Craft@Hrs	Unit	Material $	Labor $	Equipment $	Total $
4" butterfly valve	SL@.550	Ea	350.00	18.90	—	368.90
6" butterfly valve	SL@.850	Ea	455.00	29.20	—	484.20
8" butterfly valve	SL@1.25	Ea	687.00	42.90	—	729.90

Alarm valves (flanged or grooved)

Description	Craft@Hrs	Unit	Material $	Labor $	Equipment $	Total $
4" alarm valve	SL@3.50	Ea	478.00	120.00	—	598.00
6" alarm valve	SL@4.00	Ea	587.00	137.00	—	724.00
8" alarm valve	SL@4.75	Ea	856.00	163.00	—	1,019.00
4" alarm vlv trim	SL@1.25	Ea	321.00	42.90	—	363.90
6" alarm vlv trim	SL@1.25	Ea	321.00	42.90	—	363.90
8" alarm vlv trim	SL@1.25	Ea	321.00	42.90	—	363.90
4" alarm vlv pkg	SL@4.75	Ea	1,500.00	163.00	—	1,663.00
6" alarm vlv pkg	SL@5.50	Ea	1,660.00	189.00	—	1,849.00
8" alarm vlv pkg	SL@6.00	Ea	2,030.00	206.00	—	2,236.00

Dry valves and trim (deluge/pre-action system)

Description	Craft@Hrs	Unit	Material $	Labor $	Equipment $	Total $
2" dry valve	SL@2.25	Ea	894.00	77.20	—	971.20
3" dry valve	SL@2.75	Ea	925.00	94.40	—	1,019.40
4" dry valve	SL@3.05	Ea	1,050.00	105.00	—	1,155.00
6" dry valve	SL@3.65	Ea	1,340.00	125.00	—	1,465.00
2" dry valve trim	SL@1.25	Ea	436.00	42.90	—	478.90
3" dry valve trim	SL@1.25	Ea	436.00	42.90	—	478.90
4" dry valve trim	SL@1.25	Ea	436.00	42.90	—	478.90
6" dry valve trim	SL@1.25	Ea	436.00	42.90	—	478.90

Check valves, grooved

Description	Craft@Hrs	Unit	Material $	Labor $	Equipment $	Total $
2½"	SL@.450	Ea	173.00	15.40	—	188.40
3"	SL@.500	Ea	190.00	17.20	—	207.20
4"	SL@.550	Ea	171.00	18.90	—	189.90
6"	SL@.850	Ea	336.00	29.20	—	365.20

Check valves, wafer type, flanged

Description	Craft@Hrs	Unit	Material $	Labor $	Equipment $	Total $
2½"	SL@1.65	Ea	214.00	56.60	—	270.60
3"	SL@1.70	Ea	224.00	58.30	—	282.30
4"	SL@2.10	Ea	241.00	72.10	—	313.10
6"	SL@2.60	Ea	396.00	89.20	—	485.20
8"	SL@3.20	Ea	561.00	110.00	—	671.00

Double check detector valve assembly (flanged)

Description	Craft@Hrs	Unit	Material $	Labor $	Equipment $	Total $
2½"	SL@4.00	Ea	2,250.00	137.00	—	2,387.00
3"	SL@4.35	Ea	2,400.00	149.00	—	2,549.00
4"	SL@4.95	Ea	2,620.00	170.00	—	2,790.00
6"	SL@6.25	Ea	4,100.00	214.00	—	4,314.00
8"	SL@6.95	Ea	7,410.00	238.00	—	7,648.00

Fire Protection Sprinklers

Description	Craft@Hrs	Unit	Material $	Labor $	Equipment $	Total $
Switches, flow, supervisory, monitor, pressure						
Flow switch	SL@1.00	Ea	156.00	34.30	—	190.30
Pressure switch	SL@1.00	Ea	117.00	34.30	—	151.30
Monitor switch	SL@1.00	Ea	113.00	34.30	—	147.30
Supervisory sw.	SL@1.00	Ea	104.00	34.30	—	138.30
Sprinkler heads, 155 degree						
Pendent, brass	SL@.350	Ea	6.84	12.00	—	18.84
Pendent, chrome	SL@.350	Ea	7.32	12.00	—	19.32
Upright, brass	SL@.350	Ea	6.84	12.00	—	18.84
Upright, chrome	SL@.350	Ea	17.20	12.00	—	29.20
Sidewall, brass	SL@.350	Ea	8.88	12.00	—	20.88
Sidewall, chrome	SL@.350	Ea	9.51	12.00	—	21.51
Sprinkler heads, dry, 165 degree						
Dry pendent	SL@.450	Ea	68.20	15.40	—	83.60
Dry sidewall	SL@.450	Ea	95.80	15.40	—	111.20
Sprinkler heads, 200 degree						
Pendent, brass	SL@.350	Ea	6.84	12.00	—	18.84
Pendent, chrome	SL@.350	Ea	7.32	12.00	—	19.32
Upright, brass	SL@.350	Ea	6.84	12.00	—	18.84
Upright, chrome	SL@.350	Ea	17.20	12.00	—	29.20
Sidewall, brass	SL@.350	Ea	8.88	12.00	—	20.88
Sidewall, chrome	SL@.350	Ea	9.51	12.00	—	21.51
Sprinkler heads, 286 degree						
Pendent, brass	SL@.350	Ea	6.84	12.00	—	18.84
Pendent, chrome	SL@.350	Ea	7.32	12.00	—	19.32
Upright, brass	SL@.350	Ea	6.84	12.00	—	18.84
Upright, chrome	SL@.350	Ea	17.20	12.00	—	29.20
Sidewall, brass	SL@.350	Ea	8.88	12.00	—	20.88
Sidewall, chrome	SL@.350	Ea	9.51	12.00	—	21.51
Sprinkler heads, 360 degree						
Pendent, brass	SL@.350	Ea	4.60	12.00	—	16.60
Upright, brass	SL@.350	Ea	4.60	12.00	—	16.60
Sprinkler heads, 400 degree						
Pendent, brass	SL@.350	Ea	20.40	12.00	—	32.40
Upright, brass	SL@.350	Ea	20.40	12.00	—	32.40

Description	Craft@Hrs	Unit	Material $	Labor $	Equipment $	Total $

Fire hose cabinet complete assembly. Includes recessed steel cabinet, 2½" and 1½" angle valves, 100' fire hose, hose rack and fog nozzle.

Description	Craft@Hrs	Unit	Material $	Labor $	Equipment $	Total $
FHC, chrome trim	SL@1.95	Ea	411.00	66.90	—	477.90
FHC, brass trim	SL@1.95	Ea	401.00	66.90	—	467.90
FHC, plastic trim	SL@1.95	Ea	389.00	66.90	—	455.90

Fire hose cabinet components

Description	Craft@Hrs	Unit	Material $	Labor $	Equipment $	Total $
Recessed cabinet	SL@1.00	Ea	184.00	34.30	—	218.30
Surface cabinet	SL@.850	Ea	214.00	29.20	—	243.20
Cabinet glass	SL@.350	Ea	13.70	12.00	—	25.70
100' fire hose	SL@.250	Ea	174.00	8.58	—	182.58
75' hose rack	SL@.350	Ea	53.60	12.00	—	65.60
100' hose rack	SL@.350	Ea	72.60	12.00	—	84.60
1½" brass fire hose angle valve	SL@.350	Ea	83.30	12.00	—	95.30
1½" chrome fire hose angle valve	SL@.350	Ea	139.00	12.00	—	151.00
2½" brass fire hose angle valve	SL@.450	Ea	160.00	15.40	—	175.40
2½" chrome fire hose angle valve	SL@.450	Ea	63.10	15.40	—	78.50
Brass fog nozzle	SL@.150	Ea	64.90	5.15	—	70.05
Plastic fog nozzle	SL@.150	Ea	17.90	5.15	—	23.05
Chrome fog nozzle	SL@.150	Ea	66.60	5.15	—	71.75

Description	Unit	Material $	Labor $	Equipment $	Total $

Electric fire pump, skid mounted with controller and jockey pump

Description	Unit	Material $	Labor $	Equipment $	Total $
15 KW, 500 gpm	Ea	—	—	—	40,000.00
22 KW, 500 gpm	Ea	—	—	—	42,840.00
30 KW, 750 gpm	Ea	—	—	—	45,260.00
38 KW, 1000 gpm	Ea	—	—	—	50,190.00
56 KW, 1000 gpm	Ea	—	—	—	50,900.00

Diesel fire pump, skid mounted with controller and jockey pump

Description	Unit	Material $	Labor $	Equipment $	Total $
250 gpm	Ea	—	—	—	59,600.00
500 gpm	Ea	—	—	—	62,300.00
750 gpm	Ea	—	—	—	63,100.00
1,000 gpm	Ea	—	—	—	64,500.00

Description	Craft@Hrs	Unit	Material $	Labor $	Equipment $	Total $

Excess pressure pump

Description	Craft@Hrs	Unit	Material $	Labor $	Equipment $	Total $
1/4 hp	SL@1.35	Ea	443.00	46.30	—	489.30
1/3 hp	SL@1.35	Ea	458.00	46.30	—	504.30
1/2 hp	SL@1.50	Ea	476.00	51.50	—	527.50

Siamese connection, flush, fire dept. connection

Description	Craft@Hrs	Unit	Material $	Labor $	Equipment $	Total $
4" brass	SL@4.00	Ea	681.00	137.00	—	818.00
4" chrome	SL@4.00	Ea	734.00	137.00	—	871.00
6" brass	SL@4.50	Ea	791.00	154.00	—	945.00
6" chrome	SL@4.50	Ea	805.00	154.00	—	959.00

Siamese connection, surface, fire dept. connection

Description	Craft@Hrs	Unit	Material $	Labor $	Equipment $	Total $
4" brass	SL@2.85	Ea	161.00	97.80	—	258.80
6" brass	SL@3.25	Ea	305.00	112.00	—	417.00

Siamese connection, sidewalk, fire dept. connection

Description	Craft@Hrs	Unit	Material $	Labor $	Equipment $	Total $
4" brass	SL@3.25	Ea	616.00	112.00	—	728.00
6" brass	SL@3.75	Ea	870.00	129.00	—	999.00

Description	Craft@Hrs	Unit	Material $	Labor $	Equipment $	Total $

Water motor gong

Description	Craft@Hrs	Unit	Material $	Labor $	Equipment $	Total $
gong	SL@1.50	Ea	283.00	51.50	—	334.50

Multi-purpose fire extinguisher

Description	Craft@Hrs	Unit	Material $	Labor $	Equipment $	Total $
2 lb	SL@.500	Ea	33.60	17.20	—	50.80
5 lb	SL@.500	Ea	47.10	17.20	—	64.30
10 lb	SL@.500	Ea	67.20	17.20	—	84.40
20 lb	SL@.500	Ea	142.00	17.20	—	159.20

Fire hydrant with spool

Description	Craft@Hrs	Unit	Material $	Labor $	Equipment $	Total $
6"	P1@5.00	Ea	1,290.00	173.00	—	1,463.00

Indicator post

Description	Craft@Hrs	Unit	Material $	Labor $	Equipment $	Total $
6"	P1@6.50	Ea	748.00	225.00	—	973.00

Fire Protection Sprinkler Pipe and Fittings (Roll Grooved)

Description	Craft@Hrs	Unit	Material $	Labor $	Equipment $	Total $

Black steel pipe, (A53) installed horizontal, roll grooved, schedule 40.
Standard weight, including hangers every 10' and a fitting every 33'. Use these figures for preliminary estimates.

Description	Craft@Hrs	Unit	Material $	Labor $	Equipment $	Total $
2" (50mm)	SL@.160	LF	7.09	5.49	—	12.58
2½" (65mm)	SL@.180	LF	11.40	6.18	—	17.58
3" (75mm)	SL@.210	LF	14.60	7.21	—	21.81
4" (10cm)	SL@.300	LF	19.80	10.30	—	30.10
6" (15cm)	SK@.450	LF	41.00	16.50	4.20	61.70
8" (20cm)	SK@.630	LF	60.80	23.20	5.90	89.90
10" (25cm)	SK@.750	LF	118.00	27.60	7.10	152.70
12" (30cm)	SK@.800	LF	155.00	29.40	7.50	191.90

Black steel pipe, (A53) installed riser, roll grooved, schedule 40.
Standard weight, including a riser clamp every other floor and a tee at every floor. Make additional allowances for sleeving or coring as required. Use these figures for preliminary estimates.

Description	Craft@Hrs	Unit	Material $	Labor $	Equipment $	Total $
2" (50mm)	SL@.110	LF	7.32	3.77	—	11.09
2½" (65mm)	SL@.120	LF	11.80	4.12	—	15.92
3" (75mm)	SL@.150	LF	14.00	5.15	—	19.15
4" (10cm)	SL@.190	LF	20.10	6.52	—	26.62
6" (15cm)	SK@.300	LF	39.60	11.00	2.90	53.50
8" (20cm)	SK@.400	LF	61.60	14.70	3.80	80.10
10" (25cm)	SK@.510	LF	96.20	18.70	4.80	119.70
12" (30cm)	SK@.560	LF	139.00	20.60	5.30	164.90

Black steel pipe, (A53) installed horizontal, roll grooved, thin wall, schedule 10.
Light weight, including hangers every 10' and a fitting every 33'. Use these figures for preliminary estimates.

Description	Craft@Hrs	Unit	Material $	Labor $	Equipment $	Total $
2" (50mm)	SL@.160	LF	5.89	5.49	—	11.38
2½" (65mm)	SL@.180	LF	8.58	6.18	—	14.76
3" (75mm)	SL@.210	LF	10.10	7.21	—	17.31
4" (10cm)	SL@.300	LF	14.50	10.30	—	24.80
6" (15cm)	SK@.450	LF	29.10	16.50	4.20	49.80
8" (20cm)	SK@.630	LF	53.90	23.20	5.90	83.00

Black steel pipe, (A53) installed riser, roll grooved, thin wall, schedule 10.
Light weight, including a riser clamp every other floor and a tee at every floor. Make additional allowances for sleeving or coring as required. Use these figures for preliminary estimates.

Description	Craft@Hrs	Unit	Material $	Labor $	Equipment $	Total $
2" (50mm)	SL@.110	LF	6.63	3.77	—	10.40
2½" (65mm)	SL@.120	LF	9.58	4.12	—	13.70
3" (75mm)	SL@.150	LF	11.10	5.15	—	16.25
4" (10cm)	SL@.190	LF	15.60	6.52	—	22.12
6" (15cm)	SK@.300	LF	31.30	11.00	2.90	45.20
8" (20cm)	SK@.400	LF	60.80	14.70	3.80	79.30

Description	Craft@Hrs	Unit	Material $	Labor $	Equipment $	Total $

Black steel pipe only, (A53) roll grooved, schedule 40. Standard weight, no hangers or fittings.

Description	Craft@Hrs	Unit	Material $	Labor $	Equipment $	Total $
2" (50mm)	SL@.070	LF	3.14	2.40	—	5.54
2½" (65mm)	SL@.070	LF	6.69	2.40	—	9.09
3" (75mm)	SL@.090	LF	7.44	3.09	—	10.53
4" (10cm)	SL@.130	LF	10.60	4.46	—	15.06
6" (15cm)	SK@.160	LF	16.00	5.88	1.50	23.38
8" (20cm)	SK@.210	LF	24.20	7.72	2.00	33.92
10" (25cm)	SK@.280	LF	35.10	10.30	2.60	48.00
12" (30cm)	SK@.340	LF	59.40	12.50	3.20	75.10
14" (36cm)	SK@.400	LF	68.50	14.70	3.80	87.00
16" (41cm)	SK@.550	LF	79.40	20.20	5.20	104.80

Black steel pipe only, (A53) roll grooved, thin wall, schedule 10. Light weight, no hangers or fittings.

Description	Craft@Hrs	Unit	Material $	Labor $	Equipment $	Total $
2" (50mm)	SL@.070	LF	2.37	2.40	—	4.77
2½" (65mm)	SL@.070	LF	5.00	2.40	—	7.40
3" (75mm)	SL@.090	LF	5.55	3.09	—	8.64
4" (10cm)	SL@.130	LF	7.95	4.46	—	12.41
6" (15cm)	SK@.160	LF	12.00	5.88	1.50	19.38
8" (20cm)	SK@.210	LF	20.50	7.72	2.00	30.22
10" (25cm)	SK@.280	LF	29.80	10.30	2.60	42.70
12" (30cm)	SK@.340	LF	50.40	12.50	3.20	66.10
14" (36cm)	SK@.400	LF	58.30	14.70	3.80	76.80
16" (41cm)	SK@.550	LF	67.80	20.20	5.20	93.20

90 degree elbow, roll grooved, style #10, (Victaulic)

Description	Craft@Hrs	Unit	Material $	Labor $	Equipment $	Total $
2"	SL@.410	Ea	29.60	14.10	—	43.70
2½"	SL@.430	Ea	29.60	14.80	—	44.40
3"	SL@.500	Ea	39.20	17.20	—	56.40
4"	SL@.690	Ea	61.10	23.70	—	84.80
6"	SL@1.19	Ea	152.00	40.80	—	192.80
8"	SL@1.69	Ea	260.00	58.00	—	318.00
10"	SL@2.23	Ea	501.00	76.50	—	577.50
12"	SL@2.48	Ea	793.00	85.10	—	878.10

45 degree elbow, roll grooved, style #11, (Victaulic)

Description	Craft@Hrs	Unit	Material $	Labor $	Equipment $	Total $
2"	SL@.410	Ea	29.60	14.10	—	43.70
2½"	SL@.430	Ea	29.60	14.80	—	44.40
3"	SL@.500	Ea	39.20	17.20	—	56.40
4"	SL@.690	Ea	61.10	23.70	—	84.80
6"	SL@1.19	Ea	152.00	40.80	—	192.80
8"	SL@1.69	Ea	260.00	58.00	—	318.00
10"	SL@2.23	Ea	501.00	76.50	—	577.50
12"	SL@2.48	Ea	793.00	85.10	—	878.10

Fire Protection Sprinkler Pipe and Fittings (Roll Grooved)

Description	Craft@Hrs	Unit	Material $	Labor $	Equipment $	Total $
22-1/2 degree elbow, roll grooved, style #12, (Victaulic)						
2"	SL@.410	Ea	35.30	14.10	—	49.40
2½"	SL@.430	Ea	35.30	14.80	—	50.10
3"	SL@.500	Ea	37.00	17.20	—	54.20
4"	SL@.690	Ea	69.60	23.70	—	93.30
6"	SL@1.19	Ea	174.00	40.80	—	214.80
8"	SL@1.69	Ea	358.00	58.00	—	416.00
10"	SL@2.23	Ea	504.00	76.50	—	580.50
12"	SL@2.48	Ea	541.00	85.10	—	626.10
Tee, roll grooved, style #20, (Victaulic)						
2"	SL@.510	Ea	57.30	17.50	—	74.80
2½"	SL@.540	Ea	57.30	18.50	—	75.80
3"	SL@.630	Ea	69.00	21.60	—	90.60
4"	SL@.860	Ea	96.70	29.50	—	126.20
6"	SL@1.49	Ea	257.00	51.10	—	308.10
8"	SL@2.11	Ea	432.00	72.40	—	504.40
10"	SL@2.79	Ea	765.00	95.70	—	860.70
12"	SL@3.10	Ea	895.00	106.00	—	1,001.00
Reducing tee, roll grooved, style #25, (Victaulic)						
2"	SL@.510	Ea	57.30	17.50	—	74.80
2½"	SL@.540	Ea	75.30	18.50	—	93.80
3"	SL@.630	Ea	68.00	21.60	—	89.60
4"	SL@.860	Ea	117.00	29.50	—	146.50
6"	SL@1.49	Ea	247.00	51.10	—	298.10
8"	SL@2.11	Ea	449.00	72.40	—	521.40
10"	SL@2.79	Ea	594.00	95.70	—	689.70
12"	SL@3.10	Ea	656.00	106.00	—	762.00
Reducer, roll grooved, style #50, (Victaulic)						
2"	SL@.410	Ea	19.00	14.10	—	33.10
2½"	SL@.430	Ea	19.00	14.80	—	33.80
3"	SL@.500	Ea	26.60	17.20	—	43.80
4"	SL@.690	Ea	44.40	23.70	—	68.10
6"	SL@1.19	Ea	74.20	40.80	—	115.00
8"	SL@1.69	Ea	131.00	58.00	—	189.00
10"	SL@2.23	Ea	273.00	76.50	—	349.50
Cap, roll grooved, style #60, (Victaulic)						
2"	SL@.270	Ea	16.70	9.26	—	25.96
2½"	SL@.280	Ea	16.70	9.61	—	26.31
3"	SL@.330	Ea	21.00	11.30	—	32.30
4"	SL@.450	Ea	24.40	15.40	—	39.80
6"	SL@.770	Ea	54.60	26.40	—	81.00
8"	SL@1.10	Ea	88.10	37.70	—	125.80
10"	SL@1.61	Ea	377.00	55.20	—	432.20

Description	Craft@Hrs	Unit	Material $	Labor $	Equipment $	Total $

Mechanical tee (saddle tee), roll grooved, style #920, (Victaulic)

Description	Craft@Hrs	Unit	Material $	Labor $	Equipment $	Total $
3"	SL@.750	Ea	57.80	25.70	—	83.50
4"	SL@1.00	Ea	65.60	34.30	—	99.90
6"	SL@1.30	Ea	89.80	44.60	—	134.40
8"	SL@1.50	Ea	142.00	51.50	—	193.50

Coupling, roll grooved, 800 PSI, style #77, (Victaulic). Labor included with fittings.

Description	Craft@Hrs	Unit	Material $	Labor $	Equipment $	Total $
3"	SL@.000	Ea	29.10	—	—	29.10
4"	SL@.000	Ea	48.40	—	—	48.40
6"	SL@.000	Ea	83.80	—	—	83.80
8"	SL@.000	Ea	125.00	—	—	125.00
10"	SL@.000	Ea	167.00	—	—	167.00
12"	SL@.000	Ea	223.00	—	—	223.00

Coupling, roll grooved, light weight, style #75, (Victaulic). Labor included with fittings.

Description	Craft@Hrs	Unit	Material $	Labor $	Equipment $	Total $
3"	SL@.000	Ea	23.60	—	—	23.60
4"	SL@.000	Ea	25.50	—	—	25.50
6"	SL@.000	Ea	52.30	—	—	52.30
8"	SL@.000	Ea	80.20	—	—	80.20

Coupling, roll grooved, zeroflex, style #07, (Victaulic). Labor included with fittings.

Description	Craft@Hrs	Unit	Material $	Labor $	Equipment $	Total $
3"	SL@.000	Ea	27.30	—	—	27.30
4"	SL@.000	Ea	35.80	—	—	35.80
6"	SL@.000	Ea	60.50	—	—	60.50
8"	SL@.000	Ea	92.20	—	—	92.20
10"	SL@.000	Ea	135.00	—	—	135.00
12"	SL@.000	Ea	186.00	—	—	186.00

Flange, roll grooved, style #741, (Victaulic)

Description	Craft@Hrs	Unit	Material $	Labor $	Equipment $	Total $
3"	SL@.500	Ea	88.60	17.20	—	105.80
4"	SL@.690	Ea	125.00	23.70	—	148.70
6"	SL@1.19	Ea	175.00	40.80	—	215.80
8"	SL@1.69	Ea	203.00	58.00	—	261.00
10"	SL@2.23	Ea	302.00	76.50	—	378.50
12"	SL@2.48	Ea	411.00	85.10	—	496.10

Fire Protection Branch Pipe & Fittings

Description	Craft@Hrs	Unit	Material $	Labor $	Equipment $	Total $

Schedule 40 carbon steel pipe, threaded and coupled, pipe only. Add for hangers, fittings etc.

Description	Craft@Hrs	Unit	Material $	Labor $	Equipment $	Total $
1"	P1@.090	LF	2.60	3.11	—	5.71
1¼"	P1@.100	LF	3.39	3.46	—	6.85
1½"	P1@.110	LF	4.04	3.80	—	7.84
2"	P1@.120	LF	5.46	4.15	—	9.61

125# cast iron 90 degree ell, threaded joints

Description	Craft@Hrs	Unit	Material $	Labor $	Equipment $	Total $
1" x 3/4"	P1@.130	Ea	4.47	4.49	—	8.96
1"	P1@.180	Ea	4.15	6.22	—	10.37
1¼"	P1@.240	Ea	5.85	8.29	—	14.14
1½"	P1@.300	Ea	8.17	10.40	—	18.57
2"	P1@.380	Ea	12.40	13.10	—	25.50

125# cast iron 45 degree ell, threaded joints

Description	Craft@Hrs	Unit	Material $	Labor $	Equipment $	Total $
1"	P1@.180	Ea	5.44	6.22	—	11.66
1¼"	P1@.240	Ea	7.74	8.29	—	16.03
1½"	P1@.300	Ea	9.96	10.40	—	20.36
2"	P1@.380	Ea	13.50	13.10	—	26.60

125# cast iron tee, threaded joints

Description	Craft@Hrs	Unit	Material $	Labor $	Equipment $	Total $
1"	P1@.230	Ea	5.70	7.95	—	13.65
1¼"	P1@.310	Ea	10.40	10.70	—	21.10
1½"	P1@.390	Ea	13.20	13.50	—	26.70
2"	P1@.490	Ea	18.30	16.90	—	35.20

125# cast iron reducing tee, threaded joints

Description	Craft@Hrs	Unit	Material $	Labor $	Equipment $	Total $
1" x 3/4"	P1@.220	Ea	7.29	7.60	—	14.89
1¼" x 3/4"	P1@.290	Ea	9.28	10.00	—	19.28
1¼" x 1"	P1@.290	Ea	10.20	10.00	—	20.20
1½" x 3/4"	P1@.370	Ea	12.80	12.80	—	25.60
1½" x 1"	P1@.370	Ea	14.10	12.80	—	26.90
1½" x 1¼"	P1@.370	Ea	15.50	12.80	—	28.30
2" x 1"	P1@.460	Ea	20.30	15.90	—	36.20
2" x 1¼"	P1@.460	Ea	21.60	15.90	—	37.50
2" x 1½"	P1@.460	Ea	23.30	15.90	—	39.20

125# cast iron reducer, threaded joints

Description	Craft@Hrs	Unit	Material $	Labor $	Equipment $	Total $
1" x 3/4"	P1@.200	Ea	5.70	6.91	—	12.61
1¼" x 1"	P1@.210	Ea	6.86	7.26	—	14.12
1½" x 1"	P1@.270	Ea	8.43	9.33	—	17.76
1½" x 1¼"	P1@.270	Ea	8.91	9.33	—	18.24
2" x 1¼"	P1@.340	Ea	13.30	11.70	—	25.00
2" x 1½"	P1@.340	Ea	14.00	11.70	—	25.70

Description	Craft@Hrs	Unit	Material $	Labor $	Equipment $	Total $

125# cast iron cross, threaded joints

Description	Craft@Hrs	Unit	Material $	Labor $	Equipment $	Total $
1"	P1@.360	Ea	13.30	12.40	—	25.70
1¼"	P1@.480	Ea	21.90	16.60	—	38.50
1½"	P1@.600	Ea	26.60	20.70	—	47.30
2"	P1@.700	Ea	44.10	24.20	—	68.30

125# cast iron cap, threaded joint

Description	Craft@Hrs	Unit	Material $	Labor $	Equipment $	Total $
3/4"	P1@.100	Ea	2.81	3.46	—	6.27
1"	P1@.140	Ea	3.40	4.84	—	8.24
1¼"	P1@.180	Ea	4.34	6.22	—	10.56
1½"	P1@.230	Ea	5.51	7.95	—	13.46
2"	P1@.290	Ea	8.64	10.00	—	18.64

125# cast iron plug, threaded joint

Description	Craft@Hrs	Unit	Material $	Labor $	Equipment $	Total $
3/4"	P1@.100	Ea	1.84	3.46	—	5.30
1"	P1@.140	Ea	2.42	4.84	—	7.26
1¼"	P1@.180	Ea	3.77	6.22	—	9.99
1½"	P1@.230	Ea	4.79	7.95	—	12.74
2"	P1@.290	Ea	5.92	10.00	—	15.92

125# cast iron coupling, threaded joints

Description	Craft@Hrs	Unit	Material $	Labor $	Equipment $	Total $
1"	P1@.180	Ea	4.95	6.22	—	11.17
1¼"	P1@.240	Ea	6.10	8.29	—	14.39
1½"	P1@.300	Ea	7.67	10.40	—	18.07
2"	P1@.380	Ea	10.40	13.10	—	23.50

Fire Protection Sprinkler Branch Fittings (Threaded)

Description	Craft@Hrs	Unit	Material $	Labor $	Equipment $	Total $

Steel pipe nipples — 3" long, standard right hand thread

Description	Craft@Hrs	Unit	Material $	Labor $	Equipment $	Total $
1"	P1@.025	Ea	1.91	.86	—	2.77
1¼"	P1@.025	Ea	2.47	.86	—	3.33
1½"	P1@.025	Ea	2.92	.86	—	3.78
2"	P1@.030	Ea	3.64	1.04	—	4.68

Steel pipe nipples — 4" long, standard right hand thread

Description	Craft@Hrs	Unit	Material $	Labor $	Equipment $	Total $
1"	P1@.025	Ea	2.28	.86	—	3.14
1¼"	P1@.030	Ea	2.85	1.04	—	3.89
1½"	P1@.030	Ea	3.53	1.04	—	4.57
2"	P1@.030	Ea	4.54	1.04	—	5.58

Steel pipe nipples — 6" long, standard right hand thread

Description	Craft@Hrs	Unit	Material $	Labor $	Equipment $	Total $
1"	P1@.030	Ea	2.92	1.04	—	3.96
1¼"	P1@.030	Ea	3.66	1.04	—	4.70
1½"	P1@.030	Ea	4.47	1.04	—	5.51
2"	P1@.035	Ea	6.00	1.21	—	7.21

Description	Craft@Hrs	Unit	Material $	Labor $	Equipment $	Total $

Chlorinated Polyvinyl Chloride pipe (CPVC), CPVC pipe only, solvent weld. No hangers or fittings.

Description	Craft@Hrs	Unit	Material $	Labor $	Equipment $	Total $
3/4"	SL@.055	LF	1.02	1.89	—	2.91
1"	SL@.055	LF	1.48	1.89	—	3.37
1¼"	SL@.065	LF	2.34	2.23	—	4.57
1½"	SL@.075	LF	3.26	2.57	—	5.83
2"	SL@.085	LF	4.84	2.92	—	7.76
2½"	SL@.110	LF	7.49	3.77	—	11.26
3"	SL@.125	LF	11.40	4.29	—	15.69

CPVC 90 degree elbow, solvent weld

Description	Craft@Hrs	Unit	Material $	Labor $	Equipment $	Total $
3/4"	SL@.100	Ea	2.32	3.43	—	5.75
1"	SL@.120	Ea	3.49	4.12	—	7.61
1¼"	SL@.170	Ea	4.46	5.83	—	10.29
1½"	SL@.180	Ea	6.72	6.18	—	12.90
2"	SL@.200	Ea	7.81	6.86	—	14.67

CPVC 45 degree elbow, solvent weld

Description	Craft@Hrs	Unit	Material $	Labor $	Equipment $	Total $
3/4"	SL@.100	Ea	2.40	3.43	—	5.83
1"	SL@.120	Ea	3.13	4.12	—	7.25
1¼"	SL@.170	Ea	4.12	5.83	—	9.95
1½"	SL@.180	Ea	5.55	6.18	—	11.73
2"	SL@.200	Ea	6.91	6.86	—	13.77

CPVC tee, solvent weld

Description	Craft@Hrs	Unit	Material $	Labor $	Equipment $	Total $
3/4"	SL@.150	Ea	2.55	5.15	—	7.70
1"	SL@.170	Ea	4.36	5.83	—	10.19
1¼"	SL@.230	Ea	6.86	7.89	—	14.75
1½"	SL@.250	Ea	9.08	8.58	—	17.66
2"	SL@.280	Ea	14.10	9.61	—	23.71

CPVC reducing tee, solvent weld

Description	Craft@Hrs	Unit	Material $	Labor $	Equipment $	Total $
1"	SL@.170	Ea	3.74	5.83	—	9.57
1¼"	SL@.230	Ea	6.81	7.89	—	14.70
1½"	SL@.250	Ea	9.09	8.58	—	17.67
2"	SL@.280	Ea	14.50	9.61	—	24.11
3"	SL@.350	Ea	22.90	12.00	—	34.90

CPVC coupling, solvent weld

Description	Craft@Hrs	Unit	Material $	Labor $	Equipment $	Total $
3/4"	SL@.100	Ea	1.69	3.43	—	5.12
1"	SL@.120	Ea	2.27	4.12	—	6.39
1¼"	SL@.170	Ea	3.60	5.83	—	9.43
1½"	SL@.180	Ea	4.55	6.18	—	10.73
2"	SL@.200	Ea	5.72	6.86	—	12.58
3"	SL@.280	Ea	11.70	9.61	—	21.31

Fire Protection Sprinkler Fittings (CPVC)

Description	Craft@Hrs	Unit	Material $	Labor $	Equipment $	Total $

CPVC head adapter, solvent weld

Description	Craft@Hrs	Unit	Material $	Labor $	Equipment $	Total $
3/4" x 1/2"	SL@.150	Ea	3.80	5.15	—	8.95
1" x 1/2"	SL@.165	Ea	4.06	5.66	—	9.72

CPVC cap, solvent weld

Description	Craft@Hrs	Unit	Material $	Labor $	Equipment $	Total $
3/4"	SL@.060	Ea	1.25	2.06	—	3.31
1"	SL@.065	Ea	1.74	2.23	—	3.97
1¼"	SL@.075	Ea	2.98	2.57	—	5.55
1½"	SL@.085	Ea	3.83	2.92	—	6.75
2"	SL@.095	Ea	4.45	3.26	—	7.71

CPVC flange, solvent weld

Description	Craft@Hrs	Unit	Material $	Labor $	Equipment $	Total $
1"	SL@.165	Ea	4.45	5.66	—	10.11
1¼"	SL@.175	Ea	5.72	6.00	—	11.72
1½"	SL@.185	Ea	8.86	6.35	—	15.21
2"	SL@.200	Ea	13.40	6.86	—	20.26
3"	SL@.225	Ea	22.20	7.72	—	29.92

CPVC female adapter, solvent weld

Description	Craft@Hrs	Unit	Material $	Labor $	Equipment $	Total $
1"	SL@.065	Ea	11.00	2.23	—	13.23
1¼"	SL@.075	Ea	18.20	2.57	—	20.77
1½"	SL@.085	Ea	23.50	2.92	—	26.42
2"	SL@.095	Ea	30.30	3.26	—	33.56

Boilers for industrial, commercial and institutional applications. ASME "H" or "U" stamped, LFUE (Levelized Fuel Utilization Efficiency) certified 90% or better. U.S. Green Building council certified. Cleaver-Brooks or equal. Shipped factory assembled and skid mounted. Includes the boiler shell and structure, I-beam skids, combustion chamber, fire tubes, crown sheet, tube sheets (for fire tube), water tubes, mud drum(s), steam drum (for water tube boiler), finned water tubes and check valves (for hot water generators), refractory brick lining, explosion doors, combustion air inlets and stack outlet. Add the cost of the fuel train piping, electrical wiring, refractory, stack, feedwater system, combustion controls, water treatment, expansion tanks (if hot water) or condensate return (if steam) and system start-up. See the sections following packaged boilers. Costs are based on boiler horsepower rating (BHP). Add the cost of commissioning, insurance inspection, permit, permit inspection, hydraulic test, calibration and lockout sealing of emissions monitor, and final run test. Equipment cost assumes a 10-ton hydraulic truck-mounted crane (at $110 per hour). LEED (Leadership in Energy & Environmental Design) certification requires 88% boiler efficiency, recording controls, compliance with SCAQMD 1146.2 emission standards and zone recording thermostats. A LEED certified boiler with a U.S. Green Building Council rating will add 4% to 15% to the cost of the boiler, as identified in the cost tables that follow.

Description	Craft@Hrs	Unit	Material $	Labor $	Equipment $	Total $

Hot water or steam cast iron gas boiler, 30 PSIG. Costs shown are based on boiler horsepower rating (BHP). On site assembly. Includes allowances for associated appurtenances and pipe connections.

Description	Craft@Hrs	Unit	Material $	Labor $	Equipment $	Total $
4.5 BHP	SN@8.50	Ea	4,430.00	311.00	134.00	4,875.00
5.9 BHP	SN@9.50	Ea	5,530.00	348.00	149.00	6,027.00
9.0 BHP	SN@10.0	Ea	8,240.00	366.00	157.00	8,763.00
15.0 BHP	SN@12.0	Ea	12,800.00	439.00	189.00	13,428.00
20.0 BHP	SN@14.0	Ea	17,000.00	512.00	220.00	17,732.00
30.0 BHP	SN@16.0	Ea	21,900.00	585.00	251.00	22,736.00
45.0 BHP	SN@18.0	Ea	31,800.00	658.00	283.00	32,741.00
60.0 BHP	SN@20.0	Ea	41,300.00	732.00	314.00	42,346.00
Add for LEED certified boiler		Ea	6%	—	—	—
Add for LEED inspection		Ea	—	—	—	2,000.00
Add for central monitor/ recorder		Ea	1,530.00	—	—	1,530.00
Add for recording Thermostat		Ea	357.00	—	—	357.00

Commercial Boilers

Description	Craft@Hrs	Unit	Material $	Labor $	Equipment $	Total $

Hot water Scotch marine firetube gas boiler, 30 PSIG. Costs shown are based on boiler horsepower rating (BHP) Set in place only. Make additional allowances for associated appurtenances and pipe connections.

Description	Craft@Hrs	Unit	Material $	Labor $	Equipment $	Total $
30 BHP	SN@10.0	Ea	31,600.00	366.00	157.00	32,123.00
40 BHP	SN@10.0	Ea	33,600.00	366.00	157.00	34,123.00
50 BHP	SN@10.0	Ea	34,800.00	366.00	157.00	35,323.00
60 BHP	SN@12.0	Ea	38,900.00	439.00	189.00	39,528.00
70 BHP	SN@12.0	Ea	41,900.00	439.00	189.00	42,528.00
80 BHP	SN@14.0	Ea	44,600.00	512.00	220.00	45,332.00
100 BHP	SN@14.0	Ea	53,200.00	512.00	220.00	53,932.00
125 BHP	SN@16.0	Ea	57,100.00	585.00	251.00	57,936.00
150 BHP	SN@18.0	Ea	61,100.00	658.00	283.00	62,041.00
200 BHP	SN@18.0	Ea	72,100.00	658.00	283.00	73,041.00
250 BHP	SN@26.0	Ea	79,400.00	951.00	409.00	80,760.00
300 BHP	SN@26.0	Ea	85,300.00	951.00	409.00	86,660.00
350 BHP	SN@26.0	Ea	96,800.00	951.00	409.00	98,160.00
400 BHP	SN@32.0	Ea	99,500.00	1,170.00	503.00	101,173.00
500 BHP	SN@32.0	Ea	118,000.00	1,170.00	503.00	119,673.00
600 BHP	SN@32.0	Ea	134,000.00	1,170.00	503.00	135,673.00
750 BHP	SN@40.0	Ea	140,000.00	1,460.00	629.00	142,089.00
Add for LEED certified boiler		Ea	4%	—	—	—
Add for LEED inspection		Ea	—	—	—	2,000.00
Add for central monitor/ recorder		Ea	3,570.00	—	—	3,570.00
Add for recording Thermostat		Ea	357.00	—	—	357.00

Description	Craft@Hrs	Unit	Material $	Labor $	Equipment $	Total $

Packaged Scotch marine firetube oil or gas fired boiler, 150 PSIG.
Costs shown are based on boiler horsepower rating (BHP). Set in place only.
Make additional allowances for associated appurtenances and pipe connections.

Description	Craft@Hrs	Unit	Material $	Labor $	Equipment $	Total $
60 BHP	SN@12.0	Ea	44,600.00	439.00	189.00	45,228.00
70 BHP	SN@12.0	Ea	48,000.00	439.00	189.00	48,628.00
80 BHP	SN@14.0	Ea	51,500.00	512.00	220.00	52,232.00
100 BHP	SN@14.0	Ea	61,600.00	512.00	220.00	62,332.00
125 BHP	SN@16.0	Ea	65,300.00	585.00	251.00	66,136.00
150 BHP	SN@18.0	Ea	69,900.00	658.00	283.00	70,841.00
200 BHP	SN@18.0	Ea	91,900.00	658.00	283.00	92,841.00
250 BHP	SN@26.0	Ea	98,200.00	951.00	409.00	99,560.00
300 BHP	SN@26.0	Ea	111,000.00	951.00	409.00	112,360.00
350 BHP	SN@26.0	Ea	114,000.00	951.00	409.00	115,360.00
400 BHP	SN@32.0	Ea	137,000.00	1,170.00	503.00	138,673.00
500 BHP	SN@32.0	Ea	152,000.00	1,170.00	503.00	153,673.00
600 BHP	SN@32.0	Ea	156,000.00	1,170.00	503.00	157,673.00
700 BHP	SN@40.0	Ea	161,000.00	1,460.00	629.00	163,089.00
Add for LEED certified boiler		Ea	4%	—	—	—
Add for LEED inspection		Ea	—	—	—	2,000.00
Add for central monitor/ recorder		Ea	3,570.00	—	—	3,570.00
Add for recording Thermostat		Ea	357.00	—	—	357.00

Packaged hot water firebox oil or gas fired boiler.
Costs shown are based on boiler horsepower rating (BHP). Set in place only. Make additional allowances for associated appurtenances and pipe connections.

Description	Craft@Hrs	Unit	Material $	Labor $	Equipment $	Total $
13 BHP	SN@8.00	Ea	16,700.00	293.00	129.00	17,122.00
16 BHP	SN@8.00	Ea	17,000.00	293.00	129.00	17,422.00
19 BHP	SN@8.00	Ea	17,500.00	293.00	129.00	17,922.00
22 BHP	SN@8.00	Ea	18,000.00	293.00	129.00	18,422.00
28 BHP	SN@8.00	Ea	19,000.00	293.00	129.00	19,422.00
34 BHP	SN@8.00	Ea	21,600.00	293.00	129.00	22,022.00
40 BHP	SN@8.00	Ea	23,900.00	293.00	129.00	24,322.00
46 BHP	SN@8.00	Ea	27,300.00	293.00	129.00	27,722.00
52 BHP	SN@8.00	Ea	31,900.00	293.00	129.00	32,322.00
61 BHP	SN@8.00	Ea	35,100.00	293.00	129.00	35,522.00
70 BHP	SN@8.00	Ea	37,600.00	293.00	129.00	38,022.00
80 BHP	SN@8.00	Ea	38,900.00	293.00	129.00	39,322.00
100 BHP	SN@8.00	Ea	43,800.00	293.00	129.00	44,222.00
125 BHP	SN@16.0	Ea	52,100.00	585.00	256.00	52,941.00
150 BHP	SN@16.0	Ea	56,000.00	585.00	256.00	56,841.00
Add for LEED certified boiler		Ea	4%	—	—	—
Add for LEED inspection		Ea	—	—	—	2,000.00
Add for central monitor/ recorder		Ea	2,550.00	—	—	2,550.00
Add for recording Thermostat		Ea	357.00	—	—	357.00

Commercial Boilers

Description	Craft@Hrs	Unit	Material $	Labor $	Equipment $	Total $

Packaged watertube industrial high pressure boilers. Costs shown are based on boiler horsepower rating (BHP). Set in place only. Make additional allowances for associated appurtenances and pipe connections.

Description	Craft@Hrs	Unit	Material $	Labor $	Equipment $	Total $
480 BHP	SN@32.0	Ea	316,000.00	1,170.00	504.00	317,674.00
526 BHP	SN@32.0	Ea	324,000.00	1,170.00	504.00	325,674.00
572 BHP	SN@32.0	Ea	342,000.00	1,170.00	504.00	343,674.00
618 BHP	SN@32.0	Ea	347,000.00	1,170.00	504.00	348,674.00
664 BHP	SN@32.0	Ea	364,000.00	1,170.00	504.00	365,674.00
710 BHP	SN@64.0	Ea	369,000.00	2,340.00	1,010.00	372,350.00
747 BHP	SN@64.0	Ea	374,000.00	2,340.00	1,010.00	377,350.00
792 BHP	SN@64.0	Ea	387,000.00	2,340.00	1,010.00	390,350.00
838 BHP	SN@64.0	Ea	398,000.00	2,340.00	1,010.00	401,350.00
884 BHP	SN@64.0	Ea	409,000.00	2,340.00	1,010.00	412,350.00
930 BHP	SN@64.0	Ea	415,000.00	2,340.00	1,010.00	418,350.00
1,000 BHP	SN@64.0	Ea	422,000.00	2,340.00	1,010.00	425,350.00
Add for LEED certified boiler		Ea	4%	—	—	—
Add for LEED inspection		Ea	—	—	—	2,000.00
Add for central monitor/ recorder		Ea	4,390.00	—	—	4,390.00
Add for recording Thermostat		Ea	357.00	—	—	357.00

Gas fired hot water steel boilers, 12 PSIG Mid-efficiency (82%) atmospheric draft, standing pilot light, c/w primary loop circulating pump. Labor includes setting in place and connecting pump and controls. Make additional allowances for distribution piping connections, safety devices, flue, gas connections, wiring, etc.

Description	Craft@Hrs	Unit	Material $	Labor $	Equipment $	Total $
50,000 Btu	P1@4.00	Ea	1,200.00	138.00	504.00	1,842.00
70,000 Btu	P1@4.25	Ea	1,380.00	147.00	504.00	2,031.00
105,000 Btu	P1@4.50	Ea	1,520.00	155.00	504.00	2,179.00
140,000 Btu	P1@4.75	Ea	1,730.00	164.00	504.00	2,398.00
175,000 Btu	P1@5.00	Ea	1,940.00	173.00	504.00	2,617.00
210,000 Btu	P1@5.50	Ea	2,450.00	190.00	1,010.00	3,650.00
245,000 Btu	P1@7.00	Ea	2,730.00	242.00	1,010.00	3,982.00
Electronic spark ignition Add		Ea	270.00			270.00
Add for LEED certified boiler		Ea	15%	—	—	—
Add for LEED inspection		Ea	—	—	—	2,000.00
Add for central monitor/ recorder		Ea	1,120.00	—	—	1,120.00
Add for recording Thermostat		Ea	153.00	—	—	153.00

Description	Craft@Hrs	Unit	Material $	Labor $	Equipment $	Total $

Gas fired hot water cast iron boilers, 12 PSIG Mid-efficiency (82%) direct vent, forced draft electronic spark ignition, c/w primary loop circulating pump. Labor includes setting in place and connecting pump and controls. Make additional allowances for distribution piping connections, safety devices, flue, gas connections, wiring, etc.

Description	Craft@Hrs	Unit	Material $	Labor $	Equipment $	Total $
50,000 Btu	P1@4.00	Ea	1,510.00	138.00	504.00	2,152.00
65,000 Btu	P1@4.25	Ea	1,680.00	147.00	504.00	2,331.00
100,000 Btu	P1@4.50	Ea	1,840.00	155.00	504.00	2,499.00
130,000 Btu	P1@4.75	Ea	2,040.00	164.00	504.00	2,708.00
170,000 Btu	P1@5.00	Ea	2,350.00	173.00	504.00	3,027.00
200,000 Btu	P1@5.50	Ea	2,600.00	190.00	1,010.00	3,800.00
235,000 Btu	P1@7.00	Ea	2,860.00	242.00	1,010.00	4,112.00
Add for LEED certified boiler		Ea	15%	—	—	—
Add for LEED inspection		Ea	—	—	—	2,000.00
Add for central monitor/ recorder		Ea	1,120.00	—	—	1,120.00
Add for recording Thermostat		Ea	153.00	—	—	153.00

Description	Craft@Hrs	Unit	Material $	Labor $	Total $

Steam heating boilers for residential and light commercial applications. Parker or equal 15 PSIG Spiral watertube type, with ASTM SA-53 grade tubing, full American Society of Mechanical Engineers "M", "H" and "S" ratings and Underwriters Laboratories certifications. Specifically designed for "twinning" and multiple unit additions and retrofits. Packaged type units with ASME rated pressure relief valve, low water cutoff valve, main and check valves, pressure gauge, and pre-wired Fireye/McDonnell Miller combustion and steam regulator controls. Also includes pre-assembled FM/IRI approved natural gas combustion train w/Fisher or equal diaphragm regulator valve, check trim and vent line fittings or pre-assembled FM/IRI fuel oil combustion train with oil preheater, valved recirculation loop, filter check trim and fuel oil pump. Does not include sheet metal stack or vents, installation permits and approvals, or inspection costs. (bhp = boiler horse power)

Description	Craft@Hrs	Unit	Material $	Labor $	Total $
37,500 Btu (1 bhp)	P1@3.00	Ea	1,840.00	104.00	1,944.00
50,000 Btu (1.5 bhp)	P1@3.00	Ea	2,240.00	104.00	2,344.00
100,000 Btu (2.0 bhp)	P1@4.00	Ea	2,750.00	138.00	2,888.00
150,000 Btu (2.5 bhp)	P1@4.25	Ea	3,470.00	147.00	3,617.00
200,000 Btu (3.0 bhp)	P1@5.00	Ea	3,670.00	173.00	3,843.00
Add for LEED certified boiler		Ea	15%	—	—
Add for LEED inspection		Ea	—	—	2,000.00
Add for central monitor/ recorder		Ea	1,170.00	—	1,170.00
Add for recording Thermostat		Ea	153.00	—	153.00

Commercial Boiler Connections

Description	Craft@Hrs	Unit	Material $	Labor $	Equipment $	Total $

Commercial hot water boiler connection. Includes pipe, fittings, water feed and pressure relief (drains), pipe insulation, valves, gauges, vents and thermometers to connect boiler to distribution system.

Description	Craft@Hrs	Unit	Material $	Labor $	Equipment $	Total $
2½" supply	SN@18.0	Ea	1,930.00	658.00	283.00	2,871.00
3" supply	SN@20.5	Ea	2,430.00	750.00	322.00	3,502.00
4" supply	SN@26.0	Ea	3,530.00	951.00	409.00	4,890.00
6" supply	SN@32.0	Ea	5,160.00	1,170.00	503.00	6,833.00
8" supply	SN@39.5	Ea	6,890.00	1,440.00	613.00	8,943.00
10" supply	SN@48.0	Ea	9,870.00	1,760.00	754.00	12,384.00
12" supply	SN@54.0	Ea	12,200.00	1,980.00	849.00	15,029.00

Commercial steam boiler connection. Includes pipe, fittings, water feed and pressure relief (drains), pipe insulation, valves, gauges, vents and thermometers to connect boiler to distribution system.

Description	Craft@Hrs	Unit	Material $	Labor $	Equipment $	Total $
2½" supply	SN@34.0	Ea	3,710.00	1,240.00	534.00	5,484.00
3" supply	SN@38.0	Ea	3,910.00	1,390.00	597.00	5,897.00
4" supply	SN@43.0	Ea	4,540.00	1,570.00	677.00	6,787.00
6" supply	SN@53.0	Ea	6,230.00	1,940.00	833.00	9,003.00
8" supply	SN@62.0	Ea	8,020.00	2,270.00	974.00	11,264.00
10" supply	SN@70.0	Ea	10,900.00	2,560.00	1,100.00	14,560.00
12" supply	SN@82.0	Ea	13,800.00	3,000.00	1,290.00	18,090.00

Additional costs for industrial, commercial and institutional packaged boilers. See more detailed installation costs and boiler trim costs in the sections that follow.

Description	Craft@Hrs	Unit	Material $	Labor $	Equipment $	Total $
Form and pour an interior slab	CF@0.15	SF	4.85	5.08	—	9.93
Place vibration pad and anchors	CF@.10	SF	5.00	3.39	—	8.39
Boltdown of boiler	P1@3.00	Ea	—	104.00	—	104.00
Fuel train and feedwater lines	P1@0.20	LF	10.00	6.91	—	16.91
Mount interior boiler drain	P1@.500	LF	7.76	17.30	—	25.06
Bore pipe hole in concrete wall	P1@.250	Ea	—	8.64	—	8.64
Bore stack vent in concrete wall	P1@.250	Ea	—	8.64	—	8.64
Mount and edge-seal stack	SN@0.10	LF	8.50	3.66	110.00	122.16
Mount circulating pump	P1@.450	Ea	10.00	15.50	—	25.50
Expansion tank or condensate return lines	P1@0.25	LF	3.25	8.64	—	11.89
Electrical wiring	BE@0.15	LF	1.85	5.74	—	7.59
Combustion controls	BE@0.20	LF	3.50	7.66	—	11.16
Install flue gas monitoring system	BE@0.20	LF	3.50	7.66	—	11.16

Description	Craft@Hrs	Unit	Material $	Labor $	Equipment $	Total $

Additional costs for steam heating boilers for residential and light commercial applications. See more detailed installation costs and boiler trim costs in the sections that follow.

Description	Craft@Hrs	Unit	Material $	Labor $	Equipment $	Total $
Form and pour a 4' x 4' interior slab	CF@3.00	Ea	97.00	102.00	—	199.00
Place 4' x 4' x 1/2" vibration pads	CF@.750	Ea	38.80	25.40	—	64.20
Boltdown of boiler	P1@1.00	Ea	—	34.60	—	34.60
Fuel train and feedwater lines	P1@2.50	Ea	—	86.40	16.00	102.40
Mount interior boiler drain	P1@.500	LF	7.76	17.30	—	25.06
Bore piping hole in basement wall	P1@.250	Ea	—	8.64	—	8.64
Bore stack vent in concrete wall	P1@.250	Ea	—	8.64	—	8.64
Mount and edge-seal stack	P1@.500	Ea	40.00	17.30	—	57.30
Mount circulating pump	P1@.450	Ea	—	15.50	—	15.50
Install expansion tank						
2.1 gallon	P1@.300	Ea	32.59	10.40	21.00	63.99
4.5 gallon	P1@.300	Ea	54.32	10.40	21.00	85.72

Commercial Boiler Components and Accessories

Costs for Combustion Trains for Boilers. Factory Mutual, Industrial Risk Insurers, and Underwriters' Laboratories certified, U.S. Green Building Council rated, LFUE (Levelized Fuel Utilization Efficiency) rated at 90% or better. Includes the burner, burner head, burner mount flange, associated refractory and gasketing, main fuel valve, draft damper and fan (for a power burner), or burner face plate (for an atmospheric or induced-draft burner). Note: BHP multiplied by 33.5 is the approximate required 1,000 Btu per hour input (MBH input). Cost of fuel line relief vent piping and trip valve to outside of the building are not required in all jurisdictions and are not assumed in these costs.

Description	Craft@Hrs	Unit	Material $	Labor $	Equipment $	Total $

Combustion train for Scotch marine firetube boilers. Costs shown are based on boiler horsepower rating (BHP).

Description	Craft@Hrs	Unit	Material $	Labor $	Equipment $	Total $
20 BHP	SN@8.00	Ea	2,590.00	293.00	127.00	3,010.00
30 BHP	SN@8.00	Ea	3,520.00	293.00	127.00	3,940.00
40 BHP	SN@8.00	Ea	4,810.00	293.00	127.00	5,230.00
50 BHP	SN@8.00	Ea	5,960.00	293.00	127.00	6,380.00
60 BHP	SN@8.00	Ea	6,630.00	293.00	127.00	7,050.00
70 BHP	SN@8.00	Ea	7,250.00	293.00	127.00	7,670.00
80 BHP	SN@8.00	Ea	7,400.00	293.00	127.00	7,820.00
100 BHP	SN@8.00	Ea	8,070.00	293.00	127.00	8,490.00
125 BHP	SN@8.00	Ea	8,380.00	293.00	127.00	8,800.00
150 BHP	SN@8.00	Ea	9,280.00	293.00	127.00	9,700.00
200 BHP	SN@8.00	Ea	9,670.00	293.00	127.00	10,090.00
250 BHP	SN@8.00	Ea	10,600.00	293.00	127.00	11,020.00
300 BHP	SN@8.00	Ea	12,000.00	293.00	127.00	12,420.00
350 BHP	SN@8.00	Ea	12,200.00	293.00	127.00	12,620.00
400 BHP	SN@8.00	Ea	12,500.00	293.00	127.00	12,920.00
500 BHP	SN@16.0	Ea	13,600.00	585.00	251.00	14,436.00
600 BHP	SN@16.0	Ea	14,600.00	585.00	251.00	15,436.00
750 BHP	SN@32.0	Ea	15,500.00	1,170.00	347.00	17,017.00
800 BHP	SN@32.0	Ea	16,200.00	1,170.00	347.00	17,717.00

Combustion train for package firebox boilers. Costs shown are based on boiler horsepower rating (BHP).

Description	Craft@Hrs	Unit	Material $	Labor $	Equipment $	Total $
13.4 BHP	SN@8.00	Ea	1,340.00	293.00	127.00	1,760.00
16.4 BHP	SN@8.00	Ea	1,770.00	293.00	127.00	2,190.00
17.4 BHP	SN@8.00	Ea	2,100.00	293.00	127.00	2,520.00
22.4 BHP	SN@8.00	Ea	2,510.00	293.00	127.00	2,930.00
28.4 BHP	SN@8.00	Ea	2,670.00	293.00	127.00	3,090.00
34.4 BHP	SN@8.00	Ea	2,950.00	293.00	127.00	3,370.00
40.3 BHP	SN@8.00	Ea	3,200.00	293.00	127.00	3,620.00
46.3 BHP	SN@8.00	Ea	3,540.00	293.00	127.00	3,960.00
52.3 BHP	SN@8.00	Ea	3,940.00	293.00	127.00	4,360.00
61.1 BHP	SN@8.00	Ea	4,280.00	293.00	127.00	4,700.00
70.0 BHP	SN@8.00	Ea	4,370.00	293.00	127.00	4,790.00
80.0 BHP	SN@8.00	Ea	4,540.00	293.00	127.00	4,960.00
100.0 BHP	SN@8.00	Ea	4,810.00	293.00	127.00	5,230.00
125.0 BHP	SN@8.00	Ea	5,140.00	293.00	127.00	5,560.00
150.0 BHP	SN@8.00	Ea	5,580.00	293.00	127.00	6,000.00

Description	Craft@Hrs	Unit	Material $	Labor $	Equipment $	Total $

Natural gas fuel train piping for firetube and watertube boilers. Meets requirements of Underwriters' Laboratories. Shipped pre-assembled. Add the cost of venting and piping to a gas meter. Costs shown are based on boiler horsepower rating (BHP).

Description	Craft@Hrs	Unit	Material $	Labor $	Equipment $	Total $
20 BHP	SN@8.00	Ea	677.00	293.00	127.00	1,097.00
30 BHP	SN@8.00	Ea	927.00	293.00	127.00	1,347.00
40 BHP	SN@8.00	Ea	1,420.00	293.00	127.00	1,840.00
50 BHP	SN@8.00	Ea	1,690.00	293.00	127.00	2,110.00
60 BHP	SN@8.00	Ea	1,850.00	293.00	127.00	2,270.00
70 BHP	SN@8.00	Ea	1,950.00	293.00	127.00	2,370.00
80 BHP	SN@8.00	Ea	2,120.00	293.00	127.00	2,540.00
100 BHP	SN@8.00	Ea	2,460.00	293.00	127.00	2,880.00
125 BHP	SN@8.00	Ea	2,930.00	293.00	127.00	3,350.00
150 BHP	SN@8.00	Ea	3,480.00	293.00	127.00	3,900.00
200 BHP	SN@8.00	Ea	4,150.00	293.00	127.00	4,570.00
250 BHP	SN@8.00	Ea	5,140.00	293.00	127.00	5,560.00
300 BHP	SN@8.00	Ea	5,410.00	293.00	127.00	5,830.00
350 BHP	SN@8.00	Ea	5,800.00	293.00	127.00	6,220.00
400 BHP	SN@8.00	Ea	6,240.00	293.00	127.00	6,660.00
500 BHP	SN@16.0	Ea	7,000.00	585.00	251.00	7,836.00
600 BHP	SN@16.0	Ea	8,070.00	585.00	251.00	8,906.00
750 BHP	SN@16.0	Ea	8,730.00	585.00	251.00	9,566.00
800 BHP	SN@16.0	Ea	9,140.00	585.00	251.00	9,976.00

Natural gas fuel train piping for package firebox boilers.
Costs shown are based on boiler horsepower rating (BHP).

Description	Craft@Hrs	Unit	Material $	Labor $	Equipment $	Total $
13 BHP	SN@8.00	Ea	905.00	293.00	127.00	1,325.00
16 BHP	SN@8.00	Ea	1,040.00	293.00	127.00	1,460.00
19 BHP	SN@8.00	Ea	1,110.00	293.00	127.00	1,530.00
22 BHP	SN@8.00	Ea	1,220.00	293.00	127.00	1,640.00
28 BHP	SN@8.00	Ea	1,290.00	293.00	127.00	1,710.00
34 BHP	SN@8.00	Ea	1,420.00	293.00	127.00	1,840.00
40 BHP	SN@8.00	Ea	1,690.00	293.00	127.00	2,110.00
45 BHP	SN@8.00	Ea	1,770.00	293.00	127.00	2,190.00
50 BHP	SN@8.00	Ea	2,120.00	293.00	127.00	2,540.00
60 BHP	SN@8.00	Ea	2,410.00	293.00	127.00	2,830.00
70 BHP	SN@8.00	Ea	2,710.00	293.00	127.00	3,130.00
80 BHP	SN@8.00	Ea	2,840.00	293.00	127.00	3,260.00
100 BHP	SN@8.00	Ea	3,400.00	293.00	127.00	3,820.00
125 BHP	SN@8.00	Ea	3,530.00	293.00	127.00	3,950.00
150 BHP	SN@8.00	Ea	3,850.00	293.00	127.00	4,270.00
Add for code approval:						
Factory Mutual	—	%	7.0	—	—	—
Industrial Risk	—	%	10.0	—	—	—

Commercial Boiler Components and Accessories

Oil Fuel Train Piping. Costs shown include recirculating pump, electric oil preheater, regulating valve, check valves, isolating pump stop cocks, oil line pressure relief valve and pressure gauges. Add the cost of concrete pump pad, electrical connections, relief line piping back to the oil tank and tank connecting piping. Add for number 4-6 fuel oil as shown.

Description	Craft@Hrs	Unit	Material $	Labor $	Equipment $	Total $

Oil fuel train piping for boilers. Costs shown are based on boiler horsepower rating (BHP) using number 2 fuel oil.

Description	Craft@Hrs	Unit	Material $	Labor $	Equipment $	Total $
20 to 30 BHP	SN@4.00	Ea	1,440.00	146.00	62.40	1,648.40
40 to 60 BHP	SN@4.00	Ea	1,620.00	146.00	62.40	1,828.40
70 to 80 BHP	SN@4.00	Ea	1,760.00	146.00	62.40	1,968.40
100 BHP	SN@8.00	Ea	2,270.00	293.00	127.00	2,690.00
125 to 150 BHP	SN@8.00	Ea	2,930.00	293.00	127.00	3,350.00
200 BHP	SN@8.00	Ea	3,860.00	293.00	127.00	4,280.00
250 BHP	SN@8.00	Ea	4,570.00	293.00	127.00	4,990.00
300 BHP	SN@16.0	Ea	4,880.00	585.00	251.00	5,716.00
350 BHP	SN@16.0	Ea	5,460.00	585.00	251.00	6,296.00
400 BHP	SN@16.0	Ea	6,560.00	585.00	251.00	7,396.00
500 BHP	SN@32.0	Ea	6,640.00	1,170.00	503.00	8,313.00
600 BHP	SN@32.0	Ea	6,960.00	1,170.00	503.00	8,633.00
750 to 800 BHP	SN@32.0	Ea	7,600.00	1,170.00	503.00	9,273.00
900 to 1,000 BHP	SN@32.0	Ea	8,990.00	1,170.00	503.00	10,663.00
Add for #4-6 oil	—	%	10.0	—	—	—
Add for tie-in with:						
dual-fuel burner	—	%	5.0	—	—	—

Dual-fuel boiler burners For a new installation or retrofit for Scotch marine firetube, firebox or package watertube boilers. Rated at the best available control technology (BACT) for natural gas. Complies with SCAQMD rules 1146.2, 222 and 219 and the Clean Air Act section 307(d). Includes control of CO_2 emissions as well as NOx, SOx, VM's. Cleaver Brooks or equal. Factory Mutual, Industrial Risk Insurers, and Underwriters' Laboratories certified, U.S. Green Building Council rated, LFUE (Levelized Fuel Utilization Efficiency) rated at 90% or better. Includes the burner, burner head, burner mount flange, associated refractory and gasketing, main natural gas and oil fuel valves, draft damper and fan (for a power burner), or burner face plate (for an atmospheric or induced-draft burner) and the natural gas fuel train. Add the cost of an oil fuel train to complete dual-fuel bid. The control panel includes the control circuit, burner mounted control panel, motor starter(s), panel signal lights and full modulation with manual potentiometer, flame safeguard controls, flue gas recirculator air inlet butterfly valve and relay actuator, combustion air proving switch and high fire air interlock switch. Note: BHP multiplied by 33.5 is the approximate required 1,000 Btu per hour input (MBH input). Add the installation costs below and the cost of natural gas fuel line relief vent piping and a trip valve to outside of the building if required.

Description	Craft@Hrs	Unit	Material $	Labor $	Equipment $	Total $

Dual-fuel boiler burners. Costs shown are based on boiler horsepower rating (BHP).

Description	Craft@Hrs	Unit	Material $	Labor $	Equipment $	Total $
20 BHP	SN@8.00	Ea	4,580.00	293.00	—	4,873.00
30 BHP	SN@8.00	Ea	5,320.00	293.00	—	5,613.00
40 BHP	SN@8.00	Ea	6,575.00	293.00	—	6,868.00
50 BHP	SN@8.00	Ea	7,500.00	293.00	—	7,793.00
60 BHP	SN@8.00	Ea	8,525.00	293.00	—	8,818.00
70 BHP	SN@8.00	Ea	9,340.00	293.00	—	9,633.00
80 BHP	SN@8.00	Ea	10,750.00	293.00	—	11,043.00
100 BHP	SN@8.00	Ea	12,580.00	293.00	—	12,873.00
125 BHP	SN@8.00	Ea	14,250.00	293.00	—	14,543.00
150 BHP	SN@8.00	Ea	14,750.00	293.00	—	15,043.00
200 BHP	SN@8.00	Ea	18,925.00	293.00	—	19,218.00
250 BHP	SN@8.00	Ea	24,220.00	293.00	—	24,513.00
300 BHP	SN@8.00	Ea	28,575.00	293.00	—	28,868.00
350 BHP	SN@8.00	Ea	31,642.00	293.00	—	31,935.00
400 BHP	SN@8.00	Ea	33,750.00	293.00	—	34,043.00
500 BHP	SN@16.0	Ea	34,600.00	585.00	—	35,185.00
600 BHP	SN@16.0	Ea	38,800.00	585.00	—	39,385.00
750 BHP	SN@32.0	Ea	41,650.00	1,170.00	—	42,820.00
800 BHP	SN@32.0	Ea	42,300.00	1,170.00	—	43,470.00

Commercial Boiler Components and Accessories

Description	Craft@Hrs	Unit	Material $	Labor $	Equipment $	Total $
Additional costs for installing dual-fuel boiler burners						
Form and pour 4' x 4' x 2" interior slab	ER@3.00	Ea	97.00	111.00	—	208.00
Bore fuel line hole through wall or pad	P1@.250	Ea	—	8.64	—	8.64
Bore flue gas hole through wall or pad	P1@.250	Ea	—	8.64	—	8.64
Place burner and control panel enclosure	ER@8.00	Ea	—	296.00	—	296.00
Mount, level and grout burner, duct and control panel	P1@.450	Ea	400.00	15.60	—	415.60
Piping for fuel lines and flue gas recirculator	P1@.500	LF	7.76	17.30	—	25.06
Electrical wiring	BE@.300	LF	3.18	11.50	—	14.68
Wire control panel	BE@.300	LF	1.50	11.50	—	13.00
Ground fault protection wiring	BE@.300	LF	5.00	11.50	—	16.50
Commission and test	BE@8.00	Ea	—	306.00	—	306.00

Costs for Electrical Service for Boilers, Subcontract. Costs shown include typical main power tie-in and fusing, circuit breaker panel, and main bus. Assumes controls, fan, blower switchgear and control console are pre-wired electrical service. These costs include the electrical subcontractor's overhead and profit.

Description	Craft@Hrs	Unit	Material $	Labor $	Total $
Electrical service for firetube and watertube boilers. Costs shown are based on boiler horsepower rating (BHP).					
20 to 100 BHP	—	Ea	—	—	1,290.00
125 to 200 BHP	—	Ea	—	—	1,550.00
250 to 350 BHP	—	Ea	—	—	1,760.00
400 to 500 BHP	—	Ea	—	—	2,020.00
500 to 600 BHP	—	Ea	—	—	2,920.00
750 to 800 BHP	—	Ea	—	—	5,260.00

Electrical service for package firebox boilers. Costs shown are based on boiler horsepower rating (BHP).

Description	Craft@Hrs	Unit	Material $	Labor $	Total $
13 to 70 BHP	—	Ea	—	—	1,250.00
80 to 125 BHP	—	Ea	—	—	1,330.00
150 BHP	—	Ea	—	—	1,570.00

Commercial Boiler Components and Accessories

Costs for Refractory for Boilers, Subcontract. For package Scotch marine firetube, firebox and watertube boilers. Most new boilers are shipped from the factory with the refractory brick installed. If refractory brick is installed on the job site to repair shipping damage or to create firedoor seals, use the figures below. These costs include the refractory subcontractor's overhead and profit. Costs shown are per 100 pounds of refractory used.

Description	Craft@Hrs	Unit	Material $	Labor $	Equipment $	Total $
Repairs and seals	—	100lb	—	—	—	215.00

Costs for Boiler Feedwater Pumps. Costs shown are for the pump only. Add the cost of piping, pump actuating valves and concrete pump base.

Feedwater pumps for firetube and watertube boilers. Costs shown are based on boiler horsepower rating (BHP).

20 to 40 BHP	SN@8.00	Ea	9,600.00	293.00	127.00	10,020.00
50 to 80 BHP	SN@8.00	Ea	11,600.00	293.00	127.00	12,020.00
100 BHP	SN@8.00	Ea	12,900.00	293.00	127.00	13,320.00
125 to 200 BHP	SN@16.0	Ea	13,300.00	585.00	251.00	14,136.00
250 to 400 BHP	SN@32.0	Ea	14,600.00	1,170.00	503.00	16,273.00
500 BHP	SN@32.0	Ea	15,500.00	1,170.00	503.00	17,173.00
600 BHP	SN@32.0	Ea	16,000.00	1,170.00	503.00	17,673.00
750 BHP	SN@32.0	Ea	16,500.00	1,170.00	503.00	18,173.00
800 BHP	SN@32.0	Ea	22,400.00	1,170.00	503.00	24,073.00

Feedwater pumps for package firebox boilers. Costs shown are based on boiler horsepower rating (BHP).

13 to 35 BHP	SN@8.00	Ea	5,160.00	293.00	127.00	5,580.00
40 to 45 BHP	SN@8.00	Ea	6,060.00	293.00	127.00	6,480.00
50 to 60 BHP	SN@8.00	Ea	7,600.00	293.00	127.00	8,020.00
70 to 80 BHP	SN@8.00	Ea	9,050.00	293.00	127.00	9,470.00
100 BHP	SN@8.00	Ea	11,600.00	293.00	127.00	12,020.00
125 BHP	SN@16.0	Ea	11,600.00	585.00	251.00	12,436.00
150 BHP	SN@16.0	Ea	12,900.00	585.00	251.00	13,736.00

Costs for Natural Gas Combustion Controls for Boilers. Instrumentation Society of America, Underwriters' Laboratories, Factory Mutual, and Industrial Risk Insurers certified. Fireye or equal. Includes automatic recycling or continuous pilot, spark igniter and coil (for electric ignition), timer to control the purge cycle, pilot, main burner (hi-lo-off) or main burner (proportional control), flame safeguard and sensor and combustion control panel.

Natural gas combustion controls for firetube and watertube boilers.
Costs shown are based on boiler horsepower rating (BHP).

20 to 80 BHP	SN@4.00	Ea	3,940.00	146.00	62.40	4,148.40
100 BHP	SN@4.00	Ea	4,370.00	146.00	62.40	4,578.40
125 to 200 BHP	SN@8.00	Ea	4,370.00	293.00	127.00	4,790.00
250 BHP	SN@16.0	Ea	4,370.00	585.00	251.00	5,206.00
300 BHP	SN@16.0	Ea	5,230.00	585.00	251.00	6,066.00
350 or 400 BHP	SN@16.0	Ea	6,140.00	585.00	251.00	6,976.00
500 BHP	SN@32.0	Ea	6,140.00	1,170.00	503.00	7,813.00
600 BHP	SN@32.0	Ea	7,330.00	1,170.00	503.00	9,003.00
750 BHP	SN@64.0	Ea	8,550.00	2,340.00	1,010.00	11,900.00
800 BHP	SN@64.0	Ea	9,940.00	2,340.00	1,010.00	13,290.00

Commercial Boiler Components and Accessories

Description	Craft@Hrs	Unit	Material $	Labor $	Equipment $	Total $

Natural gas combustion controls for firebox boilers. Costs shown are based on boiler horsepower rating (BHP).

Description	Craft@Hrs	Unit	Material $	Labor $	Equipment $	Total $
13.4-80 BHP	SN@4.00	Ea	3,770.00	146.00	62.40	3,978.40
100.0 BHP	SN@4.00	Ea	4,370.00	146.00	62.40	4,578.40
126.9 BHP	SN@8.00	Ea	4,370.00	293.00	127.00	4,790.00
150.0 BHP	SN@8.00	Ea	8,140.00	293.00	127.00	8,560.00
Add if burner controls are for:						
#2 oil-fired	—	%	—	—	—	+10.0
Heavy oil-fired	—	%	—	—	—	+20.0
Dual fuel burners	—	%	—	—	—	+70.0

Costs for Water Softening Systems for Use with Boilers. Costs shown include the metering valve, tank, pump, and zeolite media. Add the cost of piping to connect the water softening system to the main feedwater tank and pump.

Water softening system for firetube and watertube boilers. Costs shown are based on boiler horsepower rating (BHP).

Description	Craft@Hrs	Unit	Material $	Labor $	Equipment $	Total $
20 to 80 BHP	SN@4.00	Ea	6,300.00	146.00	62.40	6,508.40
100 BHP	SN@4.00	Ea	7,390.00	146.00	62.40	7,598.40
125 BHP	SN@8.00	Ea	8,560.00	293.00	127.00	8,980.00
150 or 200 BHP	SN@8.00	Ea	10,900.00	293.00	127.00	11,320.00
250 BHP	SN@8.00	Ea	12,900.00	293.00	127.00	13,320.00
300 or 350 BHP	SN@16.0	Ea	16,500.00	585.00	251.00	17,336.00
400 or 500 BHP	SN@16.0	Ea	20,600.00	585.00	251.00	21,436.00
600 BHP	SN@32.0	Ea	24,900.00	1,170.00	503.00	26,573.00
750 or 800 BHP	SN@64.0	Ea	29,000.00	2,340.00	1,010.00	32,350.00

Water softening system for package firebox boilers. Costs shown are based on boiler horsepower rating (BHP).

Description	Craft@Hrs	Unit	Material $	Labor $	Equipment $	Total $
13.4 to 80 BHP	SN@4.00	Ea	7,410.00	146.00	62.40	7,618.40
100.0 BHP	SN@4.00	Ea	7,410.00	146.00	62.40	7,618.40
126.9 BHP	SN@8.00	Ea	8,710.00	293.00	127.00	9,130.00
150.0 BHP	SN@8.00	Ea	10,100.00	293.00	127.00	10,520.00

Costs for Start-up, Shakedown, and Calibration of Boilers. Costs shown include minor changes and adjustments to meet requirements of the boiler inspector, adjustment of combustion efficiency at the burner by a control technician, pump and metering calibration testing and steam or hot water metering on start-up.

Start-up, shakedown & calibration of firetube and watertube boilers. Costs shown are based on boiler horsepower rating (BHP.) If a factory technician performs the start-up, add this cost at a minimum of $800 (8 hours at $100.00 per hour).

Description	Craft@Hrs	Unit	Material $	Labor $	Equipment $	Total $
13.4 to 100 BHP	S2@4.00	Ea	—	137.00	—	137.00
125 to 200 BHP	S2@8.00	Ea	—	273.00	—	273.00
250 to 400 BHP	S2@16.0	Ea	—	547.00	—	547.00
500 to 600 BHP	S2@24.0	Ea	—	820.00	—	820.00
750 to 800 BHP	S2@30.0	Ea	—	1,020.00	—	1,020.00

Commercial Boiler Components and Accessories

Costs for Stack Economizer Units for Boilers. Costs shown include piping connection to existing boiler, economizer fin tube coils, feedwater pump, check valves, thermostatic regulating valve, stack dampers, pressure relief valve, stack mount flanges and insulating enclosure, but no architectural modifications.

Description	Craft@Hrs	Unit	Material $	Labor $	Equipment $	Total $

Stack waste heat recovery system for boilers. Costs shown are based on boiler horsepower rating (BHP).

Description	Craft@Hrs	Unit	Material $	Labor $	Equipment $	Total $
500 BHP	SN@40.0	Ea	36,700.00	1,460.00	624.00	38,784.00
750 BHP	SN@48.0	Ea	45,800.00	1,760.00	751.00	48,311.00
800 BHP	SN@48.0	Ea	49,400.00	1,760.00	751.00	51,911.00
1,000 BHP	SN@56.0	Ea	61,600.00	2,050.00	880.00	64,530.00

Pollution control modules for gas-fired industrial package watertube boilers. NOx, SOx, VM (volatile materials) and particulates emissions reduction module. Free-standing unit. Verantis, Croll-Reynolds or equal. Designed to meet or exceed 2010 California Code, Tier IV, EPA and European ISO standards. Either vertical counter-flow or packed-bed type. For multi-dwelling, process and industrial applications. By boiler rating in millions of Btu's per hour (MMBtu/hr). See installation and efficiency optimizing control costs below. Oil-fired boilers will add about 15% to the installed cost, including a second stage reduction module, second stage pump, sulfur extraction, venturi particulate separator and sludge tank. To calculate the annual lease rate for a complete installation, divide the total installed cost by five. Then add 2% per year to cover vendor-supplied maintenance.

Description	Craft@Hrs	Unit	Material $	Labor $	Equipment $	Total $
1.0 MMBtu/Hr	—	Ea	35,500.00	—	—	35,500.00
1.7 MMBtu/Hr	—	Ea	63,000.00	—	—	63,000.00
3.4 MMBtu/Hr	—	Ea	112,500.00	—	—	112,500.00
4.1 MMBtu/Hr	—	Ea	117,000.00	—	—	117,000.00
5.0 MMBtu/Hr	—	Ea	125,750.00	—	—	125,750.00
6.7 MMBtu/Hr	—	Ea	135,200.00	—	—	135,200.00
13.4 MMBtu/Hr	—	Ea	140,000.00	—	—	140,000.00
20.1 MMBtu/Hr	—	Ea	155,000.00	—	—	155,000.00
26.8 MMBtu/Hr	—	Ea	165,000.00	—	—	165,000.00
33.5 MMBtu/Hr	—	Ea	180,000.00	—	—	180,000.00

Installation costs for pollution control modules for gas-fired industrial package watertube boilers.

Description	Craft@Hrs	Unit	Material $	Labor $	Equipment $	Total $
Form and pour foundation	ER@.040	SF	2.05	1.48	—	3.53
Position main housing, fans and pumps	ER@4.00	Ea	—	148.00	—	148.00
Tie-down and leveling	ER@4.00	Ea	500.00	148.00	—	648.00
Mount piping system frame supports	ER@6.00	Ea	1.50	222.00	—	223.50
Rig and mount plenum and ducts	SN@5.00	Ea	—	183.00	—	183.00
Rig and mount tank for emission reduction, fluid and housing inlet metering valve	ER@4.00	Ea	—	148.00	—	148.00

Description	Craft@Hrs	Unit	Material $	Labor $	Equipment $	Total $

Installation costs for pollution control modules for gas-fired industrial package watertube boilers – (continued).

Description	Craft@Hrs	Unit	Material $	Labor $	Equipment $	Total $
Weld systems piping	ER@8.00	Ea	2.10	296.00	—	298.10
Wire electrical system	BE@8.00	Ea	1.80	306.00	—	307.80
Wire controls system	BE@16.0	Ea	1.90	612.00	—	613.90
Level and balance rotating equipment	P1@8.00	Ea	200.00	276.00	—	476.00
Calibration and test	ER@2.00	Ea	—	74.00	—	74.00
Witnessed run trials (add the permit fee)	P1@4.00	Ea	—	138.00	—	138.00

Efficiency-optimizing centralized boiler burner controls. Retrofit or new construction. Preferred Instruments or equal. For use with emissions monitoring and digital reporting pollution control equipment installed for a gas-fired industrial boiler. Complies with the Clean Air Act section 307(d), California and Massachusetts boiler codes and NFPA 85. Includes a boiler-mounted control panel with chassis, servo motor controls for burner fuel line valves, LCD touchpad control panel, ultra-violet, infra-red or self-checking flame scanner, operator interface panel and interface to a remote PC (not included). Controls variable speed drives for burner forced-draft fans, induced draft fans and feedwater pumps.

Description	Craft@Hrs	Unit	Material $	Labor $	Equipment $	Total $
Mount automation module, less wiring	BE@.250	Ea	1,100.00	9.57	—	1,109.57
Mount flame safety sensors less wiring	BE@.250	Ea	175.00	9.57	—	184.57
Servomotor mounting less wiring	BE@.250	Ea	468.00	9.57	140.00	617.57
Mount operator interface terminal with power supply less wiring	BE@.250	Ea	80.00	9.57	140.00	229.57
Operator interface terminal bridge, less wiring	BE@.250	Ea	3,800.00	9.57	—	3,809.57
Bore control wiring hole through basement wall	CF@.250	Ea	—	8.47	—	8.47
Twisted pair Cat 6, 1 GBPS wire 4 pair	BE@.008	LF	0.47	.31	—	.78
Panel wiring to emissions monitoring array	BE@.250	LF	2.50	9.57	—	12.07
Sensor wiring to controller	BE@.300	LF	2.30	11.50	—	13.80
Electric servomotor wiring to controller	BE@.400	LF	2.10	15.30	—	17.40
Mount and wire PC module	BE@2.00	LF	20.00	76.60	—	96.60
Ground fault protection wiring	BE@1.25	LF	125.00	47.90	—	172.90
Startup, programming and system test	BE@3.00	Ea	—	115.00	175.26	290.26
Commissioning and final test	BE@8.00	Ea	—	306.00	—	306.00

Costs for Condensate Receiver and Pumping Units for Boilers. Costs shown include a stainless steel factory assembled tank and pump with motor, float switch, condensate inlet, feedwater tank, connection, level gauge, thermometer, solenoid valve for direct boiler feed. No concrete mounting pad required.

Description	Craft@Hrs	Unit	Material $	Labor $	Equipment $	Total $

Condensate receiver and pumping unit for boilers. Unit sizing and costs are based on storage for one minute at the designed steam return rate. Set in place only. Make additional allowances for pipe and electrical connections.

Description	Craft@Hrs	Unit	Material $	Labor $	Equipment $	Total $
750 lbs per hour	SN@4.00	Ea	4,800.00	146.00	62.40	5,008.40
1,500 lbs per hour	SN@4.00	Ea	4,800.00	146.00	62.40	5,008.40
3,000 lbs per hour	SN@4.00	Ea	6,090.00	146.00	62.40	6,298.40
5,000 lbs per hour	SN@6.00	Ea	6,720.00	219.00	93.50	7,032.50
6,250 lbs per hour	SN@6.00	Ea	7,490.00	219.00	93.50	7,802.50

Costs for Deaerator/Condenser Units for Boilers. Pressurized jet spray type. Costs shown include an ASME storage receiver, stand, jet spray deaerator head, makeup control valve, makeup controller, pressure control valve, level controls, pressure and temperature controls, pumped condensate inlet, pumps and motor, steam inlet and system accessories. Add for a concrete mounting pad and piping to the condensate return line (inlet) and piping to the boiler feedwater system (outlet).

Deaerator/condenser unit for boilers. Costs shown are based on boiler horsepower rating (BHP).

Description	Craft@Hrs	Unit	Material $	Labor $	Equipment $	Total $
100 BHP	SN@8.00	Ea	50,300.00	293.00	127.00	50,720.00
200 BHP	SN@12.0	Ea	52,000.00	439.00	189.00	52,628.00
300 BHP	SN@14.0	Ea	55,400.00	512.00	220.00	56,132.00
400 BHP	SN@16.0	Ea	62,700.00	585.00	256.00	63,541.00
600 BHP	SN@24.0	Ea	67,200.00	878.00	385.00	68,463.00
800 BHP	SN@36.0	Ea	73,500.00	1,320.00	569.00	75,389.00
1,000 BHP	SN@48.0	Ea	85,700.00	1,760.00	751.00	88,211.00

Rolairtrol type air separators. Priced by capacity in gallons per minute (GPM) and by pipe connection size. Includes hanging separator but no connection, (2" is a screwed connection, 2-1/2" and up are flanged connections) using small tools.

Description	Craft@Hrs	Unit	Material $	Labor $	Equipment $	Total $
56 GPM, 2"	S2@2.50	Ea	902.00	85.40	39.60	1,027.00
90 GPM, 2½"	S2@2.50	Ea	980.00	85.40	39.60	1,105.00
170 GPM, 3"	S2@3.00	Ea	1,290.00	102.00	47.10	1,439.10
300 GPM, 4"	S2@3.50	Ea	1,930.00	120.00	55.00	2,105.00
500 GPM, 6"	S2@4.75	Ea	2,510.00	162.00	74.70	2,746.70
700 GPM, 6"	S2@4.75	Ea	3,260.00	162.00	74.70	3,496.70
1,300 GPM, 8	SN@6.00	Ea	4,380.00	219.00	94.30	4,693.30
2,000 GPM, 10"	SN@6.00	Ea	6,130.00	219.00	94.30	6,443.30
2,750 GPM, 12"	SN@12.0	Ea	7,950.00	439.00	189.00	8,578.00

Commercial Boiler Components and Accessories

Description	Craft@Hrs	Unit	Material $	Labor $	Equipment $	Total $

Costs for Chemical Feed Duplex Pump, Packaged Units for Boilers. Costs shown include the chemical tanks, electronic metering, valve and stand. Add the cost of piping to the feedwater tank.

Chemical feed duplex pump for boilers. Costs shown are based on boiler horsepower rating (BHP).

20 to 100 BHP	SN@3.00	Ea	1,850.00	110.00	47.60	2,007.60
25 to 200 BHP	SN@3.00	Ea	2,410.00	110.00	47.60	2,567.60
200 to 400 BHP	SN@6.00	Ea	2,410.00	219.00	93.50	2,722.50
500 to 600 BHP	SN@6.00	Ea	5,480.00	219.00	93.50	5,792.50
700 to 800 BHP	SN@8.00	Ea	6,120.00	293.00	127.00	6,540.00
1,000 BHP	SN@10.0	Ea	8,270.00	366.00	157.00	8,793.00

Chemical feed simple in-line system for hot water heating system.
Costs shown include 3 gallon pot feeder, two 3/4" isolation valves, 10' of 3/4" pipe and two 3/4" threadolets. Chemicals are drawn in through suction created by hot water system circulation pumps.

50 to 20 BHP	SN@3.00	Ea	428.00	110.00	47.60	585.60

Packaged Boiler Feedwater Systems for Boilers. Costs shown include duplex pumps with heater assembly, thermal lining, pressure gauges, makeup feeder valve, ASME feedwater tank and stand, single phase electric motor and level gauge. Add the costs for a concrete mounting pad and piping to the boilers.

Description	Craft@Hrs	Unit	Material $	Labor $	Equipment $	Total $

Packaged boiler feedwater systems. Costs shown are based on boiler horsepower rating (BHP).

15 to 50 BHP	SN@5.00	Ea	12,900.00	183.00	78.90	13,161.90
60 to 80 BHP	SN@5.00	Ea	14,200.00	183.00	78.90	14,461.90
100 BHP	SN@6.00	Ea	14,500.00	219.00	93.50	14,812.50
125 to 150 BHP	SN@6.00	Ea	15,500.00	219.00	93.50	15,812.50
200 BHP	SN@8.00	Ea	15,800.00	293.00	127.00	16,220.00
250 BHP	SN@8.00	Ea	16,600.00	293.00	127.00	17,020.00
300 BHP	SN@8.00	Ea	17,600.00	293.00	127.00	18,020.00
400 BHP	SN@8.00	Ea	18,200.00	293.00	127.00	18,620.00
500 BHP	SN@8.00	Ea	22,200.00	293.00	127.00	22,620.00
600 BHP	SN@12.0	Ea	23,100.00	439.00	189.00	23,728.00
750 BHP	SN@12.0	Ea	23,000.00	439.00	189.00	23,628.00

Continuous Blowdown Heat Recovery System. Includes a flash receiver (50 PSI ASME rated tank), plate and frame heat exchanger, pneumatic level controller and valve, air filter regulator, water gauge, pressure gauge, backflush piping, pressure relief valve connected to mud drum and drain. Add for concrete pad mount, piping and electrical wiring. Add the cost of automatic controls from the following section.

Continuous blowdown heat recovery systems. Costs shown by pounds per hour (lbs per hr) of rated makeup capacity.

5,000 lbs per hr	SN@8.00	Ea	43,300.00	293.00	127.00	43,720.00
10,000 lbs per hr	SN@8.00	Ea	85,500.00	293.00	127.00	85,920.00
25,000 lbs per hr	SN@8.00	Ea	108,000.00	293.00	127.00	108,420.00
50,000 lbs per hr	SN@8.00	Ea	173,000.00	293.00	127.00	173,420.00

Boiler blowdown waste heat recovery system controls. Typical costs in rated pounds per hour for high-efficiency commercial or industrial controls for a manually-operated boiler blowdown waste heat recovery system. Wilson Equipment, Spirax Sarco, or equal. Meets EPA efficiency specifications and liquid waste control requirements. For use with package industrial watertube, firebox and firetube boilers up to 250 PSIG and up to 800 boiler horsepower. Includes timer, total dissolved solids sensor, digital control minipanel, valve, valve actuator and T-type security key for manual actuation. For new construction, add the appropriately sized blowdown waste heat recovery system shown above. The equipment cost includes rental of an appliance dolly, 3,000 lb. come-a-long and a 1/2-ton chain hoist.

Description	Craft@Hrs	Unit	Material $	Labor $	Equipment $	Total $
5,000 lbs per hr	SN@8.00	Ea	11,000.00	293.00	127.00	11,420.00
10,000 lbs per hr	SN@8.00	Ea	15,000.00	293.00	127.00	15,420.00
25,000 lbs per hr	SN@8.00	Ea	26,500.00	293.00	127.00	26,920.00
50,000 lbs per hr	SN@8.00	Ea	32,000.00	293.00	127.00	32,420.00
Add for piping for blowdown valve	P1@.500	LF	7.76	17.30	—	25.06
Add for wiring the valve actuator	BE@.300	LF	3.18	11.50	—	14.68
Add for control panel wiring	BE@.300	LF	1.50	11.50	—	13.00
Add for ground fault protection wiring	BE@.300	LF	5.00	11.50	—	16.50
Add for commissioning and tests	BE@8.00	Ea	—	306.00	—	306.00

Boiler Stacks. Costs shown assume a 20-foot stack height and include rigging, breeching, connection of stack sections, guy wires where required, vendor-supplied stack supports and insulation. Add the cost of a concrete base.

Boiler stack. Costs shown assume a 20-foot stack height.

Description	Craft@Hrs	Unit	Material $	Labor $	Equipment $	Total $
10" diameter	SN@12.0	Ea	3,070.00	439.00	189.00	3,698.00
12" diameter	SN@12.0	Ea	3,830.00	439.00	189.00	4,458.00
16" diameter	SN@16.0	Ea	4,580.00	585.00	251.00	5,416.00
20" diameter	SN@20.0	Ea	5,760.00	732.00	314.00	6,806.00
24" diameter	SN@24.0	Ea	7,600.00	878.00	377.00	8,855.00
30" diameter	SN@32.0	Ea	9,020.00	1,170.00	503.00	10,693.00
56" diameter	SN@40.0	Ea	17,800.00	1,460.00	629.00	19,889.00
Add for each 10' section (or portion thereof) beyond 20' high per 10' sect.	—	%	—	—	—	15.0

Costs for Tankless Indirect Water Heater. Provides domestic hot water from boiler coil insert. Costs shown include heat exchanger, coil, circulating pump, thermostatically controlled valve, bypass piping and air bleeder valve. Add the cost of an equipment base, electrical wiring, piping and an insulated hot water storage tank.

Tankless indirect water heater. Costs by gallons per hour (GPH).

Description	Craft@Hrs	Unit	Material $	Labor $	Equipment $	Total $
240 GPH	SN@8.00	Ea	17,800.00	293.00	127.00	18,220.00
360 GPH	SN@8.00	Ea	22,400.00	293.00	127.00	22,820.00
480 GPH	SN@10.0	Ea	22,900.00	366.00	157.00	23,423.00
840 GPH	SN@12.0	Ea	51,900.00	439.00	189.00	52,528.00
920 GPH	SN@16.0	Ea	57,900.00	585.00	251.00	58,736.00
1,240 GPH	SN@20.0	Ea	64,800.00	732.00	314.00	65,846.00

Commercial Boiler Components and Accessories

Costs for Boiler Trim. Costs shown include the pressure relief valve, level gauge (for steam systems), level controller & low water cutoff, pressure and temperature gauge, feedwater valve & actuator, main valve, blowdown valve, cleanout manholes and gaskets.

Description	Craft@Hrs	Unit	Material $	Labor $	Equipment $	Total $

Boiler trim. Costs shown are per boiler horsepower rating (BHP).

Description	Craft@Hrs	Unit	Material $	Labor $	Equipment $	Total $
20 to 100 BHP	SN@4.00	Ea	2,860.00	146.00	62.40	3,068.40
100 to 200 BHP	SN@6.00	Ea	3,220.00	219.00	93.50	3,532.50
200 to 400 BHP	SN@8.00	Ea	3,970.00	293.00	127.00	4,390.00
400 to 600 BHP	SN@8.00	Ea	6,050.00	293.00	127.00	6,470.00
600 to 800 BHP	SN@8.00	Ea	7,140.00	293.00	127.00	7,560.00
800 to 1,000 BHP	SN@10.0	Ea	7,150.00	366.00	157.00	7,673.00

Heat reclaimer condensate return & feedwater system, stainless steel non-siphon, including flash tank with level control and vacuum breaker, overflow relief drain, simplex centrifugal pump, pre-assembled piping to feedwater tank, structural steel stand and frame, check trim and pre-wired controls. Also provides potable hot water as part of the condensed steam return cycle. Capacity rating is in GPH (gallons per hour of condensate)

Description	Craft@Hrs	Unit	Material $	Labor $	Total $
33 gal. ½ HP pump	P1@3.00	Ea	900.00	104.00	1,004.00
46 gal, ¾ HP pump	P1@4.00	Ea	1,100.00	138.00	1,238.00

Vacuum breakers, rough brass, threaded, to be mounted on finned radiation tube inlet valve fitting

Description	Craft@Hrs	Unit	Material $	Labor $	Total $
1/2" vacuum breaker	P1@.25	Ea	42.00	8.64	50.64

Steam traps, float valve Sarco type or equal w/drain fitting, brazed

Description	Craft@Hrs	Unit	Material $	Labor $	Total $
3/4" with check valve	P1@.25	Ea	40.00	8.64	48.64
1.0" with check valve	P1@.45	Ea	64.00	15.50	79.50

Baseboard fin tube radiation, per linear foot, 15 PSIG test thinwall copper tube with aluminum fins, braze fitted wall mounted

Description	Craft@Hrs	Unit	Material $	Labor $	Total $
¾" element with 8" cover	P1@.280	LF	10.20	9.67	19.87
1" element with 8" cover	P1@.350	LF	16.55	12.10	28.65
Add for corners, fillers and caps, average per foot			—	15.0%	

Solenoid valves, zone thermostatically-controlled steam electric, 15 PSIG rating, braze fitting. Thermostatic Honeywell-type or equal solenoid relay valves

Description	Craft@Hrs	Unit	Material $	Labor $	Total $
3/4", brazed	P1@.25	Ea	12.60	8.64	—	21.24
1" brazed	P1@.25	Ea	12.60	8.64	—	21.24

Description	Craft@Hrs	Unit	Material $	Labor $	Equipment $	Total $

Additional costs for boiler pumps, condenser units, feedwater systems, heat recovery and oil fuel train piping.

Description	Craft@Hrs	Unit	Material $	Labor $	Equipment $	Total $
Form and pour concrete pad	CF@2.50	Ea	97.00	84.70	—	181.70
Place vibration pads	CF@.750	Ea	38.80	25.40	—	64.20
Mount interior drain	P1@.500	LF	7.76	17.30	—	25.06
Bore hole through wall or pad	P1@.250	Ea	—	8.64	—	8.64
Piping to load (typical)	P1@.500	LF	7.76	17.30	—	25.06
Bore burner stack vent in exterior wall	P1@.250	Ea	—	8.64	—	8.64
Mounting and edge-sealing stack	P1@.500	Ea	40.00	17.30	—	57.30

Emissions sensing and recording equipment. For stack gas combustion monitoring of boilers. Monitors and records NOx, SOx, CO, H2S, volatile materials and particulates emissions to meet 2011 EPA greenhouse gas regulations. CO_2 monitoring and recording is required on boilers producing 25,000 tons or more a year of carbon emissions. Signal Group Limited or equal. Includes a stack-mounted pulse type infra-red single-beam light source with solid-state detector. Sensitivity range is variable between .1 ppm and 1,000 ppm. Includes a hot-wire radiation source, rotating shutter with reference target for continuous unmanned recalibration, 240 x 64 pixel LCD display with remote panel-mounted solid-state digital analyzer and lockout type inspector-only access recording circuitry. Cost includes calibration and testing by a factory technician. Add the cost of the permit, inspection, test and documentation.

Description	Craft@Hrs	Unit	Material $	Labor $	Equipment $	Total $
Analyzer and recorder installation to remote panel	BE@3.00	Ea	25,500.00	115.00	—	25,615.00
Infrared sensor unit installation to stack	BE@2.00	Ea	8,000.00	76.60	—	8,076.60
Wiring of sensor to analyzer and recorder	BE@8.00	Ea	500.00	306.00	—	806.00
Circuit testing and grounding	BE@2.00	Ea	—	76.60	—	76.60

Centrifugal Pumps and Pump Connections

Description	Craft@Hrs	Unit	Material $	Labor $	Equipment $	Total $

Base mounted, bronze fitted centrifugal pump, set in place only. Make additional allowances for pipe connection assembly.

Description	Craft@Hrs	Unit	Material $	Labor $	Equipment $	Total $
1/2 HP	P1@1.50	Ea	1,200.00	51.80	—	1,251.80
3/4 HP	P1@1.75	Ea	1,520.00	60.50	—	1,580.50
1 HP	P1@2.00	Ea	1,860.00	69.10	—	1,929.10
1½ HP	P1@2.40	Ea	2,260.00	82.90	—	2,342.90
2 HP	P1@2.70	Ea	2,780.00	93.30	—	2,873.30
3 HP	P1@3.00	Ea	3,320.00	104.00	—	3,424.00
5 HP	P1@3.50	Ea	3,780.00	121.00	—	3,901.00
7½ HP	P1@4.00	Ea	4,180.00	138.00	—	4,318.00
10 HP	P1@4.50	Ea	6,100.00	155.00	—	6,255.00
15 HP	ER@5.00	Ea	7,060.00	185.00	79.20	7,324.20
20 HP	ER@6.00	Ea	8,170.00	222.00	93.50	8,485.50
25 HP	ER@7.00	Ea	8,520.00	259.00	110.00	8,889.00
30 HP	ER@7.40	Ea	10,100.00	274.00	116.00	10,490.00
40 HP	ER@7.70	Ea	10,000.00	285.00	121.00	10,406.00
50 HP	ER@8.00	Ea	12,200.00	296.00	127.00	12,623.00

Base mounted centrifugal pump connection assembly. Includes pipe, fittings, pipe insulation, valves, strainers, suction guides and gauges.

Description	Craft@Hrs	Unit	Material $	Labor $	Equipment $	Total $
2½" supply	P1@12.0	Ea	2,060.00	415.00	—	2,475.00
3" supply	P1@13.5	Ea	2,380.00	466.00	—	2,846.00
4" supply	P1@16.0	Ea	3,270.00	553.00	—	3,823.00
6" supply	P1@22.0	Ea	5,400.00	760.00	—	6,160.00
8" supply	P1@28.0	Ea	7,840.00	967.00	—	8,807.00
10" supply	P1@35.0	Ea	12,900.00	1,210.00	—	14,110.00
12" supply	P1@42.0	Ea	17,200.00	1,450.00	—	18,650.00

Cast iron line-mounted centrifugal pump, including connection and supports.

Description	Craft@Hrs	Unit	Material $	Labor $	Equipment $	Total $
1/6 HP	P1@1.25	Ea	309.00	43.20	—	352.20
1/4 HP	P1@1.40	Ea	395.00	48.40	—	443.40
1/3 HP	P1@1.50	Ea	489.00	51.80	—	540.80
1/2 HP	P1@1.70	Ea	624.00	58.70	—	682.70
3/4 HP	P1@1.80	Ea	841.00	62.20	—	903.20
1 HP	P1@2.00	Ea	998.00	69.10	—	1,067.10

Description	Craft@Hrs	Unit	Material $	Labor $	Equipment $	Total $

2-pass shell and tube type heat exchanger, set in place only. Make additional allowances for pipe connection assembly.

Description	Craft@Hrs	Unit	Material $	Labor $	Equipment $	Total $
4" dia. x 30"	SN@2.00	Ea	1,450.00	73.20	31.10	1,554.30
4" dia. x 60"	SN@2.50	Ea	1,640.00	91.50	38.50	1,770.00
6" dia. x 30"	SN@3.25	Ea	2,030.00	119.00	51.40	2,200.40
6" dia. x 60"	SN@3.50	Ea	2,510.00	128.00	55.00	2,693.00
8" dia. x 30"	SN@4.25	Ea	3,110.00	155.00	66.00	3,331.00
8" dia. x 60"	SN@4.50	Ea	4,020.00	165.00	71.50	4,256.50
10" dia. x 30"	SN@5.50	Ea	4,610.00	201.00	86.20	4,897.20
10" dia. x 60"	SN@5.75	Ea	6,100.00	210.00	89.90	6,399.90
10" dia. x 90"	SN@6.00	Ea	7,600.00	219.00	93.50	7,912.50
12" dia. x 60"	SN@6.50	Ea	7,990.00	238.00	103.00	8,331.00
12" dia. x 90"	SN@7.00	Ea	10,200.00	256.00	110.00	10,566.00
12" dia. x 120"	SN@7.25	Ea	12,400.00	265.00	113.00	12,778.00
14" dia. x 60"	SN@7.50	Ea	11,800.00	274.00	118.00	12,192.00
14" dia. x 90"	SN@8.00	Ea	14,700.00	293.00	127.00	15,120.00
14" dia. x 120"	SN@8.25	Ea	17,700.00	302.00	130.00	18,132.00
16" dia. x 60"	SN@8.50	Ea	14,600.00	311.00	134.00	15,045.00
16" dia. x 90"	SN@9.00	Ea	18,200.00	329.00	141.00	18,670.00
16" dia. x 120"	SN@9.25	Ea	20,600.00	338.00	145.00	21,083.00

Heat exchanger connection assembly, hot water to hot water. Includes pipe, fittings, pipe insulation, valves, thermometers gauges and vents.

Description	Craft@Hrs	Unit	Material $	Labor $	Equipment $	Total $
1½" supply	P1@32.0	Ea	3,220.00	1,110.00	1,760.00	6,090.00
2" supply	P1@38.0	Ea	3,940.00	1,310.00	2,090.00	7,340.00
2½" supply	P1@50.0	Ea	5,150.00	1,730.00	2,750.00	9,630.00
3" supply	P1@55.0	Ea	5,410.00	1,900.00	3,030.00	10,340.00
4" supply	P1@62.0	Ea	6,580.00	2,140.00	3,410.00	12,130.00
6" supply	P1@85.0	Ea	10,700.00	2,940.00	4,680.00	18,320.00
8" supply	P1@102.	Ea	15,100.00	3,520.00	5,610.00	24,230.00
10" supply	P1@130.	Ea	19,800.00	4,490.00	7,150.00	31,440.00

Heat exchanger connection assembly, steam to hot water. Includes pipe, fittings, pipe insulation, valves, thermometers gauges and vents.

Description	Craft@Hrs	Unit	Material $	Labor $	Equipment $	Total $
1½" supply	P1@22.0	Ea	3,680.00	760.00	1,210.00	5,650.00
2" supply	P1@26.0	Ea	4,290.00	898.00	1,430.00	6,618.00
2½" supply	P1@41.0	Ea	5,320.00	1,420.00	2,260.00	9,000.00
3" supply	P1@44.0	Ea	6,170.00	1,520.00	2,420.00	10,110.00
4" supply	P1@54.5	Ea	7,020.00	1,880.00	2,990.00	11,890.00
6" supply	P1@67.0	Ea	11,200.00	2,310.00	3,690.00	17,200.00
8" supply	P1@80.0	Ea	15,800.00	2,760.00	4,400.00	22,960.00

Fan Coil Units and Connections

Description	Craft@Hrs	Unit	Material $	Labor $	Equipment $	Total $

Ceiling-hung horizontal, 2 pipe hydronic fan coil unit with cabinet, set in place only. Make additional allowances for pipe connection assembly.

Description	Craft@Hrs	Unit	Material $	Labor $	Equipment $	Total $
200 CFM	P1@2.00	Ea	767.00	69.10	—	836.10
400 CFM	P1@2.50	Ea	909.00	86.40	—	995.40
600 CFM	P1@3.00	Ea	1,070.00	104.00	—	1,174.00
800 CFM	P1@3.25	Ea	1,350.00	112.00	—	1,462.00
1,000 CFM	P1@3.50	Ea	1,690.00	121.00	—	1,811.00

Less cabinet: Deduct 20% from material cost.
Floor-mounted (vertical): Add 10% to material cost.

Vertical, 4 pipe hydronic fan coil unit, set in place only. Make additional allowances for pipe connection assembly.

Description	Craft@Hrs	Unit	Material $	Labor $	Equipment $	Total $
200 CFM	P1@2.15	Ea	872.00	74.30	—	946.30
400 CFM	P1@2.75	Ea	1,010.00	95.00	—	1,105.00
600 CFM	P1@3.25	Ea	1,190.00	112.00	—	1,302.00
800 CFM	P1@3.45	Ea	1,470.00	119.00	—	1,589.00
1,000 CFM	P1@3.60	Ea	1,850.00	124.00	—	1,974.00

2 pipe fan coil unit connection. Coil connection includes type L copper pipe and wrought fittings, pipe insulation, condensate drain, isolation valves and 2-way control valve.

Description	Craft@Hrs	Unit	Material $	Labor $	Equipment $	Total $
1/2" supply	P1@2.50	Ea	129.00	86.40	—	215.40
3/4" supply	P1@2.80	Ea	155.00	96.70	—	251.70
1" supply	P1@3.40	Ea	235.00	117.00	—	352.00

4 pipe fan coil unit connection. Coil connection includes type L copper pipe and wrought fittings, pipe insulation, condensate drain, isolation valves and 3-way control valve.

Description	Craft@Hrs	Unit	Material $	Labor $	Equipment $	Total $
1/2" supply	P1@2.75	Ea	155.00	95.00	—	250.00
3/4" supply	P1@2.95	Ea	180.00	102.00	—	282.00

Description	Craft@Hrs	Unit	Material $	Labor $	Equipment $	Total $

Duct-mounted flanged hot water reheat coil, set in place only. Make
additional allowances for pipe connection assembly.

Description	Craft@Hrs	Unit	Material $	Labor $	Equipment $	Total $
12" x 6"	SN@1.00	Ea	320.00	36.60	15.70	372.30
12" x 8"	SN@1.00	Ea	336.00	36.60	15.70	388.30
12" x 10"	SN@1.00	Ea	352.00	36.60	15.70	404.30
12" x 12"	SN@1.00	Ea	382.00	36.60	15.70	434.30
18" x 6"	SN@1.25	Ea	405.00	45.70	19.60	470.30
18" x 12"	SN@1.25	Ea	416.00	45.70	19.60	481.30
18" x 18"	SN@1.25	Ea	446.00	45.70	19.60	511.30
24" x 12"	SN@1.50	Ea	483.00	54.90	23.70	561.60
24" x 18"	SN@1.50	Ea	506.00	54.90	23.70	584.60
24" x 24"	SN@1.75	Ea	568.00	64.00	27.50	659.50

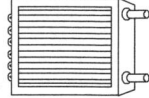

Duct-mounted hot water reheat coil connection assembly. Includes
pipe, fittings, pipe insulation, valves and strainers.

Description	Craft@Hrs	Unit	Material $	Labor $	Equipment $	Total $
1/2" steel	P1@2.25	Ea	164.00	77.70	—	241.70
3/4" steel	P1@2.35	Ea	194.00	81.20	—	275.20
1" steel	P1@2.65	Ea	253.00	91.60	—	344.60
1¼" steel	P1@3.00	Ea	307.00	104.00	—	411.00
1½" steel	P1@3.25	Ea	327.00	112.00	—	439.00
2" steel	P1@3.75	Ea	365.00	130.00	—	495.00

Duct-mounted slip-in electric reheat coil, set in place only. Make
additional allowances for electrical connection.

Description	Craft@Hrs	Unit	Material $	Labor $	Equipment $	Total $
12" x 6"	SN@1.10	Ea	713.00	40.20	17.30	770.50
12" x 8"	SN@1.20	Ea	812.00	43.90	18.90	874.80
12" x 10"	SN@1.30	Ea	987.00	47.60	20.40	1,055.00
12" x 12"	SN@1.40	Ea	1,070.00	51.20	22.00	1,143.20
18" x 6"	SN@1.50	Ea	1,190.00	54.90	23.70	1,268.60
18" x 12"	SN@1.60	Ea	1,290.00	58.50	25.10	1,373.60
18" x 18"	SN@1.70	Ea	1,380.00	62.20	26.70	1,468.90
24" x 12"	SN@1.90	Ea	1,460.00	69.50	29.90	1,559.40
24" x 18"	SN@2.10	Ea	1,540.00	76.80	33.00	1,649.80
24" x 24"	SN@2.40	Ea	1,900.00	87.80	37.70	2,025.50

Unit Heaters and Connections

Description	Craft@Hrs	Unit	Material $	Labor $	Equipment $	Total $

Gas-fired unit heater, hang in place only. Make additional allowances for gas connection assembly.

Description	Craft@Hrs	Unit	Material $	Labor $	Equipment $	Total $
60mbh, 200cfm	P1@2.00	Ea	1,420.00	69.10	—	1,489.10
100mbh, 400cfm	P1@2.50	Ea	1,660.00	86.40	—	1,746.40
150mbh, 600cfm	P1@3.00	Ea	2,010.00	104.00	—	2,114.00
175mbh, 800cfm	P1@3.25	Ea	2,180.00	112.00	—	2,292.00
200mbh, 1,000cfm	P1@3.50	Ea	2,340.00	121.00	—	2,461.00
250mbh, 1,500cfm	P1@3.75	Ea	2,740.00	130.00	—	2,870.00
300mbh, 2,000cfm	P1@4.00	Ea	3,060.00	138.00	—	3,198.00

Hot water unit heater, hang in place only. Make additional allowances for pipe connection assembly.

Description	Craft@Hrs	Unit	Material $	Labor $	Equipment $	Total $
8 mbh, 400cfm	P1@2.00	Ea	377.00	69.10	110.00	556.10
12 mbh, 400cfm	P1@2.00	Ea	485.00	69.10	110.00	664.10
16 mbh, 400 cfm	P1@2.00	Ea	510.00	69.10	110.00	689.10
30mbh, 700cfm	P1@3.00	Ea	684.00	104.00	165.00	953.00
43mbh, 1,040cfm	P1@3.50	Ea	841.00	121.00	193.00	1,155.00
57mbh, 1,370cfm	P1@4.00	Ea	906.00	138.00	220.00	1,264.00
68mbh, 1,715cfm	P1@4.00	Ea	1,420.00	138.00	220.00	1,778.00
105mbh, 2,360cfm	P1@5.00	Ea	1,690.00	173.00	275.00	2,138.00
123mbh, 2,900cfm	P1@6.00	Ea	2,170.00	207.00	330.00	2,707.00
140mbh, 3,530cfm	P1@6.00	Ea	2,510.00	207.00	330.00	3,047.00
156mbh, 4,250cfm	P1@6.00	Ea	2,640.00	207.00	330.00	3,177.00
210mbh, 4,450cfm	P1@8.00	Ea	4,690.00	276.00	440.00	5,406.00
123mbh, 5,200cfm	P1@6.00	Ea	3,870.00	207.00	330.00	4,407.00
257mbh 5,350cfm	P1@8.00	Ea	7,930.00	276.00	440.00	8,646.00

Hot water unit heater connection. Includes schedule 40 threaded and coupled supply and return piping with malleable iron fittings, pipe insulation, valves and vents Make additional allowances for electrical connection.

Description	Craft@Hrs	Unit	Material $	Labor $	Equipment $	Total $
3/4" supply	P1@2.50	Ea	218.00	86.40	138.00	442.40
1" supply	P1@3.00	Ea	256.00	104.00	165.00	525.00
1¼" supply	P1@3.30	Ea	304.00	114.00	182.00	600.00
1½" supply	P1@3.75	Ea	352.00	130.00	207.00	689.00
2" supply	P1@4.10	Ea	456.00	142.00	226.00	824.00

Gas-fired unit heater flue connection

Description	Craft@Hrs	Unit	Material $	Labor $	Equipment $	Total $
2" b vent	SN@.090	LF	4.51	3.29	—	7.80
3" b vent	SN@.100	LF	5.61	3.66	—	9.27
4" b vent	SN@.110	LF	7.48	4.02	—	11.50
6" b vent	SN@.130	LF	8.51	4.76	—	13.27

Gas-fired unit heater fuel connection. Assembly includes 8' of black steel pipe, malleable fittings, plug valve and regulator.

Description	Craft@Hrs	Unit	Material $	Labor $	Equipment $	Total $
3/4" gas conn.	P1@1.30	Ea	79.10	44.90	—	124.00
1" gas conn.	P1@1.60	Ea	86.10	55.30	—	141.40
1¼" gas conn.	P1@2.10	Ea	154.00	72.60	—	226.60
1½" gas conn.	P1@2.50	Ea	177.00	86.40	—	263.40

Description	Craft@Hrs	Unit	Material $	Labor $	Equipment $	Total $

Centrifugal water-cooled chiller, set in place only. Unit comes factory assembled complete. Make additional allowances for cooling tower and pipe connections.

Description	Craft@Hrs	Unit	Material $	Labor $	Equipment $	Total $
100 tons	SN@20.0	Ea	81,700.00	732.00	314.00	82,746.00
150 tons	SN@20.0	Ea	123,000.00	732.00	314.00	124,046.00
200 tons	SN@20.0	Ea	132,000.00	732.00	314.00	133,046.00
250 tons	SN@20.0	Ea	156,000.00	732.00	393.00	157,125.00
300 tons	SN@25.0	Ea	168,000.00	915.00	393.00	169,308.00
350 tons	SN@25.0	Ea	172,000.00	915.00	393.00	173,308.00
400 tons	SN@25.0	Ea	204,000.00	915.00	393.00	205,308.00
500 tons	SN@25.0	Ea	256,000.00	915.00	393.00	257,308.00

Reciprocating water-cooled chiller, set in place only. Unit comes factory assembled complete. Make additional allowances for cooling tower and pipe connections.

Description	Craft@Hrs	Unit	Material $	Labor $	Equipment $	Total $
20 tons	SN@12.0	Ea	25,000.00	439.00	189.00	25,628.00
25 tons	SN@12.0	Ea	28,600.00	439.00	189.00	29,228.00
30 tons	SN@12.0	Ea	31,100.00	439.00	189.00	31,728.00
40 tons	SN@12.0	Ea	37,500.00	439.00	189.00	38,128.00
50 tons	SN@16.0	Ea	53,000.00	585.00	251.00	53,836.00
60 tons	SN@16.0	Ea	68,100.00	585.00	251.00	68,936.00
75 tons	SN@16.0	Ea	73,000.00	585.00	251.00	73,836.00
100 tons	SN@20.0	Ea	77,800.00	732.00	314.00	78,846.00
125 tons	SN@20.0	Ea	93,200.00	732.00	314.00	94,246.00
150 tons	SN@20.0	Ea	108,000.00	732.00	314.00	109,046.00

Water-cooled chiller connection assembly. Includes condenser and chilled water pipe, fittings, pipe insulation, valves, thermometers and gauges.

Description	Craft@Hrs	Unit	Material $	Labor $	Equipment $	Total $
2½" chiller conn.	SN@36.0	Ea	2,610.00	1,320.00	567.00	4,497.00
3" chiller conn.	SN@38.0	Ea	2,870.00	1,390.00	603.00	4,863.00
4" chiller conn.	SN@51.0	Ea	3,820.00	1,870.00	801.00	6,491.00
6" chiller conn.	SN@65.0	Ea	6,420.00	2,380.00	1,020.00	9,820.00
8" chiller conn.	SN@77.0	Ea	9,730.00	2,820.00	1,210.00	13,760.00
10" chiller conn.	SN@100.	Ea	17,900.00	3,660.00	1,570.00	23,130.00
12" chiller conn.	SN@125.	Ea	20,700.00	4,570.00	1,960.00	27,230.00

Condensing Units and Cooling Towers

Description	Craft@Hrs	Unit	Material $	Labor $	Equipment $	Total $

Air-cooled condensing unit, set in place only. Unit comes factory assembled complete. Make additional allowances for pipe and electrical connections.

Description	Craft@Hrs	Unit	Material $	Labor $	Equipment $	Total $
3 tons	SN@2.00	Ea	3,110.00	73.20	31.40	3,214.60
5 tons	SN@3.00	Ea	5,320.00	110.00	47.10	5,477.10
7½ tons	SN@4.00	Ea	6,880.00	146.00	62.90	7,088.90
10 tons	SN@4.50	Ea	9,190.00	165.00	70.80	9,425.80
12½ tons	SN@5.00	Ea	10,800.00	183.00	78.70	11,061.70
15 tons	SN@5.50	Ea	12,400.00	201.00	86.40	12,687.40
20 tons	SN@6.00	Ea	16,400.00	219.00	94.30	16,713.30
25 tons	SN@7.00	Ea	20,700.00	256.00	110.00	21,066.00
30 tons	SN@8.00	Ea	24,900.00	293.00	125.00	25,318.00
40 tons	SN@9.00	Ea	32,300.00	329.00	142.00	32,771.00
50 tons	SN@10.0	Ea	40,600.00	366.00	157.00	41,123.00

Galvanized steel cooling tower. Assemble and set in place only. Add for pipe connections.

Description	Craft@Hrs	Unit	Material $	Labor $	Equipment $	Total $
10 tons	SN@16.0	Ea	3,150.00	585.00	251.00	3,986.00
15 tons	SN@16.0	Ea	3,570.00	585.00	251.00	4,406.00
20 tons	SN@18.0	Ea	5,610.00	658.00	283.00	6,551.00
25 tons	SN@20.0	Ea	6,920.00	732.00	314.00	7,966.00
30 tons	SN@25.0	Ea	7,890.00	915.00	393.00	9,198.00
40 tons	SN@30.0	Ea	10,100.00	1,100.00	471.00	11,671.00
50 tons	SN@35.0	Ea	11,000.00	1,280.00	550.00	12,830.00
60 tons	SN@40.0	Ea	11,600.00	1,460.00	629.00	13,689.00
80 tons	SN@45.0	Ea	12,700.00	1,650.00	707.00	15,057.00
100 tons	SN@50.0	Ea	15,000.00	1,830.00	787.00	17,617.00
125 tons	SN@60.0	Ea	18,200.00	2,190.00	943.00	21,333.00
150 tons	SN@65.0	Ea	21,100.00	2,380.00	1,020.00	24,500.00
175 tons	SN@70.0	Ea	23,800.00	2,560.00	1,100.00	27,460.00
200 tons	SN@70.0	Ea	26,300.00	2,560.00	1,100.00	29,960.00
300 tons	SN@75.0	Ea	37,800.00	2,740.00	1,180.00	41,720.00
400 tons	SN@80.0	Ea	47,900.00	2,930.00	1,260.00	52,090.00
500 tons	SN@80.0	Ea	57,500.00	2,930.00	1,260.00	61,690.00

Redwood or fir induced-draft cooling tower. Assemble and set in place only. Add for pipe connections.

Description	Craft@Hrs	Unit	Material $	Labor $	Equipment $	Total $
100 tons	SN@75.0	Ea	9,770.00	2,740.00	1,180.00	13,690.00
200 tons	SN@80.0	Ea	16,400.00	2,930.00	1,260.00	20,590.00
300 tons	SN@85.0	Ea	23,600.00	3,110.00	1,340.00	28,050.00
400 tons	SN@90.0	Ea	26,800.00	3,290.00	1,410.00	31,500.00
500 tons	SN@90.0	Ea	31,300.00	3,290.00	1,410.00	36,000.00

Description	Craft@Hrs	Unit	Material $	Labor $	Equipment $	Total $

Redwood or fir forced-draft cooling tower. Assemble and set in place only. Add for pipe connections.

Description	Craft@Hrs	Unit	Material $	Labor $	Equipment $	Total $
100 tons	SN@75.0	Ea	16,100.00	2,740.00	1,180.00	20,020.00
200 tons	SN@80.0	Ea	30,700.00	2,930.00	1,260.00	34,890.00
300 tons	SN@85.0	Ea	35,800.00	3,110.00	1,340.00	40,250.00
400 tons	SN@90.0	Ea	47,400.00	3,290.00	1,410.00	52,100.00
500 tons	SN@90.0	Ea	57,600.00	3,290.00	1,410.00	62,300.00

Cooling tower connection assembly. Includes condenser water pipe, fittings, valves, thermometers and gauges.

Description	Craft@Hrs	Unit	Material $	Labor $	Equipment $	Total $
2½" connection	SN@42.0	Ea	4,700.00	1,540.00	660.00	6,900.00
3" connection	SN@47.0	Ea	5,340.00	1,720.00	734.00	7,794.00
4" connection	SN@62.0	Ea	7,680.00	2,270.00	972.00	10,922.00
6" connection	SN@96.0	Ea	12,100.00	3,510.00	1,510.00	17,120.00
8" connection	SN@118	Ea	17,500.00	4,320.00	1,850.00	23,670.00
10" connection	SN@150	Ea	23,900.00	5,490.00	2,370.00	31,760.00
12" connection	SN@215	Ea	29,200.00	7,860.00	3,370.00	40,430.00
14" connection	SN@260	Ea	33,600.00	9,510.00	4,090.00	47,200.00

Carbon Steel, Schedule 40 with 150# Fittings & Butt-Welded Joints

Schedule 40 carbon steel (ASTM A-53 and A-120) pipe with 150 pound carbon steel welding fittings is commonly used for heating hot water, chilled water, glycol and low pressure steam systems where operating pressures do not exceed 250 PSIG.

Schedule 40 (ASTM A-53B SML) steel pipe with carbon steel welding fittings can also be used for refrigerant piping systems.

The cost estimates in this section are based on the conditions, limitations and wage rates described in the section "How to Use This Book" beginning on page 5.

Equipment cost, where shown, is $110 per hour for a 10-ton hydraulic truck-mounted crane.

Description	Craft@Hrs	Unit	Material $	Labor $	Equipment $	Total $

Schedule 40 carbon steel butt-welded horizontal pipe assembly.

Horizontally hung in a building. Assembly includes fittings and hanger assemblies. Based on a reducing tee and a 45 degree elbow every 16 feet for 1/2" pipe. A reducing tee and a 45 degree elbow every 50 feet for 12" pipe. Hangers spaced to meet plumbing code. *(Distance between fittings in the pipe assembly increases as pipe diameter increases.)* Use these figures for preliminary estimates.

Description	Craft@Hrs	Unit	Material $	Labor $	Equipment $	Total $
1/2"	P1@.144	LF	1.66	4.98	—	6.64
3/4"	P1@.170	LF	1.80	5.87	—	7.67
1"	P1@.206	LF	2.19	7.12	—	9.31
1¼"	P1@.208	LF	2.92	7.19	—	10.11
1½"	P1@.238	LF	3.14	8.22	—	11.36
2"	P1@.286	LF	4.15	9.88	—	14.03
2½"	P1@.344	LF	7.29	11.90	—	19.19
3"	P1@.390	LF	9.11	13.50	—	22.61
4"	P1@.507	LF	12.60	17.50	—	30.10
6"	ER@.712	LF	20.30	26.40	11.20	57.90
8"	ER@.847	LF	35.20	31.40	13.30	79.90
10"	ER@1.02	LF	51.30	37.80	16.10	105.20
12"	ER@1.25	LF	65.70	46.30	19.60	131.60

Schedule 40 carbon steel butt-welded vertical pipe assembly.
Riser assembly, including fittings and riser clamps. Based on a reducing tee, and a riser clamp on every floor. Use these figures for preliminary estimates.

Description	Craft@Hrs	Unit	Material $	Labor $	Equipment $	Total $
1/2"	P1@.104	LF	1.25	3.59	—	4.84
3/4"	P1@.128	LF	1.41	4.42	—	5.83
1"	P1@.162	LF	1.81	5.60	—	7.41
1¼"	P1@.184	LF	3.14	6.36	—	9.50
1½"	P1@.204	LF	3.51	7.05	—	10.56
2"	P1@.247	LF	4.66	8.53	—	13.19
2½"	P1@.304	LF	7.61	10.50	—	18.11
3"	P1@.351	LF	9.19	12.10	—	21.29
4"	P1@.505	LF	12.20	17.40	—	29.60
6"	ER@.737	LF	21.80	27.30	11.60	60.70
8"	ER@.878	LF	39.40	32.50	13.90	85.80
10"	ER@1.07	LF	60.00	39.60	16.80	116.40
12"	ER@1.32	LF	79.10	48.90	20.70	148.70

Carbon Steel, Schedule 40 with 150# Fittings & Butt-Welded Joints

Description	Craft@Hrs	Unit	Material $	Labor $	Equipment $	Total $

Schedule 40 carbon steel pipe, plain end, butt-welded joints, pipe only

Description	Craft@Hrs	Unit	Material $	Labor $	Equipment $	Total $
1/2"	P1@.070	LF	.75	2.42	—	3.17
3/4"	P1@.080	LF	.85	2.76	—	3.61
1"	P1@.100	LF	1.25	3.46	—	4.71
1¼"	P1@.110	LF	1.63	3.80	—	5.43
1½"	P1@.120	LF	1.96	4.15	—	6.11
2"	P1@.140	LF	2.64	4.84	—	7.48
2½"	P1@.170	LF	4.92	5.87	—	10.79
3"	P1@.190	LF	6.47	6.56	—	13.03
4"	P1@.300	LF	9.21	10.40	—	19.61
6"	ER@.420	LF	15.90	15.50	6.60	38.00
8"	ER@.510	LF	20.70	18.90	8.10	47.70
10"	ER@.600	LF	29.50	22.20	9.40	61.10
12"	ER@.760	LF	35.60	28.10	11.90	75.60

Schedule 40 carbon steel 45 degree ell, butt-welded joints

Description	Craft@Hrs	Unit	Material $	Labor $	Equipment $	Total $
1/2"	P1@.220	Ea	2.55	7.60	—	10.15
3/4"	P1@.330	Ea	2.55	11.40	—	13.95
1"	P1@.440	Ea	2.55	15.20	—	17.75
1¼"	P1@.560	Ea	2.69	19.30	—	21.99
1½"	P1@.710	Ea	2.69	24.50	—	27.19
2"	P1@.890	Ea	2.77	30.70	—	33.47
2½"	P1@1.11	Ea	4.01	38.40	—	42.41
3"	P1@1.33	Ea	4.85	46.00	—	50.85
4"	P1@1.78	Ea	7.14	61.50	—	68.64
6"	ER@2.67	Ea	18.40	98.80	42.10	159.30
8"	ER@3.20	Ea	43.50	118.00	50.30	211.80
10"	ER@4.00	Ea	66.80	148.00	62.90	277.70
12"	ER@4.80	Ea	97.00	178.00	75.40	350.40

Schedule 40 carbon steel 90 degree ell, butt-welded joints

Description	Craft@Hrs	Unit	Material $	Labor $	Equipment $	Total $
1/2"	P1@.220	Ea	2.49	7.60	—	10.09
3/4"	P1@.330	Ea	2.49	11.40	—	13.89
1"	P1@.440	Ea	2.49	15.20	—	17.69
1¼"	P1@.560	Ea	2.64	19.30	—	21.94
1½"	P1@.670	Ea	2.64	23.10	—	25.74
2"	P1@.890	Ea	2.90	30.70	—	33.60
2½"	P1@1.11	Ea	4.60	38.40	—	43.00
3"	P1@1.33	Ea	6.16	46.00	—	52.16
4"	P1@1.78	Ea	9.92	61.50	—	71.42
6"	ER@2.67	Ea	28.00	98.80	42.10	168.90
8"	ER@3.20	Ea	64.10	118.00	50.30	232.40
10"	ER@4.00	Ea	114.00	148.00	62.90	324.90
12"	ER@4.80	Ea	170.00	178.00	75.40	423.40

Carbon Steel, Schedule 40 with 150# Fittings & Butt-Welded Joints

Description	Craft@Hrs	Unit	Material $	Labor $	Equipment $	Total $
Schedule 40 carbon steel tee, butt-welded joints						
1/2"	P1@.330	Ea	7.86	11.40	—	19.26
3/4"	P1@.500	Ea	7.86	17.30	—	25.16
1"	P1@.670	Ea	7.86	23.10	—	30.96
1¼"	P1@.830	Ea	8.75	28.70	—	37.45
1½"	P1@1.00	Ea	9.19	34.60	—	43.79
2"	P1@1.33	Ea	10.10	46.00	—	56.10
2½"	P1@1.67	Ea	14.10	57.70	—	71.80
3"	P1@2.00	Ea	15.60	69.10	—	84.70
4"	P1@2.67	Ea	21.40	92.20	—	113.60
6"	ER@4.00	Ea	39.20	148.00	62.90	250.10
8"	ER@4.80	Ea	91.10	178.00	75.40	344.50
10"	ER@6.00	Ea	156.00	222.00	94.30	472.30
12"	ER@7.20	Ea	235.00	267.00	113.00	615.00
Schedule 40 carbon steel reducing tee, butt-welded joints						
1½" x 1/2"	P1@.940	Ea	12.00	32.50	—	44.50
1½" x 3/4"	P1@.940	Ea	12.00	32.50	—	44.50
1½" x 1"	P1@.940	Ea	12.00	32.50	—	44.50
1½" x 1¼"	P1@.940	Ea	12.00	32.50	—	44.50
2" x 3/4"	P1@1.22	Ea	16.00	42.20	—	58.20
2" x 1"	P1@1.22	Ea	16.00	42.20	—	58.20
2" x 1¼"	P1@1.22	Ea	16.00	42.20	—	58.20
2" x 1½"	P1@1.22	Ea	16.00	42.20	—	58.20
2½" x 1"	P1@1.56	Ea	20.00	53.90	—	73.90
2½" x 1¼"	P1@1.56	Ea	20.00	53.90	—	73.90
2½" x 1½"	P1@1.56	Ea	20.00	53.90	—	73.90
2½" x 2"	P1@1.56	Ea	20.00	53.90	—	73.90
3" x 1¼"	P1@1.89	Ea	20.40	65.30	—	85.70
3" x 2"	P1@1.89	Ea	20.40	65.30	—	85.70
3" x 2½"	P1@1.89	Ea	20.40	65.30	—	85.70
4" x 1½"	P1@2.44	Ea	21.80	84.30	—	106.10
4" x 2"	P1@2.44	Ea	21.80	84.30	—	106.10
4" x 2½"	P1@2.44	Ea	21.80	84.30	—	106.10
4" x 3"	P1@2.44	Ea	21.80	84.30	—	106.10
6" x 2½"	ER@3.78	Ea	49.20	140.00	59.40	248.60
6" x 3"	ER@3.78	Ea	49.20	140.00	59.40	248.60
6" x 4"	ER@3.78	Ea	49.20	140.00	59.40	248.60
8" x 3"	ER@4.40	Ea	122.00	163.00	69.20	354.20
8" x 4"	ER@4.40	Ea	122.00	163.00	69.20	354.20
8" x 6"	ER@4.40	Ea	122.00	163.00	69.20	354.20
10" x 4"	ER@5.60	Ea	205.00	207.00	88.00	500.00
10" x 6"	ER@5.60	Ea	205.00	207.00	88.00	500.00
10" x 8"	ER@5.60	Ea	205.00	207.00	88.00	500.00
12" x 6"	ER@6.80	Ea	306.00	252.00	106.90	664.90
12" x 8"	ER@6.80	Ea	306.00	252.00	106.90	664.90
12" x 10"	ER@6.80	Ea	306.00	252.00	106.90	664.90

Carbon Steel, Schedule 40 with 150# Fittings & Butt-Welded Joints

Description	Craft@Hrs	Unit	Material $	Labor $	Equipment $	Total $

Schedule 40 carbon steel concentric reducer, butt-welded joints

Description	Craft@Hrs	Unit	Material $	Labor $	Equipment $	Total $
3/4"	P1@.295	Ea	5.33	10.20	—	15.53
1"	P1@.395	Ea	6.36	13.60	—	19.96
1¼"	P1@.500	Ea	6.73	17.30	—	24.03
1½"	P1@.600	Ea	7.49	20.70	—	28.19
2"	P1@.800	Ea	6.98	27.60	—	34.58
2½"	P1@1.00	Ea	11.00	34.60	—	45.60
3"	P1@1.20	Ea	8.81	41.50	—	50.31
4"	P1@1.60	Ea	12.50	55.30	—	67.80
6"	ER@2.40	Ea	23.10	88.80	37.70	149.60
8"	ER@2.88	Ea	44.20	107.00	45.30	196.50
10"	ER@3.60	Ea	67.50	133.00	56.70	257.20
12"	ER@4.30	Ea	104.00	159.00	67.70	330.70

Schedule 40 carbon steel eccentric reducer, butt-welded joints

Description	Craft@Hrs	Unit	Material $	Labor $	Equipment $	Total $
3/4"	P1@.295	Ea	6.54	10.20	—	16.74
1"	P1@.395	Ea	8.82	13.60	—	22.42
1¼"	P1@.500	Ea	10.20	17.30	—	27.50
1½"	P1@.600	Ea	10.80	20.70	—	31.50
2"	P1@.800	Ea	8.34	27.60	—	35.94
2½"	P1@1.00	Ea	13.30	34.60	—	47.90
3"	P1@1.20	Ea	11.90	41.50	—	53.40
4"	P1@1.60	Ea	16.80	55.30	—	72.10
6"	ER@2.40	Ea	33.50	88.80	37.70	160.00
8"	ER@2.88	Ea	61.60	107.00	45.30	213.90
10"	ER@3.60	Ea	106.00	133.00	56.70	295.70
12"	ER@4.30	Ea	161.00	159.00	67.70	387.70

Schedule 40 carbon steel cap, butt-welded joints

Description	Craft@Hrs	Unit	Material $	Labor $	Equipment $	Total $
1/2"	P1@.150	Ea	6.03	5.18	—	11.21
3/4"	P1@.230	Ea	6.46	7.95	—	14.41
1"	P1@.300	Ea	6.89	10.40	—	17.29
1¼"	P1@.390	Ea	8.61	13.50	—	22.11
1½"	P1@.470	Ea	8.61	16.20	—	24.81
2"	P1@.620	Ea	8.61	21.40	—	30.01
2½"	P1@.770	Ea	10.70	26.60	—	37.30
3"	P1@.930	Ea	10.20	32.10	—	42.30
4"	P1@1.25	Ea	13.10	43.20	—	56.30
6"	ER@1.87	Ea	15.20	69.20	29.40	113.80
8"	ER@2.24	Ea	27.40	82.90	35.20	145.50
10"	ER@2.80	Ea	46.30	104.00	44.00	194.30
12"	ER@3.36	Ea	58.00	124.00	52.80	234.80

Carbon Steel, Schedule 40 with 150# Fittings & Butt-Welded Joints

Description	Craft@Hrs	Unit	Material $	Labor $	Equipment $	Total $

Schedule 40 carbon steel union, butt-welded joints

Description	Craft@Hrs	Unit	Material $	Labor $	Equipment $	Total $
1/2"	P1@.220	Ea	4.34	7.60	—	11.94
3/4"	P1@.330	Ea	5.62	11.40	—	17.02
1"	P1@.440	Ea	7.76	15.20	—	22.96
1¼"	P1@.560	Ea	16.40	19.30	—	35.70
1½"	P1@.670	Ea	18.00	23.10	—	41.10
2"	P1@.890	Ea	24.00	30.70	—	54.70
2½"	P1@1.11	Ea	64.10	38.40	—	102.50
3"	P1@1.33	Ea	76.10	46.00	—	122.10

Carbon steel weldolet, Schedule 40

Description	Craft@Hrs	Unit	Material $	Labor $	Equipment $	Total $
1/2"	P1@.330	Ea	6.05	11.40	—	17.45
3/4"	P1@.500	Ea	6.67	17.30	—	23.97
1"	P1@.670	Ea	7.44	23.10	—	30.54
1¼"	P1@.830	Ea	11.30	28.70	—	40.00
1½"	P1@1.00	Ea	11.30	34.60	—	45.90
2"	P1@1.33	Ea	12.40	46.00	—	58.40
2½"	P1@1.67	Ea	33.70	57.70	—	91.40
3"	P1@2.00	Ea	36.40	69.10	—	105.50
4"	P1@2.67	Ea	47.30	92.20	—	139.50
6"	P1@4.00	Ea	193.00	138.00	—	331.00
8"	P1@4.80	Ea	368.00	166.00	—	534.00
10"	P1@6.00	Ea	503.00	207.00	—	710.00
12"	P1@7.20	Ea	616.00	249.00	—	865.00

Carbon steel threadolet, Schedule 40

Description	Craft@Hrs	Unit	Material $	Labor $	Equipment $	Total $
3/4"	P1@.330	Ea	4.02	11.40	—	15.42
1"	P1@.440	Ea	4.77	15.20	—	19.97
1¼"	P1@.560	Ea	8.25	19.30	—	27.55
1½"	P1@.670	Ea	9.30	23.10	—	32.40
2"	P1@.890	Ea	10.80	30.70	—	41.50
2½"	P1@1.11	Ea	41.50	38.40	—	79.90
3"	P1@1.33	Ea	45.50	46.00	—	91.50
4"	P1@1.78	Ea	89.30	61.50	—	150.80

150# forged steel companion flange, weld neck

Description	Craft@Hrs	Unit	Material $	Labor $	Equipment $	Total $
2½"	P1@.610	Ea	23.90	21.10	—	45.00
3"	P1@.730	Ea	22.30	25.20	—	47.50
4"	P1@.980	Ea	30.80	33.90	—	64.70
6"	ER@1.47	Ea	49.40	54.40	23.10	126.90
8"	ER@1.77	Ea	99.80	65.50	27.80	193.10
10"	ER@2.20	Ea	165.00	81.40	34.70	281.10
12"	ER@2.64	Ea	239.00	97.70	41.50	378.20

Carbon Steel, Schedule 40 with 150# Fittings & Butt-Welded Joints

Description	Craft@Hrs	Unit	Material $	Labor $	Equipment $	Total $

Class 125 bronze body gate valve, threaded ends

Description	Craft@Hrs	Unit	Material $	Labor $	Equipment $	Total $
1/2"	P1@.210	Ea	16.20	7.26	—	23.46
3/4"	P1@.250	Ea	20.30	8.64	—	28.94
1"	P1@.300	Ea	28.50	10.40	—	38.90
1¼"	P1@.400	Ea	36.00	13.80	—	49.80
1½"	P1@.450	Ea	48.40	15.50	—	63.90
2"	P1@.500	Ea	80.90	17.30	—	98.20
2½"	P1@.750	Ea	134.00	25.90	—	159.90
3"	P1@.950	Ea	193.00	32.80	—	225.80

Class 125 iron body gate valve, flanged ends

Description	Craft@Hrs	Unit	Material $	Labor $	Equipment $	Total $
2"	P1@.500	Ea	310.00	17.30	—	327.30
2½"	P1@.600	Ea	418.00	20.70	—	438.70
3"	P1@.750	Ea	454.00	25.90	—	479.90
4"	P1@1.35	Ea	666.00	46.60	—	712.60
6"	ER@2.50	Ea	1,270.00	92.60	39.30	1,401.90
8"	ER@3.00	Ea	2,090.00	111.00	47.10	2,248.10
10"	ER@4.00	Ea	3,410.00	148.00	62.90	3,620.90
12"	ER@4.50	Ea	4,730.00	167.00	70.80	4,967.80

Class 125 bronze body globe valve, threaded ends

Description	Craft@Hrs	Unit	Material $	Labor $	Equipment $	Total $
1/2"	P1@.210	Ea	30.00	7.26	—	37.26
3/4"	P1@.250	Ea	40.00	8.64	—	48.64
1"	P1@.300	Ea	57.40	10.40	—	67.80
1¼"	P1@.400	Ea	80.70	13.80	—	94.50
1½"	P1@.450	Ea	109.00	15.50	—	124.50
2"	P1@.500	Ea	176.00	17.30	—	193.30

Class 125 iron body globe valve, flanged ends

Description	Craft@Hrs	Unit	Material $	Labor $	Equipment $	Total $
2½"	P1@.600	Ea	351.00	20.70	—	371.70
3"	P1@.750	Ea	421.00	25.90	—	446.90
4"	P1@1.35	Ea	565.00	46.60	—	611.60
6"	ER@2.50	Ea	990.00	92.60	—	1,082.60
8"	ER@3.00	Ea	1,520.00	111.00	—	1,631.00
10"	ER@4.00	Ea	2,320.00	148.00	—	2,468.00

200 PSIG iron body butterfly valve, lug type, lever operated

Description	Craft@Hrs	Unit	Material $	Labor $	Equipment $	Total $
2"	P1@.450	Ea	134.00	15.50	—	149.50
2½"	P1@.450	Ea	139.00	15.50	—	154.50
3"	P1@.550	Ea	146.00	19.00	—	165.00
4"	P1@.550	Ea	182.00	19.00	—	201.00
6"	ER@.800	Ea	293.00	29.60	12.70	335.30
8"	ER@.800	Ea	401.00	29.60	12.70	443.30
10"	ER@.900	Ea	557.00	33.30	14.10	604.40
12"	ER@1.00	Ea	729.00	37.00	15.70	781.70

Carbon Steel, Schedule 40 with 150# Fittings & Butt-Welded Joints

Description	Craft@Hrs	Unit	Material $	Labor $	Equipment $	Total $

200 PSIG iron body butterfly valve, wafer type, lever operated

Description	Craft@Hrs	Unit	Material $	Labor $	Equipment $	Total $
2"	P1@.450	Ea	122.00	15.50	—	137.50
2½"	P1@.450	Ea	125.00	15.50	—	140.50
3"	P1@.550	Ea	134.00	19.00	—	153.00
4"	P1@.550	Ea	163.00	19.00	—	182.00
6"	ER@.800	Ea	272.00	29.60	12.70	314.30
8"	ER@.800	Ea	377.00	29.60	12.70	419.30
10"	ER@.900	Ea	527.00	33.30	14.10	574.40
12"	ER@1.00	Ea	692.00	37.00	15.70	744.70

Class 125 bronze body swing check valve, threaded

Description	Craft@Hrs	Unit	Material $	Labor $	Equipment $	Total $
1/2"	P1@.210	Ea	17.70	7.26	—	24.96
3/4"	P1@.250	Ea	25.40	8.64	—	34.04
1"	P1@.300	Ea	33.30	10.40	—	43.70
1¼"	P1@.400	Ea	47.30	13.80	—	61.10
1½"	P1@.450	Ea	66.70	15.50	—	82.20
2"	P1@.500	Ea	111.00	17.30	—	128.30

Class 125 iron body swing check valve, flanged joints

Description	Craft@Hrs	Unit	Material $	Labor $	Equipment $	Total $
2"	P1@.500	Ea	155.00	17.30	—	172.30
2½"	P1@.600	Ea	197.00	20.70	—	217.70
3"	P1@.750	Ea	245.00	25.90	—	270.90
4"	P1@1.35	Ea	360.00	46.60	—	406.60
6"	ER@2.50	Ea	699.00	92.60	39.30	830.90
8"	ER@3.00	Ea	1,250.00	111.00	47.10	1,408.10
10"	ER@4.00	Ea	2,060.00	148.00	62.90	2,270.90
12"	ER@4.50	Ea	2,790.00	167.00	70.80	3,027.80

Class 125 iron body silent check valve, flanged joints

Description	Craft@Hrs	Unit	Material $	Labor $	Equipment $	Total $
2"	P1@.500	Ea	113.00	17.30	—	130.30
2½"	P1@.600	Ea	131.00	20.70	—	151.70
3"	P1@.750	Ea	147.00	25.90	—	172.90
4"	P1@1.35	Ea	193.00	46.60	—	239.60
6"	ER@2.50	Ea	347.00	92.60	39.30	478.90
8"	ER@3.00	Ea	625.00	111.00	47.10	783.10
10"	ER@4.00	Ea	970.00	148.00	62.90	1,180.90

Class 125 bronze body strainer, threaded ends

Description	Craft@Hrs	Unit	Material $	Labor $	Equipment $	Total $
1/2"	P1@.210	Ea	27.70	7.26	—	34.96
3/4"	P1@.250	Ea	36.40	8.64	—	45.04
1"	P1@.300	Ea	44.60	10.40	—	55.00
1¼"	P1@.400	Ea	62.30	13.80	—	76.10
1½"	P1@.450	Ea	93.80	15.50	—	109.30
2"	P1@.500	Ea	162.00	17.30	—	179.30

Carbon Steel, Schedule 40 with 150# Fittings & Butt-Welded Joints

Description	Craft@Hrs	Unit	Material $	Labor $	Equipment $	Total $
Class 125 iron body strainer, flanged						
2"	P1@.500	Ea	124.00	17.30	—	141.30
2½"	P1@.600	Ea	139.00	20.70	—	159.70
3"	P1@.750	Ea	160.00	25.90	—	185.90
4"	P1@1.35	Ea	273.00	46.60	—	319.60
6"	ER@2.50	Ea	554.00	92.60	39.30	685.90
8"	ER@3.00	Ea	937.00	111.00	47.10	1,095.10
Installation of 2-way control valve, threaded joints						
1/2"	P1@.210	Ea	—	7.26	—	7.26
3/4"	P1@.250	Ea	—	8.64	—	8.64
1"	P1@.300	Ea	—	10.40	—	10.40
1¼"	P1@.400	Ea	—	13.80	—	13.80
1½"	P1@.450	Ea	—	15.50	—	15.50
2"	P1@.500	Ea	—	17.30	—	17.30
2½"	P1@.830	Ea	—	28.70	—	28.70
3"	P1@.990	Ea	—	34.20	—	34.20
Installation of 2-way control valve, flanged joints						
2"	P1@.500	Ea	—	17.30	—	17.30
2½"	P1@.600	Ea	—	20.70	—	20.70
3"	P1@.750	Ea	—	25.90	—	25.90
4"	P1@1.35	Ea	—	46.60	—	46.60
6"	P1@2.50	Ea	—	86.40	—	86.40
8"	P1@3.00	Ea	—	104.00	—	104.00
10"	P1@4.00	Ea	—	138.00	—	138.00
12"	P1@4.50	Ea	—	155.00	—	155.00
Installation of 3-way control valve, threaded joints						
1/2"	P1@.260	Ea	—	8.98	—	8.98
3/4"	P1@.365	Ea	—	12.60	—	12.60
1"	P1@.475	Ea	—	16.40	—	16.40
1¼"	P1@.575	Ea	—	19.90	—	19.90
1½"	P1@.680	Ea	—	23.50	—	23.50
2"	P1@.910	Ea	—	31.40	—	31.40
2½"	P1@1.12	Ea	—	38.70	—	38.70
3"	P1@1.33	Ea	—	46.00	—	46.00
Installation of 3-way control valve, flanged joints						
2"	P1@.910	Ea	—	31.40	—	31.40
2½"	P1@1.12	Ea	—	38.70	—	38.70
3"	P1@1.33	Ea	—	46.00	—	46.00
4"	P1@2.00	Ea	—	69.10	—	69.10
6"	P1@3.70	Ea	—	128.00	—	128.00
8"	P1@4.40	Ea	—	152.00	—	152.00
10"	P1@5.90	Ea	—	204.00	—	204.00
12"	P1@6.50	Ea	—	225.00	—	225.00

Carbon Steel, Schedule 40 with 150# Fittings & Butt-Welded Joints

Description	Craft@Hrs	Unit	Material $	Labor $	Equipment $	Total $
Bolt and gasket sets						
2"	P1@.500	Ea	3.86	17.30	—	21.16
2½"	P1@.650	Ea	4.51	22.50	—	27.01
3"	P1@.750	Ea	7.64	25.90	—	33.54
4"	P1@1.00	Ea	12.70	34.60	—	47.30
6"	P1@1.20	Ea	21.20	41.50	—	62.70
8"	P1@1.25	Ea	23.80	43.20	—	67.00
10"	P1@1.70	Ea	40.90	58.70	—	99.60
12"	P1@2.20	Ea	46.20	76.00	—	122.20
Thermometer with well						
7"	P1@.250	Ea	164.00	8.64	—	172.64
9"	P1@.250	Ea	217.00	8.64	—	225.64
Dial type pressure gauge						
2½"	P1@.200	Ea	33.10	6.91	—	40.01
3½"	P1@.200	Ea	43.80	6.91	—	50.71
Pressure/temperature tap						
tap	P1@.150	Ea	15.70	5.18	—	20.88
Hanger with swivel assembly						
2"	P1@.300	Ea	6.05	10.40	—	16.45
2½"	P1@.350	Ea	7.82	12.10	—	19.92
3"	P1@.350	Ea	9.67	12.10	—	21.77
4"	P1@.350	Ea	14.90	12.10	—	27.00
5"	P1@.450	Ea	16.70	15.50	—	32.20
6"	P1@.450	Ea	21.80	15.50	—	37.30
8"	P1@.450	Ea	28.90	15.50	—	44.40
10"	P1@.550	Ea	39.70	19.00	—	58.70
12"	P1@.600	Ea	52.80	20.70	—	73.50
Riser clamp						
2"	P1@.115	Ea	4.84	3.97	—	8.81
2½"	P1@.120	Ea	5.09	4.15	—	9.24
3"	P1@.120	Ea	5.52	4.15	—	9.67
4"	P1@.125	Ea	7.03	4.32	—	11.35
5"	P1@.180	Ea	10.10	6.22	—	16.32
6"	P1@.200	Ea	12.20	6.91	—	19.11
8"	P1@.200	Ea	19.80	6.91	—	26.71
10"	P1@.250	Ea	29.40	8.64	—	38.04
12"	P1@.250	Ea	34.90	8.64	—	43.54

Carbon Steel, Schedule 40 with 150# M.I. Fittings & Threaded Joints

Schedule 40 carbon steel (ASTM A-53 and A-120) pipe with 150 pound malleable iron threaded fittings is commonly used for heating hot water, chilled water, glycol and low pressure steam systems where operating pressures do not exceed 125 PSIG and temperatures are below 250 degrees F., for pipe sizes 2" and smaller. For pipe sizes 2 ½" and larger, wrought steel fittings with either welded or grooved joints should be used.

Schedule 40 (ASTM A-53B SML) steel pipe with carbon steel welding fittings can also be used for refrigerant piping systems.

This section has been arranged to save the estimator's time by including all normally-used system components such as pipe, fittings, valves, hanger assemblies, riser clamps and miscellaneous items under one heading. Additional items can be found under "Plumbing and Piping Specialties." The cost estimates in this section are based on the conditions, limitations and wage rates described in the section "How to Use This Book" beginning on page 5.

Description	Craft@Hrs	Unit	Material $	Labor $	Equipment $	Total $

Schedule 40 carbon steel threaded horizontal pipe assembly.

Horizontally hung in a building. Assembly includes fittings and hanger assemblies. Based on a reducing tee and a 45 degree elbow every 16 feet for 1/2" pipe. A reducing tee and a 45 degree elbow every 30 feet for 4" pipe. Hangers spaced to meet plumbing code. *(Distance between fittings in the pipe assembly increases as pipe diameter increases.)* Use these figures for preliminary estimates.

Description	Craft@Hrs	Unit	Material $	Labor $	Equipment $	Total $
1/2"	P1@.119	LF	1.48	4.11	—	5.59
3/4"	P1@.132	LF	1.74	4.56	—	6.30
1"	P1@.144	LF	2.38	4.98	—	7.36
1¼"	P1@.160	LF	3.11	5.53	—	8.64
1½"	P1@.184	LF	3.45	6.36	—	9.81
2"	P1@.200	LF	5.24	6.91	—	12.15
2½"	P1@.236	LF	10.30	8.15	—	18.45
3"	P1@.271	LF	14.20	9.36	—	23.56
4"	P1@.398	LF	21.10	13.80	—	34.90

Schedule 40 carbon steel threaded vertical pipe assembly.

Riser assembly, including fittings and riser clamps. Based on a reducing tee, and a riser clamp on every floor. Use these figures for preliminary estimates.

Description	Craft@Hrs	Unit	Material $	Labor $	Equipment $	Total $
1/2"	P1@.082	LF	1.13	2.83	—	3.96
3/4"	P1@.096	LF	1.44	3.32	—	4.76
1"	P1@.121	LF	2.02	4.18	—	6.20
1¼"	P1@.138	LF	2.90	4.77	—	7.67
1½"	P1@.156	LF	3.29	5.39	—	8.68
2"	P1@.173	LF	4.92	5.98	—	10.90
2½"	P1@.200	LF	10.10	6.91	—	17.01
3"	P1@.236	LF	14.80	8.15	—	22.95
4"	P1@.354	LF	19.50	12.20	—	31.70

Carbon Steel, Schedule 40 with 150# M.I. Fittings & Threaded Joints

Description	Craft@Hrs	Unit	Material $	Labor $	Equipment $	Total $

Schedule 40 carbon steel pipe, threaded and coupled, pipe only

Description	Craft@Hrs	Unit	Material $	Labor $	Equipment $	Total $
1/2"	P1@.060	LF	1.02	2.07	—	3.09
3/4"	P1@.070	LF	1.13	2.42	—	3.55
1"	P1@.090	LF	1.73	3.11	—	4.84
1¼"	P1@.100	LF	2.24	3.46	—	5.70
1½"	P1@.110	LF	2.66	3.80	—	6.46
2"	P1@.120	LF	3.94	4.15	—	8.09
2½"	P1@.130	LF	6.07	4.49	—	10.56
3"	P1@.150	LF	8.05	5.18	—	13.23
4"	P1@.260	LF	11.40	8.98	—	20.38

150# malleable iron 45 degree ell, threaded joints

Description	Craft@Hrs	Unit	Material $	Labor $	Equipment $	Total $
1/2"	P1@.120	Ea	1.60	4.15	—	5.75
3/4"	P1@.130	Ea	1.96	4.49	—	6.45
1"	P1@.180	Ea	2.50	6.22	—	8.72
1¼"	P1@.240	Ea	4.41	8.29	—	12.70
1½"	P1@.300	Ea	5.44	10.40	—	15.84
2"	P1@.380	Ea	8.14	13.10	—	21.24
2½"	P1@.510	Ea	23.50	17.60	—	41.10
3"	P1@.640	Ea	30.60	22.10	—	52.70
4"	P1@.850	Ea	59.50	29.40	—	88.90

150# malleable iron 90 degree ell, threaded joints

Description	Craft@Hrs	Unit	Material $	Labor $	Equipment $	Total $
1/2"	P1@.120	Ea	.98	4.15	—	5.13
3/4"	P1@.130	Ea	1.22	4.49	—	5.71
1"	P1@.180	Ea	2.08	6.22	—	8.30
1¼"	P1@.240	Ea	3.40	8.29	—	11.69
1½"	P1@.300	Ea	4.49	10.40	—	14.89
2"	P1@.380	Ea	7.67	13.10	—	20.77
2½"	P1@.510	Ea	16.80	17.60	—	34.40
3"	P1@.640	Ea	25.00	22.10	—	47.10
4"	P1@.850	Ea	58.10	29.40	—	87.50

150# malleable iron tee, threaded joints

Description	Craft@Hrs	Unit	Material $	Labor $	Equipment $	Total $
1/2"	P1@.180	Ea	1.32	6.22	—	7.54
3/4"	P1@.190	Ea	1.91	6.56	—	8.47
1"	P1@.230	Ea	3.24	7.95	—	11.19
1¼"	P1@.310	Ea	5.32	10.70	—	16.02
1½"	P1@.390	Ea	6.53	13.50	—	20.03
2"	P1@.490	Ea	11.00	16.90	—	27.90
2½"	P1@.660	Ea	23.40	22.80	—	46.20
3"	P1@.830	Ea	34.20	28.70	—	62.90
4"	P1@1.10	Ea	82.10	38.00	—	120.10

Carbon Steel, Schedule 40 with 150# M.I. Fittings & Threaded Joints

Description	Craft@Hrs	Unit	Material $	Labor $	Equipment $	Total $

150# malleable iron reducing tee, threaded joints

Description	Craft@Hrs	Unit	Material $	Labor $	Equipment $	Total $
3/4" x 1/2"	P1@.180	Ea	2.82	6.22	—	9.04
1" x 1/2"	P1@.220	Ea	3.59	7.60	—	11.19
1" x 3/4"	P1@.220	Ea	3.59	7.60	—	11.19
1¼" x 1/2"	P1@.290	Ea	6.53	10.00	—	16.53
1¼" x 3/4"	P1@.290	Ea	5.73	10.00	—	15.73
1¼" x 1"	P1@.290	Ea	6.21	10.00	—	16.21
1½" x 1/2"	P1@.370	Ea	7.65	12.80	—	20.45
1½" x 3/4"	P1@.370	Ea	7.22	12.80	—	20.02
1½" x 1"	P1@.370	Ea	7.22	12.80	—	20.02
1½" x 1¼"	P1@.370	Ea	8.94	12.80	—	21.74
2" x 1"	P1@.460	Ea	11.30	15.90	—	27.20
2" x 1¼"	P1@.460	Ea	12.30	15.90	—	28.20
2" x 1½"	P1@.460	Ea	12.30	15.90	—	28.20
4" x 1½"	P1@1.05	Ea	84.90	36.30	—	121.20
4" x 2"	P1@1.05	Ea	84.90	36.30	—	121.20
4" x 3"	P1@1.05	Ea	84.90	36.30	—	121.20

150# malleable iron reducer, threaded joints

Description	Craft@Hrs	Unit	Material $	Labor $	Equipment $	Total $
3/4" x 1/2"	P1@.130	Ea	1.80	4.49	—	6.29
1" x 1/2"	P1@.160	Ea	2.79	5.53	—	8.32
1" x 3/4"	P1@.160	Ea	2.79	5.53	—	8.32
1¼" x 3/4"	P1@.210	Ea	2.79	7.26	—	10.05
1¼" x 1"	P1@.210	Ea	3.48	7.26	—	10.74
1½" x 1"	P1@.270	Ea	5.09	9.33	—	14.42
1½" x 1¼"	P1@.270	Ea	4.41	9.33	—	13.74
2" x 1¼"	P1@.340	Ea	7.29	11.70	—	18.99
2" x 1½"	P1@.340	Ea	6.39	11.70	—	18.09
3" x 2"	P1@.530	Ea	19.00	18.30	—	37.30
3" x 2½"	P1@.530	Ea	22.10	18.30	—	40.40
4" x 3"	P1@.750	Ea	22.10	25.90	—	48.00

150# malleable iron cross, threaded joints

Description	Craft@Hrs	Unit	Material $	Labor $	Equipment $	Total $
1/2"	P1@.280	Ea	4.81	9.67	—	14.48
3/4"	P1@.320	Ea	5.88	11.10	—	16.98
1"	P1@.360	Ea	7.22	12.40	—	19.62
1¼"	P1@.480	Ea	11.60	16.60	—	28.20
1½"	P1@.600	Ea	14.40	20.70	—	35.10
2"	P1@.700	Ea	23.80	24.20	—	48.00
2½"	P1@1.02	Ea	44.00	35.20	—	79.20
3"	P1@1.28	Ea	61.00	44.20	—	105.20

Carbon Steel, Schedule 40 with 150# M.I. Fittings & Threaded Joints

Description	Craft@Hrs	Unit	Material $	Labor $	Equipment $	Total $

150# malleable iron cap, threaded joint

1/2"	P1@.090	Ea	1.00	3.11	—	4.11
3/4"	P1@.100	Ea	1.33	3.46	—	4.79
1"	P1@.140	Ea	1.66	4.84	—	6.50
1¼"	P1@.180	Ea	2.13	6.22	—	8.35
1½"	P1@.230	Ea	2.90	7.95	—	10.85
2"	P1@.290	Ea	4.27	10.00	—	14.27
2½"	P1@.380	Ea	9.56	13.10	—	22.66
3"	P1@.480	Ea	14.10	16.60	—	30.70
4"	P1@.640	Ea	24.00	22.10	—	46.10

150# malleable iron plug, threaded joint

1/2"	P1@.090	Ea	.79	3.11	—	3.90
3/4"	P1@.100	Ea	.85	3.46	—	4.31
1"	P1@.140	Ea	.85	4.84	—	5.69
1¼"	P1@.180	Ea	1.34	6.22	—	7.56
1½"	P1@.230	Ea	1.94	7.95	—	9.89
2"	P1@.290	Ea	2.25	10.00	—	12.25
2½"	P1@.380	Ea	5.47	13.10	—	18.57
3"	P1@.480	Ea	6.36	16.60	—	22.96
4"	P1@.640	Ea	11.60	22.10	—	33.70

150# malleable iron union, threaded joints

1/2"	P1@.140	Ea	4.37	4.84	—	9.21
3/4"	P1@.150	Ea	5.01	5.18	—	10.19
1"	P1@.210	Ea	6.54	7.26	—	13.80
1¼"	P1@.280	Ea	9.36	9.67	—	19.03
1½"	P1@.360	Ea	11.60	12.40	—	24.00
2"	P1@.450	Ea	13.40	15.50	—	28.90
2½"	P1@.610	Ea	40.10	21.10	—	61.20
3"	P1@.760	Ea	48.30	26.30	—	74.60

150# malleable iron coupling, threaded joints

1/2"	P1@.120	Ea	1.33	4.15	—	5.48
3/4"	P1@.130	Ea	1.58	4.49	—	6.07
1"	P1@.180	Ea	2.39	6.22	—	8.61
1¼"	P1@.240	Ea	3.07	8.29	—	11.36
1½"	P1@.300	Ea	4.11	10.40	—	14.51
2"	P1@.380	Ea	5.97	13.10	—	19.07

Carbon Steel, Schedule 40 with 150# M.I. Fittings & Threaded Joints

Description	Craft@Hrs	Unit	Material $	Labor $	Equipment $	Total $

Steel pipe nipples — Close nipple, standard right hand thread

Description	Craft@Hrs	Unit	Material $	Labor $	Equipment $	Total $
1/2"	P1@.025	Ea	.54	.86	—	1.40
3/4"	P1@.025	Ea	.64	.86	—	1.50
1"	P1@.025	Ea	.98	.86	—	1.84
1¼"	P1@.025	Ea	1.22	.86	—	2.08
1½"	P1@.025	Ea	1.46	.86	—	2.32
2"	P1@.025	Ea	1.86	.86	—	2.72
2½"	P1@.030	Ea	7.29	1.04	—	8.33
3"	P1@.030	Ea	7.89	1.04	—	8.93
4"	P1@.040	Ea	12.50	1.38	—	13.88
6"	P1@.050	Ea	63.60	1.73	—	65.33
8"	P1@.065	Ea	111.00	2.25	—	113.25

Steel pipe nipples — 1-1/2" long, standard right hand thread

Description	Craft@Hrs	Unit	Material $	Labor $	Equipment $	Total $
1/2"	P1@.025	Ea	.58	.86	—	1.44
3/4"	P1@.025	Ea	.65	.86	—	1.51

Steel pipe nipples — 2" long, standard right hand thread

Description	Craft@Hrs	Unit	Material $	Labor $	Equipment $	Total $
1/2"	P1@.025	Ea	.58	.86	—	1.44
3/4"	P1@.025	Ea	.65	.86	—	1.51
1"	P1@.025	Ea	.98	.86	—	1.84
1¼"	P1@.025	Ea	1.22	.86	—	2.08
1½"	P1@.025	Ea	1.46	.86	—	2.32

Steel pipe nipples — 2-1/2" long, standard right hand thread

Description	Craft@Hrs	Unit	Material $	Labor $	Equipment $	Total $
1/2"	P1@.025	Ea	.60	.86	—	1.46
3/4"	P1@.025	Ea	.69	.86	—	1.55
1"	P1@.025	Ea	1.12	.86	—	1.98
1¼"	P1@.025	Ea	1.44	.86	—	2.30
1½"	P1@.025	Ea	1.80	.86	—	2.66
2"	P1@.025	Ea	2.10	.86	—	2.96

Steel pipe nipples — 3" long, standard right hand thread

Description	Craft@Hrs	Unit	Material $	Labor $	Equipment $	Total $
1/2"	P1@.025	Ea	.68	.86	—	1.54
3/4"	P1@.025	Ea	.80	.86	—	1.66
1"	P1@.025	Ea	1.17	.86	—	2.03
1¼"	P1@.025	Ea	1.52	.86	—	2.38
1½"	P1@.025	Ea	1.81	.86	—	2.67
2"	P1@.030	Ea	2.25	1.04	—	3.29
2½"	P1@.030	Ea	7.58	1.04	—	8.62
3"	P1@.035	Ea	8.53	1.21	—	9.74

Carbon Steel, Schedule 40 with 150# M.I. Fittings & Threaded Joints

Description	Craft@Hrs	Unit	Material $	Labor $	Equipment $	Total $
Steel pipe nipples — 3-1/2" long, standard right hand thread						
1/2"	P1@.025	Ea	.78	.86	—	1.64
3/4"	P1@.025	Ea	.93	.86	—	1.79
1"	P1@.025	Ea	1.33	.86	—	2.19
1¼"	P1@.025	Ea	1.72	.86	—	2.58
1½"	P1@.030	Ea	2.16	1.04	—	3.20
2"	P1@.030	Ea	2.65	1.04	—	3.69
2½"	P1@.035	Ea	9.99	1.21	—	11.20
3"	P1@.035	Ea	11.60	1.21	—	12.81
4"	P1@.040	Ea	15.80	1.38	—	17.18
Steel pipe nipples — 4" long, standard right hand thread						
1/2"	P1@.025	Ea	.83	.86	—	1.69
3/4"	P1@.025	Ea	.98	.86	—	1.84
1"	P1@.025	Ea	1.42	.86	—	2.28
1¼"	P1@.030	Ea	1.76	1.04	—	2.80
1½"	P1@.030	Ea	2.21	1.04	—	3.25
2"	P1@.030	Ea	2.79	1.04	—	3.83
2½"	P1@.035	Ea	8.72	1.21	—	9.93
3"	P1@.040	Ea	9.78	1.38	—	11.16
4"	P1@.040	Ea	14.20	1.38	—	15.58
Steel pipe nipples — 4-1/2" long, standard right hand thread						
1/2"	P1@.025	Ea	.98	.86	—	1.84
3/4"	P1@.025	Ea	1.11	.86	—	1.97
1"	P1@.025	Ea	1.52	.86	—	2.38
1¼"	P1@.030	Ea	2.38	1.04	—	3.42
1½"	P1@.030	Ea	2.89	1.04	—	3.93
2"	P1@.030	Ea	3.10	1.04	—	4.14
2½"	P1@.035	Ea	11.10	1.21	—	12.31
3"	P1@.040	Ea	14.00	1.38	—	15.38
4"	P1@.050	Ea	17.70	1.73	—	19.43
6"	P1@.070	Ea	76.40	2.42	—	78.82
Steel pipe nipples — 5" long, standard right hand thread						
1/2"	P1@.025	Ea	1.00	.86	—	1.86
3/4"	P1@.025	Ea	1.11	.86	—	1.97
1"	P1@.030	Ea	1.66	1.04	—	2.70
1¼"	P1@.030	Ea	2.14	1.04	—	3.18
1½"	P1@.030	Ea	2.57	1.04	—	3.61
2"	P1@.035	Ea	3.22	1.21	—	4.43
2½"	P1@.040	Ea	11.80	1.38	—	13.18
3"	P1@.045	Ea	12.30	1.55	—	13.85
4"	P1@.050	Ea	19.20	1.73	—	20.93
6"	P1@.075	Ea	77.60	2.59	—	80.19
8"	P1@.100	Ea	129.00	3.46	—	132.46

Carbon Steel, Schedule 40 with 150# M.I. Fittings & Threaded Joints

Description	Craft@Hrs	Unit	Material $	Labor $	Equipment $	Total $

Steel pipe nipples — 6" long, standard right hand thread

Description	Craft@Hrs	Unit	Material $	Labor $	Equipment $	Total $
1/2"	P1@.025	Ea	1.11	.86	—	1.97
3/4"	P1@.025	Ea	1.35	.86	—	2.21
1"	P1@.030	Ea	1.81	1.04	—	2.85
1¼"	P1@.030	Ea	2.26	1.04	—	3.30
1½"	P1@.030	Ea	2.73	1.04	—	3.77
2"	P1@.035	Ea	3.69	1.21	—	4.90
2½"	P1@.040	Ea	10.60	1.38	—	11.98
3"	P1@.045	Ea	11.80	1.55	—	13.35
4"	P1@.060	Ea	17.70	2.07	—	19.77
6"	P1@.085	Ea	86.70	2.94	—	89.64
8"	P1@.120	Ea	138.00	4.15	—	142.15

Steel pipe nipples — 8" long, standard right hand thread

Description	Craft@Hrs	Unit	Material $	Labor $	Equipment $	Total $
2½"	P1@.050	Ea	13.80	1.73	—	15.53
3"	P1@.055	Ea	17.00	1.90	—	18.90
4"	P1@.070	Ea	27.20	2.42	—	29.62
6"	P1@.100	Ea	91.00	3.46	—	94.46
8"	P1@.150	Ea	155.00	5.18	—	160.18

Steel pipe nipples — 10" long, standard right hand thread

Description	Craft@Hrs	Unit	Material $	Labor $	Equipment $	Total $
2½"	P1@.055	Ea	16.70	1.90	—	18.60
3"	P1@.060	Ea	20.20	2.07	—	22.27
4"	P1@.080	Ea	32.90	2.76	—	35.66
6"	P1@.115	Ea	101.00	3.97	—	104.97
8"	P1@.165	Ea	175.00	5.70	—	180.70

Steel pipe nipples — 12" long, standard right hand thread

Description	Craft@Hrs	Unit	Material $	Labor $	Equipment $	Total $
2½"	P1@.060	Ea	16.20	2.07	—	18.27
3"	P1@.065	Ea	20.00	2.25	—	22.25
4"	P1@.080	Ea	32.30	2.76	—	35.06
6"	P1@.130	Ea	116.00	4.49	—	120.49
8"	P1@.190	Ea	192.00	6.56	—	198.56

Class 125 bronze body gate valve, threaded ends

Description	Craft@Hrs	Unit	Material $	Labor $	Equipment $	Total $
1/2"	P1@.210	Ea	16.20	7.26	—	23.46
3/4"	P1@.250	Ea	20.30	8.64	—	28.94
1"	P1@.300	Ea	28.50	10.40	—	38.90
1¼"	P1@.400	Ea	36.00	13.80	—	49.80
1½"	P1@.450	Ea	48.40	15.50	—	63.90
2"	P1@.500	Ea	80.90	17.30	—	98.20
2½"	P1@.750	Ea	134.00	25.90	—	159.90
3"	P1@.950	Ea	192.00	32.80	—	224.80

Carbon Steel, Schedule 40 with 150# M.I. Fittings & Threaded Joints

Description	Craft@Hrs	Unit	Material $	Labor $	Equipment $	Total $

Class 125 iron body gate valve, flanged ends

2"	P1@.500	Ea	277.00	17.30	—	294.30
2½"	P1@.600	Ea	418.00	20.70	—	438.70
3"	P1@.750	Ea	454.00	25.90	—	479.90
4"	P1@1.35	Ea	666.00	46.60	—	712.60

Class 125 bronze body globe valve, threaded ends

1/2"	P1@.210	Ea	30.00	7.26	—	37.26
3/4"	P1@.250	Ea	40.00	8.64	—	48.64
1"	P1@.300	Ea	57.40	10.40	—	67.80
1¼"	P1@.400	Ea	80.70	13.80	—	94.50
1½"	P1@.450	Ea	109.00	15.50	—	124.50
2"	P1@.500	Ea	176.00	17.30	—	193.30

Class 125 iron body globe valve, flanged ends

2"	P1@.500	Ea	226.00	17.30	—	243.30
2½"	P1@.600	Ea	351.00	20.70	—	371.70
3"	P1@.750	Ea	421.00	25.90	—	446.90
4"	P1@1.35	Ea	565.00	46.60	—	611.60

200 PSIG iron body butterfly valve, lug type, lever operated

2"	P1@.450	Ea	134.00	15.50	—	149.50
2½"	P1@.450	Ea	139.00	15.50	—	154.50
3"	P1@.550	Ea	146.00	19.00	—	165.00
4"	P1@.550	Ea	182.00	19.00	—	201.00

200 PSIG iron body butterfly valve, wafer type, lever operated

2"	P1@.450	Ea	122.00	15.50	—	137.50
2½"	P1@.450	Ea	125.00	15.50	—	140.50
3"	P1@.550	Ea	134.00	19.00	—	153.00
4"	P1@.550	Ea	163.00	19.00	—	182.00

Class 125 bronze body 2-piece ball valve, threaded ends

1/2"	P1@.210	Ea	7.91	7.26	—	15.17
3/4"	P1@.250	Ea	10.50	8.64	—	19.14
1"	P1@.300	Ea	18.20	10.40	—	28.60
1¼"	P1@.400	Ea	30.30	13.80	—	44.10
1½"	P1@.450	Ea	41.00	15.50	—	56.50
2"	P1@.500	Ea	51.90	17.30	—	69.20
3"	P1@.625	Ea	355.00	21.60	—	376.60
4"	P1@.690	Ea	465.00	23.80	—	488.80

Carbon Steel, Schedule 40 with 150# M.I. Fittings & Threaded Joints

Description	Craft@Hrs	Unit	Material $	Labor $	Equipment $	Total $

Class 125 bronze body swing check valve, threaded

1/2"	P1@.210	Ea	17.70	7.26	—	24.96
3/4"	P1@.250	Ea	25.40	8.64	—	34.04
1"	P1@.300	Ea	33.30	10.40	—	43.70
1¼"	P1@.400	Ea	47.30	13.80	—	61.10
1½"	P1@.450	Ea	66.70	15.50	—	82.20
2"	P1@.500	Ea	111.00	17.30	—	128.30

Class 125 iron body swing check valve, flanged ends

2"	P1@.500	Ea	155.00	17.30	—	172.30
2½"	P1@.600	Ea	197.00	20.70	—	217.70
3"	P1@.750	Ea	245.00	25.90	—	270.90
4"	P1@1.35	Ea	360.00	46.60	—	406.60

Class 125 iron body silent check valve, wafer type

2"	P1@.500	Ea	113.00	17.30	—	130.30
2½"	P1@.600	Ea	126.00	20.70	—	146.70
3"	P1@.750	Ea	145.00	25.90	—	170.90
4"	P1@1.35	Ea	194.00	46.60	—	240.60

Class 125 bronze body strainer, threaded ends

1/2"	P1@.210	Ea	27.70	7.26	—	34.96
3/4"	P1@.250	Ea	36.40	8.64	—	45.04
1"	P1@.300	Ea	44.60	10.40	—	55.00
1¼"	P1@.400	Ea	62.30	13.80	—	76.10
1½"	P1@.450	Ea	93.80	15.50	—	109.30
2"	P1@.500	Ea	162.00	17.30	—	179.30

Class 125 iron body strainer, flanged ends

2"	P1@.500	Ea	124.00	17.30	—	141.30
2½"	P1@.600	Ea	139.00	20.70	—	159.70
3"	P1@.750	Ea	160.00	25.90	—	185.90
4"	P1@1.35	Ea	481.00	46.60	—	527.60

Installation of 2-way control valve, threaded joints

1/2"	P1@.210	Ea	—	7.26	—	7.26
3/4"	P1@.275	Ea	—	9.50	—	9.50
1"	P1@.350	Ea	—	12.10	—	12.10
1¼"	P1@.430	Ea	—	14.90	—	14.90
1½"	P1@.505	Ea	—	17.40	—	17.40
2"	P1@.675	Ea	—	23.30	—	23.30
2½"	P1@.830	Ea	—	28.70	—	28.70
3"	P1@.990	Ea	—	34.20	—	34.20

Carbon Steel, Schedule 40 with 150# M.I. Fittings & Threaded Joints

Description	Craft@Hrs	Unit	Material $	Labor $	Equipment $	Total $
Installation of 3-way control valve, threaded joints						
1/2"	P1@.260	Ea	—	8.98	—	8.98
3/4"	P1@.365	Ea	—	12.60	—	12.60
1"	P1@.475	Ea	—	16.40	—	16.40
1¼"	P1@.575	Ea	—	19.90	—	19.90
1½"	P1@.680	Ea	—	23.50	—	23.50
2"	P1@.910	Ea	—	31.40	—	31.40
2½"	P1@1.12	Ea	—	38.70	—	38.70
3"	P1@1.33	Ea	—	46.00	—	46.00
Companion flange, threaded						
2"	P1@.290	Ea	39.90	10.00	—	49.90
2½"	P1@.380	Ea	61.60	13.10	—	74.70
3"	P1@.460	Ea	66.50	15.90	—	82.40
4"	P1@.600	Ea	91.40	20.70	—	112.10
Bolt and gasket sets						
2"	P1@.500	Ea	3.86	17.30	—	21.16
2½"	P1@.650	Ea	4.51	22.50	—	27.01
3"	P1@.750	Ea	7.64	25.90	—	33.54
4"	P1@1.00	Ea	12.70	34.60	—	47.30
Thermometer with well						
7"	P1@.250	Ea	159.00	8.64	—	167.64
9"	P1@.250	Ea	164.00	8.64	—	172.64
Dial type pressure gauge						
2½"	P1@.200	Ea	33.10	6.91	—	40.01
3½"	P1@.200	Ea	43.80	6.91	—	50.71
Pressure/temperature tap						
tap	P1@.150	Ea	15.70	5.18	—	20.88
Hanger with swivel assembly						
1/2"	P1@.250	Ea	4.13	8.64	—	12.77
3/4"	P1@.250	Ea	4.33	8.64	—	12.97
1"	P1@.250	Ea	4.57	8.64	—	13.21
1¼"	P1@.300	Ea	4.77	10.40	—	15.17
1½"	P1@.300	Ea	5.51	10.40	—	15.91
2"	P1@.300	Ea	6.05	10.40	—	16.45
2½"	P1@.350	Ea	7.82	12.10	—	19.92
3"	P1@.350	Ea	9.67	12.10	—	21.77
4"	P1@.350	Ea	15.20	12.10	—	27.30

Carbon Steel, Schedule 40 with 150# M.I. Fittings & Threaded Joints

Description	Craft@Hrs	Unit	Material $	Labor $	Equipment $	Total $
Riser clamp						
1/2"	P1@.100	Ea	2.41	3.46	—	5.87
3/4"	P1@.100	Ea	3.55	3.46	—	7.01
1"	P1@.100	Ea	3.59	3.46	—	7.05
1¼"	P1@.105	Ea	4.33	3.63	—	7.96
1½"	P1@.110	Ea	4.58	3.80	—	8.38
2"	P1@.115	Ea	4.84	3.97	—	8.81
2½"	P1@.120	Ea	5.09	4.15	—	9.24
3"	P1@.120	Ea	5.52	4.15	—	9.67
4"	P1@.125	Ea	7.03	4.32	—	11.35

Carbon Steel, Schedule 5 with Pressfit Fittings

Schedule 5 carbon steel (ASTM A-53, A135 and A-795) pipe with pressfit fittings. The pressfit jointing method offers economy, speed and reliability for joining 3/4" to 2" diameter pipe for fire protection, heating and cooling water systems. *(Use roll-grooved pipe and fittings for 2½" and larger pipe diameters.)*

The pressfit system for carbon steel is BOCA approved. Listed by SBCCI PST and ESI and is UL/ULC listed and FM approved for 175 PSI (1200 kPa) on fire protection services and is rated to 300 PSI (2065 kPa) for heating water systems.

The pressfit system requires no special preparation of the pipe ends before assembly. Pipe should be square cut (+/−0.030") and de-burred. Pressfit system products are designed only for use on approved Schedule 5 carbon steel pipe.

O-ring selection as specified by the mechanical design engineer. Type O o-rings are rated for application temperatures of +20 degrees F to +300 degrees F. Type O o-rings are recommended for many oxidizing acids, petroleum oils, halogenated hydrocarbons, lubricants, hydraulic fluids, organic liquids and air with hydrocarbons within the specified temperature range. Not recommended for steam services.

Standard type E o-rings are rated for application temperatures of −30 degrees F to +230 degrees F. Type E o-rings are recommended for hot water service within the specified temperature range plus a variety of dilute acids, oil free air and many chemical services.

Type T o-rings are rated for application temperatures of −20 degrees F to +180 degrees F. Type T o-rings are recommended for petroleum products, air with oil vapors, vegetable or mineral oils within the specified temperature range. Not recommended for hot water services over 150 degrees F., or steam, or hot dry air over 140 degrees F.

A specialized hand held electric pressfit tool is required to make the pipe/fitting connections. Allow a rental of $300.00 per month or $2,900.00 to purchase the tool.

Description	Craft@Hrs	Unit	Material $	Labor $	Equipment $	Total $

Schedule 5 carbon steel pipe, plain end, pressfit joints, pipe only. No hangers or fittings.

Description	Craft@Hrs	Unit	Material $	Labor $	Equipment $	Total $
3/4"	P1@.030	LF	1.36	1.04	—	2.40
1"	P1@.040	LF	1.85	1.38	—	3.23
1¼"	P1@.040	LF	2.37	1.38	—	3.75
1½"	P1@.050	LF	2.82	1.73	—	4.55
2"	P1@.050	LF	3.40	1.73	—	5.13

45 degree pressfit ell, with Type O o-ring (P x P)

Description	Craft@Hrs	Unit	Material $	Labor $	Equipment $	Total $
3/4"	P1@.170	Ea	22.50	5.87	—	28.37
1"	P1@.180	Ea	27.10	6.22	—	33.32
1¼"	P1@.190	Ea	37.40	6.56	—	43.96
1½"	P1@.200	Ea	47.50	6.91	—	54.41
2"	P1@.200	Ea	64.30	6.91	—	71.21

Description	Craft@Hrs	Unit	Material $	Labor $	Equipment $	Total $

90 degree standard radius pressfit ell, with Type O o-ring (P x P)

Description	Craft@Hrs	Unit	Material $	Labor $	Equipment $	Total $
3/4"	P1@.170	Ea	23.70	5.87	—	29.57
1"	P1@.180	Ea	26.70	6.22	—	32.92
1¼"	P1@.190	Ea	37.40	6.56	—	43.96
1½"	P1@.200	Ea	45.70	6.91	—	52.61
2"	P1@.200	Ea	63.30	6.91	—	70.21

90 degree short radius pressfit ell, with Type O o-ring (P x P)

Description	Craft@Hrs	Unit	Material $	Labor $	Equipment $	Total $
3/4"	P1@.170	Ea	27.10	5.87	—	32.97
1"	P1@.180	Ea	32.80	6.22	—	39.02
1¼"	P1@.190	Ea	49.90	6.56	—	56.46
1½"	P1@.200	Ea	61.80	6.91	—	68.71
2"	P1@.200	Ea	80.80	6.91	—	87.71

90 degree standard radius reducing pressfit x FIP ell, with Type O o-ring (P x F)

Description	Craft@Hrs	Unit	Material $	Labor $	Equipment $	Total $
1" x 1/2"	P1@.185	Ea	30.60	6.39	—	36.99
1" x 3/4"	P1@.185	Ea	30.90	6.39	—	37.29
1¼" x 1/2"	P1@.195	Ea	40.80	6.74	—	47.54
1¼" x 1/2"	P1@.195	Ea	42.00	6.74	—	48.74
1½" x 1/2"	P1@.215	Ea	51.20	7.43	—	58.63
1½" x 3/4"	P1@.215	Ea	51.80	7.43	—	59.23

90 degree short radius reducing pressfit x FIP ell, with Type O o-ring (P x F)

Description	Craft@Hrs	Unit	Material $	Labor $	Equipment $	Total $
1" x 3/4"	P1@.185	Ea	27.90	6.39	—	34.29
3/4" x 1"	P1@.185	Ea	28.10	6.39	—	34.49
1¼" x 3/4"	P1@.195	Ea	39.00	6.74	—	45.74
1½" x 3/4"	P1@.215	Ea	49.50	7.43	—	56.93

Standard coupling, pressfit, with Type O o-ring (P x P)

Description	Craft@Hrs	Unit	Material $	Labor $	Equipment $	Total $
3/4"	P1@.170	Ea	17.60	5.87	—	23.47
1"	P1@.180	Ea	23.00	6.22	—	29.22
1¼"	P1@.190	Ea	31.90	6.56	—	38.46
1½"	P1@.200	Ea	39.10	6.91	—	46.01
2"	P1@.200	Ea	52.60	6.91	—	59.51

Carbon Steel, Schedule 5 with Pressfit Fittings

Description	Craft@Hrs	Unit	Material $	Labor $	Equipment $	Total $

Slip coupling, pressfit, with Type O o-ring (P x P)

Description	Craft@Hrs	Unit	Material $	Labor $	Equipment $	Total $
3/4"	P1@.170	Ea	23.90	5.87	—	29.77
1"	P1@.180	Ea	30.60	6.22	—	36.82
1¼"	P1@.190	Ea	40.80	6.56	—	47.36
1½"	P1@.200	Ea	50.50	6.91	—	57.41
2"	P1@.200	Ea	67.20	6.91	—	74.11

Tee, pressfit, with Type O o-ring (P x P)

Description	Craft@Hrs	Unit	Material $	Labor $	Equipment $	Total $
3/4"	P1@.190	Ea	27.00	6.56	—	33.56
1"	P1@.220	Ea	32.00	7.60	—	39.60
1¼"	P1@.240	Ea	42.30	8.29	—	50.59
1½"	P1@.255	Ea	51.60	8.81	—	60.41
2"	P1@.270	Ea	70.50	9.33	—	79.83

Reducing tee, pressfit, with Type O o-ring (P x P x P)

Description	Craft@Hrs	Unit	Material $	Labor $	Equipment $	Total $
1" x 3/4"	P1@.220	Ea	21.50	7.60	—	29.10
1¼" x 3/4"	P1@.240	Ea	43.40	8.29	—	51.69
1¼" x 1"	P1@.240	Ea	51.80	8.29	—	60.09
1½" x 3/4"	P1@.255	Ea	50.50	8.81	—	59.31
1½" x 1"	P1@.255	Ea	58.40	8.81	—	67.21
2" x 3/4"	P1@.270	Ea	66.70	9.33	—	76.03
2" x 1"	P1@.270	Ea	76.90	9.33	—	86.23
2" x 1½"	P1@.270	Ea	80.80	9.33	—	90.13

Male threaded pressfit adapter with Type O o-ring (P x M)

Description	Craft@Hrs	Unit	Material $	Labor $	Equipment $	Total $
3/4" x 1/2"	P1@.180	Ea	16.40	6.22	—	22.62
3/4" x 3/4"	P1@.190	Ea	17.60	6.56	—	24.16
3/4" x 1"	P1@.190	Ea	19.60	6.56	—	26.16
1" x 3/4"	P1@.190	Ea	22.90	6.56	—	29.46
1" x 1"	P1@.190	Ea	24.50	6.56	—	31.06
1¼" x 1¼"	P1@.200	Ea	34.00	6.91	—	40.91
1½" x 1½"	P1@.215	Ea	42.40	7.43	—	49.83
2" x 2"	P1@.225	Ea	55.00	7.77	—	62.77

Female threaded pressfit adapter with Type O o-ring (P x F)

Description	Craft@Hrs	Unit	Material $	Labor $	Equipment $	Total $
3/4" x 1/2"	P1@.180	Ea	16.40	6.22	—	22.62
3/4" x 3/4"	P1@.190	Ea	17.60	6.56	—	24.16
1" x 1/2"	P1@.190	Ea	18.30	6.56	—	24.86
1" x 3/4"	P1@.190	Ea	24.50	6.56	—	31.06
1" x 1"	P1@.200	Ea	25.20	6.91	—	32.11

Carbon Steel, Schedule 80 with 300# Fittings & Butt-Welded Joints

Schedule 80 carbon steel (ASTM A-53 and A-120) pipe with 300 pound carbon steel welding fittings is commonly used for steam condensate and re-circulating water systems where operating pressures do not exceed 700 PSIG.

The cost estimates in this section are based on the conditions, limitations and wage rates described in the section "How to Use This Book" beginning on page 5.

Equipment cost, where shown, is $110 per hour for a 10-ton hydraulic truck-mounted crane.

Description	Craft@Hrs	Unit	Material $	Labor $	Equipment $	Total $

Schedule 80 carbon steel butt-welded horizontal pipe assembly.

Horizontally hung in a building. Assembly includes fittings and hanger assemblies. Based on a reducing tee and a 45 degree elbow every 16 feet for 1/2" pipe. A reducing tee and a 45 degree elbow every 50 feet for 12" pipe. Hangers spaced to meet plumbing code. *(Distance between fittings in the pipe assembly increases as pipe diameter increases.)* Use these figures for preliminary estimates.

Description	Craft@Hrs	Unit	Material $	Labor $	Equipment $	Total $
1/2"	P1@.183	LF	4.27	6.32	—	10.59
3/4"	P1@.203	LF	4.76	7.01	—	11.77
1"	P1@.241	LF	5.44	8.33	—	13.77
1¼"	P1@.246	LF	6.11	8.50	—	14.61
1½"	P1@.271	LF	6.63	9.36	—	15.99
2"	P1@.350	LF	8.62	12.10	—	20.72
2½"	P1@.437	LF	12.80	15.10	—	27.90
3"	P1@.532	LF	16.70	18.40	—	35.10
4"	P1@.601	LF	24.20	20.80	—	45.00
6"	ER@.833	LF	33.80	30.80	13.00	77.60
8"	ER@.994	LF	52.20	36.80	15.60	104.60
10"	ER@1.20	LF	88.40	44.40	18.90	151.70
12"	ER@1.43	LF	104.00	52.90	22.60	179.50

Schedule 80 carbon steel butt-welded vertical pipe assembly.

Riser assembly, including fittings and riser clamps. Based on a reducing tee, and a riser clamp on every floor. Use these figures for preliminary estimates.

Description	Craft@Hrs	Unit	Material $	Labor $	Equipment $	Total $
1/2"	P1@.153	LF	4.21	5.29	—	9.50
3/4"	P1@.163	LF	4.71	5.63	—	10.34
1"	P1@.196	LF	5.40	6.77	—	12.17
1¼"	P1@.229	LF	6.73	7.91	—	14.64
1½"	P1@.240	LF	7.19	8.29	—	15.48
2"	P1@.310	LF	8.97	10.70	—	19.67
2½"	P1@.395	LF	13.10	13.60	—	26.70
3"	P1@.190	LF	16.80	6.56	—	23.36
4"	P1@.610	LF	24.20	21.10	—	45.30
6"	ER@.877	LF	35.70	32.50	13.80	82.00
8"	ER@1.04	LF	56.90	38.50	16.30	111.70
10"	ER@1.28	LF	95.80	47.40	20.10	163.30
12"	ER@1.58	LF	118.00	58.50	24.80	201.30

Carbon Steel, Schedule 80 with 300# Fittings & Butt-Welded Joints

Description	Craft@Hrs	Unit	Material $	Labor $	Equipment $	Total $

Schedule 80 carbon steel pipe, plain end, butt-welded

Description	Craft@Hrs	Unit	Material $	Labor $	Equipment $	Total $
1/2"	P1@.080	LF	1.70	2.76	—	4.46
3/4"	P1@.090	LF	2.11	3.11	—	5.22
1"	P1@.110	LF	2.89	3.80	—	6.69
1¼"	P1@.120	LF	3.85	4.15	—	8.00
1½"	P1@.130	LF	4.64	4.49	—	9.13
2"	P1@.170	LF	6.44	5.87	—	12.31
2½"	P1@.220	LF	9.88	7.60	—	17.48
3"	P1@.280	LF	13.10	9.67	—	22.77
4"	P1@.340	LF	19.30	11.70	—	31.00
6"	ER@.460	LF	29.00	17.00	7.20	53.20
8"	ER@.560	LF	43.80	20.70	8.80	73.30
10"	ER@.660	LF	75.90	24.40	10.50	110.80
12"	ER@.840	LF	87.30	31.10	13.20	131.60

Schedule 80 carbon steel 45 degree ell, butt-welded

Description	Craft@Hrs	Unit	Material $	Labor $	Equipment $	Total $
1/2"	P1@.300	Ea	5.96	10.40	—	16.36
3/4"	P1@.440	Ea	5.96	15.20	—	21.16
1"	P1@.590	Ea	5.96	20.40	—	26.36
1¼"	P1@.740	Ea	6.57	25.60	—	32.17
1½"	P1@.890	Ea	6.84	30.70	—	37.54
2"	P1@1.18	Ea	6.42	40.80	—	47.22
2½"	P1@1.49	Ea	8.76	51.50	—	60.26
3"	P1@1.77	Ea	11.00	61.20	—	72.20
4"	P1@2.37	Ea	16.70	81.90	—	98.60
6"	ER@3.55	Ea	46.90	131.00	55.90	233.80
8"	ER@4.26	Ea	76.10	158.00	67.00	301.10
10"	ER@5.32	Ea	122.00	197.00	83.60	402.60
12"	ER@6.38	Ea	183.00	236.00	100.30	519.30

Schedule 80 carbon steel 90 degree ell, butt-welded

Description	Craft@Hrs	Unit	Material $	Labor $	Equipment $	Total $
1/2"	P1@.300	Ea	6.02	10.40	—	16.42
3/4"	P1@.440	Ea	6.02	15.20	—	21.22
1"	P1@.590	Ea	6.02	20.40	—	26.42
1¼"	P1@.740	Ea	6.91	25.60	—	32.51
1½"	P1@.890	Ea	7.42	30.70	—	38.12
2"	P1@1.18	Ea	11.10	40.80	—	51.90
2½"	P1@1.49	Ea	11.10	51.50	—	62.60
3"	P1@1.77	Ea	14.50	61.20	—	75.70
4"	P1@2.37	Ea	34.70	81.90	—	116.60
6"	ER@3.55	Ea	65.90	131.00	55.90	252.80
8"	ER@4.26	Ea	121.00	158.00	67.00	346.00
10"	ER@5.32	Ea	219.00	197.00	83.60	499.60
12"	ER@6.38	Ea	309.00	236.00	100.30	645.30

Carbon Steel, Schedule 80 with 300# Fittings & Butt-Welded Joints

Description	Craft@Hrs	Unit	Material $	Labor $	Equipment $	Total $

Schedule 80 carbon steel tee, butt-welded

Description	Craft@Hrs	Unit	Material $	Labor $	Equipment $	Total $
1/2"	P1@.440	Ea	20.20	15.20	—	35.40
3/4"	P1@.670	Ea	20.20	23.10	—	43.30
1¼"	P1@1.11	Ea	20.20	38.40	—	58.60
1½"	P1@1.33	Ea	22.80	46.00	—	68.80
2"	P1@1.77	Ea	19.60	61.20	—	80.80
2½"	P1@2.22	Ea	47.10	76.70	—	123.80
3"	P1@2.66	Ea	51.80	91.90	—	143.70
4"	P1@3.55	Ea	54.60	123.00	—	177.60
6"	ER@5.32	Ea	87.60	197.00	83.60	368.20
8"	ER@6.38	Ea	176.00	236.00	100.30	512.30
10"	ER@7.98	Ea	284.00	295.00	125.40	704.40
12"	ER@9.58	Ea	411.00	355.00	150.70	916.70

Carbon Steel, Schedule 80 with 300# Fittings & Butt-Welded Joints

Description	Craft@Hrs	Unit	Material $	Labor $	Equipment $	Total $
Schedule 80 carbon steel reducing tee, butt-welded						
1" x 3/4"	P1@.810	Ea	24.70	28.00	—	52.70
1¼" x 1/2"	P1@1.04	Ea	24.70	35.90	—	60.60
1¼" x 3/4"	P1@1.04	Ea	24.70	35.90	—	60.60
1¼" x 1"	P1@1.04	Ea	24.70	35.90	—	60.60
1½" x 1/2"	P1@1.26	Ea	24.70	43.50	—	68.20
1½" x 3/4"	P1@1.26	Ea	24.70	43.50	—	68.20
1½" x 1"	P1@1.26	Ea	24.70	43.50	—	68.20
1½" x 1¼"	P1@1.26	Ea	24.70	43.50	—	68.20
2" x 3/4"	P1@1.63	Ea	26.70	56.30	—	83.00
2" x 1"	P1@1.63	Ea	26.70	56.30	—	83.00
2" x 1¼"	P1@1.63	Ea	26.70	56.30	—	83.00
2" x 1½"	P1@1.63	Ea	26.70	56.30	—	83.00
2½" x 1"	P1@2.07	Ea	37.30	71.50	—	108.80
2½" x 1¼"	P1@2.07	Ea	37.30	71.50	—	108.80
2½" x 1½"	P1@2.07	Ea	37.30	71.50	—	108.80
2½" x 2"	P1@2.07	Ea	37.30	71.50	—	108.80
3" x 1¼"	P1@2.51	Ea	37.30	86.70	—	124.00
3" x 2"	P1@2.51	Ea	37.30	86.70	—	124.00
3" x 2½"	P1@2.51	Ea	37.30	86.70	—	124.00
4" x 1½"	P1@3.25	Ea	58.30	112.00	—	170.30
4" x 2"	P1@3.25	Ea	58.30	112.00	—	170.30
4" x 2½"	P1@3.25	Ea	58.30	112.00	—	170.30
4" x 3"	P1@3.25	Ea	58.30	112.00	—	170.30
6" x 2½"	ER@5.03	Ea	108.00	186.00	79.20	373.20
6" x 3"	ER@5.03	Ea	108.00	186.00	79.20	373.20
6" x 4"	ER@5.03	Ea	108.00	186.00	79.20	373.20
8" x 3"	ER@5.85	Ea	192.00	217.00	92.40	501.40
8" x 4"	ER@5.85	Ea	192.00	217.00	92.40	501.40
8" x 6"	ER@5.85	Ea	192.00	217.00	92.40	501.40
10" x 4"	ER@7.45	Ea	305.00	276.00	117.70	698.70
10" x 6"	ER@7.45	Ea	305.00	276.00	117.70	698.70
10" x 8"	ER@7.45	Ea	305.00	276.00	117.70	698.70
12" x 6"	ER@9.04	Ea	558.00	335.00	141.90	1,034.90
12" x 8"	ER@9.04	Ea	558.00	335.00	141.90	1,034.90
12" x 10"	ER@9.04	Ea	558.00	335.00	141.90	1,034.90
Schedule 80 carbon steel concentric reducer, butt-welded						
3/4"	P1@.360	Ea	12.00	12.40	—	24.40
1"	P1@.500	Ea	12.80	17.30	—	30.10
1¼"	P1@.665	Ea	11.10	23.00	—	34.10
1½"	P1@.800	Ea	11.90	27.60	—	39.50
2"	P1@1.00	Ea	10.20	34.60	—	44.80
2½"	P1@1.33	Ea	13.40	46.00	—	59.40
3"	P1@1.63	Ea	12.80	56.30	—	69.10
4"	P1@2.00	Ea	17.00	69.10	—	86.10
6"	ER@2.96	Ea	37.30	110.00	46.50	193.80
8"	ER@3.90	Ea	55.00	144.00	61.30	260.30
10"	ER@4.79	Ea	76.10	177.00	75.40	328.50
12"	ER@5.85	Ea	111.00	217.00	92.10	420.10

Carbon Steel, Schedule 80 with 300# Fittings & Butt-Welded Joints

Description	Craft@Hrs	Unit	Material $	Labor $	Equipment $	Total $

Schedule 80 carbon steel eccentric reducer, butt-welded

Description	Craft@Hrs	Unit	Material $	Labor $	Equipment $	Total $
3/4"	P1@.360	Ea	14.80	12.40	—	27.20
1"	P1@.500	Ea	19.20	17.30	—	36.50
1¼"	P1@.665	Ea	15.40	23.00	—	38.40
1½"	P1@.800	Ea	18.30	27.60	—	45.90
2"	P1@1.00	Ea	14.60	34.60	—	49.20
2½"	P1@1.33	Ea	17.70	46.00	—	63.70
3"	P1@1.63	Ea	17.00	56.30	—	73.30
4"	P1@2.00	Ea	23.90	69.10	—	93.00
6"	ER@2.96	Ea	54.70	110.00	46.50	211.20
8"	ER@3.90	Ea	81.50	144.00	61.30	286.80
10"	ER@4.79	Ea	143.00	177.00	75.40	395.40
12"	ER@5.85	Ea	221.00	217.00	94.30	532.30

Schedule 80 carbon steel cap, butt-welded

Description	Craft@Hrs	Unit	Material $	Labor $	Equipment $	Total $
1/2"	P1@.180	Ea	11.90	6.22	—	18.12
3/4"	P1@.270	Ea	16.60	9.33	—	25.93
1"	P1@.360	Ea	7.68	12.40	—	20.08
1¼"	P1@.460	Ea	7.68	15.90	—	23.58
1½"	P1@.560	Ea	8.40	19.30	—	27.70
2"	P1@.740	Ea	7.27	25.60	—	32.87
2½"	P1@.920	Ea	8.15	31.80	—	39.95
3"	P1@1.11	Ea	8.68	38.40	—	47.08
4"	P1@1.50	Ea	11.60	51.80	—	63.40
6"	ER@2.24	Ea	21.60	82.90	35.20	139.70
8"	ER@2.68	Ea	33.50	99.20	42.10	174.80
10"	ER@3.36	Ea	49.60	124.00	52.80	226.40
12"	ER@4.00	Ea	65.70	148.00	62.90	276.60

Schedule 80 carbon steel union, butt-welded

Description	Craft@Hrs	Unit	Material $	Labor $	Equipment $	Total $
1/2"	P1@.300	Ea	10.00	10.40	—	20.40
3/4"	P1@.440	Ea	12.00	15.20	—	27.20
1"	P1@.590	Ea	15.80	20.40	—	36.20
1¼"	P1@.740	Ea	26.70	25.60	—	52.30
1½"	P1@.890	Ea	29.00	30.70	—	59.70
2"	P1@1.18	Ea	38.60	40.80	—	79.40
2½"	P1@1.49	Ea	84.20	51.50	—	135.70
3"	P1@1.77	Ea	105.00	61.20	—	166.20

Carbon steel weldolet

Description	Craft@Hrs	Unit	Material $	Labor $	Equipment $	Total $
1/2"	P1@.440	Ea	10.90	15.20	—	26.10
3/4"	P1@.670	Ea	11.20	23.10	—	34.30
1"	P1@.890	Ea	12.20	30.70	—	42.90
1¼"	P1@1.11	Ea	15.80	38.40	—	54.20
1½"	P1@1.33	Ea	15.80	46.00	—	61.80
2"	P1@1.77	Ea	16.30	61.20	—	77.50
2½"	P1@2.22	Ea	37.20	76.70	—	113.90
3"	P1@2.66	Ea	38.30	91.90	—	130.20
4"	P1@3.55	Ea	85.10	123.00	—	208.10

Carbon Steel, Schedule 80 with 300# Fittings & Butt-Welded Joints

Description	Craft@Hrs	Unit	Material $	Labor $	Equipment $	Total $

Carbon steel threadolet

Description	Craft@Hrs	Unit	Material $	Labor $	Equipment $	Total $
1/2"	P1@.300	Ea	8.01	10.40	—	18.41
3/4"	P1@.440	Ea	8.85	15.20	—	24.05
1"	P1@.590	Ea	10.90	20.40	—	31.30
1¼"	P1@.740	Ea	49.00	25.60	—	74.60
1½"	P1@.890	Ea	49.00	30.70	—	79.70
2"	P1@1.18	Ea	64.70	40.80	—	105.50

300# forged steel slip-on companion flange, welding type

Description	Craft@Hrs	Unit	Material $	Labor $	Equipment $	Total $
2½"	P1@.810	Ea	27.30	28.00	—	55.30
3"	P1@.980	Ea	27.30	33.90	—	61.20
4"	P1@1.30	Ea	40.20	44.90	—	85.10
6"	ER@1.95	Ea	73.00	72.20	30.60	175.80
8"	ER@2.35	Ea	103.00	87.00	37.10	227.10
10"	ER@2.90	Ea	170.00	107.00	45.70	322.70
12"	ER@3.50	Ea	272.00	130.00	55.00	457.00

Class 300 bronze body gate valve, threaded joints

Description	Craft@Hrs	Unit	Material $	Labor $	Equipment $	Total $
1/2"	P1@.210	Ea	37.90	7.26	—	45.16
3/4"	P1@.250	Ea	49.50	8.64	—	58.14
1"	P1@.300	Ea	60.10	10.40	—	70.50
1¼"	P1@.400	Ea	81.90	13.80	—	95.70
1½"	P1@.450	Ea	103.00	15.50	—	118.50
2"	P1@.500	Ea	152.00	17.30	—	169.30
2½"	P1@.750	Ea	311.00	25.90	—	336.90
3"	P1@.950	Ea	441.00	32.80	—	473.80

Class 250 iron body gate valve, flanged

Description	Craft@Hrs	Unit	Material $	Labor $	Equipment $	Total $
2½"	P1@.600	Ea	944.00	20.70	—	964.70
3"	P1@.750	Ea	681.00	25.90	—	706.90
4"	P1@1.35	Ea	991.00	46.60	—	1,037.60
6"	ER@2.50	Ea	1,350.00	92.60	39.30	1,481.90
8"	ER@3.00	Ea	4,590.00	111.00	47.10	4,748.10
10"	ER@4.00	Ea	7,500.00	148.00	62.90	7,710.90
12"	ER@4.50	Ea	12,300.00	167.00	70.80	12,537.80

Class 300 bronze body globe valve, threaded

Description	Craft@Hrs	Unit	Material $	Labor $	Equipment $	Total $
1/2"	P1@.210	Ea	56.50	7.26	—	63.76
3/4"	P1@.250	Ea	71.80	8.64	—	80.44
1"	P1@.300	Ea	102.00	10.40	—	112.40
1¼"	P1@.400	Ea	148.00	13.80	—	161.80
1½"	P1@.450	Ea	197.00	15.50	—	212.50
2"	P1@.500	Ea	273.00	17.30	—	290.30

Carbon Steel, Schedule 80 with 300# Fittings & Butt-Welded Joints

Description	Craft@Hrs	Unit	Material $	Labor $	Equipment $	Total $

Class 250 iron body globe valve, flanged

Description	Craft@Hrs	Unit	Material $	Labor $	Equipment $	Total $
2"	P1@.500	Ea	497.00	17.30	—	514.30
2½"	P1@.600	Ea	617.00	20.70	—	637.70
3"	P1@.750	Ea	735.00	25.90	—	760.90
4"	P1@1.35	Ea	1,010.00	46.60	—	1,056.60
6"	ER@2.50	Ea	2,000.00	92.60	39.30	2,131.90
8"	ER@3.00	Ea	4,420.00	111.00	47.10	4,578.10

200 PSIG iron body butterfly valve, lug type, lever operated

Description	Craft@Hrs	Unit	Material $	Labor $	Equipment $	Total $
2"	P1@.450	Ea	134.00	15.50	—	149.50
2½"	P1@.450	Ea	139.00	15.50	—	154.50
3"	P1@.550	Ea	146.00	19.00	—	165.00
4"	P1@.550	Ea	182.00	19.00	—	201.00
6"	ER@.800	Ea	293.00	29.60	12.70	335.30
8"	ER@.800	Ea	401.00	29.60	12.70	443.30
10"	ER@.900	Ea	557.00	33.30	14.10	604.40
12"	ER@1.00	Ea	729.00	37.00	15.70	781.70

200 PSIG iron body butterfly valve, wafer type, lever operated

Description	Craft@Hrs	Unit	Material $	Labor $	Equipment $	Total $
2"	P1@.450	Ea	122.00	15.50	—	137.50
2½"	P1@.450	Ea	125.00	15.50	—	140.50
3"	P1@.550	Ea	134.00	19.00	—	153.00
4"	P1@.550	Ea	163.00	19.00	—	182.00
6"	ER@.800	Ea	272.00	29.60	12.70	314.30
8"	ER@.800	Ea	377.00	29.60	12.70	419.30
10"	ER@.900	Ea	527.00	33.30	14.10	574.40
12"	ER@1.00	Ea	692.00	37.00	15.70	744.70

Class 300 bronze body swing check valve, threaded

Description	Craft@Hrs	Unit	Material $	Labor $	Equipment $	Total $
1/2"	P1@.210	Ea	120.00	7.26	—	127.26
3/4"	P1@.250	Ea	142.00	8.64	—	150.64
1"	P1@.300	Ea	218.00	10.40	—	228.40
1¼"	P1@.400	Ea	250.00	13.80	—	263.80
1½"	P1@.450	Ea	358.00	15.50	—	373.50
2"	P1@.500	Ea	500.00	17.30	—	517.30

Class 250 iron body swing check valve, flanged

Description	Craft@Hrs	Unit	Material $	Labor $	Equipment $	Total $
2"	P1@.500	Ea	401.00	17.30	—	418.30
2½"	P1@.600	Ea	467.00	20.70	—	487.70
3"	P1@.750	Ea	581.00	25.90	—	606.90
4"	P1@1.35	Ea	712.00	46.60	—	758.60
6"	ER@2.50	Ea	1,390.00	92.60	39.30	1,521.90
8"	ER@3.00	Ea	2,590.00	111.00	47.10	2,748.10

Description	Craft@Hrs	Unit	Material $	Labor $	Equipment $	Total $

Class 250 iron body silent check valve, flanged

Description	Craft@Hrs	Unit	Material $	Labor $	Equipment $	Total $
2"	P1@.500	Ea	168.00	17.30	—	185.30
2½"	P1@.600	Ea	193.00	20.70	—	213.70
3"	P1@.750	Ea	215.00	25.90	—	240.90
4"	P1@1.35	Ea	292.00	46.60	—	338.60
6"	ER@2.50	Ea	512.00	92.60	39.30	643.90
8"	ER@3.00	Ea	932.00	111.00	47.10	1,090.10
10"	ER@4.00	Ea	1,470.00	148.00	62.90	1,680.90

Class 250 bronze body strainer, threaded

Description	Craft@Hrs	Unit	Material $	Labor $	Equipment $	Total $
1/2"	P1@.210	Ea	36.80	7.26	—	44.06
3/4"	P1@.250	Ea	49.80	8.64	—	58.44
1"	P1@.300	Ea	63.20	10.40	—	73.60
1¼"	P1@.400	Ea	89.40	13.80	—	103.20
1½"	P1@.450	Ea	116.00	15.50	—	131.50
2"	P1@.500	Ea	198.00	17.30	—	215.30

Class 250 iron body strainer, flanged

Description	Craft@Hrs	Unit	Material $	Labor $	Equipment $	Total $
2"	P1@.500	Ea	212.00	17.30	—	229.30
2½"	P1@.600	Ea	232.00	20.70	—	252.70
3"	P1@.750	Ea	271.00	25.90	—	296.90
4"	P1@1.35	Ea	481.00	46.60	—	527.60
6"	ER@2.50	Ea	770.00	92.60	39.30	901.90
8"	ER@3.00	Ea	1,410.00	111.00	47.10	1,568.10

Installation of 2-way control valve, threaded joints

Description	Craft@Hrs	Unit	Material $	Labor $	Equipment $	Total $
1/2"	P1@.210	Ea	—	7.26	—	7.26
3/4"	P1@.250	Ea	—	8.64	—	8.64
1"	P1@.300	Ea	—	10.40	—	10.40
1¼"	P1@.400	Ea	—	13.80	—	13.80
1½"	P1@.450	Ea	—	15.50	—	15.50
2"	P1@.500	Ea	—	17.30	—	17.30
2½"	P1@.830	Ea	—	28.70	—	28.70
3"	P1@.990	Ea	—	34.20	—	34.20

Installation of 2-way control valve, flanged joints

Description	Craft@Hrs	Unit	Material $	Labor $	Equipment $	Total $
2"	P1@.500	Ea	—	17.30	—	17.30
2½"	P1@.600	Ea	—	20.70	—	20.70
3"	P1@.750	Ea	—	25.90	—	25.90
4"	P1@1.35	Ea	—	46.60	—	46.60
6"	P1@2.50	Ea	—	86.40	—	86.40
8"	P1@3.00	Ea	—	104.00	—	104.00
10"	P1@4.00	Ea	—	138.00	—	138.00
12"	P1@4.50	Ea	—	155.00	—	155.00

Carbon Steel, Schedule 80 with 300# Fittings & Butt-Welded Joints

Description	Craft@Hrs	Unit	Material $	Labor $	Equipment $	Total $

Installation of 3-way control valve, threaded joints

Description	Craft@Hrs	Unit	Material $	Labor $	Equipment $	Total $
1/2"	P1@.260	Ea	—	8.98	—	8.98
3/4"	P1@.365	Ea	—	12.60	—	12.60
1"	P1@.475	Ea	—	16.40	—	16.40
1¼"	P1@.575	Ea	—	19.90	—	19.90
1½"	P1@.680	Ea	—	23.50	—	23.50
2"	P1@.910	Ea	—	31.40	—	31.40
2½"	P1@1.12	Ea	—	38.70	—	38.70
3"	P1@1.33	Ea	—	46.00	—	46.00

Installation of 3-way control valve, flanged joints

Description	Craft@Hrs	Unit	Material $	Labor $	Equipment $	Total $
2"	P1@.910	Ea	—	31.40	—	31.40
2½"	P1@1.12	Ea	—	38.70	—	38.70
3"	P1@1.33	Ea	—	46.00	—	46.00
4"	P1@2.00	Ea	—	69.10	—	69.10
6"	P1@3.70	Ea	—	128.00	—	128.00
8"	P1@4.40	Ea	—	152.00	—	152.00
10"	P1@5.90	Ea	—	204.00	—	204.00
12"	P1@6.50	Ea	—	225.00	—	225.00

Bolt and gasket set

Description	Craft@Hrs	Unit	Material $	Labor $	Equipment $	Total $
2"	P1@.500	Ea	3.86	17.30	—	21.16
2½"	P1@.650	Ea	4.51	22.50	—	27.01
3"	P1@.750	Ea	7.64	25.90	—	33.54
4"	P1@1.00	Ea	12.70	34.60	—	47.30
6"	P1@1.20	Ea	21.20	41.50	—	62.70
8"	P1@1.25	Ea	23.80	43.20	—	67.00
10"	P1@1.70	Ea	40.90	58.70	—	99.60
12"	P1@2.20	Ea	46.20	76.00	—	122.20

Thermometer with well

Description	Craft@Hrs	Unit	Material $	Labor $	Equipment $	Total $
7"	P1@.250	Ea	159.00	8.64	—	167.64
9"	P1@.250	Ea	164.00	8.64	—	172.64

Dial type pressure gauge

Description	Craft@Hrs	Unit	Material $	Labor $	Equipment $	Total $
2½"	P1@.200	Ea	33.10	6.91	—	40.01
3½"	P1@.200	Ea	43.80	6.91	—	50.71

Pressure/temperature tap

Description	Craft@Hrs	Unit	Material $	Labor $	Equipment $	Total $
tap	P1@.150	Ea	15.70	5.18	—	20.88

Carbon Steel, Schedule 80 with 300# Fittings & Butt-Welded Joints

Description	Craft@Hrs	Unit	Material $	Labor $	Equipment $	Total $
Hanger with swivel assembly						
1/2"	P1@.250	Ea	5.62	8.64	—	14.26
3/4"	P1@.250	Ea	6.16	8.64	—	14.80
1"	P1@.250	Ea	6.67	8.64	—	15.31
1½"	P1@.300	Ea	6.99	10.40	—	17.39
2"	P1@.300	Ea	9.09	10.40	—	19.49
2½"	P1@.350	Ea	11.70	12.10	—	23.80
3"	P1@.350	Ea	14.70	12.10	—	26.80
4"	P1@.350	Ea	25.20	12.10	—	37.30
5"	P1@.450	Ea	29.50	15.50	—	45.00
6"	P1@.450	Ea	32.80	15.50	—	48.30
8"	P1@.450	Ea	43.30	15.50	—	58.80
10"	P1@.550	Ea	59.30	19.00	—	78.30
12"	P1@.600	Ea	78.50	20.70	—	99.20

Description	Craft@Hrs	Unit	Material $	Labor $	Equipment $	Total $
Riser clamp						
1/2"	P1@.100	Ea	2.41	3.46	—	5.87
3/4"	P1@.100	Ea	3.55	3.46	—	7.01
1"	P1@.100	Ea	3.59	3.46	—	7.05
1¼"	P1@.105	Ea	4.33	3.63	—	7.96
1½"	P1@.110	Ea	4.58	3.80	—	8.38
2"	P1@.115	Ea	4.84	3.97	—	8.81
2½"	P1@.120	Ea	5.09	4.15	—	9.24
3"	P1@.120	Ea	5.52	4.15	—	9.67
4"	P1@.125	Ea	7.03	4.32	—	11.35
5"	P1@.180	Ea	10.10	6.22	—	16.32
6"	P1@.200	Ea	12.20	6.91	—	19.11
8"	P1@.200	Ea	19.80	6.91	—	26.71
10"	P1@.250	Ea	29.40	8.64	—	38.04
12"	P1@.250	Ea	34.90	8.64	—	43.54

Carbon Steel, Schedule 80 with 300# M.I. Fittings & Threaded Joints

Schedule 80 carbon steel (ASTM A-53 and A-120) pipe with 300 pound malleable iron threaded fittings is commonly used for heating hot water, chilled water, steam and steam condensate systems where operating pressures do not exceed 250 PSIG for pipe sized 2 inches and smaller. For pipe sizes 2½ inches and larger wrought steel fittings either welded or grooved should be used.

The cost estimates in this section are based on the conditions, limitations and wage rates described in the section "How to Use This Book" beginning on page 5.

Equipment cost, where shown, is $110 per hour for a 10-ton hydraulic truck-mounted crane.

Description	Craft@Hrs	Unit	Material $	Labor $	Equipment $	Total $

Schedule 80 carbon steel threaded horizontal pipe assembly.
Horizontally hung in a building. Assembly includes fittings and hanger assemblies. Based on a reducing tee and a 45 degree elbow every 16 feet for 1/2" pipe and a reducing tee and a 45 degree elbow every 30 feet for 4" pipe. Hangers spaced to meet plumbing code. *(Distance between fittings in the pipe assembly increases as pipe diameter increases.)* Use these figures for preliminary estimates.

Description	Craft@Hrs	Unit	Material $	Labor $	Equipment $	Total $
1/2"	P1@.121	LF	3.53	4.18	—	7.71
3/4"	P1@.125	LF	4.02	4.32	—	8.34
1"	P1@.149	LF	5.04	5.15	—	10.19
1¼"	P1@.163	LF	5.81	5.63	—	11.44
1½"	P1@.186	LF	6.02	6.43	—	12.45
2"	P1@.210	LF	7.37	7.26	—	14.63
2½"	P1@.297	LF	9.84	10.30	—	20.14
3"	P1@.340	LF	20.90	11.70	—	32.60
4"	P1@.409	LF	31.70	14.10	—	45.80

Schedule 80 carbon steel threaded vertical pipe assembly.
Riser assembly, including fittings and riser clamps. Based on a reducing tee, and a riser clamp on every floor. Use these figures for preliminary estimates.

Description	Craft@Hrs	Unit	Material $	Labor $	Equipment $	Total $
1/2"	P1@.094	LF	2.89	3.25	—	6.14
3/4"	P1@.104	LF	3.31	3.59	—	6.90
1"	P1@.124	LF	4.35	4.28	—	8.63
1¼"	P1@.143	LF	5.08	4.94	—	10.02
1½"	P1@.161	LF	5.62	5.56	—	11.18
2"	P1@.179	LF	6.69	6.18	—	12.87
2½"	P1@.257	LF	9.36	8.88	—	18.24
3"	P1@.296	LF	28.00	10.20	—	38.20
4"	P1@.373	LF	46.70	12.90	—	59.60

Carbon Steel, Schedule 80 with 300# M.I. Fittings & Threaded Joints

Description	Craft@Hrs	Unit	Material $	Labor $	Equipment $	Total $
Schedule 80 carbon steel pipe, threaded and coupled joints						
1/2"	P1@.070	LF	1.79	2.42	—	4.21
3/4"	P1@.080	LF	2.24	2.76	—	5.00
1"	P1@.100	LF	3.05	3.46	—	6.51
1¼"	P1@.110	LF	3.99	3.80	—	7.79
1½"	P1@.120	LF	4.73	4.15	—	8.88
2"	P1@.130	LF	6.45	4.49	—	10.94
2½"	P1@.190	LF	10.10	6.56	—	16.66
3"	P1@.220	LF	13.30	7.60	—	20.90
4"	P1@.290	LF	19.30	10.00	—	29.30
300# malleable iron 45 degree ell, threaded joints						
1/2"	P1@.132	Ea	8.18	4.56	—	12.74
3/4"	P1@.143	Ea	9.08	4.94	—	14.02
1"	P1@.198	Ea	10.10	6.84	—	16.94
1¼"	P1@.264	Ea	15.50	9.12	—	24.62
1½"	P1@.330	Ea	20.30	11.40	—	31.70
2"	P1@.418	Ea	30.30	14.40	—	44.70
2½"	P1@.561	Ea	47.70	19.40	—	67.10
3"	P1@.704	Ea	63.60	24.30	—	87.90
4"	P1@.935	Ea	123.00	32.30	—	155.30
300# malleable iron 90 degree ell, threaded joints						
1/2"	P1@.132	Ea	6.29	4.56	—	10.85
3/4"	P1@.143	Ea	7.27	4.94	—	12.21
1"	P1@.198	Ea	9.27	6.84	—	16.11
1¼"	P1@.264	Ea	12.90	9.12	—	22.02
1½"	P1@.330	Ea	15.50	11.40	—	26.90
2"	P1@.418	Ea	21.70	14.40	—	36.10
2½"	P1@.561	Ea	41.30	19.40	—	60.70
3"	P1@.704	Ea	56.60	24.30	—	80.90
4"	P1@.935	Ea	113.00	32.30	—	145.30

Carbon Steel, Schedule 80 with 300# M.I. Fittings & Threaded Joints

Description	Craft@Hrs	Unit	Material $	Labor $	Equipment $	Total $

300# malleable iron tee, threaded joints

Description	Craft@Hrs	Unit	Material $	Labor $	Equipment $	Total $
1/2"	P1@.198	Ea	8.85	6.84	—	15.69
3/4"	P1@.209	Ea	9.72	7.22	—	16.94
1"	P1@.253	Ea	11.70	8.74	—	20.44
1¼"	P1@.341	Ea	15.50	11.80	—	27.30
1½"	P1@.429	Ea	19.30	14.80	—	34.10
2"	P1@.539	Ea	28.10	18.60	—	46.70
2½"	P1@.726	Ea	53.80	25.10	—	78.90
3"	P1@.913	Ea	90.10	31.50	—	121.60
4"	P1@1.21	Ea	153.00	41.80	—	194.80

300# malleable iron reducing tee, threaded joints

Description	Craft@Hrs	Unit	Material $	Labor $	Equipment $	Total $
3/4" x 1/2"	P1@.205	Ea	12.20	7.08	—	19.28
1" x 1/2"	P1@.205	Ea	15.30	7.08	—	22.38
1" x 3/4"	P1@.205	Ea	15.30	7.08	—	22.38
1¼" x 1/2"	P1@.310	Ea	19.80	10.70	—	30.50
1¼" x 3/4"	P1@.310	Ea	19.80	10.70	—	30.50
1¼" x 1"	P1@.310	Ea	19.80	10.70	—	30.50
1½" x 1/2"	P1@.400	Ea	24.40	13.80	—	38.20
1½" x 3/4"	P1@.400	Ea	24.40	13.80	—	38.20
1½" x 1"	P1@.400	Ea	24.40	13.80	—	38.20
1½" x 1¼"	P1@.400	Ea	24.40	13.80	—	38.20
2" x 1"	P1@.500	Ea	36.20	17.30	—	53.50
2" x 1¼"	P1@.500	Ea	36.20	17.30	—	53.50
2" x 1½"	P1@.500	Ea	36.20	17.30	—	53.50
3" x 1¼"	P1@.830	Ea	187.00	28.70	—	215.70
3" x 1½"	P1@.830	Ea	187.00	28.70	—	215.70
3" x 2"	P1@.830	Ea	187.00	28.70	—	215.70

300# malleable iron reducer, threaded joints

Description	Craft@Hrs	Unit	Material $	Labor $	Equipment $	Total $
3/4" x 1/2"	P1@.135	Ea	7.23	4.66	—	11.89
1" x 1/2"	P1@.170	Ea	8.64	5.87	—	14.51
1" x 3/4"	P1@.170	Ea	8.64	5.87	—	14.51
1¼" x 3/4"	P1@.220	Ea	10.90	7.60	—	18.50
1¼" x 1"	P1@.220	Ea	10.90	7.60	—	18.50
1½" x 1"	P1@.285	Ea	15.00	9.85	—	24.85
1½" x 1¼"	P1@.285	Ea	15.00	9.85	—	24.85
2" x 1¼"	P1@.360	Ea	21.60	12.40	—	34.00
2" x 1½"	P1@.360	Ea	21.60	12.40	—	34.00
3" x 2"	P1@.550	Ea	52.50	19.00	—	71.50
3" x 2½"	P1@.550	Ea	52.50	19.00	—	71.50

Carbon Steel, Schedule 80 with 300# M.I. Fittings & Threaded Joints

Description	Craft@Hrs	Unit	Material $	Labor $	Equipment $	Total $

300# malleable iron cross, threaded joints

Description	Craft@Hrs	Unit	Material $	Labor $	Equipment $	Total $
1/2"	P1@.310	Ea	21.20	10.70	—	31.90
3/4"	P1@.350	Ea	23.20	12.10	—	35.30
1"	P1@.400	Ea	26.30	13.80	—	40.10
1¼"	P1@.530	Ea	32.40	18.30	—	50.70
1½"	P1@.660	Ea	42.50	22.80	—	65.30
2"	P1@.770	Ea	60.90	26.60	—	87.50

300# malleable iron cap, threaded joint

Description	Craft@Hrs	Unit	Material $	Labor $	Equipment $	Total $
1/2"	P1@.100	Ea	4.25	3.46	—	7.71
3/4"	P1@.110	Ea	5.66	3.80	—	9.46
1"	P1@.155	Ea	7.30	5.36	—	12.66
1¼"	P1@.200	Ea	9.91	6.91	—	16.82
1½"	P1@.250	Ea	11.80	8.64	—	20.44
2"	P1@.320	Ea	16.30	11.10	—	27.40
3"	P1@.530	Ea	33.90	18.30	—	52.20
4"	P1@.705	Ea	62.30	24.40	—	86.70

300# malleable iron plug, threaded joint

Description	Craft@Hrs	Unit	Material $	Labor $	Equipment $	Total $
1/2"	P1@.090	Ea	1.05	3.11	—	4.16
3/4"	P1@.100	Ea	1.43	3.46	—	4.89
1"	P1@.140	Ea	1.70	4.84	—	6.54
1¼"	P1@.180	Ea	1.83	6.22	—	8.05
1½"	P1@.230	Ea	2.34	7.95	—	10.29
2"	P1@.290	Ea	3.62	10.00	—	13.62
2½"	P1@.380	Ea	5.10	13.10	—	18.20
3"	P1@.480	Ea	8.51	16.60	—	25.11
4"	P1@.640	Ea	24.40	22.10	—	46.50

300# malleable iron union, threaded joints

Description	Craft@Hrs	Unit	Material $	Labor $	Equipment $	Total $
1/2"	P1@.150	Ea	7.79	5.18	—	12.97
3/4"	P1@.165	Ea	8.78	5.70	—	14.48
1"	P1@.230	Ea	11.40	7.95	—	19.35
1¼"	P1@.310	Ea	17.60	10.70	—	28.30
1½"	P1@.400	Ea	19.10	13.80	—	32.90
2"	P1@.500	Ea	24.40	17.30	—	41.70
2½"	P1@.670	Ea	53.80	23.10	—	76.90
3"	P1@.840	Ea	90.40	29.00	—	119.40
4"	P1@.960	Ea	254.00	33.20	—	287.20

Carbon Steel, Schedule 80 with 300# M.I. Fittings & Threaded Joints

Description	Craft@Hrs	Unit	Material $	Labor $	Equipment $	Total $

300# malleable iron coupling, threaded joints

1/2"	P1@.132	Ea	4.74	4.56	—	9.30
3/4"	P1@.143	Ea	5.53	4.94	—	10.47
1"	P1@.198	Ea	6.52	6.84	—	13.36
1¼"	P1@.264	Ea	7.79	9.12	—	16.91
1½"	P1@.330	Ea	11.70	11.40	—	23.10
2"	P1@.418	Ea	16.30	14.40	—	30.70
2½"	P1@.561	Ea	20.80	19.40	—	40.20
3"	P1@.704	Ea	33.90	24.30	—	58.20
4"	P1@.935	Ea	81.00	32.30	—	113.30

Class 300 bronze body gate valve, threaded joints

1/2"	P1@.210	Ea	37.90	7.26	—	45.16
3/4"	P1@.250	Ea	49.20	8.64	—	57.84
1"	P1@.300	Ea	60.00	10.40	—	70.40
1¼"	P1@.400	Ea	81.70	13.80	—	95.50
1½"	P1@.450	Ea	103.00	15.50	—	118.50
2"	P1@.500	Ea	151.00	17.30	—	168.30

Class 250 iron body gate valve, flanged joints

2"	P1@.500	Ea	944.00	17.30	—	961.30
2½"	P1@.600	Ea	681.00	20.70	—	701.70
3"	P1@.750	Ea	862.00	25.90	—	887.90
4"	P1@1.35	Ea	1,460.00	46.60	—	1,506.60

Class 300 bronze body globe valve, threaded joints

1/2"	P1@.210	Ea	56.50	7.26	—	63.76
3/4"	P1@.250	Ea	71.80	8.64	—	80.44
1"	P1@.300	Ea	102.00	10.40	—	112.40
1¼"	P1@.400	Ea	148.00	13.80	—	161.80
1½"	P1@.450	Ea	197.00	15.50	—	212.50
2"	P1@.500	Ea	273.00	17.30	—	290.30

Class 250 iron body globe valve, flanged joints

2"	P1@.500	Ea	497.00	17.30	—	514.30
2½"	P1@.600	Ea	617.00	20.70	—	637.70
3"	P1@.750	Ea	735.00	25.90	—	760.90
4"	P1@1.35	Ea	1,010.00	46.60	—	1,056.60

200 PSIG iron body butterfly valve, lug type, lever operated

2"	P1@.450	Ea	134.00	15.50	—	149.50
2½"	P1@.450	Ea	139.00	15.50	—	154.50
3"	P1@.550	Ea	146.00	19.00	—	165.00
4"	P1@.550	Ea	182.00	19.00	—	201.00

Carbon Steel, Schedule 80 with 300# M.I. Fittings & Threaded Joints

Description	Craft@Hrs	Unit	Material $	Labor $	Equipment $	Total $

200 PSIG iron body butterfly valve, wafer type, lever operated

2"	P1@.450	Ea	122.00	15.50	—	137.50
2½"	P1@.450	Ea	125.00	15.50	—	140.50
3"	P1@.550	Ea	134.00	19.00	—	153.00
4"	P1@.550	Ea	163.00	19.00	—	182.00

Class 150 bronze body 2-piece ball valve, threaded joints

1/2"	P1@.210	Ea	11.80	7.26	—	19.06
3/4"	P1@.250	Ea	19.10	8.64	—	27.74
1"	P1@.300	Ea	24.30	10.40	—	34.70
1¼"	P1@.400	Ea	30.30	13.80	—	44.10
1½"	P1@.450	Ea	41.00	15.50	—	56.50
2"	P1@.500	Ea	51.90	17.30	—	69.20
3"	P1@.625	Ea	355.00	21.60	—	376.60
4"	P1@.690	Ea	465.00	23.80	—	488.80

Class 300 bronze body swing check valve, threaded joints

1/2"	P1@.210	Ea	120.00	7.26	—	127.26
3/4"	P1@.250	Ea	142.00	8.64	—	150.64
1"	P1@.300	Ea	218.00	10.40	—	228.40
1¼"	P1@.400	Ea	250.00	13.80	—	263.80
1½"	P1@.450	Ea	358.00	15.50	—	373.50
2"	P1@.500	Ea	500.00	17.30	—	517.30

Class 250 iron body swing check valve, flanged joints

2"	P1@.500	Ea	401.00	17.30	—	418.30
2½"	P1@.600	Ea	467.00	20.70	—	487.70
3"	P1@.750	Ea	581.00	25.90	—	606.90
4"	P1@1.35	Ea	712.00	46.60	—	758.60

Class 250 iron body silent check valve, wafer type

2"	P1@.500	Ea	168.00	17.30	—	185.30
2½"	P1@.600	Ea	193.00	20.70	—	213.70
3"	P1@.750	Ea	215.00	25.90	—	240.90
4"	P1@1.35	Ea	292.00	46.60	—	338.60

Class 250 bronze body wye strainer, threaded joints

1/2"	P1@.210	Ea	36.80	7.26	—	44.06
3/4"	P1@.250	Ea	49.80	8.64	—	58.44
1"	P1@.300	Ea	63.20	10.40	—	73.60
1¼"	P1@.400	Ea	89.40	13.80	—	103.20
1½"	P1@.450	Ea	116.00	15.50	—	131.50
2"	P1@.500	Ea	198.00	17.30	—	215.30

Carbon Steel, Schedule 80 with 300# M.I. Fittings & Threaded Joints

Description	Craft@Hrs	Unit	Material $	Labor $	Equipment $	Total $

Class 250 iron body strainer, flanged ends

2"	P1@.500	Ea	212.00	17.30	—	229.30
2½"	P1@.600	Ea	232.00	20.70	—	252.70
3"	P1@.750	Ea	271.00	25.90	—	296.90
4"	P1@1.35	Ea	481.00	46.60	—	527.60

Installation of 2-way control valve, threaded joints

1/2"	P1@.210	Ea	—	7.26	—	7.26
3/4"	P1@.275	Ea	—	9.50	—	9.50
1"	P1@.350	Ea	—	12.10	—	12.10
1¼"	P1@.430	Ea	—	14.90	—	14.90
1½"	P1@.505	Ea	—	17.40	—	17.40
2"	P1@.675	Ea	—	23.30	—	23.30
2½"	P1@.830	Ea	—	28.70	—	28.70
3"	P1@.990	Ea	—	34.20	—	34.20

Installation of 3-way control valve, threaded joints

1/2"	P1@.260	Ea	—	8.98	—	8.98
3/4"	P1@.365	Ea	—	12.60	—	12.60
1"	P1@.475	Ea	—	16.40	—	16.40
1¼"	P1@.575	Ea	—	19.90	—	19.90
1½"	P1@.680	Ea	—	23.50	—	23.50
2"	P1@.910	Ea	—	31.40	—	31.40
2½"	P1@1.12	Ea	—	38.70	—	38.70
3"	P1@1.33	Ea	—	46.00	—	46.00

Threaded companion flange, 300# malleable iron

2"	P1@.290	Ea	87.50	10.00	—	97.50
2½"	P1@.380	Ea	120.00	13.10	—	133.10
3"	P1@.460	Ea	113.00	15.90	—	128.90
4"	P1@.600	Ea	211.00	20.70	—	231.70

Bolt and gasket sets

2"	P1@.500	Ea	3.86	17.30	—	21.16
2½"	P1@.650	Ea	4.51	22.50	—	27.01
3"	P1@.750	Ea	7.67	25.90	—	33.57
4"	P1@1.00	Ea	12.80	34.60	—	47.40

Carbon Steel, Schedule 80 with 300# M.I. Fittings & Threaded Joints

Description	Craft@Hrs	Unit	Material $	Labor $	Equipment $	Total $
Thermometer with well						
7"	P1@.250	Ea	159.00	8.64	—	167.64
9"	P1@.250	Ea	164.00	8.64	—	172.64
Dial type pressure gauge						
2½"	P1@.200	Ea	33.10	6.91	—	40.01
3½"	P1@.200	Ea	43.80	6.91	—	50.71
Pressure/temperature tap						
tap	P1@.150	Ea	15.70	5.18	—	20.88
Hanger with swivel assembly						
1/2"	P1@.250	Ea	4.13	8.64	—	12.77
3/4"	P1@.250	Ea	4.33	8.64	—	12.97
1"	P1@.250	Ea	4.57	8.64	—	13.21
1¼"	P1@.300	Ea	4.77	10.40	—	15.17
1½"	P1@.300	Ea	5.51	10.40	—	15.91
2"	P1@.300	Ea	6.05	10.40	—	16.45
2½"	P1@.350	Ea	7.82	12.10	—	19.92
3"	P1@.350	Ea	9.67	12.10	—	21.77
4"	P1@.350	Ea	14.90	12.10	—	27.00
Riser clamp						
1/2"	P1@.100	Ea	2.41	3.46	—	5.87
3/4"	P1@.100	Ea	3.55	3.46	—	7.01
1"	P1@.100	Ea	3.59	3.46	—	7.05
1¼"	P1@.105	Ea	4.33	3.63	—	7.96
1½"	P1@.110	Ea	4.58	3.80	—	8.38
2"	P1@.115	Ea	4.84	3.97	—	8.81
2½"	P1@.120	Ea	5.09	4.15	—	9.24
3"	P1@.120	Ea	5.52	4.15	—	9.67
4"	P1@.125	Ea	7.03	4.32	—	11.35

Schedule 160 carbon steel (ASTM A-106) pipe with steel fittings is commonly used for steam, steam condensate and recirculating systems.

The cost estimates in this section are based on the conditions, limitations and wage rates described in the section "How to Use This Book" beginning on page 5.

Description	Craft@Hrs	Unit	Material $	Labor $	Equipment $	Total $

Schedule 160 carbon steel threaded horizontal pipe assembly.

Horizontally hung in a building. Assembly includes fittings and hanger assemblies. Based on a reducing tee and a 45 degree elbow every 16 feet for 1/2" pipe. A reducing tee and a 45 degree elbow every 30 feet for 4" pipe. Hangers spaced to meet plumbing code. *(Distance between fittings in the pipe assembly increases as pipe diameter increases.)* Use these figures for preliminary estimates.

Description	Craft@Hrs	Unit	Material $	Labor $	Equipment $	Total $
1/2"	P1@.140	LF	5.15	4.84	—	9.99
3/4"	P1@.145	LF	6.03	5.01	—	11.04
1"	P1@.172	LF	8.27	5.94	—	14.21
1¼"	P1@.184	LF	9.06	6.36	—	15.42
1½"	P1@.207	LF	10.50	7.15	—	17.65
2"	P1@.272	LF	15.80	9.40	—	25.20
2½"	P1@.388	LF	24.30	13.40	—	37.70
3"	P1@.434	LF	36.20	15.00	—	51.20
4"	P1@.530	LF	59.30	18.30	—	77.60

Schedule 160 carbon steel socket weld horizontal pipe assembly.

Horizontally hung in a building. Assembly includes fittings and hanger assemblies. Based on a reducing tee and a 45 degree elbow every 16 feet for 1/2" pipe. A reducing tee and a 45 degree elbow every 30 feet for 4" pipe Hangers spaced to meet plumbing code. *(Distance between fittings in the pipe assembly increases as pipe diameter increases.)* Use these figures for preliminary estimates.

Description	Craft@Hrs	Unit	Material $	Labor $	Equipment $	Total $
1/2"	P1@.175	LF	5.00	6.05	—	11.05
3/4"	P1@.206	LF	5.79	7.12	—	12.91
1"	P1@.247	LF	7.97	8.53	—	16.50
1¼"	P1@.250	LF	8.84	8.64	—	17.48
1½"	P1@.284	LF	9.65	9.81	—	19.46
2"	P1@.375	LF	15.00	13.00	—	28.00
2½"	P1@.503	LF	22.60	17.40	—	40.00
3"	P1@.568	LF	35.20	19.60	—	54.80
4"	P1@.709	LF	58.10	24.50	—	82.60

Carbon Steel, Schedule 160 with 3,000-6,000# Fittings

Description	Craft@Hrs	Unit	Material $	Labor $	Equipment $	Total $

Schedule 160 carbon steel threaded vertical pipe assembly. Riser assembly, including fittings and riser clamps. Based on a reducing tee, and a riser clamp on every floor. Use these figures for preliminary estimates.

Description	Craft@Hrs	Unit	Material $	Labor $	Equipment $	Total $
1/2"	P1@.114	LF	4.52	3.94	—	8.46
3/4"	P1@.125	LF	5.42	4.32	—	9.74
1"	P1@.148	LF	7.49	5.11	—	12.60
1¼"	P1@.165	LF	9.18	5.70	—	14.88
1½"	P1@.183	LF	10.10	6.32	—	16.42
2"	P1@.242	LF	15.10	8.36	—	23.46
2½"	P1@.348	LF	22.60	12.00	—	34.60
3"	P1@.393	LF	34.90	13.60	—	48.50
4"	P1@.487	LF	55.70	16.80	—	72.50

Schedule 160 carbon steel socket weld vertical pipe assembly. Riser assembly, including fittings and riser clamps. Based on a reducing tee, and a riser clamp on every floor. Use these figures for preliminary estimates.

Description	Craft@Hrs	Unit	Material $	Labor $	Equipment $	Total $
1/2"	P1@.133	LF	4.41	4.60	—	9.01
3/4"	P1@.162	LF	5.21	5.60	—	10.81
1"	P1@.199	LF	7.31	6.88	—	14.19
1¼"	P1@.227	LF	8.52	7.84	—	16.36
1½"	P1@.255	LF	9.49	8.81	—	18.30
2"	P1@.341	LF	14.40	11.80	—	26.20
2½"	P1@.467	LF	21.00	16.10	—	37.10
3"	P1@.532	LF	35.20	18.40	—	53.60
4"	P1@.674	LF	55.00	23.30	—	78.30

Schedule 160 carbon steel plain end pipe

Description	Craft@Hrs	Unit	Material $	Labor $	Equipment $	Total $
1/2"	P1@.090	LF	4.19	3.11	—	7.30
3/4"	P1@.100	LF	4.85	3.46	—	8.31
1"	P1@.120	LF	6.89	4.15	—	11.04
1¼"	P1@.130	LF	8.11	4.49	—	12.60
1½"	P1@.140	LF	12.60	4.84	—	17.44
2"	P1@.190	LF	10.40	6.56	—	16.96
3"	P1@.310	LF	20.20	10.70	—	30.90
4"	P1@.380	LF	31.50	13.10	—	44.60

Description	Craft@Hrs	Unit	Material $	Labor $	Equipment $	Total $

3,000# carbon steel 45 degree ell, threaded joints

Description	Craft@Hrs	Unit	Material $	Labor $	Equipment $	Total $
1/2"	P1@.132	Ea	8.13	4.56	—	12.69
3/4"	P1@.143	Ea	9.31	4.94	—	14.25
1"	P1@.198	Ea	12.80	6.84	—	19.64
1¼"	P1@.264	Ea	17.60	9.12	—	26.72
1½"	P1@.330	Ea	26.70	11.40	—	38.10
2"	P1@.418	Ea	36.50	14.40	—	50.90
2½"	P1@.561	Ea	90.30	19.40	—	109.70
3"	P1@.704	Ea	147.00	24.30	—	171.30
4"	P1@.935	Ea	271.00	32.30	—	303.30

3,000# carbon steel 45 degree ell, socket-welded joints

Description	Craft@Hrs	Unit	Material $	Labor $	Equipment $	Total $
1/2"	P1@.300	Ea	6.59	10.40	—	16.99
3/4"	P1@.440	Ea	7.97	15.20	—	23.17
1"	P1@.590	Ea	10.40	20.40	—	30.80
1¼"	P1@.740	Ea	14.20	25.60	—	39.80
1½"	P1@.890	Ea	17.20	30.70	—	47.90
2"	P1@1.18	Ea	29.80	40.80	—	70.60
2½"	P1@1.49	Ea	77.00	51.50	—	128.50
3"	P1@1.77	Ea	129.00	61.20	—	190.20
4"	P1@2.37	Ea	256.00	81.90	—	337.90

6,000# carbon steel 45 degree ell, threaded joints

Description	Craft@Hrs	Unit	Material $	Labor $	Equipment $	Total $
1/2"	P1@.132	Ea	13.70	4.56	—	18.26
3/4"	P1@.143	Ea	18.70	4.94	—	23.64
1"	P1@.198	Ea	21.00	6.84	—	27.84
1¼"	P1@.264	Ea	55.80	9.12	—	64.92
1½"	P1@.330	Ea	55.80	11.40	—	67.20
2"	P1@.418	Ea	77.90	14.40	—	92.30
2½"	P1@.561	Ea	296.00	19.40	—	315.40
3"	P1@.704	Ea	305.00	24.30	—	329.30

6,000# carbon steel 45 degree ell, socket-welded joints

Description	Craft@Hrs	Unit	Material $	Labor $	Equipment $	Total $
1/2"	P1@.300	Ea	10.70	10.40	—	21.10
3/4"	P1@.440	Ea	12.30	15.20	—	27.50
1"	P1@.590	Ea	16.70	20.40	—	37.10
1¼"	P1@.740	Ea	59.90	25.60	—	85.50
1½"	P1@.890	Ea	40.40	30.70	—	71.10
2"	P1@1.18	Ea	50.20	40.80	—	91.00
2½"	P1@1.49	Ea	201.00	51.50	—	252.50
3"	P1@1.77	Ea	235.00	61.20	—	296.20
4"	P1@2.37	Ea	280.00	81.90	—	361.90

Carbon Steel, Schedule 160 with 3,000-6,000# Fittings

Description	Craft@Hrs	Unit	Material $	Labor $	Equipment $	Total $

3,000# carbon steel 90 degree ell, threaded joints

Description	Craft@Hrs	Unit	Material $	Labor $	Equipment $	Total $
1/2"	P1@.132	Ea	6.35	4.56	—	10.91
3/4"	P1@.143	Ea	7.64	4.94	—	12.58
1"	P1@.198	Ea	11.00	6.84	—	17.84
1¼"	P1@.264	Ea	18.70	9.12	—	27.82
1½"	P1@.330	Ea	28.00	11.40	—	39.40
2"	P1@.418	Ea	33.80	14.40	—	48.20
2½"	P1@.561	Ea	83.80	19.40	—	103.20
3"	P1@.704	Ea	128.00	24.30	—	152.30
4"	P1@.935	Ea	280.00	32.30	—	312.30

3,000# carbon steel 90 degree ell, socket-welded joints

Description	Craft@Hrs	Unit	Material $	Labor $	Equipment $	Total $
1/2"	P1@.300	Ea	6.29	10.40	—	16.69
3/4"	P1@.440	Ea	6.50	15.20	—	21.70
1"	P1@.590	Ea	8.35	20.40	—	28.75
1¼"	P1@.740	Ea	13.70	25.60	—	39.30
1½"	P1@.890	Ea	17.50	30.70	—	48.20
2"	P1@1.18	Ea	26.70	40.80	—	67.50
2½"	P1@1.49	Ea	64.10	51.50	—	115.60
3"	P1@1.77	Ea	106.00	61.20	—	167.20
4"	P1@2.37	Ea	311.00	81.90	—	392.90

6,000# carbon steel 90 degree ell, threaded joints

Description	Craft@Hrs	Unit	Material $	Labor $	Equipment $	Total $
1/2"	P1@.132	Ea	10.30	4.56	—	14.86
3/4"	P1@.143	Ea	13.10	4.94	—	18.04
1"	P1@.198	Ea	16.90	6.84	—	23.74
1¼"	P1@.264	Ea	28.40	9.12	—	37.52
1½"	P1@.330	Ea	44.00	11.40	—	55.40
2"	P1@.418	Ea	77.40	14.40	—	91.80
2½"	P1@.561	Ea	114.00	19.40	—	133.40
3"	P1@.704	Ea	260.00	24.30	—	284.30

6,000# carbon steel 90 degree ell, socket-welded joints

Description	Craft@Hrs	Unit	Material $	Labor $	Equipment $	Total $
1/2"	P1@.300	Ea	8.72	10.40	—	19.12
3/4"	P1@.440	Ea	10.20	15.20	—	25.40
1"	P1@.590	Ea	14.20	20.40	—	34.60
1¼"	P1@.740	Ea	20.60	25.60	—	46.20
1½"	P1@.890	Ea	31.20	30.70	—	61.90
2"	P1@1.18	Ea	45.80	40.80	—	86.60
2½"	P1@1.49	Ea	95.40	51.50	—	146.90
3"	P1@1.77	Ea	168.00	61.20	—	229.20
4"	P1@2.37	Ea	371.00	81.90	—	452.90

Description	Craft@Hrs	Unit	Material $	Labor $	Equipment $	Total $

3,000# carbon steel tee, threaded joints

Description	Craft@Hrs	Unit	Material $	Labor $	Equipment $	Total $
1/2"	P1@.198	Ea	8.38	6.84	—	15.22
3/4"	P1@.209	Ea	12.00	7.22	—	19.22
1"	P1@.253	Ea	15.20	8.74	—	23.94
1¼"	P1@.341	Ea	25.40	11.80	—	37.20
1½"	P1@.429	Ea	34.40	14.80	—	49.20
2"	P1@.539	Ea	45.90	18.60	—	64.50
2½"	P1@.726	Ea	110.00	25.10	—	135.10
3"	P1@.913	Ea	207.00	31.50	—	238.50
4"	P1@1.21	Ea	343.00	41.80	—	384.80

3,000# carbon steel tee, socket-welded joints

Description	Craft@Hrs	Unit	Material $	Labor $	Equipment $	Total $
1/2"	P1@.440	Ea	7.23	15.20	—	22.43
3/4"	P1@.670	Ea	9.12	23.10	—	32.22
1"	P1@.890	Ea	12.60	30.70	—	43.30
1¼"	P1@1.11	Ea	16.90	38.40	—	55.30
1½"	P1@1.33	Ea	26.40	46.00	—	72.40
2"	P1@1.77	Ea	37.00	61.20	—	98.20
2½"	P1@2.22	Ea	89.30	76.70	—	166.00
3"	P1@2.66	Ea	210.00	91.90	—	301.90
4"	P1@3.55	Ea	337.00	123.00	—	460.00

6,000# carbon steel tee, threaded joints

Description	Craft@Hrs	Unit	Material $	Labor $	Equipment $	Total $
1/2"	P1@.198	Ea	13.30	6.84	—	20.14
3/4"	P1@.209	Ea	17.90	7.22	—	25.12
1"	P1@.253	Ea	29.80	8.74	—	38.54
1¼"	P1@.341	Ea	37.20	11.80	—	49.00
1½"	P1@.429	Ea	50.60	14.80	—	65.40
2"	P1@.539	Ea	98.90	18.60	—	117.50
2½"	P1@.726	Ea	356.00	25.10	—	381.10
3"	P1@.913	Ea	359.00	31.50	—	390.50

6,000# carbon steel tee, socket-welded joints

Description	Craft@Hrs	Unit	Material $	Labor $	Equipment $	Total $
1/2"	P1@.440	Ea	11.60	15.20	—	26.80
3/4"	P1@.670	Ea	15.20	23.10	—	38.30
1"	P1@.890	Ea	19.10	30.70	—	49.80
1¼"	P1@1.11	Ea	54.40	38.40	—	92.80
1½"	P1@1.33	Ea	48.80	46.00	—	94.80
2"	P1@1.77	Ea	61.80	61.20	—	123.00
2½"	P1@2.22	Ea	131.00	76.70	—	207.70
3"	P1@2.66	Ea	219.00	91.90	—	310.90
4"	P1@3.55	Ea	417.00	123.00	—	540.00

Carbon Steel, Schedule 160 with 3,000-6,000# Fittings

Description	Craft@Hrs	Unit	Material $	Labor $	Equipment $	Total $

3,000# carbon steel union, threaded joints

Description	Craft@Hrs	Unit	Material $	Labor $	Equipment $	Total $
1/2"	P1@.150	Ea	9.20	5.18	—	14.38
3/4"	P1@.165	Ea	11.00	5.70	—	16.70
1"	P1@.230	Ea	14.50	7.95	—	22.45
1¼"	P1@.310	Ea	24.50	10.70	—	35.20
1½"	P1@.400	Ea	26.70	13.80	—	40.50
2"	P1@.500	Ea	35.60	17.30	—	52.90
2½"	P1@.670	Ea	77.50	23.10	—	100.60
3"	P1@.840	Ea	96.90	29.00	—	125.90

3,000# carbon steel union, socket-welded joints

Description	Craft@Hrs	Unit	Material $	Labor $	Equipment $	Total $
1/2"	P1@.300	Ea	11.00	10.40	—	21.40
3/4"	P1@.440	Ea	12.60	15.20	—	27.80
1"	P1@.590	Ea	16.20	20.40	—	36.60
1¼"	P1@.740	Ea	26.00	25.60	—	51.60
1½"	P1@.890	Ea	27.10	30.70	—	57.80
2"	P1@1.18	Ea	38.10	40.80	—	78.90
2½"	P1@1.49	Ea	89.00	51.50	—	140.50
3"	P1@1.77	Ea	113.00	61.20	—	174.20

6,000# carbon steel union, threaded joints

Description	Craft@Hrs	Unit	Material $	Labor $	Equipment $	Total $
1/2"	P1@.150	Ea	21.60	5.18	—	26.78
3/4"	P1@.165	Ea	24.50	5.70	—	30.20
1"	P1@.230	Ea	32.20	7.95	—	40.15
1¼"	P1@.310	Ea	52.60	10.70	—	63.30
1½"	P1@.400	Ea	65.10	13.80	—	78.90
2"	P1@.500	Ea	93.10	17.30	—	110.40

6,000# carbon steel union, socket-welded joints

Description	Craft@Hrs	Unit	Material $	Labor $	Equipment $	Total $
1/2"	P1@.300	Ea	22.30	10.40	—	32.70
3/4"	P1@.440	Ea	25.50	15.20	—	40.70
1"	P1@.590	Ea	37.30	20.40	—	57.70
1¼"	P1@.740	Ea	57.10	25.60	—	82.70
1½"	P1@.890	Ea	66.80	30.70	—	97.50
2"	P1@1.18	Ea	101.00	40.80	—	141.80

3,000# carbon steel reducer, socket-welded joints

Description	Craft@Hrs	Unit	Material $	Labor $	Equipment $	Total $
3/4"	P1@.360	Ea	6.01	12.40	—	18.41
1"	P1@.500	Ea	7.30	17.30	—	24.60
1¼"	P1@.665	Ea	8.45	23.00	—	31.45
1½"	P1@.800	Ea	10.60	27.60	—	38.20
2"	P1@1.00	Ea	14.50	34.60	—	49.10
2½"	P1@1.33	Ea	100.00	46.00	—	146.00
3"	P1@1.63	Ea	126.00	56.30	—	182.30

Description	Craft@Hrs	Unit	Material $	Labor $	Equipment $	Total $

6,000# carbon steel reducer, socket-welded joints

Description	Craft@Hrs	Unit	Material $	Labor $	Equipment $	Total $
3/4"	P1@.360	Ea	23.00	12.40	—	35.40
1"	P1@.500	Ea	23.90	17.30	—	41.20
1¼"	P1@.665	Ea	51.20	23.00	—	74.20
1½"	P1@.800	Ea	51.20	27.60	—	78.80
2"	P1@1.00	Ea	67.90	34.60	—	102.50

3,000# carbon steel cap, socket-welded joint

Description	Craft@Hrs	Unit	Material $	Labor $	Equipment $	Total $
1/2"	P1@.180	Ea	3.59	6.22	—	9.81
3/4"	P1@.270	Ea	4.19	9.33	—	13.52
1"	P1@.360	Ea	6.38	12.40	—	18.78
1¼"	P1@.460	Ea	7.49	15.90	—	23.39
1½"	P1@.560	Ea	10.20	19.30	—	29.50
2"	P1@.740	Ea	15.90	25.60	—	41.50
2½"	P1@.920	Ea	85.60	31.80	—	117.40
3"	P1@1.11	Ea	88.40	38.40	—	126.80
4"	P1@1.50	Ea	133.00	51.80	—	184.80

6,000# carbon steel cap, socket-welded joint

Description	Craft@Hrs	Unit	Material $	Labor $	Equipment $	Total $
1/2"	P1@.180	Ea	6.89	6.22	—	13.11
3/4"	P1@.270	Ea	10.00	9.33	—	19.33
1"	P1@.360	Ea	10.60	12.40	—	23.00
1¼"	P1@.460	Ea	24.90	15.90	—	40.80
1½"	P1@.560	Ea	32.20	19.30	—	51.50
2"	P1@.740	Ea	47.80	25.60	—	73.40

3,000# carbon steel weldolet

Description	Craft@Hrs	Unit	Material $	Labor $	Equipment $	Total $
1/2"	P1@.580	Ea	12.70	20.00	—	32.70
3/4"	P1@.890	Ea	13.00	30.70	—	43.70
1"	P1@1.18	Ea	14.30	40.80	—	55.10
1¼"	P1@1.48	Ea	17.90	51.10	—	69.00
1½"	P1@1.75	Ea	17.90	60.50	—	78.40
2"	P1@2.35	Ea	19.30	81.20	—	100.50
2½"	P1@2.90	Ea	43.50	100.00	—	143.50
3"	P1@3.50	Ea	44.70	121.00	—	165.70
4"	P1@4.75	Ea	55.40	164.00	—	219.40

6,000# carbon steel weldolet

Description	Craft@Hrs	Unit	Material $	Labor $	Equipment $	Total $
1/2"	P1@.690	Ea	55.40	23.80	—	79.20
3/4"	P1@1.05	Ea	57.80	36.30	—	94.10
1"	P1@1.40	Ea	60.60	48.40	—	109.00
1¼"	P1@1.75	Ea	73.00	60.50	—	133.50
1½"	P1@2.10	Ea	82.00	72.60	—	154.60
2"	P1@2.80	Ea	94.40	96.70	—	191.10
2½"	P1@3.50	Ea	138.00	121.00	—	259.00
3"	P1@4.20	Ea	154.00	145.00	—	299.00
4"	P1@5.70	Ea	263.00	197.00	—	460.00

Carbon Steel, Schedule 160 with 3,000-6,000# Fittings

Description	Craft@Hrs	Unit	Material $	Labor $	Equipment $	Total $

3,000# carbon steel threadolet

Description	Craft@Hrs	Unit	Material $	Labor $	Equipment $	Total $
1/2"	P1@.400	Ea	9.66	13.80	—	23.46
3/4"	P1@.580	Ea	10.70	20.00	—	30.70
1"	P1@.790	Ea	13.00	27.30	—	40.30
1¼"	P1@.980	Ea	59.10	33.90	—	93.00
1½"	P1@1.20	Ea	59.10	41.50	—	100.60
2"	P1@1.60	Ea	78.00	55.30	—	133.30

6,000# carbon steel threadolet

Description	Craft@Hrs	Unit	Material $	Labor $	Equipment $	Total $
1/2"	P1@.480	Ea	14.80	16.60	—	31.40
3/4"	P1@.690	Ea	16.00	23.80	—	39.80
1"	P1@.950	Ea	22.90	32.80	—	55.70
1¼"	P1@1.20	Ea	85.60	41.50	—	127.10
1½"	P1@1.45	Ea	85.60	50.10	—	135.70
2"	P1@1.90	Ea	140.00	65.60	—	205.60

Class 300 forged steel companion flange, weld neck

Description	Craft@Hrs	Unit	Material $	Labor $	Equipment $	Total $
1/2"	P1@.240	Ea	17.40	8.29	—	25.69
3/4"	P1@.320	Ea	17.40	11.10	—	28.50
1"	P1@.340	Ea	17.40	11.70	—	29.10
1¼"	P1@.425	Ea	22.50	14.70	—	37.20
1½"	P1@.560	Ea	22.50	19.30	—	41.80
2"	P1@.740	Ea	24.70	25.60	—	50.30
2½"	P1@.810	Ea	36.10	28.00	—	64.10
3"	P1@.980	Ea	37.10	33.90	—	71.00
4"	P1@1.30	Ea	54.60	44.90	—	99.50

Class 300 forged steel companion flange, slip on

Description	Craft@Hrs	Unit	Material $	Labor $	Equipment $	Total $
1/2"	P1@.240	Ea	13.80	8.29	—	22.09
3/4"	P1@.320	Ea	13.80	11.10	—	24.90
1"	P1@.340	Ea	13.80	11.70	—	25.50
1½"	P1@.425	Ea	20.60	14.70	—	35.30
2"	P1@.560	Ea	19.60	19.30	—	38.90
2½"	P1@.740	Ea	33.30	25.60	—	58.90
3"	P1@.810	Ea	33.30	28.00	—	61.30
4"	P1@.980	Ea	49.10	33.90	—	83.00

Class 300 cast steel gate valve, flanged

Description	Craft@Hrs	Unit	Material $	Labor $	Equipment $	Total $
2"	P1@.500	Ea	1,730.00	17.30	—	1,747.30
2½"	P1@.600	Ea	2,330.00	20.70	—	2,350.70
3"	P1@.750	Ea	2,330.00	25.90	—	2,355.90
4"	P1@1.35	Ea	3,260.00	46.60	—	3,306.60

Carbon Steel, Schedule 160 with 3,000-6,000# Fittings

Description	Craft@Hrs	Unit	Material $	Labor $	Equipment $	Total $

Class 600 cast steel gate valve, flanged

Description	Craft@Hrs	Unit	Material $	Labor $	Equipment $	Total $
2"	P1@.500	Ea	2,870.00	17.30	—	2,887.30
2½"	P1@.600	Ea	4,120.00	20.70	—	4,140.70
3"	P1@.750	Ea	4,120.00	25.90	—	4,145.90
4"	P1@1.35	Ea	6,600.00	46.60	—	6,646.60

Class 300 cast steel body globe valve, flanged

Description	Craft@Hrs	Unit	Material $	Labor $	Equipment $	Total $
2"	P1@.500	Ea	1,200.00	17.30	—	1,217.30
2½"	P1@.600	Ea	1,640.00	20.70	—	1,660.70
3"	P1@.750	Ea	1,640.00	25.90	—	1,665.90
4"	P1@1.35	Ea	2,250.00	46.60	—	2,296.60

Class 600 cast steel body globe valve, flanged

Description	Craft@Hrs	Unit	Material $	Labor $	Equipment $	Total $
2"	P1@.500	Ea	1,680.00	17.30	—	1,697.30
2½"	P1@.600	Ea	2,540.00	20.70	—	2,560.70
3"	P1@.750	Ea	2,540.00	25.90	—	2,565.90
4"	P1@1.35	Ea	4,100.00	46.60	—	4,146.60

Class 300 cast steel body swing check valve, flanged

Description	Craft@Hrs	Unit	Material $	Labor $	Equipment $	Total $
2"	P1@.500	Ea	1,170.00	17.30	—	1,187.30
2½"	P1@.600	Ea	1,760.00	20.70	—	1,780.70
3"	P1@.750	Ea	1,760.00	25.90	—	1,785.90
4"	P1@1.35	Ea	2,500.00	46.60	—	2,546.60

Class 600 cast steel body swing check valve, flanged

Description	Craft@Hrs	Unit	Material $	Labor $	Equipment $	Total $
2"	P1@.500	Ea	1,800.00	17.30	—	1,817.30
2½"	P1@.600	Ea	2,840.00	20.70	—	2,860.70
3"	P1@.750	Ea	2,840.00	25.90	—	2,865.90
4"	P1@1.35	Ea	4,500.00	46.60	—	4,546.60

Installation of cast steel body 2-way control valve, threaded joints

Description	Craft@Hrs	Unit	Material $	Labor $	Equipment $	Total $
1/2"	P1@.210	Ea	—	7.26	—	7.26
3/4"	P1@.250	Ea	—	8.64	—	8.64
1"	P1@.300	Ea	—	10.40	—	10.40
1¼"	P1@.400	Ea	—	13.80	—	13.80
1½"	P1@.450	Ea	—	15.50	—	15.50
2"	P1@.500	Ea	—	17.30	—	17.30
2½"	P1@.830	Ea	—	28.70	—	28.70
3"	P1@.990	Ea	—	34.20	—	34.20

Installation of cast steel body 2-way control valve, flanged joints

Description	Craft@Hrs	Unit	Material $	Labor $	Equipment $	Total $
2"	P1@.500	Ea	—	17.30	—	17.30
2½"	P1@.600	Ea	—	20.70	—	20.70
3"	P1@.750	Ea	—	25.90	—	25.90
4"	P1@1.35	Ea	—	46.60	—	46.60

Carbon Steel, Schedule 160 with 3,000-6,000# Fittings

Description	Craft@Hrs	Unit	Material $	Labor $	Equipment $	Total $

Installation of cast steel body 3-way control valve, threaded joints

Description	Craft@Hrs	Unit	Material $	Labor $	Equipment $	Total $
1/2"	P1@.260	Ea	—	8.98	—	8.98
3/4"	P1@.365	Ea	—	12.60	—	12.60
1"	P1@.475	Ea	—	16.40	—	16.40
1¼"	P1@.575	Ea	—	19.90	—	19.90
1½"	P1@.680	Ea	—	23.50	—	23.50
2"	P1@.910	Ea	—	31.40	—	31.40
2½"	P1@1.12	Ea	—	38.70	—	38.70
3"	P1@1.33	Ea	—	46.00	—	46.00

Installation of cast steel body 3-way control valve, flanged joints

Description	Craft@Hrs	Unit	Material $	Labor $	Equipment $	Total $
2"	P1@.910	Ea	—	31.40	—	31.40
2½"	P1@1.12	Ea	—	38.70	—	38.70
3"	P1@1.33	Ea	—	46.00	—	46.00
4"	P1@2.00	Ea	—	69.10	—	69.10

300# bolt and gasket set, ring face

Description	Craft@Hrs	Unit	Material $	Labor $	Equipment $	Total $
2"	P1@.500	Ea	7.67	17.30	—	24.97
2½"	P1@.650	Ea	8.96	22.50	—	31.46
3"	P1@.750	Ea	15.40	25.90	—	41.30
4"	P1@1.00	Ea	25.00	34.60	—	59.60

300# bolt and gasket set, full face

Description	Craft@Hrs	Unit	Material $	Labor $	Equipment $	Total $
2"	P1@.500	Ea	15.40	17.30	—	32.70
2½"	P1@.650	Ea	17.90	22.50	—	40.40
3"	P1@.750	Ea	30.80	25.90	—	56.70
4"	P1@1.00	Ea	50.20	34.60	—	84.80

Thermometer with well

Description	Craft@Hrs	Unit	Material $	Labor $	Equipment $	Total $
7"	P1@.250	Ea	159.00	8.64	—	167.64
9"	P1@.250	Ea	164.00	8.64	—	172.64

Dial type pressure gauge

Description	Craft@Hrs	Unit	Material $	Labor $	Equipment $	Total $
2½"	P1@.200	Ea	33.10	6.91	—	40.01
3½"	P1@.200	Ea	43.80	6.91	—	50.71

Pressure/temperature tap

Description	Craft@Hrs	Unit	Material $	Labor $	Equipment $	Total $
tap	P1@.150	Ea	15.70	5.18	—	20.88

Carbon Steel, Schedule 160 with 3,000-6,000# Fittings

Description	Craft@Hrs	Unit	Material $	Labor $	Equipment $	Total $
Hanger with swivel assembly						
1/2"	P1@.250	Ea	5.62	8.64	—	14.26
3/4"	P1@.250	Ea	6.16	8.64	—	14.80
1"	P1@.250	Ea	6.45	8.64	—	15.09
1¼"	P1@.300	Ea	6.99	10.40	—	17.39
1½"	P1@.300	Ea	9.09	10.40	—	19.49
2"	P1@.300	Ea	11.70	10.40	—	22.10
2½"	P1@.350	Ea	14.70	12.10	—	26.80
3"	P1@.350	Ea	25.20	12.10	—	37.30
4"	P1@.350	Ea	32.80	12.10	—	44.90
Riser clamp						
1/2"	P1@.100	Ea	2.41	3.46	—	5.87
3/4"	P1@.100	Ea	3.55	3.46	—	7.01
1¼"	P1@.105	Ea	4.33	3.63	—	7.96
1½"	P1@.110	Ea	4.58	3.80	—	8.38
2"	P1@.115	Ea	4.84	3.97	—	8.81
2½"	P1@.120	Ea	5.09	4.15	—	9.24
3"	P1@.120	Ea	5.52	4.15	—	9.67
4"	P1@.125	Ea	7.03	4.32	—	11.35

Carbon Steel, Schedule 40 with Roll-Grooved Joints

Schedule 40 carbon steel (ASTM A-53 and A-120) roll-grooved pipe with factory grooved malleable iron, ductile iron, or steel fittings is commonly used for heating hot water, chilled water and condenser water systems.

Consult the manufacturers for maximum operating temperature/pressure ratings for the various combinations of pipe and fittings and system applications.

The cost estimates in this section are based on the conditions, limitations and wage rates described in the section "How to Use This Book" beginning on page 5.

Equipment cost, where shown, is $110 per hour for a 10-ton hydraulic truck-mounted crane.

Description	Craft@Hrs	Unit	Material $	Labor $	Equipment $	Total $

Schedule 40 carbon steel roll-grooved horizontal pipe assembly.

Horizontally hung in a building. Assembly includes fittings, couplings and hanger assemblies. Based on a reducing tee and a 45 degree elbow every 16 feet for 1/2" pipe. A reducing tee and a 45 degree elbow every 50 feet for 12" pipe. Hangers spaced to meet plumbing code. *(Distance between fittings in the pipe assembly increases as pipe diameter increases.)* Use these figures for preliminary estimates.

Description	Craft@Hrs	Unit	Material $	Labor $	Equipment $	Total $
2"	P1@.183	LF	8.75	6.32	—	15.07
2½"	P1@.192	LF	11.40	6.63	—	18.03
3"	P1@.220	LF	13.10	7.60	—	20.70
4"	P1@.262	LF	18.80	9.05	—	27.85
6"	ER@.347	LF	34.90	12.80	5.50	53.20
8"	ER@.414	LF	50.70	15.30	6.40	72.40
10"	ER@.530	LF	75.50	19.60	8.30	103.40
12"	ER@.617	LF	134.00	22.80	9.70	166.50

Schedule 40 carbon steel roll-grooved vertical pipe assembly.
Riser assembly, including fittings, couplings, and riser clamps. Based on a reducing tee, and a riser clamp on every floor. Use these figures for preliminary estimates.

Description	Craft@Hrs	Unit	Material $	Labor $	Equipment $	Total $
2"	P1@.120	LF	7.68	4.15	—	11.83
2½"	P1@.123	LF	10.90	4.25	—	15.15
3"	P1@.150	LF	11.30	5.18	—	16.48
4"	P1@.209	LF	17.10	7.22	—	24.32
6"	ER@.294	LF	33.20	10.90	4.60	48.70
8"	ER@.395	LF	54.40	14.60	6.20	75.20
10"	ER@.523	LF	75.50	19.40	8.30	103.20
12"	ER@.608	LF	123.00	22.50	9.50	155.00

Schedule 40 carbon steel pipe with roll-grooved joints

Description	Craft@Hrs	Unit	Material $	Labor $	Equipment $	Total $
2"	P1@.100	LF	3.48	3.46	—	6.94
2½"	P1@.115	LF	5.46	3.97	—	9.43
3"	P1@.135	LF	7.43	4.66	—	12.09
4"	P1@.190	LF	10.70	6.56	—	17.26
5"	ER@.240	LF	20.10	8.88	3.90	32.88
6"	ER@.315	LF	30.30	11.70	5.00	47.00
8"	ER@.370	LF	30.30	13.70	5.90	49.90
10"	ER@.460	LF	42.50	17.00	7.20	66.70
12"	ER@.550	LF	67.00	20.40	8.60	96.00

Carbon Steel, Schedule 40 with Roll-Grooved Joints

Description	Craft@Hrs	Unit	Material $	Labor $	Equipment $	Total $

Schedule 40 carbon steel 45 degree ell with roll-grooved joints

Description	Craft@Hrs	Unit	Material $	Labor $	Equipment $	Total $
2"	P1@.170	Ea	24.70	5.87	—	30.57
2½"	P1@.185	Ea	33.50	6.39	—	39.89
3"	P1@.200	Ea	44.20	6.91	—	51.11
4"	P1@.230	Ea	65.30	7.95	—	73.25
5"	ER@.250	Ea	158.00	9.26	3.90	171.16
6"	ER@.350	Ea	185.00	13.00	5.50	203.50
8"	ER@.500	Ea	386.00	18.50	7.90	412.40
10"	ER@.750	Ea	523.00	27.80	11.80	562.60
12"	ER@1.00	Ea	916.00	37.00	15.70	968.70

Schedule 40 carbon steel 90 degree ell with roll-grooved joints

Description	Craft@Hrs	Unit	Material $	Labor $	Equipment $	Total $
2"	P1@.170	Ea	24.70	5.87	—	30.57
2½"	P1@.185	Ea	33.50	6.39	—	39.89
3"	P1@.200	Ea	44.20	6.91	—	51.11
4"	P1@.230	Ea	65.30	7.95	—	73.25
5"	ER@.250	Ea	158.00	9.26	3.90	171.16
6"	ER@.350	Ea	185.00	13.00	5.50	203.50
8"	ER@.500	Ea	386.00	18.50	7.90	412.40
10"	ER@.750	Ea	600.00	27.80	11.80	639.60
12"	ER@1.00	Ea	967.00	37.00	15.70	1,019.70

Schedule 40 carbon steel tee with roll-grooved joints

Description	Craft@Hrs	Unit	Material $	Labor $	Equipment $	Total $
2"	P1@.200	Ea	37.70	6.91	—	44.61
2½"	P1@.210	Ea	51.70	7.26	—	58.96
3"	P1@.230	Ea	72.00	7.95	—	79.95
4"	P1@.250	Ea	110.00	8.64	—	118.64
5"	ER@.300	Ea	260.00	11.10	4.80	275.90
6"	ER@.500	Ea	302.00	18.50	7.90	328.40
8"	ER@.750	Ea	662.00	27.80	11.80	701.60
10"	ER@1.00	Ea	1,180.00	37.00	15.70	1,232.70
12"	ER@1.50	Ea	1,630.00	55.50	23.70	1,709.20

Carbon Steel, Schedule 40 with Roll-Grooved Joints

Description	Craft@Hrs	Unit	Material $	Labor $	Equipment $	Total $

Schedule 40 carbon steel reducing tee with roll-grooved joints

Description	Craft@Hrs	Unit	Material $	Labor $	Equipment $	Total $
3" x 2"	P1@.230	Ea	97.70	7.95	—	105.65
4" x 2"	P1@.240	Ea	132.00	8.29	—	140.29
4" x 2½"	P1@.245	Ea	132.00	8.46	—	140.46
4" x 3"	P1@.250	Ea	132.00	8.64	—	140.64
5" x 2"	P1@.260	Ea	242.00	8.98	—	250.98
5" x 3"	P1@.280	Ea	265.00	9.67	—	274.67
5" x 4"	P1@.300	Ea	287.00	10.40	—	297.40
6" x 3"	ER@.400	Ea	315.00	14.80	6.20	336.00
6" x 4"	ER@.450	Ea	315.00	16.70	7.20	338.90
6" x 5"	ER@.500	Ea	315.00	18.50	7.90	341.40
8" x 3"	ER@.600	Ea	454.00	22.20	9.40	485.60
8" x 4"	ER@.650	Ea	662.00	24.10	10.30	696.40
8" x 5"	ER@.700	Ea	662.00	25.90	11.00	698.90
8" x 6"	ER@.750	Ea	662.00	27.80	11.80	701.60
10" x 4"	ER@.800	Ea	707.00	29.60	12.70	749.30
10" x 5"	ER@.900	Ea	720.00	33.30	14.10	767.40
10" x 6"	ER@1.00	Ea	720.00	37.00	15.70	772.70
10" x 8"	ER@1.10	Ea	720.00	40.70	17.30	778.00
12" x 6"	ER@1.20	Ea	105.00	44.40	18.90	168.30
12" x 8"	ER@1.35	Ea	1,080.00	50.00	21.20	1,151.20
12" x 10"	ER@1.50	Ea	1,130.00	55.50	23.70	1,209.20

Schedule 40 carbon steel male adapter

Description	Craft@Hrs	Unit	Material $	Labor $	Equipment $	Total $
2"	P1@.170	Ea	16.00	5.87	—	21.87
2½"	P1@.185	Ea	19.00	6.39	—	25.39
3"	P1@.200	Ea	23.60	6.91	—	30.51
4"	P1@.230	Ea	39.70	7.95	—	47.65
5"	ER@.290	Ea	83.60	10.70	4.60	98.90
6"	ER@.400	Ea	197.00	14.80	6.20	218.00

Schedule 40 carbon steel female adapter

Description	Craft@Hrs	Unit	Material $	Labor $	Equipment $	Total $
2"	P1@.170	Ea	36.40	5.87	—	42.27
3"	P1@.200	Ea	56.30	6.91	—	63.21
4"	P1@.230	Ea	78.50	7.95	—	86.45

Schedule 40 carbon steel reducer, roll-grooved joints

Description	Craft@Hrs	Unit	Material $	Labor $	Equipment $	Total $
2"	P1@.160	Ea	34.00	5.53	—	39.53
3"	P1@.170	Ea	47.10	5.87	—	52.97
4"	P1@.210	Ea	57.20	7.26	—	64.46
5"	ER@.260	Ea	79.70	9.63	4.00	93.33
6"	ER@.310	Ea	92.60	11.50	5.00	109.10
8"	ER@.450	Ea	242.00	16.70	7.20	265.90
10"	ER@.690	Ea	422.00	25.50	10.80	458.30
12"	ER@.920	Ea	731.00	34.10	14.50	779.60

Description	Craft@Hrs	Unit	Material $	Labor $	Equipment $	Total $

Schedule 40 carbon steel cap, roll-grooved joint

Description	Craft@Hrs	Unit	Material $	Labor $	Equipment $	Total $
2"	P1@.110	Ea	17.60	3.80	—	21.40
2½"	P1@.120	Ea	27.60	4.15	—	31.75
3"	P1@.130	Ea	27.60	4.49	—	32.09
4"	P1@.140	Ea	29.80	4.84	—	34.64
5"	ER@.150	Ea	69.10	5.55	2.40	77.05
6"	ER@.170	Ea	72.00	6.29	2.80	81.09
8"	ER@.200	Ea	138.00	7.40	3.10	148.50
10"	ER@.225	Ea	251.00	8.33	3.50	262.83
12"	ER@.250	Ea	404.00	9.26	3.90	417.16

Flange with gasket, grooved joint

Description	Craft@Hrs	Unit	Material $	Labor $	Equipment $	Total $
2"	P1@.280	Ea	52.80	9.67	—	62.47
2½"	P1@.340	Ea	62.40	11.70	—	74.10
3"	P1@.390	Ea	70.70	13.50	—	84.20
4"	P1@.560	Ea	102.00	19.30	—	121.30
6"	ER@.780	Ea	127.00	28.90	12.30	168.20
8"	ER@1.10	Ea	150.00	40.70	17.30	208.00
10"	ER@1.40	Ea	190.00	51.80	22.00	263.80
12"	ER@1.70	Ea	263.00	62.90	26.70	352.60

Roll-grooved coupling with gasket

Description	Craft@Hrs	Unit	Material $	Labor $	Equipment $	Total $
2"	P1@.300	Ea	27.30	10.40	—	37.70
2½"	P1@.350	Ea	32.70	12.10	—	44.80
3"	P1@.400	Ea	36.40	13.80	—	50.20
4"	P1@.500	Ea	52.80	17.30	—	70.10
5"	ER@.600	Ea	81.00	22.20	9.40	112.60
6"	ER@.700	Ea	95.60	25.90	11.00	132.50
8"	ER@.900	Ea	158.00	33.30	14.10	205.40
10"	ER@1.10	Ea	219.00	40.70	17.30	277.00
12"	ER@1.35	Ea	251.00	50.00	21.20	322.20

Class 125 iron body gate valve, flanged ends

Description	Craft@Hrs	Unit	Material $	Labor $	Equipment $	Total $
2"	P1@.500	Ea	310.00	17.30	—	327.30
2½"	P1@.600	Ea	418.00	20.70	—	438.70
3"	P1@.750	Ea	454.00	25.90	—	479.90
4"	P1@1.35	Ea	666.00	46.60	—	712.60
6"	ER@2.50	Ea	1,270.00	92.60	39.30	1,401.90
8"	ER@3.00	Ea	2,090.00	111.00	47.10	2,248.10
10"	ER@4.00	Ea	3,410.00	148.00	62.90	3,620.90
12"	ER@4.50	Ea	4,730.00	167.00	69.90	4,966.90

Carbon Steel, Schedule 40 with Roll-Grooved Joints

Description	Craft@Hrs	Unit	Material $	Labor $	Equipment $	Total $

Class 125 iron body globe valve, flanged joints

Description	Craft@Hrs	Unit	Material $	Labor $	Equipment $	Total $
2"	P1@.500	Ea	226.00	17.30	—	243.30
2½"	P1@.600	Ea	351.00	20.70	—	371.70
3"	P1@.750	Ea	421.00	25.90	—	446.90
4"	P1@1.35	Ea	565.00	46.60	—	611.60
6"	ER@2.50	Ea	990.00	92.60	39.30	1,121.90
8"	ER@3.00	Ea	1,520.00	111.00	47.10	1,678.10
10"	ER@4.00	Ea	2,320.00	148.00	62.90	2,530.90

200 PSIG iron body butterfly valve, lug type, lever operated

Description	Craft@Hrs	Unit	Material $	Labor $	Equipment $	Total $
2"	P1@.450	Ea	134.00	15.50	—	149.50
2½"	P1@.450	Ea	139.00	15.50	—	154.50
3"	P1@.550	Ea	146.00	19.00	—	165.00
4"	P1@.550	Ea	182.00	19.00	—	201.00
6"	ER@.800	Ea	293.00	29.60	12.70	335.30
8"	ER@.800	Ea	401.00	29.60	12.70	443.30
10"	ER@.900	Ea	557.00	33.30	14.10	604.40
12"	ER@1.00	Ea	729.00	37.00	15.70	781.70

200 PSIG iron body butterfly valve, wafer type, lever operated

Description	Craft@Hrs	Unit	Material $	Labor $	Equipment $	Total $
2"	P1@.450	Ea	122.00	15.50	—	137.50
2½"	P1@.450	Ea	125.00	15.50	—	140.50
3"	P1@.550	Ea	134.00	19.00	—	153.00
4"	P1@.550	Ea	163.00	19.00	—	182.00
6"	ER@.800	Ea	272.00	29.60	12.70	314.30
8"	ER@.800	Ea	377.00	29.60	12.70	419.30
10"	ER@.900	Ea	527.00	33.30	14.10	574.40
12"	ER@1.00	Ea	692.00	37.00	15.70	744.70

Class 125 iron body swing check valve, flanged ends

Description	Craft@Hrs	Unit	Material $	Labor $	Equipment $	Total $
2"	P1@.500	Ea	155.00	17.30	—	172.30
2½"	P1@.600	Ea	197.00	20.70	—	217.70
3"	P1@.750	Ea	245.00	25.90	—	270.90
4"	P1@1.35	Ea	360.00	46.60	—	406.60
6"	ER@2.50	Ea	699.00	92.60	39.30	830.90
8"	ER@3.00	Ea	1,250.00	111.00	47.10	1,408.10
10"	ER@4.00	Ea	2,060.00	148.00	62.90	2,270.90
12"	ER@4.50	Ea	2,790.00	167.00	69.90	3,026.90

Class 125 iron body silent check valve, flanged joints

Description	Craft@Hrs	Unit	Material $	Labor $	Equipment $	Total $
2"	P1@.500	Ea	113.00	17.30	—	130.30
2½"	P1@.600	Ea	131.00	20.70	—	151.70
3"	P1@.750	Ea	147.00	25.90	—	172.90
4"	P1@1.35	Ea	193.00	46.60	—	239.60
5"	ER@2.00	Ea	279.00	74.00	31.40	384.40
6"	ER@2.50	Ea	347.00	92.60	39.30	478.90
8"	ER@3.00	Ea	625.00	111.00	47.10	783.10
10"	ER@4.00	Ea	970.00	148.00	62.90	1,180.90

Description	Craft@Hrs	Unit	Material $	Labor $	Equipment $	Total $

Class 125 iron body strainer, flanged

Description	Craft@Hrs	Unit	Material $	Labor $	Equipment $	Total $
2"	P1@.500	Ea	124.00	17.30	—	141.30
2½"	P1@.600	Ea	139.00	20.70	—	159.70
3"	P1@.750	Ea	160.00	25.90	—	185.90
4"	P1@1.35	Ea	273.00	46.60	—	319.60
6"	ER@2.50	Ea	554.00	92.60	39.30	685.90
8"	ER@3.00	Ea	937.00	111.00	47.10	1,095.10

Installation of 2-way control valve, flanged joints

Description	Craft@Hrs	Unit	Material $	Labor $	Equipment $	Total $
2"	P1@.500	Ea	—	17.30	—	17.30
2½"	P1@.600	Ea	—	20.70	—	20.70
3"	P1@.750	Ea	—	25.90	—	25.90
4"	P1@1.35	Ea	—	46.60	—	46.60
6"	P1@2.50	Ea	—	86.40	—	86.40
8"	P1@3.00	Ea	—	104.00	—	104.00
10"	P1@4.00	Ea	—	138.00	—	138.00
12"	P1@4.50	Ea	—	155.00	—	155.00

Installation of 3-way control valve, flanged joints

Description	Craft@Hrs	Unit	Material $	Labor $	Equipment $	Total $
2"	P1@.910	Ea	—	31.40	—	31.40
2½"	P1@1.12	Ea	—	38.70	—	38.70
3"	P1@1.33	Ea	—	46.00	—	46.00
4"	P1@2.00	Ea	—	69.10	—	69.10
6"	P1@3.70	Ea	—	128.00	—	128.00
8"	P1@4.40	Ea	—	152.00	—	152.00
10"	P1@5.90	Ea	—	204.00	—	204.00
12"	P1@6.50	Ea	—	225.00	—	225.00

Bolt and gasket sets

Description	Craft@Hrs	Unit	Material $	Labor $	Equipment $	Total $
2"	P1@.500	Ea	3.86	17.30	—	21.16
2½"	P1@.650	Ea	4.51	22.50	—	27.01
3"	P1@.750	Ea	7.67	25.90	—	33.57
4"	P1@1.00	Ea	12.80	34.60	—	47.40
6"	P1@1.20	Ea	21.20	41.50	—	62.70
8"	P1@1.25	Ea	23.80	43.20	—	67.00
10"	P1@1.70	Ea	41.20	58.70	—	99.90
12"	P1@2.20	Ea	46.20	76.00	—	122.20

Thermometer with well

Description	Craft@Hrs	Unit	Material $	Labor $	Equipment $	Total $
7"	P1@.250	Ea	159.00	8.64	—	167.64
9"	P1@.250	Ea	164.00	8.64	—	172.64

Dial type pressure gauge

Description	Craft@Hrs	Unit	Material $	Labor $	Equipment $	Total $
2½"	P1@.200	Ea	33.10	6.91	—	40.01
3½"	P1@.200	Ea	43.80	6.91	—	50.71

Carbon Steel, Schedule 40 with Roll-Grooved Joints

Description	Craft@Hrs	Unit	Material $	Labor $	Equipment $	Total $

Pressure/temperature tap

Description	Craft@Hrs	Unit	Material $	Labor $	Equipment $	Total $
tap	P1@.150	Ea	15.70	5.18	—	20.88

Hanger with swivel assembly

Description	Craft@Hrs	Unit	Material $	Labor $	Equipment $	Total $
2"	P1@.300	Ea	6.05	10.40	—	16.45
2½"	P1@.350	Ea	7.82	12.10	—	19.92
3"	P1@.350	Ea	9.67	12.10	—	21.77
4"	P1@.350	Ea	14.90	12.10	—	27.00
5"	P1@.450	Ea	16.70	15.50	—	32.20
6"	P1@.450	Ea	21.80	15.50	—	37.30
8"	P1@.450	Ea	28.90	15.50	—	44.40
10"	P1@.550	Ea	39.70	19.00	—	58.70
12"	P1@.600	Ea	52.80	20.70	—	73.50

Riser clamp

Description	Craft@Hrs	Unit	Material $	Labor $	Equipment $	Total $
2"	P1@.115	Ea	4.84	3.97	—	8.81
2½"	P1@.120	Ea	5.09	4.15	—	9.24
3"	P1@.120	Ea	5.52	4.15	—	9.67
4"	P1@.125	Ea	7.03	4.32	—	11.35
5"	P1@.180	Ea	10.10	6.22	—	16.32
6"	P1@.200	Ea	12.20	6.91	—	19.11
8"	P1@.200	Ea	19.80	6.91	—	26.71
10"	P1@.250	Ea	29.90	8.64	—	38.54
12"	P1@.250	Ea	34.90	8.64	—	43.54

Schedule 10 carbon steel (ASTM A-53) roll-grooved pipe with factory grooved malleable iron, ductile iron, or steel fittings is commonly used for sprinkler systems, heating hot water, chilled water and condenser water systems.

Consult the manufacturers for maximum operating temperature/pressure ratings for the various combinations of pipe and fittings and system applications.

The cost estimates in this section are based on the conditions, limitations and wage rates described in the section "How to Use This Book" beginning on page 5.

Equipment cost, where shown, is $110 per hour for a 10-ton hydraulic truck-mounted crane.

Description	Craft@Hrs	Unit	Material $	Labor $	Equipment $	Total $

Schedule 10 carbon steel roll-grooved horizontal pipe assembly.

Horizontally hung in a building. Assembly includes fittings, couplings and hanger assemblies. Based on a reducing tee and a 45 degree elbow every 16 feet for 1/2" pipe. A reducing tee and a 45 degree elbow every 50 feet for 12" pipe. Hangers spaced to meet plumbing code. *(Distance between fittings in the pipe assembly increases as pipe diameter increases.)* Use these figures for preliminary estimates.

Description	Craft@Hrs	Unit	Material $	Labor $	Equipment $	Total $
2"	P1@.178	LF	7.78	6.15	—	13.93
2½"	P1@.188	LF	9.73	6.50	—	16.23
3"	P1@.215	LF	11.20	7.43	—	18.63
4"	P1@.255	LF	16.00	8.81	—	24.81
6"	ER@.339	LF	30.30	12.50	5.30	48.10
8"	ER@.404	LF	46.20	15.00	6.40	67.60
10"	ER@.517	LF	69.00	19.10	8.10	96.20
12"	ER@.602	LF	124.00	22.30	9.50	155.80

Schedule 10 carbon steel roll-grooved vertical pipe assembly.

Riser assembly, including fittings, couplings, and riser clamps. Based on a reducing tee, and a riser clamp on every floor. Use these figures for preliminary estimates.

Description	Craft@Hrs	Unit	Material $	Labor $	Equipment $	Total $
2"	P1@.117	LF	7.44	4.04	—	11.48
2½"	P1@.120	LF	10.10	4.15	—	14.25
3"	P1@.146	LF	10.40	5.04	—	15.44
4"	P1@.204	LF	15.90	7.05	—	22.95
6"	ER@.286	LF	31.40	10.60	4.20	46.20
8"	ER@.385	LF	55.20	14.30	6.10	75.60
10"	ER@.510	LF	76.70	18.90	8.10	103.70
12"	ER@.593	LF	124.00	22.00	9.40	155.40

Carbon Steel, Schedule 10 with Roll-Grooved Joints

Description	Craft@Hrs	Unit	Material $	Labor $	Equipment $	Total $

Schedule 10 carbon steel pipe, roll-grooved joints

Description	Craft@Hrs	Unit	Material $	Labor $	Equipment $	Total $
2"	P1@.080	LF	2.27	2.76	—	5.03
2½"	P1@.100	LF	3.09	3.46	—	6.55
3"	P1@.115	LF	3.75	3.97	—	7.72
4"	P1@.160	LF	4.97	5.53	—	10.50
5"	ER@.200	LF	8.53	7.40	3.10	19.03
6"	ER@.260	LF	9.01	9.63	4.00	22.64
8"	ER@.300	LF	12.40	11.10	4.80	28.30
10"	ER@.380	LF	16.90	14.10	6.10	37.10
12"	ER@.450	LF	23.80	16.70	7.20	47.70

Schedule 10 carbon steel 45 degree ell, roll-grooved joints

Description	Craft@Hrs	Unit	Material $	Labor $	Equipment $	Total $
2"	P1@.170	Ea	24.70	5.87	—	30.57
2½"	P1@.185	Ea	33.50	6.39	—	39.89
3"	P1@.200	Ea	44.20	6.91	—	51.11
4"	P1@.230	Ea	65.30	7.95	—	73.25
5"	ER@.250	Ea	158.00	9.26	3.90	171.16
6"	ER@.350	Ea	185.00	13.00	5.50	203.50
8"	ER@.500	Ea	386.00	18.50	7.90	412.40
10"	ER@.750	Ea	523.00	27.80	11.80	562.60
12"	ER@1.00	Ea	916.00	37.00	15.70	968.70

Schedule 10 carbon steel 90 degree ell, roll-grooved joints

Description	Craft@Hrs	Unit	Material $	Labor $	Equipment $	Total $
2"	P1@.170	Ea	24.70	5.87	—	30.57
2½"	P1@.185	Ea	33.50	6.39	—	39.89
3"	P1@.200	Ea	44.20	6.91	—	51.11
4"	P1@.230	Ea	65.30	7.95	—	73.25
5"	ER@.250	Ea	158.00	9.26	3.90	171.16
6"	ER@.350	Ea	185.00	13.00	5.50	203.50
8"	ER@.500	Ea	386.00	18.50	7.90	412.40
10"	ER@.750	Ea	600.00	27.80	11.80	639.60
12"	ER@1.00	Ea	967.00	37.00	15.70	1,019.70

Schedule 10 carbon steel tee, roll-grooved joints

Description	Craft@Hrs	Unit	Material $	Labor $	Equipment $	Total $
2"	P1@.200	Ea	37.70	6.91	—	44.61
2½"	P1@.210	Ea	51.70	7.26	—	58.96
3"	P1@.230	Ea	72.00	7.95	—	79.95
4"	P1@.250	Ea	110.00	8.64	—	118.64
5"	ER@.300	Ea	260.00	11.10	4.80	275.90
6"	ER@.500	Ea	302.00	18.50	7.90	328.40
8"	ER@.750	Ea	662.00	27.80	11.80	701.60
10"	ER@1.00	Ea	1,180.00	37.00	15.70	1,232.70
12"	ER@1.50	Ea	1,630.00	55.50	23.70	1,709.20

Description	Craft@Hrs	Unit	Material $	Labor $	Equipment $	Total $

Schedule 10 carbon steel reducing tee, roll-grooved joints

Description	Craft@Hrs	Unit	Material $	Labor $	Equipment $	Total $
3" x 2"	P1@.230	Ea	97.70	7.95	—	105.65
4" x 2"	P1@.240	Ea	132.00	8.29	—	140.29
4" x 2½"	P1@.245	Ea	132.00	8.46	—	140.46
4" x 3"	P1@.250	Ea	132.00	8.64	—	140.64
5" x 2"	P1@.260	Ea	242.00	8.98	—	250.98
5" x 3"	P1@.280	Ea	265.00	9.67	—	274.67
5" x 4"	P1@.300	Ea	287.00	10.40	—	297.40
6" x 3"	ER@.400	Ea	315.00	14.80	6.20	336.00
6" x 4"	ER@.450	Ea	315.00	16.70	7.20	338.90
6" x 5"	ER@.500	Ea	315.00	18.50	7.90	341.40
8" x 3"	ER@.600	Ea	454.00	22.20	9.40	485.60
8" x 4"	ER@.650	Ea	662.00	24.10	10.30	696.40
8" x 5"	ER@.700	Ea	662.00	25.90	11.00	698.90
8" x 6"	ER@.750	Ea	662.00	27.80	11.80	701.60
10" x 4"	ER@.800	Ea	707.00	29.60	12.70	749.30
10" x 5"	ER@.900	Ea	720.00	33.30	14.10	767.40
10" x 6"	ER@1.00	Ea	720.00	37.00	15.70	772.70
10" x 8"	ER@1.10	Ea	720.00	40.70	17.30	778.00
12" x 6"	ER@1.20	Ea	105.00	44.40	18.90	168.30
12" x 8"	ER@1.35	Ea	1,080.00	50.00	19.60	1,149.60
12" x 10"	ER@1.50	Ea	1,130.00	55.50	23.70	1,209.20

Schedule 10 carbon steel male adapter

Description	Craft@Hrs	Unit	Material $	Labor $	Equipment $	Total $
2"	P1@.170	Ea	16.00	5.87	—	21.87
2½"	P1@.185	Ea	19.00	6.39	—	25.39
3"	P1@.200	Ea	23.60	6.91	—	30.51
4"	P1@.230	Ea	39.70	7.95	—	47.65
5"	ER@.290	Ea	83.60	10.70	4.60	98.90
6"	ER@.400	Ea	197.00	14.80	6.20	218.00

Schedule 10 carbon steel female adapter

Description	Craft@Hrs	Unit	Material $	Labor $	Equipment $	Total $
2"	P1@.170	Ea	36.40	5.87	—	42.27
3"	P1@.200	Ea	56.30	6.91	—	63.21
4"	P1@.230	Ea	78.50	7.95	—	86.45

Schedule 10 carbon steel reducer, roll-grooved joints

Description	Craft@Hrs	Unit	Material $	Labor $	Equipment $	Total $
2"	P1@.160	Ea	34.00	5.53	—	39.53
3"	P1@.170	Ea	47.10	5.87	—	52.97
4"	P1@.210	Ea	57.20	7.26	—	64.46
5"	ER@.260	Ea	79.70	9.63	4.00	93.33
6"	ER@.310	Ea	92.60	11.50	5.00	109.10
8"	ER@.450	Ea	242.00	16.70	7.20	265.90
10"	ER@.690	Ea	422.00	25.50	10.80	458.30
12"	ER@.920	Ea	731.00	34.10	14.50	779.60

Carbon Steel, Schedule 10 with Roll-Grooved Joints

Description	Craft@Hrs	Unit	Material $	Labor $	Equipment $	Total $

Schedule 10 carbon steel cap, roll-grooved joints

Description	Craft@Hrs	Unit	Material $	Labor $	Equipment $	Total $
2"	P1@.110	Ea	17.60	3.80	—	21.40
2½"	P1@.120	Ea	27.60	4.15	—	31.75
3"	P1@.130	Ea	27.60	4.49	—	32.09
4"	P1@.140	Ea	29.80	4.84	—	34.64
5"	ER@.150	Ea	69.10	5.55	2.40	77.05
6"	ER@.170	Ea	72.00	6.29	2.80	81.09
8"	ER@.200	Ea	138.00	7.40	3.10	148.50
10"	ER@.225	Ea	251.00	8.33	3.50	262.83
12"	ER@.250	Ea	404.00	9.26	3.90	417.16

Flange with gasket, grooved joint

Description	Craft@Hrs	Unit	Material $	Labor $	Equipment $	Total $
2"	P1@.280	Ea	52.80	9.67	—	62.47
2½"	P1@.340	Ea	62.40	11.70	—	74.10
3"	P1@.390	Ea	70.70	13.50	—	84.20
4"	P1@.560	Ea	102.00	19.30	—	121.30
6"	ER@.780	Ea	127.00	28.90	12.30	168.20
8"	ER@1.10	Ea	150.00	40.70	17.30	208.00
10"	ER@1.40	Ea	190.00	51.80	22.00	263.80
12"	ER@1.70	Ea	263.00	62.90	26.70	352.60

Roll-grooved coupling with gasket

Description	Craft@Hrs	Unit	Material $	Labor $	Equipment $	Total $
2"	P1@.300	Ea	27.30	10.40	—	37.70
2½"	P1@.350	Ea	32.70	12.10	—	44.80
3"	P1@.400	Ea	36.40	13.80	—	50.20
4"	P1@.500	Ea	52.80	17.30	—	70.10
5"	ER@.600	Ea	81.00	22.20	9.40	112.60
6"	ER@.700	Ea	95.60	25.90	11.00	132.50
8"	ER@.900	Ea	158.00	33.30	14.10	205.40
10"	ER@1.10	Ea	219.00	40.70	17.30	277.00
12"	ER@1.35	Ea	251.00	50.00	21.20	322.20

Class 125 iron body gate valve, flanged joints

Description	Craft@Hrs	Unit	Material $	Labor $	Equipment $	Total $
2"	P1@.500	Ea	412.00	17.30	—	429.30
2½"	P1@.600	Ea	559.00	20.70	—	579.70
3"	P1@.750	Ea	605.00	25.90	—	630.90
4"	P1@1.35	Ea	886.00	46.60	—	932.60
5"	ER@2.00	Ea	1,700.00	74.00	31.40	1,805.40
6"	ER@2.50	Ea	1,700.00	92.60	39.30	1,831.90
8"	ER@3.00	Ea	2,770.00	111.00	47.10	2,928.10
10"	ER@4.00	Ea	4,600.00	148.00	62.90	4,810.90
12"	ER@4.50	Ea	6,290.00	167.00	70.80	6,527.80

Description	Craft@Hrs	Unit	Material $	Labor $	Equipment $	Total $

Class 125 iron body globe valve, flanged joints

Description	Craft@Hrs	Unit	Material $	Labor $	Equipment $	Total $
2"	P1@.500	Ea	226.00	17.30	—	243.30
2½"	P1@.600	Ea	348.00	20.70	—	368.70
3"	P1@.750	Ea	421.00	25.90	—	446.90
4"	P1@1.35	Ea	562.00	46.60	—	608.60
5"	ER@2.00	Ea	990.00	74.00	31.40	1,095.40
6"	ER@2.50	Ea	990.00	92.60	39.30	1,121.90
8"	ER@3.00	Ea	1,510.00	111.00	47.10	1,668.10
10"	ER@4.00	Ea	2,320.00	148.00	62.90	2,530.90

200 PSIG iron body butterfly valve, lug type, lever operated

Description	Craft@Hrs	Unit	Material $	Labor $	Equipment $	Total $
2"	P1@.450	Ea	134.00	15.50	—	149.50
2½"	P1@.450	Ea	139.00	15.50	—	154.50
3"	P1@.550	Ea	146.00	19.00	—	165.00
4"	P1@.550	Ea	182.00	19.00	—	201.00
5"	ER@.800	Ea	240.00	29.60	12.70	282.30
6"	ER@.800	Ea	293.00	29.60	12.70	335.30
8"	ER@.800	Ea	401.00	29.60	12.70	443.30
10"	ER@.900	Ea	557.00	33.30	14.10	604.40
12"	ER@1.00	Ea	729.00	37.00	15.70	781.70

200 PSIG iron body butterfly valve, wafer type, lever operated

Description	Craft@Hrs	Unit	Material $	Labor $	Equipment $	Total $
2"	P1@.450	Ea	122.00	15.50	—	137.50
2½"	P1@.450	Ea	125.00	15.50	—	140.50
3"	P1@.550	Ea	134.00	19.00	—	153.00
4"	P1@.550	Ea	163.00	19.00	—	182.00
5"	ER@.800	Ea	217.00	29.60	12.70	259.30
6"	ER@.800	Ea	272.00	29.60	12.70	314.30
8"	ER@.800	Ea	377.00	29.60	12.70	419.30
10"	ER@.900	Ea	527.00	33.30	14.10	574.40
12"	ER@1.00	Ea	692.00	37.00	15.70	744.70

Class 125 iron body swing check valve, flanged joints

Description	Craft@Hrs	Unit	Material $	Labor $	Equipment $	Total $
2"	P1@.500	Ea	155.00	17.30	—	172.30
2½"	P1@.600	Ea	197.00	20.70	—	217.70
3"	P1@.750	Ea	245.00	25.90	—	270.90
4"	P1@1.35	Ea	360.00	46.60	—	406.60
5"	ER@2.00	Ea	693.00	74.00	31.40	798.40
6"	ER@2.50	Ea	699.00	92.60	39.30	830.90
8"	ER@3.00	Ea	1,250.00	111.00	47.10	1,408.10
10"	ER@4.00	Ea	2,060.00	148.00	62.90	2,270.90
12"	ER@4.50	Ea	2,790.00	167.00	70.80	3,027.80

Carbon Steel, Schedule 10 with Roll-Grooved Joints

Description	Craft@Hrs	Unit	Material $	Labor $	Equipment $	Total $

Class 125 iron body silent check valve, flanged joints

Description	Craft@Hrs	Unit	Material $	Labor $	Equipment $	Total $
2"	P1@.500	Ea	113.00	17.30	—	130.30
2½"	P1@.600	Ea	131.00	20.70	—	151.70
3"	P1@.750	Ea	147.00	25.90	—	172.90
4"	P1@1.35	Ea	193.00	46.60	—	239.60
5"	ER@2.00	Ea	279.00	74.00	31.40	384.40
6"	ER@2.50	Ea	347.00	92.60	39.30	478.90
8"	ER@3.00	Ea	625.00	111.00	47.10	783.10
10"	ER@4.00	Ea	970.00	148.00	62.90	1,180.90

Class 125 iron body strainer, flanged

Description	Craft@Hrs	Unit	Material $	Labor $	Equipment $	Total $
2"	P1@.500	Ea	124.00	17.30	—	141.30
2½"	P1@.600	Ea	139.00	20.70	—	159.70
3"	P1@.750	Ea	160.00	25.90	—	185.90
4"	P1@1.35	Ea	273.00	46.60	—	319.60
5"	P1@2.00	Ea	554.00	69.10	31.40	654.50
6"	P1@2.50	Ea	554.00	86.40	39.30	679.70
8"	P1@3.00	Ea	937.00	104.00	47.10	1,088.10

Installation of 2-way control valve, flanged joints

Description	Craft@Hrs	Unit	Material $	Labor $	Equipment $	Total $
2"	P1@.500	Ea	—	17.30	—	17.30
2½"	P1@.600	Ea	—	20.70	—	20.70
3"	P1@.750	Ea	—	25.90	—	25.90
4"	P1@1.35	Ea	—	46.60	—	46.60
6"	P1@2.50	Ea	—	86.40	—	86.40
8"	P1@3.00	Ea	—	104.00	—	104.00
10"	P1@4.00	Ea	—	138.00	—	138.00
12"	P1@4.50	Ea	—	155.00	—	155.00

Installation of 3-way control valve, flanged joints

Description	Craft@Hrs	Unit	Material $	Labor $	Equipment $	Total $
2"	P1@.910	Ea	—	31.40	—	31.40
2½"	P1@1.12	Ea	—	38.70	—	38.70
3"	P1@1.33	Ea	—	46.00	—	46.00
4"	P1@2.00	Ea	—	69.10	—	69.10
6"	P1@3.70	Ea	—	128.00	—	128.00
8"	P1@4.40	Ea	—	152.00	—	152.00
10"	P1@5.90	Ea	—	204.00	—	204.00
12"	P1@6.50	Ea	—	225.00	—	225.00

Description	Craft@Hrs	Unit	Material $	Labor $	Equipment $	Total $

Bolt and gasket sets

Description	Craft@Hrs	Unit	Material $	Labor $	Equipment $	Total $
2"	P1@.500	Ea	3.86	17.30	—	21.16
2½"	P1@.650	Ea	4.51	22.50	—	27.01
3"	P1@.750	Ea	7.64	25.90	—	33.54
4"	P1@1.00	Ea	12.70	34.60	—	47.30
5"	P1@1.10	Ea	21.20	38.00	—	59.20
6"	P1@1.20	Ea	21.20	41.50	—	62.70
8"	P1@1.25	Ea	23.80	43.20	—	67.00
10"	P1@1.70	Ea	40.90	58.70	—	99.60
12"	P1@2.20	Ea	46.20	76.00	—	122.20

Thermometer with well

Description	Craft@Hrs	Unit	Material $	Labor $	Equipment $	Total $
7"	P1@.250	Ea	159.00	8.64	—	167.64
9"	P1@.250	Ea	164.00	8.64	—	172.64

Dial type pressure gauge

Description	Craft@Hrs	Unit	Material $	Labor $	Equipment $	Total $
2½"	P1@.200	Ea	33.10	6.91	—	40.01
3½"	P1@.200	Ea	43.80	6.91	—	50.71

Pressure/temperature tap

Description	Craft@Hrs	Unit	Material $	Labor $	Equipment $	Total $
tap	P1@.150	Ea	15.70	5.18	—	20.88

Hanger with swivel assembly

Description	Craft@Hrs	Unit	Material $	Labor $	Equipment $	Total $
2"	P1@.300	Ea	6.05	10.40	—	16.45
2½"	P1@.350	Ea	7.82	12.10	—	19.92
3"	P1@.350	Ea	9.67	12.10	—	21.77
4"	P1@.350	Ea	14.90	12.10	—	27.00
5"	P1@.450	Ea	16.70	15.50	—	32.20
6"	P1@.450	Ea	21.80	15.50	—	37.30
8"	P1@.450	Ea	28.90	15.50	—	44.40
10"	P1@.550	Ea	39.70	19.00	—	58.70
12"	P1@.600	Ea	52.80	20.70	—	73.50

Riser clamp

Description	Craft@Hrs	Unit	Material $	Labor $	Equipment $	Total $
2"	P1@.115	Ea	4.84	3.97	—	8.81
2½"	P1@.120	Ea	5.09	4.15	—	9.24
3"	P1@.120	Ea	5.52	4.15	—	9.67
4"	P1@.125	Ea	7.03	4.32	—	11.35
5"	P1@.180	Ea	10.10	6.22	—	16.32
6"	P1@.200	Ea	12.20	6.91	—	19.11
8"	P1@.200	Ea	19.80	6.91	—	26.71
10"	P1@.250	Ea	29.40	8.64	—	38.04
12"	P1@.250	Ea	34.90	8.64	—	43.54

Carbon Steel, Schedule 40 with Cut-Grooved Joints

Schedule 40 carbon steel (ASTM A-53 and A-120) cut-grooved pipe with factory-grooved malleable iron, ductile iron or steel fittings is commonly used for heating hot water, chilled water and condenser water systems.

Consult the manufacturers for maximum operating temperature/pressure ratings for various combinations of pipe and fittings.

This section has been arranged to save the estimator's time by including all normally-used system components such as pipe, fittings, valves, hanger assemblies, riser clamps and miscellaneous items under one heading. Additional items can be found under "Plumbing and Piping Specialties." The cost estimates in this section are based on the conditions, limitations and wage rates described in the section "How to Use This Book" beginning on page 5.

Equipment cost, where shown, is $110 per hour for a 10-ton hydraulic truck-mounted crane.

Description	Craft@Hrs	Unit	Material $	Labor $	Equipment $	Total $

Schedule 40 carbon steel pipe with cut-grooved joints

Description	Craft@Hrs	Unit	Material $	Labor $	Equipment $	Total $
2"	P1@.110	LF	3.86	3.80	—	7.66
2½"	P1@.130	LF	6.08	4.49	—	10.57
3"	P1@.150	LF	8.25	5.18	—	13.43
4"	P1@.210	LF	11.90	7.26	—	19.16
5"	ER@.270	LF	22.40	10.00	4.20	36.60
6"	ER@.350	LF	33.70	13.00	5.50	52.20
8"	ER@.410	LF	33.70	15.20	6.40	55.30
10"	ER@.510	LF	47.30	18.90	8.10	74.30
12"	ER@.610	LF	74.40	22.60	9.50	106.50

Schedule 40 carbon steel 45 degree ell with cut-grooved joints

Description	Craft@Hrs	Unit	Material $	Labor $	Equipment $	Total $
2"	P1@.170	Ea	24.70	5.87	—	30.57
2½"	P1@.185	Ea	33.70	6.39	—	40.09
3"	P1@.200	Ea	44.20	6.91	—	51.11
4"	P1@.230	Ea	65.30	7.95	—	73.25
5"	ER@.250	Ea	158.00	9.26	3.90	171.16
6"	ER@.350	Ea	185.00	13.00	5.50	203.50
8"	ER@.500	Ea	386.00	18.50	7.90	412.40
10"	ER@.750	Ea	523.00	27.80	11.80	562.60
12"	ER@1.00	Ea	916.00	37.00	15.70	968.70

Schedule 40 carbon steel 90 degree ell with cut-grooved joints

Description	Craft@Hrs	Unit	Material $	Labor $	Equipment $	Total $
2"	P1@.170	Ea	24.70	5.87	—	30.57
2½"	P1@.185	Ea	33.70	6.39	—	40.09
3"	P1@.200	Ea	44.20	6.91	—	51.11
4"	P1@.230	Ea	65.30	7.95	—	73.25
5"	ER@.250	Ea	158.00	9.26	3.90	171.16
6"	ER@.350	Ea	185.00	13.00	5.50	203.50
8"	ER@.500	Ea	386.00	18.50	7.90	412.40
10"	ER@.750	Ea	600.00	27.80	11.80	639.60
12"	ER@1.00	Ea	1,630.00	37.00	15.70	1,682.70

Carbon Steel, Schedule 40 with Cut-Grooved Joints

Description	Craft@Hrs	Unit	Material $	Labor $	Equipment $	Total $

Schedule 40 carbon steel tee with cut-grooved joints

Description	Craft@Hrs	Unit	Material $	Labor $	Equipment $	Total $
2"	P1@.200	Ea	37.70	6.91	—	44.61
2½"	P1@.210	Ea	51.70	7.26	—	58.96
3"	P1@.230	Ea	72.00	7.95	—	79.95
4"	P1@.250	Ea	110.00	8.64	—	118.64
5"	ER@.300	Ea	260.00	11.10	4.80	275.90
6"	ER@.500	Ea	302.00	18.50	7.90	328.40
8"	ER@.750	Ea	662.00	27.80	11.80	701.60
10"	ER@1.00	Ea	1,180.00	37.00	15.70	1,232.70
12"	ER@1.50	Ea	1,630.00	55.50	23.70	1,709.20

Schedule 40 carbon steel reducing tee with cut-grooved joints

Description	Craft@Hrs	Unit	Material $	Labor $	Equipment $	Total $
3" x 2"	P1@.230	Ea	97.70	7.95	—	105.65
4" x 2"	P1@.240	Ea	132.00	8.29	—	140.29
4" x 2½"	P1@.245	Ea	132.00	8.46	—	140.46
4" x 3"	P1@.250	Ea	132.00	8.64	—	140.64
5" x 2"	P1@.260	Ea	242.00	8.98	—	250.98
5" x 3"	P1@.280	Ea	265.00	9.67	—	274.67
5" x 4"	P1@.300	Ea	287.00	10.40	—	297.40
6" x 3"	ER@.400	Ea	315.00	14.80	6.20	336.00
6" x 4"	ER@.450	Ea	315.00	16.70	7.20	338.90
6" x 5"	ER@.500	Ea	315.00	18.50	7.90	341.40
8" x 3"	ER@.600	Ea	454.00	22.20	9.40	485.60
8" x 4"	ER@.650	Ea	662.00	24.10	10.30	696.40
8" x 5"	ER@.700	Ea	662.00	25.90	11.00	698.90
8" x 6"	ER@.750	Ea	662.00	27.80	11.80	701.60
10" x 4"	ER@.800	Ea	707.00	29.60	12.70	749.30
10" x 5"	ER@.900	Ea	720.00	33.30	14.10	767.40
10" x 6"	ER@1.00	Ea	720.00	37.00	15.70	772.70
10" x 8"	ER@1.10	Ea	720.00	40.70	17.30	778.00
12" x 6"	ER@1.20	Ea	105.00	44.40	18.90	168.30
12" x 8"	ER@1.35	Ea	1,080.00	50.00	21.20	1,151.20
12" x 10"	ER@1.50	Ea	1,130.00	55.50	23.70	1,209.20

Schedule 40 carbon steel male adapter

Description	Craft@Hrs	Unit	Material $	Labor $	Equipment $	Total $
2"	P1@.170	Ea	16.00	5.87	—	21.87
2½"	P1@.185	Ea	19.00	6.39	—	25.39
3"	P1@.200	Ea	23.60	6.91	—	30.51
4"	P1@.230	Ea	39.40	7.95	—	47.35
5"	ER@.290	Ea	83.60	10.70	4.60	98.90
6"	ER@.400	Ea	197.00	14.80	6.20	218.00

Schedule 40 carbon steel female adapter

Description	Craft@Hrs	Unit	Material $	Labor $	Equipment $	Total $
2"	P1@.170	Ea	36.40	5.87	—	42.27
3"	P1@.200	Ea	56.30	6.91	—	63.21
4"	P1@.230	Ea	78.50	7.95	—	86.45

Carbon Steel, Schedule 40 with Cut-Grooved Joints

Description	Craft@Hrs	Unit	Material $	Labor $	Equipment $	Total $

Schedule 40 carbon steel reducer

Description	Craft@Hrs	Unit	Material $	Labor $	Equipment $	Total $
2"	P1@.160	Ea	34.00	5.53	—	39.53
3"	P1@.170	Ea	47.10	5.87	—	52.97
4"	P1@.210	Ea	57.20	7.26	—	64.46
5"	ER@.260	Ea	79.70	9.63	4.00	93.33
6"	ER@.310	Ea	92.60	11.50	5.00	109.10
8"	ER@.450	Ea	242.00	16.70	7.20	265.90
10"	ER@.690	Ea	422.00	25.50	10.80	458.30
12"	ER@.920	Ea	731.00	34.10	14.50	779.60

Schedule 40 carbon steel cap

Description	Craft@Hrs	Unit	Material $	Labor $	Equipment $	Total $
2"	P1@.110	Ea	17.60	3.80	—	21.40
2½"	P1@.120	Ea	27.60	4.15	—	31.75
3"	P1@.130	Ea	27.60	4.49	—	32.09
4"	P1@.140	Ea	29.80	4.84	—	34.64
5"	ER@.150	Ea	69.10	5.55	2.40	77.05
6"	ER@.170	Ea	72.00	6.29	2.80	81.09
8"	ER@.200	Ea	138.00	7.40	3.10	148.50
10"	ER@.225	Ea	251.00	8.33	3.50	262.83
12"	ER@.250	Ea	404.00	9.26	3.90	417.16

Flange with gasket, grooved joint

Description	Craft@Hrs	Unit	Material $	Labor $	Equipment $	Total $
2"	P1@.280	Ea	52.80	9.67	—	62.47
2½"	P1@.340	Ea	62.40	11.70	—	74.10
3"	P1@.390	Ea	70.70	13.50	—	84.20
4"	P1@.560	Ea	102.00	19.30	—	121.30
6"	ER@.780	Ea	127.00	28.90	12.30	168.20
8"	ER@1.10	Ea	150.00	40.70	17.20	207.90
10"	ER@1.40	Ea	190.00	51.80	22.00	263.80
12"	ER@1.70	Ea	263.00	62.90	26.70	352.60

Cut-grooved joint coupling with gasket

Description	Craft@Hrs	Unit	Material $	Labor $	Equipment $	Total $
2"	P1@.300	Ea	27.30	10.40	—	37.70
2½"	P1@.350	Ea	32.70	12.10	—	44.80
3"	P1@.400	Ea	36.40	13.80	—	50.20
4"	P1@.500	Ea	52.80	17.30	—	70.10
5"	ER@.600	Ea	81.00	22.20	9.40	112.60
6"	ER@.700	Ea	95.60	25.90	11.00	132.50
8"	ER@.900	Ea	158.00	33.30	14.10	205.40
10"	ER@1.10	Ea	219.00	40.70	17.30	277.00
12"	ER@1.35	Ea	251.00	50.00	21.20	322.20

Description	Craft@Hrs	Unit	Material $	Labor $	Equipment $	Total $

Class 125 iron body gate valve, flanged ends

2"	P1@.500	Ea	442.00	17.30	—	459.30
2½"	P1@.600	Ea	599.00	20.70	—	619.70
3"	P1@.750	Ea	649.00	25.90	—	674.90
4"	P1@1.35	Ea	950.00	46.60	—	996.60
6"	ER@2.50	Ea	1,830.00	92.60	39.30	1,961.90
8"	ER@3.00	Ea	2,970.00	111.00	47.10	3,128.10
10"	ER@4.00	Ea	4,900.00	148.00	62.90	5,110.90
12"	ER@4.50	Ea	6,730.00	167.00	70.80	6,967.80

Class 125 iron body globe valve, flanged joints

2"	P1@.500	Ea	226.00	17.30	—	243.30
2½"	P1@.600	Ea	351.00	20.70	—	371.70
3"	P1@.750	Ea	421.00	25.90	—	446.90
4"	ER@1.35	Ea	565.00	50.00	21.30	636.30
6"	ER@2.50	Ea	990.00	92.60	39.30	1,121.90
8"	ER@3.00	Ea	1,520.00	111.00	47.10	1,678.10
10"	ER@4.00	Ea	2,320.00	148.00	62.90	2,530.90

200 PSIG iron body butterfly valve, lug type, lever operated

2"	P1@.450	Ea	134.00	15.50	—	149.50
2½"	P1@.450	Ea	139.00	15.50	—	154.50
3"	P1@.550	Ea	146.00	19.00	—	165.00
4"	P1@.550	Ea	182.00	19.00	—	201.00
6"	ER@.800	Ea	293.00	29.60	12.70	335.30
8"	ER@.800	Ea	401.00	29.60	12.70	443.30
10"	ER@.900	Ea	557.00	33.30	14.10	604.40
12"	ER@1.00	Ea	729.00	37.00	15.70	781.70

200 PSIG iron body butterfly valve, wafer type, lever operated

2"	P1@.450	Ea	122.00	15.50	—	137.50
2½"	P1@.450	Ea	125.00	15.50	—	140.50
3"	P1@.550	Ea	134.00	19.00	—	153.00
4"	P1@.550	Ea	163.00	19.00	—	182.00
6"	ER@.800	Ea	272.00	29.60	12.70	314.30
8"	ER@.800	Ea	377.00	29.60	12.70	419.30
10"	ER@.900	Ea	527.00	33.30	14.10	574.40
12"	ER@1.00	Ea	692.00	37.00	15.70	744.70

Class 125 iron body swing check valve, flanged ends

2"	P1@.500	Ea	155.00	17.30	—	172.30
2½"	P1@.600	Ea	197.00	20.70	—	217.70
3"	P1@.750	Ea	245.00	25.90	—	270.90
4"	P1@1.35	Ea	360.00	46.60	—	406.60
6"	ER@2.50	Ea	699.00	92.60	39.30	830.90
8"	ER@3.00	Ea	1,250.00	111.00	47.10	1,408.10
10"	ER@4.00	Ea	2,060.00	148.00	62.90	2,270.90
12"	ER@4.50	Ea	2,790.00	167.00	70.80	3,027.80

Carbon Steel, Schedule 40 with Cut-Grooved Joints

Description	Craft@Hrs	Unit	Material $	Labor $	Equipment $	Total $

Class 125 iron body silent check valve, flanged joints

Description	Craft@Hrs	Unit	Material $	Labor $	Equipment $	Total $
2"	P1@.500	Ea	113.00	17.30	—	130.30
2½"	P1@.600	Ea	131.00	20.70	—	151.70
3"	P1@.750	Ea	147.00	25.90	—	172.90
4"	P1@1.35	Ea	193.00	46.60	—	239.60
5"	ER@2.00	Ea	279.00	74.00	31.40	384.40
6"	ER@2.50	Ea	347.00	92.60	39.30	478.90
8"	ER@3.00	Ea	625.00	111.00	47.10	783.10
10"	ER@4.00	Ea	970.00	148.00	62.90	1,180.90

Class 125 iron body strainer, flanged

Description	Craft@Hrs	Unit	Material $	Labor $	Equipment $	Total $
2"	P1@.500	Ea	124.00	17.30	—	141.30
2½"	P1@.600	Ea	139.00	20.70	—	159.70
3"	P1@.750	Ea	160.00	25.90	—	185.90
4"	P1@1.35	Ea	273.00	46.60	—	319.60
6"	ER@2.50	Ea	554.00	92.60	39.30	685.90
8"	ER@3.00	Ea	937.00	111.00	47.10	1,095.10

Installation of 2-way control valve, flanged joints

Description	Craft@Hrs	Unit	Material $	Labor $	Equipment $	Total $
2"	P1@.500	Ea	—	17.30	—	17.30
2½"	P1@.600	Ea	—	20.70	—	20.70
3"	P1@.750	Ea	—	25.90	—	25.90
4"	P1@1.35	Ea	—	46.60	—	46.60
6"	P1@2.50	Ea	—	86.40	—	86.40
8"	P1@3.00	Ea	—	104.00	—	104.00
10"	P1@4.00	Ea	—	138.00	—	138.00
12"	P1@4.50	Ea	—	155.00	—	155.00

Installation of 3-way control valve, flanged joints

Description	Craft@Hrs	Unit	Material $	Labor $	Equipment $	Total $
2"	P1@.910	Ea	—	31.40	—	31.40
2½"	P1@1.12	Ea	—	38.70	—	38.70
3"	P1@1.33	Ea	—	46.00	—	46.00
4"	P1@2.00	Ea	—	69.10	—	69.10
6"	P1@3.70	Ea	—	128.00	—	128.00
8"	P1@4.40	Ea	—	152.00	—	152.00
10"	P1@5.90	Ea	—	204.00	—	204.00
12"	P1@6.50	Ea	—	225.00	—	225.00

Bolt and gasket sets

Description	Craft@Hrs	Unit	Material $	Labor $	Equipment $	Total $
2"	P1@.500	Ea	3.86	17.30	—	21.16
2½"	P1@.650	Ea	4.51	22.50	—	27.01
3"	P1@.750	Ea	7.64	25.90	—	33.54
4"	P1@1.00	Ea	12.70	34.60	—	47.30
6"	P1@1.20	Ea	21.20	41.50	—	62.70
8"	P1@1.25	Ea	23.80	43.20	—	67.00
10"	P1@1.70	Ea	40.90	58.70	—	99.60
12"	P1@2.20	Ea	46.20	76.00	—	122.20

Carbon Steel, Schedule 40 with Cut-Grooved Joints

Description	Craft@Hrs	Unit	Material $	Labor $	Equipment $	Total $
Thermometer with well						
7"	P1@.250	Ea	159.00	8.64	—	167.64
9"	P1@.250	Ea	164.00	8.64	—	172.64
Dial type pressure gauge						
2½"	P1@.200	Ea	33.10	6.91	—	40.01
3½"	P1@.200	Ea	43.80	6.91	—	50.71
Pressure/temperature tap						
tap	P1@.150	Ea	15.70	5.18	—	20.88
Hanger with swivel assembly						
2"	P1@.300	Ea	6.05	10.40	—	16.45
2½"	P1@.350	Ea	7.82	12.10	—	19.92
3"	P1@.350	Ea	9.67	12.10	—	21.77
4"	P1@.350	Ea	14.90	12.10	—	27.00
5"	P1@.450	Ea	16.70	15.50	—	32.20
6"	P1@.450	Ea	21.80	15.50	—	37.30
8"	P1@.450	Ea	28.90	15.50	—	44.40
10"	P1@.550	Ea	39.70	19.00	—	58.70
12"	P1@.600	Ea	52.80	20.70	—	73.50
Riser clamp						
2"	P1@.115	Ea	4.84	3.97	—	8.81
2½"	P1@.120	Ea	5.09	4.15	—	9.24
3"	P1@.120	Ea	5.52	4.15	—	9.67
4"	P1@.125	Ea	7.03	4.32	—	11.35
5"	P1@.180	Ea	10.10	6.22	—	16.32
6"	P1@.200	Ea	12.20	6.91	—	19.11
8"	P1@.200	Ea	19.80	6.91	—	26.71
10"	P1@.250	Ea	29.40	8.64	—	38.04
12"	P1@.250	Ea	34.90	8.64	—	43.54
Galvanized steel pipe sleeves						
2"	P1@.130	Ea	4.94	4.49	—	9.43
2½"	P1@.150	Ea	5.01	5.18	—	10.19
3"	P1@.180	Ea	5.13	6.22	—	11.35
4"	P1@.220	Ea	5.85	7.60	—	13.45
5"	P1@.250	Ea	7.25	8.64	—	15.89
6"	P1@.270	Ea	7.82	9.33	—	17.15
8"	P1@.270	Ea	9.00	9.33	—	18.33
10"	P1@.290	Ea	10.50	10.00	—	20.50
12"	P1@.310	Ea	14.20	10.70	—	24.90
14"	P1@.330	Ea	14.20	11.40	—	25.60

Description	Unit	Material $	Labor $	Equipment $	Total $

Leadership in Energy & Environmental Design (LEED).

LEED offers an incentive to building owners to install energy-efficient and environmentally sensitive HVAC equipment. The LEED program awards points for application of the best available technology. The HVAC system can earn a maximum of 17 points toward LEED certification. A LEED-certified air conditioning system must comply with ASHRAE 90.1-2004 (efficiency) and ASHRAE 62.1-2004 (indoor air quality) standards. LEED certification also requires recording controls (Carrier ComfortView 3 or equal) to measure system performance. Zone sensor thermostats (Carrier Debonair or equal) are required to provide performance and efficiency data to the digital recorder. An indoor air quality CO_2 sensor, duct-mounted aspirator modules and a refrigerant such as Puron R-410A are also required.

Description	Unit	Material $	Labor $	Equipment $	Total $
Add for a LEED certified system with USGBC rating	Ea	20%	—	—	—
Add for LEED registration and inspection	Ea	2,000.00	—	—	2,000.00
Add for LEED central digital performance monitor/recorder, ComfortView 3 or equal	Ea	2,350.00	—	—	2,350.00
Add for LEED certified zone recording thermostats, Carrier DebonAir, USB remote-ready	Ea	350.00	—	—	350.00
Add for IAQ (Indoor Air Quality) CO_2 sensor and duct-mounted aspirator box	Ea	425.00	—	—	425.00

Residential A/C Cooling System.

With remote exterior condenser/compressor, field installed DX coil in existing supply air plenum. Includes electrical & control wiring, R-22 refrigerant piping & connections, programmable digital thermostat, start up and testing. Costs based on a maximum distance between outdoor condenser and coil of 60' and include a contractor mark up of 25%. Use these figures for preliminary budget purposes. Costs are based on using 650 SF per ton as the cooling requirement with a thermal envelope of R20 or greater, i.e., a 1.5-ton A/C unit will serve a 975 SF home. Typical subcontract prices.

Description	Unit	Material $	Labor $	Equipment $	Total $
1.5 tons	Ea	—	—	—	2,700.00
2 tons	Ea	—	—	—	2,900.00
2.5 tons	Ea	—	—	—	3,600.00
3 tons	Ea	—	—	—	4,900.00
5 tons	Ea	—	—	—	7,400.00
Add for R410A Refrigerant	%	—	—	—	18.0
Add for high heat loads	%	—	—	—	12.0

Description	Unit	Material $	Labor $	Equipment $	Total $

Residential forced-air heating, cooling & ventilation system.
Including a remote exterior condenser/compressor, field installed R-22 refrigerant DX "A" coil in supply air plenum, a gas-fired high efficiency furnace, programmable digital thermostat, ductwork, grilles & registers, HRV (heat recovery ventilator), kitchen and bathroom exhaust fans, ventilation and exhaust ductwork and wall hoods, electrical & control wiring, gas, refrigerant & flue piping & associated connections, start up, testing, and a contractor mark up of 25%. Use these figures for preliminary budget purposes. Heating & cooling load calculations based on a thermal envelope of R20 or greater. Typical subcontract prices.

Description	Unit	Material $	Labor $	Equipment $	Total $
900 – 1,000 SF	Ea	—	—	—	14,000.00
1,100 – 1,400 SF	Ea	—	—	—	16,000.00
1,500 – 1,750 SF	Ea	—	—	—	19,600.00
1,800 – 2000 SF	Ea	—	—	—	21,000.00
2,200 – 2,500 SF	Ea	—	—	—	23,750.00
2,600 – 3,000 SF	Ea	—	—	—	28,500.00
Deduct for mid-efficient unit	Ea	—	—	—	250.00
Deduct for electric furnace	Ea	—	—	—	250.00
Add for R410A refrigerant	%	—	—	—	3.5

Residential HVAC Assemblies

Description	Craft@Hrs	Unit	Material $	Labor $	Equipment $	Total $

Packaged self-contained roof-top DX air conditioning units.

EnergySmart certified, ASHRAE, US Green Building Council and Underwriters Laboratories approved. Includes cooling coils, compressor, heat rejection coils, regulator valves, refrigerant tank and remote digital single-zone control package. Set in place with a 13,000 lb. truck crane. Add installation costs from the section that follows.

Description	Craft@Hrs	Unit	Material $	Labor $	Equipment $	Total $
2-T, 800 CFM	SN@5.00	Ea	3,300.00	183.00	78.70	3,561.70
2½-T, 1,000 CFM	SN@6.00	Ea	3,950.00	219.00	94.20	4,263.20
3-T, 1,200 CFM	SN@7.00	Ea	4,730.00	256.00	110.00	5,096.00
4-T, 1,600 CFM	SN@8.00	Ea	5,780.00	293.00	157.00	6,230.00
5-T, 2,000 CFM	SN@9.00	Ea	7,250.00	329.00	157.00	7,736.00
7½-T, 3,000 CFM	SN@10.0	Ea	9,880.00	366.00	314.00	10,560.00
10-T, 4,000 CFM	SN@12.0	Ea	12,400.00	439.00	314.00	13,153.00
12-T, 5,000 CFM	SN@14.0	Ea	15,000.00	512.00	377.00	15,889.00
15-T, 6,000 CFM	SN@15.0	Ea	18,400.00	549.00	377.00	19,326.00
20-T, 8,000 CFM	SN@16.0	Ea	24,300.00	585.00	550.00	25,435.00
25-T, 10,000 CFM	SN@17.0	Ea	29,500.00	622.00	550.00	30,672.00
30-T, 12,000 CFM	SN@19.0	Ea	33,600.00	695.00	707.00	35,002.00
40-T, 16,000 CFM	SN@22.0	Ea	42,100.00	805.00	707.00	43,612.00

Roof-top DX air conditioning unit, hot water coil.

EnergySmart certified, ASHRAE, US Green Building Council, and Underwriters Laboratories approved. Add for the hot water coil. Single zone controls. Add installation costs from the section that follows.

Description	Craft@Hrs	Unit	Material $	Labor $	Equipment $	Total $
2-T, 800 CFM	SN@5.00	Ea	3,210.00	183.00	79.00	3,472.00
2½-T, 1,000 CFM	SN@6.00	Ea	3,870.00	219.00	94.00	4,183.00
3-T, 1,200 CFM	SN@7.00	Ea	4,640.00	256.00	110.00	5,006.00
4-T, 1,600 CFM	SN@8.00	Ea	5,650.00	293.00	157.00	6,100.00
5-T, 2,000 CFM	SN@9.00	Ea	7,060.00	329.00	157.00	7,546.00
7½-T, 3,000 CFM	SN@10.0	Ea	10,600.00	366.00	314.00	11,280.00
10-T, 4,000 CFM	SN@12.0	Ea	12,100.00	439.00	314.00	12,853.00
12-T, 5,000 CFM	SN@14.0	Ea	14,600.00	512.00	377.00	15,489.00
15-T, 6,000 CFM	SN@15.0	Ea	17,900.00	549.00	377.00	18,826.00
20-T, 8,000 CFM	SN@16.0	Ea	23,700.00	585.00	550.00	24,835.00
25-T, 10,000 CFM	SN@17.0	Ea	28,700.00	622.00	550.00	29,872.00
30-T, 12,000 CFM	SN@19.0	Ea	33,600.00	695.00	707.00	35,002.00
40-T, 16,000 CFM	SN@22.0	Ea	42,100.00	805.00	707.00	43,612.00

Description	Craft@Hrs	Unit	Material $	Labor $	Equipment $	Total $

Installation costs for packaged rooftop cooling

Description	Craft@Hrs	Unit	Material $	Labor $	Equipment $	Total $
Cut, frame and gasket downcomer hole in roof	S2@1.00	Ea	35.00	34.20	—	69.20
Mount duct hangers	S2@.250	Ea	3.50	8.54	—	12.04
Cut and mount sheet metal duct	S2@.350	LF	5.50	12.00	—	17.50
Apply and coat duct insulation	S2@.150	LF	2.40	5.12	—	7.52
Install piping for gas line	P1@.100	LF	3.75	3.46	—	7.21
Install piping for chilled or hot water/steam line	P1@.100	LF	2.85	3.46	—	6.31
Install electrical wiring	BE@.150	LF	1.75	5.74	—	7.49
Install HVAC controls	BE@.500	Ea	—	19.10	—	19.10
Commission and test	P1@4.00	Ea	—	138.00	—	138.00
Air balance and fine-tune	P1@4.00	Ea	—	138.00	—	138.00

Packaged air handler with chilled water and hot water/steam coil.

Costs shown based on 400 CFM per ton cooling. Unit includes insulated single wall casing, fan section, cooling coil section, heating coil section, mixing plenum section, bag filter section, fan motor, variable pitch drive, vibration isolators and drain pan. Set in place only. Make additional allowances for coil connections, controls, motor starters and power wiring. (12,000 BTUs equals 1 ton cooling.) Use these costs for preliminary estimates.

Description	Craft@Hrs	Unit	Material $	Labor $	Equipment $	Total $
3-T, 1,200 CFM	SN@4.00	Ea	2,870.00	146.00	63.00	3,079.00
4-T, 1,600 CFM	SN@5.50	Ea	3,770.00	201.00	157.00	4,128.00
5-T, 2,000 CFM	SN@7.00	Ea	4,500.00	256.00	157.00	4,913.00
7½-T, 3,000 CFM	SN@9.00	Ea	6,330.00	329.00	314.00	6,973.00
10-T, 4,000 CFM	SN@11.0	Ea	8,040.00	402.00	314.00	8,756.00
12-T, 5,000 CFM	SN@13.0	Ea	9,470.00	476.00	377.00	10,323.00
15-T, 6,000 CFM	SN@14.0	Ea	10,600.00	512.00	377.00	11,489.00
20-T, 8,000 CFM	SN@15.0	Ea	12,600.00	549.00	550.00	13,699.00
25-T, 10,000 CFM	SN@16.0	Ea	12,500.00	585.00	550.00	13,635.00
30-T, 12,000 CFM	SN@18.0	Ea	16,000.00	658.00	707.00	17,365.00
40-T, 16,000 CFM	SN@21.0	Ea	19,600.00	768.00	707.00	21,075.00

Description	Craft@Hrs	Unit	Material $	Labor $	Equipment $	Total $

Air handling unit accessories and options. Use these costs for preliminary estimates.

Description	Craft@Hrs	Unit	Material $	Labor $	Equipment $	Total $
DDC controls per zone complete	SN@2.75	Ea	915.00	101.00	43.30	1,059.30
Electric controls per zone complete	SN@2.75	Ea	487.00	101.00	43.30	631.30
Pneumatic controls per zone complete	SN@2.75	Ea	458.00	101.00	43.30	602.30
Variable speed drive 5 HP	SN@4.00	Ea	3,660.00	146.00	62.90	3,868.90
Variable speed drive 7.5HP	SN@4.00	Ea	4,270.00	146.00	62.90	4,478.90
Variable speed drive 10 HP	SN@6.00	Ea	4,870.00	219.00	94.20	5,183.20
Variable speed drive 15 HP	SN@8.00	Ea	5,490.00	293.00	94.20	5,877.20
Variable speed drive 20 HP	SN@12.0	Ea	6,100.00	439.00	189.00	6,728.00
Variable speed drive 25 HP	SN@16.0	Ea	6,710.00	585.00	251.00	7,546.00
Variable speed drive 30 HP	SN@18.0	Ea	7,930.00	658.00	282.00	8,870.00
Variable speed drive 40 HP	SN@22.0	Ea	9,740.00	805.00	347.00	10,892.00
Variable speed drive 50 HP	SN@26.0	Ea	11,600.00	951.00	409.00	12,960.00
Variable Inlet vanes 1,000-1,500 CFM	SN@4.00	Ea	184.00	146.00	62.90	392.90
Variable Inlet vanes 1,600-2,500 CFM	SN@4.00	Ea	396.00	146.00	62.90	604.90
Variable Inlet vanes 2,600-5,000 CFM	SN@6.00	Ea	1,100.00	219.00	94.20	1,413.20
Variable Inlet vanes 6,000-10,000 CFM	SN@8.00	Ea	1,840.00	293.00	126.00	2,259.00
Variable Inlet vanes 11,000-20,000 CFM	SN@10.0	Ea	3,050.00	366.00	157.00	3,573.00

Heat Recovery Ventilators provide a fresh air supply to tightly sealed building envelopes. An HRV extracts heat from the stale indoor air being exhausted and transfers the heat to the fresh air being drawn into the building through the HRV. Heat recovery ventilators are also excellent dehumidifiers.

HRV unit features include energy efficient defrost cycle, cross-flow polypropylene heat exchanger, acoustically lined cabinet, outdoor air filter.

Allow 15-30 cfm per person or .04 to.05 cfm per square foot when sizing HRV unit. (ASHRAE62-19890 (cfm = cubic feet per minute)

Description	Craft@Hrs	Unit	Material $	Labor $	Equipment $	Total $

Commercial heat recovery ventilator. Set/hang in place only. Make additional allowances for duct, diffusers, controls, air balancing, electrical connections and condensate drain.

Description	Craft@Hrs	Unit	Material $	Labor $	Equipment $	Total $
HRV 700 cfm	SN@4.75	Ea	5,200.00	174.00	74.60	5,448.60
HRV 1,200 cfm	SN@5.25	Ea	5,600.00	192.00	82.50	5,874.50
HRV 2,500 cfm	SN@6.75	Ea	23,000.00	247.00	106.20	23,353.20

Swimming pool heat recovery ventilator. Set/hang in place only. Make additional allowances for duct, diffusers, controls, air balancing, electrical connections and condensate drain.

Description	Craft@Hrs	Unit	Material $	Labor $	Equipment $	Total $
HRV 700 cfm	SN@5.00	Ea	6,140.00	183.00	78.70	6,401.70
HRV 1,200 cfm	SN@5.75	Ea	6,960.00	210.00	90.40	7,260.40

Description	Craft@Hrs	Unit	Material $	Labor $	Equipment $	Total $

Conventional heat recovery ventilator. Hang in place only. Make additional allowances for duct, diffusers, controls, air balancing, electrical connections and condensate drain.

Description	Craft@Hrs	Unit	Material $	Labor $	Equipment $	Total $
HRV 65–150 cfm	S2@2.45	Ea	975.00	83.70	—	1,058.70
HRV 115–200cfm	S2@2.65	Ea	1,170.00	90.50	—	1,260.50

Compact heat recovery ventilator. Hang in place only. Make additional allowances for duct, diffusers, controls, air balancing, electrical connections and condensate drain.

Description	Craft@Hrs	Unit	Material $	Labor $	Equipment $	Total $
HRV 65–127 cfm	S2@2.45	Ea	1,030.00	83.70	—	1,113.70
HRV 115–195cfm	S2@2.65	Ea	1,170.00	90.50	—	1,260.50

High efficiency heat recovery ventilator. Hang in place only. Make additional allowances for duct, diffusers, controls, air balancing, electrical connections and condensate drain.

Description	Craft@Hrs	Unit	Material $	Labor $	Equipment $	Total $
HRV 65–127 cfm	S2@2.65	Ea	1,120.00	90.50	—	1,210.50
HRV 115–180cfm	S2@2.90	Ea	1,760.00	99.10	—	1,859.10
HRV 180–265cfm	S2@3.25	Ea	1,830.00	111.00	—	1,941.00

Heat recovery ventilator controls

Description	Craft@Hrs	Unit	Material $	Labor $	Equipment $	Total $
HRV basic control	S2@1.00	Ea	89.40	34.20	—	123.60
HRV std. control	S2@1.00	Ea	142.00	34.20	—	176.20
HRV auto control	S2@1.00	Ea	192.00	34.20	—	226.20
60 Minute timer	S2@.600	Ea	59.40	20.50	—	79.90
Interlock relay	S2@.600	Ea	70.60	20.50	—	91.10

Heat recovery ventilator accessories

Description	Craft@Hrs	Unit	Material $	Labor $	Equipment $	Total $
6" diffusers	S2@.500	Ea	15.00	17.10	—	32.10
6" wall hoods	S2@1.50	Ea	26.10	51.20	—	77.30
6" tee fittings	S2@.350	Ea	3.49	12.00	—	15.49
6" flex duct	S2@.025	LF	.82	.85	—	1.67
6" flex insul duct	S2@.025	LF	1.60	.85	—	2.45
HRV filters	S2@.450	Ea	21.40	15.40	—	36.80

Description	Craft@Hrs	Unit	Material $	Labor $	Equipment $	Total $

Installation costs for heat recovery ventilators

Description	Craft@Hrs	Unit	Material $	Labor $	Equipment $	Total $
Cut, frame and gasket, mount duct hangers	S2@.250	Ea	3.50	8.54	—	12.04
Cut and mount sheet metal duct	S2@.350	LF	5.50	12.00	—	17.50
Apply and coat duct insulation	S2@.150	LF	2.40	5.12	—	7.52
Install piping for gas line	P1@.100	LF	3.75	3.46	—	7.21
Install piping for chilled or hot water/steam	P1@.100	LF	2.85	3.46	—	6.31
Install electrical wiring	BE@.150	LF	1.75	5.74	—	7.49
Install HVAC controls	BE@.500	Ea	—	19.10	—	19.10
Commission and test	P1@4.00	Ea	—	138.00	—	138.00
Run air balance and fine tune system	P1@4.00	Ea	—	138.00	—	138.00

Water Coil Piping

Engineering drawings of coil piping details have a bad reputation among HVAC contractors and estimators. They're notorious for what they leave out. They'll rarely show more than one coil bank, no matter how big the system is. Furthermore, the drawings hardly ever call out sizes for either the piping or the control valves. Don't be taken in by the apparent simplicity of the system as shown in these drawings. It's likely to be only the tip of the iceberg. For example, unless the air handling capacity of the system is less than 16,000 CFM, the single coil bank shown won't be adequate. Add one or two more coil banks and you're looking at a lot more piping — and a more complex system that takes longer to install.

You probably haven't even decided which equipment supplier to use. This is hardly the time for you to start researching heating and cooling coils. Nevertheless, you need better, more complete and realistic data to come up with a competitive estimate.

We'll see how and where to track down the hard data that you have to take the time to find. I'll also pass along a few tips on estimating water coil piping. They'll help you avoid leaving something out of your estimates — a real pitfall for any beginner. It's those little (but essential) items, so easily overlooked, that are so deadly to a profit margin. Finally, check the next two pages of diagrams with tables. The data given there, combined with the data you collected earlier, forms the basis for informed guesswork.

The Hard Data

There are two things you absolutely must know to estimate water coil piping. First, the size of the branch piping to the coils; second, the CFM rating of the air handling units for the system.

To find the pipe sizes, look at either the floor plans or the details for the equipment room. They'll list the sizes of the branch run-out pipes. Once you know them, you can make a good guess at the right size for the control valves. (See the diagrams and tables on pages 295 and 296.) The only information you need is the CFM ratings of the air handling units and the branch piping sizes to the coils. If the system's capacity is over 16,000 CFM, you need two or three coil banks.

A Few Tips on Estimating Water Coil Piping

1) Coil connection sizes seldom match branch pipe sizes. Be sure to include the reducing fittings you'll need in any estimate.

2) Two-way and three-way control valves are both usually one pipe size smaller than the pipe where they're installed. That means you'll need either two or three reducing fittings per control valve. Be sure you include their cost in your estimates.

Using the Diagrams

In the following diagrams, for clarity, some items are not included. These items are: balance valves, shut-off valves, reducers, strainers, gauges and gauge taps. Any details you need about these items for your estimate are in the engineer's coil piping details.

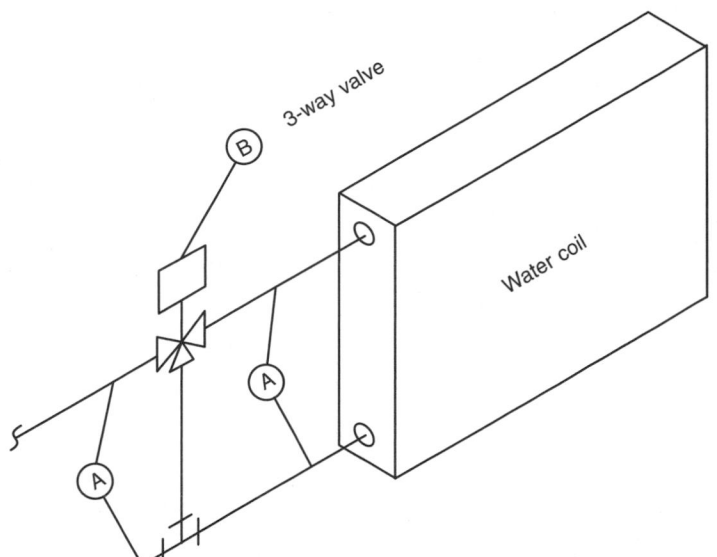

If (A) is:	Then (B) is:
1"	¾"
1¼"	1"
1½"	1¼"
2"	1½"
2½"	2"
3"	2½"

Typical water coil piping for A.H. units up to 16,000 CFM

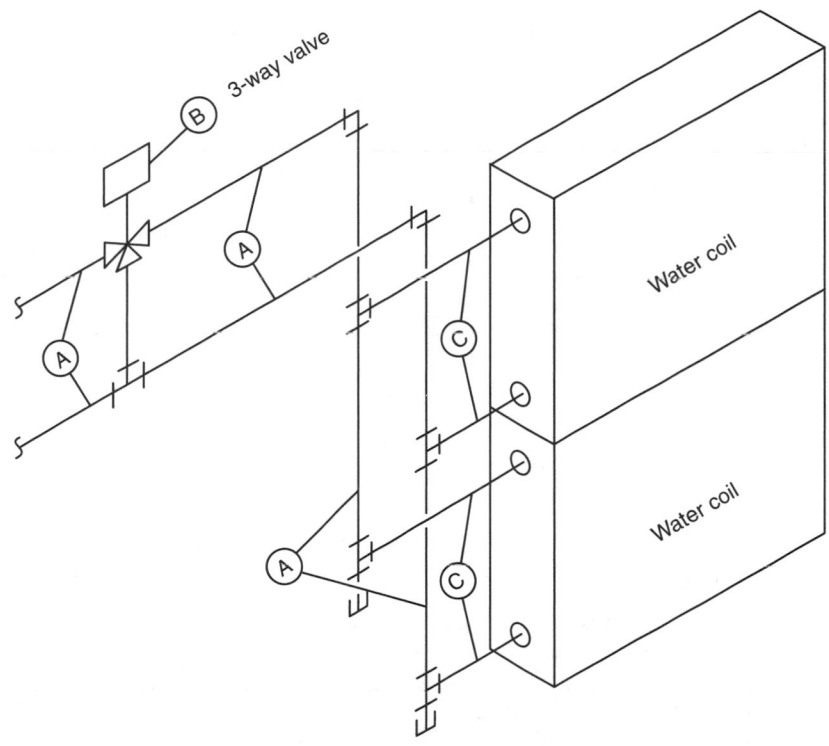

If (A) is:	Then (B) is:	And (C) is:
2½"	2"	2"
3"	2½"	2½"
4"	3"	3"

Typical water coil piping for A.H. units from 16,000 to 26,000 CFM

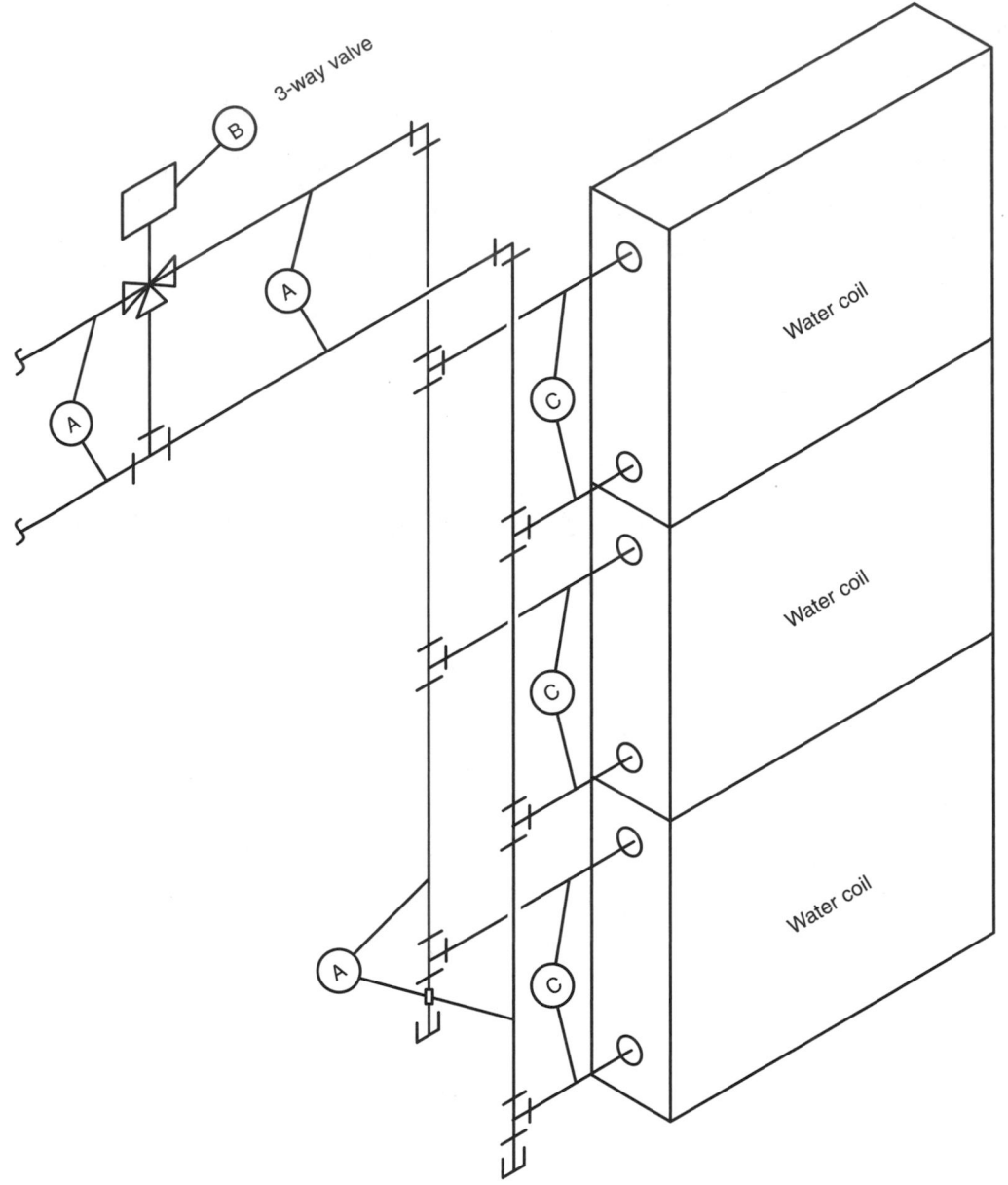

If Ⓐ is:	Then Ⓑ is:	And Ⓒ is:
4"	3"	2½"
6"	4"	3"
8"	6"	4"
10"	8"	6"

Typical water coil piping for A.H. units over 26,000 CFM

Description	Craft@Hrs	Unit	Material $	Labor $	Equipment $	Total $

Air handling unit coil connection, one row coil bank, non-regulated flow. Connection assembly includes pipe, fittings, pipe insulation, valves, gauges, thermometers and vents.

Description	Craft@Hrs	Unit	Material $	Labor $	Equipment $	Total $
1½" supply	SN@14.0	Ea	1,630.00	512.00	220.00	2,362.00
2" supply	SN@18.0	Ea	2,000.00	658.00	282.00	2,940.00
2½" supply	SN@28.0	Ea	2,670.00	1,020.00	440.00	4,130.00
3" supply	SN@31.5	Ea	2,930.00	1,150.00	495.00	4,575.00
4" supply	SN@34.0	Ea	3,140.00	1,240.00	534.00	4,914.00
6" supply	SN@41.0	Ea	4,530.00	1,500.00	644.00	6,674.00

Air handling unit coil connection, one row coil bank, 2-way control valve design. Connection assembly includes pipe and fittings, pipe insulation, valves, gauges, thermometers and vents.

Description	Craft@Hrs	Unit	Material $	Labor $	Equipment $	Total $
1½" supply	SN@16.5	Ea	1,840.00	604.00	259.00	2,703.00
2" supply	SN@21.0	Ea	2,370.00	768.00	330.00	3,468.00
2½" supply	SN@33.6	Ea	2,870.00	1,230.00	528.00	4,628.00
3" supply	SN@36.0	Ea	3,090.00	1,320.00	567.00	4,977.00
4" supply	SN@43.8	Ea	3,740.00	1,600.00	688.00	6,028.00
6" supply	SN@54.0	Ea	6,010.00	1,980.00	849.00	8,839.00

Air handling unit coil connection, one row coil bank, 3-way control valve design. Connection assembly includes pipe and fittings, pipe insulation, valves, gauges, thermometers and vents.

Description	Craft@Hrs	Unit	Material $	Labor $	Equipment $	Total $
1½" supply	SN@18.0	Ea	2,120.00	658.00	282.00	3,060.00
2" supply	SN@26.0	Ea	2,640.00	951.00	409.00	4,000.00
2½" supply	SN@41.5	Ea	3,300.00	1,520.00	653.00	5,473.00
3" supply	SN@43.8	Ea	3,640.00	1,600.00	688.00	5,928.00
4" supply	SN@54.6	Ea	4,700.00	2,000.00	858.00	7,558.00
6" supply	SN@61.4	Ea	6,690.00	2,250.00	965.00	9,905.00

Air handling unit coil connection, two row coil bank, non-regulated flow. Connection assembly includes pipe and fittings, pipe insulation, valves, gauges, thermometers and vents.

Description	Craft@Hrs	Unit	Material $	Labor $	Equipment $	Total $
2½" supply	SN@48.0	Ea	3,990.00	1,760.00	754.00	6,504.00
3" supply	SN@51.5	Ea	4,880.00	1,880.00	809.00	7,569.00
4" supply	SN@63.6	Ea	6,440.00	2,330.00	999.00	9,769.00
6" supply	SN@79.2	Ea	9,420.00	2,900.00	1,250.00	13,570.00

Air handling unit coil connection, two row coil bank, 2-way control valve design. Connection assembly includes pipe and fittings, pipe insulation, valves, gauges, thermometers and vents.

Description	Craft@Hrs	Unit	Material $	Labor $	Equipment $	Total $
2½" supply	SN@54.0	Ea	4,480.00	1,980.00	849.00	7,309.00
3" supply	SN@58.5	Ea	5,640.00	2,140.00	919.00	8,699.00
4" supply	SN@67.0	Ea	6,930.00	2,450.00	1,050.00	10,430.00
6" supply	SN@83.5	Ea	9,570.00	3,050.00	1,310.00	13,930.00

Air Handling Unit Coil Connections

Description	Craft@Hrs	Unit	Material $	Labor $	Equipment $	Total $

Air handling unit coil connection, two row coil bank, 3-way control valve design. Connection assembly includes pipe and fittings, pipe insulation, valves, gauges, thermometers and vents.

Description	Craft@Hrs	Unit	Material $	Labor $	Equipment $	Total $
2½" supply	SN@58.8	Ea	4,700.00	2,150.00	924.00	7,774.00
3" supply	SN@64.0	Ea	5,920.00	2,340.00	1,007.00	9,267.00
4" supply	SN@72.0	Ea	7,490.00	2,630.00	1,130.00	11,250.00
6" supply	SN@87.0	Ea	9,980.00	3,180.00	1,370.00	14,530.00

Air handling unit coil connection, three row coil bank, non-regulated flow. Connection assembly includes pipe and fittings, pipe insulation, valves, gauges, thermometers and vents.

Description	Craft@Hrs	Unit	Material $	Labor $	Equipment $	Total $
4" supply	SN@72.0	Ea	6,790.00	2,630.00	1,130.00	10,550.00
6" supply	SN@94.0	Ea	11,800.00	3,440.00	1,480.00	16,720.00
8" supply	SN@120.	Ea	16,000.00	4,390.00	1,890.00	22,280.00

Air handling unit coil connection, three row coil bank, 2-way control valve design. Connection assembly includes pipe and fittings, pipe insulation, valves, gauges, thermometers and vents.

Description	Craft@Hrs	Unit	Material $	Labor $	Equipment $	Total $
4" supply	SN@78.0	Ea	7,200.00	2,850.00	1,230.00	11,280.00
6" supply	SN@105.	Ea	12,900.00	3,840.00	1,650.00	18,390.00
8" supply	SN@132.	Ea	17,900.00	4,830.00	2,070.00	24,800.00

Air handling unit coil connection, three row coil bank, 3-way control valve design. Connection assembly includes pipe and fittings, pipe insulation, valves, gauges, thermometers and vents.

Description	Craft@Hrs	Unit	Material $	Labor $	Equipment $	Total $
4" supply	SN@82.0	Ea	8,360.00	3,000.00	1,290.00	12,650.00
6" supply	SN@112.	Ea	13,300.00	4,100.00	1,760.00	19,160.00
8" supply	SN@140.	Ea	20,000.00	5,120.00	2,200.00	27,320.00

Description	Craft@Hrs	Unit	Material $	Labor $	Equipment $	Total $

Residential gas-fired upflow furnace. Set in place only. Make additional allowances for gas and electrical connections. Costs shown per thousand BTU per hour (MBH) Mid-efficiency, 80% AFUE.

Description	Craft@Hrs	Unit	Material $	Labor $	Equipment $	Total $
50 MBH input	SN@2.00	Ea	809.00	73.20	31.40	913.60
75 MBH input	SN@2.00	Ea	1,060.00	73.20	31.40	1,164.60
100 MBH input	SN@2.00	Ea	1,230.00	73.20	31.40	1,334.60
125 MBH input	SN@2.00	Ea	1,400.00	73.20	31.40	1,504.60

Residential combination gas fired furnace and A/C unit. With remote exterior condenser/compressor. Set in place only. Make additional allowances for gas, electrical and DX connections. Costs shown per thousand BTU per hour (MBH) Mid-efficiency, 80% AFUE.

Description	Craft@Hrs	Unit	Material $	Labor $	Equipment $	Total $
30 MBH, 1.5 tons	SN@2.50	Ea	2,410.00	91.50	39.20	2,540.70
36 MBH, 2 tons	SN@2.75	Ea	2,860.00	101.00	43.30	3,004.30
42 MBH, 2 tons	SN@3.00	Ea	3,210.00	110.00	47.10	3,367.10
48 MBH, 2.5 tons	SN@3.50	Ea	3,750.00	128.00	55.00	3,933.00
60 MBH, 3 tons	SN@4.00	Ea	4,480.00	146.00	62.90	4,688.90

High efficiency, condensing gas furnace. Direct drive, atmospheric draft, electronic ignition. Set in place only. Make additional allowances for flue, gas and electrical connections. Costs shown per thousand BTU per hour (MBH) High efficiency 94% AFUE.

Description	Craft@Hrs	Unit	Material $	Labor $	Equipment $	Total $
40 MBH input	S2@2.00	Ea	1,670.00	68.30	—	1,738.30
60 MBH input	S2@2.00	Ea	1,670.00	68.30	—	1,738.30
70 MBH input	S2@2.00	Ea	1,610.00	68.30	—	1,678.30
90 MBH input	S2@2.00	Ea	1,610.00	68.30	—	1,678.30
100 MBH input	S2@2.00	Ea	2,290.00	68.30	—	2,358.30
120 MBH input	S2@2.00	Ea	2,370.00	68.30	—	2,438.30
2 speed fan & limit control kit	S2@1.25	Ea	32.80	42.70	—	75.50
Propane conversion kit	S2@1.75	Ea	127.00	59.80	—	186.80

Central dehumidification system.
Upflow or counterflow, 400 CFM, 30 gallon per day baseload capacity at 0.5 water column pressure differential. With inlet filter, drain pan, drain line, heater plate, cooling draft exchanger, humidistat control sensor, control relay, actuator, cabinet, two 24" by 24" by 4' long duct transitions, gaskets, hangers and ground fault protection. Whirlpool UGD160UH or equal. Installation assumes rental of an appliance dolly ($14 per day), 3,000 lb. come-a-long ($16 per day) and a 1/2-ton chain hoist ($21 per day). Add the cost of control wiring and electrical wiring.

Central dehumidification system	SW@0.50	Ea	1,500.00	19.90	51.00	1,570.90
Cut, frame and gasket hole in wall, ceiling or roof	SW@1.00	Ea	35.00	39.70	—	74.70
Mount duct hangers	SW@0.25	Ea	3.50	9.93	—	13.43
Cut and mount sheet metal duct	SW@0.35	LF	5.50	13.90	—	19.40
Apply and coat duct insulation	SW@0.15	LF	2.40	5.96	—	8.36
Install electrical wiring	BE@0.15	LF	1.75	5.74	—	7.49
Install dehumidifier controls	BE@0.50	Ea	—	19.10	—	19.10
Test and balance	SW@1.50	Ea	—	59.60	—	59.60

Wall furnace, mid efficiency, pilot light ignition.
Gas fired, atmospheric draft, (radiant heat, no fan). Set in place only. Make additional allowances for gas and flue connections. Costs shown per thousand BTU per hour (MBH). Mid efficiency 80% AFUE.

35 MBH input	S2@2.75	Ea	1,130.00	93.90	—	1,223.90
50 MBH input	S2@2.75	Ea	1,280.00	93.90	—	1,373.90
65 MBH input	S2@2.75	Ea	1,290.00	93.90	—	1,383.90
Fan blower kit	S2@1.75	Ea	183.00	59.80	—	242.80

Wall furnace, mid efficiency, electronic ignition.
Gas fired, atmospheric draft, (radiant heat, no fan). Set in place only. Make additional allowances for gas and flue connections. Costs shown per thousand BTU per hour (MBH). Mid efficiency 80% AFUE.

35 MBH input	S2@2.75	Ea	1,410.00	93.90	—	1,503.90
65 MBH input	S2@2.75	Ea	1,590.00	93.90	—	1,683.90
Fan blower kit	S2@1.75	Ea	183.00	59.80	—	242.80

Wall furnace, direct vent (included).
Gas fired, pilot light ignition, mid efficiency. (radiant heat, no fan). Set in place only. Make additional allowances for vent, gas and electrical connections. Costs shown per thousand BTU per hour (MBH). Mid efficiency 80% AFUE.

15 MBH input	S2@2.75	Ea	760.00	93.90	—	853.90
25 MBH input	S2@2.75	Ea	920.00	93.90	—	1,013.90
33 MBH input	S2@2.75	Ea	980.00	93.90	—	1,073.90
40 MBH input	S2@2.75	Ea	1,340.00	93.90	—	1,433.90
65 MBH input	S2@2.75	Ea	1,480.00	93.90	—	1,573.90
Direct vent kit	S2@2.50	Ea	129.00	85.40	—	214.40
Fan blower kit	S2@1.75	Ea	183.00	59.80	—	242.80

Description	Craft@Hrs	Unit	Material $	Labor $	Equipment $	Total $

Enthalpy energy recovery system. Steam-to-air or hot-water-to-air heat exchange. For boiler room downstream retrofits or new construction to qualify for EPA EnergyStar certification. Equipment cost is for a 40' rolling platform scissor lift. Add the cost of the energy recovery wheel ventilator.

Description	Craft@Hrs	Unit	Material $	Labor $	Equipment $	Total $
Reinforced attic joists	P1@3.00	Ea	75.50	104.00	140.00	319.50
Vibration isolators	S2@.750	LS	38.80	25.60	—	64.40
Drill and mount coil service drain	P1@.150	LF	2.91	5.18	—	8.09
Install electrical wiring	BE@.150	LF	1.75	5.74	—	7.49
Mount unit heater or enthalpy wheel	P1@.500	Ea	—	17.30	—	17.30
Connect ductwork mains to manifold	SW@4.50	Ea	145.50	179.00	—	324.50
Coil piping and condensate drain	P1@4.00	Ea	7.76	138.00	—	145.76
Zone control thermostat, manual	BE@.750	Ea	121.25	28.70	—	149.95
Master heat controller with auto change-over	BE@.750	Ea	291.00	28.70	—	319.70
Wiring of controls	BE@3.00	Ea	1.46	115.00	—	116.46
Calibration test	BE@2.00	Ea	—	76.60	—	76.60

Enthalpy energy recovery wheel. Modine Slimvent, Reznor XAWS or equal. For both heating and cooling applications in commercial and institutional buildings. Complies with the ARI Standard 1060-2000. Provides recovery of up to 75% of heat energy and 80% of cooling energy.

Description	Craft@Hrs	Unit	Material $	Labor $	Equipment $	Total $
800-1,000 CFM	SL@5.00	Ea	3,500.00	172.00	—	3,672.00
1,300-2,000 CFM	SL@5.00	Ea	4,400.00	172.00	—	4,572.00
2,400-3,000 CFM	SL@5.00	Ea	5,100.00	172.00	—	5,272.00
3,200-3,800 CFM	SL@5.00	Ea	6,700.00	172.00	—	6,872.00
4,000-4,800 CFM	SL@5.00	Ea	7,600.00	172.00	—	7,772.00
5,000-6,000 CFM	SL@5.00	Ea	8,500.00	172.00	—	8,672.00

Horizontal hot water unit heaters. Fan driven, with integral check valves, bypass piping, drain line fitting and vacuum breaker, Modine HSB series or equal.

Description	Craft@Hrs	Unit	Material $	Labor $	Equipment $	Total $
12.5 MBtu, 200 CFM	SL@2.00	Ea	400.00	68.60	140.00	608.60
17 MBtu, 300 CFM	SL@2.00	Ea	441.00	68.60	140.00	649.60
25 MBtu, 500 CFM	SL@2.50	Ea	504.00	85.80	140.00	729.80
30 MBtu, 700 CFM	SL@3.00	Ea	531.00	103.00	140.00	774.00
50 MBtu, 1,000 CFM	SL@3.50	Ea	617.00	120.00	140.00	877.00
60 MBtu, 1,300 CFM	SL@4.00	Ea	733.00	137.00	140.00	1,010.00

Unit Heaters

Description	Craft@Hrs	Unit	Material $	Labor $	Equipment $	Total $

Vertical hot water unit heaters Fan driven, with integral check valves, bypass piping, drain line fitting and vacuum breaker, Modine V500 series or equal.

Description	Craft@Hrs	Unit	Material $	Labor $	Equipment $	Total $
12.5 MBtu, 200 CFM	SL@2.00	Ea	449.00	68.60	140.00	657.60
17 MBtu, 300 CFM	SL@2.00	Ea	457.00	68.60	140.00	665.60
25 MBtu, 500 CFM	SL@2.50	Ea	593.00	85.80	140.00	818.80
30 MBtu, 700 CFM	SL@3.00	Ea	618.00	103.00	140.00	861.00
50 MBtu, 1,000 CFM	SL@3.50	Ea	745.00	120.00	140.00	1,005.00
60 MBtu, 1,300 CFM	SL@4.00	Ea	819.00	137.00	140.00	1,096.00

Horizontal steam coil unit heaters Fan driven, with integral check valves, bypass piping, drain line fitting and vacuum breaker, Modine HSB series or equal.

Description	Craft@Hrs	Unit	Material $	Labor $	Equipment $	Total $
12.5 MBtu, 200 CFM	SL@2.00	Ea	650.00	68.60	140.00	858.60
17 MBtu, 300 CFM	SL@2.00	Ea	750.00	68.60	140.00	958.60
25 MBtu, 500 CFM	SL@2.50	Ea	825.00	85.80	140.00	1,050.80
30 MBtu, 700 CFM	SL@3.00	Ea	900.00	103.00	140.00	1,143.00
50 MBtu, 1,000 CFM	SL@3.50	Ea	1,100.00	120.00	140.00	1,360.00
60 MBtu, 1,300 CFM	SL@4.00	Ea	1,350.00	137.00	140.00	1,627.00

Vertical steam coil unit heaters Fan driven, with integral check valves, bypass piping, drain line fitting and vacuum breaker, Modine V500 series or equal.

Description	Craft@Hrs	Unit	Material $	Labor $	Equipment $	Total $
12.5 MBtu, 200 CFM	SL@2.00	Ea	700.00	68.60	140.00	908.60
17 MBtu, 300 CFM	SL@2.00	Ea	770.00	68.60	140.00	978.60
25 MBtu, 500 CFM	SL@2.50	Ea	900.00	85.80	140.00	1,125.80
30 MBtu, 700 CFM	SL@3.00	Ea	1,200.00	103.00	140.00	1,443.00
50 MBtu, 1,000 CFM	SL@3.50	Ea	1,400.00	120.00	140.00	1,660.00
60 MBtu, 1,300 CFM	SL@4.00	Ea	1,500.00	137.00	140.00	1,777.00

Description	Craft@Hrs	Unit	Material $	Labor $	Equipment $	Total $

Unit heater, gas, direct fired, mid efficiency, propeller fan, atmospheric draft, single stage, standing pilot, aluminized burner and heat exchanger. Hang in place only. Make additional allowances for flue, gas and electrical connections. Costs shown per thousand BTU per hour (MBH). Mid efficiency 78% AFUE.

Description	Craft@Hrs	Unit	Material $	Labor $	Equipment $	Total $
30 MBH input	S2@4.00	Ea	933.00	137.00	—	1,070.00
50 MBH input	S2@4.00	Ea	1,030.00	137.00	—	1,167.00
75 MBH input	S2@4.00	Ea	1,150.00	137.00	—	1,287.00
100 MBH input	S2@4.00	Ea	1,280.00	137.00	—	1,417.00
125 MBH input	S2@4.00	Ea	1,520.00	137.00	—	1,657.00
145 MBH input	S2@4.00	Ea	1,580.00	137.00	—	1,717.00
175 MBH input	S2@4.00	Ea	1,730.00	137.00	—	1,867.00
200 MBH input	S2@4.00	Ea	1,910.00	137.00	—	2,047.00
250 MBH input	S2@4.00	Ea	2,010.00	137.00	—	2,147.00
300 MBH input	S2@4.00	Ea	2,610.00	137.00	—	2,747.00
350 MBH input	S2@4.00	Ea	3,080.00	137.00	—	3,217.00
400 MBH input	S2@4.00	Ea	3,500.00	137.00	—	3,637.00

Unit heater, gas fired, high efficiency, propeller fan, power vented (included), direct fired, single stage, intermittent pilot ignition, aluminized burner and heat exchanger. Hang in place and install power vent. Make additional allowances for gas and electrical connections. Costs shown per thousand BTU per hour (MBH). High efficiency 85% AFUE.

Description	Craft@Hrs	Unit	Material $	Labor $	Equipment $	Total $
30 MBH input	S2@5.25	Ea	1,380.00	179.00	—	1,559.00
50 MBH input	S2@5.25	Ea	1,470.00	179.00	—	1,649.00
75 MBH input	S2@5.25	Ea	2,350.00	179.00	—	2,529.00
100 MBH input	S2@5.25	Ea	1,780.00	179.00	—	1,959.00
125 MBH input	S2@5.25	Ea	1,980.00	179.00	—	2,159.00
145 MBH input	S2@5.25	Ea	2,100.00	179.00	—	2,279.00
175 MBH input	S2@5.25	Ea	2,220.00	179.00	—	2,399.00
200 MBH input	S2@5.25	Ea	2,370.00	179.00	—	2,549.00
250 MBH input	S2@5.25	Ea	2,740.00	179.00	—	2,919.00
300 MBH input	S2@5.25	Ea	3,230.00	179.00	—	3,409.00
350 MBH input	S2@5.25	Ea	3,610.00	179.00	—	3,789.00
400 MBH input	S2@5.25	Ea	3,960.00	179.00	—	4,139.00

Unit heater, gas, indirect fired, mid efficiency, propeller fan, power vented (included), single stage, intermittent pilot ignition, aluminized burner and heat exchanger, Hang in place and install power vent. Make additional allowances for gas and electrical connections. Costs shown per thousand BTU per hour (MBH). Mid efficiency 78% AFUE.

Description	Craft@Hrs	Unit	Material $	Labor $	Equipment $	Total $
130 MBH input	S2@5.25	Ea	2,520.00	179.00	—	2,699.00
150 MBH input	S2@5.25	Ea	2,740.00	179.00	—	2,919.00
170 MBH input	S2@5.25	Ea	2,840.00	179.00	—	3,019.00
225 MBH input	S2@5.25	Ea	3,170.00	179.00	—	3,349.00
280 MBH input	S2@5.25	Ea	3,780.00	179.00	—	3,959.00
340 MBH input	S2@5.25	Ea	4,270.00	179.00	—	4,449.00

Infrared Heaters

Description	Craft@Hrs	Unit	Material $	Labor $	Equipment $	Total $

High intensity infrared heater, gas fired. Ceramic grid. Automatic spark ignition. Including reflector. Approved for unvented commercial indoor installations. Not for use in residential applications. Labor includes hang in place only. Make additional allowances for gas and 110 volt electrical connections. Refer to local gas code for proper installation requirements.

Description	Craft@Hrs	Unit	Material $	Labor $	Equipment $	Total $
30,000 BTU	P1@1.20	Ea	461.00	41.50	66.00	568.50
60,000 BTU	P1@1.80	Ea	588.00	62.20	99.00	749.20
100,000 BTU	P1@2.50	Ea	1,390.00	86.40	138.00	1,614.40
130,000 BTU	P1@2.75	Ea	1,720.00	95.00	151.00	1,966.00
160,000 BTU	P1@2.75	Ea	1,960.00	95.00	151.00	2,206.00
Add for propane	—	Ea	106.00	—	—	106.00

High intensity infrared heater, gas fired. Ceramic grid. Millivolt standing pilot ignition. Approved for unvented commercial indoor installations. Not for use in residential applications. Labor includes hang in place only. Make additional allowances for gas connections. Millivolt standing pilot does not require electrical source.

Description	Craft@Hrs	Unit	Material $	Labor $	Equipment $	Total $
30,000 BTU	P1@1.20	Ea	1,070.00	41.50	66.00	1,177.50
60,000 BTU	P1@1.80	Ea	1,390.00	62.20	99.00	1,551.20
100,000 BTU	P1@2.50	Ea	1,740.00	86.40	138.00	1,964.40
130,000 BTU	P1@2.75	Ea	2,080.00	95.00	151.00	2,326.00
160,000 BTU	P1@2.75	Ea	2,410.00	95.00	151.00	2,656.00
Add for propane	—	Ea	120.00	—	—	120.00

Infrared tube heater, burner unit only, gas fired, negative pressure type. Labor includes hang in place only. Not for use in residential applications. Make additional allowances for burner tube, burner tube reflector, venting, gas piping and electrical requirements.

Description	Craft@Hrs	Unit	Material $	Labor $	Equipment $	Total $
30,000 BTU	P1@1.20	Ea	1,320.00	41.50	66.00	1,427.50
60,000 BTU	P1@1.80	Ea	1,250.00	62.20	99.00	1,411.20
100,000 BTU	P1@2.50	Ea	1,440.00	86.40	138.00	1,664.40
150,000 BTU	P1@2.75	Ea	1,530.00	95.00	151.00	1,776.00
175,000 BTU	P1@2.75	Ea	1,780.00	95.00	151.00	2,026.00
200,000 BTU	P1@2.75	Ea	2,050.00	95.00	151.00	2,296.00
Add for propane	—	Ea	120.00	—	—	120.00

Infrared tube heater, 4" diameter, 10' lengths. 16 gauge burner tube and .024" mill finish aluminum reflector. Labor includes hang in place only. Not for use in residential applications. Make additional allowances for burner unit, venting, gas piping and electrical requirements.

Description	Craft@Hrs	Unit	Material $	Labor $	Equipment $	Total $
Burner tubing	P1@.200	LF	5.45	6.91	—	12.36
Tubing U-bend	P1@.850	Ea	194.00	29.40	—	223.40
Reflector shield	P1@.200	LF	5.45	6.91	—	12.36
Vent terminal	P1@.600	Ea	85.70	20.70	—	106.40

Heat Pumps

In general, heat pumps are more effective in milder winter climates. In colder winter climates, secondary/supplemental electric heating elements (or equivalent heating source) are recommended.

A geothermal heat pump system's efficient operation is largely dependent upon proper design, layout, sizing and installation of the ground loop piping system for closed loop systems. In the case of well-to-well, the efficient operation of open loop systems is largely dependent upon the ability of the supply and return, or dump wells to meet the water volume demand of the heat pumps.

Rules of thumb when sizing loop & well systems:

Heating capacity, when considered or measured in tons cooling or refrigeration, is generally 3 to 4 times that of required cooling capacity for climates within 100 miles of the 49th parallel, i.e., if 2 tons of cooling is required, allow 6-8 tons of heating capacity (1 ton = 12,000 Btu).

Use 250 square feet per ton, e.g., a 2,000-square-foot home requires a 6-ton heat pump (heating capacity).

(Calculation based on R-20 wall and R-40 attic insulation, minimum dual pane argon charged windows.)

Closed Vertical Loop:

Vertical Bore Hole Loop — 3/4" or 1" diameter, socket fusioned loop = 200'-250' total bore hole depth per ton. For example, a 6-ton unit requires between 1200'-1500' (twelve to fifteen 5" bore holes, each 100' deep) with the associated 12-15 loop drops, spaced a minimum of 20' apart, connected to an adequately sized header, immersed in a bentonite slurry and applied with a tremie tube.

Closed Horizontal Loop:

Straight run — 3/4" or 1" diameter manifolded loop = 400 horizontal feet per ton. For example, a 6-ton unit requires 2,400 horizontal feet (eight 300' runs, 150' out, 150' back, minimum 2' radius return bend, placed a minimum 10' apart, minimum 4' buried depth, or buried below potential winter frost line).

Slinky — 3/4" or 1" diameter manifolded loop = 400 horizontal feet per ton. For example, a 6-ton unit requires 2,400 horizontal feet (eight 300' runs, 50' out, 50' back, coiled, placed a minimum 20' apart, minimum 4' buried depth, or buried below potential winter frost line. (Below 7' at 100 miles, or farther, north of the 49th parallel.)

Open Loop:

Well-to-Well — 2.5 gallons per minute per ton, each well (two required: supply & return). For example, a 6-ton unit requires 12-15 gallons per minute capacity per well.

Leadership in Energy & Environmental Design (LEED)

LEED offers an incentive to building owners to install energy-efficient and environmentally sensitive HVAC equipment. The LEED program awards points for application of the best available technology. The HVAC system can earn a maximum of 17 points toward LEED certification. A LEED-certified air conditioning system must comply with ASHRAE 90.1-2004 (efficiency) and ASHRAE 62.1-2004 (indoor air quality) standards. LEED certification also requires recording controls (Carrier ComfortView 3 or equal) to measure system performance. Zone sensor thermostats (Carrier Debonair or equal) are required to provide performance and efficiency data to the digital recorder. An indoor air quality CO_2 sensor, duct-mounted aspirator modules and a refrigerant such as Puron R-410A are also required.

Description	Craft@Hrs	Unit	Material $	Labor $	Equipment $	Total $

Geothermal ground or water source heat pump (open or closed loop), w/active cooling. Glycol/water mixture or water to air thermal transfer. The refrigeration circuit operates in the heating and cooling mode as required (sometimes referred to as active heating & cooling or mechanical heating & cooling). This unit is suited for both, open or closed loop systems. These units provide a higher degree of cooling capacity than the open loop, passive "free" cooling units. See table below. Optional de-superheater system provides domestic hot water temperature pre-heat or boost. Make additional allowances for the thermal source, i.e., horizontal ground loop, vertical bore hole ground loop, supply and return water wells, pond or lake source loop, etc. Make additional allowances for connections, ancillary components, start up and testing. Based on R-22 Refrigerant.

Description	Craft@Hrs	Unit	Material $	Labor $	Equipment $	Total $
Heat Pump, Open or Closed loop, 1/2 Ton	P1@2.25	Ea	1,500.00	77.70	—	1,577.70
Heat Pump, Open or Closed loop, 3/4 Ton	P1@2.25	Ea	1,550.00	77.70	—	1,627.70
Heat Pump, Open or Closed loop, 1 Ton	P1@2.25	Ea	1,630.00	77.70	—	1,707.70
Heat Pump, Open or Closed loop, 1.5 Ton	P1@2.25	Ea	1,890.00	77.70	—	1,967.70
Heat Pump, Open or Closed loop, 2 Ton	P1@2.50	Ea	1,950.00	86.40	—	2,036.40
Heat Pump, Open or Closed loop, 2.5 Ton	P1@2.50	Ea	2,420.00	86.40	—	2,506.40
Heat Pump, Open or Closed loop, 3 Ton	P1@3.00	Ea	2,510.00	104.00	—	2,614.00
Heat Pump, Open or Closed loop, 4 Ton	P1@3.50	Ea	2,880.00	121.00	—	3,001.00
Heat Pump, Open or Closed loop, 5 Ton	P1@4.00	Ea	5,650.00	138.00	—	5,788.00
Heat Pump, Open or Closed loop, 7.5Ton	P1@4.75	Ea	6,080.00	164.00	—	6,244.00
Optional de-superheater coil	P1@.000	Ea	717.00	—	—	717.00
Optional supplementary electric coil 5 KW	P1@.000	Ea	154.00	—	—	154.00
Optional supplementary electric coil 10 KW	P1@.000	Ea	182.00	—	—	182.00
Optional supplementary electric coil 15 KW	P1@.000	Ea	397.00	—	—	397.00
Optional supplementary electric coil 20 KW	P1@.000	Ea	441.00	—	—	441.00
Optional supplementary electric coil 25 KW	P1@.000	Ea	541.00	—	—	541.00
Water to water thermal transfer additional	P1@.000	Ea	353.00	—	—	353.00
R 410A Refrigerant – Add	P1@.000	LB	24.30	—	—	24.30

Description	Craft@Hrs	Unit	Material $	Labor $	Equipment $	Total $

Geothermal water source heat pump (open loop), w/free cooling.

Water to air thermal transfer. The refrigeration circuit is only operated in the heating mode while passive "free" cooling is provided by pumping cold well water directly to a unit mounted coil that by-passes the refrigeration (compressor) unit. This unit is suited to areas where the temperature of ground water supply is below 50°F. Optional de-superheater system provides domestic hot water temperature pre-heat or boost. Make additional allowances for the water source, i.e., supply and return water wells, pond or lake source, etc. Make additional allowances for connections, ancillary components, start up and testing.

Description	Craft@Hrs	Unit	Material $	Labor $	Equipment $	Total $
Heat Pump, Open Loop, Free Cooling, 2 Ton	P1@2.50	Ea	2,680.00	86.40	—	2,766.40
Heat Pump, Open Loop, Free Cooling, 3 Ton	P1@3.00	Ea	3,270.00	104.00	—	3,374.00
Heat Pump, Open Loop, Free Cooling, 4 Ton	P1@3.50	Ea	3,660.00	121.00	—	3,781.00
Heat Pump, Open Loop, Free Cooling, 5 Ton	P1@4.00	Ea	6,460.00	138.00	—	6,598.00
Heat Pump, Open Loop, Free Cooling, 7.5 Ton	P1@4.75	Ea	7,010.00	164.00	—	7,174.00
Optional de-superheater coil	P1@.000	Ea	717.00	—	—	717.00
Optional supplementary electric coil 5 KW	P1@.000	Ea	154.00	—	—	154.00
Optional supplementary electric coil 10 KW	P1@.000	Ea	182.00	—	—	182.00
Optional supplementary electric coil 15 KW	P1@.000	Ea	397.00	—	—	397.00
Optional supplementary electric coil 20 KW	P1@.000	Ea	441.00	—	—	441.00
Optional supplementary electric coil 25 KW	P1@.000	Ea	541.00	—	—	541.00
Water to water thermal transfer additional	P1@.000	Ea	353.00	—	—	353.00

Description	Craft@Hrs	Unit	Material $	Labor $	Equipment $	Total $

Geothermal water source heat pump (closed refrigerant loop). Water to air thermal transfer. Optional de-superheater system provides domestic hot water temperature pre-heat or boost. Make additional allowances for the heat transfer loop, i.e., refrigerant loop. Make additional allowances for connections, ancillary components, start up and testing.

Description	Craft@Hrs	Unit	Material $	Labor $	Equipment $	Total $
Heat Pump, 2 Ton	P1@2.50	Ea	1,600.00	86.40	—	1,686.40
Heat Pump, 3 Ton	P1@3.00	Ea	2,100.00	104.00	—	2,204.00
Heat Pump, 4 Ton	P1@3.50	Ea	2,430.00	121.00	—	2,551.00
Heat Pump, 5 Ton	P1@4.00	Ea	5,190.00	138.00	—	5,328.00
Heat Pump, 7.5 Ton	P1@4.75	Ea	5,570.00	170.00	—	5,740.00
Optional de-superheater coil	P1@.000	Ea	717.00	—	—	717.00
Optional supplementary electric coil 5 KW	P1@.000	Ea	154.00	—	—	154.00
Optional supplementary electric coil 10 KW	P1@.000	Ea	182.00	—	—	182.00
Optional supplementary electric coil 15 KW	P1@.000	Ea	397.00	—	—	397.00
Optional supplementary electric coil 20 KW	P1@.000	Ea	441.00	—	—	441.00
Optional supplementary electric coil 25 KW	P1@.000	Ea	541.00	—	—	541.00

Description	Unit	Material $	Labor $	Equipment $	Total $

LEED certification for geothermal heat pumps

Description	Unit	Material $	Labor $	Equipment $	Total $
Add for a LEED certified heat pump with USGBC rating	Ea	20%	—	—	—
Add for LEED registration and inspection	Ea	2,000.00	—	—	2,000.00
Add for LEED central digital performance monitor/recorder, ComfortView 3 or equal	Ea	2,350.00	—	—	2,350.00
Add for LEED certified zone recording thermostats, Carrier DebonAir, USB remote-ready	Ea	350.00	—	—	350.00
Add for IAQ (Indoor Air Quality) CO2 sensor and duct-mounted aspirator box	Ea	425.00	—	—	425.00

Description	Craft@Hrs	Unit	Material $	Labor $	Equipment $	Total $

Heat pump, residential air to air forced air aspirated split system.

Rated in nominal tonnage. Agency rating is ARI and CSA. Installed in with an air handling unit (mandatory) and filtration system (optional). Trane or equal. Rated at 13 SEER (Seasonal Energy Efficiency Rating). Includes an automatic reversing valve for switching between heating and cooling modes, semiconductor thermocouple sensor for monitoring indoor/outdoor temperature differential, interior thermostat, controller relay, digital controller module, centrifugal compressor and 208/230 V, 60 Hz, single phase motor drive. Must be installed with two fan-aspirated pre-charged R22 refrigerant evaporator coils, one interior in the air handling unit and one in the weatherproof enclosure mounted outside on a concrete slab. Assumes rental of an appliance dolly ($14 per day), a 3,000 lb. come-a-long ($16 per day) and a 1-ton chain hoist ($21 a day).

Description	Craft@Hrs	Unit	Material $	Labor $	Equipment $	Total $
Mounting and bolting interior heat pump unit in air handler enclosure						
2.0-ton unit	P1@.750	Ea	2,037.00	25.90	50.49	2,113.39
3.0-ton unit	P1@.750	Ea	2,231.00	25.90	50.49	2,307.39
3.5-ton unit	P1@.750	Ea	2,716.00	25.90	50.49	2,792.39
4.0-ton unit	P1@.750	Ea	2,910.00	25.90	50.49	2,986.39
5.0-ton unit	P1@.750	Ea	3,395.00	25.90	50.49	3,471.39
Mounting of interior evaporator coil in air handler						
duct	P1@1.20	Ea	—	41.50	20.79	62.29
Tie-in of connecting interior ductwork to house air ductwork manifold and						
exhaust	P1@4.50	Ea	145.50	155.00	—	300.50
Cutting and brazing of copper evaporator coil						
piping and drain	P1@4.00	Ea	7.76	138.00	—	145.76
Wiring of controls	BE@3.00	Ea	1.46	115.00	—	116.46
Calibration and test	BE@2.00	Ea	—	76.60	—	76.60
Form and pour 4' x 4' x 2" slab, exterior	CF@2.50	Ea	97.00	84.70	—	181.70
Form and pour 4' x 4' x 2" slab, interior	CF@3.00	Ea	97.00	102.00	—	199.00
Place 4' x 4' x 1/2" vibration pads	CF@.750	Ea	38.80	25.40	—	64.20
Mount interior evaporator drain	P1@.500	Ea	7.76	17.30	—	25.06
Bore piping hole through external coil	P1@.250	Ea	—	8.64	—	8.64
Mount and bolt external coil	P1@.450	Ea	29.10	15.50	—	44.60

Heat Pump Systems

Description	Craft@Hrs	Unit	Material $	Labor $	Equipment $	Total $

Heat pump, split system, single speed blower, single phase scroll compressor - 208 volt, 13 SEER (Seasonal Energy Efficiency Rating)

Air to air thermal transfer. Material costs include outdoor stat / low ambient, short cycle timer, high-pressure cut out and digital heat/cool thermostat with manual change over. Labor includes setting outdoor condenser, indoor blower and coil sections in place only. Make additional allowances for refrigerant piping / connections, electrical / temperature control wiring / connections and evaporator coil condensate drain.

Description	Craft@Hrs	Unit	Material $	Labor $	Equipment $	Total $
1.5 tons cooling	S2@4.00	Ea	2,690.00	137.00	—	2,827.00
2 tons cooling	S2@4.25	Ea	2,760.00	145.00	—	2,905.00
2.5 tons cooling	S2@4.50	Ea	3,200.00	154.00	—	3,354.00
3 tons cooling	S2@5.00	Ea	3,590.00	171.00	—	3,761.00
3.5 tons cooling	S2@5.75	Ea	3,930.00	196.00	—	4,126.00
4 tons cooling	S2@6.25	Ea	4,360.00	214.00	—	4,574.00
5 tons cooling	S2@7.50	Ea	5,050.00	256.00	—	5,306.00

Heat pump, split system, single speed blower, three phase scroll compressor - 230 volt, 13 SEER (Seasonal Energy Efficiency Rating)

Air to air thermal transfer. Material costs include outdoor stat / low ambient, short cycle timer, high-pressure cut out and digital heat/cool thermostat with manual change over. Labor includes setting outdoor condenser, indoor blower and coil sections in place only. Make additional allowances for refrigerant piping / connections, electrical / temperature control wiring / connections and evaporator coil condensate drain.

Description	Craft@Hrs	Unit	Material $	Labor $	Equipment $	Total $
3.5 tons cooling	S2@5.75	Ea	4,390.00	196.00	—	4,586.00
4 tons cooling	S2@6.25	Ea	4,790.00	214.00	—	5,004.00
5 tons cooling	S2@7.50	Ea	5,490.00	256.00	—	5,746.00

Heat pump, split system, variable speed blower, single phase scroll compressor - 208 volt, 13 SEER (Seasonal Energy Efficiency Rating)

Air to air thermal transfer. Material costs include outdoor stat / low ambient, short cycle timer, high-pressure cut out and digital heat/cool thermostat with manual change over. Labor includes setting outdoor condenser, indoor blower and coil sections in place only. Make additional allowances for refrigerant piping / connections, electrical / temperature control wiring / connections and evaporator coil condensate drain.

Description	Craft@Hrs	Unit	Material $	Labor $	Equipment $	Total $
1.5 tons cooling	S2@4.00	Ea	3,210.00	137.00	—	3,347.00
2 tons cooling	S2@4.25	Ea	3,260.00	145.00	—	3,405.00
2.5 tons cooling	S2@4.50	Ea	3,760.00	154.00	—	3,914.00
3 tons cooling	S2@5.00	Ea	4,150.00	171.00	—	4,321.00
3.5 tons cooling	S2@5.75	Ea	4,480.00	196.00	—	4,676.00
4 tons cooling	S2@6.25	Ea	5,050.00	214.00	—	5,264.00
5 tons cooling	S2@7.50	Ea	5,730.00	256.00	—	5,986.00

Description	Craft@Hrs	Unit	Material $	Labor $	Equipment $	Total $

Heat pump, split system, variable speed blower, three phase scroll compressor - 230 volt, 13 SEER (Seasonal Energy Efficiency Rating)

Air to air thermal transfer. Material costs include outdoor stat / low ambient, short cycle timer, high-pressure cut out and digital heat/cool thermostat with manual change over. Labor includes setting outdoor condenser, indoor blower and coil sections in place only. Make additional allowances for refrigerant piping / connections, electrical / temperature control wiring / connections and evaporator coil condensate drain.

Description	Craft@Hrs	Unit	Material $	Labor $	Equipment $	Total $
3.5 tons cooling	S2@5.75	Ea	4,970.00	196.00	—	5,166.00
4 tons cooling	S2@6.25	Ea	5,480.00	214.00	—	5,694.00
5 tons cooling	S2@7.50	Ea	6,200.00	256.00	—	6,456.00

Heat pump, split system, single speed blower, single phase scroll compressor - 208 volt, 14 SEER (Seasonal Energy Efficiency Rating)

Air to air thermal transfer. Material costs include outdoor stat / low ambient, short cycle timer, high-pressure cut out and digital heat/cool thermostat with manual change over. Labor includes setting outdoor condenser, indoor blower and coil sections in place only. Make additional allowances for refrigerant piping / connections, electrical / temperature control wiring / connections and evaporator coil condensate drain.

Description	Craft@Hrs	Unit	Material $	Labor $	Equipment $	Total $
2 tons cooling	S2@4.25	Ea	3,720.00	145.00	—	3,865.00
2.5 tons cooling	S2@4.50	Ea	4,200.00	154.00	—	4,354.00
3 tons cooling	S2@5.00	Ea	4,480.00	171.00	—	4,651.00
3.5 tons cooling	S2@5.75	Ea	5,120.00	196.00	—	5,316.00
4 tons cooling	S2@6.25	Ea	5,700.00	214.00	—	5,914.00
5 tons cooling	S2@7.50	Ea	6,220.00	256.00	—	6,476.00

Heat pump, split system, variable speed blower, single phase scroll compressor - 208 volt, 14 SEER (Seasonal Energy Efficiency Rating)

Air to air thermal transfer. Material costs include outdoor stat / low ambient, short cycle timer, high-pressure cut out and digital heat/cool thermostat with manual change over. Labor includes setting outdoor condenser, indoor blower and coil sections in place only. Make additional allowances for refrigerant piping / connections, electrical / temperature control wiring / connections and evaporator coil condensate drain.

Description	Craft@Hrs	Unit	Material $	Labor $	Equipment $	Total $
2 tons cooling	S2@4.25	Ea	4,230.00	145.00	—	4,375.00
2.5 tons cooling	S2@4.50	Ea	4,620.00	154.00	—	4,774.00
3 tons cooling	S2@5.00	Ea	4,980.00	171.00	—	5,151.00
3.5 tons cooling	S2@5.75	Ea	5,590.00	196.00	—	5,786.00
4 tons cooling	S2@6.25	Ea	6,050.00	214.00	—	6,264.00
5 tons cooling	S2@7.50	Ea	8,910.00	256.00	—	9,166.00

Description	Craft@Hrs	Unit	Material $	Labor $	Equipment $	Total $

Heat pump system accessories

Description	Craft@Hrs	Unit	Material $	Labor $	Equipment $	Total $
Fossil fuel kit	S2@2.50	Ea	183.00	85.40	—	268.40
High pressure cut out kit	S2@.500	Ea	63.90	17.10	—	81.00
Outdoor stat/Low ambient sensors	S2@.500	Ea	59.90	17.10	—	77.00
Short cycle protection	S2@.500	Ea	47.50	17.10	—	64.60
Digital heat/cool thermostat w/ manual change over	S2@.750	Ea	134.00	25.60	—	159.60
Digital, programmable heat/cool thermostat w/ auto change over	S2@.750	Ea	423.00	25.60	—	448.60

Heat pump, supplemental electric heating coil

Set in place only. Make additional allowances for electrical connections.

Description	Craft@Hrs	Unit	Material $	Labor $	Equipment $	Total $
5 KW, 240 Volt	S2@1.50	Ea	153.00	51.20	—	204.20
7.5 KW 240 Volt	S2@1.75	Ea	183.00	59.80	—	242.80
10 KW 240 Volt	S2@2.00	Ea	214.00	68.30	—	282.30
12.5 KW, 240 Volt	S2@2.25	Ea	358.00	76.90	—	434.90
15 KW, 240 Volt	S2@2.75	Ea	449.00	93.90	—	542.90
20 KW, 240 Volt	S2@3.50	Ea	502.00	120.00	—	622.00
25 KW 240 Volt	S2@4.25	Ea	603.00	145.00	—	748.00

Description	Unit	Material $	Labor $	Equipment $	Total $

LEED certification for geothermal heat pumps

Description	Unit	Material $	Labor $	Equipment $	Total $
Add for a LEED certified heat pump with USGBC rating	Ea	20%	—	—	—
Add for LEED registration and inspection	Ea	2,000.00	—	—	2,000.00
Add for LEED central digital performance monitor/recorder, ComfortView 3 or equal	Ea	2,350.00	—	—	2,350.00
Add for LEED certified zone recording thermostats, Carrier DebonAir, USB remote-ready	Ea	350.00	—	—	350.00
Add for IAQ (Indoor Air Quality) CO2 sensor and duct-mounted aspirator box	Ea	425.00	—	—	425.00

Description	Craft@Hrs	Unit	Material $	Labor $	Equipment $	Total $

Water pump, submersible. Domestic water, geothermal open loop, well, lake or pond applications. Stainless steel jacket with multiple stage impellers and integral foot valve.

Description	Craft@Hrs	Unit	Material $	Labor $	Equipment $	Total $
Submersible Pump, 120/240 Volt, 1/2 HP	P1@2.00	Ea	473.00	69.10	—	542.10
Submersible Pump, 240 Volt, 3/4 HP	P1@2.00	Ea	588.00	69.10	—	657.10
Submersible Pump, 240 Volt, 1 HP	P1@2.00	Ea	788.00	69.10	—	857.10
Submersible Pump, 240 Volt, 1-1/2 HP	P1@2.00	Ea	1,040.00	69.10	—	1,109.10
Submersible Pump, 240 Volt, 2 HP	P1@2.00	Ea	1,210.00	69.10	—	1,279.10
Submersible Pump, 240 Volt, 3 HP	P1@2.00	Ea	1,340.00	69.10	—	1,409.10
Submersible Pump, 240 Volt, 5 HP	P1@2.00	Ea	1,580.00	69.10	—	1,649.10
Pump Controller - Constant pressure, VSD	P1@1.50	Ea	798.00	51.80	—	849.80
Pump Control Box, 120 Volt	P1@.600	Ea	47.30	20.70	—	68.00
Pump Control Box, 240 Volt	P1@.600	Ea	57.80	20.70	—	78.50
Pump Stand, PVC	P1@1.00	Ea	126.00	34.60	—	160.60
Pump Stand, Galvanized Steel	P1@1.35	Ea	173.00	46.60	—	219.60

Water pump, jet. Domestic water well, lake and pond applications. 110 volt, cast iron body, single stage impeller, including pressure switch & pressure gauge. Use for shallow depths to 25' maximum lift. Deep well applications to 120' maximum lift.

Description	Craft@Hrs	Unit	Material $	Labor $	Equipment $	Total $
Submersible Pump, shallow depth 1/2 HP	P1@2.00	Ea	200.00	69.10	—	269.10
Submersible Pump, shallow depth 3/4 HP	P1@2.00	Ea	231.00	69.10	—	300.10
Submersible Pump, deep well 1/2 HP	P1@2.00	Ea	273.00	69.10	—	342.10
Submersible Pump, deep well 3/4 HP	P1@2.00	Ea	315.00	69.10	—	384.10
Optional pump mounted pressure tank 5 gallon	P1@.500	Ea	84.00	17.30	—	101.30

Water Pump Systems

Description	Craft@Hrs	Unit	Material $	Labor $	Equipment $	Total $

Water pump system accessories. Pressure tanks are factory pre-charged. VSD = variable speed drive. Typical subcontract costs.

Description	Craft@Hrs	Unit	Material $	Labor $	Equipment $	Total $
Pressure tank, bladder type, 5 gallon	P1@1.00	Ea	73.50	34.60	—	108.10
Pressure tank, bladder type, 10 gallon	P1@2.00	Ea	84.00	69.10	—	153.10
Pressure tank, bladder type, 20 gallon	P1@2.00	Ea	99.80	69.10	—	168.90
Pressure tank, bladder type, 30 gallon	P1@2.00	Ea	142.00	69.10	—	211.10
Pressure tank, bladder type, 40 gallon	P1@2.00	Ea	189.00	69.10	—	258.10
Brass tank tee, 3/4" or 1" w/ union	P1@.300	Ea	44.10	10.40	—	54.50
Brass tank tee, 3/4" or 1" w/o union	P1@.300	Ea	35.70	10.40	—	46.10
Constant pressure VSD pump controller	P1@1.50	Ea	798.00	51.80	—	849.80
Pressure Switch, 110/220 Volt	P1@.350	Ea	33.60	12.10	—	45.70
Pressure gauge, 0-100 psi, 1/4"	P1@.200	Ea	8.40	6.91	—	15.31
Sediment faucet (hose bibb), 1/2"	P1@1.50	Ea	6.83	51.80	—	58.63
Double injector deep well venturi, 1", Brass	P1@.600	Ea	179.00	20.70	—	199.70
Double injector deep well venturi, 1¼", Brass	P1@.650	Ea	205.00	22.50	—	227.50
Double injector deep well venturi, 1½", Brass	P1@.700	Ea	231.00	24.20	—	255.20
Double injector deep well venturi, 1", Plastic	P1@.550	Ea	57.80	19.00	—	76.80
Double injector deep well venturi, 1¼", Plastic	P1@.600	Ea	71.40	20.70	—	92.10
Double injector deep well venturi, 1½", Plastic	P1@.650	Ea	77.70	22.50	—	100.20
Foot valve, 1", Brass	P1@.400	Ea	60.90	13.80	—	74.70
Foot valve, 1¼", Brass	P1@.400	Ea	63.00	13.80	—	76.80
Foot valve, 1½", Brass	P1@.400	Ea	67.20	13.80	—	81.00
Foot valve, 1", Plastic	P1@.400	Ea	18.90	13.80	—	32.70
Foot valve, 1¼", Plastic	P1@.400	Ea	23.10	13.80	—	36.90
Foot valve, 1½", Plastic	P1@.400	Ea	25.70	13.80	—	39.50
Barbed adapter, FIP/MIP, 1" Brass	P1@.230	Ea	9.98	7.95	—	17.93
Barbed adapter, FIP/MIP, 1¼" Brass	P1@.250	Ea	11.60	8.64	—	20.24

Description	Craft@Hrs	Unit	Material $	Labor $	Equipment $	Total $
Barbed adapter, FIP/MIP, 1½" Brass	P1@.265	Ea	13.90	9.16	—	23.06
Barbed adapter, FIP/MIP, 1" Plastic	P1@.215	Ea	9.24	7.43	—	16.67
Barbed adapter, FIP/MIP, 1¼" Plastic	P1@.220	Ea	10.10	7.60	—	17.70
Barbed adapter, FIP/MIP, 1½" Plastic	P1@.235	Ea	13.40	8.12	—	21.52
Pitless adapter, 1" x 5" Brass	P1@1.25	Ea	147.00	43.20	—	190.20
Pitless adapter, 1¼" x 5" Brass	P1@1.25	Ea	160.00	43.20	—	203.20
Pitless adapter, 1½" x 5" Brass	P1@1.25	Ea	179.00	43.20	—	222.20
Pitless adapter, 2" x 6" Brass	P1@1.80	Ea	273.00	62.20	—	335.20
Poly pipe, 75 psi, 1"	P1@.020	Ea	.23	.69	—	.92
Poly pipe, 75 psi, 1¼"	P1@.021	Ea	.25	.73	—	.98
Poly pipe, 75 psi, 1½"	P1@.022	Ea	.27	.76	—	1.03
Poly pipe, 100 psi, 1"	P1@.021	Ea	.23	.73	—	.96
Poly pipe, 100 psi, 1¼"	P1@.022	Ea	.25	.76	—	1.01
Poly pipe, 100 psi, 1½"	P1@.023	Ea	.27	.79	—	1.06
Electrical wire, (110 volt) #12/4	P1@.015	Ea	.27	.52	—	.79
Electrical wire, (220 volt) #10/4	P1@.015	Ea	.29	.52	—	.81
Heat shrink kit	P1@.000	Ea	4.20	.00	—	4.20

Geothermal/Domestic Water Wells

Geothermal water wells

A geothermal water well is constructed and operates exactly as a water well used for drinking water would. In many residential applications, the supply well of the geothermal system also functions as the domestic water supply well.

The cost of a drilled well depends on many variables, such as costs to get the drilling rig and crew to the site, the type of geologic formation the well drilling rig must drill through, the depth the driller must achieve to find water in that particular location and the distance from an existing available water source to provide the water required to drill (to refill the water truck if necessary).

Well drillers charge by the foot and usually have a 100' minimum charge out fee. They can only speculate to what depth they must drill to find water. Water being found at a particular depth nearby does not always translate to finding water at another given location at the same depth. It is important to remember that when drilling a relatively small hole in the ground, and hoping to hit what is described as a vein of water as part of an underground water table, is always a gamble. As such, it is, without proper research, difficult to determine a realistic budget for well drilling. It is always prudent to call the water authority or a well driller in the area for the most accurate information on the water and geological characteristics of a given location.

Use the following to begin to formulate a budget exclusive of costs associated with factors listed above. Because of the inherent uncertainties of the process, these prices are given only as typical subcontract costs.

Description	Unit	Material $	Labor $	Equipment $	Total $

Drilled well, 5" diameter, PVC Casing, set into bedrock. Based on a 2-man crew, 1 rotary drill rig and a 1,500 gallon water truck. Minimum 100' charge in most cases. Typical subcontract costs.

Description	Unit	Material $	Labor $	Equipment $	Total $
Drilled through till, clay, sand	LF	—	—	—	31.00
Drilled through till and boulder	LF	—	—	—	40.00
Drilled through limestone soft bedrock	LF	—	—	—	45.00
Drilled through granite hard bedrock	LF	—	—	—	90.00
Add for Galvanized Steel Casing	LF	—	—	—	11.30

Drilled well, 6" diameter, PVC Casing, set into bedrock. Based on a 2-man crew, 1 rotary drill rig and a 1,500 gallon water truck. Minimum 100' charge in most cases. Typical subcontract costs.

Description	Unit	Material $	Labor $	Equipment $	Total $
Drilled through till, clay, sand	LF	—	—	—	34.40
Drilled through till and boulder	LF	—	—	—	43.80
Drilled through limestone soft bedrock	LF	—	—	—	47.50
Drilled through granite hard bedrock	LF	—	—	—	95.00
Add for Galvanized Steel Casing	LF	—	—	—	13.80

Description	Unit	Material $	Labor $	Equipment $	Total $

Drilled well, 8" diameter, PVC Casing, set into bedrock. Based on a 2-man crew, 1-rotary drill rig and a 1,500 gallon water truck. Minimum 100' charge in most cases. Typical subcontract costs.

Description	Unit	Material $	Labor $	Equipment $	Total $
Drilled through till, clay, sand	LF	—	—	—	43.80
Drilled through till and boulder	LF	—	—	—	50.00
Drilled through limestone soft bedrock	LF	—	—	—	56.30
Drilled through granite hard bedrock	LF	—	—	—	113.00
Add for Galvanized Steel Casing	LF	—	—	—	27.50

Drilled well, 10" diameter, PVC Casing, set into bedrock. Based on a 2-man crew, 1 rotary drill rig and a 1,500 gallon water truck. Minimum 100' charge in most cases. Typical subcontract costs.

Description	Unit	Material $	Labor $	Equipment $	Total $
Drilled through till, clay, sand	LF	—	—	—	52.50
Drilled through till and boulder	LF	—	—	—	58.80
Drilled through limestone soft bedrock	LF	—	—	—	65.00
Drilled through granite hard bedrock	LF	—	—	—	150.00
Add for Galvanized Steel Casing	LF	—	—	—	35.00

Geothermal bore hole (vertical loop), 3" diameter, drilled to a maximum of 30'. Includes installation of a polypropylene fluid loop using a 180-degree return bend with socket fusion joints. Bore hole filled with bentonite slurry through a tremie tube and mud pump. Includes socket fusioned header and supply & return mains to heat pump. Based on a minimum of 1,000' vertical feet (2,000' of pipe) Based on a 2-man crew, 1 skid-steer mounted rotary drill rig and a 50 gallon water tank. Typical subcontract costs.

Description	Unit	Material $	Labor $	Equipment $	Total $
3/4" vertical loop	LF	—	—	—	10.60
1" vertical loop	LF	—	—	—	11.60
Add for thermally enhanced bentonite	LF	—	—	—	2.94

Geothermal horizontal loop, directionally bored. Includes installation of a polypropylene fluid loop. Based on a minimum of 2,000 horizontal feet (2,000' of pipe). Based on a 3-man crew, 1 directional boring/horizontal drill machine. Typical subcontract costs.

Description	Unit	Material $	Labor $	Equipment $	Total $
3/4" straight horizontal loop	LF	—	—	—	6.44
1" straight horizontal loop	LF	—	—	—	7.00

Description	Unit	Material $	Labor $	Equipment $	Total $

Geothermal horizontal loop, slinky type. Includes installation of a polypropylene fluid loop. Based on a minimum of 2,000 horizontal feet (2,000' of pipe). Based on a 3-man crew, 1 excavator backhoe. Typical subcontract costs.

Description	Unit	Material $	Labor $	Equipment $	Total $
3/4" slinky loop	LF	—	—	—	4.88
1" slinky loop	LF	—	—	—	5.50
3/4" slinky pond loop	LF	—	—	—	3.81
1" slinky pond loop	LF	—	—	—	4.44

Biomass-Fired Boilers

Description	Craft@Hrs	Unit	Material $	Labor $	Equipment $	Total $

Biomass-fired hot water boilers for central heating systems. For residential, commercial and light industrial applications. 15 PSI, EPA, ASME and UL rated, with wood-pellet and/or corn fuel gravity feed hopper, ash hood cleanout, secondary natural gas or #2 oil burner, platinum stack transition emissions catalyst, forced draft fan, factory installed boiler trim, feedwater pump and valves, and tempering valve. Add the cost of the following if required: a concrete pad, optional stainless steel 2 GPM potable hot water coil insert, expansion tank and circulating pump, stack and stack liner, CO_2 fire extinguisher system and electrical connection. Add the cost of post-installation inspection by both the fire marshal and the mechanical inspector to validate federal, state and local energy tax credits or energy tax credit offsets. See pollution control stack costs below. Equipment cost is for a 2-ton capacity hydraulic crane truck. Listed by boiler horsepower (BHP) rating and input capacity in thousands of BTU per hour (MBH).

Description	Craft@Hrs	Unit	Material $	Labor $	Equipment $	Total $
3 BHP, 102 MBH	SN@24.0	Ea	8,065.000	878.00	377.00	8,091.00
3 BHP, 104 MBH	SN@24.0	Ea	8,510.00	878.00	377.00	9,765.00
6 BHP, 200 MBH	SN@28.0	Ea	11,000.00	1,020.00	440.00	12,460.00
14 BHP, 500 MBH	SN@30.0	Ea	13,000.00	1,100.00	472.00	14,572.00
27 BHP, 900 MBH	SN@44.0	Ea	18,800.00	1,610.00	692.00	21,102.00

LEED certification requires 88% boiler efficiency, recording controls, compliance with SCAQMD 1146.2 emission standards and zone thermostats.

Description	Craft@Hrs	Unit	Material $	Labor $	Equipment $	Total $
Add for LEED certified boiler with USGBC rating	—	Ea	15%	—	—	—
Add for LEED registration and inspection	—	Ea	—	—	—	2,000.00
Add for central performance monitor/ recorder	—	Ea	2,350.00	—	—	2,350.00
Add for zone recording thermostat	—	Ea	350.00	—	—	350.00

Retrofit pollution control stack for biomass hot water boilers. Stack-mounted platinum catalytic screen for biomass-fired hot water boilers for central radiant heating systems. E.P.A. and California Code standards compliant. UL rated. Includes stack mounting transition and extensions, baghouse structural steel frame, stack transition cleanout and inspection stack access bolted ports and an integral CO_2 fire extinguisher system. Add the cost of a concrete pad, electrical connection, post-installation calibration, inspection by both the fire marshal and the mechanical inspector to validate federal, state and local emission reduction tax credits and associated energy tax credit offsets. Equipment cost is for a 2-ton capacity hydraulic truck crane. Listed by boiler horsepower (BHP) rating and input capacity in thousands of BTU per hour (MBH). Use these figures to estimate the cost of adding a pollution control stack to an existing bio-mass boiler to meet environmental regulations.

Description	Craft@Hrs	Unit	Material $	Labor $	Equipment $	Total $
3 BHP, 102 MBH	SN@20.0	Ea	1,200.00	732.00	315.00	2,247.00
3 BHP, 104 MBH	SN@20.0	Ea	1,200.00	732.00	315.00	2,247.00
6 BHP, 200 MBH	SN@20.0	Ea	1,800.00	732.00	315.00	2,847.00
14 BHP, 500 MBH	SN@40.0	Ea	2,200.00	1,460.00	628.00	4,288.00
27 BHP, 900 MBH	SN@40.0	Ea	3,000.00	1,460.00	628.00	5,088.00

Biomass-Fired Boilers

Description	Craft@Hrs	Unit	Material $	Labor $	Equipment $	Total $

Biomass-fired water or steam boilers for multi-dwelling, process and industrial applications. 15 PSI, EPA, ASME and UL rated. Includes wood pellet and/or corn fuel auger feed hopper, ash auger cleanout, secondary natural gas or #2 oil burner, platinum stack transition emissions catalyst, forced draft fan, factory-installed boiler trim, feedwater pump and valves, and tempering valve. Add the following costs if required: a concrete pad, optional stainless steel 10 GPM potable hot water coil insert, circulating pump, expansion tank, shell and tube heat exchanger, stack and stack liner, CO_2 fire extinguisher system, pollution control baghouse and filter, electrical connection. Add the cost of post-installation inspection by both the fire marshal and the mechanical inspector to validate federal, state and local energy tax credits or energy tax credit offsets. See pollution control stack costs below. Equipment cost is for a 5-ton capacity forklift. Listed by boiler horsepower (BHP) rating and input capacity in thousands of BTU per hour (MBH).

Description	Craft@Hrs	Unit	Material $	Labor $	Equipment $	Total $
30 BHP, 1,000 MBH	SN@168	Ea	67,500.00	6,150.00	2,640.00	76,290.00
50 BHP, 1,700 MBH	SN@200	Ea	125,000.00	7,320.00	3,146.00	135,466.00
100 BHP, 3,400 MBH	SN@400	Ea	192,000.00	14,600.00	6,281.00	212,881.00
125 BHP, 4,100 MBH	SN@400	Ea	243,000.00	14,600.00	6,281.00	263,881.00
150 BHP, 5,000 MBH	SN@500	Ea	237,000.00	18,300.00	7,854.00	263,154.00
200 BHP, 6,700 MBH	SN@600	Ea	325,000.00	21,900.00	9,427.00	356,327.00

LEED certification requires 88% boiler efficiency, recording controls, compliance with SCAQMD 1146.2 emission standards and zone thermostats.

Description	Craft@Hrs	Unit	Material $	Labor $	Equipment $	Total $
Add for LEED certified boiler with USGBC rating	—	Ea	6%	—	—	—
Add for LEED registration and inspection	—	Ea	—	—	—	2,000.00
Add for central performance monitor/ recorder	—	Ea	2,350.00	—	—	2,350.00
Add for zone recording thermostat	—	Ea	350.00	—	—	350.00

Biomass boiler stack tie-in to baghouse filter. Ionically bonded silicon-lined carbon steel. Costs assume a 20-foot vertical stack height, connection via T-shaped connector with cleanout to the baghouse inlet plenum. Includes rigging, breeching, connecting stack sections from back "turnaround" plenum of boiler to baghouse inlet plenum, vendor-supplied structural steel stack support brackets and aluminized external coating. Equipment cost assumes rental of a 2-ton hydraulic truck crane. Biomass boilers, stoves and heaters smaller than 30 BHP can use a conventional boiler stack (without a baghouse) and require only a platinum catalytic screen. Costs shown assume a 20-foot stack height and 10' horizontal run from T-connector. Cost per 10' length, including a bolt and gasket set on each end. Add 15% for each 10' section (or portion thereof) beyond 20' vertically or horizontally.

Description	Craft@Hrs	Unit	Material $	Labor $	Equipment $	Total $
10" diameter	SN@12.0	Ea	2,500.00	439.00	188.00	3,127.00
12" diameter	SN@12.0	Ea	2,800.00	439.00	188.00	3,427.00
16" diameter	SN@16.0	Ea	3,000.00	585.00	252.00	3,837.00
20" diameter	SN@20.0	Ea	3,800.00	732.00	315.00	4,847.00
24" diameter	SN@24.0	Ea	4,200.00	878.00	377.00	5,455.00
30" diameter	SN@32.0	Ea	6,200.00	1,170.00	503.00	7,873.00
56" diameter	SN@40.0	Ea	10,500.00	1,460.00	628.00	12,588.00

Description	Craft@Hrs	Unit	Material $	Labor $	Equipment $	Total $

Retrofit pollution control stack for biomass water or steam boiler.

Stack-mounted platinum screen catalytic reactor with air filtration fabric baghouse. For use with biomass-fired hot water or low pressure steam boilers for central radiant heating or process systems. Meets EPA, NFPA, California Code and UL standards for multi-dwelling, process and industrial applications. Cost includes equipment stack transitions and fittings, transition access bolted inspection and cleanout ports, structural steel frame equipment support and ladders, bottom ash cleanout for baghouse, alarmed stack gas composition monitor and recorder, urea tank and urea pump & regulating valve and an integral CO_2 fire extinguisher system. Costs do not include the following: concrete pad, electrical tie-in, calibration and commissioning, post-installation inspection by the fire marshal and the mechanical inspector to validate federal, state and local energy tax credits or energy tax credit offsets. Equipment cost is for a 2-ton capacity hydraulic truck crane. Listed by boiler horsepower (BHP) rating and input capacity in thousands of BTU per hour (MBH). Use these figures to estimate the cost of adding a pollution control stack to an existing biomass boiler to meet environmental regulations.

Description	Craft@Hrs	Unit	Material $	Labor $	Equipment $	Total $
30 BHP, 1,000 MBH	SN@40.0	Ea	35,500.00	1,460.00	628.00	37,588.00
50 BHP, 1,700 MBH	SN@80.0	Ea	63,000.00	2,930.00	1,254.00	67,184.00
100 BHP, 3,400 MBH	SN@80.0	Ea	112,000.00	2,930.00	1,254.00	116,184.00
125 BHP, 4,100 MBH	SN@120	Ea	117,000.00	4,390.00	1,881.00	123,271.00
150 BHP, 5,000 MBH	SN@120	Ea	126,000.00	4,390.00	1,881.00	132,271.00
200 BHP, 6,700 MBH	SN@160	Ea	135,000.00	5,850.00	1,881.00	142,731.00

Biomass-fired central air space heaters for residential, multi-dwelling, and light commercial applications.

15 PSI, EPA, ASHRAE and UL rated. Includes a wood pellet and/or corn fuel gravity feed hopper, ash hood cleanout, secondary natural gas or #2 oil burner, platinum stack transition emissions catalyst, forced draft fan, ducted hot-air circulation plenum and integral three-speed circulation duct blower. Add the cost of a concrete pad, optional stainless steel 2 GPM potable hot water coil insert, expansion tank and circulating pump, stack and stack liner, CO_2 fire extinguisher system and electrical connection. These costs do not include post-installation inspection by both the fire marshal and the mechanical inspector to validate federal, state and local energy tax credits or energy tax credit offsets. Equipment cost is for a 2-ton capacity forklift. Listed by input capacity in thousands of BTU per hour (MBH).

Description	Craft@Hrs	Unit	Material $	Labor $	Equipment $	Total $
90 MBH	SN@16.0	Ea	2,750.00	585.00	252.00	3,587.00
120 MBH	SN@16.0	Ea	3,550.00	585.00	252.00	4,387.00
170 MBH	SN@20.0	Ea	6,230.00	732.00	315.00	7,277.00
500 MBH	SN@30.0	Ea	9,710.00	1,100.00	472.00	11,282.00
950 MBH	SN@44.0	Ea	11,500.00	1,610.00	692.00	13,802.00

Biomass-Fired Boilers

Description	Craft@Hrs	Unit	Material $	Labor $	Equipment $	Total $

Water mist fire extinguishing systems for biomass boilers. 20 minute full saturation cycle, with automatic reset to enable instantaneous reactivation for re-ignition. NFPA rated. Includes high pressure spray heads, piping, pumps, valves, alarm horns, emergency halogen lighting, calibration, training, insurance inspection and safety procedure documentation. Based on remote sensor relays for the fuel hopper, fuel conveyor, combustion chamber and baghouse filter.

Description	Craft@Hrs	Unit	Material $	Labor $	Equipment $	Total $
30 BHP boiler	ST@60.0	Ea	12,000.00	2,400.00	—	14,400.00
50 BHP boiler	ST@60.0	Ea	15,000.00	2,400.00	—	17,400.00
100 BHP boiler	ST@80.0	Ea	22,000.00	3,200.00	—	25,200.00
125 BHP boiler	ST@80.0	Ea	24,000.00	3,200.00	—	27,200.00
150 BHP boiler	ST@120	Ea	27,500.00	4,800.00	—	32,300.00
200 BHP boiler	ST@120	Ea	32,000.00	4,800.00	—	36,800.00
Add for CO2 based extinguishing system		%	—	—	—	20.0
Add for Halon-based extinguishing system		%	—	—	—	30.0

Pulse type boilers for central radiant heating. 15 PSI, EPA, ASME and UL rated. Modular design for multiple installations. Natural gas only. With forced draft fan, factory installed boiler trim, feedwater pump and valves, and tempering valve. For residential, commercial and light industrial radiant heating and potable water applications. Add the cost of a concrete pad, circulating pump, stack and stack liner, CO_2 fire extinguisher system, electrical connection, and post-installation inspection by both the fire marshal and the mechanical inspector to validate federal, state and local energy tax credits or energy tax credit offsets. Equipment cost is for a 1-ton capacity hydraulic truck crane. Listed by boiler horsepower (BHP) rating and input capacity in thousands of BTU per hour (MBH).

Description	Craft@Hrs	Unit	Material $	Labor $	Equipment $	Total $
3 BHP, 90 MBH	P1@24.0	Ea	3,810.00	829.00	1,320.00	5,959.00
3 BHP, 150 MBH	P1@24.0	Ea	5,510.00	829.00	1,320.00	7,659.00
6 BHP, 299 MBH	P1@28.0	Ea	7,590.00	967.00	1,540.00	10,097.00

LEED certification requires 88% boiler efficiency, recording controls, compliance with SCAQMD 1146.2 emission standards and zone thermostats.

Description	Craft@Hrs	Unit	Material $	Labor $	Equipment $	Total $
Add for LEED certified boiler with USGBC rating	—	Ea	15%	—	—	—
Add for LEED registration and inspection	—	Ea	—	—	—	2,000.00
Add for central performance monitor/ recorder	—	Ea	1,100.00	—	—	1,100.00
Add for zone recording thermostat	—	Ea	150.00	—	—	150.00

Description	Craft@Hrs	Unit	Material $	Labor $	Equipment $	Total $

Passive flat-panel solar water heater. Ambient pressure, modular design for multiple installation, EPA, DOE and UL rated, with piping, tempering valve, circulating pump, controls, storage tank and heating coil. Cost does not include electrical connection, roofing modification (bracing) to accommodate the additional weight of water-filled panels, insulation nor padding between roof and panels. Add the cost of post-installation inspection by the mechanical inspector to validate federal, state and local energy tax credits or energy tax credit offsets. For larger arrays (laundries, institutional facilities, food processing plants), develop an estimate based on required daily capacity and multiply these costs by the number of panels required. Equipment cost is for a 1-ton capacity hydraulic crane truck.

Description	Craft@Hrs	Unit	Material $	Labor $	Equipment $	Total $
One 32.3 SF solar panel, 80 gallons per day	P1@16.0	Ea	3,250.00	553.00	880.00	4,683.00
Two 32.3 SF solar panels, 120 gallons per day	P1@20.0	Ea	4,530.00	691.00	1,100.00	6,321.00

Fans and Blowers

Description	Craft@Hrs	Unit	Material $	Labor $	Equipment $	Total $

Centrifugal air-foil wheel blower, with motor, drive and isolation, set in place only.

Description	Craft@Hrs	Unit	Material $	Labor $	Equipment $	Total $
1/3 HP, 12" dia.	SN@2.50	Ea	1,280.00	91.50	39.00	1,410.50
1/2 HP, 15" dia.	SN@4.50	Ea	2,230.00	165.00	71.00	2,466.00
1 HP, 18" dia.	SN@7.00	Ea	2,580.00	256.00	110.00	2,946.00
2 HP, 18" dia.	SN@7.50	Ea	3,060.00	274.00	118.00	3,452.00
3 HP, 27" dia.	SN@9.00	Ea	4,830.00	329.00	141.00	5,300.00
5 HP, 30" dia.	SN@11.0	Ea	5,700.00	402.00	173.00	6,275.00
7½ HP, 36" dia.	SN@12.0	Ea	6,910.00	439.00	189.00	7,538.00
10 HP, 40" dia.	SN@14.0	Ea	9,630.00	512.00	220.00	10,362.00
15 HP, 44" dia.	SN@17.0	Ea	12,800.00	622.00	267.00	13,689.00
20 HP, 60" dia.	SN@20.0	Ea	14,500.00	732.00	314.00	15,546.00

Utility centrifugal blower, with motor, drive and isolation, set in place only.

Description	Craft@Hrs	Unit	Material $	Labor $	Equipment $	Total $
1/3 HP, 10" dia.	SN@2.50	Ea	834.00	91.50	39.00	964.50
1/2 HP, 12" dia.	SN@4.50	Ea	1,090.00	165.00	71.00	1,326.00
1 HP, 15" dia.	SN@6.50	Ea	1,770.00	238.00	102.00	2,110.00
2 HP, 18" dia.	SN@7.50	Ea	2,020.00	274.00	118.00	2,412.00
3 HP, 24" dia.	SN@9.00	Ea	2,900.00	329.00	141.00	3,370.00
5 HP, 27" dia.	SN@11.0	Ea	3,340.00	402.00	173.00	3,915.00
7½ HP, 36" dia.	SN@12.0	Ea	5,370.00	439.00	189.00	5,998.00
10 HP, 40" dia.	SN@14.0	Ea	6,490.00	512.00	220.00	7,222.00
15 HP, 44" dia.	SN@17.0	Ea	7,010.00	622.00	267.00	7,899.00

Vane-axial fan, set in place only.

Description	Craft@Hrs	Unit	Material $	Labor $	Equipment $	Total $
30 HP, 36" dia.	SN@16.0	Ea	17,000.00	585.00	251.00	17,836.00
50 HP, 42" dia.	SN@24.0	Ea	19,000.00	878.00	377.00	20,255.00
100 HP, 48" dia.	SN@32.0	Ea	23,600.00	1,170.00	503.00	25,273.00
200 HP, 54" dia.	SN@40.0	Ea	33,400.00	1,460.00	629.00	35,489.00

Description	Craft@Hrs	Unit	Material $	Labor $	Equipment $	Total $

Tube-axial fan, set in place only.

Description	Craft@Hrs	Unit	Material $	Labor $	Equipment $	Total $
15 HP, 24" dia.	SN@10.0	Ea	5,020.00	366.00	157.00	5,543.00
25 HP, 30" dia.	SN@13.0	Ea	7,790.00	476.00	204.00	8,470.00
30 HP, 36" dia.	SN@16.0	Ea	10,400.00	585.00	251.00	11,236.00
75 HP, 40" dia.	SN@22.0	Ea	15,600.00	805.00	346.00	16,751.00
100 HP, 48" dia.	SN@32.0	Ea	23,700.00	1,170.00	503.00	25,373.00

Roof exhaust fan, ASHRAE/American National Standards Institute specification 62.2-2007 and Air Conditioning Contractors of America standard ACCA 5QI-2007, "HVAC Indoor Air Quality Installation Specification 2007." US Green Building Council, Underwriters laboratories and CSA approved. Cost includes fan and bearing, shaft mount and power transmission assembly or direct drive, enclosure, mount plates, electric motor, 110 or 408, 3 phase, 60 Hz, switch or relay assembly, motor fusing and ground fault protection, fan blade guard. Set in place only. Add installation costs from the figures below.

Description	Craft@Hrs	Unit	Material $	Labor $	Equipment $	Total $
1/4 HP, 14" dia.	SN@2.50	Ea	1,330.00	91.50	39.00	1,460.50
1/3 HP, 22" dia.	SN@2.90	Ea	1,630.00	106.00	46.00	1,782.00
1/2 HP, 24" dia.	SN@3.50	Ea	1,860.00	128.00	55.00	2,043.00
1 HP, 30" dia.	SN@4.50	Ea	2,580.00	165.00	71.00	2,816.00
2 HP, 36" dia.	SN@5.00	Ea	3,690.00	183.00	79.00	3,952.00
3 HP, 40" dia.	SN@6.00	Ea	5,530.00	219.00	94.00	5,843.00
5 HP, 48" dia.	SN@7.00	Ea	7,670.00	256.00	110.00	8,036.00
Cut, frame and gasket downcomer hole in roof	S2@1.00	Ea	35.70	34.20	—	69.90
Mount duct hangers	S2@.250	Ea	3.57	8.54	—	12.11
Cut and mount sheet metal duct	S2@.350	LF	5.61	12.00	—	17.61
Apply and coat duct insulation	S2@.150	LF	2.45	5.12	—	7.57
Install electrical wiring	BE@.150	LF	1.79	5.74	—	7.53
Install HVAC controls	BE@.500	Ea	—	19.10	—	19.10
Commission and test	P1@2.00	Ea	—	69.10	—	69.10
Run air balance and fine-tune system	P1@1.00	Ea	—	34.60	—	34.60

Ventilators and Residential Exhaust Fans

Description	Craft@Hrs	Unit	Material $	Labor $	Equipment $	Total $

Ceiling mounted commercial ventilator. Low profile metal grille. Galvanized steel housing. Designed for continuous operation. Acoustically insulated. Can be installed horizontally, vertically or in-line. Labor includes lay-out and fasten in place only. Make additional allowances for vent duct and electrical requirements.

Description	Craft@Hrs	Unit	Material $	Labor $	Equipment $	Total $
100 CFM	P1@1.05	Ea	132.00	36.30	—	168.30
150 CFM	P1@1.15	Ea	166.00	39.70	—	205.70
200 CFM	P1@1.35	Ea	210.00	46.60	—	256.60
250 CFM	P1@1.45	Ea	264.00	50.10	—	314.10
300 CFM	P1@1.65	Ea	314.00	57.00	—	371.00
400 CFM	P1@2.15	Ea	405.00	74.30	—	479.30
500 CFM	P1@2.50	Ea	492.00	86.40	—	578.40
700 CFM	P1@2.75	Ea	685.00	95.00	—	780.00
900 CFM	P1@2.85	Ea	756.00	98.50	157.00	1,011.50
1,500 CFM	P1@3.50	Ea	1,050.00	121.00	193.00	1,364.00
2,000 CFM	P1@3.85	Ea	1,160.00	133.00	213.00	1,506.00
3,500 CFM	P1@4.25	Ea	1,320.00	147.00	235.00	1,702.00

Powered attic ventilator. Thermostatically controlled. 1/10 Hp, 120V/6-Hz motor. 8" x 24" metal housing. Labor includes lay-out and fasten in place only. Make additional allowances for electrical and roofing requirements.

Description	Craft@Hrs	Unit	Material $	Labor $	Equipment $	Total $
1,200 CFM	P1@2.00	Ea	166.00	69.10	—	235.10

Exterior wall/roof exhaust fan. Fully enclosed. Thermally protected. Lifetime lubricated 120V/6-Hz motor. Weather-resistant aluminum housing. Balance blower wheel. Neoprene vibration isolation. Includes backdraft damper, flashing plate and critter screen. 10" discharge outlet. Labor includes lay-out and fasten in place only. Make additional allowances for vent duct, electrical and roofing requirements.

Description	Craft@Hrs	Unit	Material $	Labor $	Equipment $	Total $
600 CFM	P1@2.50	Ea	492.00	86.40	—	578.40
900 CFM	P1@2.85	Ea	762.00	98.50	—	860.50

Room ventilator fan. Interior thru-wall room-to-room air transfer application. High efficiency. Manually switched operation with built-in variable speed control. 8" and 10" discharge outlets. Built in damper. Includes intake and discharge grilles. Labor includes lay-out and fasten in place only. Make additional allowances for electrical requirements.

Description	Craft@Hrs	Unit	Material $	Labor $	Equipment $	Total $
180 CFM	P1@1.25	Ea	102.00	43.20	—	145.20
270 CFM	P1@1.50	Ea	154.00	51.80	—	205.80
380 CFM	P1@1.75	Ea	210.00	60.50	—	270.50

Ceiling exhaust fan, with automatic motion response control. Adjustable (5-60 minutes) time interval operation. Manual override feature. 4" discharge outlet. Pre-wired outlet box. Balanced blower wheel. Permanently lubricated motor. Neoprene vibration isolators. Quiet operation. Suitable for washroom exhaust applications. Labor includes lay-out and fasten in place only. Make additional allowances for vent duct and electrical requirements.

Description	Craft@Hrs	Unit	Material $	Labor $	Equipment $	Total $
90 CFM	P1@1.00	Ea	158.00	34.60	—	192.60
130 CFM	P1@1.15	Ea	245.00	39.70	—	284.70

Description	Craft@Hrs	Unit	Material $	Labor $	Equipment $	Total $

Ceiling exhaust fan, with automatic humidity response control.
Adjustable time interval operation (5-60 minutes). Manual override feature. 4" discharge outlet. Pre-wired outlet box. Balanced blower wheel. Permanently lubricated motor. Neoprene vibration isolators. Quiet operation. Suitable for washroom exhaust applications. Labor includes lay-out and fasten in place only. Make additional allowances for vent duct and electrical requirements.

Description	Craft@Hrs	Unit	Material $	Labor $	Equipment $	Total $
90 CFM	P1@1.00	Ea	185.00	34.60	—	219.60
130 CFM	P1@1.15	Ea	271.00	39.70	—	310.70

Ceiling exhaust fan, manually switched operation. 4" discharge outlet.
Pre-wired outlet box. 4 pole motor. Suitable for washroom exhaust applications. Labor includes lay-out and fasten in place only. Make additional allowances for vent duct and electrical requirements.

Description	Craft@Hrs	Unit	Material $	Labor $	Equipment $	Total $
50 CFM	P1@1.00	Ea	35.10	34.60	—	69.70
70 CFM	P1@1.00	Ea	52.60	34.60	—	87.20
90 CFM	P1@1.00	Ea	61.50	34.60	—	96.10
110 CFM	P1@1.05	Ea	73.60	36.30	—	109.90

Ceiling exhaust fan, high efficiency. Manually switched operation. 8" and
10" discharge outlets. Labor includes lay-out and fasten in place only. Suitable for kitchens, laundry rooms, rec rooms and workshops. Make additional allowances for vent duct and electrical requirements.

Description	Craft@Hrs	Unit	Material $	Labor $	Equipment $	Total $
160 CFM	P1@1.25	Ea	66.60	43.20	—	109.80
180 CFM	P1@1.25	Ea	96.40	43.20	—	139.60
270 CFM	P1@1.50	Ea	141.00	51.80	—	192.80
350 CFM	P1@1.75	Ea	176.00	60.50	—	236.50

Discharge hood ducting kit. Including discharge hood, 4" x 10' of flexible
duct, duct clamps, 3" x 4" transition coupling.

Description	Craft@Hrs	Unit	Material $	Labor $	Equipment $	Total $
Wall hood, 4"	P1@2.00	Ea	17.60	69.10	—	86.70
Roof hood, 4"	P1@2.25	Ea	35.10	77.70	—	112.80
Wall hood, 6"	P1@2.55	Ea	78.90	88.10	—	167.00

Fan controls. Switch only.

Description	Craft@Hrs	Unit	Material $	Labor $	Equipment $	Total $
1 hour timer	BE@.155	Ea	56.10	5.93	—	62.03
Humidistat	BE@.155	Ea	38.60	5.93	—	44.53
Speed controller	BE@.155	Ea	52.60	5.93	—	58.53

Ventilators and Residential Exhaust Fans

Description	Craft@Hrs	Unit	Material $	Labor $	Equipment $	Total $

Air admittance valve. For ventless sanitary plumbing. Provides a water seal in traps without roof penetration and vent piping. Complies with ASHRAE/American National Standards Institute spec. 62.2-2007 and American Society for Sanitary Engineering specs 1050 and 1051.

Description	Craft@Hrs	Unit	Material $	Labor $	Equipment $	Total $
Cut, frame and gasket for wall inset and vent valve access						
door	SW@1.00	Ea	35.70	39.70	—	75.40
Mount valve	P1@.500	Ea	—	17.30	—	17.30
Connect valve to sanitary S- or						
P-trap	P1@1.00	Ea	—	34.60	—	34.60

Bathroom Fans and Heaters. Comply with ASHRAE/American National Standards Institute spec 62.2-2007 and meet new indoor air quality code requirements for dehumidification, mold and mildew prevention and radon mitigation. Continental Fan, Tamarack, Broan or equal. Includes enclosure, mount plates, 110 or 408 volt electric motor, switch or relay assembly, motor fusing, ground fault protection. Add the following installation costs, if required.

Description	Craft@Hrs	Unit	Material $	Labor $	Equipment $	Total $
Cut, frame and gasket exhaust hole in						
sidewall	SW@1.00	Ea	35.70	39.70	—	75.40
Cut and mount sheet metal						
duct	SW@.150	LF	5.61	5.96	—	11.57
Apply and coat duct						
insulation	S2@.050	LF	2.45	1.71	—	4.16
Install electrical wiring						
(typical)	BE@.150	LF	1.79	5.74	—	7.53
Install controls	BE@.500	Ea	—	19.10	—	19.10
Test and adjust	P1@.250	Ea	—	8.64	—	8.64

Bathroom exhaust fan with heater, commercial grade, Continental Fan, Broan or equal.

Description	Craft@Hrs	Unit	Material $	Labor $	Equipment $	Total $
106 CFM fan,						
4" Duct	BE@.500	Ea	189.00	19.10	—	208.10
152 CFM fan,						
4" Duct	BE@.500	Ea	214.00	19.10	—	233.10
247 CFM fan,						
6" Duct	BE@.500	Ea	357.00	19.10	—	376.10
418 CFM fan,						
8" Duct	BE@.500	Ea	459.00	19.10	—	478.10

Infrared bulb heater and fan. 4-point adjustable mounting brackets span up to 24-inches. Uses 250 watt, 120 volt R-40 infrared bulbs (not included). Heater and fan units include 70 CFM, 3.5 sones ventilator fan. Damper and duct connector included. Plastic matte-white molded grille and compact housings. CFM (cubic feet of air per minute).

Description	Craft@Hrs	Unit	Material $	Labor $	Equipment $	Total $
1-bulb, 70 CFM,						
3.5 sones	BE@1.00	Ea	53.40	38.30	—	91.70
2-bulb heater,						
7" duct	BE@1.10	Ea	67.30	42.10	—	109.40

Description	Craft@Hrs	Unit	Material $	Labor $	Equipment $	Total $

Heat-A-Lamp® bulb heater and fan. NuTone. Swivel-mount. Torsion spring holds plates firmly to ceiling. 250-watt radiant heat from one R-40 infrared heat lamp. Uses 4-inch duct. Adjustable socket for ceilings up to 1-inch thick. Adjustable hanger bars. Automatic reset for thermal protection. White polymeric finish. UL listed.

Description	Craft@Hrs	Unit	Material $	Labor $	Equipment $	Total $
2.6 amp, 1 lamp, 12-1/2" x 10"	BE@1.50	Ea	55.30	57.40	—	112.70
5.0 amp, 2 lamp, 15-3/8" x 11"	BE@1.50	Ea	71.20	57.40	—	128.60

Surface-mount ceiling bath resistance heater and fan. 1250 watt. 4,266 BTU. 120 volt. Chrome alloy wire element for instant heat. Built-in fan. Automatic overheat protection. Low-profile housing. Permanently lubricated motor. Mounts to standard 3-1/4-inch round or 4-inch octagonal ceiling electrical box. Satin-finish aluminum grille extends 2-3/4-inch from ceiling. 11" diameter x 2-3/4" deep.

Description	Craft@Hrs	Unit	Material $	Labor $	Equipment $	Total $
10.7 amp	BE@.750	Ea	56.30	28.70	—	85.00

Designer Series bath heater and exhaust fan. 1500-watt fan-forced heater. 120-watt light capacity, 7-watt night-light (bulbs not included). Permanently lubricated motor. Polymeric damper. Torsion-spring grille mount. Non-glare light diffusing glass lens. Fits single gang opening. Suitable for use with insulation. 100 CFM, 1.2 sones.

Description	Craft@Hrs	Unit	Material $	Labor $	Equipment $	Total $
4" duct, 100 watt lamp	BE@1.00	Ea	228.00	38.30	—	266.30

Ventilation exhausters. Includes all-weather enclosure, air balance control, software module and NFPA certified fusible plug-type vertical duct riser gravity dampers, and efficiency optimization arrays. Add the cost of roof curb, control wiring, electrical wiring, permits and final inspection. For wall or roof mount in single and multi-unit residences, commercial (i.e. hotels), institutional (i.e. hospitals and schools) buildings. Set in place only. Add installation costs from the section below. Costs assume rental of an appliance dolly ($14.00 per day), a 3,000 lb. come-a-long ($16.00 per day) and a 1/2-ton chain hoist ($21.00 a day).

Downblast ventilation exhausters. Rooftop mounted, direct drive, centrifugal type. Suitable for either ducted or nonducted applications.

Description	Craft@Hrs	Unit	Material $	Labor $	Equipment $	Total $
1/4 HP, 14" dia.	SN@2.50	Ea	1,330.00	91.50	39.00	1,460.50
1/3 HP, 22" dia.	SN@2.90	Ea	1,630.00	106.00	46.00	1,782.00
1/2 HP, 24" dia.	SN@3.50	Ea	1,860.00	128.00	55.00	2,043.00
1 HP, 30" dia.	SN@4.50	Ea	2,580.00	165.00	71.00	2,816.00
2 HP, 36" dia.	SN@5.00	Ea	3,690.00	183.00	79.00	3,952.00
3 HP, 40" dia.	SN@6.00	Ea	5,530.00	219.00	94.00	5,843.00
5 HP, 48" dia.	SN@7.00	Ea	7,670.00	256.00	110.00	8,036.00

Ventilators and Residential Exhaust Fans

Description	Craft@Hrs	Unit	Material $	Labor $	Equipment $	Total $

Upblast ventilation exhausters. Direct drive, centrifugal, for roof or wall mount.

Description	Craft@Hrs	Unit	Material $	Labor $	Equipment $	Total $
1/4 HP, 14" dia.	SN@2.50	Ea	1,430.00	91.50	39.00	1,560.50
1/3 HP, 22" dia.	SN@2.90	Ea	1,730.00	106.00	46.00	1,882.00
1/2 HP, 24" dia.	SN@3.50	Ea	1,990.00	128.00	55.00	2,173.00
1 HP, 30" dia.	SN@4.50	Ea	2,750.00	165.00	71.00	2,986.00
2 HP, 36" dia.	SN@5.00	Ea	3,880.00	183.00	79.00	4,142.00
3 HP, 40" dia.	SN@6.00	Ea	5,710.00	219.00	94.00	6,023.00
5 HP, 48" dia.	SN@7.00	Ea	7,850.00	256.00	110.00	8,216.00

Energy-efficient exhauster arrays. Upblast belt-drive centrifugal UL762 roof exhausters. Low profile metal grille. Galvanized steel housing. Designed for continuous operation. Acoustically insulated. Can be installed horizontally, vertically or in-line. Labor includes lay-out and fasten in place only. Make additional allowances for vent duct and electrical requirements.

Description	Craft@Hrs	Unit	Material $	Labor $	Equipment $	Total $
100 CFM	P1@1.05	Ea	204.00	36.30	—	240.30
150 CFM	P1@1.15	Ea	224.00	39.70	—	263.70
200 CFM	P1@1.35	Ea	245.00	46.60	—	291.60
250 CFM	P1@1.45	Ea	316.00	50.10	—	366.10
300 CFM	P1@1.65	Ea	357.00	57.00	—	414.00
400 CFM	P1@2.15	Ea	449.00	74.30	—	523.30
500 CFM	P1@2.50	Ea	520.00	86.40	—	606.40
700 CFM	P1@2.75	Ea	745.00	95.00	—	840.00
900 CFM	P1@2.85	Ea	806.00	98.50	157.00	1,061.50
1,500 CFM	P1@3.50	Ea	1,220.00	121.00	193.00	1,534.00
2,000 CFM	P1@3.85	Ea	1,380.00	133.00	213.00	1,726.00
3,500 CFM	P1@4.25	Ea	1,530.00	147.00	235.00	1,912.00

Installation costs for ventilation exhausters.

Description	Craft@Hrs	Unit	Material $	Labor $	Equipment $	Total $
Cut, frame and gasket downcomer hole in sidewall or roof	S2@1.00	Ea	35.70	34.20	—	69.90
Mount duct hangers	S2@.250	Ea	3.57	8.54	—	12.11
Cut & mount sheet metal duct	S2@.350	LF	5.61	12.00	—	17.61
Apply and coat duct insulation	S2@.150	LF	2.45	5.12	—	7.57
Install electrical wiring	BE@.150	LF	1.79	5.74	—	7.53
Install exhauster controls	BE@.500	Ea	—	19.10	—	19.10
Commission and test	P1@4.00	Ea	—	138.00	—	138.00
Run air balance and fine-tune system	P1@4.00	Ea	—	138.00	—	138.00

Unitary or factory-packaged air conditioning units are often too small to meet the heating and cooling needs of a large single-zone space. In such cases, engineers design what's called a "built-up" system. They're custom fitted to the client's needs and the space. A typical "built-up" system includes the following equipment:

- centrifugal blowers or axial-flow fans
- damper assemblies
- coil banks
- filter banks

Once the system is assembled, it is enclosed in a shop-fabricated housing or casing. The illustration on page 332 shows a standard apparatus housing. The walls and roof are shop-built panels. These panels consist of a layer of thermal insulation covered on one or both sides with sheets of 18 gauge galvanized steel. An interior framework of steel angles or channels supports the panels. Seal all mating surfaces to minimize air leakage, using gaskets, caulking or sealant.

Apparatus Housing

There are two types of panels used in building apparatus housings: "double-skin" panels and "single-skin" panels. Double-skin panels have a layer of thermal insulation material sandwiched between two sheets of 18 gauge galvanized steel. Single-skin panels also have a layer of insulation. However, only the outside surface is clad in 18 gauge steel sheeting. On the inside the panel insulation is exposed.

The costs of constructing and installing apparatus housings vary greatly. This is due to the wide range of possible conditions and needs that you face on each job. Some of the many factors that influence costs here include the following:

- internal operating pressures
- external wind loads
- seismic requirements
- physical locations

That's why I recommend that you always prepare a detailed cost estimate. Then, you can take all the particulars into account. However, for budget estimating purposes only, use the following cost data:

Single-skin panels	$11.30 per SF*
Double-skin panels	$19.20 per SF*
Access doors (20" x 60")	$390.00 each

*Total area of walls and roof, less doors.

When you're estimating material costs for apparatus housings, remember to add in an extra 25 percent to cover the following costs: waste, seams, gaskets, sealants and miscellaneous assembly hardware.

Labor for Shop-Fabrication and Field Assembly of Apparatus Housings. The costs listed are manhours per square foot (SF) of panel. To find the total SF of panel, add up areas for all the panels.

Description	Shop Labor (MH per SF)	Field Labor (MH per SF)
Single-skin panels	.040	.250
Double-skin panels	.085	.300
Add for access doors	.400	.240

Framed fan discharge
or duct opening

Access door

Concrete curb

Figure 1 - Typical apparatus housing

Description	Craft@Hrs	Unit	Material $	Labor $	Equipment $	Total $

Supply air side-wall register, fixed pattern, with damper. Steel construction.

Description	Craft@Hrs	Unit	Material $	Labor $	Equipment $	Total $
8" x 4"	S2@.250	Ea	8.87	8.54	—	17.41
8" x 6"	S2@.250	Ea	9.23	8.54	—	17.77
10" x 4"	S2@.250	Ea	10.00	8.54	—	18.54
10" x 6"	S2@.250	Ea	16.90	8.54	—	25.44
10" x 8"	S2@.250	Ea	16.20	8.54	—	24.74
12" x 6"	S2@.250	Ea	17.20	8.54	—	25.74
12" x 8"	S2@.250	Ea	14.10	8.54	—	22.64
14" x 6"	S2@.250	Ea	14.10	8.54	—	22.64
14" x 8"	S2@.250	Ea	16.10	8.54	—	24.64

Return air side-wall grille, fixed pattern, without damper. Steel construction.

Description	Craft@Hrs	Unit	Material $	Labor $	Equipment $	Total $
14" x 6"	S2@.250	Ea	7.66	8.54	—	16.20
14" x 8"	S2@.250	Ea	7.42	8.54	—	15.96
16" x 16"	S2@.250	Ea	22.50	8.54	—	31.04
20" x 10"	S2@.300	Ea	33.30	10.20	—	43.50
20" x 16"	S2@.300	Ea	36.50	10.20	—	46.70
20" x 20"	S2@.300	Ea	48.30	10.20	—	58.50
24" x 24"	S2@.350	Ea	62.80	12.00	—	74.80

Supply air double deflection side-wall register, adjustable pattern. Aluminum construction.

Description	Craft@Hrs	Unit	Material $	Labor $	Equipment $	Total $
8" x 4"	S2@.250	Ea	28.60	8.54	—	37.14
8" x 6"	S2@.250	Ea	31.90	8.54	—	40.44
10" x 4"	S2@.250	Ea	36.80	8.54	—	45.34
10" x 6"	S2@.250	Ea	37.80	8.54	—	46.34
10" x 8"	S2@.250	Ea	40.50	8.54	—	49.04
12" x 6"	S2@.250	Ea	42.00	8.54	—	50.54
12" x 8"	S2@.250	Ea	47.10	8.54	—	55.64
12" x 10"	S2@.250	Ea	53.20	8.54	—	61.74
14" x 6"	S2@.250	Ea	53.20	8.54	—	61.74
14" x 8"	S2@.250	Ea	53.90	8.54	—	62.44
14" x 10"	S2@.250	Ea	57.40	8.54	—	65.94
16" x 8"	S2@.250	Ea	57.40	8.54	—	65.94
16" x 10"	S2@.250	Ea	62.80	8.54	—	71.34
18" x 8"	S2@.300	Ea	65.50	10.20	—	75.70
18" x 10"	S2@.300	Ea	70.20	10.20	—	80.40
18" x 12"	S2@.300	Ea	74.10	10.20	—	84.30

Air Devices, Diffusers and Grilles

Description	Craft@Hrs	Unit	Material $	Labor $	Equipment $	Total $

Return air single deflection side-wall grille, adjustable pattern.
Aluminum construction.

Description	Craft@Hrs	Unit	Material $	Labor $	Equipment $	Total $
8" x 4"	S2@.250	Ea	26.00	8.54	—	34.54
8" x 6"	S2@.250	Ea	28.60	8.54	—	37.14
10" x 4"	S2@.250	Ea	31.50	8.54	—	40.04
10" x 6"	S2@.250	Ea	34.20	8.54	—	42.74
10" x 8"	S2@.250	Ea	36.40	8.54	—	44.94
12" x 6"	S2@.250	Ea	37.70	8.54	—	46.24
12" x 8"	S2@.250	Ea	42.30	8.54	—	50.84
12" x 10"	S2@.250	Ea	47.80	8.54	—	56.34
14" x 6"	S2@.250	Ea	47.80	8.54	—	56.34
14" x 8"	S2@.250	Ea	48.70	8.54	—	57.24
14" x 10"	S2@.250	Ea	51.30	8.54	—	59.84
16" x 8"	S2@.250	Ea	51.30	8.54	—	59.84
16" x 10"	S2@.300	Ea	56.60	10.20	—	66.80
18" x 8"	S2@.300	Ea	59.10	10.20	—	69.30
18" x 10"	S2@.300	Ea	63.40	10.20	—	73.60
18" x 12"	S2@.300	Ea	66.90	10.20	—	77.10

4-way adjustable pattern ceiling diffuser 24" x 24" with collar and volume damper. Steel construction.

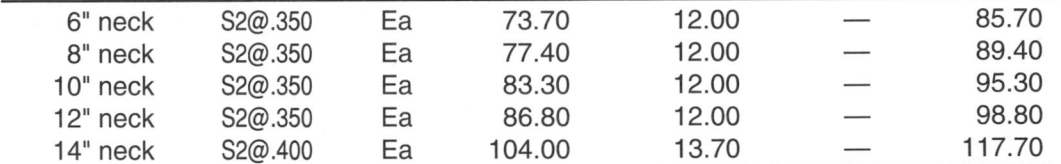

Description	Craft@Hrs	Unit	Material $	Labor $	Equipment $	Total $
6" neck	S2@.350	Ea	73.70	12.00	—	85.70
8" neck	S2@.350	Ea	77.40	12.00	—	89.40
10" neck	S2@.350	Ea	83.30	12.00	—	95.30
12" neck	S2@.350	Ea	86.80	12.00	—	98.80
14" neck	S2@.400	Ea	104.00	13.70	—	117.70

Fixed pattern ceiling diffuser 24" x 24" with collar, without volume damper. Steel construction.

Description	Craft@Hrs	Unit	Material $	Labor $	Equipment $	Total $
6" neck	S2@.350	Ea	44.40	12.00	—	56.40
8" neck	S2@.350	Ea	48.00	12.00	—	60.00
10" neck	S2@.350	Ea	53.70	12.00	—	65.70
12" neck	S2@.350	Ea	57.00	12.00	—	69.00
14" neck	S2@.350	Ea	73.70	12.00	—	85.70

Perforated ceiling diffuser 24" x 24" fixed pattern with collar, without volume damper. Steel construction.

Description	Craft@Hrs	Unit	Material $	Labor $	Equipment $	Total $
6" neck	S2@.350	Ea	59.20	12.00	—	71.20
8" neck	S2@.350	Ea	61.30	12.00	—	73.30
10" neck	S2@.350	Ea	65.70	12.00	—	77.70
12" neck	S2@.350	Ea	70.20	12.00	—	82.20
14" neck	S2@.400	Ea	78.50	13.70	—	92.20
16" neck	S2@.720	Ea	133.00	24.60	—	157.60

Description	Craft@Hrs	Unit	Material $	Labor $	Equipment $	Total $

Round 3-cone, 2-position ceiling diffuser with collar, without volume damper. Steel construction.

Description	Craft@Hrs	Unit	Material $	Labor $	Equipment $	Total $
6"	S2@.350	Ea	61.10	12.00	—	73.10
8"	S2@.350	Ea	70.20	12.00	—	82.20
10"	S2@.350	Ea	85.10	12.00	—	97.10
12"	S2@.350	Ea	99.90	12.00	—	111.90
14"	S2@.350	Ea	134.00	12.00	—	146.00

Round adjustable ceiling diffuser with collar and volume damper.
Steel construction.

Description	Craft@Hrs	Unit	Material $	Labor $	Equipment $	Total $
6"	S2@.350	Ea	92.30	12.00	—	104.30
8"	S2@.350	Ea	109.00	12.00	—	121.00
10"	S2@.350	Ea	85.10	12.00	—	97.10
12"	S2@.350	Ea	134.00	12.00	—	146.00
14"	S2@.350	Ea	249.00	12.00	—	261.00
16"	S2@.450	Ea	290.00	15.40	—	305.40
18"	S2@.450	Ea	335.00	15.40	—	350.40
20"	S2@.550	Ea	395.00	18.80	—	413.80
24"	S2@.650	Ea	544.00	22.20	—	566.20

Description	Craft@Hrs	Unit	Material $	Labor $	Equipment $	Total $

Makeup air unit. Makeup air unit Uses 100% direct-heated outdoor air for warehouse, factory and institutional applications to provide higher thermal efficiency and balanced distribution of system air while pre-heating air for use in boiler or other HVAC applications. ANSI standard Z83.4/CSA 3.7 certified. With weather-proof metal enclosure, burner, analog electric controls for burner and fan, thermostat, actuator, natural gas burner array, and either roof mount supports or sidewall external mounts and transition and gaskets. Set in place only. Add installation costs.

Description	Craft@Hrs	Unit	Material $	Labor $	Equipment $	Total $
200 to 399 CFM	SN@2.25	Ea	554.00	82.30	35.40	671.70
400 to 599 CFM	SN@2.25	Ea	610.00	82.30	35.40	727.70
600 to 799 CFM	SN@2.75	Ea	703.00	101.00	43.30	847.30
800 to 999 CFM	SN@3.00	Ea	845.00	110.00	47.10	1,002.10
1,000 to 1,499 CFM	SN@3.50	Ea	1,120.00	128.00	55.00	1,303.00
1,500 to 1,999 CFM	SN@4.00	Ea	1,420.00	146.00	62.90	1,628.90
4,000 to 5,999 CFM	SN@6.00	Ea	3,570.00	219.00	106.20	3,895.20
7,500 to 10,000 CFM	SN@8.00	Ea	6,120.00	293.00	106.20	6,519.20
15,000 to 25,000 CFM	SN@10.0	Ea	8,670.00	366.00	141.60	9,177.60
30,000 to 40,000 CFM	SN@16.0	Ea	12,800.00	585.00	283.20	13,668.20
60,000 to 80,000 CFM	SN@24.0	Ea	22,400.00	878.00	283.20	23,561.20

Installation costs for makeup air units.

Description	Craft@Hrs	Unit	Material $	Labor $	Equipment $	Total $
Cut, frame and gasket downcomer/ sidewall hole	S2@1.00	Ea	35.70	34.20	—	69.90
Mount duct hangers	S2@.250	Ea	3.57	8.54	—	12.11
Cut and mount sheet metal duct	S2@.350	LF	5.61	12.00	—	17.61
Apply and coat duct insulation	S2@.150	LF	2.45	5.12	—	7.57
Install piping for gas line	P1@.100	LF	3.83	3.46	—	7.29
Install electrical wiring	BE@.150	LF	1.79	5.74	—	7.53
Install makeup air unit controls	BE@.500	Ea	—	19.10	—	19.10
Commission and test	P1@4.00	Ea	—	138.00	—	138.00
Run air balance and fine-tune system	P1@4.00	Ea	—	138.00	—	138.00

Variable-air volume units regulate supply air to ducted air conditioning systems. These systems are certified to ANSI standard Z83.4/CSA 3.7 and can be either roof-mounted or upper sidewall externally mounted. Costs include a weather-proof metal enclosure, heater coil or electrical heater fixture, fan and fan controls, downcomer or sidewall entry transition and gaskets, and either roof mount supports or sidewall external mounts. Includes set in place only. Add installation costs from the table that follows.

Description	Craft@Hrs	Unit	Material $	Labor $	Equipment $	Total $

Variable-air volume terminal unit with analog electric controls, thermostat, actuator and controller

Description	Craft@Hrs	Unit	Material $	Labor $	Equipment $	Total $
200- 400 CFM	SN@2.00	Ea	494.00	73.20	31.40	598.60
400- 600 CFM	SN@2.00	Ea	551.00	73.20	31.40	655.60
600- 800 CFM	SN@2.50	Ea	580.00	91.50	39.20	710.70
800-1,000 CFM	SN@2.75	Ea	628.00	101.00	43.30	772.30
1,000-1,500 CFM	SN@3.00	Ea	915.00	110.00	47.10	1,072.10
1,500-2,000 CFM	SN@3.50	Ea	1,160.00	128.00	55.00	1,343.00

Variable-air volume terminal reheat unit with analog electric controls, thermostat, actuator, controller and a two row hot water coil

Description	Craft@Hrs	Unit	Material $	Labor $	Equipment $	Total $
200- 400 CFM	SN@2.25	Ea	570.00	82.30	35.40	687.70
400- 600 CFM	SN@2.25	Ea	628.00	82.30	35.40	745.70
600- 800 CFM	SN@2.75	Ea	723.00	101.00	43.30	867.30
800-1,000 CFM	SN@3.00	Ea	869.00	110.00	47.10	1,026.10
1,000-1,500 CFM	SN@3.50	Ea	1,160.00	128.00	55.00	1,343.00
1,500-2,000 CFM	SN@4.00	Ea	1,460.00	146.00	62.90	1,668.90

Installation costs for variable-air volume units.

Description	Craft@Hrs	Unit	Material $	Labor $	Equipment $	Total $
Cut, frame and gasket downcomer hole in roof	S2@1.00	Ea	35.00	34.20	—	69.20
Mount duct hangers	S2@.250	Ea	3.50	8.54	—	12.04
Cut and mount sheet metal duct	S2@.350	LF	5.50	12.00	—	17.50
Apply and coat duct insulation	S2@.150	LF	2.40	5.12	—	7.52
Install piping for chilled or hot water/steam	P1@.100	LF	2.85	3.46	—	6.31
Install electrical wiring	BE@.150	LF	1.75	5.74	—	7.49
Install VAV controls	BE@.500	Ea	—	19.10	—	19.10
Commission and test	P1@4.00	Ea	—	138.00	—	138.00
Run air balance and fine-tune system	P1@4.00	Ea	—	138.00	—	138.00

Terminal Units (VAV)

Air balance software and control modules for variable-air volume ducted zone control For commercial, institutional and industrial applications. Johnson Controls or equal. The zone and duct-mounted sensor and response unit comprises a digital controller, actuator and differential pressure transducer. These components are wired together and securely housed inside a plenum-rated enclosure which mounts directly to the VAV "serviced zone" box. Complies with Underwriters Laboratories file E107041, CCN PAZX, UL916 Energy Management Equipment. Interfaces with Windows-based commercial desktop computers per the digital control manufacturer's specifications.

Description	Craft@Hrs	Unit	Material $	Labor $	Equipment $	Total $

Fully programmable 28 point controller, 16 universal inputs,12 universal outputs, 12 HOA switches, a battery backed real time clock, plus preconfigured function blocks for a real time clock. Stores schedules and trending information.

Description	Craft@Hrs	Unit	Material $	Labor $	Equipment $	Total $
Programmable controller	BE@.500	Ea	900.00	19.10	—	919.10

Configurable variable air volume pressure independent terminal box controller with wireless transceiver (868.3 MHz)

Description	Craft@Hrs	Unit	Material $	Labor $	Equipment $	Total $
Terminal box controller	BE@.500	Ea	2,700.00	19.10	—	2,719.10

Configurable controller, preconfigured LNS plug-in, and all input devices required for typical rooftop unit application

Description	Craft@Hrs	Unit	Material $	Labor $	Equipment $	Total $
Preconfigured controller	BE@.500	Ea	1,800.00	19.10	—	1,819.10

Variable air volume controller system software for a Windows computer. Includes a software license and support for two concurrent client browser connections with no limit on the number of concurrent users and no data tag limit.

Description	Craft@Hrs	Unit	Material $	Labor $	Equipment $	Total $
System software	BE@18.0	Ea	6,800.00	689.00	—	7,489.00

Description	Craft@Hrs	Unit	Material $	Labor $	Equipment $	Total $

Opposed-blade damper for rectangular ductwork

Description	Craft@Hrs	Unit	Material $	Labor $	Equipment $	Total $
12" x 6"	S2@.600	Ea	58.00	20.50	—	78.50
12" x 10"	S2@.650	Ea	68.60	22.20	—	90.80
12" x 12"	S2@.700	Ea	84.10	23.90	—	108.00
18" x 12"	S2@.800	Ea	96.90	27.30	—	124.20
18" x 18"	S2@.850	Ea	108.00	29.00	—	137.00
24" x 12"	S2@.850	Ea	113.00	29.00	—	142.00
24" x 18"	S2@.900	Ea	124.00	30.70	—	154.70
24" x 24"	S2@1.00	Ea	139.00	34.20	—	173.20
30" x 12"	S2@.900	Ea	129.00	30.70	—	159.70
30" x 18"	S2@1.00	Ea	145.00	34.20	—	179.20
30" x 24"	S2@1.10	Ea	163.00	37.60	—	200.60
30" x 30"	S2@1.20	Ea	176.00	41.00	—	217.00
36" x 18"	S2@1.10	Ea	169.00	37.60	—	206.60
36" x 36"	S2@1.40	Ea	232.00	47.80	—	279.80
42" x 24"	S2@1.30	Ea	236.00	44.40	—	280.40
42" x 42"	S2@1.50	Ea	323.00	51.20	—	374.20
48" x 24"	S2@1.40	Ea	244.00	47.80	—	291.80
48" x 48"	S2@1.60	Ea	339.00	54.70	—	393.70
54" x 24"	S2@1.45	Ea	310.00	49.50	—	359.50
54" x 54"	S2@1.70	Ea	387.00	58.10	—	445.10

Single-blade damper for rectangular ductwork

Description	Craft@Hrs	Unit	Material $	Labor $	Equipment $	Total $
12" x 6"	S2@.600	Ea	36.40	20.50	—	56.90
12" x 8"	S2@.625	Ea	39.80	21.40	—	61.20
12" x 10"	S2@.650	Ea	44.70	22.20	—	66.90
12" x 12"	S2@.700	Ea	52.50	23.90	—	76.40
18" x 12"	S2@.800	Ea	58.40	27.30	—	85.70
18" x 18"	S2@.850	Ea	66.30	29.00	—	95.30
24" x 12"	S2@.850	Ea	70.10	29.00	—	99.10
24" x 18"	S2@.900	Ea	72.90	30.70	—	103.60
24" x 24"	S2@1.00	Ea	80.10	34.20	—	114.30

Single-blade butterfly damper for round ductwork

Description	Craft@Hrs	Unit	Material $	Labor $	Equipment $	Total $
6"	S2@.600	Ea	36.40	20.50	—	56.90
8"	S2@.550	Ea	34.20	18.80	—	53.00
10"	S2@.600	Ea	39.70	20.50	—	60.20
12"	S2@.650	Ea	44.90	22.20	—	67.10
14"	S2@.700	Ea	51.10	23.90	—	75.00
16"	S2@.765	Ea	56.60	26.10	—	82.70
18"	S2@.835	Ea	62.80	28.50	—	91.30
20"	S2@.900	Ea	70.60	30.70	—	101.30

Ductwork Specialties

Description	Craft@Hrs	Unit	Material $	Labor $	Equipment $	Total $

Curtain-type duct fire damper, 1-1/2 hour rating, U.L. label

Description	Craft@Hrs	Unit	Material $	Labor $	Equipment $	Total $
12" x 6"	S2@1.00	Ea	66.70	34.20	—	100.90
12" x 8"	S2@1.00	Ea	72.20	34.20	—	106.40
12" x 10"	S2@1.05	Ea	79.00	35.90	—	114.90
12" x 12"	S2@1.10	Ea	85.30	37.60	—	122.90
18" x 12"	S2@1.20	Ea	119.00	41.00	—	160.00
18" x 18"	S2@1.30	Ea	129.00	44.40	—	173.40
24" x 12"	S2@1.40	Ea	144.00	47.80	—	191.80
24" x 18"	S2@1.50	Ea	163.00	51.20	—	214.20
24" x 24"	S2@1.60	Ea	194.00	54.70	—	248.70
30" x 12"	S2@1.50	Ea	166.00	51.20	—	217.20
30" x 18"	S2@1.80	Ea	185.00	61.50	—	246.50
30" x 24"	S2@2.00	Ea	244.00	68.30	—	312.30
30" x 30"	S2@2.30	Ea	264.00	78.60	—	342.60
36" x 18"	S2@2.00	Ea	210.00	68.30	—	278.30
36" x 36"	S2@2.40	Ea	314.00	82.00	—	396.00
42" x 24"	S2@2.40	Ea	272.00	82.00	—	354.00
42" x 42"	S2@2.90	Ea	394.00	99.10	—	493.10
48" x 24"	S2@2.90	Ea	296.00	99.10	—	395.10
48" x 48"	S2@3.50	Ea	491.00	120.00	—	611.00
54" x 24"	S2@3.00	Ea	320.00	102.00	—	422.00
54" x 54"	S2@3.80	Ea	570.00	130.00	—	700.00

Correction factors:

(1) For 22 gauge break-away connection, multiply material cost by 1.30

(2) For blades out of air stream cap, multiply material cost by 1.25

Description	Craft@Hrs	Unit	Material $	Labor $	Equipment $	Total $

Fusible plug dampers for air duct risers. Vertical riser and header air duct fusible (melting) and heat-sensing automatic counterweight closure actuators and closure dampers. For large A/C systems in multi-story institutions such as schools, hospitals and office buildings. 1-1/2 hour rating. The liner and insulation must meet the requirements of U.L. 181 and NFPA No. 90 A-96, as modified, "Standard for the Installation of Air Conditioning and Ventilation Systems."

Description	Craft@Hrs	Unit	Material $	Labor $	Equipment $	Total $
12" x 6"	S2@1.00	Ea	88.00	34.20	—	122.20
12" x 8"	S2@1.00	Ea	90.00	34.20	—	124.20
12" x 10"	S2@1.05	Ea	93.00	35.90	—	128.90
12" x 12"	S2@1.10	Ea	95.00	37.60	—	132.60
18" x 12"	S2@1.20	Ea	120.00	41.00	—	161.00
18" x 18"	S2@1.30	Ea	155.00	44.40	—	199.40
24" x 12"	S2@1.40	Ea	165.00	47.80	—	212.80
24" x 18"	S2@1.50	Ea	185.00	51.20	—	236.20
24" x 24"	S2@1.60	Ea	210.00	54.70	—	264.70
30" x 12"	S2@1.50	Ea	200.00	51.20	—	251.20
30" x 18"	S2@1.80	Ea	250.00	61.50	—	311.50
30" x 24"	S2@2.00	Ea	290.00	68.30	—	358.30
30" x 30"	S2@2.30	Ea	350.00	78.60	—	428.60
36" x 18"	S2@2.00	Ea	280.00	68.30	—	348.30
36" x 36"	S2@2.40	Ea	375.00	82.00	—	457.00
42" x 24"	S2@2.40	Ea	350.00	82.00	—	432.00
42" x 42"	S2@2.90	Ea	425.00	99.10	—	524.10
48" x 24"	S2@2.90	Ea	380.00	99.10	—	479.10
48" x 48"	S2@3.50	Ea	850.00	120.00	—	970.00
54" x 24"	S2@3.00	Ea	1,100.00	102.00	—	1,202.00
54" x 54"	S2@3.80	Ea	1,780.00	130.00	—	1,910.00
Cut, frame and gasket access hole in sidewall	S2@1.00	Ea	65.00	34.20	—	99.20
Mount duct hangers	S2@.250	Ea	3.50	8.54	—	12.04
Cut and mount sheet metal duct	S2@.350	LF	5.50	12.00	—	17.50
Apply and coat duct insulation	S2@.150	LF	2.40	5.12	—	7.52

Ductwork Specialties

Description	Craft@Hrs	Unit	Material $	Labor $	Equipment $	Total $

Single skin 2" fixed position turning vanes for duct

Description	Craft@Hrs	Unit	Material $	Labor $	Equipment $	Total $
12" x 6"	S2@.280	Ea	7.79	9.56	—	17.35
12" x 8"	S2@.285	Ea	9.64	9.74	—	19.38
12" x 10"	S2@.290	Ea	12.40	9.91	—	22.31
12" x 12"	S2@.300	Ea	15.40	10.20	—	25.60
18" x 12"	S2@.375	Ea	23.30	12.80	—	36.10
18" x 18"	S2@.450	Ea	28.20	15.40	—	43.60
24" x 12"	S2@.450	Ea	30.90	15.40	—	46.30
24" x 18"	S2@.500	Ea	33.70	17.10	—	50.80
24" x 24"	S2@.525	Ea	38.40	17.90	—	56.30
30" x 12"	S2@.550	Ea	38.70	18.80	—	57.50
30" x 18"	S2@.750	Ea	55.80	25.60	—	81.40
30" x 24"	S2@.800	Ea	74.20	27.30	—	101.50
30" x 30"	S2@.900	Ea	94.20	30.70	—	124.90
36" x 18"	S2@.750	Ea	66.30	25.60	—	91.90
36" x 36"	S2@.800	Ea	135.00	27.30	—	162.30
42" x 24"	S2@.900	Ea	105.00	30.70	—	135.70
42" x 42"	S2@1.00	Ea	185.00	34.20	—	219.20
48" x 24"	S2@1.10	Ea	119.00	37.60	—	156.60
48" x 48"	S2@1.50	Ea	238.00	51.20	—	289.20
54" x 24"	S2@1.15	Ea	133.00	39.30	—	172.30
54" x 54"	S2@1.25	Ea	303.00	42.70	—	345.70
60" x 24"	S2@1.30	Ea	150.00	44.40	—	194.40
60" x 36"	S2@1.40	Ea	225.00	47.80	—	272.80
60" x 60"	S2@1.50	Ea	373.00	51.20	—	424.20
72" x 36"	S2@1.65	Ea	272.00	56.40	—	328.40
72" x 54"	S2@2.40	Ea	402.00	82.00	—	484.00

Note: Labor includes cost to cut, assemble and install vanes and rails. For 4-inch air-foil vanes, multiply costs by 1.80 and labor costs by .90

Description	Craft@Hrs	Unit	Material $	Labor $	Equipment $	Total $

Spin-in galvanized steel collars without volume damper

Description	Craft@Hrs	Unit	Material $	Labor $	Equipment $	Total $
4"	S2@.200	Ea	5.79	6.83	—	12.62
5"	S2@.200	Ea	6.50	6.83	—	13.33
6"	S2@.200	Ea	7.17	6.83	—	14.00
7"	S2@.200	Ea	7.88	6.83	—	14.71
8"	S2@.250	Ea	9.15	8.54	—	17.69
9"	S2@.250	Ea	10.10	8.54	—	18.64
10"	S2@.300	Ea	10.90	10.20	—	21.10
12"	S2@.350	Ea	12.90	12.00	—	24.90
14"	S2@.400	Ea	15.50	13.70	—	29.20
16"	S2@.450	Ea	18.50	15.40	—	33.90
18"	S2@.500	Ea	23.00	17.10	—	40.10

Spin-in galvanized steel collar with volume damper

Description	Craft@Hrs	Unit	Material $	Labor $	Equipment $	Total $
4"	S2@.250	Ea	19.40	8.54	—	27.94
5"	S2@.250	Ea	19.80	8.54	—	28.34
6"	S2@.250	Ea	20.00	8.54	—	28.54
7"	S2@.250	Ea	20.40	8.54	—	28.94
8"	S2@.300	Ea	20.80	10.20	—	31.00
9"	S2@.300	Ea	21.00	10.20	—	31.20
10"	S2@.350	Ea	21.50	12.00	—	33.50
12"	S2@.400	Ea	23.20	13.70	—	36.90
14"	S2@.450	Ea	24.70	15.40	—	40.10
16"	S2@.500	Ea	26.30	17.10	—	43.40
18"	S2@.550	Ea	28.20	18.80	—	47.00

Duct-to-equipment flexible connection

Description	Craft@Hrs	Unit	Material $	Labor $	Equipment $	Total $
18" x 12"	S2@.650	Ea	19.70	22.20	—	41.90
18" x 18"	S2@.850	Ea	23.70	29.00	—	52.70
24" x 12"	S2@.850	Ea	23.70	29.00	—	52.70
24" x 18"	S2@1.00	Ea	27.50	34.20	—	61.70
24" x 24"	S2@1.30	Ea	31.70	44.40	—	76.10
30" x 12"	S2@1.00	Ea	27.50	34.20	—	61.70
30" x 18"	S2@1.30	Ea	31.70	44.40	—	76.10
30" x 30"	S2@1.60	Ea	39.60	54.70	—	94.30
36" x 12"	S2@1.30	Ea	31.70	44.40	—	76.10
36" x 24"	S2@1.60	Ea	39.60	54.70	—	94.30
36" x 36"	S2@1.80	Ea	46.90	61.50	—	108.40
48" x 24"	S2@1.80	Ea	46.90	61.50	—	108.40
48" x 48"	S2@2.00	Ea	62.20	68.30	—	130.50

Galvanized Steel Ductwork

The costs for fabricating and installing galvanized steel ductwork are usually based on the total weights of the duct and fittings. Because of cost differences, fitting weights should be kept separate from straight duct weights.

Round spiral duct: Normally-used duct gauge/size relationships for low-pressure systems, up to 2 inches static pressure, are as follows:

Duct Diameter (inches)	U.S. Standard Gauge
Up to 12	26
13 through 24	24
26 through 36	22

Rectangular duct: Normally-used duct gauge/size relationships for low-pressure systems, up to 2 inches static pressure, are as follows:

Duct Size (inches)	U.S. Standard Gauge
Up to 12	26
13 through 30	24
31 through 54	22
55 through 72	20

The fitting weights in the following tables are in accordance with the above gauges.

Other material costs: All weights in the tables are net weights; they do not include bracing, cleats, scrap, hangers, end closures, sealants and miscellaneous hardware. Add 15% to calculated duct/fitting weights to cover these items if ductwork is purchased. Add 20% if ducting is manufactured in contractor's shop. The additional 5% covers the costs for scrap which is already included in an outside vendor's price.

Ductwork costs: Typical costs for purchased ductwork are as follows:

Straight duct, less than 1,000 pounds per order	$2.63/lb.
Straight duct, over 1,000 pounds per order	$2.36/lb.
Fittings, less than 1,000 pounds per order	$5.31/lb.
Fittings, over 1,000 pounds per order	$4.76/lb.
Lined ducts and fittings, add	$ 1.07/lb.*
Delivery costs	$ .15/lb.

Duct sizes shown on drawings are always inside, or net, dimensions and must be increased in size when estimating lined ductwork.

If ductwork is manufactured in the contractor's fabrication shop, the above costs can be reduced by about 20%, depending on the shop's rate of productivity.

Installation costs: An average crew can install approximately 25 pounds of duct and fittings per manhour under normal conditions. See "Applying Correction Factors" on page 6 for situations that do not conform to the definition of a standard labor unit.

EXAMPLE:

What is the cost to furnish and install 2,585 pounds of unlined duct and 560 pounds of unlined fittings? The ductwork will be purchased from an outside vendor. A 15% allowance for miscellaneous material is included in the weights.

Material:

2,585 pounds of straight duct x $2.36/lb.	=	$6,100.60
560 pounds of fittings x $5.31/lb.	=	2,973.60
Delivery cost: (2,585 + 560) x $.15/lb.	=	471.75
Total material cost	=	$9,545.95*

Labor:

$$\frac{2,585+560}{25} = 125.8 \; MH; 125.8 \; MH \cdot \$35.36 \qquad = \$4,448.29$$

Total installed cost: $9,545.95 + $4,448.29   = $13,994.24*

Sales tax not included.

Installed Ductwork Per Pound

Description	Craft@Hrs	Unit	Material $	Labor $	Equipment $	Total $

Installed ductwork per lb. (under 1,000 lbs.). Duct purchased from an independent fabrication shop, installed by this contractors' shop. Material price includes scrap, cleats, hangers, sealant, miscellaneous hardware, delivery and fabrication shop markups.

Description	Craft@Hrs	Unit	Material $	Labor $	Equipment $	Total $
Straight duct	S2@.042	Lb	2.84	1.43	—	4.27
Duct fittings	S2@.042	Lb	5.73	1.43	—	7.16
Duct & fittings	S2@.042	Lb	3.80	1.43	—	5.23

Installed ductwork per lb. (over 1,000 lbs.). Duct purchased from an independent fabrication shop, installed by this contractors' shop. Material price includes scrap, cleats, hangers, sealant, miscellaneous hardware, delivery and subcontractor markups.

Description	Craft@Hrs	Unit	Material $	Labor $	Equipment $	Total $
Straight duct	S2@.039	Lb	2.55	1.33	—	3.88
Duct fittings	S2@.039	Lb	5.14	1.33	—	6.47
Duct & fittings	S2@.039	Lb	3.43	1.33	—	4.76

Installed lined ductwork per lb. (under 1,000 lbs.). Duct purchased from an independent fabrication shop, installed by this contractors' shop. Material price includes scrap, cleats, hangers, sealant, miscellaneous hardware, delivery and subcontractor markups.

Description	Craft@Hrs	Unit	Material $	Labor $	Equipment $	Total $
Straight duct	S2@.042	Lb	4.36	1.43	—	5.79
Duct fittings	S2@.042	Lb	7.23	1.43	—	8.66
Duct & fittings	S2@.042	Lb	5.31	1.43	—	6.74

Installed lined ductwork per lb. (over 1,000 lbs.). Duct purchased from an independent fabrication shop, installed by this contractors' shop. Material price includes scrap, cleats, hangers, sealant, miscellaneous hardware, delivery and subcontractor markups.

Description	Craft@Hrs	Unit	Material $	Labor $	Equipment $	Total $
Straight duct	S2@.039	Lb	4.10	1.33	—	5.43
Duct fittings	S2@.039	Lb	6.70	1.33	—	8.03
Duct & fittings	S2@.039	Lb	4.94	1.33	—	6.27

Installed ductwork per lb. (under 1,000 lbs.). Duct fabricated and installed by this contractors' shop. Material price includes scrap, cleats, hangers, sealant, miscellaneous hardware and delivery.

Description	Craft@Hrs	Unit	Material $	Labor $	Equipment $	Total $
Straight duct	S2@.051	Lb	1.75	1.74	—	3.49
Duct fittings	S2@.074	Lb	2.00	2.53	—	4.53
Duct & fittings	S2@.059	Lb	1.84	2.02	—	3.86

Installed ductwork per lb. (over 1,000 lbs.). Duct fabricated and installed by this contractors' shop. Material price includes scrap, cleats, hangers, sealant, miscellaneous hardware and delivery.

Description	Craft@Hrs	Unit	Material $	Labor $	Equipment $	Total $
Straight duct	S2@.046	Lb	1.60	1.57	—	3.17
Duct fittings	S2@.067	Lb	1.85	2.29	—	4.14
Duct & fittings	S2@.053	Lb	1.67	1.81	—	3.48

Description	Craft@Hrs	Unit	Material $	Labor $	Equipment $	Total $

Installed lined ductwork per lb. (under 1,000 lbs.). Duct fabricated and installed by this contractors' shop. Material price includes scrap, cleats, hangers, sealant, miscellaneous hardware and delivery.

Description	Craft@Hrs	Unit	Material $	Labor $	Equipment $	Total $
Straight duct	S2@.062	Lb	2.57	2.12	—	4.69
Duct fittings	S2@.085	Lb	2.84	2.90	—	5.74
Duct & fittings	S2@.070	Lb	2.68	2.39	—	5.07

Installed lined ductwork per lb. (over 1,000 lbs.). Duct fabricated and installed by this contractors' shop. Material price includes scrap, cleats, hangers, sealant, miscellaneous hardware and delivery. Use for preliminary estimates.

Description	Craft@Hrs	Unit	Material $	Labor $	Equipment $	Total $
Straight duct	S2@.057	Lb	2.43	1.95	—	4.38
Duct fittings	S2@.078	Lb	2.72	2.66	—	5.38
Duct & fittings	S2@.064	Lb	4.41	2.19	—	6.60

Galvanized Steel Spiral Ductwork

Weights of Galvanized Steel Spiral Duct (pounds per LF)					
Diameter (inches)	U.S. Standard Gauge				
	26	24	22	20	18
3	.76	1.01	1.23	1.46	—
4	1.02	1.35	1.64	1.94	—
5	1.28	1.69	2.06	2.42	—
6	1.54	2.03	2.47	2.91	3.88
7	1.79	2.37	2.88	3.40	4.52
8	2.05	2.71	3.29	3.86	5.17
9	2.31	3.05	3.71	4.37	5.82
10	2.57	3.39	4.12	4.86	6.47
12	3.08	4.07	4.95	5.83	7.75
14	3.59	4.74	5.77	6.81	9.05
16	4.11	5.42	6.60	7.78	10.34
18	4.63	6.10	7.43	8.76	11.64
20	5.15	6.78	8.25	9.73	12.93
22	5.65	7.46	9.08	10.71	14.93
24	6.16	8.14	9.91	11.68	15.52
26	6.67	8.82	10.73	12.66	16.82
28	7.18	9.50	11.56	13.63	18.11
30	7.71	10.18	12.38	14.60	19.41
32	8.22	10.84	13.21	15.58	20.71
34	—	11.52	14.05	16.55	22.00
36	—	12.20	14.90	17.53	23.29

Weights of Galvanized Steel Round Spiral Fittings (pounds per piece)

Diameter (inches)	90° elbow	45° elbow	Coupling	Reducer
3	1.3	1.0	0.5	1.0
4	2.2	1.3	0.6	1.2
5	3.3	1.9	0.7	1.4
6	4.3	2.5	0.9	1.8
7	5.8	3.3	1.0	2.0
8	7.3	4.3	1.2	2.4
9	8.8	5.3	2.6	3.3
10	11.8	7.5	2.9	4.4
12	16.3	10.0	3.5	5.3
14	22.0	13.0	4.1	6.2
16	28.3	15.8	4.6	6.9
18	34.5	19.0	5.2	7.8
20	41.5	23.5	5.8	8.7
22	48.3	27.5	6.4	9.6
24	57.5	32.0	6.9	10.3
26	68.8	37.5	7.5	11.2
28	76.8	42.8	8.1	12.1
30	87.0	48.0	8.7	13.0
32	99.5	55.0	9.2	13.8
34	112.0	61.0	9.8	14.7
36	161.0	89.5	10.4	15.6

Weights of Galvanized Steel Round Spiral Fittings (pounds per piece)
Tee with reducing run and branch

Largest run diam. (inches)	Branch diameter (inches)													
	3	4	5	6	7	8	9	10	12	14	16	18	20	22
4	2.3													
5	2.8	3.0												
6	3.2	3.5	3.7											
7	3.7	3.9	4.1	4.5										
8	4.1	4.4	4.7	5.0	5.3									
9	4.5	4.8	5.1	5.5	5.8	6.2								
10	6.4	6.7	7.1	7.5	7.8	8.2	8.6							
12	7.7	8.1	8.5	8.9	9.4	9.9	10.3	10.7						
14	8.9	9.4	10.0	10.5	11.0	11.5	12.1	12.6	13.6					
16	10.2	10.8	11.4	12.0	12.5	13.1	13.7	14.3	15.5	16.7				
18	11.5	12.1	12.7	13.5	14.1	14.8	15.5	16.1	17.5	18.8	19.2			
20	12.7	13.4	14.2	14.9	17.7	16.4	17.2	17.9	19.4	20.9	22.4	23.9		
22	14.0	14.8	15.6	16.4	17.2	18.1	18.9	19.7	21.3	23.0	24.6	26.2	27.9	
24	15.3	16.1	17.0	17.8	18.7	19.6	20.5	21.4	23.2	25.0	26.8	28.5	30.3	32.1
26	16.5	17.5	18.5	19.5	20.4	21.3	22.3	23.3	25.2	26.2	29.1	31.1	33.0	34.9
28	17.7	18.7	19.8	20.8	21.9	22.9	23.9	25.0	27.0	29.2	31.2	33.2	35.4	37.4
30	18.9	20.0	21.1	22.2	23.3	24.5	25.5	26.7	28.9	31.1	33.3	35.5	37.7	40.0
32	20.4	21.6	22.6	24.0	25.2	26.4	27.6	28.8	31.2	33.6	36.0	38.4	40.8	42.2
34	21.6	22.9	24.2	25.4	26.7	28.0	29.3	30.5	33.1	35.6	38.1	40.7	42.2	45.6
36	29.6	31.4	33.1	34.8	36.6	38.6	40.1	41.8	45.3	48.8	52.2	55.7	59.2	62.7

Galvanized Steel Round Spiral Fittings

Run diam. (inches)	Weights of Galvanized Steel Round Spiral Fittings (pounds per piece) Cross with reducing run and branch — Branch diameter (inches)													
	3	4	5	6	7	8	9	10	12	14	16	18	20	22
4	2.6													
5	3.2	3.6												
6	3.8	4.2	4.6											
7	4.4	4.9	5.4	5.8										
8	4.9	5.4	6.0	6.5	7.0									
9	5.4	6.0	6.6	7.2	7.7	8.3								
10	7.6	8.2	8.9	9.5	10.2	10.8	11.4							
12	8.8	9.6	10.3	11.0	11.7	12.5	13.2	13.8						
14	10.1	10.9	11.7	12.6	13.4	14.2	15.1	15.9	17.5					
16	11.3	12.2	13.1	14.0	15.0	15.9	16.8	17.7	19.5	21.4				
18	12.5	13.5	14.5	15.5	16.5	17.5	18.5	19.5	21.5	23.5	25.5			
20	13.8	15.0	16.1	17.2	18.2	19.4	20.6	21.7	23.9	26.2	28.4	30.6		
22	15.2	16.4	17.7	18.9	20.1	21.4	22.6	23.8	26.2	28.7	31.2	33.6	36.1	
24	16.6	17.9	19.3	20.6	22.0	23.3	24.6	26.0	28.7	31.5	34.1	36.7	39.4	42.1
26	18.0	19.4	20.9	22.3	23.8	25.2	26.7	28.2	31.1	33.9	36.9	39.8	42.7	45.6
28	19.3	20.8	22.4	24.0	25.5	27.1	28.6	30.2	32.3	36.4	39.6	42.7	45.8	48.9
30	20.6	22.3	23.9	25.6	27.3	28.9	30.6	32.3	35.6	38.9	42.3	45.6	49.9	52.2
32	22.2	24.0	25.8	27.6	29.4	31.2	33.0	34.8	38.4	42.0	45.6	49.1	52.8	56.5
34	23.5	25.4	27.3	29.2	31.1	33.1	34.9	36.9	40.7	44.5	48.3	52.1	55.9	59.8
36	32.2	34.8	37.4	40.0	42.8	45.3	48.0	50.5	55.7	61.0	66.2	71.5	76.7	82.0

Weights of 26 Gauge Galvanized Steel Rectangular Duct (pounds per LF)									
Size (inches)	4	5	6	7	8	9	10	11	12
4	1.21								
5	1.36	1.51							
6	1.51	1.66	1.81						
7	1.66	1.81	1.96	2.11					
8	1.81	1.96	2.11	2.27	2.42				
9	1.96	2.11	2.27	2.42	2.57	2.72			
10	2.11	2.27	2.42	2.57	2.72	2.87	3.02		
11	2.27	2.42	2.57	2.72	2.87	3.02	3.17	3.32	
12	2.42	2.57	2.72	2.87	3.02	3.17	3.32	3.47	3.62

Weights of 24 Gauge Galvanized Steel Rectangular Duct (pounds per LF)									
Size (inches)	14	16	18	20	22	24	26	28	30
6	3.85	4.24	4.62	5.01	5.40	5.78	6.17	6.55	6.94
8	4.24	4.62	5.01	5.40	5.78	6.17	6.55	6.94	7.32
10	4.62	5.01	5.40	5.78	6.17	6.55	6.94	7.32	7.71
12	5.01	5.40	5.78	6.17	6.55	6.94	7.32	7.71	8.09
14	5.40	5.78	6.17	6.55	6.94	7.32	7.71	8.09	8.48
16	5.78	6.17	6.55	6.94	7.32	7.71	8.09	8.48	8.86
18	6.17	6.55	6.94	7.32	7.71	8.09	8.48	8.86	9.25
20	6.55	6.94	7.32	7.71	8.09	8.48	8.86	9.25	9.64
22	6.94	7.32	7.71	8.09	8.48	8.86	9.25	9.64	10.00
24	7.32	7.71	8.09	8.48	8.86	9.25	9.64	10.00	10.40
26	7.71	8.09	8.48	8.86	9.25	9.64	10.00	10.40	10.80
28	8.09	8.48	8.86	9.25	9.64	10.00	10.40	10.80	11.20
30	8.48	8.86	9.25	9.64	10.00	10.40	10.80	11.20	11.60

Weights of 22 Gauge Galvanized Steel Rectangular Duct (pounds per LF)											
Size (inches)	32	34	36	38	40	42	44	46	48	50	52	54
8	9.37	9.84	10.3	10.8	11.3	11.7	12.2	12.7	13.1	13.6	14.1	14.5
10	9.84	10.3	10.8	11.3	11.7	12.2	12.7	13.1	13.6	14.1	14.5	15.0
12	10.3	10.8	11.3	11.7	12.2	12.7	13.1	13.6	14.1	14.5	15.0	15.5
14	10.8	11.3	11.7	12.2	12.7	13.1	13.6	14.1	14.5	15.0	15.5	15.9
16	11.3	11.7	12.2	12.7	13.1	13.6	14.1	14.5	15.0	15.5	15.9	16.4
18	11.7	12.2	12.7	13.1	13.6	14.1	14.5	15.0	15.5	15.9	16.4	16.9
20	12.2	12.7	13.1	13.6	14.1	14.5	15.0	15.5	15.9	16.4	16.9	17.3
22	12.7	13.1	13.6	14.1	14.5	15.0	15.5	15.9	16.4	16.9	17.3	17.8
24	13.1	13.6	14.1	14.5	15.0	15.5	15.9	16.4	16.9	17.3	17.8	18.3
26	13.6	14.1	14.5	15.0	15.5	15.9	16.4	16.9	17.3	17.8	18.3	18.7
28	14.1	14.5	15.0	15.5	15.9	16.4	16.9	17.3	17.8	18.3	18.7	19.2
30	14.5	15.0	15.5	15.9	16.4	16.9	17.3	17.8	18.3	18.7	19.2	19.7
32	15.0	15.5	15.9	16.4	16.9	17.3	17.8	18.3	18.7	19.2	19.7	20.2
34	15.5	15.9	16.4	16.9	17.3	17.8	18.3	18.7	19.2	19.7	20.2	20.6
36	15.9	16.4	16.9	17.3	17.8	18.3	18.7	19.2	19.7	20.2	20.6	21.1
38	16.4	16.9	17.3	17.8	18.3	18.7	19.2	19.7	20.2	20.6	21.1	21.6
40	16.9	17.3	17.8	18.3	18.7	19.2	19.7	20.2	20.6	21.1	21.6	22.0
42	17.3	17.8	18.3	18.7	19.2	19.7	20.2	20.6	21.1	21.6	22.0	22.5
44	17.8	18.3	18.7	19.2	19.7	20.2	20.6	21.1	21.6	22.0	22.5	23.0
46	18.3	18.7	19.2	19.7	20.2	20.6	21.1	21.6	22.0	22.5	23.0	23.4
48	18.7	19.2	19.7	20.2	20.6	21.1	21.6	22.0	22.5	23.0	23.4	23.9
50	19.2	19.7	20.2	20.6	21.1	21.6	22.0	22.5	23.0	23.4	23.9	24.4
52	19.7	20.2	20.6	21.1	21.6	22.0	22.5	23.0	23.4	23.9	24.4	24.8
54	20.2	20.6	21.1	21.6	22.0	22.5	23.0	23.4	23.9	24.4	24.8	25.3

Galvanized Steel Rectangular Ductwork

Weights of 20 Gauge Galvanized Steel Rectangular Duct (pounds per LF)									
Size (inches)	56	58	60	62	64	66	68	70	72
18	20.4	21.0	21.5	22.1	22.6	23.2	23.7	24.3	24.8
20	21.0	21.5	22.1	22.6	23.2	23.7	24.3	24.8	25.4
22	21.5	22.1	22.6	23.2	23.7	24.3	24.8	25.4	25.9
24	22.1	22.6	23.2	23.7	24.3	24.8	25.4	25.9	26.5
26	22.6	23.2	23.7	24.3	24.8	25.4	25.9	26.5	27.0
28	23.2	23.7	24.3	24.8	25.4	25.9	26.5	27.0	27.6
30	23.7	24.3	24.8	25.4	25.9	26.5	27.0	27.6	28.2
32	24.3	24.8	25.4	25.9	26.5	27.0	27.6	28.2	28.7
34	24.8	25.4	25.9	26.5	27.0	27.6	28.2	28.7	29.3
36	25.4	25.9	26.5	27.0	27.6	28.2	28.7	29.3	29.8
38	25.9	26.5	27.0	27.6	28.2	28.7	29.3	29.8	30.4
40	26.5	27.0	27.6	28.2	28.7	29.3	29.8	30.4	30.9
42	27.0	27.6	28.2	28.7	29.3	29.8	30.4	30.9	31.5
44	27.6	28.2	28.7	29.3	29.8	30.4	30.9	31.5	32.0
46	28.2	28.7	29.3	29.8	30.4	30.9	31.5	32.0	32.6
48	28.7	29.3	29.8	30.4	30.9	31.5	32.0	32.6	33.1
50	29.3	29.8	30.4	30.9	31.5	32.0	32.6	33.1	33.7
52	29.8	30.4	30.9	31.5	32.0	32.6	33.1	33.7	34.2
54	30.4	30.9	31.5	32.0	32.6	33.1	33.7	34.2	34.8
56	30.9	31.5	32.0	32.6	33.1	33.7	34.2	34.8	35.3
58	31.5	32.0	32.6	33.1	33.7	34.2	34.8	35.3	35.9
60	32.0	32.6	33.1	33.7	34.2	34.8	35.3	35.9	36.4
62	32.6	33.1	33.7	34.2	34.8	35.3	35.9	36.4	37.0
64	33.1	33.7	34.2	34.8	35.3	35.9	36.4	37.0	37.5
66	33.7	34.2	34.8	35.3	35.9	36.4	37.0	37.5	38.1
68	34.2	34.8	35.3	35.9	36.4	37.0	37.5	38.1	38.6
70	34.8	35.3	35.9	36.4	37.0	37.5	38.1	38.6	39.2
72	35.3	35.9	36.4	37.0	37.5	38.1	38.6	39.2	39.7

Size (inches)	4	6	8	10	12	14	16	18	20
4	1.05	1.45	1.95	2.60	3.30	5.30	6.50	7.80	9.25
6	1.45	1.95	2.60	3.30	3.70	5.80	7.75	8.75	9.75
8	1.95	2.60	3.30	3.70	4.25	6.50	8.50	9.75	10.4
10	2.60	3.30	3.70	4.25	4.85	7.30	9.50	10.7	11.2
12	3.30	3.70	4.25	4.85	5.60	8.20	10.5	11.7	12.2
14	5.30	5.80	6.50	7.30	8.20	9.25	11.5	12.6	13.2
16	6.50	7.50	8.50	9.50	10.5	11.5	12.5	13.4	14.4
18	7.80	8.75	9.75	10.7	11.7	12.6	13.4	14.5	15.7
20	9.25	9.75	10.4	11.2	12.2	13.8	14.4	15.7	17.2
22	10.8	11.8	12.8	13.8	14.8	25.8	16.8	17.8	18.8
24	12.6	13.6	14.6	15.6	16.6	17.6	18.6	19.6	20.5
26	14.4	15.4	16.4	17.4	18.4	19.4	20.4	21.4	22.3
28	16.4	17.4	18.4	19.4	20.4	21.4	22.4	23.4	24.3
30	18.5	19.5	20.5	21.5	22.5	23.5	24.5	25.5	26.4
32	24.3	25.7	27.0	28.4	29.7	31.1	32.4	33.7	35.0
34	28.2	29.4	30.6	31.8	33.0	34.3	35.5	36.7	37.9
36	31.3	32.5	33.7	34.9	36.1	37.3	38.5	39.7	40.9
38	34.5	35.7	36.9	38.1	39.3	40.5	41.7	42.9	44.1
40	37.9	39.1	40.3	41.5	42.7	43.9	45.1	46.3	47.5
42	41.4	42.6	43.8	45.0	46.2	47.4	48.6	49.8	51.0
44	45.1	46.4	47.6	48.8	50.0	51.2	52.4	53.6	54.8
46	49.0	50.2	51.4	52.6	53.8	55.0	56.2	57.4	58.6
48	53.0	54.2	55.4	56.6	57.8	59.0	60.2	61.4	62.6
50	57.2	58.5	59.7	60.9	62.1	63.3	64.5	65.7	66.9

Weights of Galvanized Steel Rectangular 90 Degree Elbow (pounds per piece)

Note: Elbow weights do not include turning vanes.

Galvanized Steel Rectangular 90 Degree Elbows

Size (inches)	22	24	26	28	30	32	34	36	38
Weights of Galvanized Steel Rectangular 90 Degree Elbows (pounds per piece)									
22	19.6	21.9	24.1	26.3	28.5	37.0	40.8	44.5	48.3
24	21.9	24.2	26.4	28.6	30.9	39.5	43.6	47.2	50.8
26	24.1	26.4	28.7	30.9	33.2	42.0	46.4	49.8	53.3
28	26.3	28.6	30.9	33.3	35.6	44.5	49.2	52.5	55.8
30	28.5	30.9	33.2	35.6	37.9	47.0	52.0	55.1	58.3
32	37.0	39.5	42.0	44.5	47.0	49.5	52.0	57.8	60.8
34	40.8	43.6	46.4	49.2	52.0	54.8	57.6	60.5	63.3
36	44.5	47.2	49.8	52.5	55.1	57.8	60.5	63.1	65.8
38	48.3	50.8	53.3	55.8	58.3	60.8	63.3	65.8	68.3
40	52.1	54.6	57.1	59.6	62.1	64.6	67.1	69.6	72.1
42	55.9	58.4	60.9	63.4	65.9	68.4	70.9	73.4	75.9
44	59.6	62.1	64.6	67.1	69.6	72.1	74.6	77.1	79.6
46	63.4	65.9	68.4	70.9	73.4	75.9	78.4	80.9	83.4
48	67.2	69.7	72.2	74.7	77.2	79.7	82.2	84.7	87.2
50	70.9	73.4	75.9	78.4	80.9	83.4	85.9	88.4	90.9
52	74.8	77.3	79.8	82.3	84.8	87.3	89.8	92.3	94.7
54	78.5	81.0	83.5	86.0	88.5	91.0	93.5	96.0	98.5
56	97.2	100	103	106	109	112	115	118	121
58	103	106	109	112	115	118	121	124	127
60	110	113	116	119	122	125	128	131	134
62	116	119	122	125	128	131	134	137	140
64	122	125	129	132	135	138	141	144	147
66	128	131	135	138	141	144	148	151	154
68	135	138	142	145	148	151	154	157	160
70	141	144	148	151	154	157	160	163	166
72	147	150	154	157	160	163	166	169	172

Note: Elbow weights do not include turning vanes.

Size (inches)	40	42	44	46	48	50	52	54	56
Weights of Galvanized Steel Rectangular 90 Degree Elbows (pounds per piece)									
40	74.6	78.4	82.1	85.9	89.7	93.4	97.2	102	125
42	78.4	82.3	86.2	90.1	94.0	97.9	102	106	130
44	82.1	86.2	90.3	94.4	98.5	102	106	110	135
46	85.9	90.1	94.4	98.7	102	106	110	113	140
48	89.7	94.0	98.5	102	106	110	113	117	144
50	93.4	97.9	102	106	110	113	117	122	149
52	97.2	102	106	110	113	117	122	126	154
54	102	106	110	113	117	122	126	131	159
56	126	130	134	139	145	150	155	160	165
58	132	137	142	147	151	156	161	166	170
60	137	142	147	152	157	162	167	172	176
62	143	148	153	158	163	168	173	178	182
64	150	155	160	165	169	174	179	184	188
66	156	161	166	171	176	181	186	191	195
68	163	168	173	178	182	187	192	197	201
70	170	175	180	185	189	194	199	204	208
72	176	181	185	190	194	199	204	210	215

Note: Elbow weights do not include turning vanes.

Weights of Galvanized Steel Rectangular 90 Degree Elbows (pounds per piece)

Size (inches)	58	60	62	64	66	68	70	72
58	176	182	187	194	200	207	214	221
60	182	187	194	200	207	214	221	227
62	187	194	200	207	214	221	227	233
64	194	200	207	214	221	227	233	239
66	200	207	214	221	227	233	239	246
68	207	214	221	227	233	239	246	252
70	214	221	227	233	239	246	252	259
72	221	227	233	239	246	252	259	266

Note: Elbow weights do not include turning vanes.

Weights of Galvanized Steel Rectangular Drops and Tap-In Tees (pounds per piece)

Size (inches)	6	8	10	12	16	20	24	28	32
6	1.81	2.11	2.42	2.72	4.24	5.01	5.78	6.55	8.90
8	2.11	2.42	2.72	3.02	4.62	5.40	6.17	6.94	9.37
10	2.42	2.72	3.02	3.32	5.01	5.78	6.55	7.32	9.84
12	2.72	3.02	3.32	3.62	5.40	6.17	6.94	7.71	10.3
16	4.24	4.62	5.01	5.40	6.17	6.94	7.71	8.48	11.3
20	5.01	5.40	5.78	6.17	6.94	7.71	8.48	9.25	12.2
24	5.78	6.17	6.55	6.94	7.71	8.48	9.25	10.0	13.1
28	6.55	6.94	7.32	7.71	8.48	9.25	10.0	10.8	14.1
32	8.90	9.37	9.84	10.3	11.3	12.2	13.1	14.1	15.0
36	9.84	10.3	10.8	11.3	12.2	13.1	14.1	15.0	15.9
40	10.8	11.3	11.7	12.2	13.1	14.1	15.0	15.9	16.9
44	11.7	12.2	12.7	13.1	14.1	15.0	15.9	16.9	17.8
48	12.7	13.1	13.6	14.1	15.0	15.9	16.9	17.8	18.7
52	13.6	14.1	14.5	15.0	15.9	16.9	17.8	18.7	19.7
56	16.0	17.6	18.2	18.8	19.6	21.0	22.1	23.2	24.3
60	18.7	19.0	19.3	19.9	21.0	22.1	23.2	24.3	25.4

Note: Weights of drops and tap-in tees do not include splitter dampers.

Galvanized Steel Spiral Duct

Costs for Steel Spiral Duct. Costs per linear foot of duct, based on quantities less than 1,000 pounds. Add 50% to the material cost for lined duct. These costs include delivery, typical bracing, cleats, scrap, hangers, end closures, sealants and miscellaneous hardware.

Description	Craft@Hrs	Unit	Material $	Labor $	Equipment $	Total $

Galvanized steel spiral duct 26 gauge

Description	Craft@Hrs	Unit	Material $	Labor $	Equipment $	Total $
3"	S2@.030	LF	2.35	1.02	—	3.37
4"	S2@.041	LF	3.19	1.40	—	4.59
5"	S2@.051	LF	4.00	1.74	—	5.74
6"	S2@.061	LF	4.76	2.08	—	6.84
7"	S2@.072	LF	5.53	2.46	—	7.99
8"	S2@.082	LF	6.35	2.80	—	9.15
9"	S2@.092	LF	7.16	3.14	—	10.30
10"	S2@.103	LF	7.94	3.52	—	11.46
12"	S2@.123	LF	9.49	4.20	—	13.69
14" - 16"	S2@.174	LF	11.90	5.94	—	17.84
18" - 20"	S2@.195	LF	15.20	6.66	—	21.86
22" - 24"	S2@.236	LF	18.30	8.06	—	26.36
26" - 28"	S2@.277	LF	21.60	9.46	—	31.06
30" - 32"	S2@.318	LF	24.80	10.90	—	35.70

Galvanized steel spiral duct 24 gauge

Description	Craft@Hrs	Unit	Material $	Labor $	Equipment $	Total $
3"	S2@.041	LF	3.18	1.40	—	4.58
4"	S2@.054	LF	4.16	1.84	—	6.00
5"	S2@.067	LF	5.21	2.29	—	7.50
6"	S2@.081	LF	6.28	2.77	—	9.05
7"	S2@.095	LF	7.29	3.25	—	10.54
8"	S2@.108	LF	8.39	3.69	—	12.08
9"	S2@.122	LF	9.45	4.17	—	13.62
10"	S2@.135	LF	10.50	4.61	—	15.11
12"	S2@.163	LF	12.50	5.57	—	18.07
14" - 16"	S2@.203	LF	15.60	6.93	—	22.53
18" - 20"	S2@.257	LF	19.90	8.78	—	28.68
22" - 24"	S2@.312	LF	24.10	10.70	—	34.80
26" - 28"	S2@.366	LF	28.40	12.50	—	40.90
30" - 32"	S2@.419	LF	32.50	14.30	—	46.80
34" - 36"	S2@.474	LF	37.10	16.20	—	53.30

Description	Craft@Hrs	Unit	Material $	Labor $	Equipment $	Total $

Galvanized steel spiral duct 22 gauge

Description	Craft@Hrs	Unit	Material $	Labor $	Equipment $	Total $
3"	S2@.049	LF	3.84	1.67	—	5.51
4"	S2@.065	LF	5.09	2.22	—	7.31
5"	S2@.082	LF	6.41	2.80	—	9.21
6"	S2@.099	LF	7.62	3.38	—	11.00
7"	S2@.115	LF	8.90	3.93	—	12.83
8"	S2@.132	LF	10.10	4.51	—	14.61
9"	S2@.148	LF	11.40	5.06	—	16.46
10"	S2@.165	LF	12.80	5.64	—	18.44
12"	S2@.198	LF	15.40	6.76	—	22.16
14" - 16"	S2@.247	LF	19.00	8.44	—	27.44
18" - 20"	S2@.313	LF	24.30	10.70	—	35.00
22" - 24"	S2@.380	LF	29.30	13.00	—	42.30
26" - 28"	S2@.444	LF	34.70	15.20	—	49.90
30" - 32"	S2@.491	LF	39.90	16.80	—	56.70
34" - 36"	S2@.576	LF	45.20	19.70	—	64.90

Galvanized steel spiral duct 20 gauge

Description	Craft@Hrs	Unit	Material $	Labor $	Equipment $	Total $
3"	S2@.058	LF	4.55	1.98	—	6.53
4"	S2@.078	LF	6.04	2.66	—	8.70
5"	S2@.097	LF	7.50	3.31	—	10.81
6"	S2@.116	LF	9.01	3.96	—	12.97
7"	S2@.136	LF	10.50	4.65	—	15.15
8"	S2@.154	LF	12.00	5.26	—	17.26
9"	S2@.175	LF	13.40	5.98	—	19.38
10"	S2@.194	LF	15.10	6.63	—	21.73
12"	S2@.233	LF	18.20	7.96	—	26.16
14" - 16"	S2@.291	LF	22.30	9.94	—	32.24
18" - 20"	S2@.369	LF	28.60	12.60	—	41.20
22" - 24"	S2@.446	LF	34.70	15.20	—	49.90
26" - 28"	S2@.525	LF	40.80	17.90	—	58.70
30" - 32"	S2@.604	LF	46.50	20.60	—	67.10
34" - 36"	S2@.681	LF	52.60	23.30	—	75.90

Galvanized steel spiral duct 18 gauge

Description	Craft@Hrs	Unit	Material $	Labor $	Equipment $	Total $
6"	S2@.155	LF	12.00	5.29	—	17.29
7"	S2@.181	LF	14.00	6.18	—	20.18
8"	S2@.207	LF	15.80	7.07	—	22.87
9"	S2@.233	LF	18.00	7.96	—	25.96
10"	S2@.259	LF	19.90	8.85	—	28.75
12"	S2@.310	LF	24.10	10.60	—	34.70
14" - 16"	S2@.387	LF	30.00	13.20	—	43.20
18" - 20"	S2@.491	LF	38.30	16.80	—	55.10
22" - 24"	S2@.608	LF	46.90	20.80	—	67.70
26" - 28"	S2@.696	LF	53.90	23.80	—	77.70
30" - 32"	S2@.803	LF	62.00	27.40	—	89.40
34" - 36"	S2@.905	LF	70.10	30.90	—	101.00

Galvanized Steel Spiral Duct Fittings

Costs for Steel Spiral Duct Fittings. Costs per fitting, based on quantities less than 1,000 pounds. For quantities over 1,000 pounds, deduct 15% from material costs. For lined duct add 50%. These costs include delivery, typical bracing, cleats, scrap, hangers, end closures, sealants and miscellaneous hardware.

Description	Craft@Hrs	Unit	Material $	Labor $	Equipment $	Total $

Galvanized steel spiral duct 90 degree elbows

Description	Craft@Hrs	Unit	Material $	Labor $	Equipment $	Total $
3"	S2@.052	Ea	2.90	1.78	—	4.68
4"	S2@.088	Ea	4.90	3.01	—	7.91
5"	S2@.132	Ea	7.35	4.51	—	11.86
6"	S2@.172	Ea	9.65	5.88	—	15.53
7"	S2@.232	Ea	13.00	7.93	—	20.93
8"	S2@.292	Ea	16.50	9.97	—	26.47
9"	S2@.352	Ea	19.80	12.00	—	31.80
10"	S2@.470	Ea	26.40	16.10	—	42.50
12"	S2@.653	Ea	36.50	22.30	—	58.80
14" - 16"	S2@1.01	Ea	56.00	34.50	—	90.50
18" - 20"	S2@1.52	Ea	84.70	51.90	—	136.60
22" - 24"	S2@2.11	Ea	118.00	72.10	—	190.10
26" - 28"	S2@2.91	Ea	165.00	99.40	—	264.40
30" - 32"	S2@3.73	Ea	209.00	127.00	—	336.00
34" - 36"	S2@5.47	Ea	305.00	187.00	—	492.00

Galvanized steel spiral duct 45 degree elbows

Description	Craft@Hrs	Unit	Material $	Labor $	Equipment $	Total $
3"	S2@.040	Ea	2.23	1.37	—	3.60
4"	S2@.052	Ea	2.90	1.78	—	4.68
5"	S2@.076	Ea	4.24	2.60	—	6.84
6"	S2@.100	Ea	5.60	3.42	—	9.02
7"	S2@.132	Ea	7.35	4.51	—	11.86
8"	S2@.172	Ea	9.65	5.88	—	15.53
9"	S2@.212	Ea	11.80	7.24	—	19.04
10"	S2@.300	Ea	16.70	10.20	—	26.90
12"	S2@.400	Ea	22.30	13.70	—	36.00
14" - 16"	S2@.576	Ea	32.00	19.70	—	51.70
18" - 20"	S2@.850	Ea	47.50	29.00	—	76.50
22" - 24"	S2@1.19	Ea	66.30	40.70	—	107.00
26" - 28"	S2@1.61	Ea	89.90	55.00	—	144.90
30" - 32"	S2@2.06	Ea	116.00	70.40	—	186.40
34" - 36"	S2@3.01	Ea	168.00	103.00	—	271.00

Description	Craft@Hrs	Unit	Material $	Labor $	Equipment $	Total $

Galvanized steel spiral duct coupling

Description	Craft@Hrs	Unit	Material $	Labor $	Equipment $	Total $
3"	S2@.020	Ea	2.22	.68	—	2.90
4"	S2@.024	Ea	2.72	.82	—	3.54
5"	S2@.028	Ea	3.10	.96	—	4.06
6"	S2@.036	Ea	4.00	1.23	—	5.23
7"	S2@.040	Ea	4.48	1.37	—	5.85
8"	S2@.048	Ea	5.36	1.64	—	7.00
9"	S2@.104	Ea	11.60	3.55	—	15.15
10"	S2@.116	Ea	13.00	3.96	—	16.96
12"	S2@.140	Ea	15.60	4.78	—	20.38
14" - 16"	S2@.174	Ea	19.60	5.94	—	25.54
18" - 20"	S2@.220	Ea	24.20	7.52	—	31.72
22" - 24"	S2@.266	Ea	29.70	9.09	—	38.79
26" - 28"	S2@.312	Ea	34.80	10.70	—	45.50
30" - 32"	S2@.357	Ea	40.00	12.20	—	52.20
34" - 36"	S2@.403	Ea	45.10	13.80	—	58.90

Galvanized steel spiral duct with reducer

Description	Craft@Hrs	Unit	Material $	Labor $	Equipment $	Total $
3"	S2@.040	Ea	4.48	1.37	—	5.85
4"	S2@.048	Ea	5.36	1.64	—	7.00
5"	S2@.056	Ea	6.26	1.91	—	8.17
6"	S2@.072	Ea	8.07	2.46	—	10.53
7"	S2@.080	Ea	8.90	2.73	—	11.63
8"	S2@.096	Ea	10.70	3.28	—	13.98
9"	S2@.132	Ea	14.70	4.51	—	19.21
10"	S2@.176	Ea	19.60	6.01	—	25.61
12"	S2@.212	Ea	23.70	7.24	—	30.94
14" - 16"	S2@.262	Ea	29.30	8.95	—	38.25
18" - 20"	S2@.330	Ea	37.00	11.30	—	48.30
22" - 24"	S2@.398	Ea	44.40	13.60	—	58.00
26" - 28"	S2@.465	Ea	52.00	15.90	—	67.90
30" - 32"	S2@.536	Ea	59.50	18.30	—	77.80
34" - 36"	S2@.606	Ea	67.50	20.70	—	88.20

Galvanized Steel Spiral Tees

Costs for Steel Spiral Tees with Reducing Branch. Costs per tee, based on quantities less than 1,000 pounds. Deduct 15% from the material cost for quantities over 1,000 pounds. Add 50% to the material cost for lined duct. These costs include delivery, typical bracing, cleats, scrap, hangers, end closures, sealants and miscellaneous hardware.

Description	Craft@Hrs	Unit	Material $	Labor $	Equipment $	Total $
Galvanized steel spiral duct tees with 3" reducing branch						
4"	S2@.109	Ea	9.96	3.72	—	13.68
5"	S2@.112	Ea	11.70	3.83	—	15.53
6"	S2@.128	Ea	13.40	4.37	—	17.77
7"	S2@.148	Ea	15.20	5.06	—	20.26
8"	S2@.164	Ea	17.10	5.60	—	22.70
9"	S2@.180	Ea	18.20	6.15	—	24.35
10"	S2@.256	Ea	28.70	8.74	—	37.44
12"	S2@.308	Ea	34.10	10.50	—	44.60
14" - 16"	S2@.382	Ea	43.10	13.00	—	56.10
18" - 20"	S2@.485	Ea	54.10	16.60	—	70.70
22" - 24"	S2@.585	Ea	65.30	20.00	—	85.30
26" - 28"	S2@.683	Ea	76.20	23.30	—	99.50
30" - 32"	S2@.786	Ea	87.90	26.80	—	114.70
34" - 36"	S2@1.02	Ea	114.00	34.80	—	148.80
Galvanized steel spiral duct tees with 4" reducing branch						
5"	S2@.120	Ea	12.90	4.10	—	17.00
6"	S2@.140	Ea	15.20	4.78	—	19.98
7"	S2@.156	Ea	16.50	5.33	—	21.83
8"	S2@.176	Ea	18.70	6.01	—	24.71
9"	S2@.192	Ea	19.90	6.56	—	26.46
10"	S2@.268	Ea	30.40	9.15	—	39.55
12"	S2@.324	Ea	37.00	11.10	—	48.10
14" - 16"	S2@.403	Ea	45.90	13.80	—	59.70
18" - 20"	S2@.508	Ea	57.90	17.40	—	75.30
22" - 24"	S2@.619	Ea	70.30	21.10	—	91.40
26" - 28"	S2@.724	Ea	82.40	24.70	—	107.10
30" - 32"	S2@.830	Ea	94.40	28.40	—	122.80
34" - 36"	S2@1.08	Ea	123.00	36.90	—	159.90
Galvanized steel spiral duct tees with 5" reducing branch						
6"	S2@.148	Ea	16.50	5.06	—	21.56
7"	S2@.164	Ea	18.20	5.60	—	23.80
8"	S2@.188	Ea	20.50	6.42	—	26.92
9"	S2@.204	Ea	22.20	6.97	—	29.17
10"	S2@.284	Ea	33.00	9.70	—	42.70
12"	S2@.340	Ea	39.30	11.60	—	50.90
14" - 16"	S2@.428	Ea	49.40	14.60	—	64.00
18" - 20"	S2@.538	Ea	62.80	18.40	—	81.20
22" - 24"	S2@.651	Ea	75.00	22.20	—	97.20
26" - 28"	S2@.764	Ea	88.00	26.10	—	114.10
30" - 32"	S2@.873	Ea	102.00	29.80	—	131.80
34" - 36"	S2@1.15	Ea	132.00	39.30	—	171.30

Description	Craft@Hrs	Unit	Material $	Labor $	Equipment $	Total $

Galvanized steel spiral duct tees with 6" reducing branch

Description	Craft@Hrs	Unit	Material $	Labor $	Equipment $	Total $
7"	S2@.180	Ea	20.50	6.15	—	26.65
8"	S2@.200	Ea	22.20	6.83	—	29.03
9"	S2@.220	Ea	24.00	7.52	—	31.52
10"	S2@.300	Ea	35.30	10.20	—	45.50
12"	S2@.356	Ea	42.20	12.20	—	54.40
14" - 16"	S2@.449	Ea	52.70	15.30	—	68.00
18" - 20"	S2@.566	Ea	66.70	19.30	—	86.00
22" - 24"	S2@.683	Ea	80.10	23.30	—	103.40
26" - 28"	S2@.807	Ea	94.10	27.60	—	121.70
30" - 32"	S2@.924	Ea	109.00	31.60	—	140.60
34" - 36"	S2@1.20	Ea	141.00	41.00	—	182.00

Galvanized steel spiral duct tees with 7" reducing branch

Description	Craft@Hrs	Unit	Material $	Labor $	Equipment $	Total $
8"	S2@.164	Ea	24.00	5.60	—	29.60
9"	S2@.180	Ea	26.20	6.15	—	32.35
10"	S2@.252	Ea	37.00	8.61	—	45.61
12"	S2@.304	Ea	44.80	10.40	—	55.20
14" - 16"	S2@.381	Ea	56.10	13.00	—	69.10
18" - 20"	S2@.482	Ea	70.30	16.50	—	86.80
22" - 24"	S2@.579	Ea	84.70	19.80	—	104.50
26" - 28"	S2@.683	Ea	101.00	23.30	—	124.30
30" - 32"	S2@.784	Ea	114.00	26.80	—	140.80
34" - 36"	S2@1.02	Ea	150.00	34.80	—	184.80

Galvanized steel spiral duct tees with 8" reducing branch

Description	Craft@Hrs	Unit	Material $	Labor $	Equipment $	Total $
9"	S2@.228	Ea	33.60	7.79	—	41.39
10"	S2@.268	Ea	39.30	9.15	—	48.45
12"	S2@.324	Ea	47.30	11.10	—	58.40
14" - 16"	S2@.401	Ea	58.90	13.70	—	72.60
18" - 20"	S2@.508	Ea	74.60	17.40	—	92.00
22" - 24"	S2@.617	Ea	90.30	21.10	—	111.40
26" - 28"	S2@.722	Ea	106.00	24.70	—	130.70
30" - 32"	S2@.830	Ea	121.00	28.40	—	149.40
34" - 36"	S2@1.08	Ea	157.00	36.90	—	193.90

Galvanized steel spiral duct tees with 9" reducing branch

Description	Craft@Hrs	Unit	Material $	Labor $	Equipment $	Total $
10"	S2@.284	Ea	41.90	9.70	—	51.60
12"	S2@.340	Ea	49.70	11.60	—	61.30
14" - 16"	S2@.426	Ea	62.80	14.60	—	77.40
18" - 20"	S2@.540	Ea	78.70	18.40	—	97.10
22" - 24"	S2@.649	Ea	94.90	22.20	—	117.10
26" - 28"	S2@.760	Ea	111.00	26.00	—	137.00
30" - 32"	S2@.875	Ea	129.00	29.90	—	158.90
34" - 36"	S2@1.15	Ea	167.00	39.30	—	206.30

Galvanized Steel Spiral Tees

Description	Craft@Hrs	Unit	Material $	Labor $	Equipment $	Total $
Galvanized steel spiral duct tees with 10" reducing branch						
12"	S2@.360	Ea	52.70	12.30	—	65.00
14" - 16"	S2@.447	Ea	65.30	15.30	—	80.60
18" - 20"	S2@.564	Ea	82.90	19.30	—	102.20
22" - 24"	S2@.683	Ea	101.00	23.30	—	124.30
26" - 28"	S2@.805	Ea	118.00	27.50	—	145.50
30" - 32"	S2@.924	Ea	134.00	31.60	—	165.60
34" - 36"	S2@1.20	Ea	177.00	41.00	—	218.00
Galvanized steel spiral duct tees with 12" reducing branch						
14" - 16"	S2@.572	Ea	72.10	19.50	—	91.60
18" - 20"	S2@.681	Ea	91.10	23.30	—	114.40
22" - 24"	S2@.820	Ea	110.00	28.00	—	138.00
26" - 28"	S2@.965	Ea	129.00	33.00	—	162.00
30" - 32"	S2@1.11	Ea	149.00	37.90	—	186.90
34" - 36"	S2@1.44	Ea	196.00	49.20	—	245.20
Galvanized steel spiral duct tees with 14" reducing branch						
14" - 16"	S2@.572	Ea	83.60	19.50	—	103.10
18" - 20"	S2@.681	Ea	99.60	23.30	—	122.90
22" - 24"	S2@.820	Ea	120.00	28.00	—	148.00
26" - 28"	S2@.965	Ea	141.00	33.00	—	174.00
30" - 32"	S2@1.11	Ea	163.00	37.90	—	200.90
34" - 36"	S2@1.44	Ea	213.00	49.20	—	262.20
Galvanized steel spiral duct tees with 16" reducing branch						
18" - 20"	S2@.739	Ea	109.00	25.20	—	134.20
22" - 24"	S2@.888	Ea	131.00	30.30	—	161.30
26" - 28"	S2@1.04	Ea	153.00	35.50	—	188.50
30" - 32"	S2@1.20	Ea	175.00	41.00	—	216.00
34" - 36"	S2@1.56	Ea	230.00	53.30	—	283.30
Galvanized steel spiral duct tees with 18" reducing branch						
18" - 20"	S2@.837	Ea	122.00	28.60	—	150.60
22" - 24"	S2@.954	Ea	140.00	32.60	—	172.60
26" - 28"	S2@1.12	Ea	165.00	38.30	—	203.30
30" - 32"	S2@1.29	Ea	189.00	44.10	—	233.10
34" - 36"	S2@1.68	Ea	249.00	57.40	—	306.40
Galvanized steel spiral duct tees with 20" reducing branch						
22" - 24"	S2@1.02	Ea	151.00	34.80	—	185.80
26" - 28"	S2@1.20	Ea	177.00	41.00	—	218.00
30" - 32"	S2@1.38	Ea	202.00	47.10	—	249.10
34" - 36"	S2@1.81	Ea	265.00	61.80	—	326.80
Galvanized steel spiral duct tees with 22" reducing branch						
22" - 24"	S2@1.57	Ea	167.00	53.60	—	220.60
26" - 28"	S2@1.32	Ea	196.00	45.10	—	241.10
30" - 32"	S2@1.48	Ea	217.00	50.60	—	267.60
34" - 36"	S2@1.92	Ea	285.00	65.60	—	350.60

Costs for Steel Spiral Tees with Reducing Run and Branch. Costs per tee, based on quantities less than 1,000 pounds. Deduct 15% from the material cost for quantities over 1,000 pounds. Add 50% to the material cost for lined duct. These costs include delivery, typical bracing, cleats, scrap, hangers, end closures, sealants and miscellaneous hardware.

Description	Craft@Hrs	Unit	Material $	Labor $	Equipment $	Total $

Galvanized steel spiral duct tees with 3" run and branch

Description	Craft@Hrs	Unit	Material $	Labor $	Equipment $	Total $
4"	S2@.109	Ea	16.20	3.72	—	19.92
5"	S2@.112	Ea	16.50	3.83	—	20.33
6"	S2@.128	Ea	18.70	4.37	—	23.07
7"	S2@.148	Ea	21.70	5.06	—	26.76
8"	S2@.164	Ea	24.00	5.60	—	29.60
9"	S2@.180	Ea	26.20	6.15	—	32.35
10"	S2@.256	Ea	37.70	8.74	—	46.44
12"	S2@.308	Ea	45.00	10.50	—	55.50
14" - 16"	S2@.382	Ea	56.10	13.00	—	69.10
18" - 20"	S2@.485	Ea	70.80	16.60	—	87.40
22" - 24"	S2@.585	Ea	85.90	20.00	—	105.90
26" - 28"	S2@.683	Ea	101.00	23.30	—	124.30
30" - 32"	S2@.786	Ea	116.00	26.80	—	142.80
34" - 36"	S2@1.02	Ea	150.00	34.80	—	184.80

Galvanized steel spiral duct tees with 4" run and branch

Description	Craft@Hrs	Unit	Material $	Labor $	Equipment $	Total $
5"	S2@.120	Ea	17.50	4.10	—	21.60
6"	S2@.140	Ea	20.50	4.78	—	25.28
7"	S2@.156	Ea	23.00	5.33	—	28.33
8"	S2@.176	Ea	25.60	6.01	—	31.61
9"	S2@.192	Ea	27.90	6.56	—	34.46
10"	S2@.268	Ea	39.30	9.15	—	48.45
12"	S2@.324	Ea	47.30	11.10	—	58.40
14" - 16"	S2@.403	Ea	59.20	13.80	—	73.00
18" - 20"	S2@.508	Ea	74.60	17.40	—	92.00
22" - 24"	S2@.619	Ea	90.40	21.10	—	111.50
26" - 28"	S2@.724	Ea	106.00	24.70	—	130.70
30" - 32"	S2@.830	Ea	121.00	28.40	—	149.40
34" - 36"	S2@1.08	Ea	158.00	36.90	—	194.90

Galvanized steel spiral duct tees with 5" run and branch

Description	Craft@Hrs	Unit	Material $	Labor $	Equipment $	Total $
6"	S2@.148	Ea	21.70	5.06	—	26.76
7"	S2@.164	Ea	24.00	5.60	—	29.60
8"	S2@.188	Ea	27.50	6.42	—	33.92
9"	S2@.204	Ea	29.90	6.97	—	36.87
10"	S2@.284	Ea	41.90	9.70	—	51.60
12"	S2@.340	Ea	49.70	11.60	—	61.30
14" - 16"	S2@.428	Ea	62.80	14.60	—	77.40
18" - 20"	S2@.538	Ea	78.50	18.40	—	96.90
22" - 24"	S2@.651	Ea	95.70	22.20	—	117.90
26" - 28"	S2@.764	Ea	112.00	26.10	—	138.10
30" - 32"	S2@.873	Ea	129.00	29.80	—	158.80
34" - 36"	S2@1.15	Ea	167.00	39.30	—	206.30

Galvanized Steel Spiral Tees

Description	Craft@Hrs	Unit	Material $	Labor $	Equipment $	Total $

Galvanized steel spiral duct tees with 6" run and branch

Description	Craft@Hrs	Unit	Material $	Labor $	Equipment $	Total $
7"	S2@.180	Ea	26.20	6.15	—	32.35
8"	S2@.200	Ea	29.20	6.83	—	36.03
9"	S2@.220	Ea	31.90	7.52	—	39.42
10"	S2@.300	Ea	44.00	10.20	—	54.20
12"	S2@.356	Ea	52.40	12.20	—	64.60
14" - 16"	S2@.449	Ea	65.70	15.30	—	81.00
18" - 20"	S2@.566	Ea	82.90	19.30	—	102.20
22" - 24"	S2@.683	Ea	101.00	23.30	—	124.30
26" - 28"	S2@.807	Ea	118.00	27.60	—	145.60
30" - 32"	S2@.924	Ea	134.00	31.60	—	165.60
34" - 36"	S2@1.20	Ea	177.00	41.00	—	218.00

Galvanized steel spiral duct tees with 7" run and branch

Description	Craft@Hrs	Unit	Material $	Labor $	Equipment $	Total $
8"	S2@.212	Ea	31.00	7.24	—	38.24
9"	S2@.232	Ea	34.10	7.93	—	42.03
10"	S2@.312	Ea	45.50	10.70	—	56.20
12"	S2@.376	Ea	55.10	12.80	—	67.90
14" - 16"	S2@.470	Ea	69.00	16.10	—	85.10
18" - 20"	S2@.636	Ea	93.10	21.70	—	114.80
22" - 24"	S2@.717	Ea	106.00	24.50	—	130.50
26" - 28"	S2@.845	Ea	123.00	28.90	—	151.90
30" - 32"	S2@.969	Ea	144.00	33.10	—	177.10
34" - 36"	S2@1.27	Ea	186.00	43.40	—	229.40

Galvanized steel spiral duct tees with 8" run and branch

Description	Craft@Hrs	Unit	Material $	Labor $	Equipment $	Total $
9"	S2@.248	Ea	36.50	8.47	—	44.97
10"	S2@.328	Ea	48.40	11.20	—	59.60
12"	S2@.396	Ea	57.80	13.50	—	71.30
14" - 16"	S2@.493	Ea	71.70	16.80	—	88.50
18" - 20"	S2@.623	Ea	91.10	21.30	—	112.40
22" - 24"	S2@.751	Ea	110.00	25.70	—	135.70
26" - 28"	S2@.882	Ea	130.00	30.10	—	160.10
30" - 32"	S2@1.02	Ea	149.00	34.80	—	183.80
34" - 36"	S2@1.33	Ea	196.00	45.40	—	241.40

Galvanized steel spiral duct tees with 9" run and branch

Description	Craft@Hrs	Unit	Material $	Labor $	Equipment $	Total $
10"	S2@.344	Ea	50.20	11.80	—	62.00
12"	S2@.412	Ea	60.20	14.10	—	74.30
14" - 16"	S2@.515	Ea	75.60	17.60	—	93.20
18" - 20"	S2@.653	Ea	95.70	22.30	—	118.00
22" - 24"	S2@.779	Ea	116.00	26.60	—	142.60
26" - 28"	S2@.924	Ea	134.00	31.60	—	165.60
30" - 32"	S2@1.06	Ea	155.00	36.20	—	191.20
34" - 36"	S2@1.39	Ea	202.00	47.50	—	249.50

Description	Craft@Hrs	Unit	Material $	Labor $	Equipment $	Total $

Galvanized steel spiral duct tees with 10" run and branch

Description	Craft@Hrs	Unit	Material $	Labor $	Equipment $	Total $
12"	S2@.427	Ea	31.50	14.60	—	46.10
14" - 16"	S2@.538	Ea	39.60	18.40	—	58.00
18" - 20"	S2@.681	Ea	99.40	23.30	—	122.70
22" - 24"	S2@.820	Ea	120.00	28.00	—	148.00
26" - 28"	S2@.965	Ea	141.00	33.00	—	174.00
30" - 32"	S2@1.11	Ea	163.00	37.90	—	200.90
34" - 36"	S2@1.44	Ea	211.00	49.20	—	260.20

Galvanized steel spiral duct tees with 12" run and branch

Description	Craft@Hrs	Unit	Material $	Labor $	Equipment $	Total $
14" - 16"	S2@.581	Ea	84.80	19.80	—	104.60
18" - 20"	S2@.739	Ea	109.00	25.20	—	134.20
22" - 24"	S2@.888	Ea	131.00	30.30	—	161.30
26" - 28"	S2@1.04	Ea	153.00	35.50	—	188.50
30" - 32"	S2@1.20	Ea	175.00	41.00	—	216.00
34" - 36"	S2@1.57	Ea	230.00	53.60	—	283.60

Galvanized steel spiral duct tees with 14" run and branch

Description	Craft@Hrs	Unit	Material $	Labor $	Equipment $	Total $
14" - 16"	S2@.666	Ea	97.80	22.80	—	120.60
18" - 20"	S2@.794	Ea	117.00	27.10	—	144.10
22" - 24"	S2@.959	Ea	140.00	32.80	—	172.80
26" - 28"	S2@1.11	Ea	163.00	37.90	—	200.90
30" - 32"	S2@1.29	Ea	189.00	44.10	—	233.10
34" - 36"	S2@1.69	Ea	249.00	57.70	—	306.70

Galvanized steel spiral duct tees with 16" run and branch

Description	Craft@Hrs	Unit	Material $	Labor $	Equipment $	Total $
18" - 20"	S2@.833	Ea	121.00	28.50	—	149.50
22" - 24"	S2@1.03	Ea	151.00	35.20	—	186.20
26" - 28"	S2@1.20	Ea	177.00	41.00	—	218.00
30" - 32"	S2@1.39	Ea	202.00	47.50	—	249.50
34" - 36"	S2@1.81	Ea	265.00	61.80	—	326.80

Galvanized steel spiral duct tees with 18" run and branch

Description	Craft@Hrs	Unit	Material $	Labor $	Equipment $	Total $
18" - 20"	S2@.956	Ea	140.00	32.70	—	172.70
22" - 24"	S2@1.09	Ea	158.00	37.20	—	195.20
26" - 28"	S2@1.29	Ea	188.00	44.10	—	232.10
30" - 32"	S2@1.48	Ea	217.00	50.60	—	267.60
34" - 36"	S2@1.93	Ea	285.00	65.90	—	350.90

Galvanized steel spiral duct tees with 20" run and branch

Description	Craft@Hrs	Unit	Material $	Labor $	Equipment $	Total $
22" - 24"	S2@1.16	Ea	171.00	39.60	—	210.60
26" - 28"	S2@1.37	Ea	201.00	46.80	—	247.80
30" - 32"	S2@1.57	Ea	230.00	53.60	—	283.60
34" - 36"	S2@2.03	Ea	299.00	69.30	—	368.30

Galvanized steel spiral duct tees with 22" run and branch

Description	Craft@Hrs	Unit	Material $	Labor $	Equipment $	Total $
22" - 24"	S2@1.28	Ea	188.00	43.70	—	231.70
26" - 28"	S2@1.45	Ea	213.00	49.50	—	262.50
30" - 32"	S2@1.64	Ea	241.00	56.00	—	297.00
34" - 36"	S2@2.16	Ea	316.00	73.80	—	389.80

Galvanized Steel Spiral Crosses

Costs for Steel Spiral Crosses with Reducing Branches. Costs per cross, based on quantities less than 1,000 pounds. Deduct 15% from the material cost for quantities over 1,000 pounds. Add 50% to the material cost for lined duct. These costs include delivery, typical bracing, cleats, scrap, hangers, end closures, sealants and miscellaneous hardware.

Description	Craft@Hrs	Unit	Material $	Labor $	Equipment $	Total $

Galvanized steel spiral duct crosses with 3" branch

Description	Craft@Hrs	Unit	Material $	Labor $	Equipment $	Total $
4"	S2@.104	Ea	15.20	3.55	—	18.75
5"	S2@.128	Ea	18.70	4.37	—	23.07
6"	S2@.152	Ea	22.20	5.19	—	27.39
7"	S2@.176	Ea	25.60	6.01	—	31.61
8"	S2@.196	Ea	28.70	6.70	—	35.40
9"	S2@.216	Ea	31.50	7.38	—	38.88
10"	S2@.304	Ea	44.80	10.40	—	55.20
12"	S2@.352	Ea	52.00	12.00	—	64.00
14" - 16"	S2@.428	Ea	63.10	14.60	—	77.70
18" - 20"	S2@.525	Ea	77.00	17.90	—	94.90
22" - 24"	S2@.634	Ea	93.10	21.70	—	114.80
26" - 28"	S2@.745	Ea	109.00	25.40	—	134.40
30" - 32"	S2@.856	Ea	124.00	29.20	—	153.20
34" - 36"	S2@1.11	Ea	164.00	37.90	—	201.90

Galvanized steel spiral duct crosses with 4" branch

Description	Craft@Hrs	Unit	Material $	Labor $	Equipment $	Total $
5"	S2@.144	Ea	21.10	4.92	—	26.02
6"	S2@.168	Ea	24.90	5.74	—	30.64
7"	S2@.196	Ea	28.70	6.70	—	35.40
8"	S2@.216	Ea	31.50	7.38	—	38.88
9"	S2@.240	Ea	35.30	8.20	—	43.50
10"	S2@.328	Ea	48.40	11.20	—	59.60
12"	S2@.384	Ea	56.80	13.10	—	69.90
14" - 16"	S2@.461	Ea	67.70	15.70	—	83.40
18" - 20"	S2@.568	Ea	83.40	19.40	—	102.80
22" - 24"	S2@.685	Ea	101.00	23.40	—	124.40
26" - 28"	S2@.805	Ea	118.00	27.50	—	145.50
30" - 32"	S2@.927	Ea	136.00	31.70	—	167.70
34" - 36"	S2@1.20	Ea	177.00	41.00	—	218.00

Galvanized steel spiral duct crosses with 5" branch

Description	Craft@Hrs	Unit	Material $	Labor $	Equipment $	Total $
6"	S2@.184	Ea	27.10	6.29	—	33.39
7"	S2@.216	Ea	31.50	7.38	—	38.88
8"	S2@.240	Ea	35.30	8.20	—	43.50
9"	S2@.264	Ea	38.90	9.02	—	47.92
10"	S2@.356	Ea	52.40	12.20	—	64.60
12"	S2@.412	Ea	60.20	14.10	—	74.30
14" - 16"	S2@.497	Ea	72.30	17.00	—	89.30
18" - 20"	S2@.613	Ea	89.30	20.90	—	110.20
22" - 24"	S2@.741	Ea	109.00	25.30	—	134.30
26" - 28"	S2@.867	Ea	128.00	29.60	—	157.60
30" - 32"	S2@.993	Ea	146.00	33.90	—	179.90
34" - 36"	S2@1.29	Ea	189.00	44.10	—	233.10

Description	Craft@Hrs	Unit	Material $	Labor $	Equipment $	Total $

Galvanized steel spiral duct crosses with 6" branch

Description	Craft@Hrs	Unit	Material $	Labor $	Equipment $	Total $
7"	S2@.232	Ea	34.10	7.93	—	42.03
8"	S2@.260	Ea	38.20	8.88	—	47.08
9"	S2@.288	Ea	42.20	9.84	—	52.04
10"	S2@.380	Ea	56.00	13.00	—	69.00
12"	S2@.440	Ea	64.60	15.00	—	79.60
14" - 16"	S2@.532	Ea	77.70	18.20	—	95.90
18" - 20"	S2@.653	Ea	95.70	22.30	—	118.00
22" - 24"	S2@.790	Ea	117.00	27.00	—	144.00
26" - 28"	S2@.927	Ea	136.00	31.70	—	167.70
30" - 32"	S2@1.06	Ea	155.00	36.20	—	191.20
34" - 36"	S2@1.38	Ea	202.00	47.10	—	249.10

Galvanized steel spiral duct crosses with 7" branch

Description	Craft@Hrs	Unit	Material $	Labor $	Equipment $	Total $
8"	S2@.280	Ea	40.80	9.56	—	50.36
9"	S2@.308	Ea	45.00	10.50	—	55.50
10"	S2@.408	Ea	59.80	13.90	—	73.70
12"	S2@.470	Ea	68.50	16.10	—	84.60
14" - 16"	S2@.566	Ea	82.90	19.30	—	102.20
18" - 20"	S2@.692	Ea	102.00	23.60	—	125.60
22" - 24"	S2@.841	Ea	122.00	28.70	—	150.70
26" - 28"	S2@.986	Ea	145.00	33.70	—	178.70
30" - 32"	S2@1.13	Ea	166.00	38.60	—	204.60
34" - 36"	S2@1.48	Ea	217.00	50.60	—	267.60

Galvanized steel spiral duct crosses with 8" branch

Description	Craft@Hrs	Unit	Material $	Labor $	Equipment $	Total $
9"	S2@.310	Ea	48.70	10.60	—	59.30
10"	S2@.403	Ea	63.80	13.80	—	77.60
12"	S2@.470	Ea	72.70	16.10	—	88.80
14" - 16"	S2@.561	Ea	88.00	19.20	—	107.20
18" - 20"	S2@.690	Ea	109.00	23.60	—	132.60
22" - 24"	S2@.835	Ea	131.00	28.50	—	159.50
26" - 28"	S2@.980	Ea	153.00	33.50	—	186.50
30" - 32"	S2@1.12	Ea	177.00	38.30	—	215.30
34" - 36"	S2@1.47	Ea	230.00	50.20	—	280.20

Galvanized steel spiral duct crosses with 9" branch

Description	Craft@Hrs	Unit	Material $	Labor $	Equipment $	Total $
10"	S2@.427	Ea	66.70	14.60	—	81.30
12"	S2@.495	Ea	77.10	16.90	—	94.00
14" - 16"	S2@.596	Ea	93.40	20.40	—	113.80
18" - 20"	S2@.732	Ea	114.00	25.00	—	139.00
22" - 24"	S2@.882	Ea	139.00	30.10	—	169.10
26" - 28"	S2@1.04	Ea	163.00	35.50	—	198.50
30" - 32"	S2@1.19	Ea	186.00	40.70	—	226.70
34" - 36"	S2@1.55	Ea	241.00	52.90	—	293.90

Galvanized Steel Spiral Crosses

Description	Craft@Hrs	Unit	Material $	Labor $	Equipment $	Total $

Galvanized steel spiral duct crosses with 12" branch

Description	Craft@Hrs	Unit	Material $	Labor $	Equipment $	Total $
14" - 16"	S2@.692	Ea	109.00	23.60	—	132.60
18" - 20"	S2@.850	Ea	133.00	29.00	—	162.00
22" - 24"	S2@1.03	Ea	162.00	35.20	—	197.20
26" - 28"	S2@1.18	Ea	186.00	40.30	—	226.30
30" - 32"	S2@1.38	Ea	217.00	47.10	—	264.10
34" - 36"	S2@1.80	Ea	285.00	61.50	—	346.50

Galvanized steel spiral duct crosses with 14" branch

Description	Craft@Hrs	Unit	Material $	Labor $	Equipment $	Total $
14" - 16"	S2@1.81	Ea	55.10	61.80	—	116.90
18" - 20"	S2@2.11	Ea	64.10	72.10	—	136.20
22" - 24"	S2@2.55	Ea	77.70	87.10	—	164.80
26" - 28"	S2@2.98	Ea	90.80	102.00	—	192.80
30" - 32"	S2@3.43	Ea	104.00	117.00	—	221.00
34" - 36"	S2@4.47	Ea	136.00	153.00	—	289.00

Galvanized steel spiral duct crosses with 16" branch

Description	Craft@Hrs	Unit	Material $	Labor $	Equipment $	Total $
18" - 20"	S2@1.08	Ea	157.00	36.90	—	193.90
22" - 24"	S2@1.30	Ea	190.00	44.40	—	234.40
26" - 28"	S2@1.53	Ea	224.00	52.30	—	276.30
30" - 32"	S2@1.76	Ea	256.00	60.10	—	316.10
34" - 36"	S2@2.31	Ea	339.00	78.90	—	417.90

Galvanized steel spiral duct crosses with 18" branch

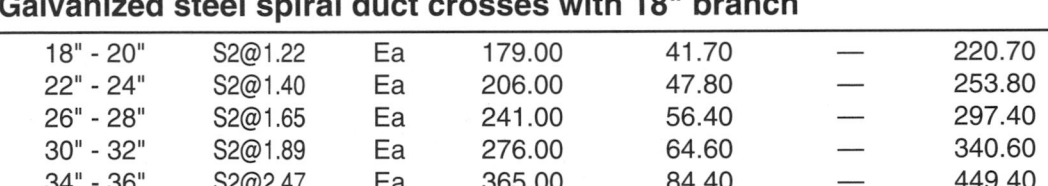

Description	Craft@Hrs	Unit	Material $	Labor $	Equipment $	Total $
18" - 20"	S2@1.22	Ea	179.00	41.70	—	220.70
22" - 24"	S2@1.40	Ea	206.00	47.80	—	253.80
26" - 28"	S2@1.65	Ea	241.00	56.40	—	297.40
30" - 32"	S2@1.89	Ea	276.00	64.60	—	340.60
34" - 36"	S2@2.47	Ea	365.00	84.40	—	449.40

Galvanized steel spiral duct crosses with 20" branch

Description	Craft@Hrs	Unit	Material $	Labor $	Equipment $	Total $
22" - 24"	S2@1.51	Ea	221.00	51.60	—	272.60
26" - 28"	S2@1.77	Ea	260.00	60.50	—	320.50
30" - 32"	S2@2.05	Ea	303.00	70.00	—	373.00
34" - 36"	S2@2.65	Ea	389.00	90.50	—	479.50

Galvanized steel spiral duct crosses with 22" branch

Description	Craft@Hrs	Unit	Material $	Labor $	Equipment $	Total $
22" - 24"	S2@1.68	Ea	249.00	57.40	—	306.40
26" - 28"	S2@1.89	Ea	276.00	64.60	—	340.60
30" - 32"	S2@2.17	Ea	316.00	74.10	—	390.10
34" - 36"	S2@2.84	Ea	419.00	97.00	—	516.00

Costs for Steel 26 Gauge Rectangular Duct. Costs per linear foot of duct, based on quantities less than 1,000 pounds of prefabricated duct. Deduct 15% from the material cost for quantities over 1,000 pounds. Add 50% to the material cost for lined duct. These costs include delivery, typical bracing, cleats, scrap, hangers, end closures, sealants and miscellaneous hardware.

Description	Craft@Hrs	Unit	Material $	Labor $	Equipment $	Total $

Galvanized steel 4" rectangular duct 26 gauge

Description	Craft@Hrs	Unit	Material $	Labor $	Equipment $	Total $
4"	S2@.048	LF	3.63	1.64	—	5.27
5"	S2@.054	LF	4.00	1.84	—	5.84
6"	S2@.060	LF	4.48	2.05	—	6.53
7"	S2@.066	LF	4.93	2.25	—	7.18
8"	S2@.072	LF	5.38	2.46	—	7.84
9"	S2@.078	LF	5.78	2.66	—	8.44
10"	S2@.084	LF	6.25	2.87	—	9.12
11"	S2@.091	LF	6.72	3.11	—	9.83
12"	S2@.097	LF	7.16	3.31	—	10.47

Galvanized steel 5" rectangular duct 26 gauge

Description	Craft@Hrs	Unit	Material $	Labor $	Equipment $	Total $
5"	S2@.060	LF	4.48	2.05	—	6.53
6"	S2@.066	LF	4.93	2.25	—	7.18
7"	S2@.072	LF	5.38	2.46	—	7.84
8"	S2@.078	LF	5.78	2.66	—	8.44
9"	S2@.084	LF	6.25	2.87	—	9.12
10"	S2@.091	LF	6.72	3.11	—	9.83
11"	S2@.097	LF	7.16	3.31	—	10.47
12"	S2@.103	LF	7.59	3.52	—	11.11

Galvanized steel 6" rectangular duct 26 gauge

Description	Craft@Hrs	Unit	Material $	Labor $	Equipment $	Total $
6"	S2@.072	LF	5.38	2.46	—	7.84
7"	S2@.078	LF	5.78	2.66	—	8.44
8"	S2@.084	LF	6.25	2.87	—	9.12
9"	S2@.091	LF	6.72	3.11	—	9.83
10"	S2@.097	LF	7.16	3.31	—	10.47
11"	S2@.103	LF	7.59	3.52	—	11.11
12"	S2@.109	LF	8.02	3.72	—	11.74

Galvanized steel 7" rectangular duct 26 gauge

Description	Craft@Hrs	Unit	Material $	Labor $	Equipment $	Total $
7"	S2@.084	LF	6.25	2.87	—	9.12
8"	S2@.091	LF	6.72	3.11	—	9.83
9"	S2@.097	LF	7.16	3.31	—	10.47
10"	S2@.103	LF	7.59	3.52	—	11.11
11"	S2@.109	LF	8.02	3.72	—	11.74
12"	S2@.115	LF	8.47	3.93	—	12.40

Galvanized Steel Rectangular Ductwork

Description	Craft@Hrs	Unit	Material $	Labor $	Equipment $	Total $

Galvanized steel 8" rectangular duct 26 gauge

Description	Craft@Hrs	Unit	Material $	Labor $	Equipment $	Total $
8"	S2@.097	LF	7.16	3.31	—	10.47
9"	S2@.103	LF	7.59	3.52	—	11.11
10"	S2@.109	LF	8.02	3.72	—	11.74
11"	S2@.115	LF	8.47	3.93	—	12.40
12"	S2@.121	LF	8.91	4.13	—	13.04

Galvanized steel 9" rectangular duct 26 gauge

Description	Craft@Hrs	Unit	Material $	Labor $	Equipment $	Total $
9"	S2@.109	LF	8.02	3.72	—	11.74
10"	S2@.115	LF	8.47	3.93	—	12.40
11"	S2@.121	LF	8.91	4.13	—	13.04
12"	S2@.127	LF	9.34	4.34	—	13.68

Galvanized steel 10" rectangular duct 26 gauge

Description	Craft@Hrs	Unit	Material $	Labor $	Equipment $	Total $
10"	S2@.129	LF	8.91	4.41	—	13.32
11"	S2@.127	LF	9.34	4.34	—	13.68
12"	S2@.133	LF	9.80	4.54	—	14.34

Galvanized steel 11" rectangular duct 26 gauge

Description	Craft@Hrs	Unit	Material $	Labor $	Equipment $	Total $
11"	S2@.133	LF	9.80	4.54	—	14.34
12"	S2@.139	LF	10.20	4.75	—	14.95

Galvanized steel 12" rectangular duct 26 gauge

Description	Craft@Hrs	Unit	Material $	Labor $	Equipment $	Total $
12"	S2@.145	LF	10.70	4.95	—	15.65

Costs for Galvanized 24 Gauge Rectangular Duct. Costs per linear foot of duct, based on quantities less than 1,000 pounds of prefabricated duct. Deduct 15% from the material cost for over 1,000 pounds. Add 50% to the material cost for lined duct. These costs include delivery, typical bracing, cleats, scrap, hangers, end closures.

Description	Craft@Hrs	Unit	Material $	Labor $	Equipment $	Total $

Galvanized steel 14" rectangular duct 24 gauge

Description	Craft@Hrs	Unit	Material $	Labor $	Equipment $	Total $
6"	S2@.154	LF	11.40	5.26	—	16.66
8"	S2@.170	LF	12.50	5.81	—	18.31
10"	S2@.184	LF	13.80	6.29	—	20.09
12"	S2@.200	LF	15.00	6.83	—	21.83
14" - 16"	S2@.223	LF	16.60	7.62	—	24.22
18" - 20"	S2@.254	LF	18.90	8.68	—	27.58
22" - 24"	S2@.285	LF	21.30	9.74	—	31.04
26" - 28"	S2@.316	LF	23.70	10.80	—	34.50
30"	S2@.339	LF	25.30	11.60	—	36.90

Galvanized steel 16" rectangular duct 24 gauge

Description	Craft@Hrs	Unit	Material $	Labor $	Equipment $	Total $
6"	S2@.170	LF	12.50	5.81	—	18.31
8"	S2@.184	LF	13.80	6.29	—	20.09
10"	S2@.200	LF	15.00	6.83	—	21.83
12"	S2@.216	LF	16.20	7.38	—	23.58
14" - 16"	S2@.239	LF	17.80	8.16	—	25.96
18" - 20"	S2@.269	LF	20.10	9.19	—	29.29
22" - 24"	S2@.300	LF	22.20	10.20	—	32.40
26" - 28"	S2@.331	LF	24.90	11.30	—	36.20
30"	S2@.354	LF	26.70	12.10	—	38.80

Galvanized steel 18" rectangular duct 24 gauge

Description	Craft@Hrs	Unit	Material $	Labor $	Equipment $	Total $
6"	S2@.184	LF	13.80	6.29	—	20.09
8"	S2@.200	LF	15.00	6.83	—	21.83
10"	S2@.216	LF	16.20	7.38	—	23.58
12"	S2@.231	LF	17.30	7.89	—	25.19
14" - 16"	S2@.254	LF	18.90	8.68	—	27.58
18" - 20"	S2@.285	LF	21.30	9.74	—	31.04
22" - 24"	S2@.316	LF	23.70	10.80	—	34.50
26" - 28"	S2@.346	LF	25.60	11.80	—	37.40
30"	S2@.370	LF	27.60	12.60	—	40.20

Galvanized Steel Rectangular Ductwork

Description	Craft@Hrs	Unit	Material $	Labor $	Equipment $	Total $

Galvanized steel 20" rectangular duct 24 gauge

Description	Craft@Hrs	Unit	Material $	Labor $	Equipment $	Total $
6"	S2@.200	LF	15.00	6.83	—	21.83
8"	S2@.216	LF	16.20	7.38	—	23.58
10"	S2@.231	LF	17.30	7.89	—	25.19
12"	S2@.247	LF	18.40	8.44	—	26.84
14" - 16"	S2@.269	LF	20.10	9.19	—	29.29
18" - 20"	S2@.300	LF	22.20	10.20	—	32.40
22" - 24"	S2@.331	LF	24.90	11.30	—	36.20
26" - 28"	S2@.362	LF	27.10	12.40	—	39.50
30"	S2@.385	LF	28.70	13.20	—	41.90

Galvanized steel 22" rectangular duct 24 gauge

Description	Craft@Hrs	Unit	Material $	Labor $	Equipment $	Total $
6"	S2@.216	LF	16.20	7.38	—	23.58
8"	S2@.231	LF	17.30	7.89	—	25.19
10"	S2@.247	LF	18.40	8.44	—	26.84
12"	S2@.262	LF	19.60	8.95	—	28.55
14" - 16"	S2@.285	LF	21.30	9.74	—	31.04
18" - 20"	S2@.316	LF	23.70	10.80	—	34.50
22" - 24"	S2@.346	LF	25.60	11.80	—	37.40
26" - 28"	S2@.377	LF	28.50	12.90	—	41.40
30"	S2@.400	LF	29.90	13.70	—	43.60

Galvanized steel 24" rectangular duct 24 gauge

Description	Craft@Hrs	Unit	Material $	Labor $	Equipment $	Total $
6"	S2@.231	LF	17.30	7.89	—	25.19
8"	S2@.247	LF	18.40	8.44	—	26.84
10"	S2@.262	LF	19.60	8.95	—	28.55
12"	S2@.278	LF	20.60	9.50	—	30.10
14" - 16"	S2@.300	LF	22.20	10.20	—	32.40
18" - 20"	S2@.331	LF	24.90	11.30	—	36.20
22" - 24"	S2@.362	LF	27.10	12.40	—	39.50
26" - 28"	S2@.392	LF	29.20	13.40	—	42.60
30"	S2@.415	LF	31.00	14.20	—	45.20

Galvanized steel 26" rectangular duct 24 gauge

Description	Craft@Hrs	Unit	Material $	Labor $	Equipment $	Total $
6"	S2@.247	LF	18.40	8.44	—	26.84
8"	S2@.262	LF	19.60	8.95	—	28.55
10"	S2@.278	LF	20.60	9.50	—	30.10
12"	S2@.292	LF	21.80	9.97	—	31.77
14" - 16"	S2@.316	LF	23.70	10.80	—	34.50
18" - 20"	S2@.346	LF	25.60	11.80	—	37.40
22" - 24"	S2@.377	LF	28.50	12.90	—	41.40
26" - 28"	S2@.407	LF	30.40	13.90	—	44.30
30"	S2@.431	LF	31.90	14.70	—	46.60

Description	Craft@Hrs	Unit	Material $	Labor $	Equipment $	Total $

Galvanized steel 28" rectangular duct 24 gauge

Description	Craft@Hrs	Unit	Material $	Labor $	Equipment $	Total $
6"	S2@.262	LF	19.60	8.95	—	28.55
8"	S2@.278	LF	20.60	9.50	—	30.10
10"	S2@.292	LF	21.80	9.97	—	31.77
12"	S2@.308	LF	23.00	10.50	—	33.50
14" - 16"	S2@.331	LF	24.90	11.30	—	36.20
18" - 20"	S2@.362	LF	27.10	12.40	—	39.50
22" - 24"	S2@.392	LF	29.20	13.40	—	42.60
26" - 28"	S2@.423	LF	31.60	14.40	—	46.00
30"	S2@.448	LF	33.60	15.30	—	48.90

Galvanized steel 30" rectangular duct 24 gauge

Description	Craft@Hrs	Unit	Material $	Labor $	Equipment $	Total $
6"	S2@.278	LF	20.60	9.50	—	30.10
8"	S2@.292	LF	21.80	9.97	—	31.77
10"	S2@.308	LF	23.00	10.50	—	33.50
12"	S2@.323	LF	24.10	11.00	—	35.10
14" - 16"	S2@.346	LF	25.60	11.80	—	37.40
18" - 20"	S2@.377	LF	28.50	12.90	—	41.40
22" - 24"	S2@.407	LF	30.40	13.90	—	44.30
26" - 28"	S2@.440	LF	32.70	15.00	—	47.70
30"	S2@.465	LF	34.50	15.90	—	50.40

Costs for Galvanized 22 Gauge Rectangular Duct. Costs per linear foot of duct, based on quantities less than 1,000 pounds of prefabricated duct. Deduct 15% from the material cost for over 1,000 pounds. Add 50% to the material cost for lined duct. These costs include delivery, typical bracing, cleats, scrap, hangers, end closures.

Description	Craft@Hrs	Unit	Material $	Labor $	Equipment $	Total $

Galvanized steel 32" rectangular duct 22 gauge

Description	Craft@Hrs	Unit	Material $	Labor $	Equipment $	Total $
8"	S2@.374	LF	27.90	12.80	—	40.70
10"	S2@.393	LF	29.20	13.40	—	42.60
12"	S2@.412	LF	30.60	14.10	—	44.70
14" - 16"	S2@.442	LF	33.00	15.10	—	48.10
18" - 20"	S2@.478	LF	35.90	16.30	—	52.20
22" - 24"	S2@.517	LF	38.50	17.70	—	56.20
26" - 28"	S2@.553	LF	41.30	18.90	—	60.20
30" - 32"	S2@.589	LF	44.20	20.10	—	64.30
34" - 36"	S2@.628	LF	46.80	21.50	—	68.30
38" - 40"	S2@.664	LF	49.70	22.70	—	72.40
42" - 44"	S2@.702	LF	52.10	24.00	—	76.10
46" - 48"	S2@.739	LF	55.10	25.20	—	80.30
50" - 52"	S2@.777	LF	57.80	26.50	—	84.30
54"	S2@.807	LF	60.00	27.60	—	87.60

Galvanized Steel Rectangular Ductwork

Description	Craft@Hrs	Unit	Material $	Labor $	Equipment $	Total $

Galvanized steel 34" rectangular duct 22 gauge

Description	Craft@Hrs	Unit	Material $	Labor $	Equipment $	Total $
8"	S2@.393	LF	29.20	13.40	—	42.60
10"	S2@.412	LF	30.60	14.10	—	44.70
12"	S2@.431	LF	31.90	14.70	—	46.60
14" - 16"	S2@.461	LF	34.20	15.70	—	49.90
18" - 20"	S2@.497	LF	37.60	17.00	—	54.60
22" - 24"	S2@.534	LF	39.60	18.20	—	57.80
26" - 28"	S2@.572	LF	42.80	19.50	—	62.30
30" - 32"	S2@.608	LF	45.40	20.80	—	66.20
34" - 36"	S2@.645	LF	48.40	22.00	—	70.40
38" - 40"	S2@.683	LF	51.00	23.30	—	74.30
42" - 44"	S2@.722	LF	54.00	24.70	—	78.70
46" - 48"	S2@.758	LF	56.80	25.90	—	82.70
50" - 52"	S2@.796	LF	59.20	27.20	—	86.40
54"	S2@.824	LF	61.60	28.10	—	89.70

Galvanized steel 36" rectangular duct 22 gauge

Description	Craft@Hrs	Unit	Material $	Labor $	Equipment $	Total $
8"	S2@.412	LF	30.60	14.10	—	44.70
10"	S2@.431	LF	31.90	14.70	—	46.60
12"	S2@.453	LF	33.90	15.50	—	49.40
14" - 16"	S2@.478	LF	35.90	16.30	—	52.20
18" - 20"	S2@.517	LF	38.50	17.70	—	56.20
22" - 24"	S2@.553	LF	41.30	18.90	—	60.20
26" - 28"	S2@.589	LF	44.20	20.10	—	64.30
30" - 32"	S2@.628	LF	46.80	21.50	—	68.30
34" - 36"	S2@.664	LF	49.70	22.70	—	72.40
38" - 40"	S2@.702	LF	52.10	24.00	—	76.10
42" - 44"	S2@.739	LF	55.10	25.20	—	80.30
46" - 48"	S2@.777	LF	57.80	26.50	—	84.30
50" - 52"	S2@.816	LF	60.30	27.90	—	88.20
54"	S2@.841	LF	63.10	28.70	—	91.80

Galvanized steel 38" rectangular duct 22 gauge

Description	Craft@Hrs	Unit	Material $	Labor $	Equipment $	Total $
8"	S2@.431	LF	31.90	14.70	—	46.60
10"	S2@.453	LF	33.90	15.50	—	49.40
12"	S2@.470	LF	34.90	16.10	—	51.00
14" - 16"	S2@.497	LF	37.60	17.00	—	54.60
18" - 20"	S2@.534	LF	39.60	18.20	—	57.80
22" - 24"	S2@.572	LF	42.80	19.50	—	62.30
26" - 28"	S2@.608	LF	45.40	20.80	—	66.20
30" - 32"	S2@.645	LF	48.40	22.00	—	70.40
34" - 36"	S2@.683	LF	51.00	23.30	—	74.30
38" - 40"	S2@.722	LF	54.00	24.70	—	78.70
42" - 44"	S2@.758	LF	56.80	25.90	—	82.70
46" - 48"	S2@.796	LF	59.20	27.20	—	86.40
50" - 52"	S2@.833	LF	62.30	28.50	—	90.80
54"	S2@.863	LF	64.20	29.50	—	93.70

Galvanized Steel Rectangular Ductwork

Description	Craft@Hrs	Unit	Material $	Labor $	Equipment $	Total $

Galvanized steel 40" rectangular duct 22 gauge

Description	Craft@Hrs	Unit	Material $	Labor $	Equipment $	Total $
8"	S2@.453	LF	33.90	15.50	—	49.40
10"	S2@.470	LF	34.90	16.10	—	51.00
12"	S2@.487	LF	36.60	16.60	—	53.20
14" - 16"	S2@.517	LF	38.50	17.70	—	56.20
18" - 20"	S2@.553	LF	41.30	18.90	—	60.20
22" - 24"	S2@.589	LF	44.20	20.10	—	64.30
26" - 28"	S2@.628	LF	46.80	21.50	—	68.30
30" - 32"	S2@.664	LF	49.70	22.70	—	72.40
34" - 36"	S2@.702	LF	52.10	24.00	—	76.10
38" - 40"	S2@.739	LF	55.10	25.20	—	80.30
42" - 44"	S2@.777	LF	57.80	26.50	—	84.30
46" - 48"	S2@.816	LF	60.30	27.90	—	88.20
50" - 52"	S2@.852	LF	63.80	29.10	—	92.90
54"	S2@.880	LF	65.30	30.10	—	95.40

Galvanized steel 42" rectangular duct 22 gauge

Description	Craft@Hrs	Unit	Material $	Labor $	Equipment $	Total $
8"	S2@.470	LF	34.90	16.10	—	51.00
10"	S2@.487	LF	36.60	16.60	—	53.20
12"	S2@.508	LF	38.10	17.40	—	55.50
14" - 16"	S2@.534	LF	39.60	18.20	—	57.80
18" - 20"	S2@.572	LF	42.80	19.50	—	62.30
22" - 24"	S2@.611	LF	45.40	20.90	—	66.30
26" - 28"	S2@.645	LF	48.40	22.00	—	70.40
30" - 32"	S2@.683	LF	51.00	23.30	—	74.30
34" - 36"	S2@.722	LF	54.00	24.70	—	78.70
38" - 40"	S2@.758	LF	56.80	25.90	—	82.70
42" - 44"	S2@.798	LF	59.20	27.30	—	86.50
46" - 48"	S2@.833	LF	62.30	28.50	—	90.80
50" - 52"	S2@.871	LF	65.00	29.80	—	94.80
54"	S2@.901	LF	66.90	30.80	—	97.70

Galvanized steel 44" rectangular duct 22 gauge

Description	Craft@Hrs	Unit	Material $	Labor $	Equipment $	Total $
8"	S2@.487	LF	36.50	16.60	—	53.10
10"	S2@.508	LF	37.70	17.40	—	55.10
12"	S2@.525	LF	38.90	17.90	—	56.80
14" - 16"	S2@.555	LF	40.80	19.00	—	59.80
18" - 20"	S2@.589	LF	44.00	20.10	—	64.10
22" - 24"	S2@.628	LF	46.30	21.50	—	67.80
26" - 28"	S2@.666	LF	49.40	22.80	—	72.20
30" - 32"	S2@.705	LF	52.00	24.10	—	76.10
34" - 36"	S2@.739	LF	54.90	25.20	—	80.10
38" - 40"	S2@.777	LF	57.50	26.50	—	84.00
42" - 44"	S2@.816	LF	60.20	27.90	—	88.10
46" - 48"	S2@.852	LF	63.40	29.10	—	92.50
50" - 52"	S2@.890	LF	65.80	30.40	—	96.20
54"	S2@.918	LF	68.00	31.40	—	99.40

Galvanized Steel Rectangular Ductwork

Description	Craft@Hrs	Unit	Material $	Labor $	Equipment $	Total $

Galvanized steel 46" rectangular duct 22 gauge

Description	Craft@Hrs	Unit	Material $	Labor $	Equipment $	Total $
8"	S2@.508	LF	38.10	17.40	—	55.50
10"	S2@.525	LF	38.90	17.90	—	56.80
12"	S2@.542	LF	40.50	18.50	—	59.00
14" - 16"	S2@.572	LF	42.80	19.50	—	62.30
18" - 20"	S2@.611	LF	45.40	20.90	—	66.30
22" - 24"	S2@.649	LF	48.40	22.20	—	70.60
26" - 28"	S2@.683	LF	51.00	23.30	—	74.30
30" - 32"	S2@.722	LF	54.00	24.70	—	78.70
34" - 36"	S2@.758	LF	56.80	25.90	—	82.70
38" - 40"	S2@.796	LF	59.20	27.20	—	86.40
42" - 44"	S2@.833	LF	62.30	28.50	—	90.80
46" - 48"	S2@.871	LF	65.00	29.80	—	94.80
50" - 52"	S2@.909	LF	67.70	31.10	—	98.80
54"	S2@.935	LF	69.60	31.90	—	101.50

Galvanized steel 48" rectangular duct 22 gauge

Description	Craft@Hrs	Unit	Material $	Labor $	Equipment $	Total $
8"	S2@.525	LF	38.90	17.90	—	56.80
10"	S2@.542	LF	40.50	18.50	—	59.00
12"	S2@.564	LF	42.00	19.30	—	61.30
14" - 16"	S2@.589	LF	44.20	20.10	—	64.30
18" - 20"	S2@.628	LF	46.80	21.50	—	68.30
22" - 24"	S2@.664	LF	49.70	22.70	—	72.40
26" - 28"	S2@.702	LF	52.10	24.00	—	76.10
30" - 32"	S2@.739	LF	55.10	25.20	—	80.30
34" - 36"	S2@.777	LF	57.80	26.50	—	84.30
38" - 40"	S2@.816	LF	60.30	27.90	—	88.20
42" - 44"	S2@.852	LF	63.80	29.10	—	92.90
46" - 48"	S2@.890	LF	66.20	30.40	—	96.60
50" - 52"	S2@.927	LF	69.30	31.70	—	101.00
54"	S2@.956	LF	70.80	32.70	—	103.50

Galvanized steel 50" rectangular duct 22 gauge

Description	Craft@Hrs	Unit	Material $	Labor $	Equipment $	Total $
8"	S2@.542	LF	40.50	18.50	—	59.00
10"	S2@.564	LF	42.00	19.30	—	61.30
12"	S2@.581	LF	43.30	19.80	—	63.10
14" - 16"	S2@.611	LF	45.40	20.90	—	66.30
18" - 20"	S2@.645	LF	48.40	22.00	—	70.40
22" - 24"	S2@.683	LF	51.00	23.30	—	74.30
26" - 28"	S2@.722	LF	54.00	24.70	—	78.70
30" - 32"	S2@.758	LF	56.80	25.90	—	82.70
34" - 36"	S2@.798	LF	59.20	27.30	—	86.50
38" - 40"	S2@.833	LF	62.30	28.50	—	90.80
42" - 44"	S2@.871	LF	65.00	29.80	—	94.80
46" - 48"	S2@.909	LF	67.70	31.10	—	98.80
50" - 52"	S2@.946	LF	70.30	32.30	—	102.60
54"	S2@.974	LF	72.30	33.30	—	105.60

Description	Craft@Hrs	Unit	Material $	Labor $	Equipment $	Total $

Galvanized steel 52" rectangular duct 22 gauge

Description	Craft@Hrs	Unit	Material $	Labor $	Equipment $	Total $
8"	S2@.564	LF	42.00	19.30	—	61.30
10"	S2@.581	LF	43.30	19.80	—	63.10
12"	S2@.598	LF	44.80	20.40	—	65.20
14" - 16"	S2@.628	LF	46.80	21.50	—	68.30
18" - 20"	S2@.662	LF	49.70	22.60	—	72.30
22" - 24"	S2@.700	LF	52.10	23.90	—	76.00
26" - 28"	S2@.739	LF	55.10	25.20	—	80.30
30" - 32"	S2@.777	LF	57.80	26.50	—	84.30
34" - 36"	S2@.816	LF	60.30	27.90	—	88.20
38" - 40"	S2@.852	LF	63.80	29.10	—	92.90
42" - 44"	S2@.890	LF	66.20	30.40	—	96.60
46" - 48"	S2@.927	LF	69.30	31.70	—	101.00
50" - 52"	S2@.976	LF	71.70	33.30	—	105.00
54"	S2@.991	LF	73.50	33.90	—	107.40

Galvanized steel 54" rectangular duct 22 gauge

Description	Craft@Hrs	Unit	Material $	Labor $	Equipment $	Total $
8"	S2@.581	LF	43.30	19.80	—	63.10
10"	S2@.598	LF	44.80	20.40	—	65.20
12"	S2@.619	LF	46.00	21.10	—	67.10
14" - 16"	S2@.645	LF	48.40	22.00	—	70.40
18" - 20"	S2@.683	LF	51.00	23.30	—	74.30
22" - 24"	S2@.722	LF	54.00	24.70	—	78.70
26" - 28"	S2@.758	LF	56.80	25.90	—	82.70
30" - 32"	S2@.796	LF	59.20	27.20	—	86.40
34" - 36"	S2@.833	LF	62.30	28.50	—	90.80
38" - 40"	S2@.871	LF	65.00	29.80	—	94.80
42" - 44"	S2@.909	LF	67.70	31.10	—	98.80
46" - 48"	S2@.946	LF	70.30	32.30	—	102.60
50" - 52"	S2@.982	LF	72.70	33.50	—	106.20
54"	S2@1.01	LF	75.60	34.50	—	110.10

Galvanized Steel Rectangular Ductwork

Costs for Galvanized 20 Gauge Rectangular Duct. Costs per linear foot of duct, based on quantities less than 1,000 pounds of prefabricated duct. Deduct 15% from the material cost for over 1,000 pounds. Add 50% to the material cost for lined duct. These costs include delivery, typical bracing, cleats, scrap, hangers, end closures, sealants and miscellaneous hardware.

Description	Craft@Hrs	Unit	Material $	Labor $	Equipment $	Total $
Galvanized steel 56" rectangular duct 20 gauge						
18" - 20"	S2@.828	LF	62.30	28.30	—	90.60
22" - 24"	S2@.871	LF	65.30	29.80	—	95.10
26" - 28"	S2@.916	LF	68.50	31.30	—	99.80
30" - 32"	S2@.959	LF	72.10	32.80	—	104.90
34" - 36"	S2@1.00	LF	75.60	34.20	—	109.80
38" - 40"	S2@1.05	LF	78.70	35.90	—	114.60
42" - 44"	S2@1.09	LF	82.20	37.20	—	119.40
46" - 48"	S2@1.14	LF	85.40	38.90	—	124.30
50" - 52"	S2@1.18	LF	88.80	40.30	—	129.10
54" - 56"	S2@1.23	LF	91.90	42.00	—	133.90
58" - 60"	S2@1.27	LF	95.40	43.40	—	138.80
62" - 64"	S2@1.31	LF	98.90	44.70	—	143.60
66" - 68"	S2@1.36	LF	102.00	46.50	—	148.50
70" - 72"	S2@1.40	LF	106.00	47.80	—	153.80
Galvanized steel 58" rectangular duct 20 gauge						
18" - 20"	S2@.850	LF	63.90	29.00	—	92.90
22" - 24"	S2@.895	LF	67.20	30.60	—	97.80
26" - 28"	S2@.937	LF	70.30	32.00	—	102.30
30" - 32"	S2@.980	LF	73.80	33.50	—	107.30
34" - 36"	S2@1.02	LF	77.00	34.80	—	111.80
38" - 40"	S2@1.07	LF	80.20	36.60	—	116.80
42" - 44"	S2@1.11	LF	83.70	37.90	—	121.60
46" - 48"	S2@1.16	LF	86.80	39.60	—	126.40
50" - 52"	S2@1.02	LF	90.60	34.80	—	125.40
54" - 56"	S2@1.25	LF	93.80	42.70	—	136.50
58" - 60"	S2@1.29	LF	96.50	44.10	—	140.60
62" - 64"	S2@1.33	LF	101.00	45.40	—	146.40
66" - 68"	S2@1.38	LF	104.00	47.10	—	151.10
70" - 72"	S2@1.42	LF	107.00	48.50	—	155.50
Galvanized steel 60" rectangular duct 20 gauge						
18" - 20"	S2@.871	LF	65.30	29.80	—	95.10
22" - 24"	S2@.916	LF	68.50	31.30	—	99.80
26" - 28"	S2@.959	LF	72.10	32.80	—	104.90
30" - 32"	S2@1.00	LF	75.60	34.20	—	109.80
34" - 36"	S2@1.05	LF	78.70	35.90	—	114.60
38" - 40"	S2@1.09	LF	82.20	37.20	—	119.40
42" - 44"	S2@1.14	LF	85.40	38.90	—	124.30
46" - 48"	S2@1.18	LF	88.80	40.30	—	129.10
50" - 52"	S2@1.23	LF	91.90	42.00	—	133.90
54" - 56"	S2@1.27	LF	95.40	43.40	—	138.80
58" - 60"	S2@1.31	LF	98.90	44.70	—	143.60
62" - 64"	S2@1.36	LF	102.00	46.50	—	148.50
66" - 68"	S2@1.40	LF	106.00	47.80	—	153.80
70" - 72"	S2@1.45	LF	109.00	49.50	—	158.50

Description	Craft@Hrs	Unit	Material $	Labor $	Equipment $	Total $

Galvanized steel 62" rectangular duct 20 gauge

Description	Craft@Hrs	Unit	Material $	Labor $	Equipment $	Total $
18" - 20"	S2@.895	LF	67.20	30.60	—	97.80
22" - 24"	S2@.937	LF	70.30	32.00	—	102.30
26" - 28"	S2@.980	LF	73.80	33.50	—	107.30
30" - 32"	S2@1.02	LF	77.00	34.80	—	111.80
34" - 36"	S2@1.07	LF	80.20	36.60	—	116.80
38" - 40"	S2@1.11	LF	83.70	37.90	—	121.60
42" - 44"	S2@1.16	LF	86.80	39.60	—	126.40
46" - 48"	S2@1.20	LF	90.60	41.00	—	131.60
50" - 52"	S2@1.25	LF	93.80	42.70	—	136.50
54" - 56"	S2@1.29	LF	96.50	44.10	—	140.60
58" - 60"	S2@1.33	LF	101.00	45.40	—	146.40
62" - 64"	S2@1.38	LF	104.00	47.10	—	151.10
66" - 68"	S2@1.42	LF	107.00	48.50	—	155.50
70" - 72"	S2@1.47	LF	110.00	50.20	—	160.20

Galvanized steel 64" rectangular duct 20 gauge

Description	Craft@Hrs	Unit	Material $	Labor $	Equipment $	Total $
18" - 20"	S2@.916	LF	68.50	31.30	—	99.80
22" - 24"	S2@.959	LF	72.10	32.80	—	104.90
26" - 28"	S2@1.00	LF	75.60	34.20	—	109.80
30" - 32"	S2@1.05	LF	78.70	35.90	—	114.60
34" - 36"	S2@1.09	LF	82.20	37.20	—	119.40
38" - 40"	S2@1.14	LF	85.40	38.90	—	124.30
42" - 44"	S2@1.18	LF	88.80	40.30	—	129.10
46" - 48"	S2@1.23	LF	91.90	42.00	—	133.90
50" - 52"	S2@1.27	LF	95.40	43.40	—	138.80
54" - 56"	S2@1.31	LF	98.90	44.70	—	143.60
58" - 60"	S2@1.36	LF	102.00	46.50	—	148.50
62" - 64"	S2@1.40	LF	106.00	47.80	—	153.80
66" - 68"	S2@1.45	LF	109.00	49.50	—	158.50
70" - 72"	S2@1.49	LF	112.00	50.90	—	162.90

Galvanized steel 66" rectangular duct 20 gauge

Description	Craft@Hrs	Unit	Material $	Labor $	Equipment $	Total $
18" - 20"	S2@.937	LF	70.30	32.00	—	102.30
22" - 24"	S2@.980	LF	73.80	33.50	—	107.30
26" - 28"	S2@1.02	LF	77.00	34.80	—	111.80
30" - 32"	S2@1.07	LF	80.20	36.60	—	116.80
34" - 36"	S2@1.11	LF	83.70	37.90	—	121.60
38" - 40"	S2@1.16	LF	86.80	39.60	—	126.40
42" - 44"	S2@1.20	LF	90.60	41.00	—	131.60
46" - 48"	S2@1.25	LF	93.80	42.70	—	136.50
50" - 52"	S2@1.29	LF	96.50	44.10	—	140.60
54" - 56"	S2@1.33	LF	101.00	45.40	—	146.40
58" - 60"	S2@1.38	LF	104.00	47.10	—	151.10
62" - 64"	S2@1.42	LF	107.00	48.50	—	155.50
66" - 68"	S2@1.47	LF	110.00	50.20	—	160.20
70" - 72"	S2@1.51	LF	113.00	51.60	—	164.60

Galvanized Steel Rectangular Ductwork

Description	Craft@Hrs	Unit	Material $	Labor $	Equipment $	Total $

Galvanized steel 68" rectangular duct 20 gauge

Description	Craft@Hrs	Unit	Material $	Labor $	Equipment $	Total $
18" - 20"	S2@.959	LF	72.10	32.80	—	104.90
22" - 24"	S2@1.00	LF	75.60	34.20	—	109.80
26" - 28"	S2@1.05	LF	78.70	35.90	—	114.60
30" - 32"	S2@1.09	LF	82.20	37.20	—	119.40
34" - 36"	S2@1.14	LF	85.40	38.90	—	124.30
38" - 40"	S2@1.18	LF	88.80	40.30	—	129.10
42" - 44"	S2@1.23	LF	91.90	42.00	—	133.90
46" - 48"	S2@1.27	LF	95.40	43.40	—	138.80
50" - 52"	S2@1.31	LF	98.90	44.70	—	143.60
54" - 56"	S2@1.36	LF	102.00	46.50	—	148.50
58" - 60"	S2@1.40	LF	106.00	47.80	—	153.80
62" - 64"	S2@1.45	LF	109.00	49.50	—	158.50
66" - 68"	S2@1.49	LF	112.00	50.90	—	162.90
70" - 72"	S2@1.53	LF	116.00	52.30	—	168.30

Galvanized steel 70" rectangular duct 20 gauge

Description	Craft@Hrs	Unit	Material $	Labor $	Equipment $	Total $
18" - 20"	S2@.980	LF	73.80	33.50	—	107.30
22" - 24"	S2@1.02	LF	77.00	34.80	—	111.80
26" - 28"	S2@1.07	LF	80.20	36.60	—	116.80
30" - 32"	S2@1.11	LF	83.70	37.90	—	121.60
34" - 36"	S2@1.16	LF	86.80	39.60	—	126.40
38" - 40"	S2@1.20	LF	90.60	41.00	—	131.60
42" - 44"	S2@1.25	LF	93.80	42.70	—	136.50
46" - 48"	S2@1.29	LF	96.50	44.10	—	140.60
50" - 52"	S2@1.33	LF	101.00	45.40	—	146.40
54" - 56"	S2@1.38	LF	104.00	47.10	—	151.10
58" - 60"	S2@1.42	LF	107.00	48.50	—	155.50
62" - 64"	S2@1.47	LF	110.00	50.20	—	160.20
66" - 68"	S2@1.51	LF	113.00	51.60	—	164.60
70" - 72"	S2@1.55	LF	117.00	52.90	—	169.90

Galvanized steel 72" rectangular duct 20 gauge

Description	Craft@Hrs	Unit	Material $	Labor $	Equipment $	Total $
18" - 20"	S2@1.00	LF	75.60	34.20	—	109.80
22" - 24"	S2@1.05	LF	78.70	35.90	—	114.60
26" - 28"	S2@1.09	LF	82.20	37.20	—	119.40
30" - 32"	S2@1.14	LF	85.40	38.90	—	124.30
34" - 36"	S2@1.18	LF	88.80	40.30	—	129.10
38" - 40"	S2@1.23	LF	91.90	42.00	—	133.90
42" - 44"	S2@1.27	LF	95.40	43.40	—	138.80
46" - 48"	S2@1.31	LF	98.90	44.70	—	143.60
50" - 52"	S2@1.36	LF	102.00	46.50	—	148.50
54" - 56"	S2@1.40	LF	106.00	47.80	—	153.80
58" - 60"	S2@1.45	LF	109.00	49.50	—	158.50
62" - 64"	S2@1.49	LF	112.00	50.90	—	162.90
66" - 68"	S2@1.53	LF	116.00	52.30	—	168.30
70" - 72"	S2@1.58	LF	118.00	54.00	—	172.00

Costs for Galvanized Rectangular 90 Degree Elbows. Costs per elbow, based on quantities less than 1,000 pounds. Deduct 15% from the material cost for over 1,000 pounds. Add 50% to the material cost for lined duct. These costs include delivery, typical bracing, cleats, scrap, hangers, end closures, sealants and miscellaneous hardware. For turning vanes, please see page 342.

Description	Craft@Hrs	Unit	Material $	Labor $	Equipment $	Total $

Galvanized steel 4" rectangular duct 90 degree elbow

Description	Craft@Hrs	Unit	Material $	Labor $	Equipment $	Total $
4"	S2@.042	Ea	6.31	1.43	—	7.74
6"	S2@.058	Ea	8.67	1.98	—	10.65
8"	S2@.078	Ea	11.70	2.66	—	14.36
10"	S2@.104	Ea	15.50	3.55	—	19.05
12"	S2@.132	Ea	19.80	4.51	—	24.31
14" - 16"	S2@.236	Ea	35.30	8.06	—	43.36
18" - 20"	S2@.339	Ea	51.00	11.60	—	62.60
22" - 24"	S2@.468	Ea	69.60	16.00	—	85.60
26" - 28"	S2@.615	Ea	91.40	21.00	—	112.40
30" - 32"	S2@.854	Ea	129.00	29.20	—	158.20
34" - 36"	S2@1.19	Ea	178.00	40.70	—	218.70
38" - 40"	S2@1.45	Ea	217.00	49.50	—	266.50
42" - 44"	S2@1.73	Ea	256.00	59.10	—	315.10
46" - 48"	S2@2.04	Ea	304.00	69.70	—	373.70
50"	S2@2.28	Ea	342.00	77.90	—	419.90

Galvanized steel 6" rectangular duct 90 degree elbow

Description	Craft@Hrs	Unit	Material $	Labor $	Equipment $	Total $
4"	S2@.058	Ea	8.67	1.98	—	10.65
6"	S2@.078	Ea	11.70	2.66	—	14.36
8"	S2@.104	Ea	15.50	3.55	—	19.05
10"	S2@.132	Ea	19.80	4.51	—	24.31
12"	S2@.148	Ea	22.10	5.06	—	27.16
14" - 16"	S2@.266	Ea	40.00	9.09	—	49.09
18" - 20"	S2@.370	Ea	55.10	12.60	—	67.70
22" - 24"	S2@.506	Ea	75.80	17.30	—	93.10
26" - 28"	S2@.655	Ea	97.80	22.40	—	120.20
30" - 32"	S2@.905	Ea	134.00	30.90	—	164.90
34" - 36"	S2@1.24	Ea	186.00	42.40	—	228.40
38" - 40"	S2@1.49	Ea	222.00	50.90	—	272.90
42" - 44"	S2@1.78	Ea	265.00	60.80	—	325.80
46" - 48"	S2@2.09	Ea	312.00	71.40	—	383.40
50"	S2@2.34	Ea	351.00	79.90	—	430.90

Galvanized Steel Rectangular Elbows

Description	Craft@Hrs	Unit	Material $	Labor $	Equipment $	Total $
Galvanized steel 8" rectangular duct 90 degree elbow						
4"	S2@.078	Ea	11.70	2.66	—	14.36
6"	S2@.104	Ea	15.50	3.55	—	19.05
8"	S2@.132	Ea	19.80	4.51	—	24.31
10"	S2@.148	Ea	22.10	5.06	—	27.16
12"	S2@.170	Ea	25.50	5.81	—	31.31
14" - 16"	S2@.300	Ea	44.80	10.20	—	55.00
18" - 20"	S2@.403	Ea	60.20	13.80	—	74.00
22" - 24"	S2@.549	Ea	82.10	18.80	—	100.90
26" - 28"	S2@.694	Ea	104.00	23.70	—	127.70
30" - 32"	S2@.950	Ea	144.00	32.50	—	176.50
34" - 36"	S2@1.28	Ea	191.00	43.70	—	234.70
38" - 40"	S2@1.54	Ea	232.00	52.60	—	284.60
42" - 44"	S2@1.83	Ea	273.00	62.50	—	335.50
46" - 48"	S2@2.13	Ea	319.00	72.80	—	391.80
50"	S2@2.39	Ea	363.00	81.60	—	444.60
Galvanized steel 10" rectangular duct 90 degree elbow						
4"	S2@.104	Ea	15.50	3.55	—	19.05
6"	S2@.132	Ea	19.80	4.51	—	24.31
8"	S2@.148	Ea	22.10	5.06	—	27.16
10"	S2@.170	Ea	25.50	5.81	—	31.31
12"	S2@.194	Ea	28.80	6.63	—	35.43
14" - 16"	S2@.336	Ea	49.80	11.50	—	61.30
18" - 20"	S2@.438	Ea	65.30	15.00	—	80.30
22" - 24"	S2@.587	Ea	87.90	20.10	—	108.00
26" - 28"	S2@.737	Ea	110.00	25.20	—	135.20
30" - 32"	S2@.997	Ea	150.00	34.10	—	184.10
34" - 36"	S2@1.33	Ea	199.00	45.40	—	244.40
38" - 40"	S2@1.59	Ea	238.00	54.30	—	292.30
42" - 44"	S2@1.87	Ea	279.00	63.90	—	342.90
46" - 48"	S2@2.18	Ea	327.00	74.50	—	401.50
50"	S2@2.43	Ea	366.00	83.00	—	449.00
Galvanized steel 12" rectangular duct 90 degree elbow						
4"	S2@.132	Ea	19.80	4.51	—	24.31
6"	S2@.148	Ea	22.10	5.06	—	27.16
8"	S2@.170	Ea	25.50	5.81	—	31.31
10"	S2@.194	Ea	28.80	6.63	—	35.43
12"	S2@.224	Ea	33.60	7.65	—	41.25
18" - 20"	S2@.478	Ea	70.80	16.30	—	87.10
22" - 24"	S2@.628	Ea	93.80	21.50	—	115.30
26" - 28"	S2@.775	Ea	117.00	26.50	—	143.50
30" - 32"	S2@1.04	Ea	155.00	35.50	—	190.50
34" - 36"	S2@1.38	Ea	206.00	47.10	—	253.10
38" - 40"	S2@1.64	Ea	243.00	56.00	—	299.00
42" - 44"	S2@1.92	Ea	287.00	65.60	—	352.60
46" - 48"	S2@2.23	Ea	336.00	76.20	—	412.20
50"	S2@2.48	Ea	370.00	84.70	—	454.70

Description	Craft@Hrs	Unit	Material $	Labor $	Equipment $	Total $

Galvanized steel 14" rectangular duct 90 degree elbow

Description	Craft@Hrs	Unit	Material $	Labor $	Equipment $	Total $
4"	S2@.212	Ea	31.60	7.24	—	38.84
6"	S2@.232	Ea	34.90	7.93	—	42.83
8"	S2@.260	Ea	38.80	8.88	—	47.68
10"	S2@.292	Ea	43.60	9.97	—	53.57
12"	S2@.328	Ea	49.00	11.20	—	60.20
14" - 16"	S2@.415	Ea	62.30	14.20	—	76.50
18" - 20"	S2@.527	Ea	78.70	18.00	—	96.70
22" - 24"	S2@.867	Ea	99.60	29.60	—	129.20
26" - 28"	S2@.816	Ea	121.00	27.90	—	148.90
30" - 32"	S2@1.09	Ea	164.00	37.20	—	201.20
34" - 36"	S2@1.43	Ea	215.00	48.80	—	263.80
38" - 40"	S2@1.69	Ea	252.00	57.70	—	309.70
42" - 44"	S2@1.97	Ea	296.00	67.30	—	363.30
46" - 48"	S2@2.28	Ea	341.00	77.90	—	418.90
50"	S2@2.53	Ea	381.00	86.40	—	467.40

Galvanized steel 16" rectangular duct 90 degree elbow

Description	Craft@Hrs	Unit	Material $	Labor $	Equipment $	Total $
4"	S2@.260	Ea	38.80	8.88	—	47.68
6"	S2@.310	Ea	46.30	10.60	—	56.90
8"	S2@.340	Ea	50.90	11.60	—	62.50
10"	S2@.380	Ea	57.10	13.00	—	70.10
12"	S2@.420	Ea	62.80	14.30	—	77.10
14" - 16"	S2@.480	Ea	71.60	16.40	—	88.00
18" - 20"	S2@.555	Ea	82.90	19.00	—	101.90
22" - 24"	S2@.707	Ea	106.00	24.20	—	130.20
26" - 28"	S2@.856	Ea	128.00	29.20	—	157.20
30" - 32"	S2@1.14	Ea	171.00	38.90	—	209.90
34" - 36"	S2@1.48	Ea	221.00	50.60	—	271.60
38" - 40"	S2@1.73	Ea	260.00	59.10	—	319.10
42" - 44"	S2@2.02	Ea	303.00	69.00	—	372.00
46" - 48"	S2@2.32	Ea	351.00	79.30	—	430.30
50"	S2@2.58	Ea	385.00	88.10	—	473.10

Galvanized steel 18" rectangular duct 90 degree elbow

Description	Craft@Hrs	Unit	Material $	Labor $	Equipment $	Total $
4"	S2@.312	Ea	46.80	10.70	—	57.50
6"	S2@.350	Ea	52.50	12.00	—	64.50
8"	S2@.390	Ea	58.50	13.30	—	71.80
10"	S2@.427	Ea	64.10	14.60	—	78.70
12"	S2@.470	Ea	69.60	16.10	—	85.70
14" - 16"	S2@.519	Ea	77.70	17.70	—	95.40
18" - 20"	S2@.604	Ea	90.40	20.60	—	111.00
22" - 24"	S2@.747	Ea	112.00	25.50	—	137.50
26" - 28"	S2@.895	Ea	133.00	30.60	—	163.60
30" - 32"	S2@1.18	Ea	177.00	40.30	—	217.30
34" - 36"	S2@1.53	Ea	230.00	52.30	—	282.30
38" - 40"	S2@1.78	Ea	265.00	60.80	—	325.80
42" - 44"	S2@2.07	Ea	310.00	70.70	—	380.70
46" - 48"	S2@2.37	Ea	359.00	81.00	—	440.00
50"	S2@2.63	Ea	393.00	89.80	—	482.80

Galvanized Steel Rectangular Elbows

Description	Craft@Hrs	Unit	Material $	Labor $	Equipment $	Total $

Galvanized steel 20" rectangular duct 90 degree elbow

Description	Craft@Hrs	Unit	Material $	Labor $	Equipment $	Total $
4"	S2@.370	Ea	55.10	12.60	—	67.70
6"	S2@.390	Ea	58.50	13.30	—	71.80
8"	S2@.415	Ea	62.30	14.20	—	76.50
10"	S2@.448	Ea	67.00	15.30	—	82.30
12"	S2@.487	Ea	72.40	16.60	—	89.00
14" - 16"	S2@.553	Ea	82.50	18.90	—	101.40
18" - 20"	S2@.658	Ea	98.50	22.50	—	121.00
22" - 24"	S2@.786	Ea	118.00	26.80	—	144.80
26" - 28"	S2@.931	Ea	139.00	31.80	—	170.80
30" - 32"	S2@1.23	Ea	183.00	42.00	—	225.00
34" - 36"	S2@1.58	Ea	237.00	54.00	—	291.00
38" - 40"	S2@1.83	Ea	275.00	62.50	—	337.50
42" - 44"	S2@2.11	Ea	316.00	72.10	—	388.10
46" - 48"	S2@2.42	Ea	365.00	82.70	—	447.70
50"	S2@2.67	Ea	404.00	91.20	—	495.20

Galvanized steel rectangular 22" duct 90 degree elbow

Description	Craft@Hrs	Unit	Material $	Labor $	Equipment $	Total $
22" - 24"	S2@.828	Ea	123.00	28.30	—	151.30
26" - 28"	S2@1.01	Ea	151.00	34.50	—	185.50
30" - 32"	S2@1.31	Ea	196.00	44.70	—	240.70
34" - 36"	S2@1.71	Ea	255.00	58.40	—	313.40
38" - 40"	S2@2.01	Ea	303.00	68.70	—	371.70
42" - 44"	S2@2.31	Ea	342.00	78.90	—	420.90
46" - 48"	S2@2.61	Ea	389.00	89.20	—	478.20
50" - 52"	S2@2.91	Ea	436.00	99.40	—	535.40
54" - 56"	S2@3.51	Ea	525.00	120.00	—	645.00
58" - 60"	S2@4.26	Ea	639.00	146.00	—	785.00
62" - 64"	S2@4.76	Ea	707.00	163.00	—	870.00
66" - 68"	S2@5.25	Ea	785.00	179.00	—	964.00
70" - 72"	S2@5.76	Ea	859.00	197.00	—	1,056.00

Galvanized steel 24" rectangular duct 90 degree elbow

Description	Craft@Hrs	Unit	Material $	Labor $	Equipment $	Total $
22" - 24"	S2@.922	Ea	138.00	31.50	—	169.50
26" - 28"	S2@1.10	Ea	165.00	37.60	—	202.60
30" - 32"	S2@1.41	Ea	211.00	48.20	—	259.20
34" - 36"	S2@1.81	Ea	271.00	61.80	—	332.80
38" - 40"	S2@2.10	Ea	316.00	71.70	—	387.70
42" - 44"	S2@2.41	Ea	363.00	82.30	—	445.30
46" - 48"	S2@2.71	Ea	405.00	92.60	—	497.60
50" - 52"	S2@3.01	Ea	448.00	103.00	—	551.00
54" - 56"	S2@3.62	Ea	541.00	124.00	—	665.00
58" - 60"	S2@4.38	Ea	653.00	150.00	—	803.00
62" - 64"	S2@4.87	Ea	724.00	166.00	—	890.00
66" - 68"	S2@5.38	Ea	801.00	184.00	—	985.00
70" - 72"	S2@5.87	Ea	879.00	201.00	—	1,080.00

Description	Craft@Hrs	Unit	Material $	Labor $	Equipment $	Total $

Galvanized steel 26" rectangular duct 90 degree elbow

Description	Craft@Hrs	Unit	Material $	Labor $	Equipment $	Total $
22" - 24"	S2@1.01	Ea	151.00	34.50	—	185.50
26" - 28"	S2@1.19	Ea	178.00	40.70	—	218.70
30" - 32"	S2@1.50	Ea	224.00	51.20	—	275.20
34" - 36"	S2@1.92	Ea	287.00	65.60	—	352.60
38" - 40"	S2@2.21	Ea	330.00	75.50	—	405.50
42" - 44"	S2@2.51	Ea	377.00	85.70	—	462.70
46" - 48"	S2@2.81	Ea	419.00	96.00	—	515.00
50" - 52"	S2@3.11	Ea	468.00	106.00	—	574.00
54" - 56"	S2@3.73	Ea	561.00	127.00	—	688.00
58" - 60"	S2@4.50	Ea	672.00	154.00	—	826.00
62" - 64"	S2@5.02	Ea	746.00	171.00	—	917.00
66" - 68"	S2@5.53	Ea	829.00	189.00	—	1,018.00
70" - 72"	S2@6.04	Ea	904.00	206.00	—	1,110.00

Galvanized steel 28" rectangular duct 90 degree elbow

Description	Craft@Hrs	Unit	Material $	Labor $	Equipment $	Total $
22" - 24"	S2@1.10	Ea	164.00	37.60	—	201.60
26" - 28"	S2@1.28	Ea	191.00	43.70	—	234.70
30" - 32"	S2@1.60	Ea	240.00	54.70	—	294.70
34" - 36"	S2@2.03	Ea	304.00	69.30	—	373.30
38" - 40"	S2@2.31	Ea	342.00	78.90	—	420.90
42" - 44"	S2@2.61	Ea	389.00	89.20	—	478.20
46" - 48"	S2@2.91	Ea	436.00	99.40	—	535.40
50" - 52"	S2@3.21	Ea	484.00	110.00	—	594.00
54" - 56"	S2@3.84	Ea	575.00	131.00	—	706.00
58" - 60"	S2@4.61	Ea	692.00	157.00	—	849.00
62" - 64"	S2@5.15	Ea	762.00	176.00	—	938.00
66" - 68"	S2@5.66	Ea	840.00	193.00	—	1,033.00
70" - 72"	S2@6.15	Ea	914.00	210.00	—	1,124.00

Galvanized steel 30" rectangular duct 90 degree elbow

Description	Craft@Hrs	Unit	Material $	Labor $	Equipment $	Total $
22" - 24"	S2@1.19	Ea	177.00	40.70	—	217.70
26" - 28"	S2@1.37	Ea	206.00	46.80	—	252.80
30" - 32"	S2@1.70	Ea	253.00	58.10	—	311.10
34" - 36"	S2@2.14	Ea	319.00	73.10	—	392.10
38" - 40"	S2@2.41	Ea	363.00	82.30	—	445.30
42" - 44"	S2@2.71	Ea	405.00	92.60	—	497.60
46" - 48"	S2@3.01	Ea	448.00	103.00	—	551.00
50" - 52"	S2@3.31	Ea	494.00	113.00	—	607.00
54" - 56"	S2@3.95	Ea	589.00	135.00	—	724.00
58" - 60"	S2@4.74	Ea	705.00	162.00	—	867.00
62" - 64"	S2@5.25	Ea	785.00	179.00	—	964.00
66" - 68"	S2@5.79	Ea	860.00	198.00	—	1,058.00
70" - 72"	S2@6.28	Ea	938.00	215.00	—	1,153.00

Galvanized Steel Rectangular Elbows

Description	Craft@Hrs	Unit	Material $	Labor $	Equipment $	Total $

Galvanized steel 32" rectangular duct 90 degree elbow

Description	Craft@Hrs	Unit	Material $	Labor $	Equipment $	Total $
22" - 24"	S2@1.53	Ea	230.00	52.30	—	282.30
26" - 28"	S2@1.73	Ea	256.00	59.10	—	315.10
30" - 32"	S2@1.93	Ea	288.00	65.90	—	353.90
34" - 36"	S2@2.25	Ea	339.00	76.90	—	415.90
38" - 40"	S2@2.51	Ea	377.00	85.70	—	462.70
42" - 44"	S2@2.81	Ea	419.00	96.00	—	515.00
46" - 48"	S2@3.11	Ea	463.00	106.00	—	569.00
50" - 52"	S2@3.41	Ea	510.00	116.00	—	626.00
54" - 56"	S2@4.06	Ea	603.00	139.00	—	742.00
58" - 60"	S2@4.85	Ea	723.00	166.00	—	889.00
62" - 64"	S2@5.38	Ea	801.00	184.00	—	985.00
66" - 68"	S2@5.89	Ea	880.00	201.00	—	1,081.00
70" - 72"	S2@6.40	Ea	957.00	219.00	—	1,176.00

Galvanized steel 34" rectangular duct 90 degree elbow

Description	Craft@Hrs	Unit	Material $	Labor $	Equipment $	Total $
22" - 24"	S2@1.67	Ea	250.00	57.00	—	307.00
26" - 28"	S2@1.91	Ea	287.00	65.20	—	352.20
30" - 32"	S2@2.12	Ea	316.00	72.40	—	388.40
34" - 36"	S2@2.36	Ea	353.00	80.60	—	433.60
38" - 40"	S2@2.60	Ea	389.00	88.80	—	477.80
42" - 44"	S2@2.91	Ea	436.00	99.40	—	535.40
46" - 48"	S2@3.21	Ea	474.00	110.00	—	584.00
50" - 52"	S2@3.51	Ea	525.00	120.00	—	645.00
54" - 56"	S2@4.17	Ea	625.00	142.00	—	767.00
58" - 60"	S2@4.97	Ea	744.00	170.00	—	914.00
62" - 64"	S2@5.49	Ea	822.00	188.00	—	1,010.00
66" - 68"	S2@6.04	Ea	904.00	206.00	—	1,110.00
70" - 72"	S2@6.51	Ea	968.00	222.00	—	1,190.00

Galvanized steel 36" rectangular duct 90 degree elbow

Description	Craft@Hrs	Unit	Material $	Labor $	Equipment $	Total $
22" - 24"	S2@1.83	Ea	275.00	62.50	—	337.50
26" - 28"	S2@2.04	Ea	306.00	69.70	—	375.70
30" - 32"	S2@2.26	Ea	339.00	77.20	—	416.20
34" - 36"	S2@2.47	Ea	370.00	84.40	—	454.40
38" - 40"	S2@2.70	Ea	405.00	92.20	—	497.20
42" - 44"	S2@3.01	Ea	448.00	103.00	—	551.00
46" - 48"	S2@3.31	Ea	494.00	113.00	—	607.00
50" - 52"	S2@3.61	Ea	540.00	123.00	—	663.00
54" - 56"	S2@4.27	Ea	639.00	146.00	—	785.00
58" - 60"	S2@5.10	Ea	759.00	174.00	—	933.00
62" - 64"	S2@5.61	Ea	837.00	192.00	—	1,029.00
66" - 68"	S2@6.15	Ea	914.00	210.00	—	1,124.00
70" - 72"	S2@6.64	Ea	992.00	227.00	—	1,219.00

Description	Craft@Hrs	Unit	Material $	Labor $	Equipment $	Total $

Galvanized steel 38" rectangular duct 90 degree elbow

Description	Craft@Hrs	Unit	Material $	Labor $	Equipment $	Total $
22" - 24"	S2@1.98	Ea	296.00	67.60	—	363.60
26" - 28"	S2@2.18	Ea	327.00	74.50	—	401.50
30" - 32"	S2@2.38	Ea	359.00	81.30	—	440.30
34" - 36"	S2@2.58	Ea	388.00	88.10	—	476.10
38" - 40"	S2@2.81	Ea	419.00	96.00	—	515.00
42" - 44"	S2@3.11	Ea	463.00	106.00	—	569.00
46" - 48"	S2@3.41	Ea	510.00	116.00	—	626.00
50" - 52"	S2@3.71	Ea	552.00	127.00	—	679.00
54" - 56"	S2@4.38	Ea	653.00	150.00	—	803.00
58" - 60"	S2@5.21	Ea	781.00	178.00	—	959.00
62" - 64"	S2@5.74	Ea	854.00	196.00	—	1,050.00
66" - 68"	S2@6.28	Ea	938.00	215.00	—	1,153.00
70" - 72"	S2@6.75	Ea	1,010.00	231.00	—	1,241.00

Galvanized steel 40" rectangular duct 90 degree elbow

Description	Craft@Hrs	Unit	Material $	Labor $	Equipment $	Total $
40" - 42"	S2@3.06	Ea	459.00	105.00	—	564.00
44" - 46"	S2@3.36	Ea	498.00	115.00	—	613.00
48" - 50"	S2@3.66	Ea	548.00	125.00	—	673.00
52" - 54"	S2@3.98	Ea	594.00	136.00	—	730.00
56" - 58"	S2@5.17	Ea	770.00	177.00	—	947.00
60" - 62"	S2@5.59	Ea	836.00	191.00	—	1,027.00
64" - 66"	S2@6.11	Ea	911.00	209.00	—	1,120.00
68" - 70"	S2@6.66	Ea	996.00	228.00	—	1,224.00
72"	S2@7.05	Ea	1,050.00	241.00	—	1,291.00

Galvanized steel 42" rectangular duct 90 degree elbow

Description	Craft@Hrs	Unit	Material $	Labor $	Equipment $	Total $
40" - 42"	S2@3.21	Ea	484.00	110.00	—	594.00
44" - 46"	S2@3.52	Ea	527.00	120.00	—	647.00
48" - 50"	S2@3.83	Ea	575.00	131.00	—	706.00
52" - 54"	S2@4.16	Ea	623.00	142.00	—	765.00
56" - 58"	S2@5.34	Ea	796.00	182.00	—	978.00
60" - 62"	S2@5.81	Ea	864.00	198.00	—	1,062.00
64" - 66"	S2@6.32	Ea	944.00	216.00	—	1,160.00
68" - 70"	S2@6.85	Ea	1,020.00	234.00	—	1,254.00
72"	S2@7.22	Ea	1,090.00	247.00	—	1,337.00

Galvanized steel 44" rectangular duct 90 degree elbow

Description	Craft@Hrs	Unit	Material $	Labor $	Equipment $	Total $
40" - 42"	S2@3.36	Ea	498.00	115.00	—	613.00
44" - 46"	S2@3.69	Ea	551.00	126.00	—	677.00
48" - 50"	S2@4.01	Ea	598.00	137.00	—	735.00
52" - 54"	S2@4.32	Ea	646.00	148.00	—	794.00
56" - 58"	S2@5.51	Ea	825.00	188.00	—	1,013.00
60" - 62"	S2@6.00	Ea	893.00	205.00	—	1,098.00
64" - 66"	S2@6.51	Ea	968.00	222.00	—	1,190.00
68" - 70"	S2@7.05	Ea	1,060.00	241.00	—	1,301.00
72"	S2@7.39	Ea	1,100.00	252.00	—	1,352.00

Galvanized Steel Rectangular Elbows

Description	Craft@Hrs	Unit	Material $	Labor $	Equipment $	Total $

Galvanized steel 46" rectangular duct 90 degree elbow

Description	Craft@Hrs	Unit	Material $	Labor $	Equipment $	Total $
40" - 42"	S2@3.52	Ea	527.00	120.00	—	647.00
44" - 46"	S2@3.86	Ea	578.00	132.00	—	710.00
48" - 50"	S2@4.16	Ea	623.00	142.00	—	765.00
52" - 54"	S2@4.32	Ea	669.00	148.00	—	817.00
56" - 58"	S2@5.72	Ea	851.00	195.00	—	1,046.00
60" - 62"	S2@6.19	Ea	922.00	211.00	—	1,133.00
64" - 66"	S2@6.70	Ea	1,010.00	229.00	—	1,239.00
68" - 70"	S2@7.26	Ea	1,090.00	248.00	—	1,338.00
72"	S2@7.60	Ea	1,130.00	260.00	—	1,390.00

Galvanized steel 48" rectangular duct 90 degree elbow

Description	Craft@Hrs	Unit	Material $	Labor $	Equipment $	Total $
40" - 42"	S2@3.67	Ea	549.00	125.00	—	674.00
44" - 46"	S2@4.01	Ea	598.00	137.00	—	735.00
48" - 50"	S2@4.32	Ea	646.00	148.00	—	794.00
52" - 54"	S2@4.61	Ea	685.00	157.00	—	842.00
56" - 58"	S2@5.91	Ea	887.00	202.00	—	1,089.00
60" - 62"	S2@6.40	Ea	957.00	219.00	—	1,176.00
64" - 66"	S2@6.90	Ea	1,030.00	236.00	—	1,266.00
68" - 70"	S2@7.41	Ea	1,110.00	253.00	—	1,363.00
72"	S2@7.77	Ea	1,170.00	265.00	—	1,435.00

Galvanized steel 50" rectangular duct 90 degree elbow

Description	Craft@Hrs	Unit	Material $	Labor $	Equipment $	Total $
40" - 42"	S2@3.82	Ea	575.00	130.00	—	705.00
44" - 46"	S2@4.16	Ea	623.00	142.00	—	765.00
48" - 50"	S2@4.46	Ea	669.00	152.00	—	821.00
52" - 54"	S2@4.78	Ea	708.00	163.00	—	871.00
56" - 58"	S2@6.11	Ea	911.00	209.00	—	1,120.00
60" - 62"	S2@6.60	Ea	986.00	225.00	—	1,211.00
64" - 66"	S2@7.09	Ea	1,060.00	242.00	—	1,302.00
68" - 70"	S2@7.62	Ea	1,140.00	260.00	—	1,400.00
72"	S2@7.94	Ea	1,190.00	271.00	—	1,461.00

Galvanized steel 52" rectangular duct 90 degree elbow

Description	Craft@Hrs	Unit	Material $	Labor $	Equipment $	Total $
40" - 42"	S2@3.98	Ea	594.00	136.00	—	730.00
44" - 46"	S2@4.32	Ea	646.00	148.00	—	794.00
48" - 50"	S2@4.61	Ea	685.00	157.00	—	842.00
52" - 54"	S2@4.95	Ea	738.00	169.00	—	907.00
56" - 58"	S2@6.32	Ea	944.00	216.00	—	1,160.00
60" - 62"	S2@6.79	Ea	1,020.00	232.00	—	1,252.00
64" - 66"	S2@7.30	Ea	1,090.00	249.00	—	1,339.00
68" - 70"	S2@7.81	Ea	1,170.00	267.00	—	1,437.00
72"	S2@8.16	Ea	1,210.00	279.00	—	1,489.00

Galvanized Steel Rectangular Elbows

Description	Craft@Hrs	Unit	Material $	Labor $	Equipment $	Total $

Galvanized steel 54" rectangular duct 90 degree elbow

Description	Craft@Hrs	Unit	Material $	Labor $	Equipment $	Total $
40" - 42"	S2@4.16	Ea	623.00	142.00	—	765.00
44" - 46"	S2@4.46	Ea	669.00	152.00	—	821.00
48" - 50"	S2@4.78	Ea	708.00	163.00	—	871.00
52" - 54"	S2@5.15	Ea	762.00	176.00	—	938.00
56" - 58"	S2@6.51	Ea	968.00	222.00	—	1,190.00
60" - 62"	S2@7.00	Ea	1,050.00	239.00	—	1,289.00
64" - 66"	S2@7.49	Ea	1,120.00	256.00	—	1,376.00
68" - 70"	S2@8.01	Ea	1,200.00	274.00	—	1,474.00
72"	S2@8.41	Ea	1,240.00	287.00	—	1,527.00

Galvanized steel 56" rectangular duct 90 degree elbow

Description	Craft@Hrs	Unit	Material $	Labor $	Equipment $	Total $
40" - 42"	S2@5.10	Ea	759.00	174.00	—	933.00
44" - 46"	S2@5.49	Ea	822.00	188.00	—	1,010.00
48" - 50"	S2@5.85	Ea	876.00	200.00	—	1,076.00
52" - 54"	S2@6.26	Ea	934.00	214.00	—	1,148.00
56" - 58"	S2@6.68	Ea	1,000.00	228.00	—	1,228.00
60" - 62"	S2@7.15	Ea	1,070.00	244.00	—	1,314.00
64" - 66"	S2@7.66	Ea	1,140.00	262.00	—	1,402.00
68" - 70"	S2@8.18	Ea	1,210.00	279.00	—	1,489.00
72"	S2@8.58	Ea	1,290.00	293.00	—	1,583.00

Galvanized steel 58" rectangular duct 90 degree elbow

Description	Craft@Hrs	Unit	Material $	Labor $	Equipment $	Total $
58" - 60"	S2@7.15	Ea	1,090.00	244.00	—	1,334.00
62" - 64"	S2@7.62	Ea	1,140.00	260.00	—	1,400.00
66" - 68"	S2@8.13	Ea	1,220.00	278.00	—	1,498.00
70" - 72"	S2@8.69	Ea	1,310.00	297.00	—	1,607.00

Galvanized steel 60" rectangular duct 90 degree elbow

Description	Craft@Hrs	Unit	Material $	Labor $	Equipment $	Total $
58" - 60"	S2@7.37	Ea	1,110.00	252.00	—	1,362.00
62" - 64"	S2@7.88	Ea	1,190.00	269.00	—	1,459.00
66" - 68"	S2@8.41	Ea	1,280.00	287.00	—	1,567.00
70" - 72"	S2@8.95	Ea	1,340.00	306.00	—	1,646.00

Galvanized steel 62" rectangular duct 90 degree elbow

Description	Craft@Hrs	Unit	Material $	Labor $	Equipment $	Total $
58" - 60"	S2@7.62	Ea	1,140.00	260.00	—	1,400.00
62" - 64"	S2@8.13	Ea	1,210.00	278.00	—	1,488.00
66" - 68"	S2@8.69	Ea	1,300.00	297.00	—	1,597.00
70" - 72"	S2@9.18	Ea	1,380.00	314.00	—	1,694.00

Galvanized steel 64" rectangular duct 90 degree elbow

Description	Craft@Hrs	Unit	Material $	Labor $	Equipment $	Total $
58" - 60"	S2@7.88	Ea	1,180.00	269.00	—	1,449.00
62" - 64"	S2@8.41	Ea	1,250.00	287.00	—	1,537.00
66" - 68"	S2@8.95	Ea	1,330.00	306.00	—	1,636.00
70" - 72"	S2@9.44	Ea	1,410.00	322.00	—	1,732.00

Galvanized Steel Rectangular Elbows

Description	Craft@Hrs	Unit	Material $	Labor $	Equipment $	Total $

Galvanized steel 66" rectangular duct 90 degree elbow

Description	Craft@Hrs	Unit	Material $	Labor $	Equipment $	Total $
58" - 60"	S2@8.13	Ea	1,210.00	278.00	—	1,488.00
62" - 64"	S2@8.69	Ea	1,300.00	297.00	—	1,597.00
66" - 68"	S2@9.18	Ea	1,380.00	314.00	—	1,694.00
70" - 72"	S2@9.69	Ea	1,460.00	331.00	—	1,791.00

Galvanized steel 68" rectangular duct 90 degree elbow

Description	Craft@Hrs	Unit	Material $	Labor $	Equipment $	Total $
58" - 60"	S2@8.41	Ea	1,250.00	287.00	—	1,537.00
62" - 64"	S2@8.95	Ea	1,330.00	306.00	—	1,636.00
66" - 68"	S2@9.44	Ea	1,410.00	322.00	—	1,732.00
70" - 72"	S2@9.95	Ea	1,500.00	340.00	—	1,840.00

Galvanized steel 70" rectangular duct 90 degree elbow

Description	Craft@Hrs	Unit	Material $	Labor $	Equipment $	Total $
58" - 60"	S2@8.69	Ea	1,300.00	297.00	—	1,597.00
62" - 64"	S2@9.18	Ea	1,380.00	314.00	—	1,694.00
66" - 68"	S2@9.69	Ea	1,460.00	331.00	—	1,791.00
70" - 72"	S2@10.2	Ea	1,530.00	348.00	—	1,878.00

Galvanized steel 72" rectangular duct 90 degree elbow

Description	Craft@Hrs	Unit	Material $	Labor $	Equipment $	Total $
58" - 60"	S2@8.95	Ea	1,330.00	306.00	—	1,636.00
62" - 64"	S2@9.44	Ea	1,410.00	322.00	—	1,732.00
66" - 68"	S2@9.95	Ea	1,500.00	340.00	—	1,840.00
70" - 72"	S2@10.5	Ea	1,560.00	359.00	—	1,919.00

Galvanized Steel Rectangular Drops and Tees

Costs for Galvanized Rectangular Drops and Tap-in Tees. Costs per drop or tap-in tee, based on quantities less than 1,000 pounds. Deduct 15% from the material cost for over 1,000 pounds. Add 50% to the material cost for the lined duct. These costs include delivery, typical bracing, cleats, scrap, hangers, end closures, sealants and miscellaneous hardware. For turning vanes, please see page 342.

Description	Craft@Hrs	Unit	Material $	Labor $	Equipment $	Total $

Galvanized steel 6" rectangular duct drops and tap-in tees

Description	Craft@Hrs	Unit	Material $	Labor $	Equipment $	Total $
6"	S2@.072	Ea	11.80	2.46	—	14.26
8"	S2@.084	Ea	13.80	2.87	—	16.67
10"	S2@.097	Ea	15.60	3.31	—	18.91
12" - 16"	S2@.139	Ea	22.60	4.75	—	27.35
20" - 24"	S2@.216	Ea	35.10	7.38	—	42.48
28" - 32"	S2@.309	Ea	49.80	10.60	—	60.40
36" - 40"	S2@.412	Ea	67.00	14.10	—	81.10
44" - 48"	S2@.489	Ea	79.40	16.70	—	96.10
52" - 56"	S2@.591	Ea	95.80	20.20	—	116.00
60"	S2@.747	Ea	121.00	25.50	—	146.50

Galvanized steel 8" rectangular duct drops and tap-in tees

Description	Craft@Hrs	Unit	Material $	Labor $	Equipment $	Total $
6"	S2@.084	Ea	13.80	2.87	—	16.67
8"	S2@.097	Ea	15.60	3.31	—	18.91
10"	S2@.109	Ea	17.70	3.72	—	21.42
12" - 16"	S2@.152	Ea	25.00	5.19	—	30.19
20" - 24"	S2@.231	Ea	37.70	7.89	—	45.59
28" - 32"	S2@.326	Ea	53.40	11.10	—	64.50
36" - 40"	S2@.432	Ea	70.30	14.80	—	85.10
44" - 48"	S2@.506	Ea	82.20	17.30	—	99.50
52" - 56"	S2@.634	Ea	103.00	21.70	—	124.70
60"	S2@.760	Ea	123.00	26.00	—	149.00

Galvanized steel 10" rectangular duct drops and tap-in tees

Description	Craft@Hrs	Unit	Material $	Labor $	Equipment $	Total $
6"	S2@.097	Ea	15.60	3.31	—	18.91
8"	S2@.109	Ea	17.70	3.72	—	21.42
10"	S2@.121	Ea	19.80	4.13	—	23.93
12" - 16"	S2@.167	Ea	27.10	5.70	—	32.80
20" - 24"	S2@.246	Ea	40.40	8.40	—	48.80
28" - 32"	S2@.343	Ea	56.10	11.70	—	67.80
36" - 40"	S2@.450	Ea	72.70	15.40	—	88.10
44" - 48"	S2@.525	Ea	85.10	17.90	—	103.00
52" - 56"	S2@.653	Ea	106.00	22.30	—	128.30
60"	S2@.773	Ea	124.00	26.40	—	150.40

Galvanized Steel Rectangular Drops and Tees

Description	Craft@Hrs	Unit	Material $	Labor $	Equipment $	Total $

Galvanized steel 12" rectangular duct drops and tap-in tees

Description	Craft@Hrs	Unit	Material $	Labor $	Equipment $	Total $
6"	S2@.109	Ea	17.70	3.72	—	21.42
8"	S2@.121	Ea	19.80	4.13	—	23.93
10"	S2@.133	Ea	21.70	4.54	—	26.24
12" - 16"	S2@.180	Ea	29.20	6.15	—	35.35
20" - 24"	S2@.262	Ea	42.80	8.95	—	51.75
28" - 32"	S2@.360	Ea	58.50	12.30	—	70.80
36" - 40"	S2@.470	Ea	75.90	16.10	—	92.00
44" - 48"	S2@.544	Ea	88.00	18.60	—	106.60
52" - 56"	S2@.675	Ea	110.00	23.10	—	133.10
60"	S2@.794	Ea	129.00	27.10	—	156.10

Galvanized steel 16" rectangular duct drops and tap-in tees

Description	Craft@Hrs	Unit	Material $	Labor $	Equipment $	Total $
6"	S2@.170	Ea	27.50	5.81	—	33.31
8"	S2@.184	Ea	30.30	6.29	—	36.59
10"	S2@.200	Ea	32.70	6.83	—	39.53
12" - 16"	S2@.231	Ea	37.70	7.89	—	45.59
20" - 24"	S2@.293	Ea	47.30	10.00	—	57.30
28" - 32"	S2@.396	Ea	64.10	13.50	—	77.60
36" - 40"	S2@.506	Ea	82.20	17.30	—	99.50
44" - 48"	S2@.581	Ea	94.40	19.80	—	114.20
52" - 56"	S2@.709	Ea	116.00	24.20	—	140.20
60"	S2@.841	Ea	136.00	28.70	—	164.70

Galvanized steel 20" rectangular duct drops and tap-in tees

Description	Craft@Hrs	Unit	Material $	Labor $	Equipment $	Total $
6"	S2@.200	Ea	32.70	6.83	—	39.53
8"	S2@.216	Ea	35.10	7.38	—	42.48
10"	S2@.231	Ea	37.70	7.89	—	45.59
12" - 16"	S2@.262	Ea	42.80	8.95	—	51.75
20" - 24"	S2@.324	Ea	52.70	11.10	—	63.80
28" - 32"	S2@.428	Ea	69.50	14.60	—	84.10
36" - 40"	S2@.544	Ea	88.00	18.60	—	106.60
44" - 48"	S2@.617	Ea	100.00	21.10	—	121.10
52" - 56"	S2@.758	Ea	122.00	25.90	—	147.90
60"	S2@.884	Ea	144.00	30.20	—	174.20

Description	Craft@Hrs	Unit	Material $	Labor $	Equipment $	Total $

Galvanized steel 24" rectangular duct drops and tap-in tees

Description	Craft@Hrs	Unit	Material $	Labor $	Equipment $	Total $
6"	S2@.231	Ea	37.70	7.89	—	45.59
8"	S2@.247	Ea	40.40	8.44	—	48.84
10"	S2@.262	Ea	42.80	8.95	—	51.75
12" - 16"	S2@.293	Ea	47.30	10.00	—	57.30
20" - 24"	S2@.354	Ea	57.50	12.10	—	69.60
28" - 32"	S2@.462	Ea	74.40	15.80	—	90.20
36" - 40"	S2@.581	Ea	94.40	19.80	—	114.20
44" - 48"	S2@.655	Ea	106.00	22.40	—	128.40
52" - 56"	S2@.798	Ea	130.00	27.30	—	157.30
60"	S2@.927	Ea	151.00	31.70	—	182.70

Galvanized steel 28" rectangular duct drops and tap-in tees

Description	Craft@Hrs	Unit	Material $	Labor $	Equipment $	Total $
6"	S2@.262	Ea	42.80	8.95	—	51.75
8"	S2@.278	Ea	44.80	9.50	—	54.30
10"	S2@.292	Ea	47.30	9.97	—	57.27
12" - 16"	S2@.324	Ea	52.70	11.10	—	63.80
20" - 24"	S2@.385	Ea	62.50	13.20	—	75.70
28" - 32"	S2@.497	Ea	80.60	17.00	—	97.60
36" - 40"	S2@.617	Ea	100.00	21.10	—	121.10
44" - 48"	S2@.694	Ea	112.00	23.70	—	135.70
52" - 56"	S2@.837	Ea	136.00	28.60	—	164.60
60"	S2@.969	Ea	157.00	33.10	—	190.10

Galvanized steel 32" rectangular duct drops and tap-in tees

Description	Craft@Hrs	Unit	Material $	Labor $	Equipment $	Total $
6"	S2@.356	Ea	57.80	12.20	—	70.00
8"	S2@.374	Ea	61.50	12.80	—	74.30
10"	S2@.393	Ea	63.90	13.40	—	77.30
12" - 16"	S2@.432	Ea	70.30	14.80	—	85.10
20" - 24"	S2@.506	Ea	82.20	17.30	—	99.50
28" - 32"	S2@.581	Ea	94.40	19.80	—	114.20
36" - 40"	S2@.655	Ea	106.00	22.40	—	128.40
44" - 48"	S2@.730	Ea	118.00	24.90	—	142.90
52" - 56"	S2@.877	Ea	144.00	30.00	—	174.00
60"	S2@1.02	Ea	165.00	34.80	—	199.80

Galvanized Steel Round Ductwork

Description	Craft@Hrs	Unit	Material $	Labor $	Equipment $	Total $

Galvanized steel round duct snap-lock with slip joints

Description	Craft@Hrs	Unit	Material $	Labor $	Equipment $	Total $
3"	S2@.080	LF	2.67	2.73	—	5.40
4"	S2@.090	LF	2.75	3.07	—	5.82
5"	S2@.095	LF	2.95	3.25	—	6.20
6"	S2@.100	LF	3.45	3.42	—	6.87
7"	S2@.110	LF	5.30	3.76	—	9.06
8"	S2@.120	LF	5.47	4.10	—	9.57
9"	S2@.140	LF	5.73	4.78	—	10.51
10"	S2@.160	LF	5.97	5.47	—	11.44

Galvanized steel round duct 90 degree adjustable elbow

Description	Craft@Hrs	Unit	Material $	Labor $	Equipment $	Total $
3"	S2@.250	Ea	5.18	8.54	—	13.72
4"	S2@.300	Ea	7.13	10.20	—	17.33
5"	S2@.350	Ea	8.61	12.00	—	20.61
6"	S2@.400	Ea	11.20	13.70	—	24.90
7"	S2@.450	Ea	38.20	15.40	—	53.60
8"	S2@.500	Ea	42.80	17.10	—	59.90
9"	S2@.600	Ea	46.30	20.50	—	66.80
10"	S2@.700	Ea	50.70	23.90	—	74.60

Galvanized steel round duct 45 degree adjustable elbow

Description	Craft@Hrs	Unit	Material $	Labor $	Equipment $	Total $
3"	S2@.250	Ea	5.18	8.54	—	13.72
4"	S2@.300	Ea	7.13	10.20	—	17.33
5"	S2@.350	Ea	8.61	12.00	—	20.61
6"	S2@.400	Ea	11.20	13.70	—	24.90
7"	S2@.450	Ea	38.20	15.40	—	53.60
8"	S2@.500	Ea	42.80	17.10	—	59.90
9"	S2@.600	Ea	46.30	20.50	—	66.80
10"	S2@.700	Ea	50.70	23.90	—	74.60

Standard fiberglass ductwork, or duct board, should not be used in systems where air velocities exceed 2,500 feet per minute, or where static pressures are higher than 2 inches of water gauge.

Additionally, it should not be used for the following applications:

1) Equipment rooms

2) Underground or outdoors

3) Final connections to air handling equipment

4) Plenums or casings

5) Fume, heat or moisture exhaust systems

The costs for manufacturing and installing fiberglass ductwork are based on the net areas of the duct and fittings.

Here are approximate current material costs, per square foot:

Fiberglass Type	Up to 2,500 SF Material $/SF	Over 2,500 SF Material $/SF
475	4.04	3.68
800	4.43	4.02
1400	5.40	5.21

Additional costs: Approximately 25 cents per square foot should be added for the cost of tie rods, hangers, staples, tape and waste.

Type 475 fiberglass board is used almost exclusively for residential and small commercial air systems, while Types 800 and 1400 are used in larger commercial and industrial systems.

Fiberglass Ductwork Fabrication Labor*						
Size ranges (inches)						
	Up through 16		17 through 32		33 through 48	
Activity	SF/Hour Output	Labor $/SF	SF/Hour Output	Labor $/SF	SF/Hour Output	Labor $/SF
Duct only	60	.58	58	.60	56	.62
Fittings only	40	.87	38	.91	35	.99
Duct & 15% fittings	55	.63	53	.65	50	.69
Duct & 25% fittings	53	.65	51	.68	48	.72
Duct & 35% fittings	51	.68	49	.71	46	.75

Labor rates are based on using a standard grooving machine and include all tie-rod reinforcing.

Labor correction factors:

1) Hand grooving in lieu of machine grooving: 1.58

2) Use of an auto-closer: .82

3) Tie-rods enclosed in conduit: 1.36

4) T-bar or channel reinforcing in lieu of tie-rods: 1.25

In the following installation table the measurements refer to the "semi-perimeter", the width plus depth of the ductwork. Example – 12" duct (8" wide plus 4" high) has 2.00 SF of area for each linear foot.

Fiberglass Ductwork

Description	Craft@Hrs	Unit	Material $	Labor $	Equipment $	Total $
Fiberglass ductwork installation						
12" (2.00 SF/LF)	S2@.070	LF	—	2.39	—	2.39
14" (2.35 SF/LF)	S2@.082	LF	—	2.80	—	2.80
16" (2.65 SF/LF)	S2@.093	LF	—	3.18	—	3.18
18" (3.00 SF/LF)	S2@.105	LF	—	3.59	—	3.59
20" (3.35 SF/LF)	S2@.117	LF	—	4.00	—	4.00
22" (3.65 SF/LF)	S2@.128	LF	—	4.37	—	4.37
24" (4.00 SF/LF)	S2@.140	LF	—	4.78	—	4.78
26" (4.35 SF/LF)	S2@.152	LF	—	5.19	—	5.19
28" (4.65 SF/LF)	S2@.163	LF	—	5.57	—	5.57
30" (5.00 SF/LF)	S2@.175	LF	—	5.98	—	5.98
32" (5.35 SF/LF)	S2@.187	LF	—	6.39	—	6.39
34" (5.65 SF/LF)	S2@.198	LF	—	6.76	—	6.76
36" (6.00 SF/LF)	S2@.210	LF	—	7.17	—	7.17
38" (6.35 SF/LF)	S2@.222	LF	—	7.58	—	7.58
40" (6.65 SF/LF)	S2@.232	LF	—	7.93	—	7.93
42" (7.00 SF/LF)	S2@.245	LF	—	8.37	—	8.37
44" (7.35 SF/LF)	S2@.257	LF	—	8.78	—	8.78
46" (7.65 SF/LF)	S2@.268	LF	—	9.15	—	9.15
48" (8.00 SF/LF)	S2@.280	LF	—	9.56	—	9.56
50" (8.35 SF/LF)	S2@.292	LF	—	9.97	—	9.97
52" (8.65 SF/LF)	S2@.303	LF	—	10.40	—	10.40
54" (9.00 SF/LF)	S2@.315	LF	—	10.80	—	10.80
56" (9.35 SF/LF)	S2@.327	LF	—	11.20	—	11.20
58" (9.65 SF/LF)	S2@.338	LF	—	11.50	—	11.50
60" (10.0 SF/LF)	S2@.350	LF	—	12.00	—	12.00
64" (10.6 SF/LF)	S2@.373	LF	—	12.70	—	12.70
68" (11.4 SF/LF)	S2@.397	LF	—	13.60	—	13.60
72" (12.0 SF/LF)	S2@.420	LF	—	14.30	—	14.30
76" (12.6 SF/LF)	S2@.443	LF	—	15.10	—	15.10
80" (13.4 SF/LF)	S2@.467	LF	—	16.00	—	16.00
84" (14.0 SF/LF)	S2@.490	LF	—	16.70	—	16.70
88" (14.6 SF/LF)	S2@.513	LF	—	17.50	—	17.50
92" (15.4 SF/LF)	S2@.537	LF	—	18.30	—	18.30
96" (16.0 SF/LF)	S2@.560	LF	—	19.10	—	19.10

For estimating purposes, when measuring the length of ductwork, include the fitting.
Then apply the labor per run foot to the total.

1-1/4" thick wire reinforced flexible fiberglass duct with vinyl cover

Description	Craft@Hrs	Unit	Material $	Labor $	Equipment $	Total $
4"	S2@.060	LF	7.23	2.05	—	9.28
5"	S2@.070	LF	7.50	2.39	—	9.89
6"	S2@.080	LF	8.19	2.73	—	10.92
8"	S2@.090	LF	10.40	3.07	—	13.47
9"	S2@.100	LF	11.10	3.42	—	14.52
10"	S2@.120	LF	11.70	4.10	—	15.80
12"	S2@.140	LF	15.00	4.78	—	19.78
14"	S2@.160	LF	18.00	5.47	—	23.47
16"	S2@.180	LF	20.80	6.15	—	26.95
18"	S2@.200	LF	23.80	6.83	—	30.63

Fiberglass Pipe Insulation with AP-T Plus (all purpose self sealing) Jacket. By nominal pipe diameter. R factor equals 2.56 at 300 degrees F. These costs do not include scaffolding, add for same, if required. Also see fittings, flanges and valves at the end of this section.

Description	Craft@Hrs	Unit	Material $	Labor $	Equipment $	Total $

Jacketed fiberglass insulation for 1/2" pipe

Description	Craft@Hrs	Unit	Material $	Labor $	Equipment $	Total $
1/2" thick	P1@.038	LF	2.31	1.31	—	3.62
1" thick	P1@.038	LF	2.71	1.31	—	4.02
1½" thick	P1@.040	LF	5.53	1.38	—	6.91

Jacketed fiberglass insulation for 3/4" pipe

Description	Craft@Hrs	Unit	Material $	Labor $	Equipment $	Total $
1/2" thick	P1@.038	LF	2.50	1.31	—	3.81
1" thick	P1@.038	LF	3.08	1.31	—	4.39
1½" thick	P1@.040	LF	5.73	1.38	—	7.11

Jacketed fiberglass insulation for 1" pipe

Description	Craft@Hrs	Unit	Material $	Labor $	Equipment $	Total $
1/2" thick	P1@.040	LF	2.66	1.38	—	4.04
1" thick	P1@.040	LF	3.53	1.38	—	4.91
1½" thick	P1@.042	LF	6.05	1.45	—	7.50

Jacketed fiberglass insulation for 1-1/4" pipe

Description	Craft@Hrs	Unit	Material $	Labor $	Equipment $	Total $
1/2" thick	P1@.040	LF	2.96	1.38	—	4.34
1" thick	P1@.040	LF	3.56	1.38	—	4.94
1½" thick	P1@.042	LF	6.44	1.45	—	7.89

Jacketed fiberglass insulation for 1-1/2" pipe

Description	Craft@Hrs	Unit	Material $	Labor $	Equipment $	Total $
1/2" thick	P1@.042	LF	3.16	1.45	—	4.61
1" thick	P1@.042	LF	4.02	1.45	—	5.47
1½" thick	P1@.044	LF	6.94	1.52	—	8.46

Jacketed fiberglass insulation for 2" pipe

Description	Craft@Hrs	Unit	Material $	Labor $	Equipment $	Total $
1/2" thick	P1@.044	LF	3.32	1.52	—	4.84
1" thick	P1@.044	LF	4.61	1.52	—	6.13
1½" thick	P1@.046	LF	7.46	1.59	—	9.05

Jacketed fiberglass insulation for 2-1/2" pipe

Description	Craft@Hrs	Unit	Material $	Labor $	Equipment $	Total $
1" thick	P1@.047	LF	4.75	1.62	—	6.37
1½" thick	P1@.048	LF	6.74	1.66	—	8.40
2" thick	P1@.050	LF	10.70	1.73	—	12.43

Jacketed fiberglass insulation for 3" pipe

Description	Craft@Hrs	Unit	Material $	Labor $	Equipment $	Total $
1" thick	P1@.051	LF	5.23	1.76	—	6.99
1½" thick	P1@.054	LF	7.37	1.87	—	9.24
2" thick	P1@.056	LF	11.80	1.93	—	13.73

Fiberglass Pipe Insulation

Description	Craft@Hrs	Unit	Material $	Labor $	Equipment $	Total $

Jacketed fiberglass insulation for 4" pipe

Description	Craft@Hrs	Unit	Material $	Labor $	Equipment $	Total $
1" thick	P1@.063	LF	6.16	2.18	—	8.34
1½" thick	P1@.066	LF	8.21	2.28	—	10.49
2" thick	P1@.069	LF	13.20	2.38	—	15.58

Jacketed fiberglass insulation for 6" pipe

Description	Craft@Hrs	Unit	Material $	Labor $	Equipment $	Total $
1" thick	P1@.077	LF	7.18	2.66	—	9.84
1½" thick	P1@.080	LF	9.88	2.76	—	12.64
2" thick	P1@.085	LF	16.60	2.94	—	19.54

Jacketed fiberglass insulation for 8" pipe

Description	Craft@Hrs	Unit	Material $	Labor $	Equipment $	Total $
1" thick	P1@.117	LF	9.88	4.04	—	13.92
1½" thick	P1@.123	LF	12.00	4.25	—	16.25
2" thick	P1@.129	LF	19.50	4.46	—	23.96

Jacketed fiberglass insulation for 10" pipe

Description	Craft@Hrs	Unit	Material $	Labor $	Equipment $	Total $
1" thick	P1@.140	LF	11.70	4.84	—	16.54
1½" thick	P1@.147	LF	14.70	5.08	—	19.78
2" thick	P1@.154	LF	23.50	5.32	—	28.82

Jacketed fiberglass insulation for 12" pipe

Description	Craft@Hrs	Unit	Material $	Labor $	Equipment $	Total $
1" thick	P1@.155	LF	13.50	5.36	—	18.86
1½" thick	P1@.163	LF	16.60	5.63	—	22.23
2" thick	P1@.171	LF	25.60	5.91	—	31.51
Add for .016" aluminum jacket						
Per SF of surface	P1@.035	SF	1.93	1.21	—	3.14

Pipe fittings and flanges
For each fitting or flange use the cost for 3 LF of pipe of the same pipe size

Valves
Body only: for each valve body use the cost for 5 LF of pipe of the same pipe size

Body and bonnet or yoke: for each valve use the cost for 10 LF of pipe of the same pipe size

Flanged valves: add the cost for flanges per above

Calcium Silicate Pipe Insulation with Aluminum Jacket

Calcium Silicate Pipe Insulation with .016" Aluminum Jacket. By nominal pipe diameter. R factor equals 2.20 at 300 degrees F. Manufactured by Pabco. These costs do not include scaffolding, add for same, if required. Also see fittings, flanges and valves below.

Description	Craft@Hrs	Unit	Material $	Labor $	Equipment $	Total $

Jacketed calcium silicate insulation for 6" pipe

Description	Craft@Hrs	Unit	Material $	Labor $	Equipment $	Total $
2" thick	P1@.183	LF	31.40	6.32	—	37.72
4" thick	P1@.218	LF	68.00	7.53	—	75.53
6" thick	P1@.288	LF	96.40	9.95	—	106.35

Jacketed calcium silicate insulation for 8" pipe

Description	Craft@Hrs	Unit	Material $	Labor $	Equipment $	Total $
2" thick	P1@.194	LF	37.60	6.70	—	44.30
4" thick	P1@.228	LF	79.90	7.88	—	87.78
6" thick	P1@.308	LF	121.00	10.60	—	131.60

Jacketed calcium silicate insulation for 10" pipe

Description	Craft@Hrs	Unit	Material $	Labor $	Equipment $	Total $
2" thick	P1@.202	LF	44.00	6.98	—	50.98
4" thick	P1@.239	LF	93.20	8.26	—	101.46
6" thick	P1@.337	LF	145.00	11.60	—	156.60

Jacketed calcium silicate insulation for 12" pipe

Description	Craft@Hrs	Unit	Material $	Labor $	Equipment $	Total $
2" thick	P1@.208	LF	51.00	7.19	—	58.19
4" thick	P1@.261	LF	104.00	9.02	—	113.02
6" thick	P1@.388	LF	164.00	13.40	—	177.40

Pipe fittings and flanges
For each fitting or flange use the cost for 3 LF of pipe of the same pipe size

Valves
Body only: for each valve body use the cost for 5 LF of pipe of the same pipe size

Body and bonnet or yoke: for each valve use the cost for 10 LF of pipe of the same pipe size

Flanged valves: add the cost for flanges per above

Closed Cell Elastomeric Pipe Insulation

Description	Craft@Hrs	Unit	Material $	Labor $	Equipment $	Total $

Closed Cell Elastomeric Pipe and Tubing Insulation. Semi split, by nominal pipe or tube diameter with insulation wall thickness as shown, no cover. R factor equals 3.58 at 220 degrees F. Manufactured by Rubatex. These costs do not include scaffolding, add for same, if required. Also see fittings, flanges and valves below.

Description	Craft@Hrs	Unit	Material $	Labor $	Equipment $	Total $
1/4", 1/2" thick	P1@.039	LF	.92	1.35	—	2.27
3/8", 1/2" thick	P1@.039	LF	.95	1.35	—	2.30
1/2", 1/2" thick	P1@.039	LF	1.06	1.35	—	2.41
3/4", 1/2" thick	P1@.039	LF	1.21	1.35	—	2.56
1", 1/2" thick	P1@.042	LF	1.35	1.45	—	2.80
1¼", 1/2" thick	P1@.042	LF	1.52	1.45	—	2.97
1½", 1/2" thick	P1@.042	LF	1.78	1.45	—	3.23
2", 1/2" thick	P1@.046	LF	2.24	1.59	—	3.83
2½", 3/8" thick	P1@.056	LF	2.85	1.93	—	4.78
2½", 1/2" thick	P1@.056	LF	3.83	1.93	—	5.76
2½", 3/4" thick	P1@.056	LF	4.94	1.93	—	6.87
3", 3/8" thick	P1@.062	LF	3.27	2.14	—	5.41
3", 1/2" thick	P1@.062	LF	4.30	2.14	—	6.44
3", 3/4" thick	P1@.062	LF	5.60	2.14	—	7.74
4", 3/8" thick	P1@.068	LF	3.83	2.35	—	6.18
4", 1/2" thick	P1@.068	LF	5.05	2.35	—	7.40
4", 3/4" thick	P1@.068	LF	6.57	2.35	—	8.92

Pipe fittings and flanges

For each fitting or flange use the cost for 3 LF of pipe of the same pipe size

Valves

Body only: for each valve body use the cost for 5 LF of pipe of the same pipe size

Body and bonnet or yoke: for each valve use the cost for 10 LF of pipe of the same pipe size

Flanged valves: add the cost for flanges per above

Description	Craft@Hrs	Unit	Material $	Labor $	Equipment $	Total $

Fiberglass flexible wrap duct insulation with foil facing vapor barrier to 250 degrees F

Description	Craft@Hrs	Unit	Material $	Labor $	Equipment $	Total $
1"	S2@.023	SF	1.00	.79	—	1.79
1½"	S2@.023	SF	1.20	.79	—	1.99
2"	S2@.025	SF	1.62	.85	—	2.47
Deduct foil facing	—	%	-30.0	—	—	—

Fiberglass rigid board duct insulation plain, *without* foil facing vapor barrier to 450 degrees F

Description	Craft@Hrs	Unit	Material $	Labor $	Equipment $	Total $
1"	S2@.067	SF	1.23	2.29	—	3.52
1½"	S2@.067	SF	2.07	2.29	—	4.36
2"	S2@.075	SF	2.46	2.56	—	5.02
3"	S2@.085	SF	3.66	2.90	—	6.56

Fiberglass rigid board duct insulation with FSK (foil) facing vapor barrier to 250 degrees F

Description	Craft@Hrs	Unit	Material $	Labor $	Equipment $	Total $
1"	S2@.067	SF	1.62	2.29	—	3.91
1½"	S2@.067	SF	1.97	2.29	—	4.26
2"	S2@.075	SF	2.37	2.56	—	4.93
3"	S2@.085	SF	3.39	2.90	—	6.29

Fiberglass flexible blanket duct lining to 250 degrees F

Description	Craft@Hrs	Unit	Material $	Labor $	Equipment $	Total $
1/2"	S2@.032	SF	.75	1.09	—	1.84
1"	S2@.032	SF	.97	1.09	—	2.06
1½"	S2@.035	SF	1.38	1.20	—	2.58
2"	S2@.035	SF	1.82	1.20	—	3.02

Fiberglass rigid duct lining to 250 degrees F

Description	Craft@Hrs	Unit	Material $	Labor $	Equipment $	Total $
5/8"	S2@.032	SF	1.64	1.09	—	2.73
1"	S2@.032	SF	2.13	1.09	—	3.22
1½"	S2@.035	SF	2.81	1.20	—	4.01
2"	S2@.035	SF	3.58	1.20	—	4.78

Note: Material prices include all necessary tape, pins, mastic and 15% waste.

Balancing of HVAC Systems

Description	Craft@Hrs	Unit	Material $	Labor $	Equipment $	Total $
Air balancing – air handling units						
Central station	S2@6.00	Ea	—	205.00	—	205.00
Multi-zone A/C	S2@4.00	Ea	—	137.00	—	137.00
Single-zone A/C	S2@3.00	Ea	—	102.00	—	102.00
Packaged A/C	S2@2.50	Ea	—	85.40	—	85.40
Built-up low pressure	S2@4.50	Ea	—	154.00	—	154.00
Built-up high pres.	S2@6.00	Ea	—	205.00	—	205.00
Built-up VAV	S2@6.00	Ea	—	205.00	—	205.00
Built-up dual duct	S2@6.00	Ea	—	205.00	—	205.00
Air balancing – terminal boxes						
Variable air volume	S2@0.40	Ea	—	13.70	—	13.70
Constant volume	S2@0.40	Ea	—	13.70	—	13.70
Dual duct box	S2@0.70	Ea	—	23.90	—	23.90
Terminal box and all downstream diffusers						
Cost per zone	S2@1.75	Ea	—	59.80	—	59.80
Air balancing – diffusers						
Ceiling diffusers to 500 CFM	S2@.250	Ea	—	8.54	—	8.54
Ceiling diffusers over 500 CFM	S2@.350	Ea	—	12.00	—	12.00
Ceiling diffusers perforated	S2@.370	Ea	—	12.60	—	12.60
Sidewall diffusers double deflection	S2@.250	Ea	—	8.54	—	8.54
Linear slot diffusers 2 slot	S2@.060	LF	—	2.05	—	2.05
Linear slot diffusers 3 slot	S2@.070	LF	—	2.39	—	2.39
Linear slot diffusers 4 slot	S2@.080	LF	—	2.73	—	2.73
Plug-in diffuser	S2@.250	Ea	—	8.54	—	8.54
Light troffers 1 slot	S2@.195	Ea	—	6.66	—	6.66
Light troffers 2 slot	S2@.220	Ea	—	7.52	—	7.52
Laminar flow diff.	S2@.750	Ea	—	25.60	—	25.60
Laminar flow diffusers with HEPA filter	S2@3.00	Ea	—	102.00	—	102.00

Description	Craft@Hrs	Unit	Material $	Labor $	Equipment $	Total $

Air balancing – grilles

Description	Craft@Hrs	Unit	Material $	Labor $	Equipment $	Total $
Return air grilles to 800 CFM	S2@.250	Ea	—	8.54	—	8.54
Return air grilles over 800 CFM	S2@.350	Ea	—	12.00	—	12.00
Bar type return air grilles 2 slot	S2@.060	LF	—	2.05	—	2.05
Bar type return air grilles 4 slot	S2@.070	LF	—	2.39	—	2.39
Bar type return air grilles 6 slot	S2@.080	LF	—	2.73	—	2.73

Air balancing – centrifugal fans

Description	Craft@Hrs	Unit	Material $	Labor $	Equipment $	Total $
Supply and return air to 3,000 CFM	S2@1.00	Ea	—	34.20	—	34.20
Supply and return air to 5,000 CFM	S2@1.50	Ea	—	51.20	—	51.20
Supply and return air to 10,000 CFM	S2@2.00	Ea	—	68.30	—	68.30
Supply and return air to 20,000 CFM	S2@2.75	Ea	—	93.90	—	93.90
Roof exhaust to 6,000 CFM	S2@.725	Ea	—	24.80	—	24.80
Roof exhaust to 10,000 CFM	S2@.925	Ea	—	31.60	—	31.60
Roof exhaust to 20,000 CFM	S2@1.50	Ea	—	51.20	—	51.20
Range hood exhaust to 10,000 CFM	S2@1.75	Ea	—	59.80	—	59.80
Range hood exhaust to 20,000 CFM	S2@2.50	Ea	—	85.40	—	85.40

Air balancing – fan coil units

Description	Craft@Hrs	Unit	Material $	Labor $	Equipment $	Total $
Vertical floor model	S2@.500	Ea	—	17.10	—	17.10
Horiz. ceiling mtd	S2@.650	Ea	—	22.20	—	22.20

Air balancing – fume hoods

Description	Craft@Hrs	Unit	Material $	Labor $	Equipment $	Total $
Lab fume hood	S2@2.00	Ea	—	68.30	—	68.30
General purpose	S2@.450	Ea	—	15.40	—	15.40
Dust collectors	S2@1.50	Ea	—	51.20	—	51.20

Description	Craft@Hrs	Unit	Material $	Labor $	Equipment $	Total $
Wet balancing						
Boiler	S2@1.65	Ea	—	56.40	—	56.40
Chiller	S2@3.50	Ea	—	120.00	—	120.00
Cooling tower	S2@2.00	Ea	—	68.30	—	68.30
Circulating pump	S2@1.65	Ea	—	56.40	—	56.40
Heat exchanger	S2@1.75	Ea	—	59.80	—	59.80
AHU water coil	S2@2.50	Ea	—	85.40	—	85.40
Reheat coil	S2@.450	Ea	—	15.40	—	15.40
Wall fin radiation	S2@.350	Ea	—	12.00	—	12.00
Radiant heat panel	S2@.450	Ea	—	15.40	—	15.40
Fan coil unit, 2 pipe	S2@.350	Ea	—	12.00	—	12.00
Fan coil unit, 4 pipe	S2@.450	Ea	—	15.40	—	15.40
Cabinet heater	S2@.350	Ea	—	12.00	—	12.00
Unit ventilator	S2@.450	Ea	—	15.40	—	15.40
Unit heater	S2@.350	Ea	—	12.00	—	12.00

Commercial HVAC controls. Temperature, pressure and humidity control for any device. 0-10 Volts DC or 4-20 milliamp input. Honeywell T775U or equal. Complies with ANSI/ACCA standard 5QI-2007. With two modulating and two relay outputs, each with their own setpoint.

Description	Craft@Hrs	Unit	Material $	Labor $	Equipment $	Total $
Install control module enclosure	B5@1.00	Ea	—	34.50	—	34.50
Twisted pair category 6 PVC cable	BE@.008	LF	0.47	.31	—	.78
Panel wiring	BE@.250	Ea	2.50	9.57	—	12.07
Relay and damper actuator wiring	BE@.250	Ea	2.25	9.57	—	11.82
Sensor wiring	BE@.300	Ea	2.25	11.50	—	13.75
Zone control module wiring	BE@.400	Ea	2.10	15.30	—	17.40
Control module and wiring	BE@2.00	Ea	400.00	76.60	—	476.60
Ground fault protection wiring	BE@1.25	Ea	125.00	47.90	—	172.90
Programming and system test	BE@3.00	Ea	—	115.00	—	115.00
Commissioning and final test	BE@8.00	Ea	—	306.00	—	306.00

Sensor and zone control modules. Honeywell Webstat TR23 or equal. 20K non-linear sensor with setpoint adjust 55-85, and override LED. With LonWorks interface card and power supply. Add the cost of control wiring.

Description	Craft@Hrs	Unit	Material $	Labor $	Equipment $	Total $
Room sensor	BE@.500	Ea	75.00	19.10	—	94.10

Damper actuators. Modutrol IV or equal. For rectangular volume control dampers. Add the cost of wiring and the damper from the section Ductwork Specialties.

Description	Craft@Hrs	Unit	Material $	Labor $	Equipment $	Total $
Lever arm actuator	BE@.500	Ea	468.00	19.10	—	487.10

Description	Craft@Hrs	Unit	Material $	Labor $	Equipment $	Total $

Remote CO2 sensors. Honeywell C72321 or equal, with LonWorks interface card and power supply. Add the cost of wiring.

Description	Craft@Hrs	Unit	Material $	Labor $	Equipment $	Total $
Panel mount	BE@.500	Ea	80.00	19.10	—	99.10

Monitoring and recording equipment. Honeywell DR4500A digital circular chart recorder or equal, with LonWorks card and power supply. Add the cost of wiring.

Description	Craft@Hrs	Unit	Material $	Labor $	Equipment $	Total $
Panel mount	BE@.500	Ea	3,800.00	19.10	—	3,819.10

Thermostat, electric. Install and connect. Make additional allowances for sub-subcontractor markups and control wiring as required.

Description	Craft@Hrs	Unit	Material $	Labor $	Equipment $	Total $
Heat/cool						
Low voltage	BE@.575	Ea	40.00	22.00	—	62.00
Heat Only						
Low voltage	BE@.500	Ea	33.30	19.10	—	52.40
Heat /cool						
Line voltage	BE@.650	Ea	121.00	24.90	—	145.90
Programmable – Residential						
Low voltage	BE@.850	LF	183.00	32.50	—	215.50
Programmable – commercial w/ subbase						
Low voltage	BE@1.10	LF	377.00	42.10	—	419.10

Thermostat, pneumatic. Install and connect. Make additional allowances for sub-subcontractor markups and pneumatic tubing as required.

Description	Craft@Hrs	Unit	Material $	Labor $	Equipment $	Total $
Direct acting						
55 to 85 Deg. F.	BE@.675	Ea	104.00	25.80	—	129.80
Reverse acting						
55 to 85 Deg. F.	BE@.675	Ea	86.20	25.80	—	112.00
Floating	BE@.675	Ea	183.00	25.80	—	208.80

Control valve, 2 way, electric. 6.9 Volt Input. Proportional Spring Return. Connect only. N.O. means: "normally open." Make additional allowances for sub-subcontractor markups, control wiring and valve installation by piping trades as required. (See Plumbing and Piping Specialties)

Description	Craft@Hrs	Unit	Material $	Labor $	Equipment $	Total $
1/2", 2 way, N.O.	BE@.400	Ea	466.00	15.30	—	481.30
3/4", 2 way, N.O.	BE@.400	Ea	495.00	15.30	—	510.30
1", 2 way, N.O.	BE@.400	Ea	534.00	15.30	—	549.30
1¼" 2 way, N.O.	BE@.400	Ea	583.00	15.30	—	598.30
1½" 2 way, N.O.	BE@.400	Ea	1,250.00	15.30	—	1,265.30
2", 2 way, N.O.	BE@.400	Ea	1,370.00	15.30	—	1,385.30

Control valve, 3 way, electric. 6.9 Volt Input, Proportional Spring Return. Connect only. Make additional allowances for sub-subcontractor markups, control wiring and valve installation by piping trades as required. (See Plumbing and Piping Specialties)

Description	Craft@Hrs	Unit	Material $	Labor $	Equipment $	Total $
1/2", 3 way	BE@.450	Ea	486.00	17.20	—	503.20
3/4", 3 way	BE@.450	Ea	529.00	17.20	—	546.20
1", 3 way	BE@.450	Ea	634.00	17.20	—	651.20

Description	Craft@Hrs	Unit	Material $	Labor $	Equipment $	Total $

Control valve, 2 way, pneumatic. Proportional Spring Return, 3 to 7 psi Input, Connect only. N.O. means "normally open." Make additional allowances for sub-subcontractor markups, pneumatic tubing and valve installation by piping trades as required. (See Plumbing and Piping Specialties)

Description	Craft@Hrs	Unit	Material $	Labor $	Equipment $	Total $
1/2", 2 way, N.O.	BE@.400	Ea	191.00	15.30	—	206.30
3/4", 2 way, N.O.	BE@.400	Ea	224.00	15.30	—	239.30
1", 2 way, N.O.	BE@.400	Ea	263.00	15.30	—	278.30
1¼" 2 way, N.O.	BE@.400	Ea	313.00	15.30	—	328.30
1½" 2 way, N.O.	BE@.400	Ea	557.00	15.30	—	572.30
2", 2 way, N.O.	BE@.400	Ea	665.00	15.30	—	680.30

Control valve, 3 way, pneumatic. Proportional Spring Return, 3 to 7 psi Input, Connect only. Make additional allowances for sub-subcontractor markups, pneumatic tubing and valve installation by piping trades as required. (See Plumbing and Piping Specialties)

Description	Craft@Hrs	Unit	Material $	Labor $	Equipment $	Total $
1/2", 3 way	BE@.450	Ea	214.00	17.20	—	231.20
3/4", 3 way	BE@.450	Ea	257.00	17.20	—	274.20
1", 3 way	BE@.450	Ea	359.00	17.20	—	376.20
1¼", 3 way	BE@.450	Ea	414.00	17.20	—	431.20
1½", 3 way	BE@.450	Ea	595.00	17.20	—	612.20
2", 3 way	BE@.450	Ea	695.00	17.20	—	712.20

Air compressor. Reciprocating piston type. Larger systems include HVAC actuator controls. Underwriters Laboratories and CSA rated. With ASME "U"-stamped pressure tank, pressure safety relief valve, silencer, lubrication system with lube cooling radiator and fan. Single phase 110 volt electric motor, drive belt and OSHA-rated safety belt guard. Add the cost of compressor hose and fittings and hose reel, if required. Set in place only. Add installation costs from the table below.

Description	Craft@Hrs	Unit	Material $	Labor $	Equipment $	Total $
1/2 hp	SL@3.00	Ea	360.00	103.00	—	463.00
3/4 hp	SL@3.00	Ea	393.00	103.00	—	496.00
1 hp	SL@3.50	Ea	456.00	120.00	—	576.00
1½ hp	SL@3.50	Ea	505.00	120.00	—	625.00
2 hp	SL@3.50	Ea	537.00	120.00	—	657.00

Installation of air compressors.

Description	Craft@Hrs	Unit	Material $	Labor $	Equipment $	Total $
Cut, frame support and gasket hole in sidewall	S2@1.00	Ea	35.00	34.20	—	69.20
Install piping for compressor line	P1@.100	LF	3.75	3.46	—	7.21
Install electrical wiring	BE@.150	LF	1.75	5.74	—	7.49
Install compressor controls	BE@.500	Ea	—	19.10	—	19.10
Commission and test	P1@2.00	Ea	—	69.10	—	69.10
Fine-tune system	P1@1.00	Ea	—	34.60	—	34.60

Ductile Iron, Class 153, Cement-Lined with Mechanical Joints

Description	Craft@Hrs	Unit	Material $	Labor $	Equipment $	Total $

Cement-lined Class 153 ductile iron pipe with mechanical joints

Description	Craft@Hrs	Unit	Material $	Labor $	Equipment $	Total $
4"	P1@.140	LF	10.80	4.84	—	15.64
6"	ER@.180	LF	15.60	6.66	1.70	23.96
8"	ER@.200	LF	21.40	7.40	1.80	30.60
10"	ER@.230	LF	31.80	8.51	2.10	42.41
12"	ER@.270	LF	43.30	10.00	2.50	55.80
14"	ER@.310	LF	65.70	11.50	2.80	80.00
16"	ER@.350	LF	84.80	13.00	3.20	101.00

Cement-lined Class 153 ductile iron 1/16 bend with mechanical joints

Description	Craft@Hrs	Unit	Material $	Labor $	Equipment $	Total $
4"	P1@.900	Ea	42.70	31.10	—	73.80
6"	ER@1.30	Ea	66.10	48.10	11.90	126.10
8"	ER@1.70	Ea	104.00	62.90	15.60	182.50
10"	ER@2.15	Ea	142.00	79.60	19.80	241.40
12"	ER@2.40	Ea	196.00	88.80	22.00	306.80
14"	ER@2.70	Ea	430.00	100.00	24.80	554.80
16"	ER@3.00	Ea	487.00	111.00	27.50	625.50

Cement-lined Class 153 ductile iron 1/8 bend with mechanical joints

Description	Craft@Hrs	Unit	Material $	Labor $	Equipment $	Total $
4"	P1@.900	Ea	44.20	31.10	—	75.30
6"	ER@1.30	Ea	65.70	48.10	11.90	125.70
8"	ER@1.70	Ea	105.00	62.90	15.60	183.50
10"	ER@2.15	Ea	144.00	79.60	19.80	243.40
12"	ER@2.40	Ea	199.00	88.80	22.00	309.80
14"	ER@2.70	Ea	427.00	100.00	24.80	551.80
16"	ER@3.00	Ea	501.00	111.00	27.50	639.50

Cement-lined Class 153 ductile iron 1/4 bend with mechanical joints

Description	Craft@Hrs	Unit	Material $	Labor $	Equipment $	Total $
4"	P1@.900	Ea	47.40	31.10	—	78.50
6"	ER@1.30	Ea	77.00	48.10	11.90	137.00
8"	ER@1.70	Ea	161.00	62.90	15.60	239.50
10"	ER@2.15	Ea	242.00	79.60	19.80	341.40
12"	ER@2.40	Ea	331.00	88.80	22.00	441.80
14"	ER@2.70	Ea	852.00	100.00	24.80	976.80
16"	ER@3.00	Ea	894.00	111.00	27.50	1,032.50

Cement-lined Class 153 ductile iron tee with mechanical joints

Description	Craft@Hrs	Unit	Material $	Labor $	Equipment $	Total $
4"	P1@1.65	Ea	71.80	57.00	—	128.80
6"	ER@2.35	Ea	105.00	87.00	21.60	213.60
8"	ER@3.15	Ea	161.00	117.00	29.00	307.00
10"	ER@4.00	Ea	242.00	148.00	36.70	426.70
12"	ER@4.45	Ea	331.00	165.00	40.90	536.90
14"	ER@4.90	Ea	852.00	181.00	44.90	1,077.90
16"	ER@5.30	Ea	894.00	196.00	48.60	1,138.60

Ductile Iron, Class 153, Cement-Lined with Mechanical Joints

Description	Craft@Hrs	Unit	Material $	Labor $	Equipment $	Total $

Cement-lined Class 153 ductile iron wye with mechanical joints

Description	Craft@Hrs	Unit	Material $	Labor $	Equipment $	Total $
4"	P1@1.65	Ea	161.00	57.00	—	218.00
6"	ER@2.35	Ea	200.00	87.00	21.60	308.60
8"	ER@3.15	Ea	302.00	117.00	29.00	448.00
10"	ER@4.00	Ea	563.00	148.00	36.70	747.70
12"	ER@4.45	Ea	847.00	165.00	40.90	1,052.90
14"	ER@4.90	Ea	1,730.00	181.00	45.70	1,956.70
16"	ER@5.30	Ea	2,160.00	196.00	48.60	2,404.60

Cement-lined Class 153 ductile iron reducer with mechanical joints

Description	Craft@Hrs	Unit	Material $	Labor $	Equipment $	Total $
6"	ER@1.45	Ea	52.60	53.70	13.30	119.60
8"	ER@2.00	Ea	83.20	74.00	18.30	175.50
10"	ER@2.55	Ea	110.00	94.40	23.50	227.90
12"	ER@3.05	Ea	142.00	113.00	28.10	283.10
14"	ER@3.60	Ea	318.00	133.00	33.00	484.00
16"	ER@4.20	Ea	386.00	155.00	38.50	579.50

Ductile Iron, 153, Double Cement-Lined with Mechanical Joints

Description	Craft@Hrs	Unit	Material $	Labor $	Equipment $	Total $

Double cement-lined Class 153 ductile iron pipe with mechanical joints

4"	P1@.140	LF	11.40	4.84	—	16.24
6"	ER@.180	LF	16.50	6.66	1.70	24.86
8"	ER@.200	LF	22.70	7.40	1.80	31.90
10"	ER@.230	LF	33.80	8.51	2.10	44.41
12"	ER@.270	LF	46.00	10.00	2.50	58.50
14"	ER@.310	LF	69.90	11.50	2.80	84.20
16"	ER@.350	LF	89.90	13.00	3.20	106.10

Double cement-lined Class 153 ductile iron 1/16 bend with mechanical joints

4"	P1@.900	Ea	50.40	31.10	—	81.50
6"	ER@1.30	Ea	78.10	48.10	11.90	138.10
8"	ER@1.70	Ea	124.00	62.90	15.60	202.50
10"	ER@2.15	Ea	167.00	79.60	19.80	266.40
12"	ER@2.40	Ea	229.00	88.80	22.00	339.80
14"	ER@2.70	Ea	511.00	100.00	24.80	635.80
16"	ER@3.00	Ea	579.00	111.00	27.50	717.50

Double cement-lined Class 153 ductile iron 1/8 bend with mechanical joints

4"	P1@.900	Ea	50.40	31.10	—	81.50
6"	ER@1.30	Ea	76.10	48.10	11.90	136.10
8"	ER@1.70	Ea	121.00	62.90	15.60	199.50
10"	ER@2.15	Ea	166.00	79.60	19.80	265.40
12"	ER@2.40	Ea	227.00	88.80	22.00	337.80
14"	ER@2.70	Ea	497.00	100.00	24.80	621.80
16"	ER@3.00	Ea	579.00	111.00	27.50	717.50

Double cement-lined Class 153 ductile iron 1/4 bend with mechanical joints

4"	P1@.900	Ea	54.60	31.10	—	85.70
6"	ER@1.30	Ea	88.40	48.10	11.90	148.40
8"	ER@1.70	Ea	137.00	62.90	15.60	215.50
10"	ER@2.15	Ea	214.00	79.60	19.80	313.40
12"	ER@2.40	Ea	278.00	88.80	22.00	388.80
14"	ER@2.70	Ea	661.00	100.00	24.80	785.80
16"	ER@3.00	Ea	751.00	111.00	27.50	889.50

Ductile Iron, Class 153, Double Cement-Lined with Mechanical Joints

Description	Craft@Hrs	Unit	Material $	Labor $	Equipment $	Total $

Double cement-lined Class 153 ductile iron tee with mechanical joints

Description	Craft@Hrs	Unit	Material $	Labor $	Equipment $	Total $
4"	P1@1.65	Ea	83.50	57.00	—	140.50
6"	ER@2.35	Ea	121.00	87.00	21.60	229.60
8"	ER@3.15	Ea	184.00	117.00	29.00	330.00
10"	ER@4.00	Ea	278.00	148.00	36.70	462.70
12"	ER@4.45	Ea	379.00	165.00	40.90	584.90
14"	ER@4.90	Ea	976.00	181.00	44.90	1,201.90
16"	ER@5.30	Ea	1,030.00	196.00	48.60	1,274.60

Double cement-lined Class 153 ductile iron wye with mechanical joints

Description	Craft@Hrs	Unit	Material $	Labor $	Equipment $	Total $
4"	P1@1.65	Ea	184.00	57.00	—	241.00
6"	ER@2.35	Ea	235.00	87.00	21.60	343.60
8"	ER@3.15	Ea	348.00	117.00	29.00	494.00
10"	ER@4.00	Ea	655.00	148.00	36.70	839.70
12"	ER@4.45	Ea	971.00	165.00	40.90	1,176.90
14"	ER@4.90	Ea	2,000.00	181.00	44.90	2,225.90
16"	ER@5.30	Ea	2,470.00	196.00	48.60	2,714.60

Double cement-lined Class 153 ductile iron reducer with mechanical joints

Description	Craft@Hrs	Unit	Material $	Labor $	Equipment $	Total $
6"	ER@1.45	Ea	60.60	53.70	13.30	127.60
8"	ER@2.00	Ea	86.30	74.00	18.30	178.60
10"	ER@2.55	Ea	112.00	94.40	23.50	229.90
12"	ER@3.05	Ea	164.00	113.00	28.10	305.10
14"	ER@3.60	Ea	353.00	133.00	27.50	513.50
16"	ER@4.20	Ea	443.00	155.00	38.50	636.50

Ductile Iron, Class 110, Cement-Lined with Mechanical Joints

Description	Craft@Hrs	Unit	Material $	Labor $	Equipment $	Total $
Cement-lined Class 110 ductile iron pipe with mechanical joints						
4"	P1@.180	LF	12.50	6.22	—	18.72
6"	ER@.220	LF	17.80	8.14	2.00	27.94
8"	ER@.240	LF	24.60	8.88	2.20	35.68
10"	ER@.270	LF	36.80	10.00	2.50	49.30
12"	ER@.320	LF	49.90	11.80	2.90	64.60
16"	ER@.400	LF	97.40	14.80	3.70	115.90
Cement-lined Class 110 ductile iron 1/16 bend with mechanical joints						
4"	P1@1.40	Ea	125.00	48.40	—	173.40
6"	ER@2.00	Ea	167.00	74.00	18.30	259.30
8"	ER@2.50	Ea	230.00	92.60	22.90	345.50
10"	ER@3.20	Ea	350.00	118.00	29.30	497.30
12"	ER@3.60	Ea	445.00	133.00	33.00	611.00
16"	ER@4.50	Ea	1,150.00	167.00	41.30	1,358.30
Cement-lined Class 110 ductile iron 1/8 bend with mechanical joints						
4"	P1@1.40	Ea	122.00	48.40	—	170.40
6"	ER@2.00	Ea	165.00	74.00	18.30	257.30
8"	ER@2.50	Ea	230.00	92.60	22.90	345.50
10"	ER@3.20	Ea	337.00	118.00	29.30	484.30
12"	ER@3.60	Ea	444.00	133.00	33.00	610.00
16"	ER@4.50	Ea	1,130.00	167.00	41.30	1,338.30
Cement-lined Class 110 ductile iron 1/4 bend with mechanical joints						
4"	P1@1.40	Ea	135.00	48.40	—	183.40
6"	ER@2.00	Ea	182.00	74.00	18.30	274.30
8"	ER@2.50	Ea	262.00	92.60	22.90	377.50
10"	ER@3.20	Ea	406.00	118.00	29.30	553.30
12"	ER@3.60	Ea	608.00	133.00	33.00	774.00
16"	ER@4.50	Ea	1,470.00	167.00	41.30	1,678.30
Cement-lined Class 110 ductile iron tee with mechanical joints						
4"	P1@2.50	Ea	205.00	86.40	—	291.40
6"	ER@3.50	Ea	273.00	130.00	32.10	435.10
8"	ER@4.70	Ea	389.00	174.00	43.10	606.10
10"	ER@6.00	Ea	671.00	222.00	55.00	948.00
12"	ER@6.70	Ea	852.00	248.00	60.50	1,160.50
16"	ER@8.00	Ea	2,240.00	296.00	73.30	2,609.30
Cement-lined Class 110 ductile iron reducer with mechanical joints						
6"	ER@2.20	Ea	135.00	81.40	20.20	236.60
8"	ER@3.00	Ea	188.00	111.00	27.50	326.50
10"	ER@3.80	Ea	308.00	141.00	34.80	483.80
12"	ER@4.60	Ea	363.00	170.00	42.20	575.20
16"	ER@6.30	Ea	994.00	233.00	57.80	1,284.80

Cast Iron, Class 150 with Mechanical Joints

Description	Craft@Hrs	Unit	Material $	Labor $	Equipment $	Total $
Class 150 cast iron pipe with mechanical joints						
1½"	P1@.080	LF	6.09	2.76	—	8.85
2"	P1@.100	LF	5.95	3.46	—	9.41
3"	P1@.120	LF	8.23	4.15	—	12.38
4"	P1@.140	LF	10.70	4.84	—	15.54
6"	ER@.180	LF	18.30	6.66	1.70	26.66
8"	ER@.200	LF	29.50	7.40	1.80	38.70
Class 150 cast iron 1/8 bend with mechanical joints						
1½"	P1@.750	Ea	6.71	25.90	—	32.61
2"	P1@.800	Ea	7.48	27.60	—	35.08
3"	P1@1.00	Ea	10.10	34.60	—	44.70
4"	P1@1.20	Ea	12.80	41.50	—	54.30
6"	ER@1.70	Ea	30.00	62.90	15.60	108.50
8"	ER@2.25	Ea	85.80	83.30	20.70	189.80
Class 150 cast iron 1/4 bend with mechanical joints						
2"	P1@.800	Ea	10.80	27.60	—	38.40
3"	P1@1.00	Ea	15.50	34.60	—	50.10
4"	P1@1.20	Ea	24.30	41.50	—	65.80
6"	ER@1.70	Ea	50.40	62.90	15.60	128.90
8"	ER@2.25	Ea	136.00	83.30	20.70	240.00
Class 150 cast iron sanitary tee with mechanical joints						
1½"	P1@.750	Ea	11.20	25.90	—	37.10
2"	P1@1.00	Ea	12.20	34.60	—	46.80
3"	P1@1.20	Ea	14.80	41.50	—	56.30
4"	P1@1.65	Ea	22.90	57.00	—	79.90
6"	ER@2.35	Ea	65.30	87.00	21.60	173.90
8"	ER@3.15	Ea	208.00	117.00	29.00	354.00
Class 150 cast iron wye with mechanical joints						
1½"	P1@.750	Ea	11.40	25.90	—	37.30
2"	P1@1.00	Ea	11.40	34.60	—	46.00
3"	P1@1.20	Ea	16.10	41.50	—	57.60
4"	P1@1.65	Ea	26.20	57.00	—	83.20
6"	ER@2.35	Ea	70.20	87.00	21.60	178.80
8"	ER@3.15	Ea	165.00	117.00	29.00	311.00
Class 150 cast iron reducer						
2" x 1½"	P1@.600	Ea	6.14	20.70	—	26.84
3" x 2"	P1@.800	Ea	6.08	27.60	—	33.68
4" x 2"	P1@1.00	Ea	9.48	34.60	—	44.08
6" x 4"	ER@1.45	Ea	25.30	53.70	13.30	92.30
8" x 6"	ER@2.00	Ea	43.30	74.00	18.30	135.60

Asbestos-Cement, Class 2400 or 3000 with Mechanical Joints

Description	Craft@Hrs	Unit	Material $	Labor $	Equipment $	Total $

Asbestos-cement pipe with mechanical joints

Description	Craft@Hrs	Unit	Material $	Labor $	Equipment $	Total $
4"	ER@.080	LF	10.20	2.96	.70	13.86
6"	ER@.100	LF	6.46	3.70	.90	11.06
8"	ER@.140	LF	10.20	5.18	1.30	16.68
10"	ER@.200	LF	15.90	7.40	1.80	25.10
12"	ER@.260	LF	21.10	9.63	2.40	33.13
14"	ER@.300	LF	28.30	11.10	2.80	42.20
16"	ER@.350	LF	35.00	13.00	3.20	51.20

Asbestos-cement 1/16 bend with mechanical joints

Description	Craft@Hrs	Unit	Material $	Labor $	Equipment $	Total $
4"	ER@1.00	Ea	144.00	37.00	9.20	190.20
6"	ER@1.25	Ea	191.00	46.30	11.50	248.80
8"	ER@1.70	Ea	264.00	62.90	15.60	342.50
10"	ER@2.20	Ea	402.00	81.40	20.20	503.60
12"	ER@2.70	Ea	460.00	100.00	24.80	584.80
14"	ER@3.40	Ea	923.00	126.00	31.20	1,080.20
16"	ER@3.90	Ea	1,330.00	144.00	35.80	1,509.80

Asbestos-cement 1/8 bend with mechanical joints

Description	Craft@Hrs	Unit	Material $	Labor $	Equipment $	Total $
4"	ER@1.00	Ea	139.00	37.00	9.20	185.20
6"	ER@1.25	Ea	190.00	46.30	11.50	247.80
8"	ER@1.70	Ea	264.00	62.90	15.60	342.50
10"	ER@2.20	Ea	386.00	81.40	20.20	487.60
12"	ER@2.70	Ea	514.00	100.00	24.80	638.80
14"	ER@3.40	Ea	913.00	126.00	31.20	1,070.20
16"	ER@3.90	Ea	1,320.00	144.00	35.80	1,499.80

Asbestos-cement 1/4 bend with mechanical joints

Description	Craft@Hrs	Unit	Material $	Labor $	Equipment $	Total $
4"	ER@1.00	Ea	156.00	37.00	9.20	202.20
6"	ER@1.25	Ea	211.00	46.30	11.50	268.80
8"	ER@1.70	Ea	302.00	62.90	15.60	380.50
10"	ER@2.20	Ea	459.00	81.40	20.20	560.60
12"	ER@2.70	Ea	608.00	100.00	24.80	732.80
14"	ER@3.40	Ea	1,130.00	126.00	31.20	1,287.20
16"	ER@3.90	Ea	1,670.00	144.00	35.80	1,849.80

Asbestos-Cement, Class 2400 or 3000 with Mechanical Joints

Description	Craft@Hrs	Unit	Material $	Labor $	Equipment $	Total $
Asbestos-cement tee or wye with mechanical joints						
4"	ER@1.40	Ea	235.00	51.80	12.80	299.60
6"	ER@1.75	Ea	311.00	64.80	16.00	391.80
8"	ER@2.40	Ea	444.00	88.80	22.00	554.80
10"	ER@3.10	Ea	765.00	115.00	28.40	908.40
12"	ER@3.80	Ea	974.00	141.00	34.80	1,149.80
14"	ER@4.75	Ea	1,760.00	176.00	43.60	1,979.60
16"	ER@5.45	Ea	2,540.00	202.00	50.10	2,792.10
Asbestos-cement reducer with mechanical joints						
6" x 4"	ER@1.20	Ea	165.00	44.40	11.00	220.40
8" x 6"	ER@1.50	Ea	242.00	55.50	13.80	311.30
10" x 8"	ER@1.95	Ea	353.00	72.20	17.90	443.10
12" x 10"	ER@2.45	Ea	491.00	90.70	22.60	604.30

Description	Craft@Hrs	Unit	Material $	Labor $	Equipment $	Total $

Fiberglass septic tank. 2 compartments. Shallow burial (2 feet of earth cover). 32" manway entrance. One piece construction. Including excavation, backfill and equipment costs.

Description	Craft@Hrs	Unit	Material $	Labor $	Equipment $	Total $
750 gallon	P1@8.00	Ea	1,410.00	276.00	440.00	2,126.00
1,000 gallon	P1@9.00	Ea	1,880.00	311.00	495.00	2,686.00
1,250 gallon	P1@10.0	Ea	2,330.00	346.00	550.00	3,226.00
1,500 gallon	P1@11.5	Ea	2,810.00	397.00	633.00	3,840.00
1,750 gallon	P1@12.0	Ea	3,290.00	415.00	660.00	4,365.00
2,000 gallon	P1@12.5	Ea	3,750.00	432.00	688.00	4,870.00

Fiberglass septic tank. 2 compartments. Deep burial (7 feet of earth cover). 32" x 40" manway extension. One piece construction. Including excavation, backfill and equipment costs.

Description	Craft@Hrs	Unit	Material $	Labor $	Equipment $	Total $
750 gallon	P1@8.00	Ea	1,580.00	276.00	440.00	2,296.00
1,000 gallon	P1@9.00	Ea	2,020.00	311.00	495.00	2,826.00
1,250 gallon	P1@10.0	Ea	2,680.00	346.00	550.00	3,576.00
1,500 gallon	P1@11.5	Ea	3,200.00	397.00	633.00	4,230.00
1,750 gallon	P1@12.0	Ea	3,730.00	415.00	660.00	4,805.00
2,000 gallon	P1@12.5	Ea	4,270.00	432.00	688.00	5,390.00
Manway extension						
	P1@.350	LF	75.00	12.10	—	87.10

Fiberglass holding tank. Single compartment. Shallow burial (2 feet of earth cover). 32" manway entrance. One piece construction. Including excavation, backfill and equipment costs. Can be used for drink water storage or sewage holding.

Description	Craft@Hrs	Unit	Material $	Labor $	Equipment $	Total $
750 gallon	P1@8.00	Ea	1,260.00	276.00	440.00	1,976.00
1,000 gallon	P1@9.00	Ea	1,620.00	311.00	495.00	2,426.00
1,250 gallon	P1@10.0	Ea	2,070.00	346.00	550.00	2,966.00
1,500 gallon	P1@11.5	Ea	2,490.00	397.00	633.00	3,520.00
1,750 gallon	P1@12.0	Ea	2,890.00	415.00	660.00	3,965.00
2,000 gallon	P1@12.5	Ea	3,310.00	432.00	688.00	4,430.00

Fiberglass holding tank. Single compartment. Deep burial (7 feet of earth cover). 32" x 40" manway extension. One piece construction. Including excavation, backfill and equipment costs. Can be used for drink water storage or sewage holding.

Description	Craft@Hrs	Unit	Material $	Labor $	Equipment $	Total $
750 gallon	P1@8.00	Ea	1,350.00	276.00	440.00	2,066.00
1,000 gallon	P1@9.00	Ea	2,000.00	311.00	495.00	2,806.00
1,250 gallon	P1@10.0	Ea	2,680.00	346.00	550.00	3,576.00
1,500 gallon	P1@11.5	Ea	2,840.00	397.00	633.00	3,870.00
1,750 gallon	P1@12.0	Ea	3,380.00	415.00	660.00	4,455.00
2,000 gallon	P1@12.5	Ea	3,700.00	432.00	688.00	4,820.00
Manway extension						
	P1@.350	LF	75.00	12.10	—	87.10

Plastic Tanks

Description	Craft@Hrs	Unit	Material $	Labor $	Equipment $	Total $

Plastic water tank. Suitable for potable water. Labor includes setting in place only. Freight, hoisting & rigging excluded.

Description	Craft@Hrs	Unit	Material $	Labor $	Equipment $	Total $
Vertical tank, D31" x H55"						
165 gallon	P1@2.00	Ea	589.00	69.10	—	658.10
Vertical tank, D48" x H102"						
500 gallon	P1@4.00	Ea	1,080.00	138.00	—	1,218.00
Vertical tank, D64" x H79"						
1,000 gallon	P1@4.00	Ea	1,550.00	138.00	—	1,688.00
Vertical tank, D87" x H65"						
1,500 gallon	P1@5.00	Ea	2,030.00	173.00	—	2,203.00
Vertical tank, D95" x H89"						
2,500 gallon	P1@5.00	Ea	2,120.00	173.00	—	2,293.00
Vertical tank, D95" x H107"						
3,000 gallon	P1@6.00	Ea	3,320.00	207.00	—	3,527.00
Vertical tank, D102" x H125"						
4,000 gallon	P1@6.00	Ea	3,540.00	207.00	—	3,747.00
Vertical tank, D102" x H150"						
5,000 gallon	P1@8.00	Ea	6,640.00	276.00	—	6,916.00
Vertical tank, D141" x H192"						
12,000 gallon	P1@9.00	Ea	10,300.00	311.00	—	10,611.00

Plastic holding tank. Single compartment. One piece polyethylene construction. Shallow burial (2 feet of earth cover). 28" manway entrance. Including excavation, backfill and equipment costs. Used for drink water storage.

Description	Craft@Hrs	Unit	Material $	Labor $	Equipment $	Total $
30 gallon	P1@3.00	Ea	197.00	104.00	165.00	466.00
40 gallon	P1@3.00	Ea	224.00	104.00	165.00	493.00
75 gallon	P1@3.00	Ea	250.00	104.00	165.00	519.00
300 gallon	P1@5.00	Ea	1,090.00	173.00	275.00	1,538.00
525 gallon	P1@6.00	Ea	1,590.00	207.00	330.00	2,127.00
1,150 gallon	P1@8.00	Ea	2,770.00	276.00	440.00	3,486.00
1,700 gallon	P1@11.0	Ea	3,570.00	380.00	605.00	4,555.00
1,950 gallon	P1@12.0	Ea	3,800.00	415.00	660.00	4,875.00

Plastic holding tank. Single compartment. One piece polyethylene construction. Above ground applications only. Used for drink water storage.

Description	Craft@Hrs	Unit	Material $	Labor $	Equipment $	Total $
180 gallon	P1@3.00	Ea	512.00	104.00	165.00	781.00
200 gallon	P1@3.75	Ea	761.00	130.00	207.00	1,098.00
300 gallon	P1@4.25	Ea	984.00	147.00	207.00	1,338.00
525 gallon	P1@5.00	Ea	1,450.00	173.00	275.00	1,898.00
1,000 gallon	P1@5.75	Ea	1,970.00	199.00	317.00	2,486.00
1,150 gallon	P1@6.25	Ea	2,420.00	216.00	345.00	2,981.00
1,700 gallon	P1@7.00	Ea	3,210.00	242.00	385.00	3,837.00

Plastic septic tank. 750 gallon. Single compartment. One piece polyethylene construction. Including excavation, backfill and equipment costs.

Description	Craft@Hrs	Unit	Material $	Labor $	Equipment $	Total $
Trickle tank	P1@8.00	Ea	2,240.00	276.00	440.00	2,956.00
Shallow buried	P1@8.00	Ea	2,240.00	276.00	440.00	2,956.00
Deep buried	P1@8.00	Ea	2,360.00	276.00	440.00	3,076.00
Manway extension						
	P1@.350	LF	89.40	12.10	—	101.50

Description	Craft@Hrs	Unit	Material $	Labor $	Equipment $	Total $

Plastic sump pit. One piece polyethylene construction. Complete with radon gasket electrical and discharge grommets. Including excavation, backfill and equipment costs.

Description	Craft@Hrs	Unit	Material $	Labor $	Equipment $	Total $
30 gallon	P1@3.00	Ea	183.00	104.00	165.00	452.00
40 gallon	P1@3.00	Ea	224.00	104.00	165.00	493.00
75 gallon	P1@3.00	Ea	263.00	104.00	165.00	532.00
110 gallon	P1@3.25	Ea	419.00	112.00	180.00	711.00
150 gallon	P1@3.75	Ea	566.00	130.00	207.00	903.00
250 gallon	P1@4.75	Ea	894.00	164.00	262.00	1,320.00
380 gallon	P1@5.50	Ea	1,390.00	190.00	303.00	1,883.00

Plastic sewage lift tank. One piece polyethylene construction. Complete with radon gasket, inlet, vent, electrical and discharge grommets. Including excavation, backfill and equipment costs.

Description	Craft@Hrs	Unit	Material $	Labor $	Equipment $	Total $
30 gallon	P1@3.00	Ea	231.00	104.00	165.00	500.00
40 gallon	P1@3.00	Ea	256.00	104.00	165.00	525.00
75 gallon	P1@3.00	Ea	288.00	104.00	165.00	557.00
110 gallon	P1@3.25	Ea	485.00	112.00	180.00	777.00
150 gallon	P1@3.75	Ea	590.00	130.00	207.00	927.00
250 gallon	P1@4.75	Ea	970.00	164.00	262.00	1,396.00
380 gallon	P1@5.50	Ea	1,430.00	190.00	303.00	1,923.00

Plastic grey water treatment tank. 75 gallon. One piece polyethylene construction. Including excavation, backfill and equipment costs.

Description	Craft@Hrs	Unit	Material $	Labor $	Equipment $	Total $
Buried	P1@3.00	Ea	460.00	104.00	165.00	729.00
Non-buried	P1@1.50	Ea	419.00	51.80	83.00	553.80

Trenching

Because of varying soil compositions and densities, trenching costs can sometimes be difficult to accurately estimate. The tables in this section are based on average soil conditions, which are loosely defined as dirt, soft clay or gravel mixed with rocks. The costs for trenching through limestone, sandstone or shale can increase by as much as 1,000 percent. For these conditions, it is best to consult with experts or to subcontract the work to specialists.

The primary consideration in excavations is to ensure the safety of the pipe layers. Current OSHA statutes require all excavations over 5 feet deep to be sloped, shored, sheeted or braced to prevent cave-ins. The use of shoring minimizes trenching costs by eliminating the need to slope the trench walls, but increases pipe-laying costs because of the difficulty in working between cross-bracing.

The estimator should carefully compare the costs for installing and removing shoring, and reduced pipe installation productivity, against the additional excavation costs for sloping the walls of the trench. For average soil conditions, not exceeding 6 to 8 feet in depth, it is usually more economical to slope the trench walls.

The current average cost for a backhoe with operator is $95.90 per hour. Some trenching contractors additionally charge $25.00 move-on and $25.00 move-off costs, particularly for small projects.

Total trenching, backfill and compaction costs are calculated by multiplying the backhoe hours from the following charts by $95.90 per hour, and adding move-on and move-off charges, if applicable.

Backhoe Trenching						
Trench walls at a 90 degree angle, based on average soil, including trenching, backfill and compaction. Hours per 100 linear feet of trench						
Trench depth (feet)	Trench width (feet)					
	1	2	3	4	5	6
2	2.6	5.1	7.7	10.2	12.8	15.3
3	3.8	7.7	11.5	15.3	19.2	23.0
4	5.1	10.2	15.3	20.4	25.6	30.7
5	6.4	12.8	19.2	25.6	32.0	38.3
6	7.7	15.3	23.0	30.7	38.3	46.0
7	8.9	17.9	26.8	35.8	44.7	53.7
8	10.2	20.4	30.7	40.9	51.1	61.3
9	11.5	23.0	34.5	46.0	57.5	69.0
10	12.8	25.5	38.3	51.1	63.9	76.6

Notes:
1) Compaction is based on the use of a compactor wheel.
2) Additional labor costs must be added if watering-in, stone removal or excess spoil removal is required.

Backhoe Trenching Trench walls at a 45 degree angle, based on average soil including trenching, backfill and compaction. Hours per 100 linear feet of trench						
Trench depth (feet)	**Trench width (feet)**					
	1	**2**	**3**	**4**	**5**	**6**
2	7.6	10.3	12.6	15.5	17.9	20.3
3	15.2	22.6	22.6	26.6	30.7	34.5
4	25.5	30.7	35.5	40.7	45.9	51.0
5	38.3	44.5	51.0	57.6	63.8	70.0
6	53.4	61.0	69.0	76.6	84.1	91.7
7	71.4	80.3	89.3	98.3	107.2	115.9
8	92.1	102.1	112.4	122.4	132.8	143.1
9	114.8	126.6	137.9	149.3	161.0	172.4
10	140.3	153.1	165.9	178.6	191.4	204.5

Notes:

1) Compaction is based on the use of a compactor wheel.
2) Additional labor costs must be added if watering-in, stone removal or excess spoil removal is required.

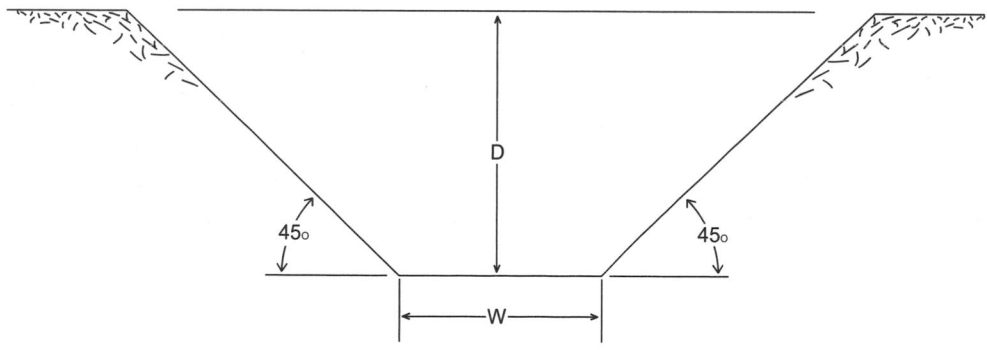

Equipment Rental

Equipment Rental			
Description	**Per day ($)**	**Per week ($)**	**Per month ($)**
Air compressor, gas or diesel, 100-125 CFM with 100' hose, air tool and 4 bits	171.00	487.00	1,360.00
Air compressor, gas or diesel, 165-185 CFM with 100' hose, air tool and 4 bits	203.00	585.00	1,650.00
Air compressor, gas or diesel, 100-125 CFM, no accessories	97.90	292.00	877.00
Air compressor, gas or diesel, 165-185 CFM, no accessories	130.00	390.00	1,170.00
Backhoe with bucket, 55 HP	375.00	1,050.00	3,400.00
Backhoe with bucket, 100 HP	485.00	1,480.00	4,300.00
Backhoe hydraulic compactor, 5-10 ton	150.00	460.00	1,350.00
Bender, hydraulic	75.00	300.00	800.00
Bevel machine with torch	20.00	61.00	177.00
Boom lift, 31' - 40'	220.00	630.00	1,700.00
Boom lift, 51' - 60'	210.00	625.00	1,900.00
Chain hoist, to 2 tons	40.00	140.00	325.00
Chain-hoist, 10 tons	80.00	160.00	480.00
Come-along, ½ to 1 ton	20.00	59.00	177.00
Come-along, 1½ to 2 tons	35.00	104.00	311.00
Come-along, 4-ton	56.00	166.00	499.00
Compactor, soil, gas or diesel, 125 lb	70.00	218.00	610.00
Crane, truck-mounted, 13,000 lb capacity	380.00	1,110.00	3,450.00
Crane, truck-mounted, 30,000 lb capacity	450.00	1,340.00	3,860.00
Forklift, 2,000 pound capacity	130.00	490.00	1,420.00
Forklift, 4,000 pound capacity	95.00	375.00	1,100.00
Forklift, 6,000 pound capacity	120.00	440.00	1,330.00
Front-end loader, 1 yard capacity	290.00	850.00	2,480.00
Front-end loader, 2 yard capacity	340.00	1,050.00	3,300.00
Front-end loader, 3¼ yard capacity	700.00	2,200.00	6,500.00
Pipe machine, up to 2" capacity	56.00	166.00	462.00
Pipe machine, 2½" to 4" capacity	62.00	215.00	659.00
Ramset (nail gun)	32.00	130.00	375.00
Scissors-lift, to 20', diesel, self-propelled	110.00	280.00	675.00
Scissors-lift, 21' – 30'	165.00	475.00	1,300.00
Skid Steer Loader 1,750 lb capacity	200.00	640.00	1,830.00
Trailer, office, 25'	55.00	180.00	465.00
Truck, 3/4 ton pickup	81.00	321.00	1,290.00
Truck, 1 ton pickup	132.00	418.00	1,320.00
Truck, 1 ton stake bed	169.00	507.00	1,490.00
Van, storage, 26'	—	—	321.00
Van, storage, 40'	—	—	391.00
Welding machine, gas, 200 amp, trailer-mounted with 50' bare lead	55.00	200.00	500.00
Welding machine, diesel, 400 amp, trailer-mounted with 50' bare lead	80.00	275.00	720.00

Description	Craft@Hrs	Unit	Material $	Labor $	Equipment $	Total $

1½" brass valve tags with black filled numbers

| Typical costs | P1@.150 | Ea | 3.26 | 5.18 | — | 8.44 |

1½" blank brass valve tags

| Typical costs | P1@.150 | Ea | 1.62 | 5.18 | — | 6.80 |

1½" plastic valve tags with engraved numbers

| Typical costs | P1@.150 | Ea | 2.72 | 5.18 | — | 7.90 |

Engraved plastic equipment nameplates

| Typical costs | P1@.400 | Ea | 7.02 | 13.80 | — | 20.82 |

Pipe and duct markers

| Typical costs | P1@.250 | Ea | 4.01 | 8.64 | — | 12.65 |

As-built drawings

| Typical costs | P1@.500 | Ea | — | 17.30 | — | 17.30 |

Instructing owner's operating personnel

| Typical costs | P1@8.00 | Ea | — | 276.00 | — | 276.00 |

Description	Craft@Hrs	Unit	Material $	Labor $	Equipment $	Total $

Remove rectangular galvanized ductwork. 22 to 30 gauge galvanized sheet metal (dimension/gauge per SMACNA standards). Per linear foot of sheet metal duct work. The cost of removing ductwork includes the cost of removing the support hangers. Add the cost of disconnecting and removing heating coils, air volume zone boxes, air handing units, condensate drains, motorized dampers or other associated accessories, piping or wiring. These figures assume demolished materials are piled on site. Disposal costs or salvage values excluded. (SMACNA = Sheetmetal & Air Conditioning National Association.) Equipment may be needed for some sizes and locations. Refer to the equipment rental costs at the front of this section.

Description	Craft@Hrs	Unit	Material $	Labor $	Equipment $	Total $
4" to 12" rectangular/square duct, remove	S2@.015	LF	—	.51	—	.51
14" to 24" rectangular/square duct, remove	S2@.020	LF	—	.68	—	.68
26" to 36" rectangular/square duct, remove	S2@.065	LF	—	2.22	—	2.22
38" to 60" rectangular/square duct, remove	S2@.090	LF	—	3.07	—	3.07

Remove round galvanized ductwork. 22 to 30 gauge galvanized sheet metal (dimension/gauge per SMACNA standards). Per linear foot of sheet metal duct work. The cost of removing ductwork includes the cost of removing the support hangers. Add the cost of disconnecting and removing heating coils, air volume zone boxes, air handing units, condensate drains, motorized dampers or other associated accessories, piping or wiring. These figures assume demolished materials are piled on site. Disposal costs or salvage values excluded. (SMACNA = Sheetmetal & Air Conditioning National Association.) Equipment may be needed for some sizes and locations. Refer to the equipment rental costs at the front of this section.

Description	Craft@Hrs	Unit	Material $	Labor $	Equipment $	Total $
4" to 12" round duct, remove	S2@.012	LF	—	.41	—	.41
14" to 24" round duct, remove	S2@.016	LF	—	.55	—	.55
26" to 36" round duct, remove	S2@.052	LF	—	1.78	—	1.78
38" to 60" round duct, remove	S2@.072	LF	—	2.46	—	2.46

Description	Craft@Hrs	Unit	Material $	Labor $	Equipment $	Total $

Remove welded steel ductwork. 10 to 16 gauge mild steel. Per linear foot of welded mild steel duct work. The cost of removing ductwork includes the cost of removing the support hangers. Add the cost of disconnecting and removing exhaust fans, condensate drains, sprinkler heads or other associated accessories, piping or wiring. These figures assume demolished materials are piled on site. Disposal costs or salvage values excluded. Equipment may be needed for some sizes and locations. Refer to the equipment rental costs at the front of this section.

Description	Craft@Hrs	Unit	Material $	Labor $	Equipment $	Total $
4" to 12", square or round duct,						
remove	S2@.045	LF	—	1.54	—	1.54
14" to 24", square or round duct,						
remove	S2@.060	LF	—	2.05	—	2.05
26" to 36", square or round duct,						
remove	S2@.095	LF	—	3.25	—	3.25
38" to 60", square or round duct,						
remove	S2@.150	LF	—	5.12	—	5.12

Remove diffuser or grille. These figures assume demolished materials are piled on site. Disposal costs or salvage values excluded. Equipment may be needed for some sizes and locations. Refer to the equipment rental costs at the front of this section.

Description	Craft@Hrs	Unit	Material $	Labor $	Equipment $	Total $
6" to 12", square or round diffuser/grille,						
remove	S2@.150	Ea	—	5.12	—	5.12
14" to 24", square or round diffuser/grille,						
remove	S2@.180	Ea	—	6.15	—	6.15
26" to 36", square or round diffuser/grille,						
remove	S2@.400	Ea	—	13.70	—	13.70
38" to 60" square or round diffuser/grille,						
remove	S2@.800	Ea	—	27.30	—	27.30

Remove air mixing box. These figures include isolating and disconnecting hot water, chilled water, steam, refrigerant and/or pneumatic control tube or control wiring. These figures assume demolished materials are piled on site. Disposal costs or salvage values excluded. Equipment may be needed for some sizes and locations. Refer to the equipment rental costs at the front of this section.

Description	Craft@Hrs	Unit	Material $	Labor $	Equipment $	Total $
Air Box, 50 to 150 CFM,						
remove	S2@.500	Ea	—	17.10	—	17.10
Air Box, 160 to 500 CFM,						
remove	S2@.650	Ea	—	22.20	—	22.20
Air Box, 550 to 750 CFM,						
remove	S2@.900	Ea	—	30.70	—	30.70

Description	Craft@Hrs	Unit	Material $	Labor $	Equipment $	Total $

Remove air handling unit. These figures include isolating and disconnecting hot water, chilled water, steam or gas and/or ductwork, electrical connections and unit disassembly when required for removal. Disposal costs or salvage values excluded. Equipment may be needed for some sizes and locations. Refer to the equipment rental costs at the front of this section.

Description	Craft@Hrs	Unit	Material $	Labor $	Equipment $	Total $
AHU, 2,000- 5,000 CFM, remove	P1@8.00	Ea	—	276.00	—	276.00
AHU, 5,000-10,000 CFM, remove	P1@12.0	Ea	—	415.00	—	415.00
AHU,10,000-20,000 CFM, remove	P1@18.0	Ea	—	622.00	—	622.00
AHU, over 20,000 CFM, remove	P1@28.0	Ea	—	967.00	—	967.00

Remove roof top unit. These figures include isolating and disconnecting hot water, chilled water, steam or gas and/or ductwork, electrical connections and unit disassembly when required for removal. Disposal costs or salvage values excluded. Make additional hoisting allowances for roof heights above 40'. Equipment may be needed for some sizes and locations. Refer to the equipment rental costs at the front of this section.

Description	Craft@Hrs	Unit	Material $	Labor $	Equipment $	Total $
RTU, 2,000- 5,000 CFM, remove	P1@6.00	Ea	—	207.00	—	207.00
RTU, 5,000-10,000 CFM, remove	P1@10.0	Ea	—	346.00	—	346.00
RTU. 10,000-20,000 CFM, remove	P1@16.0	Ea	—	553.00	—	553.00
RTU, over 20,000 CFM, remove	P1@26.0	Ea	—	898.00	—	898.00

Description	Craft@Hrs	Unit	Material $	Labor $	Equipment $	Total $

Remove boiler. These figures include isolating and disconnecting hot water, steam or gas and/or electrical connections and unit disassembly when required for removal. Disposal costs or salvage values excluded. Equipment may be needed for some sizes and locations. Refer to the equipment rental costs at the front of this section.

Description	Craft@Hrs	Unit	Material $	Labor $	Equipment $	Total $
10-50 KW electric boiler, remove	P1@8.00	Ea	—	276.00	—	276.00
50-100 KW electric boiler, remove	P1@12.0	Ea	—	415.00	—	415.00
100-200 KW electric boiler, remove	P1@26.0	Ea	—	898.00	—	898.00
200-500 KW electric boiler, remove	P1@36.0	Ea	—	1,240.00	—	1,240.00
over 500 KW electric boiler, remove	P1@44.0	Ea	—	1,520.00	—	1,520.00
to 150 Mbh gas fired boiler, remove	P1@9.00	Ea	—	311.00	—	311.00
150-300 Mbh gas fired boiler, remove	P1@14.0	Ea	—	484.00	—	484.00
300-750 Mbh gas fired boiler, remove	P1@30.0	Ea	—	1,040.00	—	1,040.00
750-1500 Mbh gas fired boiler, remove	P1@46.0	Ea	—	1,590.00	—	1,590.00
1500-2000 Mbh gas fired boiler, remove	P1@65.0	Ea	—	2,250.00	—	2,250.00
over 2000 Mbh gas fired boiler, remove	P1@80.0	Ea	—	2,760.00	—	2,760.00

Remove furnace. These figures include isolating and disconnecting plenums, fuel and/or electrical connections. Disposal costs or salvage values excluded. Equipment may be needed for some sizes and locations. Refer to the equipment rental costs at the front of this section.

Description	Craft@Hrs	Unit	Material $	Labor $	Equipment $	Total $
5-30 KW electric furnace, remove	P1@2.50	Ea	—	86.40	—	86.40
30-60 KW electric furnace, remove	P1@3.75	Ea	—	130.00	—	130.00
30-150 Mbh gas fired furnace, remove	P1@5.00	Ea	—	173.00	—	173.00
150-225 Mbh gas fired furnace, remove	P1@7.00	Ea	—	242.00	—	242.00

Description	Craft@Hrs	Unit	Material $	Labor $	Equipment $	Total $

Remove chiller. These figures include isolating and disconnecting chilled water and electrical connections, evacuating refrigerant to storage vessels and unit disassembly when required for removal. Disposal costs or salvage values excluded. Equipment may be needed for some sizes and locations. Refer to the equipment rental costs at the front of this section.

Description	Craft@Hrs	Unit	Material $	Labor $	Equipment $	Total $
Chiller, 20-50 tons,						
remove	P1@34.0	Ea	—	1,170.00	—	1,170.00
Chiller, 50-100 tons,						
remove	P1@48.0	Ea	—	1,660.00	—	1,660.00
Chiller, 100-150 tons,						
remove	P1@56.0	Ea	—	1,930.00	—	1,930.00
Chiller, 150-200 tons,						
remove	P1@68.0	Ea	—	2,350.00	—	2,350.00
Chiller, 200-250 tons,						
remove	P1@80.0	Ea	—	2,760.00	—	2,760.00
Chiller, over 250 tons,						
remove	P1@100	Ea	—	3,460.00	—	3,460.00

Remove air cooled condenser. These figures include isolating and disconnecting refrigerant lines and electrical connections, evacuating refrigerant to storage vessels and unit disassembly when required for removal. Disposal costs or salvage values excluded. Make additional hoisting allowances for roof heights above 40'. Equipment may be needed for some sizes and locations. Refer to the equipment rental costs at the front of this section.

Description	Craft@Hrs	Unit	Material $	Labor $	Equipment $	Total $
Air cooled condenser, 2-4 tons,						
remove	P1@4.00	Ea	—	138.00	—	138.00
Air cooled condenser, 5-10 tons,						
remove	P1@8.00	Ea	—	276.00	—	276.00
Air cooled condenser, 10-20 tons,						
remove	P1@20.0	Ea	—	691.00	—	691.00
Air cooled condenser, 20-30 tons,						
remove	P1@28.0	Ea	—	967.00	—	967.00
Air cooled condenser, 30-50 tons,						
remove	P1@36.0	Ea	—	1,240.00	—	1,240.00
Air cooled condenser, 50-150 tons,						
remove	P1@44.0	Ea	—	1,520.00	—	1,520.00
Air cooled condenser, 150-250 tons,						
remove	P1@52.0	Ea	—	1,800.00	—	1,800.00

Description	Craft@Hrs	Unit	Material $	Labor $	Equipment $	Total $

Remove cooling tower. These figures include isolating and disconnecting chilled water lines and electrical connections, and unit disassembly when required for removal. Disposal costs or salvage values excluded. Make additional hoisting allowances for roof heights above 40'. Equipment may be needed for some sizes and locations. Refer to the equipment rental costs at the front of this section.

Description	Craft@Hrs	Unit	Material $	Labor $	Equipment $	Total $
Cooling tower, 5-10 tons, remove	P1@8.00	Ea	—	276.00	—	276.00
Cooling tower, 10-20 tons, remove	P1@16.0	Ea	—	553.00	—	553.00
Cooling tower, 20-30 tons, remove	P1@24.0	Ea	—	829.00	—	829.00
Cooling tower, 30-50 tons, remove	P1@32.0	Ea	—	1,110.00	—	1,110.00
Cooling tower, 50-150 tons, remove	P1@40.0	Ea	—	1,380.00	—	1,380.00
Cooling tower, 150-250 tons, remove	P1@48.0	Ea	—	1,660.00	—	1,660.00
Cooling tower, 250-500 tons, remove	P1@70.0	Ea	—	2,420.00	—	2,420.00

Remove fan coil. These figures include isolating and disconnecting chilled water and/or hot water lines and/or duct and electrical connections, and unit disassembly when required for removal. Disposal costs or salvage values excluded. Equipment may be needed for some sizes and locations. Refer to the equipment rental costs at the front of this section.

Description	Craft@Hrs	Unit	Material $	Labor $	Equipment $	Total $
2 pipe fan coil, 300- 500 CFM, remove	P1@4.00	Ea	—	138.00	—	138.00
2 pipe fan coil, 550- 750 CFM, remove	P1@4.50	Ea	—	155.00	—	155.00
2 pipe fan coil, 800- 1200 CFM, remove	P1@6.00	Ea	—	207.00	—	207.00
4 pipe fan coil, 300- 500 CFM, remove	P1@4.50	Ea	—	155.00	—	155.00
4 pipe fan coil, 550- 750 CFM, remove	P1@5.00	Ea	—	173.00	—	173.00
4 pipe fan coil, 800- 1200 CFM, remove	P1@6.50	Ea	—	225.00	—	225.00

Description	Craft@Hrs	Unit	Material $	Labor $	Equipment $	Total $

Remove unit heater. These figures include isolating and disconnecting hot water, steam lines or gas and/or electrical connections. Disposal costs or salvage values excluded. Equipment may be needed for some sizes and locations. Refer to the equipment rental costs at the front of this section.

Description	Craft@Hrs	Unit	Material $	Labor $	Equipment $	Total $
Gas fired unit heater, 50-150 Mbh, remove	P1@2.25	Ea	—	77.70	—	77.70
Gas fired unit heater, 200-350 Mbh, remove	P1@3.50	Ea	—	121.00	—	121.00
Steam unit heater, 75–200 Mbh, remove	P1@3.25	Ea	—	112.00	—	112.00
Steam unit heater, 250– 350 Mbh, remove	P1@4.75	Ea	—	164.00	—	164.00
Electric unit heater, 5-25 KW, remove	P1@2.00	Ea	—	69.10	—	69.10
Electric unit heater, 30-50 KW, remove	P1@2.75	Ea	—	95.00	—	95.00

Remove heat pump. These figures include isolating and disconnecting pipe, duct and electrical connections and evacuating refrigerant to storage vessels when required for removal. Disposal costs or salvage values excluded. Equipment may be needed for some sizes and locations. Refer to the equipment rental costs at the front of this section.

Description	Craft@Hrs	Unit	Material $	Labor $	Equipment $	Total $
Heat pump, split system, 2-5 Ton, remove	P1@4.75	Ea	—	164.00	—	164.00
Heat pump, split system, 7.5–10 Ton, remove	P1@8.50	Ea	—	294.00	—	294.00
Heat pump, packaged system, 2-5 Ton, remove	P1@3.25	Ea	—	112.00	—	112.00
Heat pump, pkg. system, 7.5-10 Ton, remove	P1@5.50	Ea	—	190.00	—	190.00

Description	Craft@Hrs	Unit	Material $	Labor $	Equipment $	Total $

Remove heat exchanger. These figures include isolating and disconnecting chilled water, hot water and/or steam line connections. Disposal costs or salvage values excluded. Equipment may be needed for some sizes and locations. Refer to the equipment rental costs at the front of this section.

Description	Craft@Hrs	Unit	Material $	Labor $	Equipment $	Total $
Heat exchanger, 6" x 30", remove	P1@2.75	Ea	—	95.00	—	95.00
Heat exchanger, 10" x 48", remove	P1@4.00	Ea	—	138.00	—	138.00
Heat exchanger, 12" x 72", remove	P1@5.25	Ea	—	181.00	—	181.00
Heat exchanger, 16" x 90", remove	P1@6.00	Ea	—	207.00	—	207.00

Remove duct mounted coil. These figures include isolating and disconnecting steam, chilled water, hot water, condensate, refrigerant or electrical and duct connections. Disposal costs or salvage values excluded. Refrigerant coil removal costs include system refrigerant evacuation and storage. Equipment may be needed for some sizes and locations. Refer to the equipment rental costs at the front of this section.

Description	Craft@Hrs	Unit	Material $	Labor $	Equipment $	Total $
Single row water coil, 12" to 18", remove	P1@2.00	Ea	—	69.10	—	69.10
Single row water coil, 20" to 30", remove	P1@3.50	Ea	—	121.00	—	121.00
Single water coil, 32" to 60", remove	P1@8.00	Ea	—	276.00	—	276.00
Single row steam coil, 12" to 18" remove	P1@2.25	Ea	—	77.70	—	77.70
Single row steam coil, 20" to 30" remove	P1@3.75	Ea	—	130.00	—	130.00
Single row steam coil, 32" to 60" remove	P1@9.00	Ea	—	311.00	—	311.00
Electric resistance, 12" to 18" remove	P1@1.25	Ea	—	43.20	—	43.20
Electric resistance, 20" to 30" remove	P1@1.75	Ea	—	60.50	—	60.50
Electric resistance, 32" to 60" remove	P1@4.00	Ea	—	138.00	—	138.00
Refrigerant coil, 2-3 ton remove	P1@4.00	Ea	—	138.00	—	138.00
Refrigerant coil, 4-5 ton remove	P1@6.50	Ea	—	225.00	—	225.00
Refrigerant coil, 6-10 ton remove	P1@12.0	Ea	—	415.00	—	415.00
Refrigerant coil, 12-15 ton remove	P1@16.0	Ea	—	553.00	—	553.00

Description	Craft@Hrs	Unit	Material $	Labor $	Equipment $	Total $

Remove steel piping. These figures include cutting out and removing threaded or welded steel piping. These figures assume demolished materials are piled on site. Equipment, fixture or apparatus disconnection costs and salvage values excluded. Equipment may be needed for some sizes and locations. Refer to the equipment rental costs at the front of this section.

Description	Craft@Hrs	Unit	Material $	Labor $	Equipment $	Total $
Steel pipe, sch. 40, 1/2" – 1"						
remove	P1@.038	LF	—	1.31	—	1.31
Steel pipe, sch. 40, 1½" – 2"						
remove	P1@.068	LF	—	2.35	—	2.35
Steel pipe, sch. 40, 2½" – 4"						
remove	P1@.108	LF	—	3.73	—	3.73
Steel pipe, sch. 40, 6" – 8"						
remove	P1@.230	LF	—	7.95	—	7.95
Steel pipe, sch. 40, 10" – 12"						
remove	P1@.330	LF	—	11.40	—	11.40
Steel pipe, sch. 80, 1/2" – 1"						
remove	P1@.042	LF	—	1.45	—	1.45
Steel pipe, sch. 80, 1½" – 2"						
remove	P1@.075	LF	—	2.59	—	2.59
Steel pipe, sch. 80, 2½" – 4"						
remove	P1@.118	LF	—	4.08	—	4.08
Steel pipe, sch. 80, 6" – 8"						
remove	P1@.290	LF	—	10.00	—	10.00
Steel pipe, sch. 80, 10" – 12"						
remove	P1@.360	LF	—	12.40	—	12.40
Remove steel pipe, sch. 160,						
Add	—	%	—	—	—	30.00

Remove copper piping. These figures include cutting out and removing copper piping. These figures assume demolished materials are piled on site. Equipment, fixture or apparatus disconnection costs and salvage values excluded.

Description	Craft@Hrs	Unit	Material $	Labor $	Equipment $	Total $
Copper pipe, 1/2" – 1"						
remove	P1@.022	LF	—	.76	.07	.83
Copper pipe, 1½" – 2"						
remove	P1@.028	LF	—	.97	.08	1.05
Copper pipe, 2½" – 4"						
remove	P1@.044	LF	—	1.52	.11	1.63

Remove plastic piping. These figures include cutting out and removing plastic piping. These figures assume demolished materials are piled on site. Equipment, fixture or apparatus disconnection costs and salvage values excluded. Equipment may be needed for some sizes and locations. Refer to the equipment rental costs at the front of this section.

Description	Craft@Hrs	Unit	Material $	Labor $	Equipment $	Total $
plastic pipe, 1/2" – 1"						
remove	P1@.015	LF	—	.52	—	.52
plastic pipe, 1½" – 2"						
remove	P1@.030	LF	—	1.04	—	1.04
plastic pipe, 2½" – 4"						
remove	P1@.038	LF	—	1.31	—	1.31
plastic pipe, 6" – 8"						
remove	P1@.080	LF	—	2.76	—	2.76

Description	Craft@Hrs	Unit	Material $	Labor $	Equipment $	Total $

Remove pump. These figures include isolating and disconnecting pipe and electrical connections. Disposal costs or salvage values excluded. Equipment may be needed for some sizes and locations. Refer to the equipment rental costs at the front of this section.

Description	Craft@Hrs	Unit	Material $	Labor $	Equipment $	Total $
Base mounted pump, 1/2 – 1 HP, remove	P1@1.00	Ea	—	34.60	—	34.60
Base mounted pump, 1½ – 3 HP, remove	P1@1.75	Ea	—	60.50	—	60.50
Base mounted pump, 5 – 10 HP, remove	P1@2.75	Ea	—	95.00	—	95.00
Base mounted pump, 15 – 25 HP, remove	P1@3.75	Ea	—	130.00	—	130.00
Base mounted pump, 30 – 50 HP, remove	P1@4.55	Ea	—	157.00	—	157.00
In-line mounted pump, 1/12 – 1/3 HP, remove	P1@.650	Ea	—	22.50	—	22.50
In-line mounted pump, 1/2 – 1 HP, remove	P1@.750	Ea	—	25.90	—	25.90
In-line mounted pump, 3 – 5 HP, remove	P1@1.85	Ea	—	63.90	—	63.90
In-line mounted pump, 7.5 – 10 HP, remove	P1@2.55	Ea	—	88.10	—	88.10
In-line mounted pump, 15 – 25 HP, remove	P1@3.90	Ea	—	135.00	—	135.00
In-line mounted pump, 30 – 50 HP, remove	P1@4.85	Ea	—	168.00	—	168.00

Remove valve. These figures include isolation and disconnection. Disposal costs or salvage values excluded. Equipment may be needed for some sizes and locations. Refer to the equipment rental costs at the front of this section.

Description	Craft@Hrs	Unit	Material $	Labor $	Equipment $	Total $
Soldered valve, 1/2" – 1", remove	P1@.165	Ea	—	5.70	—	5.70
Soldered valve, 1½" – 2", remove	P1@.225	Ea	—	7.77	—	7.77
Soldered valve, 2-1/2" – 4", remove	P1@.650	Ea	—	22.50	—	22.50
Threaded valve, 1/2" – 1", remove	P1@.150	Ea	—	5.18	—	5.18
Threaded valve, 1½" – 2", remove	P1@.235	Ea	—	8.12	—	8.12
Threaded valve, 2½" – 4", remove	P1@.680	Ea	—	23.50	—	23.50
Flanged valve, 1/2" – 1", remove	P1@.200	Ea	—	6.91	—	6.91
Flanged valve, 1½" – 2", remove	P1@.280	Ea	—	9.67	—	9.67
Flanged valve, 2½" – 4", remove	P1@.625	Ea	—	21.60	—	21.60
Flanged valve, 6" – 8", remove	P1@1.70	Ea	—	58.70	—	58.70
Flanged valve, 10" – 12", remove	P1@2.65	Ea	—	91.60	—	91.60

HVAC & Plumbing Demolition

Description	Craft@Hrs	Unit	Material $	Labor $	Equipment $	Total $

Remove hot water tank. These figures include isolation and disconnection. Disposal costs or salvage values excluded. Equipment may be needed for some sizes and locations. Refer to the equipment rental costs at the front of this section.

Description	Craft@Hrs	Unit	Material $	Labor $	Equipment $	Total $
Gas fired hot water tank, 40 gallon, remove	P1@2.00	Ea	—	69.10	—	69.10
Gas fired hot water tank, 60 gallon, remove	P1@2.50	Ea	—	86.40	—	86.40
Gas fired hot water tank, 100 gallon, remove	P1@3.00	Ea	—	104.00	—	104.00
Electric hot water tank, 40 Gallon, remove	P1@1.60	Ea	—	55.30	—	55.30
Electric hot water tank, 60 Gallon, remove	P1@2.00	Ea	—	69.10	—	69.10
Electric hot water tank, 100 Gallon, remove	P1@2.60	Ea	—	89.80	—	89.80

Remove plumbing fixture. These figures include isolation and disconnection. Disposal costs or salvage values excluded. Equipment may be needed for some sizes and locations. Refer to the equipment rental costs at the front of this section.

Description	Craft@Hrs	Unit	Material $	Labor $	Equipment $	Total $
Floor mount, tank type water closet, remove	P1@.850	ea	—	29.40	—	29.40
Wall mount, tank type water closet, remove	P1@1.35	Ea	—	46.60	—	46.60
Floor mount, flush valve water closet, remove	P1@.950	Ea	—	32.80	—	32.80
Wall mount, flush valve water closet, remove	P1@1.55	Ea	—	53.60	—	53.60
Wall mount, flush valve urinal, remove	P1@1.15	Ea	—	39.70	—	39.70
Wall mount, tank type urinal, remove	P1@1.65	Ea	—	57.00	—	57.00
Kitchen sink, remove	P1@.850	Ea	—	29.40	—	29.40
Bathroom sink, remove	P1@.850	Ea	—	29.40	—	29.40
Bathtub, remove	P1@2.25	Ea	—	77.70	—	77.70
Shower stall, remove	P1@2.00	Ea	—	69.10	—	69.10
Tub and shower combination, remove	P1@2.85	Ea	—	98.50	—	98.50
Laundry sink, remove	P1@.950	Ea	—	32.80	—	32.80
Mop sink, remove	P1@1.50	Ea	—	51.80	—	51.80
Slop sink, remove	P1@1.75	Ea	—	60.50	—	60.50
Drinking fountain, remove	P1@1.40	Ea	—	48.40	—	48.40

Description	Craft@Hrs	Unit	Material $	Labor $	Equipment $	Total $

Disconnect plumbing fixture. These figures include isolation and disconnection only. Fixtures removed by others. Disposal costs or salvage values excluded. Equipment may be needed for some sizes and locations. Refer to the equipment rental costs at the front of this section.

Description	Craft@Hrs	Unit	Material $	Labor $	Equipment $	Total $
Floor mount, tank type water closet, disconnect	P1@.450	Ea	—	15.50	—	15.50
Wall mount, tank type water closet, disconnect	P1@.650	Ea	—	22.50	—	22.50
Floor mount, flush valve water closet, disconnect	P1@.550	Ea	—	19.00	—	19.00
Wall mount, flush valve water closet, disconnect	P1@.650	Ea	—	22.50	—	22.50
Wall mount, flush valve urinal, disconnect	P1@.650	Ea	—	22.50	—	22.50
Wall mount, tank type urinal, disconnect	P1@.950	Ea	—	32.80	—	32.80
Kitchen sink, disconnect	P1@.450	Ea	—	15.50	—	15.50
Bathroom sink, disconnect	P1@.450	Ea	—	15.50	—	15.50
Bathtub, disconnect	P1@.650	Ea	—	22.50	—	22.50
Shower stall, disconnect	P1@.650	Ea	—	22.50	—	22.50
Tub and shower combination, disconnect	P1@.650	Ea	—	22.50	—	22.50
Laundry sink, disconnect	P1@.450	Ea	—	15.50	—	15.50
Mop sink, disconnect	P1@.450	Ea	—	15.50	—	15.50
Slop sink, disconnect	P1@.750	Ea	—	25.90	—	25.90
Drinking fountain, disconnect	P1@.650	Ea	—	22.50	—	22.50
Gas fired hot water tank, 40 gallon, disconnect	P1@.900	Ea	—	31.10	—	31.10
Gas fired hot water tank, 60 gallon, disconnect	P1@1.15	Ea	—	39.70	—	39.70
Gas fired hot water tank, 100 gallon, disconnect	P1@1.35	Ea	—	46.60	—	46.60
Electric hot water tank, 40 gallon, disconnect	P1@.600	Ea	—	20.70	—	20.70
Electric hot water tank, 60 gallon, disconnect	P1@.900	Ea	—	31.10	—	31.10
Electric hot water tank, 100 gallon, disconnect	P1@1.00	Ea	—	34.60	—	34.60

Description	Craft@Hrs	Unit	Material $	Labor $	Equipment $	Total $

Remove pipe insulation. These figures assume demolished materials are piled on site. Disposal costs or salvage values excluded.

Description	Craft@Hrs	Unit	Material $	Labor $	Equipment $	Total $
Fiberglass pipe insulation, 1/2" – 1", remove	P1@.020	LF	—	.69	—	.69
Fiberglass pipe insulation, 1½" – 2", remove	P1@.025	LF	—	.86	—	.86
Fiberglass pipe insulation, 2½" – 4", remove	P1@.035	LF	—	1.21	—	1.21
Fiberglass pipe insulation, 6" – 8", remove	P1@.060	LF	—	2.07	—	2.07
Fiberglass pipe insulation, 10" – 12", remove	P1@.090	LF	—	3.11	—	3.11
Pipe insul with canvas jacket - add		%	—	10.00	—	10.00
Pipe insul. with alum. jacket - add%			—	20.00	—	20.00
Calcium silicate pipe insul. - add%			—	15.00	—	15.00

Remove duct insulation. These figures assume demolished materials are piled on site. Disposal costs or salvage values excluded.

Description	Craft@Hrs	Unit	Material $	Labor $	Equipment $	Total $
Fiberglass blanket insulation, remove	S2@.020	SF	—	.68	—	.68
Fiberglass rigid board insulation, remove	S2@.025	SF	—	.85	—	.85
Insul with canvas jacket - add	%		—	8.00	—	8.00
Insul. with alum jacket - add	%		—	10.00	—	15.00

Budget Estimates for Plumbing and HVAC Work

General contractors and owners often ask mechanical subcontractors to prepare budget cost estimates for use in planning projects. A budget estimate isn't a bid for the contract and you probably won't be paid for preparing the estimate. That's why you won't want to spend too much time on these estimates. Accuracy within 8 to 10 percent of the final bid price will usually be acceptable. Normally you'll have only preliminary architectural drawings and possibly a guide specification to work from. The tables that follow will help you prepare budget estimates for nearly any plumbing or HVAC job.

The costs in these tables are averages and will vary considerably with design requirements and by geographic area. Make it clear to the owner or architect requesting the figures that these are budget estimates and will be revised when final plans and specifications are available.

Budget Estimates for Plumbing: First, count the number of plumbing fixtures. Multiply the number of fixtures of each type by the price per fixture shown in the table below. These prices include all the usual labor and material for a complete average plumbing installation. Prices are based on branch piping lengths averaging 35 feet between the fixture and the main. Typical main piping is also included in the prices.

Description	Craft@Hrs	Unit	Material $	Labor $	Equipment $	Total $

Budget plumbing estimate, cast iron DWV, copper supply pipe

Description	Craft@Hrs	Unit	Material $	Labor $	Equipment $	Total $
Bathtubs	P1@15.0	Ea	2,120.00	518.00	—	2,638.00
Showers	P1@9.00	Ea	1,150.00	311.00	—	1,461.00
Lavatories	P1@11.0	Ea	1,990.00	380.00	—	2,370.00
Kitchen sinks	P1@12.0	Ea	2,070.00	415.00	—	2,485.00
Service sinks	P1@10.0	Ea	1,790.00	346.00	—	2,136.00
Bar sinks	P1@9.00	Ea	1,510.00	311.00	—	1,821.00
Floor sinks	P1@7.00	Ea	931.00	242.00	—	1,173.00
Water closets						
Tank-type	P1@11.0	Ea	1,510.00	380.00	—	1,890.00
Flush valve	P1@12.0	Ea	1,690.00	415.00	—	2,105.00
Urinals	P1@8.00	Ea	2,170.00	276.00	—	2,446.00
Drinking fountains						
(refrigerated)	P1@12.0	Ea	2,510.00	415.00	—	2,925.00
Wash fountains	P1@25.0	Ea	5,410.00	864.00	—	6,274.00
Can washers	P1@18.0	Ea	2,760.00	622.00	—	3,382.00
Floor drains	P1@8.00	Ea	851.00	276.00	—	1,127.00
Area drains	P1@6.00	Ea	732.00	207.00	—	939.00
Roof drains	P1@18.0	Ea	1,930.00	622.00	—	2,552.00
Overflow drains	P1@18.0	Ea	1,930.00	622.00	—	2,552.00
Deck drains	P1@4.00	Ea	602.00	138.00	—	740.00
Cleanouts	P1@5.00	Ea	651.00	173.00	—	824.00
Trap primers	P1@2.00	Ea	330.00	69.10	—	399.10
Sump pumps	P1@6.00	Ea	3,210.00	207.00	—	3,417.00
Water heaters						
Gas, 40 gal.	P1@16.0	Ea	3,800.00	553.00	—	4,353.00
Gas, 80 gal.	P1@17.0	Ea	4,210.00	587.00	—	4,797.00
Gas, 120 gal.	P1@18.0	Ea	4,910.00	622.00	—	5,532.00

Description	Craft@Hrs	Unit	Material $	Labor $	Equipment $	Total $

Budget plumbing estimate, plastic DWV and plastic supply pipe

Description	Craft@Hrs	Unit	Material $	Labor $	Equipment $	Total $
Bathtubs	P1@12.0	Ea	1,710.00	415.00	—	2,125.00
Showers	P1@7.00	Ea	828.00	242.00	—	1,070.00
Lavatories	P1@9.00	Ea	1,590.00	311.00	—	1,901.00
Kitchen sinks	P1@10.0	Ea	1,770.00	346.00	—	2,116.00
Service sinks	P1@8.00	Ea	1,420.00	276.00	—	1,696.00
Bar sinks	P1@7.00	Ea	1,190.00	242.00	—	1,432.00
Floor sinks	P1@6.00	Ea	721.00	207.00	—	928.00
Water closets						
Tank-type	P1@8.00	Ea	1,110.00	276.00	—	1,386.00
Flush valve	P1@9.00	Ea	1,340.00	311.00	—	1,651.00
Urinals	P1@6.00	Ea	1,800.00	207.00	—	2,007.00
Drinking fountains						
(refrigerated)	P1@10.0	Ea	2,080.00	346.00	—	2,426.00
Wash fountains	P1@22.0	Ea	4,770.00	760.00	—	5,530.00
Can washers	P1@15.0	Ea	2,340.00	518.00	—	2,858.00
Floor drains	P1@7.00	Ea	596.00	242.00	—	838.00
Area drains	P1@5.00	Ea	486.00	173.00	—	659.00
Roof drains	P1@16.0	Ea	1,660.00	553.00	—	2,213.00
Overflow drains	P1@16.0	Ea	1,660.00	553.00	—	2,213.00
Deck drains	P1@3.00	Ea	415.00	104.00	—	519.00
Cleanouts	P1@4.00	Ea	506.00	138.00	—	644.00
Trap primers	P1@2.00	Ea	251.00	69.10	—	320.10
Sump pumps	P1@5.00	Ea	2,920.00	173.00	—	3,093.00
Water heaters						
Gas, 40 gal.	P1@15.0	Ea	3,530.00	518.00	—	4,048.00
Gas, 80 gal.	P1@16.0	Ea	3,870.00	553.00	—	4,423.00
Gas, 120 gal.	P1@17.0	Ea	4,490.00	587.00	—	5,077.00

Budget Estimates for HVAC Work: Budget estimates for heating, ventilating and air conditioning work are figured by the square foot of floor. Multiply the area of conditioned space by the cost per square foot in the table that follows. The result is the estimated cost including a complete heating, ventilating and air conditioning system and 20 percent overhead and profit. The table also shows average heating and cooling requirements for various types of buildings.

Description	Cooling (Btu/SF)	Heating (Btu/SF)	Total Selling Price ($) Per SF	Total Selling Price ($) Per Ton
Apartments and condominiums	25	25	12.60	4,660.00
Auditoriums	40	40	32.40	7,460.00
Banks	45	30	33.60	7,440.00
Barber shops	40	40	33.60	7,690.00
Beauty shops	60	30	39.30	6,020.00
Bowling alleys	40	40	25.90	5,940.00
Churches	35	35	28.10	7,330.00
Classrooms	45	40	51.00	10,400.00
Cocktail lounges	70	30	35.50	4,660.00
Computer rooms	145	20	72.30	4,570.00
Department stores	35	30	22.70	5,980.00
Laboratories	60	45	62.90	9,650.00
Libraries	45	35	37.50	7,670.00
Manufacturing plants	40	35	14.50	3,350.00
Medical buildings	35	35	24.90	6,540.00
Motels	30	30	17.30	5,310.00
Museums	35	40	27.70	7,270.00
Nursing homes	45	35	31.90	6,570.00
Office buildings, low-rise	35	35	25.40	6,640.00
Office buildings, high-rise	40	30	34.40	7,860.00
Residences	20	30	7.75	3,580.00
Retail shops	45	30	25.90	5,270.00
Supermarkets	30	30	13.50	4,120.00
Theaters	40	40	25.40	5,850.00

Note that these are budget estimates and can vary widely with conditions which may be unique to the job site. Many of these conditions are identified below. Avoid submitting even a budget estimate without either a site walk-through, a conference with the consulting engineer or architect or a careful review of the plans.

Be alert to any of the following conditions. Any of these can have a major impact on cost:

1. Do HVAC unit dimensions exceed the size of available openings?

2. If a crane is required, is there ample clearance for crane operations?

3. Will any doors, permanent ladders, scaffolding or load-bearing supports obstruct installation?

4. Do the plans show all vents, drains and cleanouts required by the code? Many items like these are not specified by the engineer but will be required by the inspector.

5. For retrofit work, consider carefully problems associated with demolition, including removal of the existing HVAC system, structural modifications and any encased asbestos that may be present.

6. In retrofit jobs, the type and size of HVAC equipment is limited by the window area and installed insulation.

7. How will available power, gas and water lines be extended to the new HVAC equipment?

Plumbing & HVAC Forms and Letters

The following pages contain business forms and letters most plumbing and HVAC contractors can use.

- Change Orders
  Change Estimate Takeoff
  Change Estimate Worksheet
  Change Estimate Summary
  Change Order Log

- Subcontract Forms
  Standard Form Subcontract
  Subcontract Change Order

- Purchase Order

- Construction Schedule

- Letter of Intent

- Submittal Data Cover Sheet

- Submittal Index

- Billing Breakdown Worksheet

An explanation is provided on how the forms function in the contractor's office, how to fill them out, and a sample provided. Where appropriate, a blank copy of the form is provided for your use.

Permission is hereby given by the publisher for the duplication of any of the blank forms on a copy machine or at a printer, provided they are for your own use and not to be sold at a cost exceeding the actual printing and paper cost.

Space has been provided at the top of the forms so you can add your own letterhead or logo.

Change Estimates

Very few projects are completed without some changes to the original plans. Most changes in the scope of work are a result of either errors by the designer or requests by the owner.

Here's the usual sequence in handling changes.

1) The project architect usually initiates a change by sending a Request for Quotation (R.F.Q.) to the general contractor with a detailed description of the work to be modified.

2) The general contractor prepares a Change Estimate (C.E.) if the work is to be done by the general.

3) The subcontractor prepares a change estimate which shows the work to be added to or deleted from the contract and the cost of changes, including markup. The general contractor reviews the change estimate and forwards a summary to the architect for decision.

4) If the decision is to go ahead with the change, the architect issues a Change Order (C.O.) to the general contractor. This change order is authorization to proceed with the change at the price quoted.

Your costs for making changes will normally be higher than your costs for similar items on the original estimate. Here's why:

- Equipment and materials for changes are almost always purchased in smaller quantities. Volume discounts are seldom available.

- Special handling and delivery of small orders will further increase equipment and material costs.

- Scheduled work will be disrupted.

- Overhead costs will be higher because special purchase orders or subcontracts will be required.

- Vendor restocking charges for deleted items will range from 20 to 50 percent of the original cost.

- Large change orders may require additional manpower, which usually results in decreased efficiency.

- The cumulative effect of change orders will be to increase overhead costs if the project completion date is extended.

To compensate for these higher costs, most estimators use a higher markup on change estimates:

- Add an extra 10 percent markup to equipment and material costs to cover increased overhead and handling costs, prior to adding final Overhead and Profit markup.

- Increase competitive labor units (manhours required to perform a specific task) by 15 percent to compensate for inefficiencies such as disruptions in the work schedule, extra handling of equipment and material, and additional manpower.

- Mark up subcontractor prices by 10 percent.

- Figure overhead and profit markup at 15/10 or 10/10.

By following these suggestions, the mathematical gross profit will appear to be 40 to 45 percent, but the true gross will be closer to 25 percent because your costs for change order work are higher, as listed above.

Change Estimate Example

Let's assume that the general contractor on your job has sent a R.F.Q. to your attention. The extra work is a run of hot water piping that will connect to equipment being furnished and set by others. The first step is to list all material and labor required to do the work. Notice the items entered on the Change Estimate Take-off form on page 440.

When the take-off is complete, transfer the manhour total to the Change Estimate Worksheet on page 441. To complete this form:

1) Multiply manhours by the cost per hour.

2) Add the cost of supervision.

3) Total direct labor cost.

4) Add the cost of preparing the change order estimate (C.E.).

5) Add equipment and tool costs.

6) Add subcontract costs.

Then bring totals forward to the Change Estimate Summary on page 442:

1) Enter the material cost total from the Change Estimate Take-off form on page 444.

2) Enter direct and indirect labor cost totals from the Change Estimate Worksheet.

3) Enter equipment, tool and subcontract cost totals from the Change Estimate Worksheet.

Notice the additional bond charge on line M of the Change Estimate Summary. This is the extra premium charged by the bonding company to cover the increase in contract value. The next line, Service Reserve, is the allowance for service work (if any is required) during the warranty period. A sample Change Order Log, used to record the status of changes, is also included on page 443.

ACME
Mechanical Contractors

7600 Oak Avenue - Smallville, U.S.A. 12345-6789
Voice 1-234-5678 / FAX 1-234-5680

Change Estimate Take-off

Project CBC Bank Building

Take-off by DCO

Date 2-2-12

C. E. Number One

Job No 7777

	Equipment and Material			Material $		Labor Manhours	
Item	Description	Quantity	Unit	Total	Unit	Total	
1	1" Type L hard copper pipe	40 LF	3.87	154.80	.038	1.52	
2	1" 90 degree copper ell	6 Ea	4.21	25.26	.23	1.38	
3	1" copper coupling	4 Ea	2.54	10.16	.24	.96	
4	1" bronze ball valve	2 Ea	17.30	34.60	.36	.72	
5	2" x 1" reducing copper tee	2 Ea	20.60	41.20	.40	.80	
6	1" copper union	2 Ea	19.10	38.20	.26	.52	
7	1" pipe hanger	8 Ea	4.33	34.64	.25	2.00	
8	Miscellaneous material	1 Ea	LS	50.00	1.78	1.78	
		Totals		388.86		9.68	

440

ACME
Mechanical Contractors

7600 Oak Avenue - Smallville, U.S.A. 12345-6789
Voice 1-234-5678 / FAX 1-234-5680

Change Estimate Worksheet

Estimated by DCO

C. E. Number One

Date 2-3-12

Job No 7777

Direct Labor Expense (including benefits)

Plumber or pipefitter journeyman	9.68 manhours at $	41.85	per hour =	$ 405.11
Plumber or pipefitter supervisor	1.00 manhours at $	45.00	per hour =	$ 45.00
Sheet metal journeyman	manhours at $		per hour =	$
Sheet metal supervisor	manhours at $		per hour =	$
Laborer journeyman	manhours at $		per hour =	$
	manhours at $		per hour =	$

Total Direct Labor Cost $ 450.11

Indirect Costs

Travel _____ $ _____

Subsistence _____ $ _____

Labor _____ Cost Estimate Preparation (1 Hour) $ 40.00

Total Indirect Cost $ 40.00

Equipment and Tool Costs

_____ Ramset rental $ 35.00

_____ Propane $ 4.50

Total Equipment and Tool Cost $ 39.50

Subcontract Costs

_____ Quikrap Insulation Co. $ 100.00

_____ $ _____

Total Subcontract Cost $ 100.00

ACME
Mechanical Contractors

7600 Oak Avenue - Smallville, U.S.A. 12345-6789
Voice 1-234-5678 / FAX 1-234-5680

Change Estimate Summary

Quotation to   ABC General Contractors, Inc   **Date**   2-3-12

Address   380 First Street   **Change Order No.**   One

Address   **Job Number**   7777

City / State / Zip   Smallville, CA 63876

Attention: Mr. J.H. Smith

Job Name   CBC Bank Building

Reference: Your R.F.O. No. 7 Labor and Material to furnish and install additional hot
water piping.

A.	Materials and equipment:	$ 388.86		
B.	Sales tax: 7% .	$ 27.22		
C.	Direct labor:	$ 450.11		
D.	Indirect costs:	$ 40.00		
E.	Equipment and tools:	$ 39.50		
F.			Subtotal $	945.69
G.	Overhead at : 15% of line F:	$ 141.85		
H.	Subcontracts:	$ 100.00		
I.	Overhead at : 10% of line H:	$ 10.00		
J.			Subtotal $	1,197.54
K.	Profit at 10% of line J:	$ 119.75		
L.			Subtotal $	1,317.29
M.	Bond premium at 1% of line L:	$ 13.17		
N.	Service reserve at 0.5% of line L:	$ 6.59		
O.	**Total cost estimate, lines L thru N:**	Add Deduct	$	1,337.05

P.   Exclusions from this estimate: Per Base

Q.   This quotation is valid for   30   days

R.   We require   1   day(s) extension of the contract time.

S.   We are proceeding with this work per your authorization.

T.   Please forward your confirming change order.

Signed by: _____

Project Manager

Change Order Log

Job Name _____   **Job Number** _____

Change Number	Customer Number	Date	Amount	Date Approved	Amount Approved	Remarks

Use this space to insert your company logo and letterhead.

Change Estimate Take-off

Project _____   **C. E. Number** _____

Take-off by _____   **Job No** _____

Date _____

Item	Description	Quantity	Material $		Labor Manhours	
	Equipment and Material		Unit	Total	Unit	Total
	Totals					

Change Estimate Worksheet

Estimated by _____   **C. E. Number** _____

Date _____   **Job No** _____

Direct Labor Expense (including benefits)

Plumber or pipefitter journeyman   _____ manhours at $ _____ per hour = $ _____

Plumber or pipefitter supervisor   _____ manhours at $ _____ per hour = $ _____

Sheet metal journeyman   _____ manhours at $ _____ per hour = $ _____

Sheet metal supervisor   _____ manhours at $ _____ per hour = $ _____

Laborer journeyman   _____ manhours at $ _____ per hour = $ _____

_____   _____ manhours at $ _____ per hour = $ _____

Total Direct Labor Cost $ _____

Indirect Costs

Travel _____ $ _____

Subsistence _____ $ _____

Labor _____ $ _____

Total Indirect Cost $ _____

Equipment and Tool Costs

_____ $ _____

_____ $ _____

Total Equipment and Tool Cost $ _____

Subcontract Costs

_____ $ _____

_____ $ _____

Total Subcontract Cost $ _____

Use this space to insert your company logo and letterhead.

Change Estimate Summary

Quotation to _____	**Date** _____
Address _____	**Change Order No.** _____
Address _____	**Job Number** _____
City / State / Zip _____	
Attention: _____	
Job Name _____	
Reference: _____	

_____

A.   Materials and equipment: $ _____

B.   Sales tax: _____ . $ _____

C.   Direct labor: $ _____

D.   Indirect costs: $ _____

E.   Equipment and tools: $ _____

F.   **Subtotal $** _____

G.   Overhead at _____ of line F: $ _____

H.   Subcontracts: $ _____

I.   Overhead at _____ of line H: $ _____

J.   **Subtotal $** _____

K.   Profit at _____ of line J: $ _____

L.   **Subtotal $** _____

M.   Bond premium at 1% of line L: $ _____

N.   Service reserve at 0.5% of line L: $ _____

O.   **Total cost estimate, lines L thru N:**   Add   Deduct $ _____

P.   Exclusions from this estimate: _____

Q.   This quotation is valid for _____ days

R.   We require _____ day(s) extension of the contract time.

S.   We are proceeding with this work per your authorization.

T.   Please forward your confirming change order.

Signed by: _____
Project Manager

446

Another term for the general contractor is *prime contractor*. Subcontractors working directly for the prime contractor are called *second-tier subcontractors*. Contractors working for these second-tier subs are usually known as *third-tier subcontractors*. On a large job, many second-tier subs may hire third-tier subs to perform specialized work such as insulation, fireproofing, test and balance, water treatment, instrumentation and trenching.

If a portion of your work will be subcontracted to others, I recommend drawing up a subcontract agreement for that work. Any subcontractors who furnish both material and labor for a job should have a written contract.

Most larger plumbing, heating and A/C subcontractors use a two-part *Standard Form Subcontract* published by the Associated General Contractors of America. This two-part form is used to write the base subcontract. The A.G.C. also publishes a *Subcontract Change Order* form which is used when adding or deleting items after the base subcontract is signed. These forms are sold at modest cost at most A.G.C. offices.

The first section of page one of the Standard Form Subcontract identifies the two contractors entering into the agreement. The party issuing the subcontract is the *contractor*. Recipient of the agreement is the *subcontractor*.

Under *Recitals,* the contractor must affirm the right to issue a subcontract by declaring that a legal contract exists with the *owner* (general contractor).

Section 1 - Entire Contract describes the contract documents: the project plans, specifications and addenda. This list of documents should always be the same as the documents identified in the second-tier subcontractor's contract with the general contractor.

Section 2 - Scope describes the specific scope of work to be performed.

Section 3 - Contract Price. Complete this section by inserting the agreed-upon price for doing the work described.

Section 4 - Payment Schedule on page two should show the same payment terms as your contract with the general contractor.

Section 7 - Special Provisions is used to list any special agreements or exclusions.

When the contract is typed, do not sign it. Instead, forward it to the third-tier subcontractor with instructions to sign it and return it intact. When the signed contract is received, sign it and send a copy to the third-tier subcontractor.

Standard Form Subcontract

Subcontract No. 7777-1

THIS AGREEMENT, made and entered into at Smallville, CA. this 3rd day of May, 2012, by and between   Acme Mechanical Contractors hereinafter called **CONTRACTOR,** with principal office at 7600 Oak Avenue, Smallville, California, and Quikrap Insulation Co., 320 Maple Blvd., Smallville, CA hereinafter called a **SUBCONTRACTOR.**

RECITALS

On or about the_____2nd_____day of_____January_____, 20_12, CONTRACTOR entered into a prime contract with

ABC General Contractors, Inc._____ hereinafter called OWNER, whose address is 380 First Street, Smallville, California_____ to perform the following construction work: The installation of all mechanical and plumbing systems for the proposed Mile-Hi office building to be located at 2600 Second, North, Smallville, California.

Said work is to be performed in accordance with the prime contract and the plans and specifications. Said plans and specifications have been prepared by or on behalf of Quik-Draw and Associates, Smallville, California____, **ARCHITECT**

SECTION 1 - ENTIRE CONTRACT

SUBCONTRACTOR certifies and agrees that he is fully familiar with all of the terms, conditions and obligations of the Contract Documents, as hereinafter defined, the location of the job site, and the conditions under which the work is to be performed, and that he enters into this Agreement based upon his investigation of all of such matters and is in no way relying upon any opinions or representations of CONTRACTOR. It is agreed that this Agreement represents the entire agreement. It is further agreed that the Contract Documents are incorporated in this Agreement by this reference, with the same force and effect as if the same were set forth at length herein, and that SUBCONTRACTOR and his subcontractors will be and are bound by any and all of said Contract Documents insofar as they relate in any part or in any way, directly or indirectly to the work covered by this Agreement. SUBCONTRACTOR agrees to be bound to CONTRACTOR in the same manner and to the same extent as CONTRACTOR is bound to OWNER under the Contract Documents, to the extent of the work provided for in this Agreement, and that where, in the Contract Documents, reference is made to CONTRACTOR and the work or specification therein pertains to SUBCONTRACTOR'S trade, craft, or type of work, then such work or specification shall be interpreted to apply to SUBCONTRACTOR instead of CONTRACTOR. The phrase "Contract Documents" is defined to mean and include:

Drawing Nos. A-1 thru A-17, C-1 thru C-4, S-1 thru S-7, E-1 thru E-6 and M-1 thru M-7, all dated
10-4-2011, Specifications dated 10-2-11 and Addendum No. 1 dated 10-18-11.

SECTION 2 - SCOPE

SUBCONTRACTOR agrees to furnish all labor, services, materials, installation, cartage, hoisting, supplies, insurance, equipment, scaffolding, tools and other facilities of every kind and description required for the prompt and efficient execution of the work described herein and to perform the work necessary or incidental to complete thermal insulation for all plumbing, HHW, CHW and condensate piping systems, including pumps P-1, P-2 and P-3 for the project in strict accordance with the Contract Documents and as more particularly, though not exclusively, specified in:

Division 15, Section 400 entitled "Thermal Insulation systems" and General Conditions, as applicable.

SECTION 3 - CONTRACT PRICE

CONTRACTOR agrees to pay SUBCONTRACTOR for the strict performance of his work, the sum of:

Forty-two thousand, three hundred dollars ($42,300.00), subject to additions and deductions for changes in the work as may be agreed upon, and to make payment in accordance with the Payment Schedule, Section 4.

SECTION 4 - PAYMENT SCHEDULE

CONTRACTOR agrees to pay SUBCONTRACTOR in monthly payments of _____90_____% of labor and materials which have been placed in position and for which payment has been made by OWNER to CONTRACTOR. The remaining _____10_____% shall be retained by CONTRACTOR until he receives final payment from OWNER, but not less than thirty-five days after the entire work required by the prime contract has been fully completed in conformity with the Contract Documents and has been delivered and accepted by OWNER, ARCHITECT, and CONTRACTOR. Subject to the provisions of the next sentence, the retained percentage shall be paid SUBCONTRACTOR promptly after CONTRACTOR receives his final payment from OWNER. SUBCONTRACTOR agrees to furnish, if and when required by CONTRACTOR, payroll affidavits, receipts, vouchers, release of claims for labor, material and subcontractors performing work or furnishing materials under this Agreement, all in form satisfactory to CONTRACTOR, and it is agreed that no payment hereunder shall be made, except at CONTRACTOR'S option, until and unless such payroll affidavits, receipts, vouchers or release; or any or all of them, have been furnished. And payment made hereunder prior to completion and acceptance of the work, as referred to above, shall not be construed as evidence of acceptance of any part of SUBCONTRACTOR'S work.

SECTION 5 - GENERAL SUBCONTRACT PROVISIONS

General Subcontract Provisions on back of Pages 1 and 2 are an integral part of this Agreement.

SECTION 6 - GENERAL PROVISIONS

1. *SUBCONTRACTOR* agrees to begin work as soon as instructed by the CONTRACTOR, and shall carry on said work promptly, efficiently and at a speed that will not cause delay in the progress of the CONTRACTOR'S work or work of other subcontractors. If, in the opinion of the CONTRACTOR, the SUBCONTRACTOR falls behind in the progress of the work, the CONTRACTOR may direct the SUBCONTRACTOR to take such steps as the CONTRACTOR deems necessary to improve the rate of progress, including, without limitation, requiring the SUBCONTRACTOR to increase the number of shifts, personnel, overtime operations, days of work, equipment, amount of plant, or other remedies and to submit to CONTRACTOR for CONTRACTOR'S approval an outline schedule demonstrating the manner in which the required rate of progress will be regained, without additional cost to the CONTRACTOR. CONTRACTOR may require SUBCONTRACTOR to prosecute, in preference to other parts of the work, such part or parts of the work as CONTRACTOR may specify.

The SUBCONTRACTOR shall complete the work as required by the progress schedule prepared by the CONTRACTOR, which may be amended from time to time. The progress schedule may be reviewed in the office of the CONTRACTOR and sequence of construction will be as directed by the CONTRACTOR.

The SUBCONTRACTOR agrees to have an acceptable representative (an officer of SUBCONTRACTOR if requested by the CONTRACTOR) present at all job meetings and to submit weekly progress reports in writing if requested by the CONTRACTOR. Any job progress schedules are hereby made a part of and incorporated herein by reference.

2. *Reserved Gate Usage*

SUBCONTRACTOR shall notify in writing, and assign its employees, material men and suppliers, to such gates or entrances as may be established for their use by CONTRACTOR and in accordance with such conditions and at such times as may be imposed by CONTRACTOR. Strict compliance with CONTRACTOR'S gate usage procedures shall be required by the SUBCONTRACTOR who shall be responsible for such gate usage by its employees, material men, suppliers, subcontractors, and their material men and suppliers.

3. *Staggered Days and Hours of Work and for Deliveries*

SUBCONTRACTOR shall schedule the work and the presence of its employees at the jobsite and any deliveries of supplies or materials by its material men and suppliers to the jobsite on such days, and at such times and during such hours, as may be directed by CONTRACTOR. SUBCONTRACTOR shall assume responsibility for such schedule compliance not only for its employees but for all its material men, suppliers and subcontractors, and their material men and suppliers.

SECTION 7 - SPECIAL PROVISIONS

    1. Pipe hanger inserts will be furnished and installed by Contractor.
    2. All trash pickup by Subcontractor; haul-away will be by General Contractor.

Contractors are required by law to be licensed and regulated by the Contractors' State License Board. Any questions concerning a contractor may be referred to the registrar of the board whose address is:

Contractors' State License Board -- P. O. Box 26000, Sacramento, California 95826

IN WITNESS WHEREOF: The parties hereto have executed this Agreement for themselves, their heirs, executors, successors, administrators, and assignees on the day and year first above written.

SUBCONTRACTOR	CONTRACTOR
Quikrap Insulation Company	Acme Mechanical Contractors
By _____	By _____
Name Title	Name Title
☐ Corporation ☐ Partnership ☐ Proprietorship	
(Seal)	
Contractor's State License No. _____	Contractor's State License No. _____

Subcontract Change Order

Number ___One___ g

Date 6-11-12	**Subcontract Number** 7777-1
To Quickrap Insulation Co.	**Our Job Number** _____
	Our Proposal Number _____
	Architect's C.O. Number _____
	Effective Date of Charge 6-17-12

Subject to all the provisions of this Change Order, you are hereby directed to make the following change(s)

Delete HHW and CHW piping insulation located above Room No. 322 per ABC General

Contractor's Change Order No. 18, dated 6-5-12.

The following change(s) will alter the price provided in your subcontract by the ___deduction___ *of $* ___465.00___ g

*Surety Consent		
This Change is Approved Date _____	Adjusted Subcontract Price Through C.O. Number 0	$ 42,300.00
Name: _____		
By: _____	Amount this C.O. Number:	$ (465.00)
Title:	Current Adjusted Subcontract Price:	$ 41,835.00

When this Change Order is signed by both parties (and by Subcontractor's surety is subcontract is bonded), it constitutes their agreement:

(A) That the subcontract price is adjusted as shown above and that no further adjustment in that price by reason of the change(s) provided herein shall be made; and (B) That all the terms and conditions of the subcontract, except as modified by this and any previous changes, shall remain in full force and effect and apply to the work as so changed.

Accepted and Agreed:	**Date:** _____
By _____ Authorized Signature – Subcontractor	By _____ Authorized Signature – Contractor
Title	Title

* Subcontractor: Sign pink copy and return immediately. If subcontract is bonded, obtain consent of surety endorsed thereon.
   No payments on account of this Change Order will be made until you have complied with the foregoing.

Published by San Diego Chapter A.G.C.

A purchase order is a legal document used to order equipment and materials from a vendor, with the implied promise to pay for these goods within a specified time after receipt of the items. Purchase orders are sometimes used to write subcontracts whose value does not exceed one or two thousand dollars. Refer to the sample purchase order on page 452.

While most of the purchase order is self-explanatory, certain items need to be emphasized:

"Description" should include all pertinent data such as model numbers, arrangements, performance requirements, applicable standards, electrical characteristics and so on.

"Tag" is used to identify a particular piece of equipment to facilitate unloading it at the proper location at the jobsite. Tag numbers for all major equipment can usually be found on the contract drawings.

"48 hour delivery notice": This can be very important if the material or equipment being delivered is too heavy to be unloaded by hand. Time will be required to arrange for a crane or forklift to unload the truck.

"Sales tax" is the current state sales tax which must be included unless the goods are to be delivered and installed at a project located out-of-state.

"Terms": The usual payment terms are "Net 30" which means the entire amount of the purchase order must be paid within thirty days after receipt of all goods, undamaged. If items are received damaged, payment should be withheld until satisfactory repair or replacement is made.

ACME
Mechanical Contractors

7600 Oak Avenue - Smallville, U.S.A. 12345-6789
Voice 1-234-5678 / FAX 1-234-5680

Purchase Order

P.O. Number: 7777-36   **Date:** 1-6-12

Job: CBC Bank Building

Job No: 7777

Seller: Smallville Industrial Sales Co.	**Ship to:** Acme Mechanical Contractors
3657 Third Avenue Northwest	c/o CBC Bank Building
Smallville, CA 63876	465 Commercial Street
	Smallville, CA 63876

Attn: Mr. L.H. Seller   **By:** RJS

Delivery date: 2-28-12   **24 Hr. Delivery Notice Required**   **Payment terms:** Net 30

Quantity	Description	Unit	Total
Two	Big-Blo Model No. 1JN 86-13 centrifugal	$443.00	$886.00
	fans with 480/3/60 one-half H.P., O.D.P.		
	motor. 3250 CFM @ 0.50 T.S.P.		
	Tag one EF-13 and one EF-23		

Number of copies of operation and maintenance
manuals required ___2___ g

All shipments are to be F.O.B. jobsite or shop unless
otherwise noted.

Total before tax	$886.00
Sales tax	$62.02
Freight	Included
Total Order	$948.02

Buyer: RJS

Acceptance by seller _____   **Date** _____

The general contractor's construction schedule may range from a simple bar chart to a complicated computer-generated CPM (Critical Path Method) diagram. More complex jobs require more complete and detailed schedules. On larger jobs, lower-tier subcontractors may be required to prepare a bar chart showing their construction schedule.

If you have to prepare a construction schedule, make conservative estimates of the time required to complete each part of the job. A slower schedule makes it possible to use smaller crews which are usually more efficient.

You can't schedule your own work until the general contractor has supplied a schedule for the balance of the project. When you have that schedule, prepare a list of tasks your crews will perform. Show this list to the general contractor to be certain there are no conflicts with the master schedule.

When the list of tasks to be performed has been approved, begin recording the manhours required for each task. Take these manhours from your estimate. When the duration for each task has been determined, figure the crew sizes required.

For example, suppose the estimate shows that it will take 1,040 manhours to install the underground plumbing for a project. The work must be completed in two months. Assuming one worker averages 173 hours of work in one month, how many workers will be required to meet the schedule? Here's the solution:

$$\frac{1,040 \text{ manhours}}{173 \text{ MH / Mo. x 2 months}} = 3 \text{ workers}$$

The first of the two bar charts on the following pages shows the schedule a general contractor might expect to receive from a plumbing and HVAC subcontractor. The chart on page 454 is intended for use by the subcontractor. It includes information a mechanical subcontractor needs to determine proper crew sizes for each task. The *Cumulative Manhours* line shows the budgeted manhours for each month of the project. If labor costs are to be kept within budget, actual hours should not exceed estimated hours. Monitor labor costs each month by comparing the line *Actual MH Used* (actual manhours used) with the line *Cumulative MH* (estimated cumulative manhours).

Construction Schedule

Company: Acme Mechanical Contractors   **Project:** Mile-Hi Office Bldg   **Job Number:** ????   **Date:** 6/8/12

Activity	2012						2013					Crew Sizes
	Jul	Aug	Sep	Oct	Nov	Dec	Jan	Feb	Mar	Apr	May	
Submittals	▓											
Purchasing		▓	▓									
U/G Plumbing			▓	▓								
A/G Plumbing						▓	▓					
Fin. Plumbing								▓				
HVAC Piping					▓	▓						
HVAC Ducting					▓	▓	▓					
Equipment									▓			
Insulation							▓	▓	▓			
Temp. Controls					▓	▓	▓					
Start-up										▓		

Construction Schedule

Company: Acme Mechanical Contractors   **Project:** Mile-Hi Office Bldg   **Job Number:** 7777   **Date:** 6/8/12

Activity	2012 Jul	Aug	Sep	Oct	Nov	Dec	2013 Jan	Feb	Mar	Apr	May	Crew Sizes
Submittals	▓											N/A
Purchasing		▓	▓									N/A
U/G Plumbing			▓	▓								1040 MH ÷ (173 x 2) = 3
A/G Plumbing				▓	▓	▓	▓					2075 MH ÷ (173 x 4) = 3
Fin. Plumbing								▓				130 MH ÷ (173 x .5) = 1.5
HVAC Piping						▓	▓	▓				2760 MH ÷ (173 x 4) = 4
HVAC Ducting						▓	▓	▓	▓			2790 MH ÷ (173 x 4) = 4
Equipment									▓			690 MH ÷ (173 x 2) = 2
Insulation						▓	▓	▓	▓			Subcontract
Temp. Controls					▓	▓	▓	▓	▓			Subcontract
Start-up										▓		85 MH ÷ (173 x .5) = 1
Crew size/month			3	6	11	11	11	11.5	2	1		
Cumulative MH*			520	1159	3466	5373	7280	9143	9448	9573		MH Estimated = 9573
Actual MH used												
*Per estimate												
*Rounded												

455

Letter of Intent

On most large projects the contractor is required to submit drawings and technical data to the owner's representative for approval before work actually begins. Most of these submittals will be prepared by your suppliers and third-tier subs. Vendors and subs may be reluctant to prepare these documents without some assurance that they've been selected to do the work. That's the purpose of a letter of intent. It notifies a proposed vendor or subcontractor that you plan to contract with them when the owner approves the information submitted.

A letter of intent isn't a contract. It's an expressed intention to make a contract, which isn't a contract at all. But a vendor who gets your letter of intent and supplies all the information requested should get the contract. If you place the order with a different vendor, obviously, your letter of intent was worthless. That first vendor may be very reluctant to cooperate in the future.

A sample letter of intent follows this page.

ACME
Mechanical Contractors

7600 Oak Avenue - Smallville, U.S.A. 12345-6789
Voice 1-234-5678 / FAX 1-234-5680

December 20, 2011

Quikrap Insulation Company
320 Maple Boulevard
Smallville, U.S.A. 12345-6789

Attn: Mr. R. S. Quikrap

Dear Mr. Quikrap:

Acme Mechanical Contractors has been issued a subcontract to furnish and install the mechanical and plumbing systems for the proposed Mile-Hi Office Building to be located at 2600 Second Street in Smallville.

It is my intention to award your firm a subcontract to provide the thermal insulation for these systems in accordance with your proposal dated 12-13-11 in the amount of $42,300.00.

Please prepare ten copies of your submittal data and forward them to me no later than January 15, 2012. Upon approval of your submittal, I will mail you the subcontract for your review and signature.

Thank you,

Bobby Thompson
Project Manager

CC: Project file

Submittal Data

The construction specifications may require that you submit manufacturer's technical data on certain equipment you plan to install. You may have to submit six to ten copies of this technical data for approval before buying the equipment or contracting with third-tier subcontractors.

First, find out how many submittal copies will be required. Request that number of copies plus at least two additional sets for your use. A subcontractor who provides only services (no materials) may have to submit a detailed written explanation of the work to be done.

The second step is to label each submittal with the paragraph number of the specification where that equipment, material or service is described. Type or write this number in the upper right corner of each submittal sheet. From this set of numbered submittals, prepare a submittal index, a list of submittals identified by title and paragraph number. This index should be arranged in specification paragraph order. A blank submittal index form follows this section.

I prefer to use a three-ring binder to hold submittals. That makes it easier to add and delete sections as needed. Be sure to include a cover sheet, usually on company letterhead, which identifies the project, job number and scope of work being submitted. A sample submittal cover sheet follows this section.

Purchase orders and subcontracts should not be written until an approved copy of the submittal brochure has been received.

ACME
Mechanical Contractors

7600 Oak Avenue - Smallville, U.S.A. 12345-6789
Voice 1-234-5678 / FAX 1-234-5680

Division 15

Heating, Ventilating, Air Conditioning and Plumbing Systems

Submittal Data for

Mile-Hi Office Building
2600 Second Street
Smallville, U.S.A.

Submittal Index

Specification Section	Specification Paragraph	Item Description	Proposed Vendor or Sub	As Specified	See Submittal Data Page

The format to be used for monthly progress billings is seldom specified in the contract documents. In any case, your bill has to include enough detail to satisfy the owner and the lender.

Before preparing your bill, ask the general contractor how much detail is required. Some general contractors will want detailed cost breakdowns showing costs for each system on each building floor. Others will require much less detail.

Find out if billings can include the cost of equipment and materials delivered and stored either on site or off site but not yet installed. If billings can include materials stored off site, do these materials have to be stored in a bonded warehouse? Do vendor's invoices have to accompany progress billings?

When you understand what's required for monthly progress billings, prepare a billing breakdown worksheet. A sample worksheet follows this section.

Column one, Activity Lists each work item in the order work will be performed. The first item listed will usually be mobilization. This includes the cost of the job site trailer, electrical and telephone hookups, office furniture and supplies and initial labor costs. Billings for mobilization costs are sometimes denied by the lender. Many contractors minimize these costs to increase the chance of approval. It's better to receive partial payment for these costs than none at all.

Column two, Cost ($) Lists the actual contractor's costs for each activity, including labor, material, equipment and sales taxes. Markup for overhead and profit are not included.

Column three, Factor This column shows the markup assigned to each activity. Activities scheduled to be completed first are usually assigned the highest markups. This is called front loading and is common in the construction industry. Most bills won't be paid for 30 to 60 days. When the bill is paid, the amount received probably won't include the percentage allowed for retention. Generally, retention is 10 percent and isn't released until the project is complete and accepted by the owner.

Front loading helps contractors carry the financial burden of work in progress. Few subcontractors have enough cash to pay all their bills when due and still wait months to collect for work that's been completed. Employees have to be paid in full and on time. Assigning a higher markup to work completed first accelerates the payment schedule and helps spread payments more evenly over the entire project. Front loading is routine with subcontractors and unpopular with owners and lenders. In practice, subcontractors have no choice but to place a higher price or higher markup on work completed first.

Note that figures in the Factor column are less than 1.0 for work done near the end of the project. That's because front loading doesn't change the contract price. It changes only when that money is received.

Column four, Sell ($) Values for this column are the product of the cost and factor columns. Use the figures in this column when submitting monthly progress invoices.

ACME
Mechanical Contractors

7600 Oak Avenue - Smallville, U.S.A. 12345-6789
Voice 1-234-5678 / FAX 1-234-5680

Billing Breakdown Worksheet
(CBC Bank Building - Job No. 7777)

Activity	Cost ($)	Factor	Sell ($)
Mobilization	2,000	1.50	3,000
Underground chilled and heated water piping	120,000	1.35	162,000
Underground plumbing & piping	87,000	1.35	117,450
Above ground chilled and heating water piping	115,000	1.20	138,000
Above ground plumbing & piping	87,000	1.20	104,400
HVAC ducting	96,000	1.20	115,200
Equipment	312,000	1.10	343,200
Duct and pipe insulation	119,000	1.00	119,000
Temperature controls	53,000	.90	47,700
Plumbing fixtures	43,000	.65	27,950
Water treatment	1,800	.55	990
Test and balance	13,000	.55	7,150
Validation	500	.50	250
	1,049,300		1,186,290

$$\text{Estimated gross profit} = \frac{\$1,186,290 - \$1,049,300}{\$1,049,300} = 13\%$$

Index